THE DEMOCRATIC POLITICAL PROCESS

A CROSS-NATIONAL READER

The Democratic Political Process

Edited by

Kurt L. Shell

University of Frankfurt
German Federal Republic

Ginn and Company
A XEROX COMPANY

Waltham, Massachusetts | Toronto

Consulting Editor

Andrew Gyorgy

George Washington University

PREFACE

The reawakened interest in the comparative study of politics has not — so far — been matched by an equivalent number of studies using comparative approaches. As Stein Rokkan has pointed out in a recent contribution to a volume dedicated to the comparative use of quantitative data, in the pioneering phase of social science extensive efforts were made "to establish an internationally and interculturally valid body of knowledge about variation and regularities in the functioning and development of human societies."[1] But the increasing emphasis on methodological rigor, as well as a growing preoccupation with an intensive and detailed investigation of the domestic political process, led to prolonged withdrawal — particularly on the part of American political scientists — from the field of cross-national research. This contributed to regrettable parochialism just at a time when the United States was being drawn fully into the network of international relations.

At this same time, it should have become clear that generalizations on a single, culture-bound political system were necessarily limited in their range, and that hypotheses about "political life" required formulations and testing based on data from more than one political system if they were to be independent of unique cultural and historical situations. Impressionistic explanations based on lessons drawn from one country — or a cursory comparison of two or three — were suspect, and could no longer be taught with a clear conscience. Conclusions drawn from analyses — however carefully developed — remained necessarily inconclusive as long as they were not checked against analyses drawn from other political systems.

Thus, to cite but two examples (themselves reflecting two different types of political science generalizations): (1) The traditional generalization about the relation between the electoral law and the development of a

---

[1] Stein Rokkan, "Comparative Cross-National Research: The Context of Current Efforts," in Richard L. Merritt and Stein Rokkan, eds., *Comparing Nations: The Use of Quantitative Data in Cross-National Research* (New Haven: Yale University Press, 1966), p. 3.

particular party system required precise, comparative examination of diverse examples drawn from different political systems; and (2) the positive correlations again and again exhibited in American empirical investigations between level of education and "democratic" attitudes needed to be seen in the context of a particular educational system and national traditions. Only careful cross-national research could provide insight into the conditions under which education actually furthered "democratic attitudes." These insights were necessary for the practical application of research findings, as well as for further scholarly pursuits into such questions as the relation between cognitive and emotive elements in the formation of political attitudes.

Yet, it must be admitted, that the quest for "genuine" cross-national comparative studies meets, in practice, with a host of methodological and practical difficulties. This is not the place to consider them in any detail. A growing body of literature indicates both the seriousness with which the task is now being pursued, and the obstacles standing in its way, even where the attempt is addressed to those areas of political life where data are relatively easily obtainable — voting behavior studies, attitudinal data obtained by survey methods, or correlations based on aggregate statistical data.

The most serious problems of all comparative research rest in the nature of politics itself: It is a process shaped by particular historical forces within a largely national or local "culture," and structured by (within or against) a particular political system. As a consequence, the very meaning of "the political," and the terms and institutions related to it, varies from place to place. To put it simply, the same question has a very different meaning to respondents in each political context.

A second major problem is related to the first. The more emphasis put on precise *horizontal comparisons* — comparisons on the same level of institutions or behavior patterns in different political systems — the greater is the difficulty of relating that level and others to which the phenomena examined are structurally linked. The problem of "linkages" within the system, the analysis of the precise integration within a political system, has baffled scholars even where only one political system was under examination. It was always only the leg, or the trunk, or the tail, of the elephant that was grasped, never the whole beast. The late V. O. Key focused on this problem at the conclusion of *Public Opinion and American Democracy:*

> The exploration of public attitudes is a pursuit of endless fascination — and frustration. Depiction of the distribution of opinions within the public, identification of the qualities of opinon, isolation of the odd and the obvious correlates of opinion, and ascertainment of the modes of opinion formation are pursuits that excite human curiosity. Yet these endeavors are bootless unless the findings about the preferences, aspirations and prejudices of the public can be connected with the workings of the governmental system. . . . Despite their power as instruments for the observation of mass opinion, sampling procedures do not bring within their range elements of the political system

basic for the understanding of the role of mass opinion within the system . . . the pieces of the puzzle are different in form and function and . . . for the existence of a democratic opinion-oriented system each piece must possess the characteristics necessary for it to fit together in a working whole.[2]

The emphasis on the difficulties of the enterprise is not intended to prove its impossibility. Rather, it is meant to explain the nature of the volume here presented. This reader grew out of the attempt to assemble for a seminar on the political process in Western democracies, pieces that either represented significant cross-national research, or, though limited to one political system, allowed or suggested comparisons across systems. The collection is not committed to any single methodological approach; in fact, because its focus is on content — the nature of the democratic process and the problems connected with it — no attempt was made to represent all significant approaches. My major concern was not to neglect the linkages — to throw light on the political systems as wholes rather than to deal with isolated aspects. The structure of this volume bears witness to this concern: The sections follow a vertical arrangement, rising from "political culture" dispositions to more explicit political attitudes, and then to the institutional transmission belts of parties and interest organizations, which connect mass attitudes with the macro-political process.

A selection of this sort cannot, however, rise above its sources. It cannot claim to have established findings or to present verified truths that honest scholarly research so far has not provided. And it must be admitted that this research has just started, that we find ourselves at the foot of the mountain, not at its peak. The heterogeneity of this collection and the tentative nature of most conclusions are indications of this. Lastly, it should be remembered that this reader is intended for students, not for the research scholar engaged in cross-national investigations. It is designed for students who need, above all, to be made aware of the workings of democratic systems outside the United States; who need to have stereotyped notions challenged, substantive problems brought to their attention; and who must be made aware of the danger of hasty generalizations or a rigidly moralistic or too-simple and non-empirical view of democratic politics.

While a collection of predominantly empirical pieces cannot claim to take the place of a worked-out theory of democracy, it is my conviction that such a theory, if it does not take account of empirically established varieties and similarities of political behavior (in the widest sense), is empty and intellectually unsatisfactory. Of course, it cannot be denied that such a complete theory would necessarily include dimensions of inquiry and reflection other than those here tapped. Neither the problem of historical change, nor that

---

[2] V. O. Key, Jr., *Public Opinion and American Democracy* (New York: Alfred A. Knopf, 1967), pp. 535–37.

of "human nature," nor that of the relation between the political process and the social structure within which it is embedded, is reflected in this volume except marginally.

It should also be made clear that a collection of this sort bears the mark of its historical location. Most of the items included stem from the period frequently referred to as the "post-ideological" age, the years following World War II when Western democracies were characterized by spreading economic prosperity, absence of deep economic crises, the memory of Hitlerism and Stalinism, and the growth of bureaucratized welfare states — all of which combined to remove a great deal of bitterness and ideological hostility from the political arena and appeared to reduce the spectrum of political options available. Thus, problems presented by interest-politics in consumption-oriented, highly bureaucratized democracies are central to the volume. While this preface is being written, there are indications that the generalizations based on this period were premature, that the systems thought so firmly established and so unquestioningly accepted were once again being radically challenged, though in novel forms and through movements hitherto largely excluded from the scope of scholarly perception and inquiry. The concluding selections provide a hint of this challenge. The full examination of its nature and of its impact on the structure and processes of Western democracies would require another volume and would itself be premature. It is a source of both frustration and exhilaration to realize that the enterprise of analyzing an ongoing political process is marked by a profound problem of built-in obsolescence, that the systems and processes are changing in the very moment of observation, and perhaps — in a possible parallel to Heisenberg's "law of uncertainty" — as a consequence of our observation. For, the insights gained by scholars become the material and stimulus for reflection and action by those who assert their freedom in molding the processes of democratic politics to accord with their values.

KURT L. SHELL

CONTENTS

PART ONE
DIMENSIONS OF POLITICAL CULTURE   1

1. Modernity and Tradition in Britain   4
   STANLEY ROTHMAN

2. Germany: The Remaking of Political Culture   19
   SIDNEY VERBA

3. The View of Government from Eastport   28
   ROBERT E. LANE

4. "Amoral Familism" in an Italian Village   38
   EDWARD C. BANFIELD

5. A French Village — Protection Against Collective Power   49
   LAURENCE WYLIE

6. Political Culture and "Competent" Citizens   60
   SIDNEY VERBA

PART TWO
PERCEPTIONS OF POLITICS — MASSES AND ELITES   79

7. Consensus and Ideology in American Politics   82
   HERBERT MC CLOSKY

8. Politicization of the Electorate in France and the United States   109
   PHILIP E. CONVERSE AND GEORGES DUPEUX

9. Party Identification in Norway and the United States   129
   ANGUS CAMPBELL AND HENRY VALEN

ix

103019

10. Party Identification in the Federal Republic of Germany and
    the United States   148
    WERNER ZOHLNHÖFER

11. Voters' Participation in the Political Life
    of a Swiss Community   159
    JÜRG STEINER

12. Austrian Youth and Socialist Ideology   166
    ERNST GEHMACHER

13. Values, Expectations and Political Predispositions
    of Italian Youth   170
    JOSEPH LA PALOMBARA AND JERRY B. WATERS

14. Social Trends and Electoral Behavior in Britain   178
    MARK ABRAMS

15. The Political Ideas of English Party Activists   189
    RICHARD ROSE

PART THREE
POLITICAL TRANSMISSION BELTS — PARTIES   209

16. Who Makes Party Policy in the British Labour Party?   212
    LEON D. EPSTEIN

17. Policy Decision in Opposition   227
    SAUL ROSE

18. Policy Decision in Opposition: A Rejoinder   237
    ROBERT T. MC KENZIE

19. Foreign Policy and Party Discipline in the CDU   244
    ARNOLD J. HEIDENHEIMER

20. Intra-Party Conflict in a Dominant Party: The Experience of
    Italian Christian Democracy   254
    RAPHAEL ZARISKI

21. A Profile of the Japanese Conservative Party   267
    JUNNOSUKE MASUMI

22. The Socialist Party of Austria — A "Party of Integration"   276
    KURT L. SHELL

23. The Transformation of the Western European Party System   290
    OTTO KIRCHHEIMER

PART FOUR
POLITICAL TRANSMISSION BELTS — INTEREST GROUPS   309

24. Parties, Pressure Groups and the British Political Process   312
    ROBERT T. MC KENZIE

25. Pressure Group Politics in Britain   322
    HARRY ECKSTEIN

26. Pressure Politics in the Fifth Republic   329
    BERNARD E. BROWN

27. Austria: Representative Democracy or "Chamber State"?   341
    HERBERT P. SECHER

28. Group Theory and the Italian Process   357
    JOSEPH LA PALOMBARA

PART FIVE
THE CHANGING PATTERN OF DEMOCRATIC POLITICS   367

29. The Changing Class Structure and Contemporary European Politics   371
    SEYMOUR MARTIN LIPSET

30. Decline of Ideology: A Dissent and an Interpretation   394
    JOSEPH LA PALOMBARA

31. Some Further Comments on "The End of Ideology"   410
    SEYMOUR MARTIN LIPSET

32. The Trend Towards Political Consensus: The Case of Norway   413
    ULF TORGERSEN

33. Coalition Government in Austria   425
    HERBERT P. SECHER

34. Consensus and Cleavage in British Political Ideology   440
    JAMES B. CHRISTOPH

35. French Technocracy and Comparative Government   461
    F. F. RIDLEY

36. Europe's Identity Crisis: Between the Past and America   478
    STANLEY HOFFMANN

37. The Problem of the New Left   495
    TOM KAHN

THE DEMOCRATIC POLITICAL PROCESS

Part 1

DIMENSIONS OF POLITICAL CULTURE

It has long been known that political institutions and political behavior reflect attitudes and behavior patterns that are "pre-political" in nature and the result of a process of historical growth. The notion of "national character" has a long and unhappy history, for it serves as a highly impressionistic, subjective, frequently prejudiced, and all-too-facile explanation of political behavior.

Because of the easy perversion and unscientific nature of the concept, serious scholars ceased using it for a while, particularly as it ran counter to the humanist and universalist ideologies of both Liberal Democratism and Marxist Socialism. But it remained standard procedure to introduce descriptions and analyses of contemporary political institutions with a sketch of the "historical background" and the "social structure" of the polity; obviously with the assumption that some connection existed between the historically grown "culture" of a society and the workings of its political institutions. Every discussion of British government refers to Bagehot's description of the English as a "deferential" people; which is supposed to explain the continued and largely unchallenged dominance of British politics by members of a traditional elite.

The development and acceptance of the "culture concept" — first by anthropologists and later by social scientists in general — gave renewed stimulus to the insistence that the political process could not be understood as an isolated phenomenon, and that the functioning of institutions depended on perceptions, valuations, and expectations that members of society — to an unknown

1

extent — shared with each other. This "culture" expressed itself in and was transmitted and modified by institutions — family, school, factory — which could be considered more "basic" than political institutions in shaping attitudes affecting the processes in the political sphere. Political events following the First and Second World Wars — the collapse of democratic institutions in Central and Eastern Europe, the rise of a particularly brutal form of totalitarianism in the "advanced" Germany of 1933, the varied and fluid political experiments in the emergent "third" part of the world — further directed scholars' attention to the question of the relation between "national cultures" and political behavior.

The importance of the problem explains the wealth of studies that have been published in recent decades dealing with the concept of "political culture."[1] Its multidimensionality and complexity explain the extreme diversity of approaches, conceptual apparatus, and techniques that characterize various scholarly studies. "Political culture" has no clearly defined borders. It has been understood to include not only the political (and some nonpolitical) perceptions and attitudes of members of a society, but also the processes by which individuals have come to adopt them. Thus it involves the "socialization" of personality — at various levels of interaction within an environment that is "historical," changing in ways that the contemporary observer finds hard to describe precisely.[2] The methods by which these multiple and dynamically interacting variables can be accurately grasped and evaluated do not exist today, and may, given the nature of the problem, forever escape our reach.

But the difficult nature of the enterprise has not prevented scholars from gaining many insights, however diverse and unsystematized, that enlarge our horizon, make us perceive differences and similarities hitherto unexpected, challenge traditional generalizations, and — in my view most important — stimulate us to ask questions and formulate hypotheses. Because of the diversity of methodological approaches, we have to be extremely careful in making comparisons; however, a consideration of conclusions based on different methods will lead us to tentative hypotheses, and to the search for common approaches to the variables that we have observed.

The variety of approaches is clearly apparent in the selections that follow. The methods range from historical analysis to depth interviews and aggregate

---

[1] The article "National Character and Modern Political Systems," by Alex Inkeles, reprinted in Polsby, Dentler, Smith (eds.), *Politics and Social Life* (Boston: Houghton Mifflin, 1963), provides a useful introduction to and summary of work done in the field as well as an extensive bibliography. For a more recent collection mirroring the diversity of approaches, see *Political Culture and Political Development,* edited by L. W. Pye and S. Verba (Princeton, N. J.: Princeton University Press, 1965).

[2] Thus, in reviewing *Political Culture and Political Development* (see Footnote 1), Aristide R. Zolberg writes: "One comes away with the impression that the domain of

data based on large-scale, cross-national surveys. But the selections have not been chosen to illustrate the diversity of approaches. That they do so reflects my principle (admittedly a subjective criterion) to choose those statements that seem to me to provide the greatest insights, by whatever method they were gained; and to find studies dealing with common questions in various democratic systems. They succeed, in my view, in throwing light on the fundamental — and still so obscure — question of how individuals perceive their relation to the centers of political power, in what way these perceptions relate to their actions (or nonactions) in the political sphere and ultimately affect the functioning of the institutions of political decision making.

All these selections are linked to political systems described as "democracies" — systems in which citizens are legally entitled and normatively expected to participate in the process of decision making. Therefore, popular perceptions and actions affect the viability of the political system and the manner in which the "allocation of values" proceeds. It must be understood that these pieces deal with the "bottom" level of perceptions and actions — the level most remote from the ultimate center of policy making. Furthermore, the linkage between the two levels is indirect, mediated by transmission belts, elites of various kinds, and structural elements of a complex system. Therefore we cannot make simple statements about the impact of a particular form of political culture or subculture on the democratic process.

It should be added that studies that are not based on national sample surveys necessarily run up against the problem of their representativeness, or — as in historical analyses — their "validity." On the other hand, "representative" surveys necessarily neglect the differential weight of various groups, with their possibly diverse and opposed subcultures, within the political process.

The simple conclusion is that it is not now possible to provide a "valid" picture of a particular political culture, nor justified to assume a clear (not to speak of one-directional) relation between that political culture and the workings of the political system. This, however, does not relieve us of the need to be precise and imaginative (and cautious) in our inevitable speculations regarding this relation.

The following selections are meant to point up differences and similarities, and thus to raise questions — not to provide substantiated answers, which are to be found, if at all, only in full-scale investigations yet to be undertaken.

'political culture' is indeed extremely broad. . . . Political culture ultimately appears to include not only beliefs, cognitions, values, and symbols pertaining to politics, but also mechanisms for socialization and recruitment, political history, and political institutions . . ." (*American Political Science Review, LX/1*, March 1966, pp. 120–121).

1. Modernity and Tradition in Britain

STANLEY ROTHMAN

Though Professor Rothman does not explicitly use the concept of political culture, he gives a multidimensional analysis that focuses on those aspects of British society that help explain the gradual emergence of a stable democracy. His use of a historical approach allows him to integrate social, ideological, and institutional variables that probably defy integration through a more precise, "behavioral" method.

With the increasing study of non-Western societies it is becoming ever more apparent that the countries of the West, whatever differences may exist among them, form part of a common European civilization. It seems, therefore, that a fruitful approach to analysis of the social and political systems of any Western country is to seek a dynamic understanding of the particular combination of Western elements that have characterized them — and thus to develop a common set of categories for comparisons both among Western nations and between Western and non-Western nations. In this essay such an approach is applied to Britain. My thesis is that the structure and dynamics of British social and political life are to be understood in terms of the traditional society out of which modern Britain emerged, and the particular manner in which the transition to modernity developed. More specifically, it is argued that a crucial key to understanding British social and political life is the fact that Britain entered upon modernity as a *Gemeinschaft*, to use a term coined by Tönnies, that is, a collectivity whose members are bound together by *affective* ties to the collectivity itself, and to each other as members of the collectivity.

I do not, of course, maintain that the development of British social and political life is to be explained solely in terms of *Gemeinschaft*. Certainly a complex combination of variables operating over time determined the pattern that emerged; in the nineteenth century, for example, important influences were such factors as Britain's economic supremacy, the role of empire as safety valve, the role of Methodism. My point is that a particular pattern of social relations did develop, and that as such it played an autonomous causal role. In effect this pattern represented the nationalization of the class structure and attitudes that had been characteristic of the mediaeval manor. And as a result, British political and social life has been characterized, at least until recently, by a unique synthesis of traditional elements and the forces that transformed them. For example, the emergence of democratic conceptions of authority in the nineteenth and twentieth centuries was associated, as Bagehot and later

SOURCE: Reprinted by permission from *Social Research* (Autumn 1961), pp. 297–320. Footnotes are abridged.

commentators have noted, with the maintenance of a deferential society and a governing class characterized by strong feelings of *noblesse oblige*.

In what follows I shall attempt to demonstrate that these propositions systematize features of British social and political life that have heretofore been explained by ad hoc propositions or not explained at all, and that they enable us to make meaningful and systematic comparisons between the British social and political systems and those of other Western countries. For such comparisons I shall refer primarily to France and the United States. And my analysis will focus primarily on political life.

I

The British introduced Europe, and we may say the whole world, to "modernity." It was in Britain that the practical, that is, industrial, use of modern science had its beginnings, and it was there that the Calvinist sects sprang up which provided the psychological basis for capitalist entrepreneurship. It was in Britain, too, that the multiplicity of sects springing from Calvinism itself (and from the destruction of a central religious authority which was a concomitant of the break with Rome) prepared the way for the erosion of a psychologically compelling religious view of the universe, and hence for the emergence of the secular world view. Thus the modern outlook sprang naturally, as it were, from British soil. This may go a long way to explain why the rifts that developed in other countries, where the new was introduced from the outside, and where "modern" men had to struggle with far "stickier" societies, never reached full proportions in Britain. It also explains why many traditional social patterns retained their viability in the face of dramatic change. They could more easily be accommodated to the social-economic and ideological revolution to which they had given birth than was the case with other nations.

One of the key variables here is that England had developed many of the characteristics of a modern nation before the economic and social revolutions of the eighteenth and nineteenth centuries — indeed, much earlier. Henry VIII could consummate the break with Rome with relative ease, in part because he no longer had to compete with a powerful quasi-independent aristocracy, and because Britons, bound together by a common law and a set of national institutions, thought of the Roman church as a foreign church. Thus England escaped the religious upheavals that rent the continent. And, even more important, the liberal economists and political theorists of a later period felt far less need to completely transform traditional patterns than did reformers in other countries. Among the aims of all continental reformers was the development of an integrated national state under a common law. Traditional English society was characterized by both.

But the fact that England had developed national institutions before the reformers' attack on traditional modes of thought and action meant that these institutions and the modes of thought associated with them retained important traditional elements. Eighteenth-century England, in practice as well as theory, was more than a mere aggregation of atoms bound together by law or force. The "estates" of the realm were functionally related to one another by traditionally defined rights, duties, and attitudes. It was as if the state were the mediaeval manor writ large — as if the sense of mutual responsibilities which had theoretically characterized the manor had been transferred to the national level. Thus the state played a continuing role in regulating conditions of work, and secular authorities took over from the Church the care of the indigent and poor through a system of outdoor relief that reached its culmination in the Speenhamland system of 1795. And we find here a governing class willing, despite some grumbles, to support "poor rates" that were quite high. Comparison with France is instructive. As Trevelyan notes: "The worst horrors of failure, of unemployment or of unprovided old age were not suffered by the poor in England to the same extent as in the continental countries of the ancient regime. The regiments of beggars, such as continued to swarm in the streets of Italy, and of France under Louis XIV, were no longer over here . . . That is one reason . . . why through all our political, religious and social feuds from the Seventeenth to the Nineteenth Centuries the quiet and orderly habits of the people, even in times of distress, continued upon the whole as a national characteristic."[1] I certainly do not want to suggest that English social life at this point was idyllic, but for present purposes it is the comparison that is important.

Modernity, the rapid industrialization that transformed traditional societies, came to the Western world in the form of liberal capitalism, of which the intellectual grandfather was John Locke and the most systematic British exponents were the philosophic radicals. The premises of liberalism stood in direct antithesis to the assumptions of the society it sought to transform. For natural inequality it substituted natural equality, each man counting as one. For a view of secular history as a series of events it substituted a conception of history as the development toward a future in which men would become happier and more moral as they achieved increasing control over nature. For reliance on the traditional ways of doing things it substituted the method of reason and the standard of utility. It accepted and even welcomed changing patterns of social life. In economic thought it idealized the free market, and attacked all limitations on the natural play of economic laws, whether these resulted from tariffs, guilds, the regulation of wages, or poor rates. It equated the good life with the life of economic wellbeing, and subordinated other values to those of economic expansion. It expected continued technological and economic progress. The philosophic reaction to liberal capitalism came in the form of the rationalization of tradition, that is, conservative thought, and the clash between the advocates of the new and the defenders of the old took a variety of forms.

In the United States, with its general lack of traditional social patterns, no substantial conservative orientation emerged. The premises of liberal thought were regarded as natural, and were accepted almost immediately, with an interpretation that was democratic, egalitarian, and atomistic. As Hartz points

---

[1] George Trevelyan, *Illustrated English Social History*, vol. 2 (New York 1942) p. 88.

out,[2] the United States thus skipped the traditional stage of European society, and began life essentially as a modern nation. As a result, American society was never characterized by the sharp ideological conflicts that developed in European nations. Ideological conflict involves basic disagreements on the nature of legitimate political authority and the goals of political action. And sharp as labor-capital conflicts became in this country, the fact is that both groups were committed to essentially a liberal-capitalist outlook, and hence the situation cannot be described in terms of ideological conflict. Compared to developments in almost every other nation in the world since the early nineteenth century, the changes experienced by the United States have been relatively marginal.

The development in France is illustrative. While Americans drew the most radical theoretical implications from Locke, these did not produce radicalism on the practical level, for they described substantially what existed. In France too the premises of liberalism yielded radical consequences almost immediately, but there the same theoretical conclusions, and the attempt to carry them out, could only mean violent social upheaval and further radicalization. (This helps explain the ambivalence with which Americans like Jefferson regarded the French Revolution: they could not help but agree with the ideas of the revolutionaries, but they recoiled from the results of those ideas and from the kind of men whom really radical social changes generally bring to power.) In France the "stickiness" of preexisting social patterns resulted in Jacobinism, the emergence of an intransigent conservatism, and the development of a persistent fault in French society that finds its violent echoes down to the present.

British development exhibits still another pattern. Whig historians have written of the triumph of liberalism, and socialists of the triumph of the middle class and of capitalism. Actually neither of these interpretations is completely satisfactory, for the actual course of events involved an intermingling of liberal and traditional views of society. As with Calvinism itself, liberalism was transformed even as it transformed the traditional community out of which it emerged. The result was that while Britain became more and more liberal as the nineteenth century proceeded, so liberalism took on increasing traditional content. In this process the fact that Britain was already a national community played an important role: it muted the inherently radical premises of conflicting ideologies, thus permitting the pragmatic handling of issues arising from violent social changes; and in some areas it even inhibited the very conception of thought patterns that might tend to shatter the stability of the community. Thus the logical consequences of liberal premises were muted on the levels of both thought and action. The liberal attack on the Establishment was never a total attack, and conservatives never held on to the point of no return. Later, when the area of conflict shifted and a socialist movement developed, the pattern repeated itself.

The consequences of the liberal idea were many: the gradual extension of the suffrage through the great reform bills; the establishment of free trade,

---

[2] Louis Hartz, *The Liberal Tradition in America* (New York 1955).

culminating in the repeal of the Corn Laws; the new Poor Law of 1834; and so on. Politically the result was a society that was becoming more and more democratic, with consequent shifts in the distribution of power. Economically the result was the creation of a society that for a short time approached the model of laissez faire — but only for a short time and never completely, for at the same time that a new "economic" Poor Law was being introduced, so were factory acts. And the pace of social reform of this type increased as the century wore on, to culminate in the National Insurance Act of 1911, providing for universal unemployment insurance, old-age protection, and a very extensive system of free medical care.

Again it should be emphasized that the history of social and economic change cannot be associated solely with either a party or a social class. Conservatives in Britain accepted significant portions of the new economics and the new politics, and the Whigs (liberals) accepted the idea of community responsibility, despite the heavy weight they attached to the arguments of the liberal economists. Classic liberalism assigned very little role to the state aside from the maintenance of law and order (and American liberals, until the New Deal period, were committed to this point of view). But British liberals, almost from the beginning, implicitly considered the state to have a creative role in transforming the will of the community into action, if only to eliminate feudal abuses.

A notable area in which liberal theory was quickly eroded in action was its acceptance of the legitimacy of trade-union organization. In the classic liberal view, labor was a commodity to be bought as cheaply as possible, and any limitation on free contract, in the form of associations of men, was thought to be a positive evil. Here again, however, a large number of Britons, while accepting the views of the "economists" in theory, felt that workers had as much right to protect their interests as the masters — a reflection of the traditional view of society as made up of organized estates. This comes out quite clearly in the debates on the Combination Acts of 1824 and 1825, especially the latter. At neither time did the point of view that labor had no right to organize command substantial support. The only question really raised dealt with the limitations to be placed on trade-union activity. Again the capstone was the insurance act of 1911, which, by providing that benefits be paid through friendly societies, almost compelled individuals to join unions and fostered their ever more rapid growth. In contrast to the United States, where the organization of "interests" has always been regarded as somewhat sinister, all British governments have discussed proposed legislation with the interests affected, and have even encouraged the amalgamation of different organizations representing the same interest, so that consultations might be more readily completed.

Traditional histories of the working-class movement tend to emphasize the workers' "struggle" for the recognition of "rights." Without denying the fact of opposition and even sharp conflict, one is struck by the relative rapidity with which working-class organization was accepted in Britain as compared with either France or the United States. Trade unions were not legalized in France until 1884, and until 1890 the French worker had to carry a *livret* or be accounted a vagabond; he handed it to his employer when he took a job and could not take another unless his employer signed and returned the book to him, thus indicating that all obligations had been met. While legal prohibitions were not nearly so severe in the United States, there too the individualistic orientation of both employers and workers seriously inhibited the formation of trade unions. In Britain, moreover, the amount of violence attending conflicts between labor and capital was relatively small. Workers preferred letters to the *Times* and an appeal to the general will of the community to mounting the barricades. And capitalists were willing to yield under pressure rather than maintain a completely intransigent position. The willingness to compromise built on itself. British employers, in contrast to the French, did not think of trade-union leaders as irresponsible revolutionaries, and trade-union leaders came to expect the possibility of gains based on peaceful action. I am aware, of course, that this picture flies in the face of conventional discussions of the nineteenth century, but so far as I can determine, the evidence for it, if one takes a comparative view, is overwhelming.

Before turning to the development of British political life, I wish to add a word on the emergence of modern socialism. This is not simply, in my opinion, a concomitant of industrialization or of liberal capitalism. If it were, a socialist party of substantial size should have developed in the United States. It seems more reasonable to search for the origins of Western socialism in the particular relationships that characterized European society. More specifically, following Hartz and Ulam,[3] I would argue that a key factor was the emergence of liberal capitalism, that is, bourgeois society, out of a preexisting feudal society. According to this view, the class consciousness of European workers and their reaction to the imperatives of industrialism and the atomism of liberalism are related to two main factors: the tension between the continuing class consciousness of the European bourgeoisie and the promise of liberalism; and the tension between the imperatives of a liberal-capitalist society and an awareness of what had been before. Certainly socialism's intellectual attack on liberalism combines the insights of the conservative reaction to liberal society with the liberal promise of equality and affluence.

But if the class consciousness of the worker explains the ultimate attraction of a working-class party, what explains the relative moderation of British socialism as a movement? Is not part of the answer to be found in the relative muting, in Britain, of the implications of liberal thought, from which socialism took its promise, and in the social content that almost immediately infused British liberalism?

In Britain the intellectuals who embraced socialism were, by and large, far from being in total rebellion against the society they wished to change. The fact that the state constantly intervened to ameliorate economic evils took the edge off social protest. And the success of trade unions, first of the skilled and then of the unskilled, gave workers a stake in the system. Not only did it provide a career open to talents for the most dynamic of the workers, but it

---

[3] Hartz (cited above) and Adam B. Ulam, "The Historical Role of Marxism and the Soviet System," in *World Politics*, vol. 8 (October 1955) pp. 20–45.

gave them a sense of belonging to an estate whose interests were represented. Here the history of the first and second generations of the leaders of the unskilled is instructive. The pattern is typified by the career of Ernest Bevin: beginning as a member of the Social Democratic Federation, he gradually sloughed off his radicalism as he achieved power at the head of a highly successful trade union. This was not, of course, a question of betrayal or of the "aristocratic embrace," but rather an acceptance of the legitimacy of a system of which he had become part.

British radicals, even while preaching moderate socialism, refused to attack the basic communal values of the society. Contrast, for example, Clement Attlee and Léon Blum. By 1920 Blum was certainly no longer a *political* revolutionary. Yet throughout his life he mounted a fundamental attack on all of what he considered the "bourgeois" premises of French society, including conceptions of love and the family. Attlee, on the other hand, accepted all of these values; indeed he could not conceive of questioning them. Thus when Blum outlines the future that socialism will bring, his words induce the intellectual excitement of a radical and total attack, but Attlee on this subject is merely dull. In Britain fundamental criticisms of the basic values of the community are left to literati, who are always marginal politically; there, in contrast to France, literary and political criticism hardly ever meet. Radicals from other countries who find haven in England are almost always highly critical of what seems to them the insularity and stuffiness of their English comrades.

II

British politics is characterized by a disciplined two-party system. The fact of two parties it shares with the United States; the fact of disciplined parties it shares, at least in some measure, with the European continent. The combination is almost unique, and can be fully understood only in terms of the previous discussion.

It has frequently been asserted that the existence of a two-party system in Britain is primarily the result of its system of single-member electoral districts, for this system discriminates sharply against minor parties. But this essentially mechanical answer is not satisfactory in and of itself, even though it may represent a factor of significance. The electoral system did not prevent the continued existence of a party that represented a geographically segregated ethnic minority, the Irish: those who continued to support the nationalist cause felt that neither of the major British parties had anything of importance to offer them. And even if a minority were not isolated geographically, but felt strongly enough about certain kinds of issues, it might continue to support the party of its choice despite the discrimination of the electoral system. This was the experience of the Labour Party itself for a number of years, and also of the French Communist Party during 1924–36, when it was heavily discriminated against by the electoral system. In fact is can be argued that discrimination of this kind against powerful minority sentiments may have the result of turning them to violence. Thus while single-member districts may create a tendency toward two parties, the ultimate result may be the replacement of a party system by civil war. Apropos of this, it can be argued that the political polarization that occurred in the United States between 1852 and 1860 was not unrelated to the existence of an electoral system characterized by single-member districts and a popularly elected president.

In other words, if single-member electoral districts are to produce a successful (in the sense of working peacefully over time) two-party system, a precondition is necessary: the society in which the system operates must not be characterized by sharp conflicts. Only under this condition can the major parties absorb the adherents of the minor. If single-member electoral districts have served, in both Britain and the United States, to produce a successful two-party system, they have done so because in some measure the politics of the two countries is pragmatic, founded on basic social consensus.

How then do we explain the differences between the British and American systems, specifically the difference between a disciplined two-party system and one that is not disciplined? Without attempting a total explanation of this complex problem, I would emphasize that one necessary condition for the development of party discipline is that the party be more than a party: it must be a "cause," representing a particular *Weltanschauung*. It is notable that party discipline in Britain reached its maximum only after the emergence of the Labour Party; and what has held the Labour Party together has been the self-imposed discipline not only of the party but also of an electorate to whom party meant everything and the quality of individual leadership meant practically nothing. This has been partly true also of the communists in France and of the socialists and Catholics in Germany, but in the multi-party environments of the continent, where the significance of party "mission" becomes blurred by the fine shadings of political differences, even "radical" parties, or those representing a given religious or ethnic group, have found it more difficult to maintain discipline than has the Labour Party. The discipline that has characterized the British Conservative Party in recent years has been not so much the result of a positive sense of mission as a reflex to the discipline of those who have opposed it within the framework of a two-party system. And in the United States, where a radical party has not developed, for reasons already outlined, this essential ideological basis for party discipline has not existed.

But if we grant the importance of this factor we are faced with what, on the surface, appears to be something of a paradox. Among the necessary conditions of a successful two-party system is the existence of pragmatic politics, but among the necessary conditions of disciplined parties is that, in some sense, they be more than parties — that they represent *Weltanschauungen,* divergent ideologies. How can it be held that both of these seemingly contradictory conditions have obtained in Britain? The answer lies again in the fact that ideological and class conflict has always taken place in Britain within the framework of a more inclusive attachment to the community as such. I suggest that British politics cannot be understood unless these interrelations are recognized.

It has often been argued that the key to a disciplined party system in Britain lies in the continued authority of the Crown, which devolved upon the prime minister — including, and this is what is generally emphasized, the power of dissolution. The effective institutionalization of the power of dissolution in the hands of the prime minister has also been cited — especially by Frenchmen who have seen absence of this power as one of the prime sources of the weakness of the French executive — to explain why British government has effectively become cabinet government while France, at least until the Fifth Republic, remained a parliamentary regime. Undoubtedly the power of dissolution played a role, but the answer is far more complex than this, and in fact the institutionalization of the dissolution power has itself to be explained. Why did the dissolution powers of the French monarchy not devolve upon the prime minister?

Again I would suggest that the development of the dissolution power in Britain, and indeed the whole system of cabinet government, can best be understood in terms of our previous discussion. More specifically, it was *possible* for cabinet government to emerge there because Britain's transition from traditional to modern society was associated not only with the development of class and ideological conflict and hence with the emergence of a disciplined two-party system, but also with the fact that party leaders, convinced of the necessity of effective governance, continued, despite their differences, to assign a creative role to the state as the executive arm of the community. These points can be clarified by comparing British developments with those of France and the United States.

The first precondition of the emergence of cabinet government was the development of a parliamentary regime in which legislative and executive authority was derived from the same body. This occurred in all European countries as the traditional balance among king, aristocracy, and commons tipped toward the commons, and authority came to reside in the institution responsible to the people.

In the United States, however, the political separation and balance of power created by the founding fathers maintained itself. It could do so for a number of reasons. First of all it was not, as in Britain, a social balance. Thus, the president, unlike the English monarch, could combine democracy with authority. But even given this, and the constitutional fetishism that quite early came to characterize American public life, the pattern still might have been different. Had the country been sharply divided into numerous splinters, as was France, we might have slipped into Caesarism. Or had sharp class divisions yielded two disciplined parties, and had Americans felt a strong need for a state capable of carrying out a relatively integrated and active public policy, it is certainly possible that some greater integration between the president and the legislature would have developed. In other words, both the structure and the dynamics of our political system are a result of our having been born a modern nation, that is, a liberal society.

In France, as in England, dissolution was originally part of the prerogative of the monarch. Under the constitution of the Third Republic the power was assigned to the president. It was not used by him after MacMahon and *seize mai*, but there is no logical reason that the power could not have devolved upon a prime minister who was immediately responsible to a parliamentary majority. The reasons it failed to do so are not difficult to uncover. Part of the answer lies in the feeling of the "republicans" that such authority would bring with it the dangers of "reactionary" plebiscitarianism, but of great importance as well was the emergence of a multi-party system from a fragmented political culture.

Such was the nature of this system that in order to become prime minister one needed the support of the Assembly as against the support of one's party. Therefore if one wished to obtain office one did not force deputies to fight another election, in which the issues would, in any event, be unclear and nothing would be resolved. And, in general, those who obtained office were men with a sense of "balance" who, despite differences of ideological nuance, liked and were liked by a reasonably substantial number of deputies. These were men who were, by and large, more oriented to office than to policy. Even during the Fourth Republic, then, when the dissolution power was specifically given to the prime minister, it was used only once. In fact, many potential ministers were forced to promise that they would not make use of this power unless the Assembly supported them. Thus, given the existence of a multiplicity of ideological parties that found it impossible to achieve their ends, individual deputies (with the exception of the communists or the very extreme right) were always tempted to seek the satisfaction of their constituents' immediate demands through mutual backscratching and the power that comes from office. As a result, the political system was such, paradoxically enough, as to transform ideological into pragmatic politics.

In Britain, finally, it was widely agreed that, whatever the balance of political forces, effective government was required. But given the acceptance of popular sovereignty, the emergence of two disciplined parties implied that an effective government could be formed only by the party that possessed a majority, rather than, as had been the case in the middle of the nineteenth century, by intra-parliamentary negotiation. If the leader of that party lost his compact majority his only course, save in exceptional circumstances, was to dissolve the parliament since the breakdown of agreement within a party precluded effective government. And since the electoral fate of his party became bound up with the image of the government and prime minister, his authority was bound to increase, especially since, except in the most rare circumstances, one preferred one's own party in office, whatever one's disagreements with official policy.

This relationship between government and parliament, which emerged with the modern party system in Britain, is what structured the present organization of the Commons. In France and the United States legislators have, for different reasons, been primarily members of the legislature rather than members of a government or an opposition, and thus legislative policy there has been largely determined by a mutual give-and-take among legislators who are anxious both to pass what they consider to be good legislation and to satisfy the interests they represent. But if the legislation that is introduced does not come from a government of trusted colleagues who have at their disposal the bureaucratic apparatus necessary for drawing up a program, the legislature is thrown back on itself. Thus a complex system of subject-matter committees has developed, and the committees, since they acquire the authority and prestige that come from expertise and power over time tables, have drawn to themselves the most dynamic members of the legislature. This, of course, serves to further weaken executive authority. It is no accident that in Britain the subject-matter committees that existed in the eighteenth and nineteenth centuries gradually disappeared, and that all governments today exhibit an unwillingness to restore them, even in very limited areas.

If the system operates effectively in its peculiarly British manner, it is only because, tied in with all of this, are those informal agreements and attitudes that assume Parliament to be a body searching to discover and implement the general will of the community. A majority does not, as it could, ride rough-shod over a minority, but, through informal channels, tries to arrange time tables acceptable to all; and all governments, whatever the size of their major-ity, remain sensitive to minority desires. The symbol of this attitude is that continued cherishing of traditional procedures ("the dignified part of gov-ernment," to use Bagehot's delightful formulation) which never fails to delight American visitors and has always angered rising young radicals.

The importance of the view that the state is a creative instrument whose function it is to serve the general will of the community, and that public servants have a duty to carry out this will, is exemplified in the British bureaucracy. In the 1930s, when the Marxist view of history was popular, it was widely argued that the emergence of an efficient disciplined bureaucracy was tied in with the rise of the middle classes, and that if, in Britain, the bureaucracy had served several masters equally well, this was only because the masters were equally bourgeois parties. At that time it was feared that the coming to power of a Labour government could entail a serious bureaucratic crisis. The fears did not, of course, materialize; the bureaucracy continued to serve different sets of masters with equal diligence. Actually, the Marxist view was invalid in other respects as well. For example, the German bureauc-racy, on which the British reforms of the mid-nineteenth century were based, was developed not by the bourgeoisie but by an aristocratic state. And in the United States the rise of middle-class democracy was associated initially with a complete loss of interest in the ideal of a bureaucratic apparatus consisting of competent men.

But pointing to the errors of the Marxist analysis does not tell us why the British so naturally developed a bureaucracy that combined effectiveness with objectivity. After all, in both France and Germany ideological differences did lead bureaucrats to subvert the governments with whose views they violently disagreed. Again, one cannot argue that it has been *simply* a matter of basic ideological consensus, for in the United States bureaucrats have found them-selves in frequent conflict with administrations or Congressional edicts they did not like, and administrations still feel it necessary to replace top-level officials by members of their own party. Here too the difference between the United States and Britain is partly a consequence of divergent patterns of legislative-executive relationships. However, if middle-class reformers in

Britain were, from the beginning, concerned with the development of an effective bureaucracy, it was, as we have seen, because British liberals always felt the necessity for effective state action. And if they accepted the ideal of the "gentleman" as the model of the bureaucrat, it was because they had, in part, internalized the values of the society they were changing. Finally, if in fact the British public has come to assume that civil servants will carry out political mandates with which they disagree, and if civil servants have accepted this image of themselves, it has been because of a general agreement underlying sharp political differences — an agreement that bureaucrats are the servants of a community interest transcending political conflict, and that their job is to translate the "general will" of the community into effective action.[4]

To complete this discussion we can examine the symbols that serve as shorthand expressions of national unity. The symbols of American consensus, the founts at which we renew our faith, are the Declaration of Independence and the Constitution, documents that enshrine a set of abstract ideas — the "liberal" view of the world. In Britain, on the other hand, the symbol of unity remains the monarchy and all the traditional paraphernalia that go with it. One may attack the monarchy because it fosters a class society, or because, as Keir Hardy and other early Labour Party militants contended, it is a "stupid" archaic institution. Or one may defend it because of its utility as a symbol or because it serves certain psychological needs. But its possible usefulness as a "symbol" does not explain why it is a symbol, and the psychological needs it is sometimes said to fulfill (such as pageantry in a drab world) do not enable us to explain why Americans, who have similar needs, fulfill them in different ways. When all is said and done, neither defense nor attack explains the monarchy's continued attraction for the British people as a symbol of their nationality. It has no real ideological continuity with the past. At one time it was part of a certain kind of society in which it played an integral role, combining dignity with power. Today, like the smile on the Cheshire cat, only the dignity remains. Everyone knows that the prerogative of the monarchy is no more.

If the monarchy does not, like our Constitution, stand for a set of political ideas handed down from the past, what does it stand for? To raise the question in this way is to answer it. It represents the British community qua community, not only at the present moment but in its total development. Thus the attachment to monarchy is a traditional attachment, in the Weberian sense. To be sure, the monarchy could not have survived had it not relinquished political power gracefully, that is, had it not been lifted out of the realm of politics; thus the actual fact of its survival may be, in part, the result of historical accident. However, the accident could not have occurred were it not for the cultural role the monarchy played and has continued to play.

---

[4] See F. M. Marx, *The Administrative State* (Chicago 1957) p. 86. In Germany and France the members of the bureaucratic elite were also "gentlemen" serving a "creative" state; but they identified the "real" state with their own preconceptions in communities that had been shattered by social and ideological upheavals (Germany under Weimar, and France throughout the nineteenth and the first half of the twentieth century).

III

Thus the development of British social and political life has involved a uniquely British synthesis of traditional patterns and the forces that transformed them. The synthesis was possible not only because traditional British society was less "sticky" than its counterparts elsewhere, but because its patterns had taken on a national form before their transformation began. The result has been an organic community with its own peculiar political institutions. No wonder, then . . . the British tend to regard their institutions as peculiarly their own, while both Americans and Frenchmen identify themselves with universal ideas applicable to all peoples.

But what of the future of society and politics in Britain? It is quite apparent that some of the traditional patterns we have been discussing are rapidly eroding, for while traditional British society was able to transform and, in some sense, incorporate modern values and social patterns, there exists a kind of dialectical tension between modernity and tradition. Thus the continuing changes in educational patterns and in income distribution, which were accelerated by the Labour government of 1945, have broken down the barriers between social strata. Just as important has been the increasing rapidity with which Britain and other Western societies have emerged into the era of mass consumption. This breakthrough stems in part, of course, from the belief that the purpose of society is to satisfy the material wants of individuals as consumers, but it is also related to the implications of industrialization and the advance of scientific technology itself. Mass production of cars and clothing masks differences in wealth and status. The advent of radio and television contributes to an ever increasing erosion of class and regional speech patterns, as does the increased geographic mobility associated with the mass production of the automobile and the building of more and more roads.

All these fortify, and partially result from, a society that finds traditional patterns of deference and social responsibility increasingly archaic — one that participates in a more homogeneous "mass" culture, in which relationships are increasingly impersonal. The desire for increased consumption, and the expectations of possible advance, erode working-class loyalties; traditional upper-class patterns of behavior are eroded by the loss of real prestige, of real roots, and of the sense of the legitimacy of *noblesse oblige* and a certain style of life. And the advance of science itself, as well as the felt need for increasing technical competence in the interest of increasing production, erodes traditional concepts of education and culture. These social results, which have been accelerating ever more rapidly since the war, are what both Conservative and "left-wing" Labour Party critics have pointed to when they bewail the "Americanization" of British life. Actually, whatever their merits or evils, they are essentially the outcome of a revolution in economic and social patterns which was European and more specifically British in origin.

These emerging social patterns have already had a considerable effect on political life. The Labour Party has now lost three elections by increasing majorities, and partially as a result its socialism is gradually being watered down. The connection between this development and the social changes in

Britain was pointed out several years ago by G. D. H. Cole: "To one who can look back over more than sixty years, it is remarkable how conditions in Great Britain have changed. Nowadays . . . it is often impossible to tell by looking at a man — or woman — and by hearing them talk, to what class they belong. In these circumstances the struggle between classes . . . necessarily changes its human character. It becomes more and more a contest, not between unlikes, but of like with like."[5]

Paradoxically, the recent resurgence of the "left" within the Labour Party seems to stem, in part, from the very forces that have resulted in Labour's declining electoral fortunes. During the 1930s and earlier the great mass of constituency party and trade-union activists were highly class-conscious working men and women, driven by a desire to obtain greater benefits for their class. They voted for a class party because in a Britain that maintained traditional class distinctions they identified themselves as members of a class; as indicated earlier, their outlook involved an implicit acceptance of much of the traditional pattern of British society. On the whole, however, these men and women have now left or are leaving the party (or becoming relatively inactive), and they are not being replaced in equivalent numbers. Those who remain most active politically tend, therefore, to be "true believers." Their activism stems not from "interest" but from conviction. The Labour Party has always had its quota of this type, but the present situation is qualitatively different, in that their relative number has increased since the party attained the status of a national movement.

The changes have affected the Conservatives too. The Conservative Party, which has won these three victories, is no longer the party even of the interwar years. It has accepted the welfare state as a permanent part of the British scene, and within that framework is willing to compete with Labour in extending social services. Just as importantly, it is no longer — though traces of this remain and can be deceptive — a party whose appeal to the electorate is couched in terms of the natural superiority for leadership of the "better" elements in society. Rather, it is now a political organization whose professed aim is to give the voters what they want and to provide an open, not a class, society, in which individuals have equal opportunity to rise to their "natural" level.[6]

Thus as traditional elements in British life have declined they have been replaced by an "idea" consensus associated with social patterns that are more and more "modern." And it is quite likely, assuming no great depression or other catastrophe, that the political parties will move ever closer together in the nature of their appeals, and that, like American political parties, or British parties in the mid-nineteenth century, they will come to represent coalitions of "interests" (with interests also operating across party lines). In fact, there is every evidence that tendencies in this direction are gaining momentum.[7]

---

[5] G. D. H. Cole, *The Post-War Condition of Britain* (New York 1957) pp. 43–44.

[6] See the Conservative Party's 1959 Election Manifesto, *The Next Five Years.*

[7] See S. H. Beer, "Pressure Groups and Parties in Great Britain," in *American Political Science Review,* vol. 50 (March 1956) pp. 1–23.

But if this is so, what will happen to party discipline, and to a parliamentary structure that is based, according to this analysis, on vanishing social and political patterns? One certainly cannot answer this question with any assurance. If some of the factors that helped determine the shape of British political institutions are disappearing, this does not mean that the institutions themselves will go. Certainly it can be plausibly argued that institutional arrangements of a certain kind can develop an autonomy and maintain themselves, at least unless powerful forces develop which they cannot contain. Thus the bureaucratic organization of the parties, and also the position that the cabinet has attained, may tend to perpetuate present arrangements. It is also possible, however, that these patterns will be gradually replaced by a situation in which Parliament, developing subject-matter committees, begins once again to assert its prerogative, in a system not too unlike that of Sweden, for example. In this case a whole generation of American political scientists will have to radically revise its thinking.

2. Germany: The Remaking of Political Culture

SIDNEY VERBA

German political behavior presents a crucial case for the study of the rela-tion between political culture and democratic politics. How are present-day German political attitudes and practices, generally supportive of de-mocracy, related to underlying factors of personality and social structure? Sidney Verba, who directed jointly with Gabriel Almond a comparative five-nation survey that resulted in the volume The Civic Culture *(Prince-ton, N. J.: 1963), uses some data thus obtained for the present analysis. It is not possible, though, to interpret the survey data without reference to the historical dimension, which provides meaning to responses such as those relating to "pride in system."*

German Political Attitudes Since the War

Postwar prognostications of the future of Germany were gloomy. However difficult it had been to create a viable democracy in Germany after World War I, the situation after World War II was worse. Destruction and disillu-sionment were much greater. Furthermore students of Germany had come to the conclusion that the roots of Nazism and German authoritarianism were more than political; that they lay within German character and social structure. In particular the German inability to achieve democracy was traced to the family. Within the family the German child was brought up to expect relationships of domination from authority figures. The father-dominated family (one writer wrote of the mother-dominated family, but the impact on the child was the same) created submissive and dependent individuals. The expectations for the future of Germany were particularly gloomy with respect to youth. They had been raised under the Nazis and knew no other value system; yet this value system and the society based on it collapsed in 1945. And with the collapse came physical destruction and disruption of family life. The prediction for the future was a German youth made up of Nazi fanatics and aimless anomic youth bands.

One was faced then with a picture of a Germany in which a vicious ideology either lived on to create havoc for the society or had disappeared leaving a vacuum in its place; in which the basic formative institutions of society, family, and school produced citizens who yearned for domination; and in which the

SOURCE: Reprinted by permission of Princeton University Press, copyright owners, from *Political Culture and Political Development*, L. W. Pye and Sidney Verba (eds.) (1965); pp. 136–146, from Sidney Verba, "Germany: The Remaking of Political Culture." Footnotes are abridged.

physical destruction was so great as to suggest that little energy would be available for political reconstruction. Yet the gloomy predictions about the future of Germany have not been fulfilled. In this paper we shall examine some data on postwar German attitudes in order to describe how those attitudes have developed since the war, to suggest some reasons why they did not develop as predicted, and to assess the relationship of these attitudes to the potentiality for democracy in Germany.

In describing the state of German attitudes toward politics since World War II the researcher has available to him a wealth of material. The interest of the occupying powers in the potentialities for German democracy led to a long series of public opinion polls by the military government and, later, by the office of the High Commissioner for Germany. These have been supplemented by numerous studies of German political attitudes by German scholars. In fact, in terms of the amount of data about basic political attitudes the researcher is probably better equipped to deal with Germany than with any other nation. There is a large volume of survey material available for Britain and the United States as well, but little of it displays the constant, self-conscious concern with questions of basic political orientation and the acceptance of democracy. (The fact that so many introspective questions are asked about problems — attitudes toward democracy, the state, politics in general — which are presumably not considered problematic in other nations is in itself a significant bit of information about the nature of German political culture.)

But though there is no shortage of material, a few words are in order about some problems of interpreting these data. It is hard to say what the implication of the response to any particular public opinion poll question means for the problem of democracy in Germany. If one finds a substantial proportion of the population responding in ways one would assume are not supportive of democracy, one can point out that in democracies more successful than Germany one also finds political attitudes that do not fit the expectations one would have as to democratic attitudes.[1] On the other hand, the meaning of answers which indicate adherence to democratic norms and practices may also be hard to interpret. Does the expression of agreement with normative propositions of democratic theory represent lip service to what is assumed to be a proper norm, or does it involve a commitment with significant behavioral implications?[2] The former is not unimportant, but it is obviously quite differ-

---

[1] Studies of voting behavior in the United States have consistently shown relatively low levels of political knowledge and political involvement. See in particular Angus Campbell et al., *The American Voter*, New York, Wiley, 1960, Chap. 10. See also Samuel A. Stouffer, *Communism, Conformity and Civil Liberties*, Garden City, New York, Doubleday, 1955, for some disturbing data on the support among Americans of certain civil liberties. See also James W. Prothro and Charles M. Grigg, "Fundamental Principles of Democracy: Bases of Agreement and Disagreement," *Journal of Politics*, Vol. 22, 1960, pp. 275–294.

[2] How, for instance, is one to interpret the fact that 63 per cent of a sample in the American Zone of Germany in 1948 said "yes" to the question, "In the future, should the people have more influence on political activities or not?," when in the same sample 75 per cent of former members of the Nazi Party said, "yes," to the same question. See Office of

ent from the latter. There are no easy answers to these questions, but the reader is forewarned that the response to any particular question must be interpreted with caution. To give responses some framework, we shall deal at several points with some problems for which comparable data exist from other nations (particularly the data gathered by Almond and myself in *The Civic Culture*) as well as with problems for which one can trace changes over time so that we can see in what direction the system is moving.

The German Citizen Views the Political System

The most obvious characteristic of contemporary German political attitudes — especially in the light of the postwar predictions — is their conservative nature. The electorate has supported the moderate and broad-based parties of the middle, while the more radical right-wing and narrowly oriented refugee parties that appeared to be gaining strength at the beginning of the Bonn Republic have dropped in strength. The political attitude of "no experimentation" is reflected in a general security-consciousness and conservatism of German youth, the group from which one might have expected the greatest degree of volatility. In a 1956 study of German youth 79 per cent of the respondents reported that they would prefer a secure and low-paying job to a less secure but higher-paying one;[3] and in a similar survey 68 per cent of German youth said they would prefer a job with a lower salary and a pension plan than a higher salary and no pension plan.[4]

This conservatism is reflected in the lack of intensity of German attitudes toward politics. Consider for instance the attitudes toward the particular regime in power. A series of polls taken over a decade indicates a striking stability in the public's evaluation of Adenauer's performance as Chancellor. Both the proportion that considered his work "very good" and the proportion considering his work "bad" have hovered around 10 per cent going neither much higher nor much lower, while the bulk of the population fell in between.[5] These results do not indicate overwhelming support for Dr. Adenauer but neither do they indicate strong opposition. And what is most important — given the history of intense partisan rivalry in pre-Nazi Germany

---

Military Government for Germany (U.S.), Surveys Division, Report 88, January 20, 1948. (Reports of this sort will hereafter be cited as *OMGUS*, Report No. ———.)

[3] *Basic Orientation and Political Thinking of West German Youth and Their Leaders*, Frankfurt am Main, DIVO Institut, 1956, p. 31.

[4] Elisabeth Noelle Neumann and Erich Peter Neumann, *Jahrbuch der Öffentlichen Meinung, 1957*, Allensbach am Bodensee, Verlag für Demoskopie, 1957, p. 135 (hereafter referred to as *Jahrbuch, 1957*). Karl Deutsch and Lewis Edinger report a similar caution and conservatism in relation to attitudes on foreign policy. See their *Germany Rejoins the Powers*, Stanford, Stanford University Press, 1959, Chap. 2.

[5] *EMNID Information*, October 1958, No. 42. If one looks at less intensely phrased responses than the responses that Adenauer's policies were "very good" or "bad," one finds a larger proportion supporting him. Thus, during his tenure of office, the proportion saying they "generally agree" with his policies stayed around 40 to 50 per cent with only a few fluctuations above or below. See Erich P. Neumann and Elisabeth Noelle, *Statistics on Adenauer*, Allensbach, 1962, pp. 40–44.

— is the fact that expressions of support are often found among supporters of parties other than Adenauer's own CDU. Perhaps this attitude of neither strong support nor strong opposition toward Adenauer is the same as the German attitude toward the Bonn Republic and to democracy in general. Since the formation of the Bonn Republic the numbers favoring a democratic form of government or a multi-party system over a single-party system have steadily increased. The proportion saying that democracy was the best form of government for Germany increased from 57 per cent in 1953 to 74 per cent in 1960, though a fairly steady 20 per cent replied that they do not know what government is best for Germany; and the proportion thinking it is better to have more than one political party rose steadily from 61 per cent in 1951 to 76 per cent in 1956.[6] And the proportion perceiving the Bonn political system as democratic — for instance, the proportion believing that one can speak his mind freely in Germany — also consistently goes up.[7] Figures of this sort are hard to interpret. Which is the significant finding — that "as many as" 70 per cent of the German respondents say that democracy is the best form of government, or that "as many as" 30 per cent say they think some other form is better or they do not know? Information of this sort tells us little about the state of German political opinions.[8] Perhaps more important than the reaction to the word "democracy" is the nature of democracy Germans believe they have or would like to have.

In one of the first postwar sociological studies of German youth by a German, Gerhard Baumert wrote that "when the American army brought great quantities of the basic necessities that the Europeans needed for survival, the notion 'democracy' became closely connected in the minds of German youth with the notions 'food, clothing, abundance.'"[9] This quotation suggests that "democracy" and what has come to be called the "economic miracle" are closely interconnected in German attitudes, and the evidence supports this proposition. It is not so much an intellectual connection between the terms democracy and economic progress. When asked to name the most important characteristics of democracy, less than 2 per cent of respondents in each of five different polls conducted from 1953 to 1959 mentioned economic advancement, and most respondents mentioned various freedoms or rule of the people.[10] The connection between democracy and the economic miracle lies

---

[6] *EMNID Information*, May, July, September and October (Nos. 19, 28, 35, and 40) 1960, and *Jahrbuch, 1957*, p. 259.

[7] *Jahrbuch, 1957*, p. 165.

[8] Less structured questions may be more useful. The more unstructured the question, the less chance there is for individuals to answer with slogans. On unstructured questions the proportion favoring democracy tends to be quite a bit lower. In an analysis of a large series of systematic group discussions, for instance, it was found that about 10 per cent of the statements were prodemocratic; about 67 per cent were mixed, and about 27 per cent antidemocratic. See Friedrich Pollock, *Gruppenexperiment: Ein Studienbericht*, Frankfurt am Main, Europäische Verlagsanstatt, 1955, pp. 139–140.

[9] Gerhard Baumert, *Jugend der Nachkriegszeit*, Darmstadt, Edward Roether Verlag, 1952, p. 198.

[10] *EMNID Information*, January 1959, No. 5.

in the fact that a good deal of the orientation of the individual to the state in Germany is a rather pragmatic orientation in which the economic services the state can provide are considered important. In 1947 Germans were asked, "Which of these two forms of government would you personally choose as better: a government which offers people economic security and a chance to make a good living, or a government which guarantees freedom of speech, suffrage, press, and religion?" Sixty-two per cent replied that they favored a government which provided economic security, while 26 per cent preferred a government which guaranteed freedom. (The rest had no opinion.)[11] It is probable that the dichotomy is a false one and that there is hope one would not have to choose, but it is instructive to note that, forced to choose, German respondents chose economic security. When an identical question was asked at the same time in the United States, 83 per cent chose freedom, while 12 per cent chose economic security.[12] Given the state of the German economy in 1947, one would expect answers of this sort, but three years later an almost identical percentage answered the same question the same way.[13] However, this still may reflect more a postitive need for economic progress than a negative reaction to democratic government. In 1950, for instance, 58 per cent of the employed respondents wanted a government that stressed economic security, whereas 74 per cent of those unemployed considered this most important. (There is a less clear relationship with income level.)

The fact that Germans tended at the time of the founding of the Federal Republic to view the government as an economic and social service agency rather than as a guarantor of freedom and democracy has led to concern about the future of democracy in Germany. An attachment to a particular form of government based upon the economic performance of that government is too fragile. If the economic level falls, so may the government. Long-run political stability probably depends upon a more general commitment to the political system as legitimate over and above its day-to-day performance. But the fact that at the time of its founding the Bonn government was looked on as a system with mainly an economic task is not in itself cause for despair. Such a political orientation is to be expected in a situation in which economic needs are great. Furthermore it may be that through experience with the political system as an effectively functioning unit — one under which the economic demands of individuals are satisfied — a more general, positive attachment to the political system can be created. One would not, for instance, expect Germans after World War II to become suddenly converted to democracy in the normative and affective sense — that is, suddenly to come to accept democratic values as the proper ones to follow and suddenly to come to feel a strong and diffuse attachment to democracy per se. The political attitudes that would support democracy are not of a form to which one can suddenly become converted —

---

[11] *OMGUS* Report 74, October 27, 1947.

[12] National Opinion Research Center, *Opinion News,* August 1, 1948.

[13] Office of the High Commissioner for Germany, Office of Public Affairs, Reactions Analysis Staff, Report No. 50, Ser. 2, November 30, 1950 (hereafter referred to as *HICOG* Reports).

as one might be converted rather quickly to a more comprehensive and inclusive ideology. Rather, the political culture which would support democracy is a complicated mixture of norms, perceptions, and behaviors — a mixture in which many of the components are implicit and some are indeed inconsistent with others. It is not through formal teaching that one learns what is the right system (though teaching plays a role), but through a long and often indirect socialization process as well as through experience with participation in a democratic system. Thus experience over an extended period with a government which is adequately performing the task it is primarily expected to perform (in the German case maintaining the economy) may create other forms of attachment to the system over and above the pragmatic one based upon performance. If the economic recovery can retain the luster of a miracle and if the political system can operate in a way that fosters participation and adherence to democratic norms, then it may be possible to transfer the pragmatic attachment toward politics to a more thoroughgoing acceptance of the democratic system.

How long does it take for this transfer to take place? It is hard to say since it depends upon so many factors, but it may well be a slow process. The question one can ask about Germany is whether there is any evidence for the beginning of a generalization from the economic performance of the system to a more general political attachment. The decline of radical parties and of ideological politics suggests that the performance of the system has reduced any sharp rejection of the Bonn government. But it is less clear that there has been developed any more diffuse positive sense of attachment to the political system. For one thing, though economic reconstruction was considered the task of the new German government, there is less evidence that the government is given direct credit for the economic miracle. When asked to name the factors underlying the economic miracle about 12 per cent of a German sample credited it to the activities of the government. Most respondents talked of the industriousness of the Germans (41 per cent) or of foreign aid (21 per cent) — though perhaps the latter should be considered an indirect praise of the Bonn government.[14] This in itself may not be that significant. It may be more important that the economy in Germany creates a stable environment in which political attitudes can develop and change than that the government itself be given credit for the economic environment.

The kind of commitment to the political system that one finds has two characteristics: (1) it involves a certain pragmatic — perhaps even cynical — view of politics, combined with (2) the absence of the kind of intense rejection of politics that this pragmatic detachment might engender. In 1953 a sample of Germans was asked if they believed that the representatives in Bonn considered first the interests of the people or whether they considered first other interests. Thirty-nine per cent replied that Bonn considered the interests of the people first, 41 per cent mentioned other interests (personal interests, party interests, or specific interest groups), and 24 per cent said they did not know. It is hard to say how high a level of cynicism toward the Bonn government this

---

[14] *HICOG* Report, No. 236, June 19, 1956.

represents, but what is significant is that in surveys carried on in the three succeeding years the results remained remarkably stable. By 1956, 38 per cent of the respondents said that the representatives in Bonn are interested primarily in the welfare of the people, 36 per cent said they have other prime interests, and 28 per cent "do not know."[15] Unlike the responses about the desirability of democracy, which did change noticeably even within that short period, the responses that indicate respect for the actual operation of the government in Bonn do not change appreciably. Furthermore the answers about the prime interests of the representatives in Bonn appear to reflect closely the German citizen's own view of what is of prime importance. When asked how they would vote if they had to choose between a vote that would benefit themselves but not Germany, or Germany but not themselves, 37 per cent said they would vote so as to benefit themselves, 33 per cent so as to benefit Germany, and 30 per cent did not know.[16]

The pragmatic and perhaps cynical view of the political system reflected in the above data can best be appreciated in a comparative context. In our study of political attitudes in five nations Almond and I dealt with two types of attachment to the political system, what we call "output affect" and "system affect." The former refers to the level of satisfaction the individual expresses with the specific performance of the government; the latter, to his more general and diffuse attachment to the political system as a whole without reference to any particular aspect. In Germany one finds an expression of satisfaction with specific governmental performance more frequently than an expression of attachment to the system as a whole. This fact is highlighted by the comparable data from the other nations studied. In terms of output satisfaction the German data roughly resemble that in the United States and Britain; in terms of system affect the differences are sharp. The absolute levels of system affect are, however, not what is of greatest interest here. Considering recent German history, it is to be expected that a much smaller proportion of individuals would report that they take pride in the political system of their nation (to take the specific measure of system affect used) than would so report in Britain and the United States. Nor is it unexpected that the nations would be more alike in the frequency with which satisfaction with specific governmental performance is expressed; that the latter form of satisfaction can obviously develop more rapidly. What is of greatest interest is whether the level of system affect — of stable and diffuse attachment to the political system not based upon performance — is developing out of contact with the specific activities of the German government. Are contact with the government and

---

[15] *Jahrbuch, 1957*, p. 177. In 1950 a sample of 3,000 Germans in the American Zone were asked: "Do you find that the West German Government keeps the welfare of the West German people in view or do you believe that they primarily follow the aims of their parties?" At that earlier date a higher proportion answered that it kept the views of the West German people in view (52 per cent), but the different phrasing of the question makes the comparison over time a bit difficult (see *HICOG* Report, No. 28, Ser. 2, July 1950).

[16] Elisabeth Noelle and Erich Peter Neumann, *Jahrbuch der Öffentlichen Meinung 1947–1955* (Allensbach am Bodensee: Verlag für Demoskopie, 1956), p. 123.

participation within the political system leading to greater system affect? If so, one can predict that over time the stable functioning of the Bonn government will lead to the development of citizens committed to it over and above its specific performance at any particular time — a form of "rain or shine" commitment that may be necessary for long-run stability.

Data collected by Almond and me are relevant here. We divided our respondents into three groups depending upon the the extent of their subjective sense of ability to participate in and influence the government. This was done on the basis of scores on a scale of "subjective competence." Those who score high on the scale consider themselves capable of influencing the course of government action; those who score low consider themselves incapable. The question we raise is: does a citizen's satisfaction with the government increase, the more he considers himself able to participate in the government? In our data we find that those who consider themselves competent to influence the government are more likely to express satisfaction with the specific output of the government in the United States, in Britain, and in Germany as well. For instance, 75 per cent of the respondents who scored high on the subjective competence scale in Germany (n:244) reported satisfaction with governmental output, in contrast with 62 per cent (n:233) of those who scored low.[17] Thus the individual who believes he can participate in decisions is more likely to express satisfaction with the output of the governmental decision-making process. The relationship between sense of ability to participate and more general system affect produces a sharp contrast to the above pattern. In the United States and Britain general system affect (as measured by the frequency with which individuals express pride in their political system) increases with the level of sense of ability to participate. Those high in sense of competence are more likely to express pride in the political system and less likely to say they are proud of "nothing" as citizens of their nations. In Germany, on the other hand, the pattern is quite different. There is apparently little relationship between an individual's sense of political competence and the likelihood that he will express pride in the political system. High scorers on the subjective competence scale are not more likely to say that they are proud of a political aspect of their nation than are low scorers. Furthermore, although those respondents high in subjective political competence are less likely to say that they do not know what they are proud of as Germans than are those low on subjective competence; they are just as likely to give a rather alienated response that they are proud of "nothing." In Germany the sense of political competence does not appear to be related to a more general sense of system affect.[18]

In Germany, though there is some opportunity to participate and there are some respondents who consider themselves competent to participate, the participation does not lead to a greater sense of identification with the political system. This point must be qualified, however, in that there is a positive

---

[17] See Gabriel Almond and Sidney Verba, *The Civic Culture* (Princeton, N. J.: Princeton University Press, 1963).

[18] *Ibid.*, Chap. 9, Table 5.

relationship between sense of political competence and system affect among those Germans who have attained an educational level beyond the primary school. This suggests that the translation of ability to participate into attachment to the political system may be beginning among those who have attained some higher educational level. Since our data support the proposition that the attainment of a sense of political competence develops earlier among those with higher educational attainment, the fact that it is among these people that the translation into attachment to the political system takes place supports the point that time is what may be needed for experience with the performance of the Bonn government to be translated into a more stable commitment.

But in general the data for Germany suggest that whatever attachment there is to the political system is mainly a pragmatic one. The individual who believes himself capable of participating within the political system is more satisfied with the system, but his satisfaction tends to be with the specific outputs of the system. If the hypothesis about the greater significance of system affect for the long-run stability of a political system is correct, it would appear that the sense of ability to participate in governmental decision processes that has developed since the war in Germany will foster the stability of the system so long as the performance of the system remains at a high level. If the performance of the system lags, the fact that some individuals feel capable of participating may add little to its capacity for survival.

These data as to contemporary German political attitudes must be evaluated, however, in the light of recent German political history — and when seen in this light, the picture is quite a bit brighter. A purely pragmatic politics that involves no emotional or ideological commitment is not a firm basis for a stable democracy, but then neither is its polar opposite. What is needed is a combination of pragmatism and deep commitment. Given the history of Germany's first attempt at democracy during the Weimar Republic — a republic torn by politically intense, and irreconcilable ideologies — the rather stolid pragmatism of politics under Bonn can only be welcomed. The crucial point may not be the fact that there is little deep attachment to the system, but that there is little deep rejection of it. That Germans have a detached and somewhat cynical view of what goes on in politics is important, but it is more important that they do not totally reject the political system because of this — as Weimar politics was often rejected as a rather dirty form of horse trading. One of the reasons Weimar was rejected may be that it was expected to be an ideal democracy, and when it did not live up to that ideal, the rejection was total. If contemporary Germans can see the blemishes in the Bonn democracy and yet not totally reject it, they may have learned a significant political lesson indeed.

3. The View of Government from Eastport

ROBERT E. LANE

In order to obtain his data, Professor Lane intensively interviewed fifteen lower-middle-class citizens of "Eastport" (a fictional name) Connecticut. So far, the study has not been duplicated either in the United States or in other Western democracies, so there is no basis for a comparison between citizens in other parts of the United States or in European cities of similar size. Psychoanalytical techniques and interpretations are significant in Professor Lane's approach.

The political theory of the common man and his image of government focus, naturally enough, upon Congress and the President. In these institutions are gathered together the legitimate reins of power. Who runs things in government? A few said "party leaders," "big shots," "party bosses" — but generally these leaders are thought to have their seat of power on Capitol Hill; the legislature is their theater of operations. Others were more explicit about it — "the inner circle of congressmen," "the congressional leaders." Many who thought "the people" ran things saw this as done through Congress, the agent of the people. Whether it is "the bosses" or "the people" or "congressional leaders," Congress in the fifties is the center of government; it is the main location of power (though, as we shall see, not necessarily of interest). Here Max Lerner, along with others, is wrong. He says, "When the American thinks of government, he thinks first of the President as its symbol."[1] More than two-thirds of the men said that of the three institutions, Congress, the Supreme Court, and the Presidency, it is the Congress that is most important. DeAngelo puts it this way: "Well, they all got their importance. I guess Congress seems to be the important one; they pass all the legislation; they pass all the bills; and they seem to run everything. They have the power."

Making laws, it seems, is the most visible product of government. Asked, "When you think of government, what do you think about?" a common response places lawmaking at the center of things: "Well, it suggests a group of people elected by the people to formulate laws"; "Well, I think of a bunch of men; they get together and, uh, uh, they governmentize our country, lead us, make laws"; "It's a way of taking care of ourselves by choosing leaders and laws." In the fifties, it was hard to locate and appraise the President's contribution, his influence, initiative, policy, responsibility; but the enactment of a law is definite, concrete, important. And the process of *making* one in Congress is public and dramatic, often with an uncertain outcome until the

SOURCE: Reprinted by permission from Robert E. Lane, *Political Ideology* (New York: The Free Press, 1962), pp. 145–160. Footnotes are abridged.

[1] Max Lerner, *America as a Civilization: Life and Thought in the United States* (New York: Simon and Schuster, 1957), p. 377.

very end. "It's here in Congress that the ideas are brought and presented as bills," says Ferrera, "and it's here that they are discussed and either passed or voted down. . . . The President would be the least important." Thus, under Eisenhower, the President presides over government, but he has lost control. The congressional leaders, says DeAngelo, again, "they are running the country. The President is only a figurehead, y'know what I mean." But in the sixties, as in the thirties, this image surely is different.

In this view the Congress is more important than I expected it to be; the President is less important. The emphasis upon law, the deemphasis of leadership, are contrary to what is often said of the common man's personalized image of governmental institutions. The view needs modification. Speaking of the past, the men speak of Presidents, not Congresses. Speaking of the recession, they are hurt that Eisenhower has been so delinquent, rather than angry that Congress has been so slow to act. Speaking of elections, they speak of presidential elections, not congressional or senatorial elections. Speaking of their surprise and wounded feelings over the American failures in rocketry, they discuss the defective intelligence, foresight, and action of "the Administration," not the Congress. Perhaps one can reconcile their views of the current power of Congress with these other phases of their image of government in two ways. One is to allocate time periods differently: past time is for the Presidency; contemporary time is for Congress. Another is to separate responsibility for initiative and responsibility for decision: the President must initiate, the Congress must decide.

Congress, it appears, is an "oral" agency—the congressman's job is one of talking and listening, often quite informally. He is rarely pictured in debate on the floor of the Senate or the House; rather he is seen meeting the folks from back home streaming endlessly through his office; he is answering his mail, traveling to see his constituents. He seems to receive his information and advice in conversation directly from the common man, the people. Not so the President. He *studies* matters, something he can do alone. When he is with others, he *tells* them; he does not listen. Sokolsky says of the President, "Maybe he's at his desk three or four hours a day, and the rest [of the time] he's supposed to be—maybe in the White House there, in the living room, studying the different bills." The idea of presidential advisers is vaguely threatening, partly because it suggests "influence in high places" and partly because it hints at presidential uncertainty.

Congress is responsive; the President is more autonomous. This follows, in a way, from the idea that Congress has an ear cocked for the voice of the people, while the President listens to inner voices. It also follows from the idea that the President proposes, the Congress disposes. Thus DeAngelo thinks of the President as maneuvering from outside: "Most anything that has to be passed, he knows about it. He's informed of it. I suppose he's trying to push his own bills through, you know? I mean, he's got to think of *his* wants." But Congress is not passive—congressmen are positively enjoined to be active supervisors of the public wants. For O'Hara the good congressmen are "not just going along with the party . . . they're looking out for the welfare of all the people he's representing."

Congress looks inward toward the nation; the President looks outward to the world. Congressmen have special duties to their home districts; they are custodians of popular welfare. The President is the custodian of popular safety, national destiny, the conscience of the people. Congress expresses the impulsive immediate needs; the President has a longer view. Congress offers "secondary gain"; the President offers a chance to fulfill the life goals of the nation. Perhaps this is the reason that in normal times they write to their congressmen, if they write at all. In time of national emergency (major depression, conscription, humiliation, as in the missile lag) they write to the President.[2]

Congress is in no way frightening; it is comfortable. The Presidency is, if not frightening, a little awesome, calling, in the imagination, for more deference. Congressmen *have* to be nice to you; it is their job. Every agent of a powerful congressional public-relations team is devoted to presenting the image in each case of a friendly, attentive man, interested in "you." The collective image reflects this. Congress, moreover, has no police arm: the congressmen is not surrounded by policemen, secret-service men, military aides. He not only will not hurt you; he hasn't the punitive means of doing it (unless, of course, you happen to be "subversive"). But the President is the head of an executive branch with bite: FBI, armed services, secret services. He is surrounded by guards.

If the President is a conscientious, an autonomous, a nonpartisan figure, how shall he adjust to an office that is at the very focus of all the major national pressures? If others are not supposed to be privily influential to the Great Man, what shall we do with the politics that surround the office? The cabalist mind has an answer: "President Eisenhower is not a big wheel. Tom Dewey is the big boss" (Ferrera). "It really surprised us. We figured he's a general and he knows what to do. . . . But he's taking orders like anybody else" (Sokolsky). The noncabalist democrat rejects this idea: "I don't think Ike would let them tell him what to do. If he didn't think it was right, I don't think he'd let it be" (Johnson). But a congressman is *supposed* to listen to T. Dewey and J. Doe and R. Roe, although he too must pursue his own version of the public interest.

The loneliness of the President as these men see him, contributes to a suffering image; not Zeus but Prometheus, not Jehovah but Christ. In a vivid conceit Ruggiero explains his picture of the President's job:

> It would be, uh, if you take a vise, only, instead of two parts, the vise would have maybe ten or fifteen parts to put around his head, and then every once in a while giving a squeeze on each one of 'em. That's exactly what I . . . that's how I feel as far as his Cabinet, see? He's got a problem with labor, this guy's squeezin'. This other fella's havin' trouble with the War Department, or something like that, he starts squeezin'.

And Rapuano says: "He's got to satisfy everybody, let's say in all parties, whether it's his own party or the opposition, he's got to satisfy them both. And that's a tough job to do." No one ever saw a congressman suffering in this way.

---

[2] See my *Political Life: Why People Get Involved in Politics* (New York: The Free Press of Glencoe, 1959), pp. 67–74.

Without being a comic figure, he lends himself to a lighter treatment. Senator Claghorn never appeared in the Eastport interviews, but the congressman's image on the public stage is to be contrasted to *Abe Lincoln in Illinois* or *Sunrise at Campobello*. The President is a tragic figure, at least in the fifties. Not the dignity, not the eminence, not the prestige of the President's job — the crushing responsibility of it: that is what strikes these men. So badly do they want him to be responsible that they make him so — even if he is on the golf course. O'Hara, a maintenance mechanic and oiler, asked how he would describe the President's job, says: "It's too much mental strain where he's got so many people that figure he's leading them. . . . I guess a lot of them probably have a lot of trouble sleeping at night, just thinking and worrying . . . even now when you've got a lot of unemployment throughout the country, I imagine he thinks about it. I mean I think if I were, I would." The awful importance of these decisions is what strikes Woodside: "His actions would make a great deal [of difference?] in making our country a better country or a bad one by the way he handled himself in his decisions. . . . I don't think there's any goofing off on that job." Says Johnson, a mechanic, "I think it's always on his mind." Elsewhere these same men express disappointment in President Eisenhower's second-term performance: they fear that he is indifferent to their fate and, more generally, to the fate of the unemployed (this is the winter of 1957–1958), but they cannot easily accept this conclusion. The idea that *nobody* is in charge of things, the idea of leaving the economy to the "unseen hand" of the market and the polity to the play of forces around Congress, is not easy to accept. In their interpretation of government, then, these men vest the President with a responsible concern for their welfare and a capacity to decide big issues commensurate with his eminence.

Johnson says: "When I think of government, I think of [pause] security. It makes you feel secure when you get good government." This is true for all the men, though they do not say it so clearly, but the security may be of several kinds, and the psychic welfare, like its material counterpart, may be unevenly distributed. Shortly we shall examine the benignity of government, here something of the source of that general support is indicated. From the Congress, and more particularly from the idea of home-state congressmen, these men derive a sense of protection, of a friend in power, of an accessible person who is not likely to be protected by a number of secretaries. The right of petition here is expressed in personal, human contact, not through paper forms and proper channels. Flynn once petitioned for a change in civil-service rules and, with others in the same position, sent a delegation to Washington. They got what they wanted. Ruggiero sees Morrell, Eastport's congressman, on the problems his friends in the post office want taken care of; he is warmly received. The congressman's self-interest is seen as closely congruent with the economic prosperity of his district; his interests correspond to the interests of men like these Eastport fifteen, and this is true regardless of party. It could happen only in a society where class and ethnic political divisions are seen as fluid, where every Democrat is seen by a Republican congressman as a potential convert, a person worth wooing.

The President gives another kind of security; at least he does in normal times. He is a strong arm against the outside world; he is a national protector, and has the stature to be one. He does not have this soft side, this slightly lovable venality — hence he reinforces the voice of the superego; he calls for a higher morality; he is a protector against our weaker natures — the side of ourselves that might cut taxes when we should keep them high to pay for defense. He cares deeply about what happens to the nation and the people and the values for which this country stands. Part of what makes congressmen so appealing is that they are not so seriously committed in this way; they are more human. But what makes the President appealing is that he is not "all too human" like the rest of us; while not quite a hero, he is supportive of whatever small heroic qualities we have in us, at the very least, of our moral selves. Perhaps it will be misunderstood, but in a figurative sense Congress is the group-adjustment leader; the President is the task leader; Congress is the mother, the President the father. . . .[3]

No one in the Eastport group sees civil servants as having much power; certainly they do not see them as dangerous to our liberties. No one reveals a lurking sense that the bureaucrat can borrow the power of government to enhance his own failing strength in life — as Lasswell suggests may be the motives of some civil servants.[4] The bureaucrat is not dangerous, or powerful, or important. Nor is he generally embraced in the euphoric picture of a beneficent government. Almost half of the men referred at some point to the less ambitious, less hard-working qualities of men attracted to jobs that are generally seen as offering lower pay, slower advancement, and greater security. Thus Ruggiero, a bundle of nervous energy and drive with a second job in the post office, says of civil servants: "They are the persons that are afraid. . . . They're just hiding, that's all they are. Because they have no ambition." Like a *narcotic,* the civil service helps them to sleep through life.

Not everyone, of course, has the same jaundiced view of the administrative branch of government and its occupants. Costa, on the ragged edge of being laid off, says: "Maybe those people were a little smarter in picking a field where there's more security. I think that if I knew twenty years ago what I know today, I'd be working for the government." For him, employment by the government also has this "escape" motif, but it seems to be a kind of escape from the pain and troubles of this world — a happy serenity — *nirvana.*

Sorting out those who think the civil service (and often this means post office) is too confining for the ambitious, or gives security in lieu of income, or offers a haven for those who do not work so hard, we find about seven men whose own jobs are not much different from those of the other eight in the group. (These are not, for example, the white collar or the better paid — or the

---

[3] Geoffrey Gorer, who is often as exaggeratedly right and wrong as a caricature, reverses the family-state comparisons, but with the same effect: "To a certain extent the pattern of authority in the state is reproduced in the family: it is as if the father represented the executive, the mother the legislative, and the neighbors, headed by the schoolteacher, the judiciary authority. The child is in the position of the public, playing off one authority against another, invoking the system of checks and balances to maintain his independence" (*The American People* [New York: Norton, 1948], p. 44). The idea of "the public" (instead of, say, the NAM and the AMA) playing off Congress against the President is, to say the least, ridiculous.

[4] Harold Lasswell, *Psychopathology and Politics* (Chicago: University of Chicago Press, 1930).

reverse of these.) They differ from the other eight, by and large, in their expressive, emotionally charged life styles. They include the angry men we have mentioned (Rapuano, Sullivan, Ferrera, Sokolsky); the impulsive, volatile men like Johnson and, again, Sokolsky; the quick, nervous, ambitious Ruggiero.

On the other side, those who view civil servants as in no way different from others and who treat the civil service with respect are, generally speaking, the more "responsible," the more sober, the more disciplined, and the more emotionally restricted group. Their life styles seem to involve a lower affectual tone — indeed, a certain monotony; their discussion is less colorful; the words they select are rarely extreme. This group, then, includes Farrel, whose voice is captured on the tape with no force or expression; Woodside, whose conscientious earnestness prevents him from emotional outbursts: Costa, who takes back such critical thoughts as escape into language; McNamara, with his friendly, gentle, but always low-key moderation in all things. It also includes Dempsey, whose lack of energy and owlish imperturability, combined with what must be a very modest I.Q., do not support many expressions or emotion.[5]

If it is true that the men who are emotionally more expressive, more extreme, more likely in discourse to produce an opinion than a statement of a factual nature are, for one reason or another, likely to look upon the civil service with distaste, one source of this widespread negative attitude toward bureaucracy is suggested. The civil service is associated in many minds, and in these men's minds to some degree, with regulation, red tape, restrictions. In the literature on bureaucracy, much is made of the depersonalizing effect of the stress on a standardized product, of its reliance on routine and convention to protect itself from variations due to the personal values, whims, and emotions of the individuals who occupy the offices. It is clear enough, on this reading of the situation, that these expressive and less disciplined men would find such a situation a strain; the devaluation of emotional life must appear not only confining; it also suggests a kind of castration of an affective life that is an integral part of their life styles. Impatient men, they cannot easily yield to the demands of everything in triplicate and "by the numbers." Their alienation from the bureaucracy, therefore, suggests one of the sources of intemperate opinions about the welfare state, or bureaucracy, or big government on the part of the entrepreneurial class, or the self-made man. Ideology rests on temperament and its many vicarious lives. The imagination of the self now in one situation, now in another, as well as "interest" and logic, gives color and direction to a social and political point of view. . . .

For Eastport, good government is not necessarily moral government. This is not what they look for. Nor is good government characterized by any

---

[5] The coincidence is not perfect; three men who seem to accept the civil service and civil servants as relatively able and ambitious men do not share this emotionally disciplined personal style. Two of them (Kuchinsky and DeAngelo) structure the problem differently: they see civil servants as men trying to get ahead politically. The other, O'Hara, an expressive and friendly man, accepts the civil service as an area of relatively good jobs with one kind of payment — continuity in service and security — instead of higher payment per week or year. But he does not feel that the distinction between those who accept one and not the other is an invidious one in any way.

particular structure; federalism, electoral-college reform, reorganization of the executive branch (with one exception), all these are matters of considerable indifference. The American Constitution, they believe, is the last word in governmental arrangements, and the matter is eternally settled. No, good government in Eastport is *responsive* government; better government is more responsive government.

Bickering

The greatest impediment to responsive government is bickering: "The government right now should cut down on all this bickering between the Armed Forces. There's no reason for a lot of it." "There's too many people telling everybody else what to do. There's too many chiefs and no Indians." "I think he's [Eisenhower's] got a lot of people bickering along with him." "People fighting with one another and not getting together."

No doubt part of the trouble lies in the checks and balances of American government that make the amount of "bickering" greater because there are many coordinate and independently powerful authorities who may and do express views that are neither those of the Opposition nor those of the Administration. Yet there are reasons to think there is something special at work here. For one thing . . . Eastport is quite willing to believe that "democracy creates confusion and prevents important things from getting done," without being disturbed by this at all. There is almost no raillery at Congress (which is said to be the most important part of government) for its talkativeness. They do not at all accept Dempsey's view that the three branches of government "have to have someone over them to tell them whether they're stepping out of line or not . . . and [therefore] naturally the President should have more power than the other two."

The special intensity of feeling about bickering comes, I think, from its interpretation as "answering back" in a hierarchical setting where subordinates are usurping authority they should not have. Moreover, the difference between debating and bickering is that the one is sanctioned as part of expected political role performance, while the other is outside the expected role. The general feeling is that public differences outside the roles of campaign speaker and legislative debator become public quarreling, and hence unseemly, even disorderly. Finally, because they do not associate "issues" or "principles" with such reported "bickering," the men of Eastport fill in the gaps in their knowledge with an easy *ad hominem* argument — these are conflicts over power.

A Government of Words

Congressmen, as we have said, are associated with oral activity, bureaucrats with paper work. For all men, but particularly for working-class men, this wordiness has a vaguely threatening, somewhat distasteful quality. Sullivan, the truck driver, speaking of congressmen meeting their constituents, feels that in this flow of words "lots of times they've nothing to say" — a futile and embarrassing enterprise. Woodside, the railroad guard, says of the bureaucrat, "I imagine he would have the position of going through a tremendous amount of paper work." Johnson, a mechanic, and Rapuano, a clerk, distinguish between the civil servant who is out in the open doing something important and the man in the office who is shuffling papers around. Wordiness, whether spoken or written, produces among all people — but especially among working-class people — an ambivalence that, as we have seen, is likely to attach to government, particularly a democracy.

The theme is a latent one; its incidence diffused and voice muted, it is still strong enough for us to ask whence this verbophobic attitude toward government. Men who are too fluent are disliked because their pace may be too fast for the attention and grasp and emotional affectivity of their listeners, creating for these listeners a problem of timing and response. In some manner, perhaps this is also true of a government of "words" — and not of men. Probably, too, the verbosity of government is reminiscent of school, evoking first an association with painful memories for some, and for many of these men a sense of guilt that they did not go further. Folk wisdom suggests that people who "talk too much" are "trying to put something over on you," concealing ignorance, diverting attention from the crux of the matter — whatever it may be. Leaders are usually not those with greatest verbal productivity in a group. These Eastport men are men who, for the most part, work with their hands; they have — or may have — an instinct of workmanship along these lines; they may have a craftsman's pride in a job well done. They cannot easily generalize this set of values from the shops they know to a "talking shop." The verbosity of government is, like any high-level policy-making or sophisticated administration, concerned with more or less subtle distinctions. Listening in to snatches of this discussion, the working-class man with his very blunt and undifferentiated perspective on the problems under discussion may utterly fail to understand what it is all about. He will see hairsplitting where the informed may see differences with enormous consequences. Talk and discussion often, if not usually, delay action; it is of the essence in the American democracy, at least, that everyone have his "say" in the matter, and there will be a strong tendency to avoid action if a strong and articulate minority asserts itself. But "men of action," such as manual workers and hard-driving businessmen, each in his own way, are not well endowed with patience and do not bide their time gracefully. It is of such stuff as this that the verbophobic response to government is created. But it is also too useful a weapon for those who hate the government on other grounds for it to disappear with better education and understanding of the nature of government. It is entrenched as a rationalization wherever positive government has its enemies.

Defection

Nathan Leites argues that one of the main themes in French politics is the fear of abandonment, fear by the populace that the authorities will abandon them, fear by the deputies that their leaders will abandon them, fear by the prime minister that his cabinet will abandon him.[6] In Eastport the nagging

---

[6] Nathan Leites, "Images of Power in French Politics" (1960), unpublished manuscript on themes in the French political culture.

concern (rather than "fear") lest its representatives lose sight of the people's best interests is present as an important theme, subordinated as it may be to the dominant note of trust. It has several components. In its simplest form it is a concern lest the representative place self before duty; there is contempt for "the guy who is just taking the job for whatever he can get out of it, the prestige there is in it." There is a concern about loss of contact: "Congressmen know less and less about the people they are supposed to represent." Some express a concern, too, about the man who must leave his home district and go to a metropolitan, gay, seductive city: "The most important thing is to remember the things that he took with him to Congress, the ideals he was going to follow and the wishes of his people." But, curiously enough, one concern was hardly mentioned that in another era would have been central: there is little thought that the congressman will be bought off by "the interests" (although he might be helped by them now and then).

But if these fears of defection lie latent in the political mind of the upper working class and the lower middle class, rising to the surface obliquely, without that taste of bitterness characteristic of the alienated classes of Europe, they seem to be more or less forgotten when the men describe what it is that congressmen in fact do with their working days. As noted above, they are seen as reading their mail, listening to others; they are seen as receptive to communication from their constituents. The nagging fear of defection stays unobtrusively in the background. Thus it makes sense for them to *disagree*, as all but one did, with the statement, "I don't think public officials care much what people like me think." The fact seems to be that the antigovernment, anti-Congress educational campaigns of the National Association of Manufacturers, the steel, oil, and utility interests, and the medical profession, have been employing the wrong theme. The men of Eastport may — and some do — think of congressmen as spendthrift, not too efficient, talkative, and sometimes obtuse — but they do not think of them as cold, unreceptive to communication, and indifferent to their fates. And these are what matter to them.

Abandonment and defection by responsible, loved, and nurturant figures was not, for the most part, a feature of the life pattern of these men. There are, of course, exceptions: DeAngelo's father did run off — but his mother assumed a protective responsibility for him; Woodside's father did not serve as an adequate provider for the family; McNamara's father died when he was very young, and he was brought up by his mother and stepfather; O'Hara's father died when he was eleven, but his mother brought him up and protected him. Flynn's father drank heavily at times, but he loved his son and the two were very close. Throughout the lives of these men there were occasions — perhaps for half of them — when the demise, unemployment, frailty, or drunkenness of the father created situations that cause men to be generally suspicious that responsible authorities leave their charges, and defect, or lose an intetrest in them, or embrace another loyalty. But these events were not interpreted as abandonment by most of the men on most of the occasions. We have said elsewhere that the relationship of father and son is a central pillar of the foundations of political belief — and so it is. On the other hand, it is significant that all these men had their own natural mother's nurturant care for their entire infancy and youth. Perhaps the sense that responsible figures defect and abandon their followers does not grow where this is the case. If the central problem with the father emerges as authority-tension, the central problem of mother-son relations may emerge, politically speaking, as nurturance-tension. Of course, this is hopelessly schematized; both mother and father represent both authority and nurturance. But, whether it is the Old World mothering or the New World momism, these men seem to have experienced nurturant mother care sufficient to protect them against a distrust of government or a fear that their protectors in government will abandon them.[7] . . .

Because of the belief in a harmony of interests, Eastport believes that public officials serve themselves by discovering and serving the general welfare, the public interest. Because of their belief that public officials seek, somewhat imperfectly perhaps, to serve the American people, the people of Eastport, the people at Hilltop, "me," they feel that the people are sovereign, and "I" am important. It is not necessary to discover, then, how it is that the people run things — *they run things by having their welfare serve as the criterion of policy.* They do not need to manage government, if they trust it to be run along these lines.

The government has many agencies with which to serve their interests. Some are more powerful than others; some are "better" than others. A code of good and bad political power . . . would look something like this:

> Court power is good; it represents the conscience of the nation and, like a conscience, keeps people from doing what they want to do but shouldn't. The Court speaks for our better selves.
> Presidential power is good when it originates in the President; it is suspect when it originates with advisers. Advisers are likely to be self-seeking and manipulative. Strong Presidents, in some unexplained way, "make up their own minds."
> Presidential power is usually "better" than congressional power because it is less "partisan"; the President represents all the people, but congressmen represent special areas, interests, and groups. The President is "united"; Congress is divided, hence factional. But congressional power may be influenced specifically for "me."
> Popular power is ultimate; supreme, original; but the people are less trustworthy than Congress, and individually vote for foolish and irrelevant reasons.
> Party power is worse than any other kind because it is (a) partisan, and therefore divisive, and (b) selfish, that is, the party leaders are more "out for themselves" than are other leaders.

---

[7] For a discussion of the relation between politics and separation anxiety, see Sebastian De Grazia, *The Political Community* (Chicago: University of Chicago Press, 1948).

4. "Amoral Familism" in an Italian Village

EDWARD C. BANFIELD

The village of Montegrano studied by Professor Banfield is located in the South of Italy, marked by extreme poverty and alienation from the national tradition. That the attitudes exhibited there are not typical for other Italian villages is recognized by the author. The "amoral familism" he describes may, however, serve as a polar concept against which to compare other cases where integration into national systems is incomplete.

A very simple hypothesis will make intelligible all of the behavior about which questions have been raised and will enable an observer to predict how the Montegranesi will act in concrete circumstances. The hypothesis is that the Montegranesi act as if they were following this rule:

> Maximize the material, short-run advantages of the nuclear family; assume that all others will do likewise.

One whose behavior is consistent with this rule will be called an "amoral familist." The term is awkward and somewhat imprecise (one who follows the rule is without morality only in relation to persons outside the family — in relation to family members, he applies standards of right and wrong; one who has no family is of course an "amoral individualist"), but no other term seems better.

In this chapter, some logical implications of the rule are set forth. It will be seen that these describe the facts of behavior in the Montegrano district. The coincidence of facts and theory does not "prove" the theory. However, it does show that the theory will explain (in the sense of making intelligible and predictable) much behavior without being contradicted by any of the facts at hand.

1. *In a society of amoral familists, no one will further the interest of the group or community except as it is to his private advantage to do so.*

In other words, the hope of material gain in the short-run will be the only motive for concern with public affairs.

This principle is of course consistent with the entire absence of civic improvement associations, organized charities, and leading citizens who take initiative in public service.

A teacher who is a member of a leading family explained,

> I have always kept myself aloof from public questions, especially political ones. I think that all the parties are identical and those who belong to them — whether Communist, Christian Democrat, or other — are men who seek their

SOURCE: Reprinted by permission from Edward C. Banfield, *The Moral Basis of a Backward Society* (New York: The Free Press, 1958), pp. 85–104. Footnotes are abridged.

own welfare and well-being. And then too, if you want to belong to one party, you are certain to be on the outs with the people of the other party.

Giovanni Gola, a merchant of upper-class origins, has never been a member of a political party because "It isn't convenient for me — I might lose some business."

Gola does not think of running for office because:

> I have all I can do to look after my own affairs. I do enough struggling in my business not to want to add to it in any political struggling. Once in office there would be a constant demand for favors or attentions. I'd have to spend all my time looking after other people's affairs . . . my own would have to be neglected. I don't feel like working hard any more. I am no longer young. [He is in his late forties.]

Those who run for office, Gola says, do so for private advantage.

> They get the office, and then they look after themselves. Some take office so as to be able to say, "I am the mayor." But really there isn't much honor attaching to an office; people here don't even respect the President of the Republic. In F —, the mayor wants to be mayor so that he can keep the population down.

2. *In a society of amoral familists only officials will concern themselves with public affairs, for only they are paid to do so. For a private citizen to take a serious interest in a public problem will be regarded as abnormal and even improper.*

Cavalier Rossi, one of the largest landowners of Montegrano, and the mayor of the nearby town of Capa, sees the need for many local public improvements. If he went to the prefect in Potenza as mayor of Capa, they would listen to him, he says. But if he went as a private citizen of Montegrano, they would say, "Who are you?" As a private citizen he might help a worker get a pension, but as for schools, hospitals, and such things, those are for the authorities to dole out. A private citizen can do nothing.

The trouble is only partly that officials will not listen to private citizens. To a considerable extent it is also that private citizens will not take responsibility in public matters. As Rossi explains,

> There are no leaders in Montegrano. People's minds are too unstable; they aren't firm; they get excited and make a decision. Then the next day they have changed their minds and fallen away. It's more or less the same way in Capa. There is lots of talk, but no real personal interest. It always comes to this: the mayor has to do it. They expect the mayor to do everything and to get everything — to make a world.

Farmuso, the director of the school district and formerly the Communist mayor of a town in another province, is earnest, energetic, and intelligent. He listed several things which might be done to improve the situation in Montegrano, but when he was asked if he could bring influence to bear to get any of them done, he said that he could not. "I am interested only in the schools," he explained. "If I wanted to exert influence, with whom would I talk? In Vernande there are six teachers in two rooms, but no money for improvements. I have talked to the mayor and others, but I can't get anything even there."

The feeling that unofficial action is an intrusion upon the sphere of the state accounts in some measure both for Mayor Spomo's haughty officiousness and for the failure of private persons to interest themselves in making stop-gap arrangements for a school and a hospital. In nearby Basso a reclamation project will increase vegetable production and make possible the establishment of a canning factory. The large landowners of Basso will not join together to build a factory, however, even though it might be a good investment. It is the right and the duty of the state to build it.

3. *In a society of amoral familists there will be few checks on officials, for checking on officials will be the business of other officials only.*

When Farmuso, the school director, was asked what he would do if it came to his attention that a public official took bribes, he said that if the bribery were in his own department he would expose it at once. However, if it occurred outside his department, he would say nothing, for in that case it would be none of his concern.

A young school teacher, answering the same question, said that even if he could prove the bribery he would do nothing. "You are likely to be made a martyr," he explained. "It takes courage to do it. There are so many more dishonest people than honest ones that they can gang up on you . . . twist the facts so that you appear to be the guilty one. Remember Christ and the Pharisees."

A leading merchant would not expose bribery, because "Sooner or later someone would come to me and tell me it would be good if I didn't."

4. *In a society of amoral familists, organization (i.e., deliberately concerted action) will be very difficult to achieve and maintain. The inducements which lead people to contribute their activity to organizations are to an important degree unselfish (e.g., identification with the purpose of the organization) and they are often non-material (e.g., the intrinsic interest of the activity as a "game"). Moreover, it is a condition of successful organization that members have some trust in each other and some loyalty to the organization. In an organization with high morale it is taken for granted that they will make small sacrifices, and perhaps even large ones, for the sake of the organization.*

The only formal organizations which exist in Montegrano — the church and the state — are of course provided from the outside; if they were not, they could not exist. Inability to create and maintain organization is clearly of the greatest importance in retarding economic development in the region.

Despite the moral and other resources it can draw upon from the outside, the church in Montegrano suffers from the general inability to maintain organization. There are two parishes, each with its priest. Rivalry between the priests is so keen that neither can do anything out of the ordinary without having obstacles placed in his way by the other, and cooperation between them is wholly out of the question. (On one occasion they nearly came to blows in the public square; on another the saint of one parish was refused admittance to the church of the other when the *festa*-day procession stopped there on its route). When some young men tried to organize a chapter of Catholic Action, a lay association to carry Catholic principles into secular life, they encountered so much sabotage from the feuding priests, neither of whom was willing to tolerate an activity for which the other might receive some credit, that the project was soon abandoned.

The Montegranesi might be expected not to make good soldiers. However brave he may be, the amoral familist does not win battles. Soldiers fight from loyalty to an organization, especially the primary groups of "buddies," not from self-interest narrowly conceived.

Lack of attachments even to kindred has impeded emigration and indirectly economic development. In the half century prior to 1922, there was heavy emigration from Montegrano to the United States and later to Argentina. In general, however, ties between the emigrants and those who remained at home were not strong enough to support "chains" of emigration. Hundreds of Montegranesi live in the hope that a brother or uncle in America will send a "call," but such calls rarely come. People are perplexed when their relatives in America do not answer their letters. The reason is, probably, that the letters from Montegrano always ask for something, and the emigrant, whose advantage now lies elsewhere, loses patience with them. The relative absence of emigration, as well as of gifts from persons who have emigrated, is a significant impediment to economic development. Some Italian towns, whose ethos is different, have benefited enormously from continuing close ties with emigrants who have prospered in the New World.

5. *In a society of amoral familists, office-holders, feeling no identification with the purposes of the organization, will not work harder than is necessary to keep their places or (if such is within the realm of possibility) to earn promotion. Similarly, professional people and educated people generally will lack a sense of mission or calling. Indeed, official position and special training will be regarded by the possessors as weapons to be used against others for private advantage.*

In southern Italy, the indifference of the bureaucracy is notorious. "A zealous official is as rare as a white fly," a man who had retired after 49 years in the public service remarked.

"From the President of the Republic down to the last little Italian," a landowner said, "there is a complete lack of any sense of duty — especially of the sense of duty to do productive work."

The school teachers of Montegrano notably lack a sense of calling. It is not uncommon for a teacher to come late to class or to miss class altogether. At best the teacher teaches four hours a day and takes no further part in the lives of the children. An engineer from northern Italy was shocked at what he saw in Montegrano. "During the summer vacation," he said, "a teacher in the north may hold informal classes. He will take the children on walks into the country and explain a bit about nature. Or they will go on picnics and sing together. The teacher is a part of the children's lives out of school as well as in." In Montegrano, he found, teachers spend the summer loafing in the *piazza* and they do not speak to their pupils when they see them.

"Study and education," a young teacher who was himself of an artisan family explained, "has helped some people to succeed. It has helped them by giving them an advantage over the ignorant. With their knowledge, they are better able to exploit ignorance. They are able to cheat more dexterously."

With other professionals the situation is more or less the same. The pharmacist, a left-wing socialist who enjoys a government monopoly and is one of the richest men in town, feels himself under no obligation to stock the antibiotics and other new medicines which the doctor prescribes or to extend credit to those desperately in need. The doctor himself, although an outstanding man in many ways, does not feel under an obligation to provide himself with the bare essentials of equipment for modern medical practice.

6. *In a society of amoral familists, the law will be disregarded when there is no reason to fear punishment. Therefore individuals will not enter into agreements which depend upon legal processes for their enforcement unless it is likely that the law will be enforced and unless the cost of securing enforcement will not be so great as to make the undertaking unprofitable.*

This, of course, is another impediment to organization and to economic and other development.

It is taken for granted that all those who can cheat on taxes will do so. Minimum wage laws and laws which require the employer to make social security payments on the wages of domestic servants are universally ignored.

An employer who can get away with it is almost sure to cheat his employees. If the employer is a local man, the worker can get justice by appealing to the Marshal, whose informal powers are great. Otherwise the worker is usually cheated. The new municipal building was built by contractors from Matera who paid Montegrano laborers less than the legal minimum and left town owing several of them wages for their last month's work. Since the employer was not a local man, the Marshal could do nothing. In principle the workers could appeal to a labor commission in Potenza. In practice they had to reconcile themselves to the fact that they had been cheated.

Frequently the worker is prevented by self-interest from taking his case to the Marshal. He cannot afford to be on bad terms with the employer: it is better to be cheated than to be deprived of employment altogether. Accordingly, it is the custom for the employer to pay only at his convenience. A peasant may have to go, hat in hand, to the *signore* month after month to ask politely for the dollar or two that is owed.

Mutual distrust between landlords and tenants accounts in part for the number of tiny, owner-operated farms in Montegrano. Rather than work a larger unit on shares, an arrangement which would be more profitable but which would necessitate getting along with a landlord, the peasant prefers to go it alone on his uneconomic holding. Twenty-one peasants were asked which they would prefer, to own eight hectares of land or to sharecrop 40. One said he would prefer to sharecrop the larger holding "because even if I had to be under another and to work a little harder, the gain would be much more." None of the others thought the gain from the larger holding would offset the burden of having to get along with a landlord. Their explanations showed how anxiety, suspicion, and hate make cooperation burdensome.

I would prefer to be the owner of eight hectares rather than have the rental of 40 because if you are an owner no one commands you and furthermore you are not always worried that tomorrow your half may not be yours and so always under the necessity of being careful.

* * *

I would prefer to be the owner of eight hectares or even less than to work someone else's land. I've had experience with that already and it is really unbearable because the owners always think you are stealing from them.

* * *

I would prefer a little land of my own to renting 40 hectares because, as I have already said, I hate the rich who sit in the breeze all year and come around only when it is time to divide the produce which I have worked hard with so many sacrifices to grow.

7. *The amoral familist who is an office-holder will take bribes when he can get away with it. But whether he takes bribes or not, it will be assumed by the society of amoral familists that he does.*[1]

There is no way of knowing to what extent bribery actually exists in Montegrano. There is abundant evidence, however, that it is widely believed to be common. The peasants are sure that the employment officer gives preference to those who bring him presents. They believe, too, that Mayor Spomo made a fortune by selling the communal forest without competitive bids. Better informed people say that it is highly unlikely that there is graft in the administration of the commune: its affairs are too closely supervised from Potenza. However, many upper class people agree that bribery and favoritism are widespread in southern Italy at large. A teacher said,

Today one gets ahead only by bribes and recommendations. All of the

---

[1] An interview with the Communist mayor of Grottole, another village of Lucania, by E. A. Bayne of the American Universities Field Staff, reveals the same selfishness and distrust that are evident in Montegrano.

After explaining to Bayne that the peasants of Grottole would not work together — that all wanted something for themselves — the mayor asked if the Americans would give the village a tractor. After he had been discouraged in this hope, the mayor said,

"When you leave here I will go down in the street with my people, and they will ask me, 'Did you get any help for us?' And I will try to explain that you are not officials — not even rich tourists — but journalists. 'Why then,' they will say, 'have you bought them wine and coffee with our money and now have nothing to show for it?' "

At the conclusion of his interview Bayne laid a few thousand *lire* on the mayor's desk and asked if he would distribute it where it would do the most good. Perhaps there was a Christmas fund for children? The mayor's consternation was immediate. With politeness but with unmistakable firmness he refused.

"You do not understand my people [he protested]. If I were to accept this gift which *I* understand, those people in the street would soon ask if there had not been more and how much I had kept for myself. We have no Christmas fund, for who would contribute to it? . . ."

Two years later Bayne revisited Grottole and found that the mayor had been defeated for re-election and had taken to drink. "He didn't do anything for the people and they became tired of him," someone explained. "Now we have a new mayor — this one is really a fascist. He won't do anything either."

Quoted with permission from American Universities Field Staff letters of December 17, 1954, and February 21, 1957.

examinations are infected with this disease and those who get ahead are the ones with the most drag. To me this is odious. I would do anything not to have to see it.

The principal merchant is building a cinema. Before it goes into operation he must have a permit from the proper authority. After months of waiting, his request for a permit had not been acted upon. "If I took an envelope with $160 and slipped it into the right pocket, I would have my permission right away," he told an interviewer. "It's the little yellow envelope that gets things done. Big and small, they all take bribes."

"Why don't you do it, then?"

"Because I don't have $160 to spare."

8. *In a society of amoral familists the weak will favor a regime which will maintain order with a strong hand.*

Until it involved them in war, Fascism appealed to many peasants — at least so they now say — because by enforcing the laws rigorously, it protected them. Here are some answers given by peasants to the question, "What did the Fascists claim to stand for?"

> The Fascists said they wanted to be commanders of all. We had no free speech under them, but Mussolini was a good administrator. The Fascists were very bad, but you could send a child any distance unmolested when they were in power. Now you have to walk with a hand on your pocket and a hand on your hat to keep from being robbed.

* * *

> The Fascists wanted the peasants to have a better life. There was an eight-hour day and a standard rate of pay. It was a published rate. If a proprietor made you work ten hours you went to the employment office and they would force him to pay the right wage. Now it is everyone for himself, and everyone tries to get the most work for the least pay out of the peasant.

* * *

> I don't know what they wanted, but they did make severe laws. There was order and you had rights and duties. You had the right to be paid when you worked and it was a duty to pay workers for work done. They looked after the children too. There were subsidies for large families and help when a new baby was born. Nowadays there is supposed to be help, but it is not enforced.

* * *

> I do not remember what it was the Fascists wanted. I only remember that in those days one made out better than today. In those days the worker was well off and not unhappy. Also there were many more aids. Instead, today, nobody cares. If it were during the days of Fascism, the things that happen now would not happen. Today a worker must wait to be paid . . . must wait for the convenience of his employer. Many times months pass without his being paid. During Fascism, this would never have happened.

A landowner made a similar explanation:

> During Fascism, parents were really forced to send their children to school. There could be no excuses, like lack of clothes or books, because the government really provided those where necessary. There was an official who stood

outside the school building each morning at 8:30. He gave the children bread and cheese or marmalade and the children would go into the school to eat. School would begin at nine. Now if ten suits are sent to the commune for the children, we are lucky if a cuff of one suit really gets here . . . it just melts by the wayside. The laws are all there, but no one enforces them.

A merchant argued that the consumer was better off under Fascist regulation than under present-day competition. "Cloth was grade-labelled and marked with a fixed price along the selvedge. Everything was controlled. You knew what you were getting for your money. Now, unless you really understand cloth, a merchant can sell you inferior material at high prices. It was good for the customer and good for the merchant too. The customer knew what he was getting and the merchant could count on his twenty or thirty percent. Some people get one hundred percent today."

A teacher had this recollection of Fascism:

> During Fascism there was a great deal of emulation among the pupils and good discipline. Today all this is gone; children grow up very rude and the teacher in school must always have a stick in hand because the children are fighting among themselves all of the time.

9. *In a society of amoral familists, the claim of any person or institution to be inspired by zeal for public rather than private advantage will be regarded as fraud.*

A young man said,

> If I decided that I wanted to do something for Montegrano, I would enter my name on the list at election time, and everyone would ask, "Why does he want to be mayor?" If ever anyone wants to do anything, the question always is: what is he after?

Anti-clericalism is widespread in Montegrano, and the usual objection to priests is that they are "money grubbers" and "hypocrites." In fact, the priests seem to be no more concerned with gain than are other professionals, and their level of living is no higher than that of the others. They are peculiarly liable to attack, however, because the church professes to be unselfish.

Socialists and Communists, like priests, are liable to be regarded as pious frauds. "There are socialists of the mouth and socialists of the heart," a peasant woman explained.

The extraordinary bitterness and, as it seems to an outsider, unfairness with which so many peasants accuse others of hypocrisy is to be understood, in part, perhaps, as an expression of guilt feelings. As is explained elsewhere, the peasant is not unaware that charity is a virtue. Not practicing it himself, he feels some guilt therefore, and he projects this as hostility against those institutions, especially the church, which preach the virtue of charity and through which, perhaps, he would like to be vicariously virtuous.

10. *In the society of amoral familists there will be no connection between abstract political principle (i.e., ideology) and concrete behavior in the ordinary relationships of every day life.*

In Montegrano, the principal left-wing socialists are the doctor and the pharmacist, two of the town's most prosperous gentlemen. The doctor, although he has called upon the government to provide a hospital, has not arranged an emergency room or even equipped his own office. The pharmacist, a government-licensed monopolist, gives an absolute minimum of service at extremely high prices (Signora Prato paid five cents for a single aspirin tablet!) and is wholly unconcerned with local affairs, i.e., those which would have implications for action by him.

The discrepancy between ideology and behavior in practical affairs tends to discredit ideology in the eyes of the peasants. Prato was one of those who assembled in the *piazza* when Dr. Gino tried to organize a branch of the Socialist Party.

> I went a few times and it all sounded very good [he said later]. But that Spring Don Franco hired a mule to cultivate his vineyard, and I thought to myself, What can this be? What can Socialism mean? Why does Don Franco, who is such a believer in it, hire a mule instead of the ten workers he used to hire? There are ten people out of work. And it wouldn't cost him any more to use them than to use the mules.

> What ignorance! [the doctor exclaimed when he was told what Prato said]. Cultivation well done by hand is better than cultivation done with a mule. But the workers here must be watched all the time because they don't really know their jobs, and it is a nuisance to have to be on hand to keep watch. With a mule, you can at least see that the whole row has been done the same way.

11. *In a society of amoral familists there will be no leaders and no followers. No one will take the initiative in outlining a course of action and persuading others to embark upon it (except as it may be to his private advantage to do so) and, if one did offer leadership, the group would refuse it out of distrust.*

Apparently there has never been in Montegrano a peasant leader to other peasants. Objectively, there is a basis for such leadership to develop: the workers on road gangs, for example, share grievances and one would expect them to develop feelings of solidarity.

Suspicion of the would-be leader probably reduces the effectiveness of the doctor, the mid-wife, and the agricultural agent as teachers. When a peasant was asked whether she could get birth control information from the mid-wife, she replied, "Of course not. It is not to her interest that I limit the size of my family."

The nearest approximation to leadership is the patron-client relationship. By doing small favors (e.g., by lending a few bushels of grain during the winter, by giving cast-off clothing, or by taking a child from a large family as a housemaid), a well-to-do person may accumulate a clientele of persons who owe him return favors and, of course, deference. Such clients constitute a "following," perhaps, but the patron is not a "leader" in any significant sense. In Montegrano, moreover, none of the well-to-do has troubled to develop much of a clientele. One reason is, perhaps, that the leading families are not engaged in factional squabbles, and so the advantage to be had from a clientele does not outweigh the expense and inconvenience of maintaining it.

12. *The amoral familist will use his ballot to secure the greatest material gain in the short run. Although he may have decided views as to his long-run interest, his class interest, or the public interest, these will not affect his vote if the family's short-run, material advantage is in any way involved.*

Prato, for example, is a monarchist as a matter of principle: he was born and brought up one and he believes that monarchy is best because Italy is too poor to afford frequent elections. These principles do not affect his vote, however. "Before elections," he explains, "all the parties send people around who say, 'Vote for our party.' We always say 'Yes,' but when we go to vote, we vote for the party we think has given us the most." The Christian Democratic party has given Prato a few days work on the roads each year. Therefore he votes for it. If it ceased to give him work and if there were no advantage to be had from voting for another party, he would be a monarchist again. If Mayor Spomo has influence with the Minister of Agriculture, he should be kept despite his haughtiness and his stealing. But if Councilmen Viva and Lasso can get a larger project than the mayor can get, or if they can get one quicker, then down with him.

13. *The amoral familist will value gains accruing to the community only insofar as he and his are likely to share them. In fact, he will vote against measures which will help the community without helping him because, even though his position is unchanged in absolute terms, he considers himself worse off if his neighbors' position changes for the better. Thus it may happen that measures which are of decided general benefit will provoke a protest vote from those who feel that they have not shared in them or have not shared in them sufficiently.*

In 1954, the Christian Democratic party showed the voters of Basso that vast sums had been spent on local public works. Nevertheless the vote went to the Communists. There are other reasons which help to account for the vote (the Christian Democratic candidate was a merchant who would not give credit and was cordially disliked and distrusted), but it seems likely that the very effectiveness of the Christian Democratic propaganda may have helped to cause its defeat. Seeing what vast sums had been expended, the voters asked themselves: Who got it all? Why didn't they give me my fair share?

No amoral familist ever gets what he regards as his fair share.

14. *In a society of amoral familists the voter will place little confidence in the promises of the parties. He will be apt to use his ballot to pay for favors already received (assuming, of course, that more are in prospect) rather than for favors which are merely promised.*

Thus Prato, in the statement quoted above, attaches weight to past performance rather than to promises. "All the parties make promises," he says. "The Christian Democratic party had a chance and it has done a great deal. Why change?" And thus the writer of the letter quoted in Chapter One, after describing the enthusiasm with which the new mayor was received after Spomo's defeat, remarks significantly, "We will wait and see."

The principle of paying for favors received rather than for ones merely promised gives a great advantage to the party in power, of course. Its effect, however, is often more than offset by another principle, as follows:

15. *In a society of amoral familists it will be assumed that whatever group is in power is self-serving and corrupt. Hardly will an election be over before the voters will conclude that the new officials are enriching themselves at their expense and that they have no intention of keeping the promises they have*

made. Consequently, the self-serving voter will use his ballot to pay the incumbents not for benefits but for injuries, i.e., he will use it to administer punishment.

Even though he has more to gain from it than from any other, the voter may punish a party if he is confident that it will be elected despite his vote. The ballot being secret, he can indulge his taste for revenge (or justice) without incurring losses. (Of course there is some danger that too many will calculate in this way, and that the election will therefore be lost by error.)

Addo's switch from Christian Democrat to Communist and back again to Christian Democrat is to be explained in this way. The priest in Addo was slightly mad. Some of his eccentricities nobody minded (he arrayed himself as a cardinal and required a chicken as part payment for a marriage), but when he left town a few days before the election taking with him the *pasta*, sugar, and other election-day presents that had been sent them from the Vatican, the voters of Addo were outraged. Afterward, a new priest soon made matters right.

16. *Despite the willingness of voters to sell their votes, there will be no strong or stable political machines in a society of amoral familists. This will be true for at least three reasons: (a) the ballot being secret, the amoral voter cannot be depended upon to vote as he has been paid to vote; (b) there will not be enough short-run material gain from a machine to attract investment in it; and (c) for reasons explained above, it will be difficult to maintain formal organization of any kind whatever.*

Prato says "Yes" to all who ask for his vote. Since they cannot trust him to vote as he promises, none of the parties will offer to buy his vote. The *pasta* and sugar that are distributed by the parties are good-will offerings rather than bribes. The amounts given are, of course, trivial in comparison to what would be paid if there were some way of enforcing the contract.

17. *In a society of amoral familists, party workers will sell their services to the highest bidders. Their tendency to change sides will make for sudden shifts in strength of the parties at the polls.*[2]

The sudden conversion of the secretary of the Montegrano branch of the Monarchist Party to Communist occurred because Monarchist headquarters in Naples was slow in paying him for his services. When he turned Communist, the Monarchists made a settlement. He then returned to his duties as if nothing had happened.

---

[2] That voter behavior in the Montegrano district is closely similar to that in much of rural Italy is suggested by the data in an undated report by the Office of Intelligence Research, based on data secured by International Research Associates, Inc., of New York, which includes "profiles" of the political situation in 76 communities ranging in size from 200 to 7,000 electors and located in all parts of Italy. The communes described are those in which Communism made its greatest gains or suffered its greatest losses in the 1953 elections. The data was gathered in field interviews in which citizens were asked to explain the voting shift in their communes. The report shows that local economic issues were by far the most important cause of the voting shifts. Economic doctrine, it shows, was of little importance. National issues — e.g., monarchy, the church, foreign policy — were of even less importance. "Next to economic causes," the report says, "significant changes in the voting pattern appear to have been caused by corruption, graft, injustice (real or fancied), and failure to fulfill promises."

5. A French Village—Protection Against Collective Power

LAURENCE WYLIE

The people in the French village of Peyrane share with those of Monte-grano the suspicion of central power but have, in contrast, developed a communal spirit that makes them something of a community. This village community is also more "modern" in that national parties and media have penetrated local structures. The dynamics of change and integration are, therefore, different, and one must be very cautious in speaking of a common political culture even among the rural populations of Southern Europe.

Letters from Peyrane are like letters from any little town. The news is of the same order: marriages, births, deaths. People have moved away and others have moved in. A public sewage system has been installed. The old shower bath down at the soccer field has been moved into a new public bathhouse next to the public laundry. An artist from Paris is living in one of the windmills. The Charrins' cow died, and they closed up their house and moved away. Madame Pamard is now one hundred and two years old. She survived both the public celebration of her hundredth birthday and the catastrophic cold wave of January 1956. L'abbé Autrand died, and the church of Peyrane has been closed. Since the flock in Peyrane was not fervent enough to support a full-time priest, a priest is sent up from Apt to say Mass on Sundays and on special occasions.

These events seem in the order of things. They could not have been predicted, but there is nothing surprising about them, and above all there is nothing about them that would lead us to change our conception of Peyrane. When one lives in Peyrane, of course, such events take on important proportions. City events lose their impact because they fade into the surrounding activity. Even a small event in a village looms up, especially if it can qualify as drama.

Undoubtedly the most dramatic event in Peyrane in the last five years was the invasion by the Gaumont Moving Picture Company. With almost no warning a crew of actors, actresses, directors, and technicians arrived to make a movie entitled "Le Paradis retrouvé," and for several weeks the red cliffs of Peyrane became the backdrop of a romantic tale. All I have been able to learn about the tale is that it concerns Adam and Eve, who are not dead, after all. They rediscover themselves and Paradise in Peyrane. However, they bump

---

SOURCE: Reprinted by permission from Laurence Wylie, *Village in the Vaucluse* (Cambridge, Mass.: Harvard University Press, 1957), pp. 325–339.

into the Wandering Jew and this encounter touches off a series of events which make up the plot of the movie.

One can imagine what the filming of this movie did to Peyrane. Rivet wrote: "The village is upside down and has been for a month. I was named Impresario and Official Liaison Officer between Directors and Villagers. Many scenes were shot in the village and around the cliffs. I even had a rôle — I was the Postman, and I'm in several scenes in my son's uniform. Others were given rôles, too, and still others had technical jobs. The famous Moïse and young Philippe Aubenas worked with the technicians. The inside scenes were filmed in my house. Most of the actors and actresses found places to stay in the village, but some had to be lodged in Apt. The stir made by this event has changed the village completely."

The spectacular changes were temporary, but there were other changes that had lasting effects. For instance, the filming of the movie made the Voisin café go bankrupt. It had been expected that Voisin's passion for boules would ruin him, but it was his prosperity, not boules, that finally did it.

When the Gaumont company moved into Peyrane it brought actors and technicians who had time and money to spend in the café. It also brought tourists who came to the café to see the actors and actresses. Voisin was so awed by the actresses and by the flowering of his business that he was paralyzed. Madame Voison took over. She hired Jacques Leporatti to help her and sent her husband away to play boules so that he would not be behind the bar to give credit and drinks on the house. For a while the Voisins thought Peyrane was really "Paradise Regained."

Madame Avenas, the owner of the beauty shop next door, was prospering, too. Her appointment book and her extra rooms were filled with people from the movie company. She was jealous of the Voisins. It seemed to her that they were making easy money. Her tenants gave her the idea of actually cutting in on the café trade. Dissatisfied with the high price they paid for meals in Vincent's Guide Michelin restaurant, they persuaded Madame Avenas to give them board as well as room. Next they asked for apéritifs before their meals, and then for drinks at the other times of the day, and soon Madame Capel found herself in the café business. She paid her patent, hired Charles Pouget as waiter, and became a *cafetiére* in earnest. Needless to say, the relations between Madame Voisin and Madame Avenas deteriorated.

An unexpected complication made the competition ever more intense. The owner of a café in Marseille, Jean Mauron, heard of the little town where a movie company was attracting many tourists. His wife was *fatiguée* and needed a change of air, so he closed the Marseille business and moved his city fixtures and equipment into the empty shop next door to Madame Voisin's.

For a few weeks there were three cafés lined up in Peyrane's little Place de la Mairie. They all lasted through the stay of the Gaumont Company, but when the glamorous actors departed, *c'était la catastrophe*. Normal business was scarcely enough to keep one café alive. Each of the three settled down to wait for the other two to die. The first to give up were the Voisins. They had the advantage of their tobacco business, but they lacked capital to hold them over. As soon as they could make arrangements to settle the exchange of the government tobacco patent they moved away from Peyrane. That left Madame Avenas and Mauron sparring for an advantage.

This incident would hardly be worth telling if it were not for its political ramifications. Madame Avenas is the number three communist in the commune. Chanon is the leader. Léon Favre is the brains. Madame Avenas is the dynamo. Pouget, the waiter she hired for her new café, is number four, the worker and local Secretary of the Party. However, it turned out that Mauron was also an active Communist, and he brought with him the prestige, the self-assurance, and the influential relations of a big operator from Marseille. He started at once to take over the direction of the Party in Peyrane.

From reports it appears that the reaction was violent. When Madame Avenas shouts and beats her breast it seems as though something awful were about to happen. Mauron, who is a caricature of the popular conception of a Marseillais, was a match for her. The Place de la Mairie became an unpleasant place. Even the boule players were disrupted. Rather than choose between the two cafés, and consequently take part in the internecine struggle, they moved their game to another part of the village. Meetings of the Communist cell became impossible because Madame Capel and Mauron equated party loyalty with café loyalty. The party had not been in so bad shape since the dispute over the use of guns and ferrets in rabbit hunting.

It was at that moment that Prime Minister Faure called an election. The followers of Mendés-France could have been no more outraged than members of the Communist Party of Peyrane. They were caught in an awkward moment in history. It took all the patience and common sense of Léon Favre to patch up the ranks. Perhaps, of course, it was good for the Party that it came so suddenly. The surprise shocked members into a semblance of discipline.

The campaign was short, and it was more furious than any election since just after the war. The fury was stirred up by a new political force that muscled its way into the center of the traditional political situation — Poujade's middle class antitax movement. It had been said that the best way to undermine the Communist Party in Peyrane was to invent a party that would represent an even more violent protest. But since all the parties in Peyrane are protest parties, Poujadism endangered them all. Poujade was even more dangerous in the Vaucluse than elsewhere because in that départment he multiplied himself. That is, there was not one Poujade candidate, there were three — one for the tradesmen, one for the peasants, and one for the consumers. The three candidates were, of course, affiliated, so that according to the electoral law of 1951 each one was credited with the combined success of all three.

The heat of the campaign can be measured most precisely by the fact that more people turned out to vote in this election than in any other national election since the war. It may be recalled that usually about 70 per cent of the registered voters of Peyrane vote in a national election. In the election of January 1956, 79 per cent of the voters came to the polls.

The results of the election bring further confirmation of our concept of politics in Peyrane. Their meaning is clear when they are compared with the election returns of 1951. . . .

	1951	1956	Difference
Registered Voters	467	457	— 10
Votes Cast	329	361	+ 32
Invalid Votes	10	14	+ 4
Valid Votes Cast	319	347	+ 28
Communist (PC)	141	130	— 11
Socialist Radical (RGR)	77	44	— 33
Socialist (SFIO)	40	42	+ 2
Popular Republican (MRP)	37	27	— 10
de Gaulle (RPF)	21	–	— 21
Independent	6	–	— 6
Poujade	–	104	+104

Almost a third of the Peyrane voters supported Poujade's candidates! Who were these voters? We cannot answer definitely, but the preceding tabulation is suggestive. If we add the 81 votes of those who apparently deserted the traditional parties to the 32 votes of those who voted in the election of 1956 but not in the election of 1951, the total is close to the 104 votes received by the Poujade candidates.

There were three principal sources of support for Poujade. First, there was the vote of people like Figeard who have always had such contempt of politics that they did not bother to come to the polls. The destructive oversimplifications of Poujade's statements appealed to them more than any party statements had before, so they voted instead of staying at home. Then there was the support of the score or more people who always vote to the right, who had voted in 1951 for the conservative candidates on the Gaullist and Independent tickets.

The strongest support, however, seems to have come from the Socialist Radicals who deserted Daladier. Their switch is not surprising, for on the whole they are people of substantial means who bear the heaviest tax burden in the commune. Poujade's denunciation of the system of taxation appealed to them directly. He also gave them an opportunity to express their traditional feeling of extreme protest against impinging forces without at the same time associating themselves with the other extreme protesters, their Communist neighbors. So their vote for Poujade was a vote agaist taxation; it was an extremist vote against government; it was also a means of differentiating themselves still more radically from their neighbors.

For a person who is fond of Peyrane it is painful to acknowledge that it gave Poujade stronger support than did most of the other communes in the Vaucluse. Unfortunately, this is not the first time that Peyrane has distinguished itself by offering support to less admirable candidates. François Goguel, in an unpublished analysis of the electoral history of Peyrane, points out that in several elections at the turn of the century Peyrane gave proportionally more votes than did other Vaucluse villages to the ex-socialist, ex-Boulangist, nationalistic, and alcoholic adventurer Georges Laguerre. Professor Goguel warns us, however, that it is dangerous to read too much meaning into any one such fact. It might seem that Peyrane has a penchant for demagogues if we were not aware of another fact that implies a quite different motivation in the Laguerre vote. It was Laguerre who worked with the Mayor to secure for Peyrane one of the first municipal water systems in the region. Election statistics may be revealing, but they may also be misleading, especially if they are studied without regard for other factors and if the numbers involved are as small as they are in the commune of Peyrane.

The election results of 1956 as in a sense just as misleading. It is a fact that in this election, roughly one-quarter of the voters did not vote, one-quarter voted Poujadist, one-quarter voted Communist, and one-quarter voted for moderate candidates. Logically, one might conclude that revolution seethes in Peyrane since only one-fourth of the adults support the Fourth Republic, while three-fourths of them are either indifferent to it or favor its destruction.

We know that the opposite is true. Peyrane is profoundly conservative. The vote does not mean that they want to change the order of things. It means quite the contrary, that they want to be left alone so they will not have to change. Not that the state of things is good as it is. It is neither good nor bad; it is tolerable. Or rather it would be tolerable if it were not for the malevolence of human beings organized into groups. For organization means power, and power means the oppression of the individual.

Even at the local level where individuals know each other personally we have seen that the only successful organizations are coöperatives whose benefits have been concretely demonstrated to outweigh their oppressive nature. Other groups lead a precarious life, and usually they disintegrate entirely. People say they do not want to belong to an organization because they do not want to put themselves in a position where other people will spy on them, boss them, criticize them, burden them with responsibilities, make them the butt of gossip and ridicule, commit them to action against their will.

They can ignore or disrupt local organizations, but whether they like it or not they are under the control of the French Government and the hidden forces which they believe run the Government. They react characteristically. The person who does not vote pretends to ignore the Government as he pretends to ignore a person with whom he is *brouillé*. He symbolically assassinates it. The person who votes adopts an even more popular form of defense. Just as he insults and gossips about his enemy, inflicting harm on him orally, he uses the ballot as an insult to organized power. A few literal-minded voters cannot content themselves with expressing a destructive vote. They write insulting words on the ballot, even though they know the writing will cause their votes to be thrown out.

Seen in this light the political behavior of Peyrane loses its paradoxical appearance. In context it becomes understandable — if not right — that a conservative people should thus assert its will to protect the individual from collective human power.

This explanation raises three basic questions. Why should the people of Peyrane feel that collective human power is essentially baleful? Why do they not act collectively and creatively to control the power instead of simply cursing it? Why do they not make positive use of the one real weapon at their disposal — the vote?

The answers to these questions must be implicit in the facts of life in Peyrane as they have been described, but cultural, psychological, and historical information is still too fragmentary for me to think in terms of causal relationships. The best I can do is to suggest certain parallels which may have some bearing on the questions.

When I think of the individual of Peyrane faced with collective human power, an image immediately occurs to me. I see Alphonse Peretti stoically walking from school up to the church with his messy school theme pinned to his back so that people along the way will make fun of him. Or I see a little girl walking in a circle in the school yard, alone, with her hands on her head, with the sign "thief" pinned to her back, while the other children point at her and mock her. These are extreme and unusual cases, but they point forcefully to the essential disciplinary tools — shame and ridicule — which adults use with children both at home and at school. Children need not fear violence, mutilation, loss of love, separation from parents, threats of damnation or any of the other weapons which people in the world use to secure obedience from children. They are constantly faced, however, with shaming fingers and mocking laugher. To avoid the pain of public shame and ridicule children must learn to conform — on the surface at least. The revenge that is sometimes tolerated is for them to stand at a safe distance and shout insults.

How can a child avoid feeling as he grows up that people are ready to assail him collectively with the force of public scorn whenever he deviates from the behavior that is expected of him? And since no one can live without deviating from an ideal social code — both in action and in thought — almost everyone feels that society has cause to attack him. He is even further convinced that humans collectively are hostile because he assumes that they feel as hostile toward him as he feels toward them.

As the child grows up these personal feelings about collective human power are reinforced by conventional attitudes that have undoubtedly been current in Peyrane since the first individuals settled on the red hill. For there has never been a time since the beginning of Peyrane's history, when contact with organized humanity has meant anything but the exploitation and manipulation of the individual. The wandering hordes, the Romans, the feudal lords — including the neighboring papal rulers, the agents of Provençal counts and French kings, the nineteenth-century régimes set up by Paris, the twentieth-century bureaucracy centralized in Paris — all these form an unbroken past in the vague memory of the village. They all mean domination by a human power beyond the control of the individual. At best the domination has brought unsought modifications in living habits. At worst it has brought disaster. And so it has become conventional to think of human power as a plague to be classed with the plagues of nature: the odious government, the leveling mistral, the flooding Durance.

Later when adults come into actual contact with government these inner feelings and conventional attitudes toward human power, and especially toward government, seem to be confirmed. The most intimate contact a young man can have with a government agency comes through his military service. Whatever else one may say of an army, it is not designed to change the mind of a young man from Peyrane about his relationship with collective human power. He returns home changed in some respects but not in that one. And as he establishes his own family and assumes adult responsibility, he personally suffers from the direct and secondary effects of all the ills he has always heard attributed to government — war, taxation, inflation, legal restraints, administrative callousness.

But he also enjoys the benefits of government. How can he ignore the good that government accomplishes for him as an individual and for his family? Some of the benefits, like public health protection, eliminate suffering, and it is hard to feel and to appreciate an absence of suffering. Social security benefits are concrete and important, but they are obscured by inflation, red tape and charges of favoritism. Other benefits, like mail service, have become so natural a part of life that one accepts them unthinkingly. Others, like French honor in the French Union, are too abstract, too remote, and too tainted with private interests to evoke more than an indifferent or cynical reaction. The benefits of government as a whole lack the provoking immediacy of its oppressive effects. Confronted by this oppression, people want to seal themselves off so that outside authority can exert none of its malevolent control within the invisible frontier that separates the *foyer* from the rest of the world. Unable to do this, they stand back and shout insults — if only symbolically through the ballot.

To stand back and shout insults is not a constructive approach to the solution of a problem. Why do they not act instead of shouting?

The feeling of frustration does not paralyze all their activities. We have seen that when immediate family concerns are at stake there is no such despair. Members of the family participate positively in every aspect of family life. A child learns very young that he must share the problems. One after another, responsibilities are thrust on him, so that he acquires a growing sense of responsibility for the family's welfare. In this sphere he is impelled to act constructively.

But in other spheres of life, corporate responsibility and constructive participation by the individual are not stressed. We have seen that the school experience tends toward passivity and immobility. Children are not made to feel that the initiative is theirs as it is in the family. Spontaneity is not officially recognized in the educational system as it operates in Peyrane. A child who acts spontaneously risks being punished, and the punishment consists of forced immobilization of the body combined with shame. In formal learning emphasis is placed on deduction: children are not encouraged to "discover" a principle by themselves; it is presented to them as something to accept passively. Even in art class there is no place for free expression; children are asked to reproduce as realistically as possible a flower or a vase that is put before them. Recess play on the playground is unplanned, but children must behave with civilized caution. School experience does not, on the whole, develop an urge to act, to act adventurously to dominate one's own situation, to act coöperatively to improve the situation of the whole group. So far as the average student is concerned responsibility is something to be avoided. It may be recalled why Jacques Leporatti worked hard in school: "So they'll leave me alone!"

The school experience is paralleled in other spheres of life, especially in the relationship the child comes to have with his government. No government in the history of the village has tried seriously to give the individual a feeling of active, responsible participation. In the last hundred years he has been able to vote, but the centralization of the government is such that the individual still feels much more acted upon than acting. We have seen a good example of this in the episode of the new school building: the welfare of the village is frustrated by a remote centralized agency of government. Such incidents have more effect in the formation of attitudes than the "beautiful sentences" in the civics books. These sentences slide over the surface of the child's personality as smoothly as the injunction to be kind to little birds. He grows into adulthood and finds that outside the limits of the family he is treated on the whole more like a manipulated thing than a participating personality.

Of course, other peoples in the world may share this predicament and still believe individually that fate is in their individual hands. The people of Peyrane could reply only that this feeling of omnipotence is an illusion which they cannot share. They reject easy illusions and prefer to look unpleasant truths in the face. Once recognized for what they are, unpleasant truths may be accepted. One cannot act against them. Resignation is the remedy. The most common expression in Peyrane is, we have seen, "C'est comme ça."

But still there is the vote. Why do so many people throw away this one opportunity? Every vote cast has in intention the same negative meaning. Why should it not be used positively?

The attitude toward the vote may be given perspective by another aspect of the classroom situation. The immobilizing effect of the school experience is in a sense relieved by the existence of a sort of jungle area in which the formal system of punishments and rewards does not function. This, we have seen in the chapter on the school, is the area called "favors." The granting of favors is governed by unpredictable and rather mysterious feelings of one person toward another. Both parents and children expect the teacher to have pets because human likes and dislikes cannot be dictated. Spontaneity is not constrained here any more than it is in the *bien* and *brouillé* relations of the children and their parents among themselves. There is no resentment in the granting of favors so long as the official system of school laws is not infringed upon. A favor has nothing to do with laws because it has nothing to do with right and wrong. The fact that it is recognized as an exception guarantees the sanctity of the system itself.

As a child grows up he learns that this duality characterizes life. There is on the one hand the paralyzing network of official laws and regulations. Beneath this is the area of human relationships where with resourcefulness one may move freely to accomplish what may be legally unattainable. The existence of these two worlds may be amply documented with incidents that occur in Peyrane, but the most dramatic illustration is the case of Paul Rivet's hearing aid.

Through an improbable chain of efforts and coincidences Paul was sent a hearing aid by Big Joe Rosenfeld, the director of an American radio program called "Happiness Exchange." The customs officials at the Marignane airport notified Paul's father that the package could not be sent on until Rivet produced an import licence and ninety-six dollars customs duty. Since Rivet had not purchased the hearing aid he had no import licence, and he certainly could not produce the customs fee which was three times his monthly salary. He went to Marignane to explain the situation to officials. No reasoning could prod the hearing aid loose. Local officials could not or would not find a loophole in the rules and regulations so that a humanitarian purpose might be served. ("The law is the law, and we have no authority to change it. You'll have to see my superior. . . .") After weeks of frustration on different levels of official channels Rivet found a solution. He telephoned a childhood friend of his in Marseille who, he said, owns a bar and a string of racehorses. I do not know how the friend maneuvered to accomplish what he did, but I do know that he soon appeared in Peyrane with the hearing aid for Paul.

Frustrated in the area of rules and regulations, Rivet had retreated to the jungle area of human relations where he could move freely and effectively. He had utilized the "Système D" — the art of wangling, which is an essential lubricant in the stiffly functioning French legal machine. It is through this system that individual human rights may triumph over official restrictions when the two are in conflict. If one develops sufficient skill and good connections one can nullify the restricting force of rules and regulations. So a person's power depends less on his official position in society than on his skill in manipulating human relationships. Who would have thought that a little town clerk could successfully challenge the collective will incarnate in the Marignane customs clerks?

Generally speaking the people of Peyrane believe that effective action is accomplished not officially through legal channels but unofficially through personal contacts. Most people do not have contacts as powerful as Rivet's outside the commune. Without the "belles relations" necessary to maneuver in the area of favors and obligations they feel paralyzed in the area of laws and regulations. What is their power compared with the power of Rivet's friend? What is his power compared with the truly great powers in Paris? Against such forces the individual's vote is no more than an empty legal gesture. One would be naïve to take it for more than that. Offered to the individual as a gesture, the vote is used as a gesture — a gesture of defiance.

The exasperation of the citizen of Peyrane is intensified by his contradictory position. He would like to divorce himself from the rest of the world — and yet he does not want to. Monsieur Marnas cuts, cleans, and bunches his asparagus and takes it down to the edge of the road. Monsieur Borel comes along in his truck and takes it to Cavaillon where it is shipped to London. The amount of money that goes into Monsieur Marnas' wallet depends on the many factors that separate him from a London housewife who takes money out of her purse. These factors interest Monsieur Marnas. This is a bond with the outside world that he has no inclination to cut. It is a bond that is concrete and immediate, but beneficent rather than maleficent. If only for its sake, Monsieur Marnas and the people of Peyrane should be helped to think in more constructive terms of their relationship with the rest of the world.

They might be helped if there were in Peyrane a strong force to counter the traditional attitudes. Perhaps it would help if there were an agent of articulation, an Articulator who could interpret Peyrane and the outside world to each other. For this task one would need patience, sympathy, intelligence, imagination. Especially imagination, for this is probably the quality that the people of Peyrane lack most seriously — the imagination to grasp abstract goals beyond their concrete experience. They need a Complicator who could show them that oversimplified solutions do more harm than good.

But who could serve as Articulator, as Complicator? It is a tragedy that every year the two or three children who show qualities of creative leadership are encouraged to move away to the city. Their potential influence is lost to the commune. Of course, almost every village suffers the same loss, but most villages have a teacher or priest or mayor to exercise leadership. Peyrane has been unfortunate in this respect. Teachers stay only until they can secure transfer to the city where they can find intellectual companionship and supplementary sources of income. The priests who have been sent to live out their purgatory in Peyrane have been old, tired, and resigned, and now there is no resident priest at all. No mayor has served as a real leader since Monsieur Prullière. Rivet is intelligent and imaginative, but he lacks patience and confidence.

The only possible leaders in Peyrane are Chanon and Edouard Pascal. Chanon is friendly and has the confidence of people, who trust him despite his party affiliation, because "he's not so bad underneath." But Chanon lacks the intelligence and imagination to exert positive influence, and although he showed real courage in the *maquis* he curls into a ball whenever Pascal deigns to snarl at him. Pascal has imagination and intelligence, but his sour disposition, his nasty tongue, and his contempt for the villagers make him the most powerful destructive force in the community. His influence only reinforces the psychological barriers that frustrate human coöperation. Politics always leads to personalities in Peyrane, and our attempt to elucidate the political behavior of the people has led us to the gloomy personality of Edouard Pascal.

To many an American the political behavior of the people of Peyrane is the most puzzling aspect of their culture. We have dwelt on it because it needs interpretation. However, by emphasizing this one factor we risk leaving a distorted impression. After all politics is only a small part — and the least attractive part — of the general pattern of life in Peyrane. If we look at the pattern as a whole, each element falls into its proper perspective, and the little corner of political behavior assumes its proper proportion. Seen as a whole, what is life in Peyrane?

Peyrane is a place where a person can live with himself. He sees himself in the perspective of time and nature. He thinks it is important to "see things as they are," and he readily acknowledges the unpleasant along with the pleasant aspects of existence. He knows that his knowledge and experience are limited, but he respects the pursuit of knowledge both for its own sake and for the practical benefits he may derive from it. He has a clear conception of his roles in life, and he makes an effort to fulfil them without violating his inner needs. He enjoys being with himself. He can sit alone with no other entertainment than the contemplation of what goes on within him and around him. He listens to the radio occasionally and goes to the movies and to church now and then, but organized entertainment, comics, and pulp magazines do not interest him.

He also enjoys and is even stimulated by the company of other individuals. His relations with other people and his observation of their personal dramas bring warmth and excitement into his life. The somewhat tolerant regulation of sexual expression keeps a certain balance between his needs and those of society. He accepts his emotions but moderates them because he fears their extreme expression. He feels anger readily, but anger rarely results in physical violence. A tongue lashing usually brings sufficient release to calm him down, although he may feel compelled to "cut the other person dead" for years. Peyrane is a community where crime is almost unknown, a community with almost no homicide, suicide, theft, juvenile delinquency, or criminal assault. Consumption of alcohol is general, but there is almost no drunkenness.

Life in Peyrane is centered about the family, and the family is a strong, healthy organism. Children are wanted. They are treated with love, and they are carefully trained. There is little divorce. Old people are cared for. The most solemn occasion of the year is the celebration of All Souls' Day which unites the family about the family tomb. Formal religion is given formal recognition, but the deepest religious feelings relate directly to the family.

Peyrane is a hard-working, productive community. Though only one-third of the land is profitably arable, though it is inefficiently distributed, and though there are few other important natural resources in the commune, the people produce more than they consume. The wealth of the community is rather evenly divided: no one is extremely rich, and there is no misery. The health of the community is good. Housing is poor, but everyone is sheltered. Clothes may be patched, but everyone is clothed. Food is expensive, but everyone is fed.

If Adam and Eve were to return to life as they did in the Gaumont movie, they might well choose Peyrane as their Paradise Regained. Compared to most communities in the world today, Peyrane is well off. Its pattern of life seems balanced and sane. There is a bit of madness in the relationship of the Peyranais with the rest of the world. But when we look at life there and life elsewhere, it is not always clear on which side the madness lies.

6. Political Culture and "Competent" Citizens

SIDNEY VERBA

*In this article Professor Verba selects one aspect—the subjective percep-
tion of a citizen's competence to affect governmental decisions—as a variable crucial for the understanding of a democratic political culture. The
data on which the findings are based are, once again, those of the five-
nation comparative survey undertaken jointly by Verba and Gabriel
Almond. The cross-national survey method makes possible the separation and thus the refinement of variables, and helps clarify which features
are uniquely national cultural traits and which are primarily related to
citizens' position on the social pyramid.*

Democracy refers in some rough way to the degree to which power and
influence over significant decisions for a society is diffused throughout that
society. Political participation, therefore, will increase the extent to which a
nation is democratic only insofar as such participation involves at some point
influence by the participant over governmental decisions. Participatory acts
whose main function is to express support for the government are important,
but not as crucial to democracy as are acts that involve influence.

The influence of a group or individual over a governmental decision may be
defined as equal to the degree to which governmental officials act to benefit
that group or individual because the officials believe that they will risk some
deprivation (they will risk their jobs, be criticized, lose votes) if they do not so
act. Thus influence involves both the outcome of the decision (it will, to some
extent, be more advantageous to the influential groups or individual than it
would have been if that group or individual has not been influential), and the
motives of the decision-makers (they act to benefit the group because they
believe they will otherwise suffer some deprivation). The latter criterion is
important. Officials may act to benefit a particular group for a variety of
reasons; out of a feeling of paternalism, for instance. But it is only when
officials act because they fear the consequences of not so acting, that a group
may be considered to be influential and a participant in the decision.

Influence, and consequently democracy, are defined in terms of the way in
which governmental elites make decisions. But the problem of studying the
way in which such decisions are made is enormous, especially when one is
dealing with an entire nation, or as in this paper, with five nations at once.
No such attempt is made here. Rather, this paper concentrates not upon the

SOURCE: Reprinted by permission from Sidney Verba, "Political Participation and Strategies of Influence: A Comparative Study," *Acta Sociologica*, VI (1962), pp. 22–42.
Footnotes are abridged.

perceptions and behaviors of governmental elites but upon the perceptions and behaviors of the ordinary citizen. It will report some preliminary results to a series of survey questions on the amount of influence individuals believe they can exert over the government, and the ways in which they would go about it. The paper will concentrate on differences among the five nations surveyed — the United States, Britain, Germany, Italy, and Mexico. In subsequent publications, attempts will be made to explore and explain these differences further.

We are interested in the perception of the ordinary man as to how much influence he has over the decisions of his government. Thinking that one can influence the government or even attempting to influence government is not the same as actually influencing it. An individual may think he has influence over decisions or he may attempt to exert influence over decisions, and the government official may be unmoved. Conversely, he may believe that all government decisions are made without any consideration of his needs and desires and of the needs and desires of his fellow citizens, when, in fact, government officials constantly try to calculate the reactions of groups to their acts. In the latter case, an individual will exert influence without being aware he is doing so.

If the degree to which individuals believe they can influence the course of governmental decisions is not necessarily related to their actual level of influence, why study their subjective views as to their competence? There are several reasons. The perception that one can participate furthers such participation: if an individual believes he has influence, he is more likely to attempt to influence the government. A subjectively competent citizen, therefore, is more likely to be an active citizen. And if government officials do not necessarily respond to active influence attempts, they are more likely to respond to such attempts to influence than to a passive citizenry that makes no demands. If the ordinary citizen, on the other hand, perceives government policy as being far outside of his sphere of influence, he is unlikely to attempt to influence that policy and government officials are unlikely to worry about the potential pressure that can be brought to bear on them. Thus the extent to which citizens in a nation perceive themselves as competent to influence the government should be closely related to the extent of democracy in that country.

A good deal of the influence that individuals and groups exert over their government may not involve any conscious attempt on their part to influence. As our concept of influence specifies, governmental officials are being influenced if they respond to what they consider a possible deprivation. This implies that the citizen or group of citizens from whom they fear some deprivation may, at the time the government officials are acting, neither have attempted to influence these officials nor intend so to attempt. The government officials act in anticipation of certain consequences if they do not so act. They believe that if they do not act to benefit a group, that group will at some point in the future withdraw its support or its vote. In many respects a good deal of the influence that the ordinary citizen has over the decisions of the government officials may be of this anticipatory type.

But if one is interested in the extent of the perception that one can influence the government, one will have to concentrate on more overt and conscious attempts to affect actions of the government. Several questions may be asked about conscious attempts to influence the government:

1. Under what circumstances will an individual make some conscious effort to influence the government? Direct political influence attempts are rare. For the ordinary citizen, the activities of government — even local government — may seem quite distant. At the time that a decision is being made, the citizen will not be aware that it is being made or of what its consequences for him are likely to be. It is likely then, that only in situations of some stress in which a government activity is perceived to have a direct and serious impact upon the individual will a direct influence attempt be triggered off.

2. What method will be used in the influence attempt? Some major dimensions along which the method used can vary include: whether or not the attempt is made through legitimate channels; whether the attempt is violent or non-violent; whether the individual attempts to influence the government alone or attempts to enlist the support of others; and, if he seeks support, whose support does he seek.

3. What is the effect of the influence attempt? The problem of the extent to which the government official changes his behavior in response to some influence attempt on the part of a citizen is beyond the scope of this study. However, since it concentrates on the perspectives of the citizen, we shall consider his views as to the likelihood that an attempt made by him to influence the government would have any effect. That, after all, is a key question.

The Distribution of Subjective Competence

Does an individual feel he can influence his government? How would he go about it? Would it make any difference? Respondents were asked questions that attempted to place them in hypothetical stress situations. Each respondent was asked to suppose that a law were being considered by the national legislature that he considered very unjust and harmful. Could he do anything about it and, if so, what? He was then asked how much effect he thought any action he took would have, and how likely it was that he actually would do something. A similar set of questions was asked about an unjust and harmful regulation being considered by the most local governmental unit.[1] These questions attempted to get some notion of the respondent's views as to the extent of his political competence and, more important, of the strategy of influence open to him.

---

[1] The exact question wording on the national government was:
   — Suppose a law were being considered by (Appropriate national legislature specified for each nation) which you considered to be unjust or harmful, what do you think you could do?
   — If you made an effort to change this law, how likely is it that you would succeed?
   — If such a case arose, how likely is it you *would actually* try to do something about it?
The exact question wording on the local government was:
   — Suppose a regulation were being considered by (Most local governmental unit:

Table 1   *What Citizens Would Do to Try to Influence*
Their Local Government, by Nation

	U. S. %	U. K. %	Germany %	Italy %	Mexico %
Some citizens would try to enlist the support of others by:					
Organizing some informal group; arousing their friends and neighbors, getting them to write letters of protest or to sign a petition ..	56	34	13	7	26
Working through a political party	1	1	3	1	–
Working through some other formal group of which they are a member: union, church, professional group	4	3	5	1	2
TOTAL WHO WOULD ENLIST SUPPORT OF OTHERS*	59	36	22	8	28
Other citizens would, as individuals:					
Directly contact political leaders (elected officials) or the press. Write a letter to, or visit a local political leader	20	45	15	12	15
Directly contact administrative officials (nonelected officials)	1	3	31	12	18
Consult a lawyer; appeal through courts	2	1	3	2	2
Vote against offending officials at next election	14	4	1	1	–
Take some violent action	1	1	1	1	1
Just protest	–	–	–	12	–
Other	1	2	–	3	5
TOTAL WHO WOULD ACT AS INDIVIDUALS**	18	42	40	43	25
TOTAL WHO WOULD DO SOMETHING WITH OTHERS OR AS INDIVIDUALS*	77	77	62	51	52
Other respondents say they can do nothing	17	17	31	31	32
Other say they do not know if they can do anything	6	5	7	18	15
TOTAL RESPONDENTS	100	100	100	100	100
TOTAL RESPONSES	123	115	111	101	118
Number of cases	970	963	955	995	1295

* The total percentage is less than the total of the individual cells since some respondents gave more than one answer.
** This row includes only the respondents who replied that they could do something, but did not mention working with others. Hence, the total is less than some of the individual categories which contain respondents who may have mentioned both group activity and an individual activity.

Town? Village? Etc. specified) which you considered very unjust or harmful, what do you think you could do?
— If you made an effort to change this regulation how likely is it that you would succeed?
— If such a case arose, how likely is it that you *would actually* do something about it?

The question as to the amount of influence the ordinary man has is a fundamental political one and the response to it reflects an individual's perception of the nature of his government and of his own role as a citizen. Let us look at responses as to how amenable to influence is a local government. This is a good place to start because the impact of local government tends to be more immediate. And, for obvious reasons, people in all countries tend to think that one can do more about a local regulation than about a law considered by the national legislature. But what is striking are the sharp differences among nations in the number who think they can do something and in what these people think they can do. In response to the question on whether one can do anything about a local law that is unjust American and British respondents most frequently say that there is something they can do. More than three-quarters of the people interviewed in each of these two countries express the opinion that they have some recourse if they believe the local government is planning a law they consider unjust. (The data on what individuals say they can do about a local regulation is reported in Table 1. The figures we are considering here are near the bottom of the table.) In each country, only 17% say that there is nothing they can do. In the other three countries over 30% of those interviewed report that there is nothing they can do in such a situation. In Germany more people (62%) say they can do something than in Mexico and Italy (52% and 51%). In the latter two countries, respondents are more likely to say thay do not know what they can do. Clearly then the images that citizens have of their roles and potentials differ from nation to nation. Britons and Americans are more likely to think of themselves as competent to influence their local government than are people in the other three countries.

That an individual believes there is something he can do if the government is planning an unjust or unfair act does not mean that he will in fact try to do something. This was a hypothetical situation and, of course, one does not really know what respondents would do if they ever were in fact faced with such a challenging situation. But they were asked for their opinions on whether or not they actually would act. In all countries many who say they can do something about an unjust regulation report that in fact they probably would do nothing. But the number who report that there is at least some likelihood that they would make an effort, reflects the same national pattern reported above. 58% of the American respondents and 60% of those in Britain say that there is some likelihood that they would actually make an effort to influence an unjust regulation. In Germany 44% made some such affirmation, while in Italy 41% of the respondents say that they might act in these circumstances. (The question was, unfortunately, not asked in a comparable form in Mexico.) The American and British respondents express a willingness to act much more frequently than do the respondents in Germany and Italy.

Lastly, there is some evidence that the subjective estimate of one's propensity to act in such a challenging political situation is not completely unrelated to actual attempts to influence the government. In all five nations a substantially larger proportion of those respondents who say there is something they can do about a local unjust regulation (let us, for convenience, call them "local competents") report some experience in attempting to influence the local government than is reported among those who say there is nothing they can do. These data are reported in Table 2.

Table 2   *Proportion of Those Respondents Who Say They Have Attempted to Influence the Local Government Among Local Competents and Local Noncompetents*

	Proportion of respondents who have attempted to influence the government.	
	Among local competents %	Among local non-competents %
U. S.	33 (745)*	10 (225)
U. K.	18 (748)	3 (217)
Germany	21 (590)	2 (355)
Italy	13 (508)	4 (487)
Mexico	9 (677)	2 (618)

* Numbers in parentheses refer to the base upon which percentage was calculated.

At this point we are merely describing differences among nations in the political attitudes of respondents. In this connection it is clear that the frequency with which individuals report that they could have some effect upon a law contemplated by the local government differs from nation to nation. The explanation of these differences is more difficult. At least part of the explanation of the differences in the degree to which individuals believe they are politically competent rests upon the differing structures of government. The individual who says he can do nothing to oppose the local government may be making a quite realistic appraisal of his potentialities. Thus the lower frequency of subjective political competence in Italy, for instance, may be largely a reaction to a political structure — the Italian prefecture system — that does not allow the individual to be politically competent. It is not that individuals choose to be uninfluential. It may be that they have no choice.

The frequency with which individuals say they could exert some influence over the local government is clearly a case in which attitudes are affected significantly by governmental structure (although there is evidence that they are not completely determined by these structures). Let us turn to a more significant aspect of political competence than the extent to which individuals believe themselves competent; an aspect of competence that is not as clearly affected by the structure of the local government. This is the strategy an individual would use in attempting to influence the government. The way in which those individuals who report that they *could* influence the government report they *could go about* exerting this influence is, of course, important. It makes a difference whether an individual has, on the one hand, only the vaguest notion as to what he can do in such a situation or on the other, a clear and explicit view of the channels open to him for expressing his point of view. It also makes a difference what resources he believes he has available to use in such a situation. Furthermore, the strategy that an individual would use will naturally have an effect on the extent to which his subjective view of his ability to influence will represent real influence potential — that is, represent the sort of activity that has some chance of changing the behaviors of the government officials. Lastly, by concentrating on how those who think they can have influence would go about exerting that influence, we can partially eliminate (but only partially) the effect of the differing degrees to which local governments are amenable to influence. We shall deal primarily with those who think they have influence, the "local competents," and ask how they would exert that influence.

The Strategy of Influence

The strategies of influence that individuals report they would use are summarized in Table 1. Consider first the question of what social resources the individual feels he has available to him in attempting to influence the local government. When one looks at the individual and his government, one is tempted to see him as lonely, powerless, and somewhat frightened by the immensity of the powers he faces. Whatever the validity of this view may be in terms of the actual amount of power the average man has and the social resources to him, our data suggest that a large number of our respondents think of themselves neither as powerless nor, what is more important, as alone, in their relationship to the government.

This fact is reflected in the data reported in Table 1. A number of respondents believe that they can enlist the support of others in their attempts to influence the government. What is most striking is the variation from country to country in the numbers who feel they can call on others to aid them. In the United States, 59% of the respondents indicate that they would attempt to enlist the support of others if they wish to change a regulation they consider unjust. At the other extreme, only 8% of the Italian sample mention the use of this social resource. In the other countries, the percentages reporting that they would try to enlist the support of others varies from 36% in Britain, to 28% in Mexico, to 22% in Germany.[2]

Who is it that citizens would enlist to support them? Individuals as we know are members of a large number of social structures. They are not merely citizens of their nations; they are members of families, communities, churches, voluntary associations, trade unions and a myriad of other groups and organizations. Much has been written about the important role of formal organizations in the political process — in particular, the role of political parties and formal associational interest groups. But what the data show most strikingly is that when it comes to the support that individuals believe they could enlist in a challenging political situation, they think much more often of enlisting the support of the informal face-to-face groups of which they are members than they think of enlisting the support of the formal organizations with which they are affiliated.

---

[2] Since question wording can seriously affect responses, it is important to note here that the notion that one can enlist the support of others was in no way suggested by the question or by the interviewer's probing of the question. Interviewers were carefully instructed not to ask such questions as: "Is there anyone you could get to help you?" or "Would you attempt to do this alone or with other people?"

In all countries, the numbers are few who say that they would work through their political party if they were attempting to counteract some unjust regulation being considered by the local government. Less than 1% of the respondents — with the exception of Germany, where the figure is about 3% — mention that they would work through their political party. Clearly, no matter how important the role of political parties may be in democratic societies, relatively few citizens think of them first as the place where support may be enlisted for attempts to influence the government.[3]

In all countries, more individuals report that they would attempt to work through other formal organized groups than would attempt to work through political parties. But even when one considers the entire range of formal organizations to which people may belong, the numbers who report they would enlist the support of these organizations is small, in no country going above 5% of all the respondents (as seen on Table 1) or 9% of the local competents.[4] Of course, not all respondents have some formal organization at their disposal. Such organizations are most frequent in some nations than in others. And the percentage who report membership differs substantially from country to country. Furthermore, not all formal organizations are equally politically relevant. But even if one considers only those respondents who belong to some formal organization that they report is involved in politics, the percentage invoking such membership in a stress situation is much smaller than the percentage who are members. In the United States where such memberships are most frequent, 228 respondents report membership in some organization that they consider to be involved in some way with government or politics, but only 35 Americans report that they would work through such an organization if they were trying to influence a local regulation. In Italy where such memberships are least frequent, we find the same pattern. Fifty-six Italians belong to some organization they believe is involved in political affairs, but only 13 Italians would work through a formal organization if they were trying to influence a local regulation. The greatest frequency of mention of formal organization is found in Germany, but it is still only half as frequent as the frequency of membership in a politically relevant organization.

---

[3] To some extent the infrequent mention of a political party in the context probably understates the role of parties in this influence process. Many more respondents mentioned contacting government officials. If they explicitly mentioned that the partisan affiliation of the official was relevant in giving them access to him, they would be coded as working through a party. But many may have considered this affiliation relevant, even if it was not mentioned.

[4] The percentage of respondents mentioning a particular strategy of influence can be computed either as a percentage of the entire population or as a percentage of the local competents — in this latter case, that is, as a percentage of those who feel there is something they can do. Both figures are important. The first figure reflects frequency of certain types of political behavior in a nation. But if we are interested in how nations differ in the strategies their citizens will use, we must use the second figure — the percentage of local competents who would use a particular strategy — for, otherwise, differences between nations in the percentage choosing a particular strategy might be merely a reflection of the fact that there are more in one country than another who report that there is "nothing" they could do.

That formal organizations are rarely invoked as the resource that individuals would use if they were trying to enlist some support for their attempt to influence the government does not mean that these organizations are unimportant politically. They still operate on what we have called the passive level — that is, the citizen has influence over government officials by being a member of such a group, but he does not necessarily make any overt attempt to influence the government. And this sort of influence is of a great significance, perhaps of greater overall significance than the overt influence attempts that citizens from time to time will make. Furthermore though individuals would not use their formal organizations as the means to influence the government directly, such formal membership enhances the prospects that an individual will believe himself capable of influencing the government and will in fact make some such attempt. Thus, even though he does not directly use his group membership in attempting to influence the local government, an individual may, for a variety of reasons, develop greater self-confidence in his own political competence through organization membership.

Cooperative Political Behavior

If one is interested in who it is that citizens believe they can enlist to support them if they are trying directly and consciously to influence an act of their local government, one must turn to the informal face-to-face groups to which they belong. In all countries, respondents more frequently mention enlisting the support of such groups — arousing their neighbors, getting friends and acquaintances to support their position, circulating a petition — than they mention using some formal organization. This is seen in the top row of Table 1. The differences among nations are quite sharp here. These differences are highlighted if one considers the proportion of local competents (i.e., those who believe they can influence the local government) who say they would cooperate with their fellow citizens in attempting to influence the government: 73% of American local competents would use informal groups, whereas only 13% of Italian local competents and 22% of the German would do so. In Mexico, though the proportion of local competents is relatively low, the proportion of these local competents who would work through informal groups is quite high, — 50%. And in Britain, the proportion of local competents who say they would seek the cooperation of others is about as great, — 43%.

The belief that cooperation with one's fellow citizens is both a possible political action and an effective one, it may be suggested, represent a highly significant orientation from the point of view of a democratic political system. The diffusion of influence over political decisions by which we define democracy implies some cooperative ability among the citizenry. This cooperation would appear to be necessary in terms both of the amount of influence the ordinary man could otherwise expect to have and the results of the influence of the ordinary man on governmental decisions. By definition, the "average" man's influence over the government must be small. Compared with the forces of the government and the state he is a frail creature indeed, and this would apply to local as well as national government. If the ordinary man is to have any influence vis-à-vis the government, it must be in concert with his fellows. Secondly, uncooperative and completely individualistic influence attempts could only lead to dysfunctional results from the point of view of the output of a democratic government. Every individual demand cannot be met or the result will be chaos. If the government is to be responsive to the demands of the ordinary man, those demands must be aggregated, and the aggregation of interests implies cooperation among men. The aggregation of interests involved in the cooperation of groups of like-minded individuals is aggregation on a rather low level, but it does suggest a propensity to work together with one's fellows that is relevant for larger political structures as well. In any case, one may suggest that the citizen who believes that he can work cooperatively with others in his environment if he wants to engage in political activity has a quite different perspective on politics from the individual who thinks of himself as a lone political actor.

Furthermore, the notion that one can affect a government decision by bringing one's peers into the dispute is a highly political notion. It represents a fairly clear attempt to use political influence in one's relations with government officials. The invocation of others in the dispute indicates that in this way the individual hopes to bring pressure on the officials, to threaten them with some deprivation if they do not accede to his demands. The threat that many make — whether it be the threatened loss of votes or of support, or the threat of public criticism — is, other things being equal, greater than the threat that one can make. Thus the individual who mentions getting others to join him in his dispute with the government is more likely to be an individual who sees himself as able to influence his government. And the variation among the five nations in the frequencies with which such groups are mentioned reflects a varying distribution of such citizen competence.

Lastly, the importance of this propensity toward cooperation with one's fellow political actors is stressed not merely because such behavior has significant consequences for a political system, but because it is a type of behavior which cannot be understood and explained solely in terms of differences in the structure of local government. The difference between the individual who responds that he would write a letter to the local council and the individual who responds that he would write a letter to the local council *and try to induce his friends to do likewise* cannot be explained by differences among nations in the structure and powers of their respective local councils.[5] Furthermore, as

---

[5] This is not completely true. Governmental structure may be more amenable to group influence in some countries than in others. But this is more likely to be the case because of experience in the past with such groups, rather than formal structure. On the other hand, there is no doubt that certain structures of government foster such "banding together" protests more than others. Structures where power is diffused among a large number of autonomous or semi-autonomous boards and councils and the like (especially elected boards and councils) are more likely to foster such protest than structures dominated by a centrally appointed official whose domain includes a larger area (as with the Italian prefect system). But this is an example of the general proposition that there will be an interaction between political orientation and political structure. In this case, however, the explanation of the origins of this group-forming attitude in terms of formal structure alone would be quite hard. One has to look beyond the structure of the local government.

we shall see shortly, the propensity to cooperate politically cannot be explained in terms of differing levels of social and economic development in the five nations. The origin of this propensity toward political cooperation must be sought elsewhere.[6]

Though the use of primary groups as a resource for influence is most common in the United States, Britain and Mexico, several interesting differences between the United States and Britain on the one hand and Mexico on the other in this respect must be mentioned. The notion that one can mobilize an informal group to aid one in the process of attempting to influence the government, appears to be of greater significance for the actual exercise of influence in the former two countries. Earlier it was pointed out that those who report they can do something about an unjust local law (the local competents) are much more likely also to report some experience in attempting to influence the government. If we look only at the local competents and ask how those who would work through groups and those who would attempt to influence the government alone differ in terms of the extent of their experience in attempted influence, we find that in the United States and Britain those who would work through groups are more likely to be those who have had experience in attempting to influence their local government. In the United States 36% of those who report they would work through informal groups (n: 547) report experience in influence attempts, whereas only 25% of those local competents who would use some other strategy (n: 198) report such experience. In Britain the parallel figures are 23% for those who mention informal groups (n: 315) and 15% for other local competents (n: 414). On the other hand, in Mexico, those who mention informal groups are a bit less likely to be the experienced respondents — 7% report experience of those who mention informal groups (n: 339) as against 10% of the other local competents (n: 344).[7]

Furthermore, in the former two countries, the use of informal groups as a

---

[6] The relationship between social and economic groupings and the propensity to form groups will be discussed at the end of the chapter. The explanation of this group-forming propensity in terms of social values and partisan fragmentation will be attempted in forthcoming publication.

That one can show the relationship between social grouping and the propensity to form groups as well as attempt an explanation for this propensity in terms of other attitudes illustrates the advantage of "discovering" this group-forming propensity in a study based on a systematic survey rather than "discovering" this group-forming propensity through the sort of keen but unsystematic observation of a writer like Tocqueville — who certainly noticed and was impressed by the way in which political groups could be easily formed when needed in the United States.

In the first place, one now knows about the relative propensities to form groups in a new way. Those of us who work on studies of this sort like to think that the data are more reliable when systematically gathered. Secondly, the knowledge is more precise. One can not only distinguish among nations more finely, one can specify who it is within the nation who is likely to think of forming groups of this sort. And lastly, one can explore the roots of this group-forming propensity by seeing the ways in which those individuals who think of forming such groups differ from other respondents who do not. Thus, not only is the knowledge more precise, it is more useful since it can lead to further knowledge.

[7] In Germany, those local competents who mention informal groups are somewhat less likely to be experienced. 17% of those who mention informal groups (n: 126) report

means of influencing the government is seen not only as a means to protest but as the key to effective protest. In order to test the extent to which individuals felt they could influence their local government, respondents were asked another question: "If you made an effort to change this regulation, how likely is it that you would succeed?" Of interest to us here is that a large number of American and British local competents volunteered the statement that their protest would have some likelihood of success only if others joined with them. (The percentages were 30% in the United States and 20% in Britain.) In Mexico, though a good percentage felt that there was some likelihood that they would succeed if they attempted to influence their local government, fewer than 10% of the Mexican respondents suggested that this would only be the case if they had the support of others. Thus, though the use of informal groups is perceived as a means of influence in Mexico, it is not yet perceived as the key to effective influence.[8])

One further difference deserves mention. In the United States and Britain, the use of informal groups as a means of influencing a governmental decision is considered much more appropriate on the local level than on the national level. In the United States 73% of the local competents report that they would work through informal groups in attempting to influence the local government, whereas only 38% of the national competents (i.e., those who believe they could do something if the national government were considering a law they thought unjust) would work through such groups. In Britain, similarly, 43% of the local competents would work through informal groups, while only 28% of the national competents would do so. On the other hand, in Mexico, the proportion of local and national competents who would use informal groups is about the same — 50% of local competents mention informal groups as the means they would use to influence the local government and 46% of national competents say that this is the means they would use to influence the national government. The fact that the use of such groups is more closely related both to experience and to expectations of success in Britain and the United States than in Mexico, coupled with the fact that such strategy is considered more appropriate in connection with the local government in the former two countries suggests that such informal group strategy is based on a more realistic appraisal of the potentialities of such a strategy — a realistic appraisal deriving from actual experience with such groups on the local level. In Mexico, this influence strategy is less well grounded in actual local experience.

Individual Activities

Among those respondents who spoke of themselves as acting as individuals in an attempt to influence the government there is some variation, as Table 1 indicates, in the strategies they mention. In the United States and Britain respondents are more likely to say that they would approach an elected gov-

---

experience as against 23% of local competents who do not mention such groups (n: 460). In Italy, those local competents who mention groups are slightly more likely to be experienced: 16% (n: 67) as against 13% (n: 438) of those who do not mention groups.

[8] In Germany the percentage of local competents who mentioned that they would succeed only if others joined them was 12%; in Italy it was 5%.

ernment official rather than an appointed official of the bureaucracy. In Mexico and Italy, respondents are as likely to say they would direct their protest toward one type of official as toward the other. In Germany, in contrast, more respondents mention appointed officials than mention elected officials as the target of their protest. It is tempting to consider these results to be a reflection of a more highly developed political competence in the United States and Britain. A protest to an elected official would appear to be inherently more of a political protest in the sense of involving an implied threat of deprivation to the official if he does not comply — since the loss of the vote is the most usual deprivation with which the individual can threaten an offending official. To some extent this may be an explanation of the differences among the nations in the chosen targets of influence attempts, but it is more likely that these differences merely reflect differences in the relative position and importance of elected and appointed officials within the structures of local governments in the respective nations.

Lastly, in considering the strategies that local competents say they would use, it is important to note that not all those who say they could do something about a local regulation they consider unjust have any clear strategy in mind. As Table 1 indicates, 12% of the Italian respondents say that they can "protest" if faced with a regulation they consider unjust, but when asked how or to whom they can protest, give no more specific reply. The 12% who would "protest" represent about one-fourth of all Italian local competents. While this answer shows a higher level of subjective competence than the answer that one could do nothing (the right to gripe and complain being perhaps one of the last and most basic of democratic rights), it certainly reflects little awareness of the political channels through which one might effectively approach the government.[9]

Distribution Patterns of Influence and Influence Strategies

The data presented so far indicate some rather sharp differences among the nations. But the data are rather crude, representing, as they do, national totals. One would want to go further and seek some explanation for these differences. This will not be attempted in this paper, but the question will be considered of the extent to which such differences are explicable in terms of differences in the social class compositions of the samples for the various nations (and, since these were national samples, in the social class compositions of the nations.) We shall consider three questions: the extent to which the attitudes reported in the previous section are related in similar ways to social groups in the five nations (does, for instance, perceived influence increase with social class in all five nations?); the extent to which differences among nations diminish when one compares similar social groups; and the extent to which

---

[9] The data on the response to the question about the national government cannot be discussed here. In general, there is less competence expressed in connection with an unjust act of the national government, but the patterns of differences among the nations are about the same.

differences among differing social groups within a single nation are greater or less than differences among similar social groups across the nations. The answer to the last question, of course, depends on the first two. If, when one controls for some social class variable, one finds that the frequency of a political attitude varies sharply and in a similar manner with that variable from nation to nation and that the differences among nations tend to disappear, one will then find that differences among groups within a nation are greater than differences among similar groups across the nations.

The answers to these three questions will help us decide if the differences in political attitudes discussed in the earlier part of the paper are, in some sense, "real" differences in political style among the nations, or if they are explicable in terms of differing levels of social and economic development in the various nations — in terms, for instance, of the fact that there are many more respondents with no education in our Italian and Mexican samples than in the other nations. If a political attitude varies sharply with a social attribute in all the nations, if the differences among the nations tend to diminish when one controls for the social attribute, and if those of a particular social group are more like others of a similar social group in other nations than they are like their fellow citizens of a different social group one probably has a political attitude less intrinsic to the political style in a particular nation and more dependent on the level of social and economic development in the nation. On the other hand, if the attitude is not closely related to social grouping, if all groups in a nation are likely to respond the same way, and in ways that differ from similar groups in other nations; if therefore, an Italian from the upper class is more likely to respond like an Italian of the lower class than like a German of the upper class, one is probably dealing with an aspect of political style more intrinsic to a particular nation.

As an indicator of social group, we shall use the respondent's educational attainment. This is selected because it is a social attribute that is closely related to political attitudes and that differs sharply in its distribution from nation to nation. (For instance, 35% of the sample in the United States did not go beyond primary school education, in contrast with 69% of the Italian sample.) It will not be possible to report data for other social attributes, but suffice to say that the pattern of attitudes one would find if one considered such characteristics as occupation or income would be almost identical.

As Figure 1 clearly points out, in all countries the more education an individual has, the more likely is he to consider himself capable of influencing the local government; that is, to be what we have called a local competent. (The percentage of individuals who say they could affect a local law is measured on the vertical axis; the level of education on the horizontal.) Fifty-eight percent of those who did not get beyond primary school are local competents in the United States; 94% of those with some college education are. And the pattern repeats itself in each country. This then is a clear uniformity across national lines. No matter what the frequency in a nation of local competence, the incidence of this competence is greater among those with higher education.

What about the question of the differences among and within nations? The question is a bit harder to answer for differences exist both among educational groups within the same country (as the slopes of the lines indicate) and within similar educational groups among nations (as the different lengths of the lines indicate). Some differences among nations diminish significantly within matched educational groups. For instance, though the national totals for local competents are quite different as between the United States and Germany, the differences between the two countries almost disappear when similar educational groups are compared. On the other hand, the two pairs of nations that are almost similar in terms of the national totals, the United States and Britain, on the one hand, and Mexico and Italy on the other, differ somewhat more

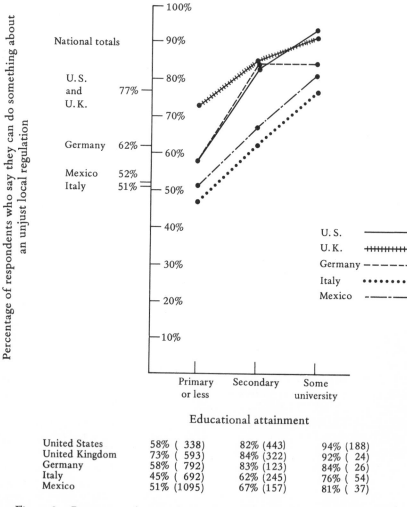

	Primary or less	Secondary	Some university
United States	58% (338)	82% (443)	94% (188)
United Kingdom	73% (593)	84% (322)	92% (24)
Germany	58% (792)	83% (123)	84% (26)
Italy	45% (692)	62% (245)	76% (54)
Mexico	51% (1095)	67% (157)	81% (37)

Figure 1   *Percentage of respondents who say they can do something about a local regulation they consider unjust, by nation and education*

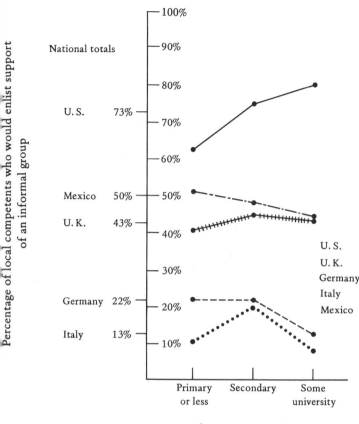

	Primary or less	Secondary	Some university
United States	63% (203)	75% (366)	81% (178)
United Kingdom	41% (433)	46% (272)	45% (22)
Germany	22% (461)	22% (102)	14% (22)
Italy	11% (310)	20% (151)	9% (44)
Mexico	51% (541)	49% (106)	46% (28)

Figure 2 *Percentage of local competents who would enlist the support of an informal group in order to influence a local regulation they consider unjust, by nation and education*

from each other within matched educational groups than they do on the national level. This is the case among those with primary school education in the case of the United States and Britain, where Britons show a higher rate of citizen competence, and in all educational groups for Italy and Mexico, with the Mexicans showing somewhat higher competence on the lower two levels and somewhat lower competence on the higher level.

What about the problem of which are greater, national differences or educational differences? The measure of this is rough, but if one compares the range between the highest and lowest nation within each educational group with the range between the highest and lowest educational group within each nation, the results suggest that there is certainly as much if not, on the average, more variation among educational groups within a single nation than among those with similar educational attainment in different nations. The range between the nation with the greatest frequency of local competents and the nation with the smallest frequency is 28 percentage points (between Britain and Italy) on the elementary school level, 22 percentage points (again between Britain and Italy) on the secondary school level, and 18 percentage points (between the United States and Italy) on the university level. Within each nation, on the other hand, there is about as much if not more difference among the differing educational levels in the frequency with which respondents believe themselves competent to influence the government. The ranges between the educational group that most frequently reports itself competent to influence the government (those with some university education in each nation) and the group that least frequently reports such competence (those with only primary education or no education in each country) are: United States, 36 percentage points; Britain, 19 percentage points; Germany, 26 percentage points; Italy, 31 percentage points; and Mexico, 30 percentage points. These figures compare extremes in terms of education and in terms of nation. But they do suggest that in terms of overall local competence, similar educational groups compared cross-nationally are at least as similar and perhaps more similar than are different educational groups within a nation.

So far we have considered the extent to which individuals believe they can influence a local unjust regulation. But the strategy an individual would use may be more important than the simple distinction of whether or not he thinks he can do anything. In particular the belief that one can cooperate with one's fellow citizen as a means of influencing the government appears to be important. Does this particular political strategy depend to as large an extent upon educational attainments as does the existence of local competence? The data in Figure 2 suggest that this is not the case. The percentage of local competents who would work through informal groups varies sharply from country to country even within each educational group, but varies very little among educational groups within the individual countries.[10] Only in the United States does the frequency with which such activity is mentioned vary directly with educational attainment, and even in this case the relationship is not as strong as that between education levels in terms of local competence in general. Consider again the contrast between the United States and Germany. When we consider similar educational groups, German and American respondents hardly differ in the frequency with which they say that there is something they can do about a local unjust regulation. But if we compare the percentage of the local competents who would cooperate with their fellow citizens, we see that on each educational level, German respondents are much less likely

---

[10] The data are calculated as a percentage of local competents not of the total population. This is to isolate the political strategy that competents would use from the fact that the frequency of competents differs from country to country.

to mention such activity. Furthermore, more highly educated Germans respondents are no more likely to talk of such activity than are less highly educated ones. In general, unlike the situation in relation to overall local competence where the range of difference among nations was no greater and perhaps a little less than the range of variation among educational groups, the variation among nations in the frequency with which political cooperation is mentioned is much greater on all educational levels than in the variation among educational groups within a nation.[11] Here, then, may be a pattern of political behavior whose existence is independent of the educational level in a nation. Education, the data suggest, may lead individuals to believe that they can influence their government, no matter what country they live in (providing, of course, that there is at least some institutional structure to support this). The data also suggest that as the overall educational levels of nations rise, they will become more similar in this respect. But education does not necessarily increase the potentiality that individuals will create groups to support them. The ability to create political structures through cooperation with one's fellow citizens in time of stress seems to be typical of some nations and not of others. It is an element of political style, not a result of educational attainment.

The data on differences among social groups in citizen competence suggest that it makes a great deal of difference who you are within your own country whether or not you believe yourself able to influence a local regulation. If you have more education, a higher status or are male, you are clearly more likely to consider yourself competent. In this sense, one's self-perceptions of one's role as a citizen vary greatly with one's social position within a nation. But whether or not the local competent believes that his friends and neighbors are available to help him in a situation of this sort depends relatively little on his social position within a nation, but depends heavily on what nation he happens to be in. Political competence, thus, grows with higher education or occupational status, but the style of political competence seems to be rooted more in general political culture.[12]

---

[11] The difference between the pattern in relation to the extent to which individuals think they have influence and that in relation to their strategy of influence is quite striking if one compares Figures 1 and 2.

[12] As mentioned earlier, a similar pattern would appear if one controlled for other indicators of social group. The intriguing question is, of course, how does one explain the differences in propensity to form groups if such social variables do not explain it.

Part 2

PERCEPTION OF POLITICS—
MASSES AND ELITES

The normative model of democracy emphasized the value of equality, stressing either the individual voter's capacity to form a rational view of public issues and the relation between these and his own interest; or the policymakers' responsiveness to "public opinion," which was conceived "as a mysterious vapor that emanated from the indifferentiated citizenry and in some way or another enveloped the apparatus of government to bring it into conformity with the public will."[1] This simple normative approach has been seriously shaken during the past three decades, with the analysis of extensive survey research into citizens' perceptions of the wide realm of politics, the values underlying democratic constitutions, of issues, parties, and candidates.

In whatever democratic polity these surveys were carried through they have revealed a highly tangled picture, in which, however, some features stand out starkly to form a unifying bond between diverse nations. These similarities include the presence of a large stratum of politically indifferent and inattentive citizens alongside groups with varying, but considerably higher, levels of political interest and activity. We lack the historical data to generalize about periods prior to our own, but at least for the present period (roughly dating from the end of World War II), this division — a relatively small number of political "attentives" and large masses of more or less passive and inattentive spectators — appears an established fact of what has come to be called "mass

---

[1] V. O. Key, Jr., *Public Opinion and American Democracy* (New York: Alfred A. Knopf, 1967), p. 536.

democracy." This has meant that a series of standard generalizations or explanations about the functioning of democratic systems — not only normative but also supposedly empirical generalizations — have had to be revised. I would like to mention but three — well known from the traditional literature — that must be questioned in the face of findings contained in some of the selections that follow:

- the existence of a basic "consensus on fundamentals" to account for the stability of American democracy (at least since the Civil War).
- the alleged French susceptibility to divisive political ideologies to explain the frequent crises that have shaken the French system.
- the assumption that where conditions provide for direct participation within a small territory — the contemporary test case is Switzerland — political knowledge, interest, and activity will be vastly greater than under conditions of mass democracy.

In all three of these cases, it was found that political knowledge, interest, and activity remained limited to minorities (varying in size), so that the generalizations held at best — and this in itself is an important finding — for the political elites that form the active core of the democratic process. Thus, the fate and functioning of democracy appears to depend largely on the values and expectations held by these elites. This is one important reason for the previous assertion that no simple linkage should be assumed between the political culture at the mass level and the functioning of the democratic process.

The attempt to make cross-national comparisons has, however, brought forth not only similarities or uniformities, but also some significant differences, both in the relative quantitative distribution between "attentive" and "indifferent" strata, and between their perceptions of and orientations toward the respective national political institutions and processes. Thus, the comparison between the degree of "politicization" in the United States and France not only explodes the myth of the "ideologized" French electorate; it also shows the contrast between a strongly ideologized, dissensus-ridden French elite, qualitatively separated from the mass electorate; and the consensual American "attentives," differing primarily on policies among each other, sloping more gradually toward the "lower" strata.

The discovery of carefully defined differences is valuable to the student of democratic politics in at least two ways: It directs his attention to variables that may account for these differences, and thus to a more precise interpretation of the interaction between institutional arrangements (themselves embedded in historically grown social structures), and the degree and nature of "politicization." This, in turn, prevents him from universalizing his national experience, and from assuming (if he is an American, for example) that voters everywhere are as ignorant of issues as the mass of Americans have been found to be — thus giving impetus to a normatively inspired urge to alter institutions toward more rationality and participation in the democratic process.

In the absence of extensive longitudinal studies, the following selections include a few rigorous cross-national investigations, though the methods employed differ among them and thus prevent genuinely multi-national comparisons. In addition, analyses dealing with individual countries are included where they appear to throw some new light on traditional assumptions or to provide information roughly comparable to that given in other studies.

7. Consensus and Ideology in American Politics

HERBERT McCLOSKY

The concept of "consensus" has been widely employed to explain the stability of democratic systems. On closer analysis it has, however, proved an extremely vague and complex concept, which requires much refinement before it can be employed as a genuinely explanatory variable. In his conclusions Professor McClosky moves beyond the American scene and questions the assumed linkage between consensus and democratic stability in other Western nations.

The belief that consensus is a prerequisite of democracy has, since deTocqueville, so often been taken for granted that it is refreshing to find the notion now being challenged. Prothro and Grigg,[1] for example, have questioned whether agreement on "fundamentals" actually exists among the electorate, and have furnished data which indicate that it may not. Dahl,[2] reviewing his study of community decision-makers, has inferred that political stability does not depend upon widespread belief in the superiority of democratic norms and procedures, but only upon their *acceptance*. From the findings turned up by Stouffer,[3] and by Prothro and Grigg, he further conjectures that agreement on democratic norms is greater among the politically active and aware — the "political stratum" as he calls them — than among the voters in general. V. O. Key,[4] going a step further, suggests that the viability of a democracy may depend less upon popular opinion than upon the activities and values of an "aristocratic" strain whose members are set off from the mass by their political influence, their attention to public affairs, and their active role as society's policy makers. "If so, any assessment of the vitality of a democratic system should rest on an examination of the outlook, the sense of purpose, and the beliefs of this sector of society."

Writers who hold consensus to be necessary to a free society have commonly failed to define it precisely or to specify what it must include. Even Tocque-

SOURCE: Reprinted by permission from *The American Political Science Review*, LVIII (June 1964), pp. 361–379. Appendices have been deleted.

[1] James W. Prothro and C. W. Grigg, "Fundamental Principles of Democracy: Bases of Agreement and Disagreement," *Journal of Politics*, Vol. 22 (Spring, 1960), pp. 276–94.

[2] Robert A. Dahl, *Who Governs?* (New Haven, 1961), ch. 28.

[3] Samuel A. Stouffer, *Communism, Conformity, and Civil Liberties* (New York, 1955).

[4] V. O. Key, "Public Opinion and the Decay of Democracy," *Virginia Q. Rev.*, Vol. 37 (Autumn, 1961), pp. 481–94. See also David B. Truman, "The American System in Crisis," *Political Science Quarterly*, Vol. 74 (Dec., 1959), pp. 481–97. John Plamenatz, "Cultural Prerequisites to a Successfully Functioning Democracy: a Symposium," *American Political Science Review*, Vol. 50 (March, 1956), p. 123.

ville[5] does not go deeply enough into the matter to satisfy these needs. He tells us that a society can exist and, *a fortiori*, prosper only when "the minds of all the citizens [are] rallied and held together by certain predominant ideas; . . . when a great number of men consider a great number of things from the same aspect, when they hold the same opinions upon many subjects, and when the same occurrences suggest the same thoughts and impressions to their minds" — and he follows this pronouncement with a list of general principles he believes Americans hold in common. Elsewhere, he speaks of the "customs" of the American nation (its "habits, opinions, usages, and beliefs") as "the peculiar cause which renders that people able to support a democratic government." But nowhere does he set forth explicitly the nature of the agreement upon which a democratic society presumably depends.

Later commentators have not clarified matters much. Some, like A. Lawrence Lowell,[6] have avoided Tocqueville's emphasis upon shared ideas, customs, and opinions in favor of the less demanding view that popular government requires agreement mainly "in regard to the legitimate character of the ruling authority and its right to decide the questions that arise." Consensus, in this view, becomes merely a synonym for legitimacy. Others speak of consensus as a sense of solidarity or social cohesion arising from a common ethos or heritage, which unites men into a community.[7] Political scientists have most frequently employed the term to designate a state of agreement about the "fundamental values" or "rules of the game" considered essential for constitutional government. Rarely, however, have writers on consensus attempted to state what the fundamentals must include, how extensive the agreement must be, and *who* must agree. Is agreement required among all men or only among certain of them? Among the entire electorate or only those who actively participate in public affairs? Is the same type of consensus essential for all democracies at all times, or is a firmer and more sweeping consensus needed for periods of crisis than for periods of calm, for newer, developing democracies than for older stable ones?

While certain of these questions are beyond the scope of this paper (no one, in any event, has done the systematic historical and comparative research needed to answer them satisfactorily), something might be learned about the relation of ideological consensus to democracy by investigating the subject in at least one major democracy, the United States. In the present paper I wish

---

[5] Alexis deTocqueville, *Democracy in America* (ed. Phillips Bradley, New York, 1945), II, p. 8; I, pp. 392, 322. The difficulty of specifying the values which underly democracy, and on which consensus is presumed to be required, is illustrated in the exchange between Ernest S. Griffith, John Plamenatz, and J. Roland Pennock, cited above, pp. 101–37. The problem of certifying the "fundamentals" of democratic consensus is directly discussed by Pennock, pp. 132–33. See also Peter Bachrach, "Elite Consensus and Democracy," *Journal of Politics*, Vol. 24 (August, 1962), pp. 449–52.

[6] A. L. Lowell, *Public Opinion and Popular Government* (New York, 1926), p. 9.

[7] *Cf.*, for example, Louis Wirth, *Community Life and Social Policy* (Chicago, 1956), pp. 201–03, 381–83. For a critique of "consensus theory" and the several definitions of consensus see Irving L. Horowitz, "Consensus, Conflict, and Cooperation: a Sociological Inventory," *Social Forces*, Vol. 41 (Dec., 1962), pp. 177–88.

to explore further some of the questions raised by the writers I have cited and to present research findings on several hypotheses relating to those questions.

I

Hypotheses and Definitions

We expected the data to furnish support for the following hypotheses, among others:

That the American electorate is often divided on "fundamental" democratic values and procedural "rules of the game" and that its understanding of politics and of political ideas is in any event too rudimentary at present to speak of ideological "consensus" among its members.

That, as Prothro and Grigg report for their samples, the electorate exhibits greater support for general, abstract statements of democratic belief than for their specific applications.

That the constituent ideas of American democratic ideology are principally held by the more "articulate" segments of the population, including the political influentials; and that people in these ranks will exhibit a more meaningful and far reaching consensus on democratic and constitutional values than will the general population.

That consensus is far from perfect even among the articulate classes, and will be evidenced on political questions more than on economic ones, on procedural rights more than on public policies, and on freedom more than equality.

That whatever increases the level of political articulateness — education, S.E.S., urban residence, intellectuality, political activity, etc. — strengthens consensus and support for American political ideology and institutions.

Whether a word like ideology can properly be employed in the American context depends, in part, on which of its many connotations one chooses to emphasize. Agreement on the meaning of the term is far from universal, but a tendency can be discerned among contemporary writers to regard ideologies as *systems* of belief that are elaborate, integrated, and coherent, that justify the exercise of power, explain and judge historical events, identify political right and wrong, set forth the interconnections (causal and moral) between politics and other spheres of activity, and furnish guides for action.[8] While liberal democracy does not fulfill perfectly the terms of this definition, it comes close enough, in my opinion, to be considered an ideology.[9] The elements of liberal

---

[8] *Cf.* Daniel Bell, *The End of Ideology* (Glencoe, 1960), pp. 369–75; Edward Shils, "Ideology and Civility: on the Politics of the Intellectual," *Sewanee Review*, Vol. 66 (Summer, 1958), pp. 450–51; Louis Wirth, *Community Life and Social Policy* (Chicago, 1956), pp. 202–03.

[9] A persuasive case for considering liberal democracy as an ideology is made by Bernard Williams, "Democracy and Ideology," *Political Science Quarterly*, Vol. 32 (October–December, 1961), pp. 374–84. The nature of ideology in America and some of the other questions addressed in the present paper are discussed by Robert G. McCloskey, "The American Ideology," in Marian D. Irish (ed.), *Continuing Crisis in American Politics* (Englewood Cliffs, N. J., 1963), pp. 10–25.

democratic thought are not nearly so vague as they are sometimes made out to be, and their coalescence into a single body of belief is by no means fortuitous. American democratic "ideology" possesses an elaborately defined theory, a body of interrelated assumptions, axioms, and principles, and a set of ideals that serve as guides for action. Its tenets, postulates, sentiments, and values inspired the great revolutions of the seventeenth and eighteenth centuries, and have been repeatedly and explicitly set forth in fundamental documents, such as the Constitution, the Declaration, and the Federalist Papers. They have been restated with remarkable unanimity in the messages of Presidents, in political speeches, in the pronouncements of judges and constitutional commentators, and in the writings of political theorists, historians, and publicists. They are so familiar that we are likely to see them not as a coherent union of ideas and principles embodying a well-defined political tendency, but as a miscellany of slogans and noble sentiments to be trotted out on ceremonial occasions.

Although scholars or Supreme Court justices might argue over fine points of interpretation, they would uniformly recognize as elements of American democratic ideology such concepts as consent, accountability, limited or constitutional government, representation, majority rule, minority rights, the principle of political opposition, freedom of thought, speech, press, and assembly, equality of opportunity, religious toleration, equality before the law, the rights of juridical defense, and individual self-determination over a broad range of personal affairs. How widely such elements of American liberal democracy are approved, by whom and with what measure of understanding, is another question — indeed, it is the central question to be addressed in this paper. But that they form an integrated body of ideas which has become part of the American inheritance seems scarcely open to debate.[10]

The term consensus will be employed in this paper to designate a state of agreement concerning the aforementioned values. It has principally to do with shared beliefs and not with feelings of solidarity, the willingness to live together, to obey the laws, or to accept the existing government as legitimate. Nor does it refer to an abstract or universal state of mind, but to a measurable state of concurrence around values that can be specified. Consensus exists in degree and can be expressed in quantitative form. No one, of course, can say how close one must come to unanimity before consensus is achieved, for the cutting point, as with any continuous variable, is arbitrary. Still, the term in ordinary usage has been reserved for fairly substantial measures of correspondence, and we shall take as a minimal requirement for consensus a level of agreement reaching 75 per cent. This figure, while also arbitrary, recommends itself by being realistically modest (falling as it does midway between

---

[10] See Gunnar Myrdal, *An American Dilemma: The Negro Problem and American Democracy* (New York, 1944), ch. I. For a comprehensive review of the American value system and evidence concerning its stability over time, see Clyde Kluckhohn, "Have There Been Discernible Shifts in American Values during the Past Generation?" in E. E. Morrison (ed.), *The American Style: Essays in Value and Performance* (New York, 1958), pp. 145–217. Kluckhohn concludes (p. 152) that despite some changes, the American value system has been "remarkably stable" since the 18th century and remains "highly influential in the life of the United States."

a bare majority and unanimity), and by having been designated in this country and elsewhere as the extraordinary majority required for certain constitutional purposes.

Since I shall in subsequent pages frequently (and interchangeably) employ such terms as the "articulate minority," the "political class," the "political elite," the "political influentials," and the "political stratum," I should also clarify what they are intended to signify. I mean them to refer to those people who occupy themselves with public affairs to an unusual degree, such as government officials, elected office holders, active party members, publicists, officers of voluntary associations, and opinion leaders. The terms do not apply to any definable social class in the usual sense, nor to a particular status group or profession. Although the people they designate can be distinguished from other citizens by their activity and concerns, they are in no sense a community, they do not act as a body, and they do not necessarily possess identical or even harmonious interests. "Articulates" or "influentials" can be found scattered throughout the society, at all income levels, in all classes, occupations, ethnic groups, and communities, although some segments of the population will doubtless yield a higher proportion of them than others. I scarcely need to add that the line between the "articulates" and the rest of the population cannot always be sharply drawn, for the qualities that distinguish them vary in form and degree and no single criterion of classification will satisfy every contingency.

The data for the present inquiry have been taken from a national study of political actives and supporters carried out in 1957–58. I have in a previous paper described the procedures of that study in some detail,[11] and will not trouble to repeat that description here. Perhaps it will suffice for present purposes merely to note the following: national surveys were carried out on two separate samples, the first a sample of over 3,000 political "actives" or "leaders" drawn from the delegates and alternates who had attended the Democratic and Republican conventions of 1956; the second a representative national sample of approximately 1,500 adults in the general population drawn by the American Institute of Public Opinion (Gallup Poll). Gallup interviewers also delivered and introduced the questionnaire to all respondents, discussed its contents with them, and furnished both oral and written instructions for its self-administration and completion. . . .

The party actives may be considered an especially pure sample of the "political stratum," for every person in the sample has marked himself off from the average citizen by his greater political involvement. Although the general population sample may be regarded as a sample of "inarticulates," to be compared with the sample of leaders, there are within it, of course, many persons who by virtue of education, profession, organizational activities, etc. can be classified as "articulates." We shall for certain purposes consider them in this light in order to provide further tests for our hypotheses.

Both samples received the same questionnaire — a lengthy instrument con-

---

[11] Herbert McClosky, Paul J. Hoffmann, and Rosemary O'Hara, "Issue Conflict and Consensus among Party Leaders and Followers," *American Political Science Review,* Vol. 44 (June, 1960), pp. 406–27.

taining questions on personal background, political experience, values, attitudes, opinions, political and economic orientation, party outlooks, and
personality characteristics. Many of the questions were direct inquiries in the
standard form, but most were single sentence "items" with which the respondent was compelled to express his agreement or disagreement. While each of
these items can stand alone and be regarded in its own right as an indicator
of a person's opinions or attitudes, each of them is simultaneously an integral
element of one of the 47 "scales" that was expressly fashioned to afford a
more refined and reliable assessment of the attitude and personality predispositions of every respondent. Each of the scales (averaging approximately nine
items) has been independently validated either by empirical validation procedures employing appropriate criterion groups, or by a modified Guttman
reproducibility procedure (supplemented, in some instances, by a "face validity" procedure utilizing item ratings by experts).

Data on the *scale* scores are presented in Table 4 and are to be distinguished
from the "percentage agree" scores for *individual items* presented in the
remaining tables.

II

Findings

"Rules of the Game" and Democratic Values

Although the so-called "rules of the game" are often separated from other
democratic values, the distinction is to some extent arbitrary. One might, for
example, reasonably regard as "rules of the game" many of the norms governing free speech, press, social and political equality, political toleration, and the
enforcement of justice. For convenience, nevertheless, we shall treat separately
those responses that stand out from the general body of democratic attitudes
by their particular emphasis upon fair play, respect for legal procedures, and
consideration for the rights of others. A sample of items expressing these values
is presented in Table 1.

The responses to these items show plainly that while a majority of the electorate support the "rules of the game," approval of such values is significantly
greater and more uniform among the influentials. The latter have achieved
consensus (as we have defined it) on eight of the twelve items and near
consensus on three of the remaining four items. The electorate, by contrast,
does not meet the criterion for consensus on a single item.

Although the *scales* (as distinguished from individual *items*) cannot appropriately be used to measure *consensus*, comparison of the scores on those scales
which most nearly embody the "rules of the game" furnishes additional
evidence that the political class responds to such norms more favorably than
does the electorate. The proportion scoring high[12] on a scale of "faith in direct

---

12 "High" refers to a score made by the upper third of the popular distribution on the
scale in question. For example, in the case of the "political indulgence" scale approximately one-third (actually 30.6%) received scores of five or above. Hence, anyone
making a score of five or above on this scale is considered to have scored high on "political
indulgence." "Low" refers to scores made by the lower third of the distribution.

action" (a scale measuring the inclination to take the law into one's own hands) is 26.1 per cent for the active political minority and 42.5 per cent for the general population. On a scale assessing the willingness to flout the rules of political integrity, the proportions scoring high are 12.2 per cent and 30.6 per cent respectively. On "totalitarianism," a scale measuring the readiness to subordinate the rights of others to the pursuit of some collective political purpose, only 9.7 per cent of the political actives score high compared with 33.8 per cent of the general population.

These and other results which could be cited support the claim advanced

Table 1   *Political Influentials vs. the Electorate: Response to Items Expressing "Rules of the Game"**

Items	Political Influentials (N=3020)	General Electorate (N=1484)
	% Agree	
There are times when it almost seems better for the people to take the law into their own hands rather than wait for the machinery of government to act.	13.3	26.9
The majority has the right to abolish minorities if it wants to.	6.8	28.4
We might as well make up our minds that in order to make the world better a lot of innocent people will have to suffer.	27.2	41.6
If congressional committees stuck strictly to the rules and gave every witness his rights, they would never succeed in exposing the many dangerous subversives they have turned up.	24.7	47.4
I don't mind a politician's methods if he manages to get the right things done.	25.6	42.4
Almost any unfairness or brutality may have to be justified when some great purpose is being carried out.	13.3	32.8
Politicians have to cut a few corners if they are going to get anywhere.	29.4	43.2
People ought to be allowed to vote even if they can't do so intelligently.	65.6	47.6
To bring about great changes for the benefit of mankind often requires cruelty and even ruthlessness.	19.4	31.3
Very few politicians have clean records, so why get excited about the mudslinging that sometimes goes on?	14.8	38.1
It is all right to get around the law if you don't actually break it.	21.2	30.2
The true American way of life is disappearing so fast that we may have to use force to save it.	12.8	34.6

* Since respondents were forced to make a choice on each item, the number of omitted or "don't know" responses was, on the average, fewer than one percent, and thus has little influence on the direction or magnitude of the results reported in this and subsequent tables.

by earlier investigators like Prothro and Grigg, and Hyman and Sheatsley,[13] that a large proportion of the electorate has failed to grasp certain of the underlying ideas and principles on which the American political system rests. Endorsement of these ideas is not unanimous among the political elite either, but is in every instance greater than that exhibited by the masses.

The picture changes somewhat when we turn from "rules of the game" to items which in a broad, general way express belief in freedom of speech and opinion. As can be seen from Table 2, support for these values is remarkably high for both samples. Both groups, in fact, respond so overwhelmingly to abstract statements about freedom that one is tempted to conclude that for these values, at least, a far-reaching consensus has been achieved.[14] These results become even more striking when we consider that the items in the table are not mere clichés but statements which in some instances closely paraphrase the arguments developed in Mill's essay, *On Liberty*. We cannot, therefore, dismiss them as mere responses to familiar, abstract sentiments which commit the respondent to nothing in particular.

Still, as can readily be discerned from the items in Table 3, previous investigators have been partially correct, at least, in observing that the principles of freedom and democracy are less widely and enthusiastically favored when they are confronted in their specific, or applied, forms.[15] As Dahl remarks, it is a "common tendency of mankind . . . to qualify universals in application while leaving them intact in rhetoric."[16] This observation, of course, also holds for the political articulates, but to a lesser degree. Not only do they exhibit stronger support for democratic values than does the electorate, but they are also more consistent in applying the general principle to the specific instance.[17] The average citizen has greater difficulty appreciating the importance of certain procedural or juridical rights, especially when he believes the country's internal security is at stake.

Findings which underscore and amplify these conclusions are yielded by a comparison of the scale scores. The data presented in Table 4 confirm that the

---

[13] James W. Prothro and C. W. Grigg, "Fundamental Principles of Democracy: Bases of Agreement and Disagreement," *Journal of Politics*, Vol. 22 (Spring, 1960), pp. 276–94; Herbert Hyman and Paul B. Sheatsley, "The Current Status of American Public Opinion," in Daniel Katz *et al.* (eds.), *Public Opinion and Propaganda* (New York, 1954), pp. 33–48.

[14] *Cf.* Robert Lane's report on his "Eastport" sample, in *Political Ideology* (New York, 1962), pp. 461–62.

[15] See Herbert Hyman and Paul B. Sheatsley, "The Current Status of American Public Opinion," in Daniel Katz *et al.* (eds.), *Public Opinion and Propaganda* (New York, 1954), pp. 40–42; James W. Prothro and C. W. Grigg, "Fundamental Principles of Democracy: Bases of Agreement and Disagreement," *Journal of Politics*, Vol. 22 (Spring, 1960), pp. 276–94.

[16] Robert A. Dahl, *Who Governs?* (New Haven, 1961), ch. 28. For data on the failure of some people to perceive the relevance of democratic principles for concrete situations see G. D. Wiebe, "The Army–McCarthy Hearings and the Public Conscience," *Public Opinion Quarterly*, Vol. 22 (Winter, 1958–59), pp. 490–502.

[17] See also Samuel A. Stouffer, *Communism, Conformity, and Civil Liberties* (New York: 1955).

Table 2   *Political Influentials vs. the Electorate: Responses to Items Expressing
Support for General Statements of Free Speech and Opinion*

Items	Political Influentials (N=3020)	General Electorate (N=1484)
	% Agree	
People who hate our way of life should still have a chance to talk and be heard.	86.9	81.8
No matter what a person's political beliefs are, he is entitled to the same legal rights and protection as anyone else.	96.4	94.3
I believe in free speech for all no matter what their views might be.	89.4	88.9
Nobody has a right to tell another person what he should and should not read.	81.4	80.7
You can't really be sure whether an opinion is true or not unless people are free to argue against it.	94.9	90.8
Unless there is freedom for many points of view to be presented, there is little chance that the truth can ever be known.	90.6	85.2
I would not trust any person or group to decide what opinions can be freely expressed and what must be silenced.	79.1	64.6
Freedom of conscience should mean freedom to be an atheist as well as freedom to worship in the church of one's choice.	87.8	77.0

influentials not only register higher scores on all the pro-democratic scales (faith in freedom, faith in democracy, procedural rights, tolerance), but are more likely to reject antidemocratic sentiments as well. Although they are themselves an elite of a sort, they display greater faith in the capacity of the mass of men to govern themselves, they believe more firmly in political equality, and they more often disdain the "extreme" beliefs embodied in the Right Wing, Left Wing, totalitarian, elitist, and authoritarian scales. Their repudiation of anti-democratic attitudes is by no means unanimous either, but their responses are more uniformly democratic than are those expressed by the electorate.

Equalitarian Values

If Americans concur most strongly about liberty in the abstract, they disagree most strongly about equality. Examples of equalitarian values are presented in Table 5. Both the political stratum and the public divide sharply on these values, a finding which holds for political, as well as for social and economic equality. Both are torn not only on the empirical question of whether men are *in fact* equal but also on the normative issue of whether they should be *regarded* as equal. Neither comes close to achieving consensus on such questions as the ability of the people to rule themselves, to know their best interests in the long run, to understand the issues, or to pick their own leaders wisely. Support for these equalitarian features of "popular" democracy, however, is greater among the elite than among the masses.

Table 3   *Political Influentials vs. the Electorate: Response to Items Expressing Support for Specific Applications of Free Speech and Procedural Rights*

Items	Political Influentials (N=3020)	General Electorate (N=1484)
	% Agree	
Freedom does not give anyone the right to teach foreign ideas in our schools.	45.5	56.7
A man oughtn't to be allowed to speak if he doesn't know what he's talking about.	17.3	36.7
A book that contains wrong political views cannot be a good book and does not deserve to be published.	17.9	50.3
When the country is in great danger we may have to force people to testify against themselves even if it violates their rights.	28.5	36.3
No matter what crime a person is accused of, he should never be convicted unless he has been given the right to face and question his accusers.	90.1	88.1
If a person is convicted of a crime by illegal evidence, he should be set free and the evidence thrown out of court.	79.6	66.1
If someone is suspected of treason or other serious crimes, he shouldn't be entitled to be let out on bail.	33.3	68.9
Any person who hides behind the laws when he is questioned about his activities doesn't deserve much consideration.	55.0	75.7
In dealing with dangerous enemies like the Communists, we can't afford to depend on the courts, the laws and their slow and unreliable methods.	7.4	25.5

The reverse is true for the values of economic equality. Among the political stratum, indeed, the weight of opinion is against equality — a result strongly though not exclusively influenced by the pronounced economic conservatism of the Republican leaders in the sample. Support for economic equality is only slightly greater among the electorate. The pattern, furthermore, is extremely spotty, with some policies strongly favored and others as strongly rejected. Thus approval is widespread for public policies (such as social security) that are designed to overcome gross inequalities, but is equally strong for certain features of economic life that promote inequality, such as private enterprise, economic competition, and unlimited pursuit of profit.[18] On social and ethnic equality, both samples are deeply split.

[18] These inferences are drawn not only from the few items presented in Table 5, but from data previously reported by Herbert McClosky, Paul J. Hoffmann, and Rosemary O'Hara, "Issue Conflict and Consensus among Party Leaders and Followers," *American Political Science Review*, Vol. 44 (June, 1960), p. 413; and from the responses to dozens of items in the present study that express attitudes and opinions toward the private enterprise system, taxes, private property, profits, socialism, etc. On the whole, little enthusiasm is registered among either the elite or the masses for a drastic revision of the economy or a major redistribution of the wealth.

In short, both the public and its leaders are uncertain and ambivalent about equality. The reason, I suspect, lies partly in the fact that the egalitarian aspects of democratic theory have been less adequately thought through than other aspects, and partly in the complications connected with the concept itself. One such complication arises from the historical association of democracy with capitalism, a commingling of egalitarian and inegalitarian elements that has never been (and perhaps never can be) perfectly reconciled. Another complication lies in the diffuse and variegated nature of the concept, a result of its application to at least four separate domains: political (e.g., universal suffrage), legal (e.g., equality before the law), economic (e.g., equal distribution of property or opportunity), and moral (e.g., every man's right to be treated as an end and not as a means). Accompanying these are the confusions which result from the common failure to distinguish equality as a *fact* from equality as a *norm*. ("All men are created equal," for example, is taken by some as an empirical statement, by others as a normative one.) Still other complications arise from the differential rewards and opportunities inevitable in any complex society, from the differences in the initial endowment individuals bring into the world, and from the symbolism and fears that so often attend the division of men into ethnic compartments. All these confound the effort to develop a satisfactory theory of democratic equality, and further serve to frustrate the realization of consensus around egalitarian values.

Table 4   *Political Influentials vs. the Electorate: Percentages Scoring High and Low on Democratic and Anti-Democratic Attitude Scales**

Scale	Political Influentials (N=3020) (%)	General Electorate (N=1484) (%)	Scale	Political Influentials (N=3020) (%)	General Electorate (N=1484) (%)
Faith in Democracy			Elitism		
High*	40.1	18.5	High	22.8	38.7
Low	14.4	29.7	Low	41.0	22.4
Procedural Rights			Totalitarianism		
High	58.1	24.1	High	9.7	33.8
Low	12.3	31.3	Low	60.1	28.4
Tolerance			Right Wing		
High	61.3	43.1	High	17.5	33.1
Low	16.4	33.2	Low	45.3	28.9
Faith in Freedom			Left Wing		
High	63.0	48.4	High	6.7	27.8
Low	17.1	28.4	Low	68.7	39.3
Ethnocentrism			California F-Scale		
High	27.5	36.5	High	14.7	33.5
Low	46.9	36.3	Low	48.0	23.5

* For explanation of % High and Low see Footnote 12. The middle group has been omitted from this table. Differences between the influentials and the electorate on all the scales in this table are, by Kolmogorov–Smirnov and chi-square tests, statistically significant at or beyond the .01 percent level of significance.

Faith in the Political System

Another perspective on the state of ideology and consensus in America may be obtained by observing how people respond to the political system. How do Americans feel about the political and social institutions by which they are ruled? Do they perceive the system as one they can reach and influence? Are they satisfied that it will govern justly and for the common good? Sample items relating to these questions are contained in Tables 6 and 7.

Table 5   *Political Influentials vs. the Electorate: Responses to Items Expressing Belief in Equality*

Items	Political Influentials (N=3020)	General Electorate (N=1484)
	% Agree	
Political Equality		
The main trouble with democracy is that most people don't really know what's best for them.	40.8	58.0
Few people really know what is in their own best interest in the long run.	42.6	61.1
"Issues" and "arguments" are beyond the understanding of most voters.	37.5	62.3
Most people don't have enough sense to pick their own leaders wisely.	28.0	47.8
It will always be necessary to have a few strong, able people actually running everything.	42.5	56.2
Social and Ethnic Equality		
We have to teach children that all men are created equal but almost everyone knows that some are better than others.	54.7	58.3
Just as is true of fine race horses, some breeds of people are just naturally better than others.	46.0	46.3
Regardless of what some people say, there are certain races in the world that just won't mix with Americans.	37.2	50.4
When it comes to the things that count most, all races are certainly not equal.	45.3	49.0
The trouble with letting certain minority groups into a nice neighborhood is that they gradually give it their own atmosphere.	49.8	57.7
Economic Equality		
Labor does not get its fair share of what it produces.	20.8	44.8
Every person should have a good house, even if the government has to build it for him.	14.9	28.2
I think the government should give a person work if he can't find another job.	23.5	47.3
The government ought to make sure that everyone has a good standard of living.	34.4	55.9
There will always be poverty, so people might as well get used to the idea.	40.4	59.4

An assessment of the responses, however, is founded by an ambivalence in our tradition. Few will question that Americans are patriotic and loyal, that they accept the political system as legitimate, and that they are inclined to shy away from radical or extreme movements which aim to alter or to overthrow the constitutional foundations of the system. Yet Americans are also presumed to have a longstanding suspicion of government — a state of mind which some historians trace back to the depredations of George III and to the habits of self-reliance forced upon our ancestors by frontier life.[19]

Table 6   *Political Influentials vs. the Electorate: Responses to Items Expressing Cynicism Toward Government and Politics*

Items	Political Influentials (N=3020)	General Electorate (N=1484)
	% Agree	
Most politicians are looking out for themselves above all else.	36.3	54.3
Both major parties in this country are controlled by the wealthy and are run for their benefit.	7.9	32.1
Many politicians are bought off by some private interest.	43.0	65.3
I avoid dealing with public officials as much as I can.	7.8	39.3
Most politicians can be trusted to do what they think is best for the country.	77.1	58.9
I usually have confidence that the government will do what is right.	81.6	89.6
The people who really "run" the country do not even get known to the voters.	40.2	60.5
The laws of this country are supposed to benefit all of us equally, but the fact is that they're almost all "rich-man's laws."	8.4	33.3
No matter what the people think, a few people will always run things anyway.	30.0	53.8
Most politicians don't seem to me to really mean what they say.	24.7	55.1
There is practically no connection between what a politician says and what he will do once he gets elected.	21.4	54.0
A poor man doesn't have the chance he deserves in the law courts.	20.3	42.9
Most political parties care only about winning elections and nothing more.	28.3	46.2
All politics is controlled by political bosses.	15.6	45.9

[19] Evidence is accumulating that the distrust of politics, often thought to be peculiar to the United States, is also found in many other countries. In fact, Gabriel Almond and Sidney Verba report in their cross-cultural study of citizenship that political interest is higher in the United States than it is in the four other countries they studied (United Kingdom, West Germany, Italy, and Mexico); and that Americans, if anything, are less negative toward politics than are the citizens of the other countries. See *The Civic Culture* (1963), chs. III–IV.

It is impossible in the present context to determine the extent to which the scores contained in these tables signify genuine frustration and political disillusionment and the extent to which they represent familiar and largely ritualistic responses. It is plain, however, that Americans are, verbally at least, both confused and divided in their reactions to the political system. Many feel themselves hopelessly ineffectual politically. Approximately half perceive government and politicians as remote, inaccessible, and largely unresponsive to the electorate's needs or opinions.[20] About the same proportion regard politics as squalid and seamy, as an activity in which the participants habitually practice deception, expediency, and self-aggrandizement. Yet by a curious inconsistency which so frequently frustrates the investigator searching the data for irregularities, 89.6 per cent express confidence that the government will do what is right. However strongly they mistrust the men and the procedures through which public policies are fashioned, most voters seem not to be greatly dissatisfied with the outcome. They may be cynical about the operation of the political system, but they do not question its legitimacy.[21]

Although the influentials do not unanimously endorse American political practices either, they are substantially less suspicious and cynical than is the

Table 7   *Political Influentials vs. the Electorate: Responses to Items Expressing a Sense of Political Futility*

Items	Political Influentials (N=3020)	General Electorate (N=1484)
	% Agree	
It's no use worrying my head about public affairs; I can't do anything about them anyhow.	2.3	20.5
The people who really "run" the country do not even get known to the voters.	40.2	60.5
I feel that my political leaders hardly care what people like myself think or want.	10.9	39.0
Nothing I ever do seems to have any effect upon what happens in politics.	8.4	61.5
Political parties are so big that the average member hasn't got much to say about what goes on.	37.8	67.5
There doesn't seem to be much connection between what I want and what my representative does.	24.0	43.7
It seems to me that whoever you vote for, things go on pretty much the same.	21.1	51.3

[20] See also the Michigan data on voters' sense of "political efficacy" in Angus Campbell, Gerald Gurin, and Warren E. Miller, *The Voter Decides* (Evanston, 1954), pp. 187–94.
[21] For other data on ambivalent attitudes toward government, see Herbert Hyman and Paul B. Sheatsley, "The Current Status of American Public Opinion," in Daniel Katz *et al.* (eds.), *Public Opinion and Propaganda* (New York, 1954), pp. 33–48.

electorate. Indeed, they have achieved consensus or come close to achieving it on most of the items in the two tables. These results are further borne out by the *scale* scores: only 10.1 per cent of the articulates score "high" on the political cynicism scale, as contrasted with 31.3 per cent of the general population; on political suspiciousness the scores are 9.0 per cent high versus 26.7 per cent; on pessimism they are 12.6 per cent versus 26.7 per cent; and on sense of political futility the influentials score (understandably enough) only 3.1 per cent high compared with 30.2 per cent high for the electorate. The active minority also exhibits a stronger sense of social responsibility than the people do (their respective percentage high scores are 40.7 per cent versus 25.8 per cent) and, as previously noted, they are less tolerant of infractions against ethical political procedures.

Should we not, however, have expected these results as a matter of course, considering that the influentials were selected for study precisely because of their political experience and involvement? Possibly, except that similar (though less pronounced) differences emerge when we distinguish articulates from inarticulates by criteria other than actual political activity. Voters, for example, who have been to college, attained high status occupations or professions, or developed strong intellectual interests are, by a significant margin, also likely to possess more affirmative attitudes toward government, politics, and politicians.[22] They display a greater sense of social and political responsibility, are more optimistic, and are less indulgent of shoddy political methods. The political actives who are highly educated exhibit these attitudes even more strongly. Familiarity, it seems, far from breeding contempt, greatly increases respect, hope and support for the nation's political institutions and practices. Inferential support for this generalization is available from the findings turned up by Almond and Verba in all five countries they investigated in their comparative study of citizenship.[23]

Coherence and Consistency of Attitudes

So far we have explored the question of ideology and consensus mainly from the point of view of agreement on particular values. This, however, is a minimum criterion. Before one can say that a class or group or nation has achieved consensus around an ideology, one should be satisfied that they understand its values in a coherent and correct way. It is a poor consensus in which generalities and slogans are merely echoed with little appreciation of their significance. It seemed appropriate, therefore, to compare the influentials and voters concerning their information and understanding, the relation of their

---

[22] Similar findings are reported by Robert E. Agger, Marshall N. Goldstein and Stanley A. Pearl, "Political Cynicism: Measurement and Meaning," *Journal of Politics,* Vol. 23 (1961), pp. 477–506.

[23] Almond and Verba, *op. cit.,* ch. IV. One can, of course, imagine circumstances, such as political disorganization or revolutionary crises, in which the generalization would not hold — in which, indeed, the political elite might lead the struggle *against* the existing governing institutions. I am speaking, in the present context, of politics under "normal" conditions in established democracies.

opinions to their party preferences, and the consistency of their views on public affairs.

To begin with, the influentials are more likely than the electorate to have opinions on public questions. For example, 28 per cent of the public are unable (though a few may only be *unwilling*) to classify themselves as liberal, middle of the road, or conservative; while only 1.1 per cent of the articulates fail to make this classification. Forty-eight per cent of the voters, compared to 15 per cent of the actives, do not know in which direction they would turn if the parties were reorganized to reflect ideological differences more clearly. Forty-five per cent of the electorate but only 10.2 per cent of the influentials cannot name any issue that divides the parties. By ratios of approximately three or four to one the electorate is less likely to know which level of government they are mainly interested in, whether they prefer their party to control Congress or the presidency, whether they believe in party discipline and of what type, whether control of the parties should rest at the national or local levels, and so on.

As these and other of our findings suggest, active political involvement heightens one's sense of intellectual order and commitment. This inference is further supported by the data on partisanship. One example may suffice to illustrate the point: when the articulates and the electorate are ranged on a scale assessing their orientation toward 14 current liberal–conservative issues, the political actives tend to bunch up at the extreme ends of the distribution (the Democratic actives at the "liberal" end, the Republican actives at the "conservative" end), while the rank and file supporters of both parties fall more frequently into the middle or conflicted category. The political influentials, in short, display issue orientations that are more partisan and more consistent with their party preferences.

Essentially the same effect is achieved among the general population by increases in education, economic status, or other factors that raise the level of articulateness. College-educated Democrats and Republicans, for example, disagree more sharply on issues than grade school Democrats and Republicans do. Partisan differences are greater between the informed than between the uninformed, between the upper-class supporters of the two parties than between the lower-class supporters, between the "intellectuals" in both parties than between those who rank low on "intellectuality."

Increases in political knowledge or involvement, hence, cause men not so much to waver as to choose sides and to identify more unswervingly with one political tendency or its opposite. Inarticulateness and distance from the sources of political decision increase intellectual uncertainty and evoke political responses that are random rather than systematic. We are thus led by the findings to a pair of conclusions that may at first appear contradictory but that in reality are not: the political class is more united than the electorate on fundamental political values but divides more sharply by party affiliation on the issues which separate the two parties.[24] Both facts — the greater consensus

---

[24] See also V. O. Key, *Public Opinion and American Democracy* (New York, 1961), pp. 51–52.

in the one instance and the sharper cleavage in the other — testify to its superior ideological sophistication.

Not only are the articulates more partisan, but they are also more consistent in their views. Their responses to a wide range of political stimuli are to a greater extent intellectually patterned and informed. They are, for example, better able to name reference groups that correspond with their party affiliation and doctrinal orientation: approximately twice as many active Democrats as ordinary Democratic voters name liberal, Democratically oriented organizations as groups they would seek advice from (*e.g.*, trade unions, Farmers Union, etc.); and by equally large or larger ratios they *reject* as sources of advice such conservative or Republican oriented organizations as the NAM, the Farm Bureau, and the Chamber of Commerce. With some variations, similar findings emerge when Republican leaders are compared with Republican voters. If we also take into account the liberal or conservative issue-orientation of the respondents, the differential ability of party leaders and followers to recognize reference groups becomes even more pronounced. Clearly, the political stratum has a better idea than the public has of who its ideological friends and enemies are. The capacity to recognize sympathetic or hostile reference groups is not highly developed among the public at large.

Compared with the influentials, ordinary voters also show up poorly in their ability to classify themselves politically. For example, among Democratic actives who score as "liberals" in their views on issues, 82.2 per cent correctly describe themselves as "liberals," while 16.7 per cent call themselves "middle of the roaders" and only 1.1 per cent misclassify themselves as "conservatives." Among Democratic *voters* who actually hold liberal views, only 37.0 per cent are able to label themselves correctly. The disparity is less striking between Republican leaders and followers but bears out no less conclusively that most voters lack the sophistication to recognize and label accurately the tendency of their own political views. Even their choice of party is frequently discrepant with their actual ideological views: as we reported in a previous paper,[25] not only do Democratic and Republican voters hold fairly similar opinions on issues, but the latter's opinions are closer to the opinions of Democratic leaders than to those of their own leaders.

Data we have gathered on patterns of support for individual political leaders yield similar conclusions: the articulates are far better able than the electorate to select leaders whose political philosophy they share. Often, in fact, voters simultaneously approve of two or more leaders who represent widely different outlooks — for example, Joseph McCarthy and Dwight D. Eisenhower. In a similar vein, a surprisingly large number of voters simultaneously score high on a Right Wing scale and a liberal issues scale, or hold other "discrepant" outlooks. Such inconsistencies are not unknown among the political actives either, but they are much less frequent. Not only does the public have less

---

[25] Herbert McClosky, Paul J. Hoffmann, and Rosemary O'Hara, "Issue Conflict and Consensus among Party Leaders and Followers," *American Political Science Review,* Vol. 44 (June 1960), pp. 406–27.

information than the political class but it does not succeed as well in sorting out and relating the information it does possess.[26]

Most of the relationships reported in the foregoing have been tested with education, occupation, and sometimes with other demographic variables controlled, but the introduction of these factors does not change the direction of the findings, although it sometimes affects the magnitude of the scores.

Comparisons of scores for the two samples have also been made with "acquiescent" response-set controlled. Acquiescence affects the results, but does not eliminate the differences reported or alter the direction or significance of the findings.

III

Summary and Discussion

Several observations can be offered by way of summarizing and commenting upon the data just reported:

1. American politics is widely thought to be innocent of ideology, but this opinion more appropriately describes the electorate than the active political minority. If American ideology is defined as that cluster of axioms, values and beliefs which have given form and substance to American democracy and the Constitution, the political influentials manifest by comparison with ordinary voters a more developed sense of ideology and a firmer grasp of its essentials. This is evidenced in their stronger approval of democratic ideas, their greater tolerance and regard for proper procedures and citizen rights, their superior understanding and acceptance of the "rules of the game," and their more affirmative attitudes toward the political system in general. The electorate displays a substantial measure of unity chiefly in its support of freedom in the abstract; on most other features of democratic belief and practice it is sharply divided.

The political views of the influentials are relatively ordered and coherent. As liberals and conservatives, Democrats and Republicans, they take stands on issues, choose reference groups, and express preferences for leaders that are far more consistent than the attitudes and preferences exhibited by the electorate. The latter's opinions do not entirely lack order but are insufficiently integrated to meet the requirements of an ideology.[27] In contrast to the political elite, which tends to be united on basic values but divided on issues by party

---

[26] For other findings on the state of ideological development among the electorate, see Angus Campbell, Philip E. Converse, Warren E. Miller and Donald E. Stokes, *The American Voter* (New York, 1960), chs. 8–10.

[27] For a similar conclusion on this point, see V. O. Key, *Public Opinion and American Democracy* (New York, 1961), pp. 41, 49. The second chapter of this volume contains an excellent discussion of opinion consensus among the electorate, and touches on a number of the points dealt with in this paper. Evidence on the infrequency of "ideological" thinking among the voters is presented in Campbell, Converse, Miller and Stokes, *op. cit.*, p. 249. By the criteria used the authors were able to classify only 3.5% of the voters as "ideologues" and 12% as "near-ideologues."

affiliation (both of which testify to a measure of ideological sophistication), the voters divide on many basic political values and adopt stands on issues with little reference to their party affiliation.

The evidence suggests that it is the articulate classes rather than the public who serve as the major repositories of the public conscience and as the carriers of the Creed. Responsibility for keeping the system going, hence, falls most heavily upon them.[28]

2. Why should consensus and support for democratic ideology be stronger among the political stratum than among the electorate? The answer plainly has to do with the differences in their political activity, involvement and articulateness.

Some observers complain that Americans have little interest in political ideas because they are exclusively concerned with their own personal affairs. Evidence is becoming available, however, that political apathy and ignorance are also widespread among the populations of other countries and may well be endemic in all societies larger than a city-state. It is difficult to imagine any circumstance, short of war or revolutionary crisis, in which the mass of men will evince more interest in the community's affairs than in their own concerns. This is not because they are selfish, thoughtless, or morally deficient, but because the stimuli they receive from public affairs are relatively remote and intangible. One can scarcely expect ordinary men to respond to them as intensely as they respond to the more palpable stimuli in their own everyday lives, which impinge upon them directly and in ways they can understand and do something about. The aphorism which holds man to be a political animal may be supportable on normative grounds but is scarcely defensible as a description of reality. Political apathy seems for most men the more "natural" state. Although political matters are in a sense "everyone's concern," it is just as unreasonable to hope that all men will sustain a lively interest in politics as it would be to expect everyone to become addicted to chamber music, electronics, poetry, or baseball. Since many voters lack education, opportunity, or even tangible and compelling reasons for busying themselves with political ideas, they respond to political stimuli (if they respond at all) without much reflection or consistency. Their life-styles, furthermore, tend to perpetuate this state of affairs, for they are likely to associate with people like themselves whose political opinions are no more informed or consistent than their own. As inarticulates, they are also inclined to avoid the very activities by which they might overcome their indifference and develop a more coherent point of view.

Many voters, in addition, feel remote from the centers of political decision and experience an acute sense of political futility. They know the political world only as a bewildering labyrinth of procedures and unceasing turmoil in which it is difficult to distinguish the just from the wicked, the deserving from the undeserving. The political questions about which they are asked to have opinions are complex and thorny; every solution is imperfect and exacts its price; measures that benefit some groups invariably aggrieve others. The prin-

---

[28] V. O. Key, "Public Opinion and the Decay of Democracy," *Virginia Q. Rev.*, Vol. 37 (Autumn, 1961), pp. 481–94.

ciples which govern the political process seem vague, recondite and impossible to relate to actual events. All this obviously deters voters from developing ideologically, from acquiring insights into the subtleties of the democratic process, and from achieving consensus even on fundamental values.

Although the influentials face some of the same obstacles, they are better able to overcome them. As a group they are distinguished from the mass of the electorate by their above-average education and economic status, their greater political interest and awareness, and their more immediate access to the command posts of community decision. Many of them participate not only in politics but in other public activities as well. This affords them, among other benefits, a more sophisticated understanding of how the society is run and a more intimate association with other men and women who are alert to political ideas and values. Political concepts and abstractions, alien to the vocabulary of many voters, are for the elite familiar items of everyday discourse.

Consider also that the political stratum is, by almost every social criterion we have examined, more homogeneous than the electorate. This promotes communication among them and increases their chances of converging around a common body of attitudes.[29] As Newcomb[30] has remarked, "The actual consequences of communication, as well as the intended ones, are consensus—increasing." Among many segments of the general population, however, communication on matters of political belief either occurs not at all or is so random and cacophonous as to have little utility for the reinforcement of political values. If Louis Wirth is correct in observing that "the limits of consensus are marked by the range of effective communication,"[31] it becomes easier to understand why the active minority achieves consensus more often than the voters do.

Compared with the electorate, whose ordinary members are submerged in an ideological babble of poorly informed and discordant opinions, the members of the political minority inhabit a world in which political ideas are vastly more salient, intellectual consistency is more frequently demanded, attitudes are related to principles, actions are connected to beliefs, "correct" opinions are rewarded and "incorrect" opinions are punished. In addition, as participants in political roles, the actives are compelled (contrary to stereotype) to adopt opinions, to take stands on issues, and to evaluate ideas and events. As articulates they are unavoidably exposed to the liberal democratic values which form the main current of our political heritage. The net effect of these influences is to heighten their sensitivity to political ideas and to unite them more firmly behind the values of the American tradition. They may, as a result, be better equipped for the role they are called upon to play in a democracy than the citizens are for *their* role.

---

[29] For additional data on the homogeneity of social characteristics and values among American elite groups, see James N. Rosenau, "Consensus-Building in the American National Community: Hypotheses and Supporting Data," *Journal of Politics,* Vol. 24 (November, 1962).

[30] Theodore M. Newcomb, "The Study of Consensus," in R. K. Merton *et al.* (eds.), *Sociology Today* (New York, 1959), pp. 277–92.

[31] Louis Wirth, *Community Life and Social Policy* (Chicago, 1956), p. 201.

The findings furnish little comfort for those who wish to believe that a passion for freedom, tolerance, justice and other democratic values springs spontaneously from the lower depths of the society, and that the plain, home-spun, uninitiated yeoman, worker and farmer are the natural hosts of demo-cratic ideology. The mystique of the simple, unworldly, "natural" democrat has been with us since at least the rise of Christianity, and has been assiduously cultivated by Rousseau, Tolstoy, Marx, and numerous lesser writers and social reformers. Usually, the simpler the man, the lower his station in life, and the greater his objective need for equality, the more we have endowed him with a capacity for understanding democracy. We are thus inclined to give the nod to the farmer over the city man, the unlearned over the educated, the poor man over the man of wealth, the "people" over their leaders, the unsophisti-cated over the sophisticated. Yet every one of these intuitive expectations turns out, upon investigation, to be questionable or false. Democratic beliefs and habits are obviously not "natural" but must be learned; and they are learned more slowly by men and women whose lives are circumscribed by apathy, ignorance, provincialism and social or physical distance from the centers of intellectual activity. In the absence of knowledge and experience — as we can readily observe from the fidgety course of growth in the newly emerging nations — the presuppositions and complex obligations of democracy, the rights it grants and the self-restraints it imposes, cannot be quickly comprehended. Even in a highly developed democratic nation like the United States, millions of people continue to possess only the most rudimentary understanding of democratic ideology.

3. While the active political minority affirms the underlying values of democracy more enthusiastically than the people do, consensus among them is far from perfect, and we might well inquire why this is so.

Despite the many forces impelling influentials toward agreement on basic ideological values, counteracting forces are also at work to divide them. Not all influentials are able to comprehend democratic ideas, to apply them to concrete contexts, or to thread their way through the complexities of modern political life. Nor is communication perfect among them either, despite their greater homogeneity. Many things divide them, not least of which are differ-ences in education, conflicting economic and group interests, party competition, factional cleavages and personal political ambitions.

In demonstrating that the influentials are better prepared than the masses to receive and reflect upon political ideas, we run the risk of overstating the case and of exaggerating their capacity for ideological reasoning. Some mem-bers of the political class obviously have no more intellectual concern with politics than the masses do; they are in it for "the game," for personal reasons, or for almost any reason except ideology.

Then, too, while most democratic ideas are in their most general form simple enough for almost all members of the elite to understand, they become con-siderably more puzzling when one sets out to explicate them, to relate them to each other, or to apply them to concrete cases. Only a few of the compli-cations need to be cited to illustrate the point: several of the ideas, such as equality, are either inherently vague or mean different things in different contexts. Some democratic (or constitutional) values turn out in certain situations to be incompatible with other democratic values (e.g., the majority's right to make and enforce the laws at times clashes with individual rights, such as the right to stand on one's religious conscience). As this suggests, democratic ideas and rules of the game are ordinarily encountered not in pure form or in isolation but in substantive contexts that are bound to influence the ways in which we react to them.[32] Many businessmen who consider the regulation of business as an unconstitutional invasion of freedom look upon the regulation of trade unions as a justifiable curb upon lawlessness; trade unionists, needless to say, lean to the opposite view.

Consider, too, what a heavy burden we place upon a man's normal impulses by asking him to submit unconditionally to democratic values and procedures. Compliance with democratic rules of the game often demands an extraordinary measure of forbearance and self-discipline, a willingness to place constraints upon the use of our collective power and to suffer opinions, actions, and groups we regard as repugnant. The need for such self-restraint is for many people intrinsically difficult to comprehend and still more difficult to honor. Small wonder, then, that consensus around democratic values is imperfect, even among the political influentials who are well situated to appreciate their importance.

4. We turn now to the most crucial question suggested by the research findings, namely, what significance must be assigned to the fact that democratic ideology and consensus are poorly developed among the electorate and only imperfectly realized among the political influentials?

Our first and most obvious conclusion is that, contrary to the familiar claim, a democratic society can survive despite widespread popular misunderstanding and disagreement about basic democratic and constitutional values. The American political system survives and even flourishes under precisely these conditions, and so, we have reason to think, do other viable democracies. What makes this possible is a more conjectural question, though several observations can be offered by way of answering it.

Democratic viability is, to begin with, saved by the fact that those who are most confused about democratic ideas are also likely to be politically apathetic and without significant influence. Their role in the nation's decision process is so small that their "misguided" opinions or non-opinions have little practical consequence for stability. If they contribute little to the vitality of the system, neither are they likely to do much harm. Lipset[33] has pointed out that "apathy undermines consensus," but to this one may add the corollary observation that apathy also furnishes its own partial corrective by keeping the doubters from acting upon their differences. In the United States, at least, their disagreements are *passive* rather than *active*, more the result of political

---

[32] For a discussion of this point, see Peter Bachrach, "Elite Consensus and Democracy," *Journal of Politics*, Vol. 24 (August, 1962), pp. 439–52.

[33] Seymour Martin Lipset, *Political Man* (New York, 1960), p. 27. Chapter I of this volume provides a stimulating and valuable discussion of the relation of conflict and consensus to the operation of democracy.

ignorance and indifference than of intellectual conviction or conscious identification with an "alien" political tendency. Most seem not even to be aware of their deviations from the established values. This suggests that there may, after all, be some utility in achieving agreement on large, abstract political sentiments, for it may satisfy men that they share common values when in fact they do not. Not only can this keep conflicts from erupting, but it also permits men who disagree to continue to communicate and thus perhaps to convert their pseudo-consensus on democratic values into a genuine consensus.

I do not mean to suggest, of course, that a nation runs no risks when a large number of its citizens fail to grasp the essential principles on which its constitution is founded. Among Americans, however, the principal danger is not that they will reject democratic ideals in favor of some hostile ideology, but that they will fail to understand the very institutions they believe themselves to be defending and may end up undermining rather than safeguarding them. Our research on "McCarthyism," for example, strongly suggests that popular support for the Senator represented less a conscious rejection of American democratic ideals than a misguided effort to defend them. We found few McCarthy supporters who genuinely shared the attitudes and values associated with his name.[34]

Whether consensus among the influentials is either a necessary or sufficient condition for democratic stability is not really known. Since the influentials act, make public decisions, are more organized, and take political ideas more seriously, agreement among them on constitutional values is widely thought to be essential for viability. At present, however, we do not have enough information (or at least we do not have it in appropriately organized form) to state with satisfactory precision what the actual relation is between elite consensus and democratic stability. Some democratic governments, e.g., Weimar Germany, crumbled when faced with ideological conflicts among their political classes; others, e.g., post-war Italy and France, have until now managed to weather pronounced ideological cleavages. The opinion has long prevailed that consensus is needed to achieve stability, but the converse may be the more correct formulation, i.e., that so long as conditions remain stable, consensus is not required; it becomes essential only when social conditions are disorganized. Consensus may strengthen democratic viability, but its absence in an otherwise stable society need not be fatal or even particularly damaging.

It should also be kept in mind that the existence of intellectual disagreements — even among the influentials — does not necessarily mean that they will be expressed or acted upon. In the United States (and doubtless elsewhere as well), numerous influences are at work to prevent ideological cleavages from assuming an important role in the nation's political life. This is certainly the tendency of such political institutions as federalism, checks and balances, separation of powers, bicameralism, the congressional committee system, the judiciary's practice of accommodating one discrepant law to another, and a

---

[34] Herbert McClosky, "McCarthyism: The Myth and the Reality," unpublished paper delivered at the American Psychological Association, New York, September, 1957. See also G. C. Wiebe, "The Army–McCarthy Hearings and the Public Conscience," *Public Opinion Quarterly*, Vol. 22 (Winter, 1958–1959), pp. 490–502.

system of elections more often fought around local issues and personalities than around urgent national questions. Our two-party system also functions to disguise or soften the genuine disagreements that distinguish active Democrats from active Republicans. The American social system contributes to the same end, for it is a model of the pluralistic society, a profuse collection of diverse groups, interests and organizations spread over a vast and variegated territory. Consensus in such a society becomes difficult to achieve, but by the same token its absence can also more easily be survived. The complexities of a highly pluralistic social and political order tend to diminish the impact of intellectual differences, to compel compromise, and to discourage the holders of divergent views from crystalizing into intransigent doctrinal camps. Thus it seems, paradoxically enough, that the need for consensus on democratic rules of the game increases as the conflict among competing political tendencies becomes sharper, and declines as their differences become more diffused. Italy, by this reasoning, has greater need of consensus than the United States, but has less chance of achieving it. A democratic nation may wisely prefer the American model to the Italian, though what is ideally desired, as Lipset observes[35] is a balance between cleavage and consensus — the one to give reality and force to the principle of opposition, the other to furnish the secure framework within which that principle might be made continuously effective. Countervailing power within a structure of shared political values would, by this logic, be the optimal conditions for the maintenance of a democratic society.

5. But even giving this much weight to consensus may exaggerate the role which intellectual factors play in the attainment of democratic stability. The temptation to assign a controlling influence to the place of ideas in the operation of democracy is very great. Partly this results from our tendency to confuse the textbook model of democracy with the reality and to assume the high order of rationality in the system that the model presupposes (e.g., an alert citizenry aware of its rights and duties, cognizant of the basic rules, exercising consent, enjoying perfect information and choosing governors after carefully weighing their qualifications, deliberating over the issues, etc.). It is not my purpose to ridicule this model but to underscore the observation that it can easily mislead us into placing more weight than the facts warrant upon cognitive elements — upon ideas, values, rational choice, consensus, etc. — as the cementing forces of a democratic society. An ad hominem consideration may also be relevant here: as intellectuals and students of politics, we are disposed both by training and sensibility to take political ideas seriously and to assign central importance to them in the operation of the state. We are therefore prone to forget that most people take them less seriously than we do, that they pay little attention to issues, rarely worry about the consistency of their opinions, and spend little or no time thinking about the values, presuppositions, and implications which distinguish one political orientation from another. If the viability of a democracy were to depend upon the satisfaction of these intellectual activities, the prognosis would be very grim indeed.

---

[35] Seymour Martin Lipset, *Political Man* (New York, 1960), pp. 21–22.

Research from many different lines of inquiry confirms unequivocally that the role heretofore assigned to ideas and to intellectual processes in general has been greatly exaggerated and cannot adequately explain many political phenomena which, on *a priori* grounds, we have expected them to explain. Witness, for example, the research on the non-rational factors which govern the voting decision, on the effects — or rather the non-effects — of ideology on the loyalty and fighting effectiveness of German and American soldiers, on the differences between the views of party leaders and followers, on the influence of personality on political belief, and on group determinants of perception.[36] We now have evidence that patriotism and the strength of one's attachment to a political community need not depend upon one's approval of its intellectual, cultural, or political values. Indeed, our present research clearly confirms that the men and women who express "patriotism" in extreme or chauvinistic form usually have the least knowledge and understanding of American democratic ideals, institutions, and practices.

Abundant anecdotal data from the observation of dictatorial and other nations further corroborates the conclusion that men may become attached to a party, a community, or a nation by forces that have nothing to do with ideology or consensus. Many of these forces are so commonplace that we often neglect them, for they include family, friends, home, employment, property, religion, ethnic attachments, a common language, and familiar surroundings and customs. These may lack the uplifting power of some political doctrines, but their ability to bind men to a society and its government may nevertheless be great. This observation, of course, is less likely to hold for the intelligentsia than for the inarticulates, but even the political behavior of intellectuals is never governed exclusively by appeals to the mind.

The effect of ideas on democratic viability may also be diminished by the obvious reluctance of most men to press their intellectual differences to the margin and to debate questions that may tear the community apart. So long as no urgent reason arises for bringing such differences to the surface, most men will be satisfied to have them remain dormant. Although there are men and women who are exceptions to this generalization, and who cannot bear to leave basic questions unresolved, they are likely to be few, for both the principles and practices of an "open society" strongly reinforce tolerance for variety, contingency and ambiguity in matters of belief and conscience. As our data on freedom of opinion suggest, few Americans expect everyone to value the same things or to hold identical views on public questions. The tendency to ignore, tolerate, or play down differences helps to create an

---

[36] Cf., for example, Angus Campbell, Philip E. Converse, Warren E. Miller, and Donald E. Stokes, *The American Voter* (New York, 1960), chs. 8–10; Bernard R. Berelson, Paul F. Lazarsfeld, and William N. McPhee, *Voting* (Chicago, 1954), especially ch. 14; Edward A. Shils and Morris Janowitz, "Cohesion and Disintegratiaon in the German Wehrmacht in World War II," *Public Opinion Quarterly*, Vol. 12 (1948), pp. 280–315; Herbert McClosky, "Conservatism and Personality," *American Political Science Review*, Vol. 52 (March, 1958), pp. 27–45; T. W. Adorno *et al.*, *The Authoritarian Personality* (New York, 1950), ch. XVII; Richard Crutchfield, "Conformity and Character," *American Psychologist*, Vol. 10 (1955), pp. 191–98.

illusion of consensus which for many purposes can be as serviceable as the reality.[37]

6. To conclude, as we have in effect, that ideological awareness and consensus are overvalued as determinants of democratic viability is not to imply that they are of no importance. While disagreements among Americans on fundamental values have tended to be passive and, owing to apathy and the relative placidity of our politics, easily tolerated; while they do not follow party lines and are rarely insinuated into the party struggle; and while no extremist movement has yet grown large enough to challenge effectively the governing principles of the American Constitution, this happy state of affairs is not permanently guaranteed. Fundamental differences could *become* activated by political and economic crises; party differences could *develop* around fundamental constitutional questions, as they have in France and other democracies; and powerful extremist movements are too familiar a phenomenon of modern political life to take for granted their eternal absence from the American scene.

Obviously a democratic nation also pays a price for an electorate that is weakly developed ideologically. Lacking the intellectual equipment to assess complex political events accurately, the unsophisticated may give support to causes that are contrary to their own or to the national interest. In the name of freedom, democracy, and the Constitution, they may favor a McCarthy, join the John Birch Society, or agitate for the impeachment of a Supreme Court Justice who has worked unstintingly to uphold their constitutional liberties. They may also have difficulty discriminating political integrity from demagoguery, maturity and balanced judgment from fanaticism, honest causes from counterfeits. Our findings on the attitudes shown by ordinary Americans toward "extreme" political beliefs (Left Wing beliefs, Right Wing beliefs, totalitarianism, isolationism, etc.) verify that the possibilities just cited are not merely hypothetical. Those who have the least understanding of American politics subscribe least enthusiastically to its principles, and are most frequently "misled" into attacking constitutional values while acting (as they see it) to defend them.

There is, however, reason to believe that ideological sophistication and the general acceptance of liberal democratic values are increasing rather than declining in the United States. Extreme ideological politics of the type associated with Marxism, fascism and other doctrinaire networks of opinion may

---

[37] Robert G. McCloskey, "The American Ideology," in Marion D. Irish (ed.), *Continuing Crisis in American Politics* (Englewood Cliffs, N. J., 1963), pp. 10–25, suggests that the American political tradition is marked by "ambivalence" toward certain of our fundamental values and that this may discourage the achievement of "consensus" in the usual sense. He believes, however, that Americans have learned to live with, and even to ignore, inconsistencies in the value system, in keeping with our "pragmatic spirit." Whether this ability is uniquely American or whether it is characteristic of all "open," democratic societies is a question well worth investigating. It could, conceivably, be a natural outgrowth of democratic ideology itself, no element of which can be conceived and enforced absolutely without infringing other elements. On this last point, see Sidney Hook, *The Paradoxes of Freedom* (Berkeley, 1962), pp. 14–62.

be waning, as many sociologists believe,[38] but the same observation does not hold for the influence of democratic ideas. On the contrary, democratic ideology in the United States, linked as it is with the articulate classes, gives promise of growing as the articulate class grows. Many developments in recent American life point to an increase in "articulateness": the extraordinary spread of education, rapid social mobility, urbanization, the proliferation of mass media that disseminate public information, the expansion of the middle class, the decline in the size and number of isolated rural groups, the reduction in the proportion of people with submarginal living standards, the incorporation of foreign and minority groups into the culture and their increasing entrance into the professions, and so on. While these developments may on the one side have the effect of reducing the tensions and conflicts on which extreme ideologies feed, they are likely on the other side to beget a more articulate population and a more numerous class of political influentials, committed to liberal democracy and aware of the rights and obligations which attend that commitment.

---

[38] Cf., Daniel Bell, *The End of Ideology* (Glencoe, 1960), pp. 369–375; S. M. Lipset, *Political Man* (New York, 1960), pp. 403–17; Edward Shils, "Ideology and Civility: on the Politics of the Intellectual," *Sewanee Review,* Vol. 66 (Summer, 1958), pp. 450–51.

8. Politicization of the Electorate in France and the United States

PHILIP E. CONVERSE AND GEORGES DUPEUX

The two authors examine the popular stereotypes of the "passionate" French and the "apolitical" American citizen. The results of their analysis not only force us to qualify these stereotypes; they also help us to understand certain puzzling features of the French political scene, such as the rise of "flash parties," the radical rhetoric accompanied by bargaining politics, and the widespread approval of De Gaulle's "above-party" appeal accompanied by continued voting support for the traditional parties.

The turbulence of French politics has long fascinated observers, particularly when comparisons have been drawn with the stability or, according to one's point of view, the dull complacency of American political life. Profound ideological cleavages in France, the occasional threat of civil war, rather strong voter turnout, the instability of governments and republics, and the rise and fall of "flash" parties like the R.P.F. in 1951, the Poujadists in 1956, and the U.N.R. in 1958 have all contributed to the impression of a peculiar intensity in the tenor of French political life.

It is a sign of progress in the study of political behavior that such symptoms no longer seem to form a self-evident whole. We feel increasingly obliged, for example, to take note of the level in the society at which the symptoms are manifest. Most of our impressions of the French scene reflect only the behavior of French political leadership. Growing familiarity with survey data from broad publics has schooled us not to assume perfect continuity between the decision-making characteristics of a leadership and the predispositions of its rank and file. The extremism of the military elite in Algeria or ideological intransigence in the French National Assembly are in themselves poor proof that the shipyard worker in Nantes has political reflexes which differ from those of the shipyard worker in Norfolk.

We feel increasingly obliged, moreover, to discriminate between some of these well-known symptoms of turbulence, for they no longer point in a common direction as clearly as was once assumed. Two signs which unquestionably reflect mass electoral behavior in France provide a case in point. Turnout levels in France are indeed high relative to those in the United States,[1] suggesting that, in the politically indifferent strata of the electorate where nonvoting is considered, political motivations are more intense. On the other hand, we now doubt that the rise and fall of "flash" parties are parallel

SOURCE: Reprinted, by permission, from *Public Opinion Quarterly*, XXVI (Spring, 1962), pp. 1–23.

[1] They are not, of course, outstanding against the backdrop provided by other Western European nations.

symptoms of intense involvement. Rather, it seems likely that such episodes represent spasms of political excitement in unusually hard times on the part of citizens whose year-in, year-out involvement in political affairs is abnormally weak.[2] Obviously, for France and the United States, the basic traditions of a two-party or a multiparty system affect the likelihood that the flash party phenomenon will occur. But other things being equal, it seems that such phenomena are hardly signals of long-term public involvement in politics but betray instead a normal weak involvement. The durably involved voter tends toward strong partisan commitments, and his behavior over time stabilizes party fortunes within a nation.

Other less direct indicators add doubt as to the high involvement of the broad French public. Demographically, French society differs from the American in its lesser urbanization and lower mean formal education. Intranational studies have persistently shown higher political involvement among urban residents and, more strongly still, among people of more advanced education. While cross-national extrapolation of such data may be precarious, it does leave further room to question our intuitive impressions.

We intend in this paper to examine comparative data on the French and American publics in an effort to determine more precisely the locus of Franco-American differences in these matters.[3] We shall consider the locus in qualitative terms, covering an extended series of political characteristics which run from expressions of involvement, acts of participation, and information seeking to orientations whereby the voter links party alternatives to the basic ideological issues in the society. We shall throughout maintain an interest as well in a vertical locus of differences. That is, we shall think of the two electorates as stratified from persistent nonvoters at the bottom, through the large middle mass of average voters, to citizens who engage in some further partisan activity, and thence by extrapolation to the higher leadership whose highly visible behavior is so frequently the source of our cross-national impressions. Such extrapolation is necessary, of course, because it is unlikely that the handful of "activists" whom we can distinguish at the top layer of both national samples include more than one or two persons who have ever had any direct hand in a leadership decision of even a parochial party organization or political interest group.

Involvement, Participation, and Information Seeking

While a relatively large number of comparisons may be drawn with regard to simple manifestations of political involvement in the two countries, these

---

[2] For a fuller discussion, see Angus Campbell, Philip E. Converse, Warren E. Miller, and Donald E. Stokes, *The American Voter* (New York: Wiley, 1960), Chap. 15.

[3] The French data were gathered in three waves of a national cross-section sample in the fall of 1958, during the constitutional referendum launching the Fifth Republic and the

comparisons vary widely in quality. Broad differences in institutions and political practices in the two societies can serve to channel public interest in different directions. The French political poster, often a full-blown campaign document, is addressed to other goals than the American political billboard, and hence the reading of such posters in the two societies is in no sense comparable activity. Similarly, the national control of the domestic airwaves in France means that the two media of communication are given a totally different cast than in the United States. This fact, coupled with reduced access to radio or television sets in France, renders the attention paid by the two publics to such political broadcasts fundamentally incomparable. Or, in a different vein, certain manifestations of involvement are known to vary widely in their frequency within a nation from one type of election to another, or for the same type of election between periods of crisis and troughs of routine politics. While an extended American time series has provided some useful norms, these were more difficult to find for the French data. In general, then, we shall elaborate upon only a few of the most solid comparisons, referring summarily to the flavor conveyed by other, looser comparisons.

Given the broad institutional differences between the two societies, it might seem useful to draw contrasts between self-estimates of psychological involvement between the two nations, however differently institutions might channel the ultimate behavioral expressions of such interest. While the data permit a number of matches between questions on political interest, posed at comparable times with comparable wording and with superficially comparable alternatives, one hesitates at comparisons which depend on crude "amount words" such as "very," "fairly," and the like. Cautiously, however, it may be observed that Americans gauge their interest in their elections at a rather higher level than do the French. Two to five times as many French respondents indicated that they were "not at all" interested in the 1958 elections as is the tendency for Americans with regard to their presidential elections; three to four times as many Americans say that they are "very" interested. Distributions from France in the more normal political year of 1953 show slightly higher levels of expressed interest, but even this distribution fails to approach the most unenthusiastic American distributions collected at the time of off-year congressional elections. For what it is worth, then, it is relatively hard to get French citizens to confess much interest in their elections.

---

ensuing legislative elections. The study was jointly supported by the Conseil Supérieur de la Recherche Scientifique, the Rockefeller Foundation, and the Fondation Nationale des Sciences Politiques. The American studies over six elections have been conducted by the Survey Research Center of the University of Michigan, under grants from the Rockefeller Foundation and the Carnegie Corporation. Informal cross-national collaboration prior to the 1958 French study led to a French interview schedule permitting more rigorous comparative analysis than unrelated studies usually offer.

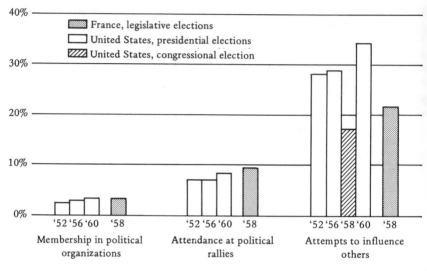

Figure 1   *Rates of several forms of political participation,
France and the United States*

More solid are comparisons of reported acts of political participation selected as involving comparable motivation in the two systems: membership in political organizations, attendance at political rallies, and attempts to influence the political choice of others through informal communication.[4] As Figure 1 suggests, the cross-national similarities on these items are impressive. Furthermore, we can examine such additional points as the number of meetings attended by those French and Americans who do attend political gatherings. Graphs of the frequency of attendance by attender are almost indistinguishable between the two countries. The mean number of meetings attended among those who attend at all is in both cases a slight fraction over two. In sum, it is hard to imagine that any slight divergencies in rates of attendance are crucial in any dramatic differences between the two systems.

---

[4] Of these three pairings, the first is technically the weakest. The American item asks about membership in "any political club or organization," while the French item focuses directly on political party membership, although the term "party" may be rather broadly construed in France. Furthermore, there were a substantial number of refusals to answer this membership item in France. These refusals have simply been removed from the calculations, since such treatment leaves the gross rate on the upper side of the range that informed estimates have suggested for total party membership in France, after realistic appraisal of the memberships claimed by the parties.

Data were collected in both countries as well with regard to dependence on the mass media for political information. Here one of the most excellent bases for comparison which the data afford is provided by reports of the regularity with which political news about the elections was followed in daily newspapers. Although the structured alternatives again involve "amount words," there is a more tangible standard for responses implicit in the rhythm of newspaper production. "Regularly" or "never," when applied to readership of daily papers, has a common meaning in any language. Furthermore, we find empirically that responses to the newspaper questions show much higher stability for individuals over time than the direct interest questions. It is clear that we are dealing here with stable habits which are reliably reported.

When we compare distributions from the two countries (Table 1), there seems little doubt of higher American devotion to newspapers as a source of political information. Furthermore, the French citizen appears also to monitor other media for political information less. Thus, for example, he is less likely to have a television or radio set than his American counterpart; but even among those French who possess sets, attention to political broadcasts is markedly less than for comparable Americans. As we have observed, these latter differences are not in themselves proof of lesser French motivation, since the choices offered through the airwaves are not comparable cross-nationally. But such facts, along with further comparisons as to magazine reading, indicate that

Table 1   *Frequency of Newspaper Reading for Political Information, in Per Cent*

	FRANCE 1958		UNITED STATES 1960	
	Post-referendum	*Post-election*	*Post-election*	
Regulièrement	19	18	44	Regularly
Souvent	12	10	12	Often
De temps en temps	25	29	16	From time to time
Très rarement	19	21	7	Just once in a great while
Jamais	25	22	21	Never
	100	100	100	

lower French attention to political material in the newspapers is not compensated for from other sources. Since elite political competition in France, even when reduced to simplest terms, is considerably more complex than two-party competition in the United States, it is ironic that the French voter exposes himself less faithfully to the flow of current political information.

Education being a strong determinant of all these information-seeking activities, it is of interest to control the substantial Franco-American differences in level of formal education. For Figure 2 we have applied a simple integer

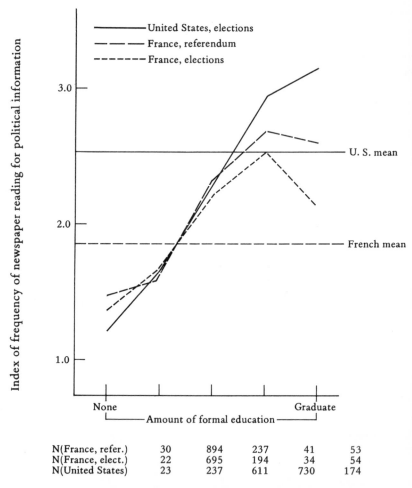

	None				Graduate
N(France, refer.)	30	894	237	41	53
N(France, elect.)	22	695	194	34	54
N(United States)	23	237	611	730	174

Figure 2   *Frequency of newspaper reading for political information in France and the United States, by education*

scoring to the five response categories of Table 1 and extracted means within education categories, the latter having been carefully tailored on the American side to match French intervals with regard to simple number of years of formal education. While the two curves do not match precisely, the main departures lie at the extremes, where case numbers are lowest, and hence where sampling error is bound to disperse results.[5] Where more than 200 cases are available from both sides, the estimates show a most remarkable convergence.

As we see, there are strong cross-national differences in total distribution of regularity of newspaper reading (as represented by the distance between the horizontal lines in Figure 2). But these differences very nearly disappear (the general proximity of the two slopes, and their essential identity when case numbers are sufficient), with education controlled. The gap in total news reading for the two electorates comes about, then, simply because the American cases are loaded heavily to the right side of the graph, while the center of gravity of the French education distribution is to the left, or low, side. The capacity to move cross-national differences out to the marginals in this fashion not only strengthens presumption of common causal factors, but also is a reassuring anchor in the unknown waters of cross-national research, where the basic comparability of data must be held to special question. We shall see a more dramatic demonstration of this circuit of empirical reasoning below.

By way of summary, then, comparisons up to this point create a general sense of Franco-American similarity, with occasional mild divergences suggesting stronger American political involvement. The locus of these differences in the vertical sense is interesting. Let us bear in mind that most of these involvement actions in both societies stand in a scalar relationship to one another, in the Guttman sense. That is, the party member who passes the "hardest" of our items is very likely to have attended meetings, monitored the media, and so on. In this sense there is an underlying involvement dimension represented here. Furthermore, we have established cutting points on this dimension in quite different ranges of the continuum, at the high end for party membership and meeting attendance, but much deeper in the middle mass where information seeking and expressions of involvement are concerned. In a rough way, we may observe that the American data seem to show somewhat higher motivation in the middle ranges, with cross-national differences narrowing near the very top, and perhaps even showing a slight French advantage. Interestingly enough, this pattern would describe as well the cumulative frequency distributions expressing differences in years of formal education in the two countries. This identity is, of course, no proof that education accounts for the involvement divergences. But it does remind us that these patterns, if they differ cross-nationally at all, may partake of the sharper discontinuities in France between a tiny elite and the remainder of the population that one suspects for a variety of characteristics, and can readily demonstrate for education.[6]

---

[5] The decline in reading among the most educated French citizens approaches statistical significance and is currently unaccounted for. We have been able to show that these people are not substituting political reviews and weekly magazines for daily news reading. The educated elite which follows the reviews also reads the newspapers faithfully; the remainder which fails to attend to the newspapers ignores political magazines as well.

[6] We shall not treat Franco-American differences in vote turnout, save to observe that they are probably more institutional than motivational. American registration requirements in many states are such that an American is persistently confronted by an institutional barrier which is rarely erected in France. It can be argued most strongly that the

Partisan Orientations

The gross similarities between the two publics in apparent political interest do not, to be sure, remove the possibility that the Frenchman in his interested moments may respond to politics in much different terms that his American counterpart. Actually, when we consider the character of partisan ties felt by citizens in the two countries, we strike upon some contrasts of great magnitude.

If Americans are asked to locate themselves relative to the American party system, 75 per cent classify themselves without further probing as psychological members of one of the two major parties, or of some minor party. In France, somewhat before the elections, less than 45 per cent of those who did not refuse to answer the questions were able to classify themselves in one of the parties or splinter groups, while another 10 to 15 per cent associated themselves with a more or less recognizable broad *tendance* ("left," "right," a labor union, etc.). The cross-national differences of 20 to 30 per cent are sufficiently large here to contribute to fundamental differences in the flavor of partisan processes in the two electorates. For a long time, we wrote off these differences as products of incomparable circumstances or of reticence on the part of the French concerning partisanship, most of which was being expressed not as refusal to answer the question, but as some other evasion. As we grew more familiar with the data, however, these differences took on vital new interest.

The hypothesis of concealed partisanship was very largely dispelled by a close reading of the actual interviews. It is undeniable that nearly 10 per cent of the French sample explicitly refused to answer the question, as compared with a tiny fraction in the United States. However, we have already subtracted this group from the accounting. Beyond the explicit refusals, the remarks and explanations which often accompanied statements classified as "no party," or as "don't know which party," had a very genuine air about them which made them hard to read as hasty evasions. No few of these respondents were obviously embarrassed at their lack of a party; some confessed that they just hadn't been able to keep track of which party was which. The phrase "je n'y ai jamais pensé" was extremely common. Others indicated that they found it too hard to choose between so many parties; some indicated preferences for a specific political leader but admitted that they did not know which party he belonged to or, more often, had no interest in the identity of his party, whatever it might be. Others, forming a tiny minority of the nonparty people, rejected the notion of parties with some hostility.

It became clear, too, that people reporting no party attachments were distinct on other grounds from those who willingly classified themselves as close to a party. On our vertical involvement dimension, for example, they tended to fall in the bottom stratum of the least involved, just as the paper-thin stratum unable to choose a party in the United Stattes consists heavily of the least

---

act of getting somewhere to register demands higher political motivation than going to the polls on Election Day. Indeed, over half the Americans who fail to vote in major elections blame such registration barriers as change in residence, failure to renew on time, etc. If such reports are credited, the registration toll in the United States would easily make up the apparent Franco-American differences.

nvolved. Demographically, these nonparty people were disproportionately
housewives, poorly educated, young, and the other familiar statuses which tend
to be uninformed and uninvolved.

Among actual party identifiers in France there was further interesting
variation in the character of the party objects to which reference was made.
A very few linked themselves with small new ideological splinter groups which
had developed during the political crises of 1958. For these people, it was not
enough to indicate that they felt closest to the Radical-Socialists, for example:
they had to specify that they were Mendesists or anti-Mendesists, Valoisiens,
and the like. Most identifiers suffered no difficulty in seeing themselves as
"Radical-Socialists," completely shattered though the party was. Others,
perceiving the system even more grossly, linked themselves only with a broad
tendance. On involvement measures these groupings showed the expected
differences: the grosser the discrimination, the lower the involvement.

In other ways as well it was clear that the extreme ideological fractionation
of parties in France has few roots in the mass population, members of which
simply pay too little attention to politics to follow the nicer discriminations
involved. When asked whether the number of parties in France was too great,
about right, or too few, 97 per cent of those responding said there were too
many parties, and less than 1 per cent said there were too few. In response
to an ensuing question as to the desirable number of parties, the mean of the
number seen as optimal was 3.5 for the handful of adherents of the new
ideological splinters, 3.0 for the partisans of the traditional mass parties, and
less than 2.8 among those who had formed no party attachments. Perhaps
the most apt expression of the problem of partisan fractionation and discrimi-
tion came from the naïve respondent who opined that France should have two
or three parties, "enough to express the differences in opinion."

The fact that large proportions of the French public have failed to form any
very strong attachments to one of the political parties should not be taken to
mean that these people are totally disoriented in the French party system. In
particular, a sensitivity to the gulf separating the Communist Party from the
remainder of French parties does pervade the mass public. There seems to be
less confusion as to the identity of the Communist Party than for any of the
other parties; and for the bulk of non-Communists, the Communist Party is a
pariah. There are some nonidentifiers who appear to shift from Communist
to non-Communist votes with abandon, and were all of these votes to fall to
the Communists in the same election, the Party would undoubtedly exceed its
previous high-water mark in its proportion of the French popular vote. At the
same time, however, one cannot help but be impressed by the number of
respondents who, while indicating they were not really sure what they were
in partisan terms, indicated as well at one point or another in the interview
that they were not only non-Communist but anti-Communist. In other words,
were the descriptions of party adherents to proceed simply in terms of a
Communist, non-Communist division, the proportion of ready self-classifications
would advance considerably toward the American figure, and would probably
exceed that which could be attained by any other two-class division in France.

Nevertheless, the limited party attachments outside the Communist camp in France retain strong theoretical interest, as they seem so obviously linked to a symptom of turbulence which is clearly not an elite phenomenon alone — the flash party. With a very large proportion of the electorate feeling no anchoring loyalty, it is not surprising that a new party can attract a large vote "overnight," or that this base can be so rapidly dissolved. Furthermore, there is a problem here that is peculiarly French, in that the low proportion of expressed attachments cannot simply be seen as a necessary consequence of a multiparty system per se. Fairly comparable data from Norway, where six parties are prominent, show party attachments as widespread as those in the two-party United States.[7]

The French sample was asked further to recall the party or *tendance* which the respondent's father had supported at the polls. Here the departure from comparable American data became even more extreme (Table 2). Of those Americans in 1958 having had a known father who had resided in the United States as an American citizen, thereby participating in American political life,

Table 2   *Respondent's Characterization of Father's Political Behavior, by Country, 1958, in Per Cent*

	France	United States
Located father in party or broad *tendance*	25	76
Recalled father as "independent," "shifting around," or as apolitical, nonvoting	3	6
Total able to characterize father's political behavior	28	82
Unable to characterize father's political behavior	68	8
Father did not reside in country or was never a citizen		3
Did not know father; question not asked about father surrogate	4	6
Refused; other		1
	100	100
(N)	(1,166)	(1,795)

86 per cent could characterize his partisanship, and another 5 per cent knew enough of his political behavior to describe him as apolitical or independent. Among comparable French respondents, only 26 per cent could link fathers with any party or with the vaguest of *tendances* (including such responses as "il a toujours voté pour la patrie"), and another 3 per cent could describe the father's disposition as variable or apolitical. In other words, among those eligible to respond to the question, 91 per cent of Americans could characterize their father's political behavior, as opposed to 29 per cent of the French.

It goes without saying that differences of this magnitude rarely emerge from individual data in social research. And they occur at a point of prime theo-

---

[7] Angus Campbell and Henry Valen, "Party Identification in Norway and the United States," *Public Opinion Quarterly,* Vol. 25, 1961, pp. 505–525 [reprinted below, Section 9].

retical interest. We have long been impressed in the United States by the degree to which partisan orientations appear to be passed hereditarily, from generation to generation, through families. It has seemed likely that such transmission is crucial in the stability of American partisan voting patterns. Therefore, we find it startling to encounter a situation in which huge discontinuities seem to appear in this transmission.

What do the French responses concerning paternal partisanship really mean? As best we can determine, they mean what they appear to mean: the French father is uncommunicative about his political behavior before his children, just as he is more reserved in the interviewing situation than Americans or Norwegians. It seems highly unlikely, for example, that Franco-American differences in recall represent French concealment: large numbers of the French willing to speak of their own party preference are unable to give the father's preference of a generation before, and explicit refusals to answer, while attaining 10 per cent or more where own partisanship is at stake, are almost nonexistent for paternal partisanship.

Furthermore, we have come to reject the possibility that the bulk of the Franco-American difference is some simple consequence of the more fluid and complex French party system. Responses to a similar question in the Norwegian multiparty system look like our American results, and not like the French. Nor is there reason to believe that the Frenchman has trouble finding comparable modern terms for the party groupings of a generation ago. As we have observed, the respondent was invited to give a rough equivalent of his father's position in terms of *tendance*. Moreover, where there are any elaborations of "I don't know" captured in the interview, the consistent theme seemed to be that the respondent did not feel he had ever known his father's position ("je n'ai jamais su"; "je ne lui ai jamais demandé"; "il ne disait rien à ses enfants"; "il n'en parlait jamais"). Finally, if special problems were occasioned on the French side by the changing party landscape over time, we should certainly expect that older French respondents would have greater difficulty locating their fathers politically than would younger respondents. They do not: the tabulation by age in France shows only the slightest of variations attributable to age, and these lend no support to the hypothesis (e.g., slightly less knowledge of father's position for children under thirty) and are variations which may be found in the comparable American table as well.

If we accept the proposition, then, that there are basic discontinuities in the familial transmission of party orientations in France, all of our theory would argue that weaker party attachments should result in the current generation. The data do indeed show a remarkable association between the two phenomena, once again involving differences of 30 per cent or more. Both French and Americans who recall their father's partisanship are much more likely themselves to have developed party loyalties than are people who were not aware of their father's position. Of still greater importance are the more absolute Franco-American similarities. Setting aside those people whose fathers were noncitizens, dead, apolitical, or floaters, or who refused to answer the question, we can focus on the core of the comparison (in per cent):

	KNOW FATHER'S PARTY		DO NOT KNOW FATHER'S PARTY	
	France	U.S.	France	U.S.
Proportion having some partisan self-location (party or vague *tendance*)	79.4	81.6	47.7	50.7
Proportion that these are of total electorate	24	75	63	8

Where the socialization processes have been the same in the two societies, the results in current behavior appear to be the same, in rates of formation of identification. The strong cross-national differences lie in the socialization processes. In other words, we have come full circle again: we have encountered large national differences but have once again succeeded in moving them to the marginals of the table. This is our best assurance that our measurements are tapping comparable phenomena.

Partisan attachments appear therefore to be very weakly developed within the less politically involved half of the French electorate. While undoubtedly a large variety of factors, including the notoriety which the French parties had acquired in the later stages of the Fourth Republic, have helped to inhibit their development, more basic discontinuities of political socialization in the French family appear to be making some persisting contribution as well.[8] Of course, similar lack of party attachment does occur among people indifferent to politics in the American and Norwegian systems as well; but the strata of unidentified people are thinner in these systems and do not extend greatly above that layer of persistent nonvoters which is present in any system.

The link between an electorate heavily populated with voters feeling no continuing party attachments and a susceptibility to "flash" parties is an obvious one. It must be recognized at the outset, of course, that such phenomena arise only under the pressure of social, political, or economic dislocations occurring in some segment of the population, thereby generating an elite which wishes to organize a movement and a public which is restive. This means that even a system highly susceptible to such phenomena is not likely to experience them when it is functioning smoothly: their prevalence in postwar France cannot be divorced from the severe dislocations the society has been undergoing. Once misfortunes breed discontent, however, the proportions of partisans in an electorate is a datum of fundamental significance. One cannot fail to be impressed by the agility with which the strong partisan can blame the opposing party for almost any misfortune or deny the political

---

[8] Among other factors, an alleged paucity of voluntary associations acting vigorously to mediate between the mass of citizens and centralized authority in France has often been cited as a crucial differentium in the quality of the political process between France and the United States. See William Kornhauser, *The Politics of Mass Society* (Glencoe, Ill.: Free Press, 1959). If such differences do exist, they may well have some bearing on the prevalence of partisan attachments, for it is clear intranationally, at least, that high rates of participation in nonpolitical voluntary associations and strong partisan attachments tend to co-occur at the individual level (although it is much less clear whether this represents a causal progression or two aspects of the same stance toward community life). In other

relevance of the misfortune if some opposing party cannot conceivably be blamed. Hence, where partisans are concerned, misfortunes do relatively little to shift voting patterns. Independents, however, have no stake in such reinforcements and defenses and move more massively in response to grievances. In France, the institutions which conduce to a multiparty system make the organization of new party movements more feasible from an elite point of view than it is likely to be under two-party traditions. At the same time, the presense of a large number of French voters who have developed no continuing attachments to a particular party provides an "available" mass base for such movements. This available base is no necessary concomitant of a multiparty system, but is rather a peculiarity of the current French scene.

Parties and Policy Controversy

Whatever differences exist in partisan orientations, no assessment of politicization would be complete without consideration of the manner in which ideological conflict is worked out through the party system. If parties are recognized at all in the classical view of democratic process, they are relegated to a distinctly secondary position: they are means to policy ends, and should be judged by the citizen accordingly. In this light, the number of Americans with strong party loyalty and a poor sense of what either party stands for in policy terms represents a distinct perversion of the democratic process. In this light, too, weaker partisan orientations in the French populace might simply mean a relegation of party to second rank, with a primary focus on policy goals.

At an elite level, of course, there are distinct Franco-American differences in the phrasing of the means-end relation between party and policy, and these contrasts weigh heavily in our impressions of differences in quality of political process between the two systems. That is, while French political elites are not insensitive to party formations as instruments toward policy goals, the fact remains that parties are split and reshaped with relative freedom in order that the party may be the purest possible expression, not only of the politician's position on a single basic issue dimension, but of the total configuration of position adopted on cross-cutting issue dimensions. On the American side, remarkable policy accommodations are made to preserve the semblance of party unity, and party competition for votes "in the middle" leads to a considerable blurring of interparty differences on policy. The crucial role of basic political institutions in stimulating either multipartite or bipartite trends has often been discussed, and whether French elite activities would survive long

contexts, however, it has been argued that ostensibly nonpolitical associations of mass membership in France tend to play more vigorous roles as parapolitical agents than do comparable associations in the United States, which so often tend to regard political entanglement with horror. Both views have some appeal on the basis of loose impressions of the two societies, and are not in the strictest sense contradictory. However, their thrusts diverge sufficiently that a confrontation would seem worthwhile if either can be borne out by any systematic evidence. Where grass-roots participation in expressly political associations is concerned, we have seen no notable differences between the nations in either membership rates or rates of attendance at political gatherings.

under American ground rules is a moot point. We may consider, however, whether the ideological clarity or intransigence associated with French political elites and the policy compromise or confusion which characterizes the American party system reflect properties of their mass publics.

Data have been collected in both countries concerning reactions to a variety of issues confronting the two systems. While both sets of items must be regarded as only the crudest samplings of hypothetical issue universes, selection on both sides was performed in an attempt to tap some of the most basic controversies of the period. In France, three items were devoted to the classic socio-economic left and right, with one concerning the role of labor and the other two the relative roles of government and private enterprise in housing; two more involved the clerical question; a sixth item had to do with military expenditures and national prestige; a seventh concerned the freedom of the press to criticize the government. Of eight American questions, two dealt with social-welfare legislation and a third with the relative role of government and private enterprise in housing and utilities, covering the classic right and left; two more dealt with the government's role in racial matters (FEPC and school desegregation); and three others were concerned with the internationalist or isolationist posture of the government in foreign affairs. All questions were in Likert scale form.

We shall focus upon three properties of these issues which we can more or less crudely measure in the two countries: (1) the degree to which public opinion is sharply crystallized on each issue; (2) the degree to which opinion within the two publics is polarized on each; and (3) for each issue, the degree to which individual opinion is associated with partisan preference.[9] Assuming the items do give fair coverage to most primary issue dimensions in the two nations, we are interested to see if opinion in France at a mass level appears more sharply crystallized or polarized, and to assess the manner in which policy concerns are linked with party preference. As before, we shall distinguish layers of both populations in terms of partisan involvement. At the top, we isolate as political "actives" those people who were either party members or reported attending two or more political rallies in the respective election campaigns, a group which amounts to 5 to 7 per cent within each population and hence is sufficiently large for analysis. We also continue to distinguish

---

[9] Of these three properties, polarization is most dependent on question wording. It is measured by the standard deviation of the response distribution, after the five steps of the scale have been assigned simple integer scores. The statistic takes high values (e.g. over 1.50) only when the distribution of opinion is relatively U-shaped. Party-relatedness is measured by a rank-order correlation between the respondent's partisan position and his issue position. In the United States, the Democratic Party was presumed to be the more liberal on domestic issues and the more internationalist in foreign affairs, and respondents were arrayed from a Democratic to a Republican pole on the basis of party loyalty for identifiers, or patterns of 1956–1958 vote for nonidentifiers. In France, a panel of expert observers arranged the many parties or fractions thereof on a socio-economic left-right continuum and again on a continuum from clerical to anticlerical. The second was used to array respondents for the two religious issues; the first was used for the other five issues. Once again, nonidentifiers were located on the basis of reports of 1956 and 1958 votes. All rank-order correlations, including those used for the crystallization measure discussed

etween party identifiers (three-quarters of the American population, but half f the French) and nonidentifiers.

In both nations, the issue items were asked again of the same respondents fter an interval of time. We take as a measure of crystallization of opinion he rank-order correlation between the two expressions of opinion. There is a ood deal of internal evidence to suggest that "change" in opinion between he two readings is almost never a matter of true conversion, but rather epresents haphazard reactions to items on which the respondent has never ormed much opinion. With minor exceptions, there is no significant change n the marginal distributions of the tables, despite the high turnover of opinion. There is a persistent relation between the proportions of people who confess hey have no opinion on any given issue and the amount of turnover shown by those who do attempt an opinion. As one might expect, too, there is a endency for high crystallization, high polarization, and high party-relatedness o co-occur, despite intriguing exceptions. Clearly both publics are more likely o have arrived at stable prior opinions on some items than on others, and this degree of crystallization has an obvious bearing on the vitality of the role the ssue dimension may play in partisan choice.

Unfortunately, the magnitude of these turnover coefficients may not be compared cross-nationally, since the interval between tests averaged little more han a month on the French side but ran twenty-six months on the American ide.[10] Nevertheless, as Table 3 indicates, the level of these coefficients is by any standard remarkably low in both populations. Taken as test-retest relia-bility coefficients, they would send the psychologist in search of a better measuring instrument. After all, on an item where the stability seems relatively high (freedom of the press), less than eight Frenchmen in ten take the same side of the issue twice in a five-week period, when five out of ten would ucceed in doing so by making entirely random choices. On the other hand, while more routine measurement error certainly imposes a rather constant eiling on these coefficients which may not greatly exceed .8, the further ncapacity of the two publics to respond reliably to these items must be considered a substantive datum of the first water. For if these items, reduced to an unusually simple vocabulary, fail to touch off well-formed opinions, the remoteness of both publics from most political and journalistic debate on such dimensions is obvious. It is not as though the items presented new contro-

---

n the text, are tau-betas, based on tables of equal rows and columns. See Hubert M. Blalock, *Social Statistics* (New York: McGraw-Hill, 1960), pp. 321 ff.

[10] In American panel studies we are beginning to fill in a picture of the manner in which these coefficients erode over time. For example, coefficients after four years show almost no decline from their two-year levels, and it seems likely that, in the infrequent instances where opinions on these issues ar truly crystallized, they are subject to little change. As the test-retest interval changes, we may suppose that the coefficient declines very rapidly in the brief period in which respondents forget their previous answers and hence are obliged to "guess again," and then stabilizes at a hard core of well-formed opinions. The French interval was so brief, however, that it is hard to imagine that the coefficients had yet dropped to their stabilized level. We would hazard the loose judgment that the French coefficients lie about where one would expect were they destined to decline to American levels in a comparable period of time.

Table 3 Selected Issue Characteristics in France and the United States

| | CRYSTALLIZATION | | POLARIZATION | | PARTY-RELATEDNESS | | | |
| | | | | | Total Sample | NON-SOUTH | | |
	Total Sample	Actives	Total Sample	Actives	Actives	Actives	Identifiers	Unidentified
France:								
State support of religious schools	.65	.74	1.54	1.62	.58		.39	.32
Strikes by government employees	.52	.69	1.60	1.70	.59		.31	.22
Current threat posed by clergy	.47	.80	1.32	1.64	.56		.34	.19
Freedom of press	.47	.68	1.50	1.60	.39		.22	.13
State responsibility for housing	.42	.34	1.39	1.45	.38		.13	.08
Level of military expenditures	.34	.46	1.36	1.56	.33		.18	.17
Private responsibility for housing	.28	.35	1.26	1.60	.37		.22	.04
United States:								
Federal school integration action	.42	.47	1.69	1.72	.00	.12	.07	—.06
Federal guarantees of employment	.35	.49	1.45	1.55	.16	.30	.19	.03
Federal FEPC	.34	.34	1.41	1.55	.00	.14	.06	.01
Federal aid to education	.34	.54	1.09	1.60	.16	.29	.21	.16
General isolationism-internationalism	.33	.25	1.48	1.48	.16	.06	.03	.04
Deployment of U.S. forces abroad	.28	.10	1.23	1.25	.07	.04	.05	—.02
Government vs. private enterprise in power and housing	.25	.41	1.37	1.45	.21	.27	.18	.21
Foreign aid	.24	.31	1.36	1.38	.11	.10	.02	—.05

versies on which opinion had not yet had time to develop. With few exceptions, they have been the basic stuff of political disagreement for decades or generations. Opinions still unformed are unlikely to develop further.

In this light, then, it is interesting to compare the stability over time of reactions to parties with the stability of responses to these "basic" controversies shown in the first column of Table 3. This assessment is rather difficult on the French side in view of the frequent indeterminacy of party locations; however, it seems that, in a comparable period of time, affective reactions to the parties are more stable than issue reactions even in France. In the United States, we know that partisan reactions show dramatically greater stability than the issue responses. Most important, perhaps, is the failure of data in Table 3 to support an image of the mass French public as remaining aloof from party sentiments while hewing dogmatically to ideological goals. Beyond the political actives, stability of issue opinion seems unimpressive, and for the majority of French voters without party attachments, the articulation of party choice with any of the issue dimensions covered here is slight indeed (Table 3, final column).

While the instability of opinion in both nations is of primary interest in Table 3, several further comparisons may be summarized. The major cross-national contrast comes in the party-relatedness column, where French actives and partisans show much higher coefficients than their American counterparts. The most obvious American phenomenon which blunts interparty policy differences is the disparity between the Southern and non-Southern wings of the Democratic Party. While setting aside the Southern Democratic rank and file does not remove the perceptual problem posed for Northern Democrats who may find the top leaders of their party at odds on many issues, we complete this exercise in Table 3 to show that, even for actives, this regional limitation does not begin to bring the American coefficients up to the French level. While the higher French coefficients are no statistical necessity, it is likely that, in practice, closer party-relatedness is inevitable in the multiparty system. The interparty differences in opinion among French *partisans* appear to lie in about the same range as those found in Norway.[11] However, as we have seen, party attachments are more prevalent in Norway than in France; when the unidentified enter the French electorate in an actual vote, it is likely that individual issue opinions receive less clear expression across the electorate as a whole than is the case in Norway.

Beyond this primary contrast, Table 3 is impressive for its cross-national similarities. Actives in both countries show more highly crystallized opinions, and usually more polarized opinions as well, although American actives differ less sharply and consistently from their mass public than do French actives. In neither country do identifiers differ reliably from nonidentifiers with regard to crystallization or polarization of opinion. In both countries, however, there are quite reliable differences in party-relatedness, not only between actives and the remaining 95 per cent of the population, but between identifiers and

---

[11] Angus Campbell and Henry Valen, "Party Identification in Norway and the United States," *Public Opinion Quarterly*, Vol. 25, 1961, pp. 505–525.

nonidentified. In other words, while the partisan manner of relating to the political process makes little difference in basic opinion formation save for the extremely active, the translation of these attitudes to some kind of party choice seems increasingly haphazard as party attachments become weaker.

Throughout these comparisons, however, we may remain struck by the fact that the "slope" is steeper on the French side: the differences between actives and mass are large relative to those in the United States. From the upper end of this steep slope, one might wish to extrapolate to the sharp and rigid cleavages on policy matters for which French elites are noted; for our purposes, it is sufficient to observe that these cleavages blur rapidly and lose their tone in the mass of the French electorate.

Finally, it should be observed that the issues seem to sort themselves into two rough categories in both nations: (1) emotional-symbol issues involving some of the more gross group conflicts within the two societies (racial in the United States, religious in France, along with items which touch in a direct way upon labor as an interest group), which show relatively high crystallization and polarization; and (2) more complex questions of relations between the state and private enterprise which, along with all foreign policy issues, tend to be less crystallized.

These differences in crystallization are scarcely surprising, as the objects and means involved in the second group of issues are clearly more remote from the common experience of the man-in-the-street. Yet the pattern is ironic, for the issues which show a stronger resonance in both mass publics tend to be those which both elites make some attempt to soft-pedal, in favor of direct debate over such more "ideological" matters as arrangements between state and private enterprise. The more resonant issues are not dead, of course, and are used for tactical advantage by elites in both countries. Calculations of vote gain are made in the United States on the basis of the religion of the nominee, and the clerical question in France has been resuscitated repeatedly as a handy crowbar to split apart government coalitions. At the same time, however, there is genuine elite effort to keep such cleavage issues in the background: the American public is told that religion is not a proper criterion for candidate choice, and the battleground for elite debate on the racial issue is usually displaced quite notably from race itself in the modern period. Similarly, much sophisticated French opinion has for some time argued that even the secondary role which the clerical question has been playing in elite debate exaggerates its importance.

Given this common background, the different manner in which the two types of controversy weave into partisan choices in the two countries is fascinating. In France, there is fair coincidence between the ordering of issues in terms of party-relatedness and the ordering on the other two properties. The clerical questions, for example, are highly crystallized and polarized, and show high levels of party-relatedness as well. The structure of party competition is such that, elite values notwithstanding, these emotional cleavages achieve prominent partisan expression. Such is not the case in the United States: there is little coincidence between the party-relatedness of issues and the other two properties. Indeed, the racial issue finds little clear party expression, while the "elite" issue concerning government and private enterprise, one of the least crystallized issues, is at the same time one of the most party-related across the full electorate.

Where mass or elite control of issue controversy is concerned, then, the two systems have rather paradoxical outcomes. By conception, the French party system is geared to elites, encouraging them to a multifaceted ideological expression which is too complex for most of the public to encompass. At the same time, the multidimensional clarity of party position serves to return a measure of control to part of the public, for the more involved citizens can single out certain dimensions to reduce the system to manageable simplicity. These reductions are naturally made in terms of issues which are more resonant in the public, even if these are not the dimensions which the elites might wish to stress. The American system is less elite in conception; it is sufficiently simple in its gross characteristics that it is easier for the common citizen to follow it with only limited attention. But this simplification requires great blurring of party differences across most of the universe of possible issues, and the differences which are maintained are those which the competing elites select as battlegrounds. Hence, control of controversy which can be given partisan expression is, paradoxically, more nearly in elite hands.

Conclusions

We have attempted to sort through a number of those characteristics of French politics which add up to vague impressions of intense French politicization, in order to identify more precise loci for Franco-American differences. It appears likely that the more notable of these differences stem from the actions of elites and require study and explanation primarily at this level, rather than at the level of the mass electorate. While certain peculiarities reminiscent of French political elites are visible in the most politically active twentieth of the French population, these peculiarities fade out rapidly as one approaches the more "representative" portions of the broad French public.

It is unlikely that the common French citizen devotes any greater portion of his attention to politics than does his American counterpart, and he may well give less. His behavior is constrained within a much different set of political institutions, and these differences have important consequences for the character of his political behavior, including the opportunity of closer articulation between any crystallized opinions he may hold and an appropriate party instrument. However, the data give no striking reason to believe that the French citizen, either through the vagaries of national character, institutions, or history, is predisposed to form political opinions which are more sharply crystallized or which embrace a more comprehensive range of political issues than do comparable Americans. On both sides, opinion formation declines as objects and arrangements become more remote from the observer; and much of politics, for both French and Americans, is remote. Hence the proliferation of choices offered by the multiparty system is itself a mixed blessing: it is capitalized upon only by the more politically interested segments of the electorate, and appears to represent "too much" choice to be managed comfortably by citizens whose political involvement is average or less.

Over the range of characteristics surveyed, only one striking difference at the level of the mass public was encountered which seemed more uniquely French than the multiparty system itself. There is evidence of a widespread absence of party loyalties, a phenomenon which can be empirically associated with peculiarities in the French socialization process. This characteristic has obvious links with the major symptom of French political turbulence, which is based on the behavior of the mass population rather than that of elites — the current availability of a mass base for flash party movements under circumstances of distress.

9. Party Identification in Norway and the United States

ANGUS CAMPBELL AND HENRY VALEN

This comparison between party identification in Norway and the United States reveals a rather surprising fact: The percentage of "strong" identifiers is—contrary to expectation—greater in the United States than in Norway. However, further information tends to confirm the traditional view that Americans are much less sharply divided on issues and more independent in their voting habits. This raises a number of important questions about the meaning of party to the voters in different countries, and about the traditional explanations for the emergence and maintenance of a two-party system.

The importance of the identification of the citizen of a democratic state with the political party of his choice has been recognized for many years. David Hume wrote of the party "affections," Washington and Madison of the "spirit of Party," and Calhoun of "party attachments."[1] Generally regarded as deplorable by these early writers, party spirit was recognized as a natural accompaniment of the development of mass parties within the electorate.

Within recent years attempts have been made in the United States to bring the concept of party identification within the purview of empirical analysis.[2] Party identification has been defined as "the sense of personal attachment or belonging which an individual feels toward a given political party," and questions have been devised to measure both the intensity and the partisanship of this identification. Its significance as an intervening variable lying causally prior to the individual's perceptions of his immediate political world has been convincingly demonstrated.[3]

As the result of certain fortunate circumstances, we now have an opportunity to compare the characteristics of party identification in two countries which resemble each other closely in their basic commitment to the principles of democratic government but differ sharply in their system of political parties.

SOURCE: Reprinted by permission from *Public Opinion Quarterly*, XXV (Winter, 1961), pp. 505–525. Footnotes are abridged.

[1] A review of the intellectual history of political parties appears in Austin Ranney and Willmoore Kendall, *Democracy and the American Party System*, New York, Harcourt, Brace, 1956, Chap. 6.

[2] George Belknap and Angus Campbell, "Political Party Identification and Attitudes toward Foreign Policy," *Public Opinion Quarterly*, Vol. 15, 1951, pp. 601–623. Angus Campbell, Gerald Gurin, and Warren E. Miller, *The Voter Decides*, Evanston, Ill., Row, Peterson, 1954.

[3] Angus Campbell, Philip E. Converse, Warren E. Miller, and Donald E. Stokes, *The American Voter*, New York, Wiley, 1960.

The availability of comparable data from Norway and the United States make
it possible to examine a number of hypotheses regarding the interaction o
party systems and party identifications which could not be tested within ;
single country.

In the following pages we will first review the major similarities and differ
ences between the political system of Norway and the United States, witl
particular reference to the characteristics of the political parties in the tw
countries. We will then present survey data intended to show commor
characteristics in the phenomenon of party identification in the two countries
Finally we will propose certain hypotheses as to differences which we expec
to find in Norway and the United States resulting from the different characte
of their political parties and relate data from surveys in the two countries t
them.

The Political Systems of Norway and the United States

The institutional arrangements within which the party systems of Norwa
and the United States function differ substantially. Most important is the fac
that Norway has a parliamentary government while the United States has ;
presidential system. Norway is a unitary state while the United States is ;
federation of states. In Norway representatives to the Storting are elected by ;
system of proportional representation; representatives in the American Congress are elected by a plurality in single-member constituencies.

The party systems which have developed within these contrasting constitutional structures differ in a number of respects which have important implications for the character of party identification in the two countries.

1. While in the United States Democrats and Republicans are the only
parties of any significance, Norway has a multiple system with six main
parties: the Communists, the Labor Party, the Liberals, the Christian People's
Party, the Agrarians, and the Conservatives. The Labor Party holds a domi-
nating position, and in the most recent elections it has obtained nearly half the
votes. Since 1935 Labor has run the government. The four nonsocialist
opposition parties carry almost all the other half of the vote. The Communists
play a rather insignificant role in Norwegian politics (in 1957 they obtained
only 3 per cent of the vote). The difference in number of parties is obviously
a basic difference between the two systems, and most other differences which
may be recorded are related to this fact.

In the American system the goal of both parties at elections is to obtain a
majority of the votes and thus gain control of the government. Each party has
to rely upon support from all sections of the population, and both parties
attempt to appeal to most social groups and interests. This tends to reduce the
differences between the policies of the two parties, since they both have to
avoid being too specific in their group appeals.

The Norwegian parties tend to appeal to distinctive clienteles. This is
especially true of the three newer parties, the Agrarians, the Christians, and
the Communists. The older parties, the Conservatives, the Liberals, and Labor,

despite their historic connections with specific segments of Norwegian society, have tended in recent years to broaden the character of their appeal and to seek support from a wide range of groups within the electorate. They are still considerably more specific in their group appeals than the American parties, however.

2. At elections Norwegian parties tend to commit themselves more clearly to specific policies than do American parties. Party platforms in Norway are rather detailed and specific compared with those in the United States. Furthermore, candidates running for election in Norway are strongly committed to the party platform. Therefore, in Norway, it is almost exclusively the parties which are made responsible for the policies, whereas in the United States a campaign is not only a contest between opposing parties, it also focuses heavily upon individual candidates.

3. Norwegian parties possess better organizational facilities than American parties for communicating to the rank and file in regard to party politics and ideologies: (a) In contrast to the American system, Norwegian parties have a regular dues-paying membership. This difference implies that there is more party activity on the local level and more frequent interaction between party militants in Norwegian parties than in American parties. (b) Norwegian parties are more centralized than American parties, i.e., central leadership is more influential in formulating party policies and decisions on organizational matters. In American parties centralization seems to be weakened by the Federal system. (c) Contrary to the practices of the Republican and the Democratic Parties, the Norwegian parties make great efforts toward organizing educational activities for their members and leaders. Through conferences, courses, and various types of group activities, the militants are trained and indoctrinated in political and organizational matters.

4. The American press is less politicized than the Norwegian press. All American papers are financially independent of the two parties. Many papers take a stand for one of the two parties during the campaign, but in the periods between campaigns they tend to be politically neutral. In Norway almost all papers are strongly committed to some party or group of parties which they continuously defend. For a great number of papers, partisan attitudes are determined by the fact that they are owned or financially supported by the parties. The Labor Party, which has the most politicized press, runs (together with trade-unions) altogether forty-one papers throughout the country. In order to provide the newspapers with partisan news and viewpoints, all Norwegian parties are equipped with a press bureau which is connected to the party headquarters. Thus the Norwegian daily press contributes much more than the American press to articulating differences between the parties.[4]

From these observations on the functioning of the party systems in the two countries, it seems justified to conclude that (1) differences between parties

---

[4] Details on the relationships between the press, the parties, and the voters are presented in an article by Stein Rokkan and P. Torsvik, "Der Wähler, der Leser und die Partei Presse," *Kölner Zs. f. Soziol.* ["The Voter, the Reader and the Party Press," *Cologne Journal of Sociology*], Vol. 12, 1960, pp. 278–301.

in stands on issues are both greater and clearer in Norway than in the United States; (2) Norwegian parties are more specific than American parties in appealing to various groups and sections of the electorate; (3) differences on policies between the parties are more effectively brought to the attention of the public in Norway than in the United States.

The Distribution of Party Identification in Norway and the United States

Although the party systems in Norway and the United States differ in important respects, the basic quality of the parties as social entities to which individual citizens may feel a greater or smaller degree of personal attachment is essentially the same. In both countries the parties have their group symbols, their prominent leaders, their historical accomplishments. As the groups most relevant to political affairs, they offer the citizen a point of reference for guidance in the confusing world of politics.

The problem of obtaining comparable measures of the degree to which people identify themselves with the political parties in the two countries is not easily solved. Differences in language make it impossible to use precisely the same wording in the questions employed to record party identification, and make it difficult to compare in an absolute sense the values obtained in the categories of the scales used in the two countries. Thus we will not be able to say that more or fewer people in Norway are strongly party-identified than in the United States, but we can contrast the characteristics of strong and weak identifiers in Norway with strong and weak identifiers in the United States.

The data to be presented from Norway were gathered as part of a comprehensive study of the 1957 elections to the Norwegian Storting. A nationwide sample of 1,546 persons, selected randomly from the Norwegian register of electors, was interviewed during October and November of 1957. An additional special sample of 1,017 persons was selected on the southwestern coast of Norway; Stavanger, an important harbor and industrial center, is its largest city. The Rogaland sample was asked a series of questions which make it possible to classify each respondent as strongly or weakly identified with a political party. The nationwide sample was not asked these questions, although each respondent was classified as a member or nonmember of a political party. Most of the Norwegian data presented in this article are based on the Rogaland sample, although they are supplemented at one point (Table 3) by data from the nationwide sample. It cannot be said that Rogaland is typical of the whole of Norway, but there is no obvious reason to believe that information regarding party identification in this area would differ substantially from information from the country as a whole.

The respondents in the Norwegian (Rogaland) sample were asked the following three questions during the course of their interview: "Are you now or have you been a member of a political party or an associated group (e.g., a political youth group or a political women's group)?" For those who were not party members: "Apart from formal party membership, would you say that you wholeheartedly support one special party; in other words, do you consider yourself a Liberal, a Conservative, a Laborite or what?" If "Yes" to either of these questions: "Suppose that your party for one reason or another was prevented from presenting a ballot at the Storting election in the Province of Rogaland, would that mean a great deal to you or would you not care at all?" If the respondent said that he was a member of a party or that he "considered himself" a Liberal or whatever, he was classified as a party identifier. If he rejected both these questions, he was classified as independent. Those respondents who did identify themselves with a party were classified as strong or weak identifiers on the basis of the third question, in answer to which they expressed the strength of their feeling about the possibility that their party might be left off the ballot.

The data from the United States are taken from the national survey of the electorate conducted in the fall of 1956 by the Survey Research Center of the University of Michigan. The sample of 1,772 respondents was drawn by methods of probability sampling from the universe of persons living in private households in the United States. In 1952 the Center developed a simple scale for the measurement of party identification, based on the following two questions: "Generally speaking, do you usually think of yourself as a Republican, a Democrat, an Independent, or what?" and, if the respondent identified himself with a party: "Would you call yourself a strong (Republican) (Democrat) or a not very strong (Republican) (Democrat)?" These questions have been used by the Center in a number of national surveys to distribute the population, first in degree of identification from strong identifier to independent and second in quality of partisanship, Republican or Democratic. Distributions of very great stability have been obtained over the period from 1952 to 1960.

We find at the outset that the concept of personal affiliation with a political party is readily comprehended by virtually the entire electorate in both Norway and the United States. Only a minor fraction of the people interviewed in the two studies (4 per cent in the United States and 9 per cent in Norway) seemed unable to relate themselves to the alternatives offered in the survey questions.[5] The rest appeared to recognize the dimension implied by the questions and to place themselves in relation to it with little difficulty. The distributions of their self-identifications are given in Table 1.

Table 1 *Extent of Party Identification in Norway and the United States, in Per Cent*

	Norway	United States
Strong identifiers (consider themselves strong supporters of a party)	25	36
Weak identifiers (consider themselves supporters of a party but not very strong)	32	37
Identifiers whose intensity was not ascertained	6	0
Independents (reject party identification)	28	23
Unpolitical (do not understand concept or do not relate themselves to it)	9	4
	100	100

[5] The Norwegian figure includes a number of people of whom the questions on party identification were not asked.

When we examine the demographic and social characteristics of those people in the two countries who identify or do not identify with the political parties, we find very striking similarities. Considering first men and women in the two electorates, we find no consistent tendency in either country for party identifiers and independents to differ in sex composition. In Norway strong identifiers are somewhat more likely to be men than are weak identifiers, but in neither country are women notably less likely to identify themselves with a party label.

In both countries strength of party identification tends to increase with age, and this is true among both men and women. In the absence of life-cycle data which would reveal the course of development of individual attitudes toward political parties, we may speculate as to the source of this tendency toward strong political identification among the older levels of the electorate in the two countries. Since there is nothing to indicate that the Norwegian and American parties have gained or lost in significance during the lifetime of our respondents, we incline to the belief that partisanship tends to become more important for the average member of the electorate as he grows older. Concerned with interests of a more personal character during his early years, he may become involved with political affairs as he becomes more fully a member of society as a parent, a worker, a neighbor, a taxpayer. Once drawn into peripheral association with a party, the strength of his attachment to the party is likely to increase as his length of membership increases. Our data from Norway and the United States appear to conform to other observations regarding the relationship between frequency and strength of group interactions.[6]

People at the different levels of party identification do not differ greatly in the number of years of formal education they have completed. Among men, strong identification tends to be associated with lower educational attainment, independence with higher. The relationship is not high and it has some irregularities, but the pattern is very similar in the two countries. Among the women there is no consistent association with education in either country.

Serious difficulties are encountered when one attempts to compare occupational groups in different societies, even when the societies are as similar as those of Norway and the United States. For the purposes of the present analysis, we have had to be satisfied with a very rough system of classification by which we have divided our samples into white-collar workers, blue-collar workers, and farmers. When the members of the three identification groups are divided into these occupation categories, we find a pattern very similar to that which appeared when we considered educational level. Among men in both countries there is some tendency, although not a strong one, for the independents to draw disproportionately from the white-collar workers at the expense of the farmers, with a converse tendency among the strong identifiers. This relationship is less clear among the women.[7]

---

[6] For example, see George Homans, *The Human Group* (London: Routledge, 1951), Chap. VI.

[7] In the United States there is a sharp difference between farmers in the North and South, with Southern farmers tending toward strong party identification and Northern farmers toward political independence (see Angus Campbell, Philip E. Converse, Warren E. Miller, and Donald E. Stokes, *The American Voter*, New York, Wiley, 1960, Chap. 15).

A final comparison of the characteristics of party identifiers in Norway and the United States may be obtained by comparing the extent of participation in the electoral process shown by identifiers and independents in the two countries. Similar questions were asked of the two samples intended to record the number of elections in which the respondent had voted "since you have been old enough to vote." As one might expect, the reported level of voting was higher in Norway than in the United States and the strong identifiers were the most faithful in their voting in both countries. In Norway the weak identifiers reported a somewhat less impressive record than the strong identifiers and the independents were considerably less likely than the other groups to have voted in all the elections. In the United States the weak identifiers and independents did not differ in their previous voting record.

We conclude from these findings that the phenomenon of party identification has similar qualities in the two countries. It is a group attachment very widely held in the population, it does not differentiate men and women, and it is only moderately related to measures of social and occupational status. The strength of this sense of attachment increases in the later decades of life, presumably as the result of long-continued association with the party. The stronger the attachment is, the more likely the individual is to be consistently active politically. These common attributes give us confidence that we are indeed measuring the same phenomenon in the two countries and that the differences which are noted in the succeeding pages derive from actual differences in the party systems in the two countries and not from ambiguities in our measures of party identification.

Party Systems and Party Followers

The comparative study of nations differing in party structure provides an opportunity to examine the relationship between the nature of political parties and the character of the popular following these parties attract. While we assume that party identification represents the same kind of psychological attachment in both Norway and the United States, we expect to find differences in the characteristics of partisans of the different parties in the two countries deriving from the differences in their party systems.

As we have seen, the Norwegian parties are considerably more ideological and class-related in their appeals to the electorate than are the American parties. In such a party system it is to be expected that the adherents of the several parties will be more homogeneous than they would be in a system where the parties have no special class character and attempt to attract followers from all levels of the electorate. Because of the distinctive quality of their appeal, the Norwegian parties are likely to recruit from a narrower range within the electorate and to exert a stronger influence on the political attitudes and behavior of their members than do the American parties. We expect then to find the following differences between party identifiers in the two countries:

1. Identifiers of the different Norwegian parties will be more distinctive in socio-economic characteristics than identifiers of the two American parties.

2. Identifiers of the Norwegian parties will perceive greater policy differ-

ences between the parties than will identifiers of the American parties.

3. In stands on issues, identifiers of the Norwegian parties will be more distinctive than identifiers of the American parties.

4. Identifiers of the Norwegian parties will be more likely to vote in accordance with their identification than will identifiers of the American parties.

5. For all of the above hypotheses we not only expect to find differences between identifiers of the different parties in the two countries, but within each country we expect party distinctiveness to be greater among those party adherents who are most strongly identified.

1. *Identifiers of the different Norwegian parties will be more distinctive in socio-economic characteristics than identifiers of the two American parties.* In testing this hypothesis we shall compare identifiers of the different parties in the two countries with regard to the following socio-economic characteristics: education, occupation, and class identification. Relationships between party identification and the demographic variables, age and sex, will also be explored, although possible differences between parties with regard to these characteristics do not necessarily reflect differences in the way in which parties are related to socio-economic groups.

Age: In both countries the parties differ with regard to age composition. In the United States, Democratic identifiers tend to be younger than Republican identifiers. In Norway, the Labor Party has the relatively youngest identifiers. The discrepancies between parties are not as large in the United States as they are in Norway. In the American sample, 43 per cent of the Democrats are forty-five years or more in age while 53 per cent of the Republicans have reached this age. In Norway one finds an increasing number of older persons (over forty-five years) as one moves from the Labor Party (37 per cent), to the Liberal Party (48 per cent), to the Agrarian Party (51 per cent), to the Conservative Party (55 per cent), to the Christian People's Party (56 per cent). In both countries, the strong identifiers of each party are somewhat older than the less strongly identified, with the exception of the Christian People's Party, which had been active in Norwegian politics for only twelve years at the time of this study. This undoubtedly reflects the tendency we have noted earlier for group association to increase in strength as tenure of association is extended.

Sex: There is a marked difference between the two countries with regard to sex composition of party identifiers. In the United States there is a small but reliable difference between the proportions of men and women in the two parties: 47 per cent of the Democratic Party identifiers are men, 43 per cent of the Republican partisans. In Norway the differences between parties are much larger. The proportions of men in Norwegian parties range from 62 per cent of the Agrarian Party to 32 per cent of the partisans of the Christian People's Party. In the United States the sex composition of the strong and weak identifiers of the two parties does not differ significantly. In Norway there is a consistent tendency in all parties for the strong identifiers to have higher proportions of men than do the weak identifiers.

Education: In both the United States and Norway the level of education reported by party identifiers differs from one party to the other. Republican identifiers are more likely to report a high educational level than Democrats; 37 per cent of the Republicans have completed high school, 26 per cent of the Democrats. In Norway the Conservatives and Liberals report relatively high educational achievement; the Agrarians, Christians, and Laborites are substantially lower. Taking attendance at the "real skole" or beyond as a mark of a high educational achievement, we find 45 per cent of the Conservatives at this level, 23 per cent of the Liberals, 7 per cent of the Agrarians, 5 per cent of the Christians and 7 per cent of the Labor Party. The Norwegian parties are clearly more variable in this respect than the American parties.

We have seen earlier that there is relatively little relationship between educational level and strength of party identification in the two countries. Within the respective parties there are various degrees of difference between the strong and weak adherents. In the United States, the educational differences between strong and weak Democrats are insignificant; among Republicans, the strong identifiers have a slightly higher educational level than the weak. In Norway, the strong partisans of the Conservatives, Liberals, and Agrarians are markedly higher in education than the weak partisans. In the Labor and Christian Parties the strong and weak identifiers do not differ in formal education. In other words, such differences as we find in education between strong and weak identifiers occur in those parties where the educational level of identifiers is generally high.

Occupation: In both countries the occupational distribution of identifiers differs among the parties. In the United States, the differences are rather small. The Democratic Party draws 30 per cent of its adherents from the white-collar occupations, 46 per cent from the blue-collar. The Republicans come 36 per cent from the white-collar occupations and 39 per cent from the blue-collar. The occupational differences are very much greater among the various Norwegian parties. Of the Labor Party identifiers 79 per cent are blue-collar workers, 17 per cent are white-collar; among the Conservatives the proportions are 19 per cent and 76 per cent. The two center parties, Liberals and Christians, whose ideologies are not primarily economic, are somewhat less extreme, but even they are clearly more distinctive in their proportions of blue-collar and white-collar workers than are the American parties.

When we compare the parties in the proportion of their adherents who are farmers, we find no difference in the United States (Democrats 10 per cent and Republicans 9 per cent) and no great difference among the Norwegian parties except for the Agrarian Party. The distinctive appeal of this party to Norwegian farmers is shown by the 77 per cent of Agrarian identifiers who are classified as farmers. None of the other parties has a proportion of farmers higher than 14 per cent.

These occupational differentials between the Norwegian parties become even more pronounced when we divide each party's followers into strong and weak identifiers. In the Conservative, Liberal, and Christian People's Parties there are relatively more white-collar workers among strong identifiers than among weak, while the proportions of blue-collar workers are higher among strong than among weak identifiers in the Labor Party. Similarly, farmers are most numerous among the strong Agrarians. In the United States the occupational levels of the strong and weak adherents of the two parties are very similar. There are minor tendencies in both parties in the expected direction but they are not significant.

Class identification: The distribution of class identification follows the same pattern as occupational distribution in the two countries. The Democrats have a majority of working-class identifiers (66 per cent), while the Republicans divide themselves about equally between middle class and working class. In Norway some 80 per cent of Labor identifiers say they belong to the working class, whereas all the nonsocialist parties are dominated by middle-class identifiers, with majorities rising as high as 86 per cent in the case of the Conservative Party.

Strong identifiers in both countries tend to be more distinctive in their class position than weak identifiers. In the Norwegian nonsocialist parties and in the Republican Party, strong identifiers more often see themselves as middle-class than do weak identifiers. In the Democratic Party there is a tendency for strong identifiers to be more working-class than weak identifiers but it is very slight. The Norwegian Labor Party forms an exception to this general pattern in that strong and weak identifiers are equally distributed in social-class position.

We see from these various comparisons that the constituencies of the Norwegian parties are considerably more distinctive in socio-economic background than are those of the American parties. The Democratic Party has a somewhat stronger working-class quality than the Republican Party, but neither party could be said to have a homogeneous membership; both draw significant numbers of followers from all the important segments of the electorate. The Labor Party and the Conservative Party, standing at the extremes of the political spectrum in Norway (excluding the Communists), do on the other hand draw their constituents from a different social-class base. The Agrarian Party also has a distinctive appeal to a particular segment of Norwegian society and is composed very largely of people from this segment. The Liberal and Christian Parties have a more heterogeneous membership, although middle-class identifiers dominate in number. In general, the Norwegian multiparty system may be said to be characterized by a relatively strong association between social class and political party, an association which is only weakly present in the American two-party system.

Our expectation that strong identifiers in the two countries would be more distinctive in social characteristics than weak identifiers (point 5 above) is only partially supported. In Norway this tendency is quite apparent for the nonsocialist parties but is hardly discernible for the Labor Party. In the United States, consistent with the smaller over-all differences between party followers, there are smaller differences between strong and weak identifiers of each party than we find in Norway. But the difference between strong and weak identifiers tends to be greater in the Republican Party than among the Democrats.[8]

2. *Identifiers of the Norwegian parties will perceive greater policy differences between the parties than will identifiers of the American parties.* Our description of the organization and activities of the parties in the two countries makes it apparent that, unless there is a general failure of communication by the parties to the electorate, the Norwegian parties must be perceived by the Norwegian public as being more distinctive in their policy positions than the American parties are in the United States. It is not possible to make a precise estimate of the difference between the two countries in this regard, but the evidence available suggests strongly that our supposition is correct. The Norwegian sample was asked the following question: "Many people think there is so much agreement between the parties on important matters that it does not matter for which party one is voting this time. Are you of this opinion?" The American sample was asked: "Do you think there are any important differences between what the Democratic and Republican Parties stand for, or do you think they are about the same?" Of the Norwegian sample, 11 per cent felt that there were no differences between the parties; an additional 8 per cent did not know whether there were differences or not. Of the American samples 40 per cent thought the two parties were about the same, and an additional 8 per cent didn't know whether they differed or not. Granting the variation in the wording of the questions, these differences are obviously sizable and in the direction of our expectation.

When we subdivide these data into the party groups, we find little difference between the parties in each country (Table 2). But in every case the strong identifiers of the party are more likely to feel that there are important differences between the parties than are the weak identifiers.

3. *In stands on issues, identifiers of the Norwegian parties will be more distinctive than identifiers of the American parties.* Both the Norwegian and American surveys contained questions intended to elicit the respondents' attitudes toward questions of national policy thought to be important in each of the two countries at the time. In Norway two questions were asked of the Rogaland sample, one dealing with the level of national taxation and the other with the level of expenditures for defense. In the nationwide sample, four additional questions were asked, one concerned with governmental activity in

---

[8] An analysis of the recruitment of party activists in Norway and the United States shows a corresponding difference between the middle-class and working-class parties of the two countries. Middle-class voters for the Republican Party and the nonsocialist parties of Norway were considerably more likely to be politically active than were working-class voters for these parties. This tendency was also found in much weaker degree among middle-class and working-class voters for the Democratic Party, but it was reversed among the supporters of the Labor Party in Norway. Perception of conflict or congruence between one's own class position and the class character of the party with which one identifies appears to discourage or support active participation in that party's activities (see Stein Rokkan and Angus Campbell, "Citizen Participation in Political Life: Norway and the United States of America," *International Social Science Journal*, Vol. 12, No. 1, 1960).

Table 2   *Relation of Party Identification to Perception of Policy Differences between the Parties, in Per Cent*

Conception of Differences	NORWEGIAN PARTY IDENTIFICATION									
	Labor		Liberal		Christian		Agrarian		Conservativ	
	Strong	Weak	Strong	Weak	Strong	Weak	Strong	Weak	Strong	Wea
No differences	2	17	4	12	6	17		2	4	15
Communists differ from other parties	2	6	8	16	6		3	6		4
Labor and Communists differ from other parties	4	5		16		4	15	16	14	11
Big differences	88	63	85	45	80	66	82	68	79	66
Don't know	3	7	3	8	6	4		4	3	
Not ascertained	1	2		3	2	9		4		4
Total	100	100	100	100	100	100	100	100	100	100
(N)	(123)	(144)	(27)	(75)	(36)	(23)	(34)	(50)	(28)	(47)

Perception of Differences	UNITED STATES PARTY IDENTIFICATION			
	Democratic		Republican	
	Strong	Weak	Strong	Weak
No differences	31	46	33	49
Minor differences	10	10	8	12
Some differences	36	24	34	23
Important differences	15	8	17	6
Don't know	6	10	5	9
Not ascertained	2	2	3	1
Total	100	100	100	100
(N)	(392)	(449)	(241)	(246)

housing construction, one with governmental regulation of private enterprise the third with governmental control of inflation, and the fourth with governmental promotion of religious values. In the American survey, sixteen questions were asked dealing with welfare legislation, foreign policy, governmental control of big business and labor unions, governmental production of power and housing, civil rights, and taxation. In both studies the issue questions were presented in such a way that the respondents answered in terms of whether they thought the government had not done enough, had gone too far, or had done about right in regard to the particular policy.

We obviously cannot make direct comparisons of distributions of attitude in the two countries. We can, however, compare the different parties within each country in order to determine the degree of interparty difference. The extensive array of data presented in Table 3 can be summarized in the following statements:

a. In Norway the adherents of the different parties differ substantially in their views on five of the six issues to which they were asked to respond, and their positions conform to the ideological positions of their party leadership. On the issue of national defense there is no consistent pattern across the party continuum, although the Laborites and Conservatives hold the extreme positions.

b. Strong and weak identifiers of the Norwegian parties do not differ significantly in their issue positions. Only in the Conservative Party is there a consistent tendency for the strong identifiers to take a more strongly partisan position than the weak identifiers.[9]

c. None of the issues presented to the American sample divides the followers of the two parties as sharply as the Norwegian sample is divided. Questions relating to various domestic economic policies bring out moderate differences between Democrats and Republicans that conform to the general posture taken by the leadership of the two parties, but questions relating to foreign affairs and civil rights result in generally small and inconsistent party differences.

d. In general, strong Democrats are most likely and strong Republicans least likely to criticize the policies of the government (which was Republican at the time of the study). The differences between strong and weak partisans are small or nonexistent on issues which do not divide the two parties, but they are relatively large when the party differences are large, particularly in the case of the economic welfare policies.

In general, we may conclude that the Norwegian parties differ not only in their publicly declared positions but in the positions held by their rank and file. The one issue on which there is not coincidence of viewpoint between the party leadership and the party followers is instructive. The question of national defense has not in fact been a partisan issue in Norway during recent years; all parties in the Storting, except the Communists, have supported the defense budget. Traditionally, however, the Conservative and Agrarian Parties have been most favorable to a strong defense program; before the Second World War the Labor Party was generally resistant to defense expenditures. Despite the fact that the Labor Party has been in power throughout the postwar period and has been responsible for the development of the present defense program of Norway, public attitudes on this issue appear to reflect strong convictions carried over from the prewar period.

It seems very likely that the relatively small differences found between Democrats and Republicans in the United States are also carried over from the depression period of the 1930's. The only issues on which partisan differences are appreciable are those which relate to the New Deal ideology and the early Roosevelt period. The strong identification of the Democratic Party with various forms of welfare legislation that came into American politics as a result

---

[9] It is not clear why the policy attitudes of the strong and weak identifiers of the Norwegian parties do not differ more sharply than they do. In the case of the nationwide sample it is possible that the division of the voters for the various parties into members and nonmembers does not catch the quality of party attachment that we assumed. This is suggested by the fact that when we divide the voters in this sample into those who were politically active beyond simply voting and those who did no more than vote, the actives were consistently more likely to support the policy positions of the party they voted for than were the voters-only. It is unfortunate for this aspect of our analysis that a clearer measure of strength of party identification was not obtained from the nationwide sample.

Table 3   *Issue Positions of Party Identifiers in Norway and the United States,* in Per Cent*

Issue†	Party Identification	Labor	Liberal‡	Christian	Agrarian	Con-servative
Government has raised	Strong	27	44	37	47	74
taxes too high	Weak	23	45	29	54	56
Government should re-	Strong	51	29	51	29	25
duce defense budget	Weak	48	52	38	52	29
Government has gone too far in slowing down	Members	26		40	50	70
building of houses	Nonmembers	27	58	45	55	68
Government has inter-fered too much in	Members	8		50	71	84
economic life	Nonmembers	9	61	50	47	74
Government has not done enough to	Members	12		44	64	75
stop inflation	Nonmembers	15	54	45	58	62
Government has done too little to promote Christian morals and	Members	17		97	60	51
Christian faith	Nonmembers	24	42	89	63	43

Issue	Party Identification	Democrats	Republicans
Government has concerned itself too much with world problems	Strong	29	16
	Weak	18	21
Government has given too much economic aid to poor countries	Strong	30	21
	Weak	24	27
Government has gone too far in keeping soldiers overseas	Strong	9	8
	Weak	8	9
Government has given too much help to neutralist nations	Strong	21	18
	Weak	17	19
Government has been too friendly with other countries	Strong	15	8
	Weak	13	10
Government has not been tough enough in dealing with Russia and China	Strong	38	25
	Weak	26	28
Government has not gone far enough in guaranteeing full employment	Strong	39	12
	Weak	22	16
Government has not done enough to help build more schools	Strong	44	28
	Weak	37	32
Government has not done enough to help provide low-cost medical care	Strong	48	21
	Weak	32	29

* Entries in the table are the proportion of the sample agreeing with the policy statement.
† The first two of the Norwegian issues were asked of the Rogaland sample. The other four were asked of the nationwide sample. In the latter case, the respondents are divided into those who identified themselves as members of one of the Norwegian parties and those who stated an intention to vote for a particular party although they were not party members.
‡ The strong Liberal group in the nationwide sample was too small to justify inclusion.

Table 3 (continued)

Issue	Party Identification	UNITED STATES Democrats	Republicans
Government is going too far in leaving electricity	Strong	15	5
and housing to private businessmen	Weak	15	9
Government is not doing enough to see that	Strong	22	16
Negroes get fair treatment in jobs and housing	Weak	22	20
Government is not doing enough to control	Strong	37	10
business influence on government	Weak	27	19
Government is not doing enough to control	Strong	21	19
union influence on government	Weak	20	19
Government has not done enough to cut taxes	Strong	34	13
	Weak	24	16
Government has not gone far enough in firing	Strong	19	15
suspected Communists	Weak	10	15
Government has concerned itself too much	Strong	22	12
with racial integration of schools	Weak	23	22

of the economic distress of the 1930's was probably less clear in 1956 than it had been twenty years earlier, but reverberations of that period still persist.

4. *Identifiers of the Norwegian parties will be more likely to vote in accordance with their identification than will identifiers of the American parties.* If the Norwegian electorate see greater differences among their parties than the Americans do between theirs, we should expect it to be more difficult for a Norwegian voter to shift his vote from one party to another than it would be for voters in the United States. We can test this hypothesis in two ways, first by comparing the lifetime voting record of the samples in the two countries, and, second, by comparing the votes of party groups in certain recent elections. Reports of votes over a period of many years are obviously subject to errors of memory, but if we assume that this type of error is no greater in one country than another we find that the Norwegians do in fact have a more consistent record of party regularity than the Americans (Table 4). In both countries the strong party identifiers are more dependable in their party loyalty than the weak identifiers.[10]

The vagaries of memory and the ambiguities of comparing a Storting

---

[10] The substantial difference in the voting history of the present followers of the Labor and Conservative parties raises an interesting question as to the character of political movement in a party system having as strong a "left-right" quality as the Norwegian system has. We have seen that the Conservative partisans as a group are considerably older than the Labor partisans, a difference which suggests the commonplace observation that people tend to grow more conservative as they grow older. We also find when we compare the first vote reported by these people with their present party preference that there has been considerably more movement from left to right on the party scale than in the other direction. The Conservative Party at the extreme of this scale apparently profits from these life-cycle changes and counts a larger proportion of erstwhile members of other parties in its numbers than does the Labor Party from which the movement mainly comes. If this exchange of personnel were the only change in the constituency of the parties, the Conservative Party would obviously increase its relative strength over the long run. Other facts at least as important, however, are the additions to the electorate of the young voters and the

Table 4   *Party Regularity in Voting in Norway and the United States,**
in Per Cent

	STRENGTH OF IDENTIFICATION	
	Strong	*Weak*
Norway:		
Have you always voted for the same party at Storting elections, or have you voted for different parties?		
Labor	83	77
Liberal	74	63
Christian†	17	22
Agrarian	81	72
Conservative	70	44
United States:		
Have you always voted for the same party or have you voted for different parties for President?		
Democrats	67	45
Republicans	65	44

* Entries in the table are the proportion of each group who say they have always voted for the same party.
† The Christian Party was founded in 1935 and has drawn its membership primarily from the Liberal and Labor parties.

election to a presidential election are considerably reduced when we look at the reported votes of the Norwegian party groups in the Storting election of 1957 and the American party groups in the congressional election of 1958. Table 5 again shows the Norwegian voters to be less likely to cross party lines than the American voters and the strong partisans in both countries to be most likely to vote their party's ticket.

Discussion

The evidence we have presented supports our general expectation that identification with the Norwegian parties would be associated with greater demographic and political distinctiveness than would identification with the American parties. Although we have been able to compare only two nations, we think it likely that similar results would be obtained from the comparison of any pair of stable multiparty and two-party systems.

It is apparent, as various scholars have observed, that in a two-party system one party draws away from the other in its position on important policy issues

---

subtractions of those who die, a continuing process of replacement which benefits the party with the greatest appeal to youth, in Norway the Labor Party.

There is some reason to believe that a similar balance of exchanges occurs between the American parties, although there is so much movement from one party's presidential candidate to that of the other for reasons having very little ideological quality that such life-cycle increases in conservatism as do occur are entirely obscured in the totals given in Table 4. We would not in any case expect to find as large a life-cycle shift in partisanship in the United States as we would in a country having strongly differentiated liberal and conservative parties.

Table 5   *Vote of Party Groups in Norway and the United States, in Per Cent*

1957 Storting Election Vote	NORWEGIAN PARTY IDENTIFICATION									
	Labor		Liberal		Christian		Agrarian		Conservative	
	Strong	Weak	Strong	Weak	Strong	Weak	Strong	Weak	Strong	Weak
Communist	1	2					2			
Labor	97	95		2						
Liberal	1	1	96	92	8	20	3			2
Christian		1	4	6	92	80	3	4		
Agrarian							94	90		
Conservative	1	1						4	100	98
Total	100	100	100	100	100	100	100	100	100	100
(N)	(120)	(130)	(26)	(67)	(35)	(21)	(34)	(46)	(27)	(41)

1958 Congressional Election Vote	UNITED STATES PARTY IDENTIFICATION			
	Democratic		Republican	
	Strong	Weak	Strong	Weak
Democratic	96	86	11	32
Republican	4	14	89	68
Total	100	100	100	100
(N)	(187)	(173)	(149)	(120)

at the risk of losing adherents in the center who now find themselves closer to the opposition party.[11] In such a situation considerations of self-preservation tend to hold the two parties close to each other, so close in the American situation that large segments of the electorate cannot distinguish any clear policy differences between the parties. In a multiparty system, the parties typically develop as the expression of special interests within the electorate and they seek to associate themselves with specific appeals to these special segments of the electorate. As Duverger remarks, "Each tries to emphasize the differences of detail which distinguish it from its nearest rivals, instead of drawing attention to their profound similarities."[12]

The question of why a two-party system develops in one country and a multiparty system in another is not illuminated by the evidence from our studies. We can only surmise from a knowledge of the political histories of Norway and the United States the sequence of forces which gave rise to the different party systems we find in the two countries at the present time. Our studies do give us some insight, however, into the manner in which the characteristics of a party system are maintained or modified once it has been established.

In the American situation, the major cohesive force which gives the party system stability and continuity is the psychological attachment of the electorate to the parties. In the absence of strong class identification and class-associated programs of political action, the parties themselves serve as the significant

---

[11] The strategy of two-party competition is discussed by Anthony Downs in his *An Economic Theory of Democracy* (New York: Harper, 1959), Chap. VIII.

[12] M. Duverger, *Political Parties* (London: Methuen, 1959), p. 388.

source of political direction for the electorate. The parties do not represent themselves as spokesmen of special social classes and do not develop strong ideologies to express special class interests. In their appeal to the electorate they tend to emphasize broad party virtues, the righteousness of party heroes past and present, and the general ineptitude, if not wickedness, of the opposition. As the electorate's major source of political education, they create a public image of politics as a competition between parties *per se* rather than a choice between alternative policies. In such a situation, politics tends to lose its ideological character: the public is not stimulated to inform itself regarding specific policies; its political role becomes one of deciding who shall manage the government, not what shall the government do. For the bulk of the electorate, this decision is determined by long-established party loyalties, loyalties to parties which, in their effort to stay close to what they take to be the political center, have reduced policy differences between themselves to a minimum.

The strength of these party attachments and the general weakness in the American electorate of ideological interest both serve to maintain the two-party system. The failure of various attempts to launch third parties appealing to the special interests of the farmers or the urban working class reflects the conserving force of these two attributes of the American party system. Deriving from the two-party system, they have become important factors in its preservation.

The party system which took shape in Norway after World War I was an extremely polarized one, and the conflict between the working-class movement and the parties in the center and to the right was at times so violent as to endanger the basic constitutional framework. Electoral statistics suggest that during the years since the depression there has been a significant decline in the intensity of this status polarization, associated with the rise to power of the Labor Party, the experience of the all-party government-in-exile during the war, and the postwar growth of the "new middle class" and other intermediary groups in the social structure. The system is still highly polarized, however and, as we have seen, the fit between class status and party preference is marked. The Norwegian electorate has learned to structure politics in terms of party representation of class interests, and despite the softening of interparty and interclass conflict in recent years its expectations regarding the interests which the different parties represent are still much clearer than comparable expectations in the United States.

In a party system having a close relationship between the parties and the social classes, it is difficult to isolate the independent influence which party identification itself has on the electorate. The Norwegian labor union member who is a member of the Labor Party may display a strong party attachment but one wonders if this does not merely express in different form his basic identification with the working class. Certainly it appears that this conjoining of party identification with more basic loyalties is more significant in Norway than it is in the United States. Because the party-class relationship is so weak in the United States, the voters are freer to move from one party to the other in successive elections and the parties are freer to exploit such opportunities as arise to induce them to do so. An examination of the history of American elections would demonstrate the frequency with which the parties have relied on outstanding personalities and contemporary embarrassments of the party in power to achieve political advantage and would reveal the extent to which the electorate has responded to these largely nonideological appeals.

It is a paradox that because of these facts the weakly organized American parties may exert a greater independent influence on political attitudes and votes than do the highly organized and more clearly class-related parties of Norway. To a voter who has not learned to interpret political events in terms of an ideology of social class, the party is likely to be the most important source of political direction available. In contrast, when a self-conscious segment of the electorate comes to see its party as the instrument for the implementation of its policy aspirations, it may exert at least as much influence on the party as the party does on it.

10. Party Identification in the Federal Republic of Germany and the United States

WERNER ZOHLNHÖFER

Any comparison between American and German attitudes toward political parties must presumably take account of recent German history: the experience with the totalitarian one-party Nazi regime; the re-emergence of a multiparty system after World War II with some new and some traditional parties; the change to a system in which two parties—both increasingly pragmatic in outlook—predominated. To someone expecting a radically different set of responses in the two nations, the following data must come as a surprise, though the expected proportionally higher share of "weak identifiers" and "nonidentifiers" in Germany obviously contains a large potential for radical and rapid shifts under changing circumstances.

I

Introduction

In this study the attempt is made to examine comparatively the phenomenon of party identification in the Federal Republic [of Germany] and the United States. By party identification we mean the feeling of belonging, an inclination, or, in other words, being a short subjective distance to a political party.[1] We have, therefore, placed in the center a comparative analysis of the frequency and intensity of respective existing political-party ties, and their relation to sociographic characteristics as well as their connection with individual electoral choices and views on everyday political questions.

The emipirical material on which the following study is based results from a representative survey of voters in both countries. The American data are part of the survey carried out by the Survey Research Center of the University of Michigan on the presidential election of 1956; the German data are taken from the Cologne research project "Election to the Federal Parliament 1961."[2]

Differences in language, society, and political culture between these two countries necessarily limit the comparability of such data. A further factor limiting comparability, which in principle is avoidable, results from the fact that the material utilized here could not be produced with a view toward its

SOURCE: Reprinted by permission from Werner Zohlnhöfer, "Parteiidentifizierung in der Bundesrepublik und den Vereinigten Staaten," *Kölner Zeitschrift für Soziologie und Sozialpsychologie*, Sonderheft 9 (1965), pp. 126–135 and 160–166. Footnotes are abridged. Translation by Kurt L. Shell.

[1] This use of concepts is identical with that used in American literature. Cf. above all Angus Campbell, Philip E. Converse, Warren E. Miller, and Donald E. Stokes, *The American Voter* (New York: Wiley, 1960), Chs. 6 and 7, where "party identification" is defined as "sense of attachment with one party or another" or as "the sense of individual

optimal comparability. Within these limits there remains, however, sufficient information to make a comparative analysis of the phenomenon of party identification in both systems appear worth while.

It is necessary to keep always in mind that diverse categories of one system cannot be compared directly with those of the other system. Comparable are primarily relations between diverse elements of the one system with relations between corresponding categories of the other system. One cannot assume, for example, that a certain number of years of education or a certain occupation has identical meanings in both countries in terms of social status. But it is possible to compare such things as connections between educational or occupational levels and the relative frequency or intensity of party preferences. Even such comparisons are meaningful, however, only when the categories . . . are based in both countries on structures of basically comparable social and political relevance. We assume that comparability (as just defined) of the type of social and political structures and processes which characterize the Federal Republic and the United States exists.

II

Conditions for the Formation of Party Identification

It is neither possible nor necessary to discuss in this connection party and governmental systems of the two countries in great detail. It is required, however, to point out, at least briefly, the differences in political-historical conditions that presumably have influenced the respective manifestations of the phenomenon of party identification.

1. Special Conditions in the Federal Republic

In 1961, when the empirical data were obtained, the party system of the Federal Republic was in a process of profound transformation from a "multi-party" to a "several-party" system. In the multiparty system, parties were differentiated by class-ideological and religious antagonisms, each party appealing to certain, clearly differentiated parts of the population. In the newer, several-party system, the parties are in considerable agreement on all major principles of constitution and politics, and try — by "pragmatic" orientation — to obtain as numerous, socially heterogeneous a following as possible. As the evolution of the German party system results from the interaction between parties and voters, the main lines of existing party ties are in turn determined in part by this transitional situation.

It seems useful to compare the postwar years in the Federal Republic with

---

attachment to party" (p. 121). Subsequently the terms "party preference," "party loyalty," and "party ties" will be used interchangeably with "party identification."

[2] As in the American survey, only persons above age 21 were considered. As the study concentrates on the voting population, it was decided for the purpose of this study to eliminate from the 1964 German sample 169 respondents because, at the time of the survey, they were not yet entitled to vote.

the periods of so-called "critical elections"[3] in American history. Similar to the latter, the period since 1949 was characterized in the Federal Republic at first by highly controversial political decisions dealing with a general situation of crisis. These decisions were reflected in the conciousness of all population strata, and led to the emergence of new parties as well as shifts in or strengthening of old party preferences. This process was somewhat impeded by the experiences many German voters had had with political parties under the Weimar Republic and the Third Reich; but the political and economic successes of the reconstruction period considerably weakened their resistances and in many cases reduced their feelings to ones of reserve toward unconditional political-party ties. At the same time, the development of party preferences was encouraged by the relatively explicit organization of German parties, their continuing programmatic integration, the parliamentary system, and the identification — a likely one from the beginning — of one of the two large parties with governmental responsibility, and the other with the role of parliamentary opposition.

The following of each German party in 1961 was thus, speaking roughly composed of two segments: followers who maintained a historically rooted loyalty based on class-ideological and religious foundations; and followers who in the postwar years felt a particular appeal of the policy, program, or leadership of a party. Because of the historical roots and ideological origin, the former is likely to be more intensive and more related to status or group membership than the latter. In any case existing party preferences are likely to show regularly at least vague political-programmatic relations.

2. Conditions in the United States

Basically, the American party system has developed continuously as a two-party system. The cause of this (among others) must be seen in the decisional situation — renewed every fourth year — in connection with presidential elections. Each of the two parties bases itself on the approval of a conglomerate of socially highly diverse voters who are connected less by detailed programs or a systematically developed ideology than by some very general and frequently unarticulated principles for the solution of political problems. By comparison, American parties thus have always shown less ideological orientation involving articulated programs; and socio-economic interest conflicts have led on the national level to no lasting parties, but rather from instance to instance to transitory formation of parties that aimed at looking after relatively narrowly defined group interests. Nevertheless, the various social groups in the United States also tend more to one party than another.

As recent empirical studies show,[4] this is explained by the fact that a lasting

---

[3] Cf. V. O. Key, Jr., "A Theory of Critical Elections," *Journal of Politics XVII* (1955), pp. 3–18.

[4] Cf. V. O. Key, *ibid.*; Bernard R. Berelson, Paul F. Lazarsfeld, and William N. McPhee, *Voting* (Chicago: University of Chicago, 1954), pp. 88–93; Angus Campbell, Gerald Gurin, and Warren E. Miller, *The Voter Decides* (Evanston: Harper, 1954), pp. 97–107 and 176–177; Angus Campbell, Philip E. Converse, Warren E. Miller, and Donald E. Stokes, *The American Voter* (New York: Wiley, 1960), pp. 146–216.

individual party preference was formed in certain historical situations in which the solutions propagated or executed by parties for acute national problems touching the majority of the population held different appeals for different social groups ("built-in group appeals"). Because historical crisis situations that effected especially deep shifts in party preferences — examples are above all the American Civil War and the economic crisis of the thirties — are located in a past so distant that all or a large part of the present voters have not consciously lived through them, the historical connection has often lost its immediate political meaning. Party loyalty formed in this way is, therefore, more frequently maintained as a matter of family tradition or as a general group tradition than as a conscious political decision. In spite of a possible lack of political content, such a traditional tie also gains in intensity over time. This adherence to traditional party preferences can largely be explained by the obscurity of the political decision-making process which, in connection with the special nature of American parties, is a consequence of the separation of power that is still effective in the American governmental system. . . . It is characteristic that enforced party discipline in Congress does not exist.

These considerations make it apparent that, at least for the majority of the American voters, it is difficult to assign political responsibility for the results of the governmental process to the political parties as such. Indeed, it is less the political parties as such that are praised or blamed in cases of important decisions than governmental organs and/or personalities. It can thus hardly be expected — except in crisis situations — that parties will gain or lose a considerable number of steady followers through the positions taken by its members in Congress, even though the candidates' voting records may, in election campaigns, be cited by themselves or their opponents as proof of their credibility (or lack of it, respectively). The president, too, cannot — as a rule — achieve much in this respect. He may lose the support of followers of his own party through his policies, or gain the votes of followers of the opposition party. These not indications of lasting changes in party preferences, but rather shows of approval or disapproval directed at the president's person and policies. These fluctuations may impair the meaning of party identification in presidential elections; but the party ties themselves remain, as a rule, unaffected by them. . . .

3. Conclusions

A comparison of the conditions under which the formation of existing party identifications has taken place shows the following important differences (among others):

1. While American parties at all times tried to attract members of various social groups, German parties oriented themselves traditionally to narrowly defined class or group interests; only recently have they increasingly begun to woo the approval of all social strata.

2. While the last period of critical developments that to a large extent caused formation of or shifts in party preferences dates back about three

decades in the United States, the Federal Republic experienced this process quite recently.

3. In contrast to the widespread satisfaction of Americans over the success and continuity of their party and governmental system, reserve toward party ties exists on the part of many Germans — particularly of the older generation — resulting from the experiences of recent German history.

4. Party structures — regionalism in the United States, centralism (in spite of federalistic features) in the Federal Republic — as well as differences in the governmental systems, bring about a different articulation of party preferences in the electoral act.

5. The party and governmental system makes it easier for the German than the American voter to assign responsibility for political decisions to the parties.

One can therefore expect that, on the whole, party identification in the Federal Republic will be more connected with group or status, and will probably be more emotionally clear-cut in the acceptance or rejection of a party, more consciously rooted in political program, and thus less intensive and stable, than in the United States. We must now support these hypotheses in detail.

III

Identification with Various Parties

Even though the differences between the German and American systems are considerable in many respects, the politico-social quality of the parties that permits them to become group formations with which the individual can identify more or less intensively is the same in both countries. In both systems the parties fulfill almost identical functions, among others that of interest aggregation. In both countries parties are probably the most important links between "public opinion" and the political decision processes. At the same time, the parties contribute significantly to the structuring of public opinion by offering the individual their concepts as keys for interpreting and evaluating politically relevant events and situations. Against this background of similarities, we first intend to examine empirically through comparative analysis the extent to which the concrete expression of party preferences in the two systems shows common characteristics or differences. For this purpose we shall now disregard the fact there are different parties in each system, and concentrate rather on a comparison of nonidentifiers with identifiers of parties and distinguish subsequently between unqualified and qualified identifiers.

Different formulations were used in the German and American surveys to elicit the respective extent and intensity of party ties. To the Americans chosen on the basis of a random sample, the following question was put: "Generally speaking do you usually think of yourself as a Republican, a Democrat, an Independent, or what?" Those who named one of the two parties (party identifiers) were then asked: "Would you call yourself a strong Republican/Democrat, or a not very strong Republican/Democrat?" The comparable German questions were: "Would you please tell me which politi-cal party you like best?" and "Would you say that you are a convinced follower of [the party mentioned], or would you rather say that you prefer [the party mentioned] because it appears the more suitable in the present situation?"

Both versions of the first question have been used in representative surveys for a considerable time, and have basically proved sound. They somewhat diverge in their formulations cognitively and emotively, and grasp different breadths of the party identification continuum, but the functional equivalence of the questions is greater than the divergence in the wording would lead us to suspect.

A German formulation of the first question that was closer to the American original version would surely have narrowed too much the meaning of "party identifiers," so that, in extreme cases, perhaps only enrolled party members would have been included. The formulation actually chosen appear to have lessened the possible effects of the previously mentioned reserve toward party ties among many German respondents, and thus to have been more adequate to the real situation. The gradations used to measure relative intensity of party preferences in both surveys are also probably comparable in principle, although the category "convinced identifier" may sound a little more com-mitted and exclusive than that of the "strong partisan." The differences in formulations thus are probably less consequential than might appear on first sight; besides, it would not have been possible in any case to make the values of intensity categories in one system exactly equivalent to those in the other system in any absolute sense.

Extent and Intensity

As Table 1 shows, 72.5 per cent of the American and 76.5 per cent of the German respondents identify with a political party. Even though we should not take these results too literally, they are fairly clear indications that the phenomena to be analyzed here are of basically comparable weight in both systems.

All the stronger, however, is the difference in intensity: American identi-fiers are composed almost equally of "strong" (49% = 35% of the sample) and "weak" identifiers (51% = 37% of the sample). In the Federal Republic, on the other hand, only about a third of those who identified themselves with a party referred to themselves as "convinced followers" (25.4% of the sample), while more than three fifths (46.3% of the sample) voiced a preference for one of the parties only because "it seemed more suitable in the present situation."

. . . Another remarkable aspect of Table 1 is the relatively high frequency of simple refusal among German respondents to answer questions about their party preferences. This refusal is presumably the expression of a certain political alienation — which may well be the aftereffect of our totalitarian past.

In view of a widespread assumption, the percentage of apolitical respondents

Table 1   *Party Identifiers in the Federal Republic and the United States*

	Federal Republic *in per cent*	USA *in per cent*
1. Party identifiers	76.5	72.5
Convinced identifiers	25.4	35.5
Qualified identifiers	46.3	37.0
N. A. (of intensity)	4.8	
2. "Independent" — but preference for *various** parties in the past		14.6
3. Nonidentifiers	23.5	12.9
Like neither party (Ger.) or "independent" and no previous preference (USA)	4.8	8.8
No opinion (apolitical)	6.8	3.8
N. A. (to party preference)	11.9	0.3
	100 (N=1794)	100 (N=1762)

* In the American survey the category "Independent" was divided between independents who in the past had preferred different parties or, depending on the kind of election (local, state, or federal) had voted for different parties; and independents who had no party preference whatsoever. The first group of Independents is essentially the same as "changers." In the United States, "Independent" is often conceived as a third-party orientation. Of the total of 23.4 per cent Independents, 14.6 per cent were of the first type (changers), and 8.8 per cent of the second type (liking no party).

in the German survey is surprisingly small: 6.8 per cent compared to 3.8 per cent of the American sample. The apolitical German is thus not a dominant type in the Federal Republic; a fact corroborated by other evidence as well. Thus it was also shown, for example, in an international comparative survey that knowledge about political institutions was quite high in Germany compared to other European countries.[5]

What is special about the Germans in the Federal Republic is the nature of their identification with political institutions and processes, not a general turning away and apathy. . . .

IV

Perception of Party Differences and Polarization of Political Opinions

Hypothesis 1: The perception of (imagined or existing) programmatic differences between the parties is comparatively more widespread among German than American identifiers.

Hypothesis 2: Polarization of political attitudes or opinions among the separate groups of Identifiers within the various parties is likely to show similar extent in both systems. (Regrettably, the material available for verification of this

[5] *Cf.* Gabriel Almond and Sidney Verba, *The Civic Culture* (Princeton, N. J.: Princeton University Press, 1963).

hypothesis is comparable only to a limited extent, as it consists of answers to two rather different questions.)

American respondents were confronted with a number of concrete policy propositions and requested to give a positive or negative answer to each; those who voiced an opinion were then asked: "Are the Democrats or Republicans loser to your own views on this question — or is there no difference?" In the German surveys the interviewers were first requested to give their views on the importance of a number of themes under every-day political discussion examples: security against a Russian attack, improvement of old-age pensions, stabilization of prices, diminution of delinquency among the young, good relations to the United States.) Then they were asked: "Quite apart from which party you personally find most attractive, what do you think: Which of the two major parties can deal with this problem best, SPD or CDU?" It is this last question on which we base our comparison with the questions put in the United States. . . .

Even if we accept the limitations inherent in the results presented in Table 2 due to the differences in the formulation of questions), one conclusion seems indubitable: Perception of programmatic differences is comparatively far higher among German than among American party identifiers. If only 35 per cent of convinced Democrats and 42 per cent of convinced Republicans perceive such differences, compared to 92 per cent convinced SPD followers and 87 per cent convinced CDU/CSU followers, this cannot be explained merely by the differing survey techniques. Here a differing social reality finds expression. This result may also express quantitatively the tendency for popularly held views of political parties to diverge from reality — but in opposite directions. This stereotype tends to dramatize party differences in the Federal Republic, while in the United States the tendency is to minimize them. At the same time, we may see here confirmation of the assumption that party identification in Western Germany is, on the whole, more politically oriented and rooted than is the case in the United States.

But what is the relation of party identifiers' views on political problems to the positions taken by the parties? As Table 2 shows clearly, the attitudes of those who do perceive party differences are more strongly polarized in favor of the positions taken by the favored party in the United States than in the Federal Republic. One similarity cannot, however, be overlooked: In each system the followers of the socially conservative party agreed with their own party on domestic (that is, primarily economic and social) issues. Conversely, the followers of the progressive party in each country show less conformity with their own party in questions of foreign policy.

Even if comparability is affected by differences in the indicators, it seems undoubtedly the case that polarization is at about the same level in the Federal Republic and in the United States. This means that the two initial hypotheses of this section can be considered verified. The thesis that convinced identifiers articulate the characteristics of a political system more clearly has been confirmed anew. What is the significance of the connections just analyzed for the stability of political development? This question will now be discussed in the entire context of the results obtained by this comparative study.

Table 2   *Extent and Distribution of Political Opinions among Party Identifiers*

1. Federal Republic

". . . Which of the two major parties can handle this problem best: SPD or CDU/CSU?"	PARTY IDENTIFICATION					
	CDU			SPD		
	Total %	Conv. %	Qual. %	Total %	Conv. %	Qual. %
Average % of those who asserted differences in respect to 15 political problems between parties	86	87	86	87	92	83
Average % of those who perceived differences and attributed to the CDU/CSU superior ability to solve of 15 diverse political problems	82	86	80	32	23	37
5 domestic problems	77	81	74	20	11	24
5 foreign problems	85	88	83	37	27	44

2. United States

"Are the Democrats closer to your own views, or the Republicans, or is there no difference?"	PARTY IDENTIFICATION					
	REPUBLICANS			DEMOCRATS		
	Total %	Conv. %	Qual. %	Total %	Conv. %	Qual. %
Average % of those who, regarding 15 policy propositions						
a) took a personal position	59	61	57	55	60	52
b) perceived party differences	38	42	33	31	35	28
Average % of those who perceived differences and considered themselves in agreement with the Republican party regarding 15 diverse political problems	91	96	85	16	6	27
5 domestic proposals	89	92	86	12	4	23
5 foreign policy proposals	95	98	92	23	8	41

V

Party Identification and Political Stability

On the basis of the preceding analysis, it can be viewed as proved that part identification in both countries corresponds to comparable socio-politic. realities. The historical developments and political experiences differing fro one country to another have their effect, so to say, within this similarity b retarding or advancing individual processes and thus articulating themselv in specific structural characteristics. Furthermore, this analysis has shown th the insights and presumptions about the emergence and growth of part preferences[6] gained in the study of American conditions apparently have mor

---

[6] Cf. V. O. Key, Jr., "A Theory of Critical Elections," *Journal of Politics XVIII* (1955 pp. 3–18.

general validity: particularly for the interpretation of West German data, they have provided plausible and powerful explanatory principles. Summarizing these insights, they could be formulated thus: (1) Potentially lasting large-scale party loyalties require for their development certain critical historical situations and/or events that immediately touch a major part of the population and that enter into general consciousness in connection with one or more parties. (2) Under conditions of political and at least minimal economic stability, party preferences thus once formed, gain over time in intensity in the form of individual ties to a party.

These results permit us to provide in a few concluding remarks some hints on the extent to which manifestations of party identification contribute to the stabilization of political processes and thus to the stabilization of the respective political systems. In view of the similarities discovered, it seems justified to draw some conclusions from American experiences and insights – modified by consideration of the differing historical background – as to the direction in which political [party] developments in the Federal Republic presumably will move. As mentioned initially, the steady decline of ideological-class orientations among West German parties has since 1949 led to a political [party] situation that exhibits characteristics similar to that of the United States since the development of modern American parties. Since under these conditions the voter is discouraged rather than encouraged to interpret political events and issues in the categories of class ideology, the parties become for him the most important source of orientation toward political behavior patterns, when he is appealed to as voter.

In view of the widespread consensus existing in both countries on constitutional fundamentals, as well as on a number of political goals; and in view of the resulting uni-modal distribution of basic political attitudes on the part of a large majority of the voters, the parties tend to move from opposite directions in their ideologies and concrete programs toward the political center. As each party must fear the loss of supporters in the center with each step it takes in important political questions away from the rival party, strategic considerations lead to a minimization of program differences between the competing parties.[7] This, however, presumes a certain flexibility among the voters appealed to, which is largely a function of existing party preferences. The example of the United States shows, for instance, that party identifications formed largely in the past, and maintained and strengthened under conditions of a convergence of the parties, inhibit a considerable part of the electorate from perceiving the subsequent growing differences between the Democratic and Republican parties, although these in part have assumed proportions of a fundamental nature. In contrast, party preference in the Federal Republic are of more recent origin, and are accompanied by a widespread perception of party differences. The frequently brief period of preference brings with it a considerably higher flexibility among German voters. If, therefore, German party supporters perceive party differences by com-

---

[7] Cf. Anthony Downs, *An Economic Theory of Democracy* (New York: Harper, 1957), pp. 133–134.

parison very frequently — and if, on the other hand, they enter relatively seldom into intensive political ties — while there is a noticeable tendency in the opposite direction in the United States, then this characteristic difference holds significant implications for the stabilization of political processes in each of the systems.

"In the American situation, the major cohesive force which gives the party system stability and continuity is the psychological attachment of the electorate to the parties. . . . In such a situation, politics tends to lose its ideological character: the public is not stimulated to inform itself regarding specific politics; its political role becomes one of deciding who shall manage the government, not what shall the government do. For the bulk of the electorate, this decision is determined by long-established party loyalties."[8]

Most of the characteristics of the American system describe tendencies, however, that are also present in the political reality of the Federal Republic, or that in outline are becoming increasingly visible. The most important and particularly characteristic difference is to be found in the fact that that segment of the electorate for which voting choice is enduringly determined by long-lasting party identification is significantly smaller in the Federal Republic than in the United States.

The implications of this situation for the stability of West Germany's political system are, on the whole, quite encouraging, though not unproblematical. It would be surely unjustified to conclude from it that in the Federal Republic "the people's attitude toward political parties again took on the familiar pattern of playful non-commitment."[9] Also, it should not rashly be seen as an indication that in the Federal Republic, once again "political parties could not find a popular base — the absolute prerequisite for any functioning democratic party system."[10]

Such undifferentiated judgements surely are no longer adequate if one wishes to characterize the political [party] situation of West Germany in the year 1961. To do justice to reality, one should attempt first of all to understand the reasons for the relatively lesser spread of intensive party ties. They are not to be found in any inflexible "national character" that just exists, but are determined by more general, in particular historical, factors. Thus, the responsibility for the limited identification with parties rests primarily with the personal experiences of a large part of the electorate with political parties in the Weimar Republic and the so-called Third Reich, as well as in the very brief history of the newly emerging party system. The noticeable decline in the influence of just these factors is, however, primarily a function of time, if only a minimum of political continuity and stability is guaranteed. But this is the decisive requisite.

---

[8] Angus Campbell and Henry Valen, "Party Identification in Norway and the United States," *Public Opinion Quarterly* XXV (1961), p. 524.

[9] Sigmund Neumann, "Germany: Changing Patterns and Lasting Problems," in Sigmund Neumann (ed.), *Modern Political Parties* (Chicago: University of Chicago, 1955), p. 377.

[10] *Ibid.*

11. Voters' Participation in the Political Life of a Swiss Community

JÜRG STEINER

This case study dealing with "politicization" in a small Swiss community tests one of the favorite generalizations of traditional democratic theory— and finds it wanting. Even under conditions where local autonomy is emphasized, where the size of the community is small and the political process transparent, interest and participation in politics remains restricted to a relatively narrow segment of the population. Apparently even under these conditions, "the political" is a realm that is frequently not perceived as relevant to the questions with which the citizen is preoccupied in his daily life.

I

Posing the Question

After "voting Sundays," again and again complaints are raised against the weak participation. In many places one fears that lack of political interest on the part of many citizens might endanger our democracy. We considered the problem sufficiently important to make it the subject of a sociological inquiry. We were concerned primarily with two questions: How strong intellectual and social participation in political life actually is; and which factors decide that some citizens participate more, others less, in political life.

We must clarify at once, however, that for reasons of time we had to limit our study to the citizens' participation in the political life of their local communities. The equally interesting question of their concern with cantonal, federal, or world politics we would like to leave to subsequent examination. Our study is further limited by the fact that we surveyed only one community, and thus, strictly speaking, our results are valid only under the special conditions of this community. We are quite aware of this fact and therefore do not wish to assert that the conclusions derived from our analysis can simply be applied to other communities. . . .

SOURCE: Reprinted by permission from Jürg Steiner, *Die Anteilnahme der Stimmbürger am politischen Leben ihrer Gemeinde* (Bern: Haupt Verlag, 1961), pp. 10, 32–45. Footnotes and text are abridged. Translation by Kurt L. Shell.

II

The Results of the Survey

1. The Intensity of Citizen Participation in the Political Life of Their Community

. . . Especially among foreigners, the Swiss local communities are often presented as the original cells of democracy. This is explained by the existence of manifold political rights that permit the entire electorate to participate actively in directing the communal political process. Three conditions are often tacitly assumed to exist for all citizens:

1. They are interested in everything occuring within their communities; they follow, in particular, the work of communal authorities and inform themselves about all political business.

2. Based on this information, they form their own opinions about all arising problems of communal politics.

3. Finally, they translate their opinions into action, at a minimum by participating in the community meeting and thus become co-responsible for communal policy.

Below we wish to show the extent to which citizens of the community of Belp meet these three conditions. First, we try to find out how great the interest of individual citizens is in the political events in their community. To the question, "To what extent are you interested in what happens in your community?" these were the responses (in per cent):

Very interested	10
Rather interested	20
Moderately interested	45
Little interested	22
Not at all	3
	100%

. . . The low interest of many citizens is clearly shown when we consider the responses to the following nine questions regarding local government rules (percentage of correct answers):

1. What is the councillors' term of office?	87%
2. Who elects the local primary school commission?	81%
3. Of how many members does the local council consist?	61%
4. How many times may a councillor be reelected?	48%
5. Who elects the town clerk (*Gemeindeschreiber*)?	45%
6. Who elects the building commission?	34%
7. How many regular town meetings are held every year?	30%
8. Up to what ceiling may the Council vote credits?	10%
9. What is the percentage of eligible voters entitled to call for a town meeting?	7%

. . . The low level of information of many citizens must unequivocally be explained by lack of interest, for all questions refer to rules that are again and again used in the daily functioning of the communal political process.

. . . Two further questions attempted to discover the citizens' information about the political parties in their community. The results were (percentages of correct answers):

1. Which local party organizations exist in Belp?   78%
2. How are the seats in the local council distributed according to
   parties?   48%

. . . We get a particularly interesting picture if we combine the results of the nine questions regarding local government rules and two about political parties, and examine how many were correctly answered by all citizens:

No correct answer	3%	
1 correct answer	4%	
2 correct answers	9%	
3 correct answers	12%	55%
4 correct answers	12%	
5 correct answers	15%	
6 correct answers	12%	
7 correct answers	9%	
8 correct answers	11%	
9 correct answers	8%	45%
10 correct answers	2%	
11 correct answers	3%	
	100%	

. . . Thus, 28 per cent of all citizens answered three or fewer questions correctly, while, on the other hand, another 24 per cent gave the answers to eight or more questions. . . . The picture thus far obtained gains even clearer contours if we next examine the relation of citizens to the councillors. We may assume that those citizens who take strong interest in the political events of their community also know exactly which men are members of the council. From the responses to the following three questions, we see here, too, that we cannot presume a maximum of interest for communal politics among all citizens:

1. What are the names of the seven councillors?

No correct answer	3%	
1 correct answer	7%	36%
2 correct answers	13%	
3 correct answers	13%	
4 correct answers	11%	
5 correct answers	12%	64%
6 correct answers	14%	
7 correct answers	27%	

2. Do you know the occupation of Council President Tannaz? [Same question for remaining six councillors.]

No correct answer	1%	
1 correct answer	3%	
2 correct answers	7%	17%
3 correct answers	6%	
4 correct answers	11%	
5 correct answers	19%	
6 correct answers	26%	83%
7 correct answers	27%	

3. Do you know in which house Council President Tannaz lives? [Same question for remaining six councillors.]

No correct answer	5%	
1 correct answer	4%	
2 correct answers	7%	27%
3 correct answers	11%	
4 correct answers	17%	
5 correct answers	16%	
6 correct answers	22%	73%
7 correct answers	18%	

Here, too, the most significant point of the analysis appears to be the striking difference between citizens, some of whom have a very close relation to the councillors while for others it is a more or less anonymous one. We consider it extraordinarily interesting that most of the citizens are better informed about the councillors than about council rules and political parties. . . . This obviously means that the citizen interest in communal politics focuses more on the human being of flesh and blood than on the purely institutional aspects.

We came up with interesting results also when we examined the citizens' relation to each councillor.

Table 1   *Citizens and Councillors*

Characteristic	Tannaz	Reinhard	Müller	Christen	Krähen-bühl	Reif	Flüc-kiger
Occupation known	98	94	93	82	68	48	43
Residence known	90	94	69	80	54	44	29
Addressed as "thou"	42	45	61	53	17	16	32
Occasional or frequent personal meeting	46	47	50	45	33	23	14

Councillors Tannaz, Reinhard, Müller, and Christen obviously have close relations to their citizens than Councillors Krähenbühl, Reif, and Flückiger

It seems to us that the intensity of relations is decisively influenced by the councillors' occupations. The three councillors with relatively loose relation to the citizens all have occupations that keep them working behind closed doors practically all the time. . . . They are part of a more dynamic, modern time and lead to few or only very superficial contacts with the outside world. The work place and residence for these occupations do not coincide, and in two of the three cases the work is pursued outside the community. The situation is entirely different regarding the four local councillors who have relatively close relations to the citizens. Two are farmers, one runs a dairy, and the fourth is employed as a plumber (usually working outside). These four all have plenty of opportunity to cultivate close contacts with the voters during their working hours: the two farmers, for instance, while cutting wood or visiting the rural co-op; the owner of the dairy when receiving milk or serving customers; the plumber on construction sites and when working on repairs in the houses of the community.

It could be stated that Councillors Tannaz, Reinhard, Müller and Christen still represent the older, more static social strata, while the other three councillors already represent the modern and dynamic Belp. Thus, within a single community our findings of a previous study comparing rural and urban milieus emerge again. Then we wrote: "The relations [between citizens and the Councillors] in urban milieus are predominantly purely functional and in large part even completely anonymous, while in rural milieus these relations are much more personal and often lead to quite close socialization."

. . . Next we turn to the question of whether we can assume that in the case of all citizens, they form their own opinions about all political matters. It is, in practice, very difficult to find out by survey methods whether people have formed an opinion regarding a particular concrete problem. Above all, there is the danger that a direct question will provoke a clear-cut opinion that previously existed only vaguely or not at all. . . . It therefore seemed much more rewarding to ask citizens on what occasions in their daily lives they talked about politics. We proceeded from the assumption that those who frequently talk about politics probably also have formed an opinion. We are aware, of course, that there may be citizens who have formed an opinion of their own who quite consciously avoid talking to other people about it. As a rule it is likely, however, that citizens who never discuss politics will not have a clear political opinion and therefore feel no need to have political conversations in which they can express their views. We think, therefore, that the following five questions indicate something about the intensity of political opinion formation.

Does it happen that you talk about politics . . .	often	occasionally	rarely	never
1. in inns of Belp?	7	17	36	40
2. in organizations?	7	10	13	70
3. with colleagues at work	19	21	24	36
4. with neighbors?	8	17	49	26
5. within the family?	24	34	33	9

First we find it interesting to show the percentage of citizens who do not discuss politics *often or occasionally* on any of the five occasions:

Frequent or occasional political discussions:	
none of the five occasions	29%
inns	24%
organizations	19%
colleagues	14%
neighbors	10%
family	4%

Thus, 29 per cent of all citizens stated that they never or rarely talk about politics on any of the five occasions, which points to a very weakly developed political opinion formation in their case . . . When analyzing the five questions separately, we find that political discussions within the family are most frequent. The number of husbands who told me, for instance, that after each town meeting they had to report to their wives about the decision taken there, was remarkable. In many families it is also a matter of course that prior to council elections, there is rather intensive discussion of the candidates, and also of current issues such as construction of a new school.

Next to discussion within the family, that with colleagues at work is of the greatest importance for political opinion formation. For the further development of our democracy, it is not unimportant to note that the opportunity for political discussion during working hours is far rarer than in the days of the old, more static occupations. The reason is that a farmer or an artisan establishes much closer relations to his fellow men in his daily working life than, for example, an employee in a large institution; above all, the former are not tied to a prescribed work tempo like the latter. In our interviews we thus heard again and again that, for example, during a business visit by a farmer to the smith or butcher, the business talk is, as a rule, followed up with a discussion of current questions of communal politics. Most of those employed in modern, dynamic occupations told me, on the other hand, that they preferred not to discuss politics in their place of work, "as one never knows what the other person is thinking." . . . Finally, it seems very interesting that group organizations are no longer centers of political discussion, as was the case in the nineteenth century, particularly in sports and choral groups. The de-politization of many of these groups appears to have been consciously carried through. This becomes clear, for example, in the case of the "Workers' Music Association" and the bourgeois "Music Society," which were in Belp fused into a politically neutral Village Music Society. . . .

The third question we wish to examine is whether one can assume in the case of all citizens that they have a need to make their political views effective and are ready to help assume responsibility for shaping communal politics by active participation. Every observer already knows, however, from the voting statistics that this third assumption is met nowhere in Switzerland, so that the responses to the following three questions probably merely confirmed facts generally accepted (figures in per cent).

1. Do you participate in town meetings?	frequently	13
	occasionally	20
	rarely	37
	never	30
2. Have you ever exercised a function in your community (particularly as member of a commission)?	frequently	8
	occasionally	6
	rarely	7
	never	79
3. Did you ever participate in a discussion at a town meeting?	frequently	3
	occasionally	3
	rarely	9
	never	85

. . . What becomes evident here is — and we wish to emphasize the point clearly once more — that we cannot assume that all citizens feel an intensive interest in the political affairs of their community, and that it is only a matter of granting them the required political rights in order for them to cooperate actively in the communal political process. In fact, the political interest within the community is frequently overlaid with other, stronger interests; the question still to be posed is under what social conditions the chances are best for these political interests to break through into the open. . . .

12. Austrian Youth and Socialist Ideology

ERNST GEHMACHER

Between the wars Austrian politics was characterized by fierce struggles between highly ideologized parties. After World War II, two parties (the Socialist party and the People's party) achieved domination, largely abandoned their radical past, and joined in a "Grand Coalition" that lasted for twenty years. The stable, low-temperature politics of this period seems reflected in the findings here presented (by a committed Socialist in a Socialist party periodical) and provide a contrast to the attitudes exhibited by Italian youth (Section 13).

As an associate of the Institute for Empirical Social Research, I had continuing opportunity to conduct interviews with employed boys and girls between 14 and 18 in the Youth Recreation Homes of the Austrian Trade Union Federation (OeGB). The interviews were not thematically aimed at the political attitudes of that sample of working youths, but many answers provided certain information about it. The results are in agreement with a number of political science surveys undertaken by the Institute, but probe more deeply the ideological conceptions held.

A few of these results are selected and presented here not only because they are typical and reveal a good deal about the attitudes of working youths, but because it was recently also possible to address identical questions at gatherings of Socialist party functionaries to a sample of party workers.

This small comparative study, which makes no demand to being comprehensive or strictly representative, shows, however, a few rather interesting tendencies in the thinking of working youths and Socialist party workers. . . .

The boys interviewed came from all over Austria, predominantly from larger industrial centers and cities weighted in favor of eastern Austria. Seventy per cent were manual workers, the remainder [white collar] employees. Only a small percentage could be clearly assigned to a basic ideological position. Four fifths appreciated the achievements of trade unions; 55 per cent considered religion important for a happy life. Political thinking among these young people had no clear articulation, but everyday political events had an echo. At the time of the survey — last autumn — wages and prices were central, yet the problems of expected military service were of greater interest.

One question in the survey dealt with nationalization of industries: Should more industries be nationalized? Should those presently nationalized be retained under public ownership, or should they rather be reprivatized? Or

SOURCE: Reprinted by permission from Ernst Gehmacher, "Haben die Sozialisten der Jugend nichts mehr zu sagen?," *Die Zukunft* (May, 1966), pp. 31–33. Footnotes and text are abridged. Translation by Kurt L. Shell.

should nationalization be entirely abolished? The same question was addressed to a smaller sample of Vienna SPOe functionaries. The answers were:

	Youths (N=534) (%)	SPOe Func. (N=34) (%)
More nationalization	21	41
Retain nationalization	37	53
Reduce nationalization	15	6
Abolish nationalization	27	–
	100	100

Only 58 per cent of working youths favor nationalization of industries. At this central point of a Socialist economic policy, the impact of conservative theses becomes evident. For if girls, rural youths (unrepresented in the sample), and students are added to the 42 per cent of young workers opposed to nationalization, it shows a massive majority of young people in favor of a policy of reprivatization.

The Socialist functionaries, among whom only 6 per cent favor a certain reduction in nationalization, are rather isolated in their opinions regarding this point. They have failed to convey to the majority of young people within their sphere of influence the meaning of nationalization. Perhaps one might assume this resulted from a total imperviousness of youth to Socialist ideas, but this is not the case. Certain Socialist principles are still popular, particularly with young people — equality, for instance.

Three questions were asked to this theme.

Question 1: "How large should the differential between highest and lowest incomes be: i.e., how much more should people in leading positions earn than an unskilled worker?"

Differential	Working Youths (%)	SPOe Func. (%)
up to double	33	18
3 to 5 times	31	24
6 to 10 times	19	30
more	5	24
N. A.	12	4
	100	100

Question 2: "How large do you estimate this differential really to be in Austria today?"

Differential	Working Youths (%)	SPOe Func. (%)
up to 5 times	14	6
6 to 10 times	32	12
11 to 50 times	30	35
50 to 100 times	5	30
more	2	12
N. A.	17	5
	100	100

The desire for equality of incomes is more radical among young workers and employees than among Socialist party functionaries. . . . The difference is great [however] in their respective estimates of existing society. While the party functionaries view sums of about 100,000 shillings ($4000) per month as peak income, the young people most frequently see the upper limit of existing incomes as between 15,000 and 30,000 shillings ($600 to $1200).

But even this appears to them unjustifiably high, as responses to Question 3 show:

"How high, would you say, should the highest income be that can be earned in the best-paid occupations?" (Figures express medians.)

	Working Youths	Party Func.
Film actor	11,200	9,300
Inventor	13,800	17,200
Politician	6,700	13,000
World sport champion	6,500	7,600
Scientist	10,300	9,900
Top manager	9,500	8,800

The opinions are here surprisingly uniform. The young people would grant a far lower income to politicians than would the functionaries (who, however, are known to criticize strongly any suspected enrichment by politicians). Very characteristic: Today's young generation, too, longs for equality, but hardly believes that it will be achieved through the actions of politicians.

It would be wrong to ascribe envy to these youths. When asked about the level of the present-day educational budget and the increases that should be voted for education, the boys showed themselves rather better informed than the functionaries — and equally ready to accept a raise in moneys spent on education. Male youths and SPOe functionaries would double the budget for education (girls, on the other hand, would decrease it). . . .

On an average the boys favored that approximately 1 per cent of all incomes be sacrificed for aid to developing nations. Only 9 per cent of the boys did not want to sacrifice anything. On the other hand, the spirit of sacrifice among Socialist functionaries showed itself very weak in this respect. Far more than half declared "give nothing," "nobody gave us anything either." . . .

The impression one gains in these youth studies is that young people in Austria today favor progress and community, but do not set their hope in political forces; rather, they believe that salvation would be found in harmonizing social life. Many survey results could be used to support this impression. Here it shall be demonstrated by means of two results of the small comparative study.

"What, in your opinion, should be the most important goal of a good Austrian policy?"

	Working Youths (%)	SPOe Func. (%)
Raising living standards	9	18
Strong economic development	18	53
Growth of Austria's power	4	–
A warm, friendly, close-knit life of people in the state	68	24

"If the Austrian national product were to rise significantly within a short period, would you favor . . .

	Working Youths (%)	SPOe Func. (%)
reducing the work week by 15%?	25	29
raising wages by 15%?	23	18
using the money to build new factories, power stations, hospitals, apartments, and schools?	50	53
N. A.	2	–
	100	100

. . . No sign of narrow egoism among these young people.

13. Values, Expectations and Political Predispositions of Italian Youth

JOSEPH LaPALOMBARA AND JERRY B. WATERS

A number of tantalizing questions are suggested by the Italian data analyzed by Professors LaPalombara and Waters. Can we assume, in the absence of precise comparative findings, that Italian youth has rejected the Fascist past far less decisively than its German counterpart? And if this impression were correct, what factors (in view of certain similarities in the two nations' recent historical experiences) would account for it? How do we explain that the apparently existing pro-fascist potential finds little expression in the Italian party system—not even in the form of flash parties such as Poujadism in France? If, as the data suggest, higher education does not, in the Italian context, correlate positively with pro-democratic attitudes and political activity, are we not forced to revise and refine the generalizations we have derived from their relation in the American context?

I

Youth's supposed allegiance to the extremes in politics is frequently identified as a central cause of Italian political instability. About the younger voters it is common to assert that their "radicalism," their alleged support of extreme political parties, is a function of many factors. Chief among these, the argument runs, is disillusionment over the failure of fascism and humiliation over Italy's betrayal of a Nazi German ally and subsequent defeat in war. Equally important is an imputed antagonism of the nation's youth toward a society that offers little material and spiritual attraction, and little prospect of social and economic betterment in the future.

Evidence offered in support of observations such as these is generally unsystematically gathered and inconclusive in its implications. Is it true, for example, that the young people lean essentially toward the Communist party and, more recently, toward the neo-Fascist Italian Social Movement? Are the Communists more successful than competitors in attracting youth to auxiliary organizations such as trade unions and athletic associations? Most Italians would answer affirmatively to both of these questions. They might add that, even within the universities, hotly-fought elections to choose representatives to student organizations reflect the influence among youth of the anti-democratic ideologies discernible in Italian politics. Indicators such as these seem to

SOURCE: Reprinted by permission from *The Midwest Journal of Political Science* (February, 1961), pp. 39–42, 47–51, 57–58. Footnotes are abridged.

:onfirm what many Italians assert — either fearfully or in glee, depending on heir own political predispositions and hopes for the future.

This paper will identify and analyze some patterns of the political orien- ation of Italian youth, relating these where possible to objective or attitudinal socio-economic factors. The data, which we subject here to "secondary analysis," were gathered in 1958 in a national survey conducted by one of Italy's reputable survey-research organizations.[1] Almost 3,000 respondents, ranging in age from 18 to 25 years, were included in the sample. The inter- viewers administered a set-schedule questionnaire of approximately fifty major tems. We are reporting only aspects of the study that are relevant to the :opic of this paper.

As we expected, not all generalizations about Italy's youth are supported by our data. Nevertheless, there is much to suggest that, if the stability of the Italian political system depends on satisfied youth who view the future with relative optimism, there is much that should gravely concern the nation's present leadership.

II

Several important patterns of values, expectations, and attitudes emerge from our analysis. First, it is clear that, except for students and housewives, Italy's young people are strongly preoccupied with economic problems and do not view the future as one in which the concern is likely to be alleviated. Thus, almost one-half (43.5%) of the 2,962 respondents identify as their most pressing personal problem the need to find a job, to earn more money, to better their living standard or to set themselves up economically. By category of respondent, the distribution of responses is given in Table 1.

Of the 1,674 persons giving responses of the "All Remaining" category,

[1] *Methodological note.* The national sample included 2,962 respondents of whom 1,982 (66.9%) were males and 980 (33.1%) were females. The total sample was deliberately skewed to overrepresent the males, who make up only 48.6% of the Italian population. This oversampling was felt to be necessitated because of the known gross lack of interest in politics and political policy characteristic of Italian women. However, in the sub-sample of 1,811, representing the *employed respondents,* 848 (46.9%) males and 963 (53.2%) females appear. Here it was felt that *working* women would be more politically aware and active and that they would have something meaningful to say about society and politics. A considerable number of questions were asked only of this sub-sample.

The sample was also controlled for geographic distribution. Thus, the following actual and sample population distributions occur:

DISTRIBUTION OF ITALIAN POPULATION BY GEOGRAPHIC REGION

Region	Percentage Census, 1951	Percentage Sample
North	44.1	43.5
Central	18.4	16.6
South	24.8	29.0
Insular	12.1	10.9

The sampling method used was that of the two-stage cluster probability sampling technique.

12.6% indicate that they are confronted by no particular problem. Most of these are married women who evidently have turned their economic concerns over to their husbands. Several of the other responses in the "All Remaining" category (e.g., marrying and having a family, 8.4%; completing one's education, 4.9%) are also economically based in part.

Not unexpectedly, those respondents from the lower socio-economic classes are more concerned than others about personal economic problems. However

Table 1   Major Personal Problem, by Category of Respondent

Type of Respondent	Economic Problem (N=1288)		All Remaining Responses (N=1674)	
	N	%	N	%
Student (N=261)	39	14.9	222	85.1
Employed Worker (N=1811)	848	46.8	963	53.2
Unemployed (N=325)	245	75.4	80	24.6
Housewife (N=499)	127	25.4	372	74.6
Other (N=66)	29	43.9	37	56.1

it is noteworthy that only one of every five respondents either indicate that they are not plagued by particular problems or list personal problems of little import.

Of the 1,811 respondents who were employed 57.3% say they are dissatisfied with present compensation, 31.5% say they are "sufficiently satisfied," and only 4.6% reply that they are "very satisfied." Roughly one-third of these same persons expect to improve their economic position notably in the future, 42.5% expect to improve their condition only a little, and 23% expect essentially no improvement at all.

The incidence of dissatisfaction corresponds consistently with the economic conditions of Italy's major geographic areas. That is, as one moves from the industrialized, relatively flourishing Northern provinces to the rural, economically depressed provinces of Southern and Insular Italy, dissatisfaction rises significantly for all categories. Table 2 provides evidence for this assertion.

The contrast between the "sufficiently satisfied" and the "not at all satisfied" is striking for all regions. The Northern and Central employed youth who are relatively at ease about their compensation outnumber their Southern and Insular brothers in the ratio of more than two to one. Alternatively, for every

Table 2   Degree of Satisfaction with Compensation, by Major Geographic Region

Degree of Satisfaction	North (N=848) (%)	Central (N=273) (%)	South (N=513) (%)	Insular (N=177) (%)
Very satisfied (N=83)	5.2	4.0	4.9	1.7
Sufficiently satisfied (N=571)	40.0	35.9	19.7	19.2
Little satisfied (N=769)	38.1	43.6	47.1	48.0
Not at all satisfied (N=269)	9.3	11.7	22.0	24.9
DK – NR (N=119)	7.4	4.8	6.3	6.2

Northern and Central person who is not at all satisfied with his compensation, there are more than two such persons in the South and closer to three on the islands. We find that future expectations are closely related to the degree of satis- faction with present compensation. . . .

III

What of the political values and level of political information evinced by the respondents? As far as national and international developments are concerned, an overwhelming 72.7% of all respondents say they have little or no interest in such matters; only 6.8% claim "great interest." Not surprising is the high degree of correspondence between lack of interest and such factors as social class, education, sex, and geographic location. In general, the most interested citizens tend to be upper class males, university trained, of higher occupational status and living in the Central and Northern provinces. That only 14% of the females claim any interest at all in these matters lends great credence to the assertion that the vast majority of women voters in Italy are essentially uninformed and incapable of making rational political decisions. However, the general lack of interest in domestic and international issues and developments suggests that much of the criticism directed against women can be equally extended to the men as well.

Another good measure of the level of political information possessed by respondents was obtained by a question that examined whether one had heard of the European Common Market, about which millions of words have been published throughout the member countries. Fifty per cent of all respondents admit to never having heard of it; only 31% have any accurate idea of what the Common Market means. Once again, the level of accurate information increases as one moves up the socio-economic scale. Nearly three-fourths of the "poor class" (69% of those with only elementary educations, 64% of workers, farmers and housewives, 62% of those from Southern and Insular Italy, and 66% of the supporters of the Communist party) have not heard of ECM. These are the outside limits of the information vacuum, but while other groups fare better, the general level of information is strikingly low.

If, as we shall later suggest in detail, the poorer, less educated and largely uninformed voters gravitate primarily to the Communist and Christian Demo- cratic parties, we are confronted with a phenomenon in which membership in voluntary associations is not primarily appealing to the most well informed voters. To begin with, most of the respondents (58.7%) indicate that they do not belong to trade unions, political parties or athletic associations. Others (28.6%) hold single memberships, as follows: trade unions, 7.9%; political parties, 8.3%; athletic associations, 12.4%. The remaining 12.7% hold multiple memberships in a combination of the above organizations.

Males join political parties in greater numbers than females (23% to 8%). The relative decline of the political party as a social organization in the larger urban centers is attested by the fact that, whereas 9% of those in cities of over 250,000 inhabitants join parties, the incidence of party membership rises to an amazing 25% in communities in the 30,001 to 50,000 population range. Within these communities, as well as throughout Italy, those from the lower-status occupational categories are more likely than others to join parties. Similarly, those who identify with the political Left are more inclined than others to take out party memberships. If our inferences are accurate, the heaviest incidence of card-carrying party membership occurs among Italy's poorest, least well educated voters from middle-sized communities, who are largely inclined, if male, to join the Communist party and, if female, to join the Christian Democratic party. To put the inverse proposition, the greater the degree of education, the higher the occupational status, the more urban the place of residence, the less likely are persons involved to join a political party.

Perhaps the general lack of interest and information is responsible for the confusion and inconsistencies we encounter when the political values of respondents are examined. At one point, those interviewed were asked to indicate with which of the following freedoms they would be most unwilling to part:

1. Freedom of personal expression   (46.2%)
2. Religious freedom   (18.5%)
3. Human dignity and respect for individual   (19.2%)
4. Independence of my country   (9.6%)
5. Freedom of private economic enterprise   (4.7%)
6. No response   (1.8%)

The figures in parentheses represent the proportion of all respondents who list each alternative as the most important freedom. Men (50%) are more attached than women (39%) to freedom of expression. Not unexpectedly, a much higher proportion of women (32%) than men (11%) score religious freedom as the one they would surrender least readily.[2] The strong concentration of females as supporters of the Christian Democratic party may be inferred in part from the fact that, whereas only 7% of those who identify with the political Left view religious freedom as most important, fully 30% of Christian Democratic supporters opt primarily for this freedom. Freedom of economic enterprise does not attract many of either sex, and this is in keeping with what we have already learned about the attitudes of young people toward the private sector of the economy.

One might infer from the above responses that most of the respondents are positively oriented toward democratic freedoms. However, we find a considerable number of these same persons supporting pro-fascist or anti-democratic positions. For example, respondents were given cards containing statements of judgment and asked to indicate with which of the statements they were most in agreement. The specific questions and the gross distribution of responses were as follows:

---

[2] It should be noted that, in Italy, "religious freedom" does not connote exactly what is meant by this symbol in the United States. Italians generally mean no interference by the government in Catholic Church affairs. They generally do not mean tolerance of many religious beliefs.

Question 30. With which of the following statements do you most agree?

1. Fascism was a regime that brought the country to ruin. (34.2%)
2. The Fascist party would have been an excellent thing for our country if it had stayed out of war. (27.5%)
3. The Fascist regime was an excellent thing for our country. (5.7%)
4. The Fascist regime would have been a blessing for Italy if there had not been so many traitorous acts committed within and against it. (26.6%)
5. No response. (6.0%)

Question 32. With which of the following statements do you most agree?

1. The democratic system is the only system that will allow us to develop economically. (32.2%)
2. The democratic system slows up development and progress in our country. (6.9%)
3. The democratic system is a political system that works well in general but is not adaptable to Italy. (16.9%)
4. The democratic systetm may have many defects, but it is still the best system of government. (40.0%)
5. No response. (4.0%)

The first response (34.2%) for Question 30 was classified as "anti-fascist," the next three (59.8%) as "pro-fascist." For Question 32, the first and fourth responses were called "pro-democratic" (72.2%), and the second and third (23.8%) "anti-democratic." When we group the response to the two questions, results are obtained as given in Table 3.

It is difficult to reconcile responses to the question on "most important freedom" with the large number of respondents who gave anti-democratic and pro-fascist choices in Questions 30 and 32. The fact is, however, that in several places in the questionnaire we find basic inconsistencies of response. Depending on which specific question is analyzed, it is possible to conclude that the Italian youth are primarily disposed toward fascism, toward democracy or, as in the case of a question not here reported, toward communism. The degree of this confusion is suggested by the 53.7% of the pro-democratic respondents who seem also to be pro-fascist. It is possible, of course, that for many respondents our questions did not discriminate ideological values. We suggest, however, that many of the young people are not concerned with logical consistency and that they can and do hold contradictory views.

Table 3 *Distribution of Pro- and Anti-Democratic Responses, by Pro- and Anti-Fascist Responses*

	Pro-Democratic	Anti-Democratic	NR
Anti-Fascist	37.6%	27.3%	15.1%
Pro-Fascist	53.7%	68.4%	26.9%
NR	8.7%	4.3%	58.0%

For all of the obvious inconsistencies of attitude to which we might point, there is enough relationship among some of these variables to suggest that the distributions of responses on Questions 30 and 32, when cross-tabulated with other questions, are significant. As an example, the incidence of pro-fascist responses ranges from 54% in the Northern and Central provinces to 72% in the islands of Sicily and Sardinia. This supports other electoral evidence that the neo-fascist movement has its roots primarily in the South of Italy where Mussolini's regime never managed to gain the degree of acceptance it secured in the North. Why the fascist revolution, if one is developing in the South, is so late in making its appearance is a problem that we cannot answer in this study.

In similar vein, those with the highest amount of education are also the most likely (65%) to express pro-fascist views. Or, to depict the situation differently, 68% of the "middle class" is pro-fascist by comparison with only 46% of the "poor class." The class concentration of pro-fascist and anti-democratic attitudes can be otherwise depicted. Thus, 94% of those who identify with the political Right are pro-fascist. This tendency is considerably lower for the political Left (44%), although a surprising 30% of Communist party supporters fall into the same category. On the other hand, those who incline toward the Left are more favorably (61%) disposed toward the World War II Resistance Movement (identified with Communist leadership) than are those of the political Right (23%).

It should be stressed again that these responses were quite inconsistent. Thus, although we can say that the "middle class" is more inclined toward fascism than is the "poor class," we do not intend to say that fully 68% of the former class is anti-democratic as compared to 46% of those in the latter class. In fact, despite the difficulties inherent in trying to interpret these variations, it is apparent that the dominant attitude expressed is pro-democratic, in the sense that it is supported by the most respondents and in the cross tabulations seems to be a much more reliable differentiating variable. Thus, only 48% of those of the political Right express pro-democratic views, compared with 53% of the Left and an overwhelming 87% of those who identify with the parties of the Center. Individually, those who support the Christian Democratic, Republican, and Radical parties (88%) are much more committed to a democratic value than the supporters of the Communist party, of whom only 35% express pro-democratic attitudes.

Even though the dominant attitude seems to be pro-democratic, it is striking to note that a very substantial number of Italians who have come of age under relatively free and democratic institutions express attitudes which demonstrate, at best, a wavering faith in democracy and, at worst, an outright dissatisfaction with the democratic system. It is important to recall that fully 25% of the youth agreed with the statements that the democratic system slows up economic progress, or that it is not adaptable to the Italian situation. This group probably more accurately reflects the basic anti-democratic attitude than do the groups that chose to support pro-fascist statements. . . .

Our findings suggest that political stability for Italy is strongly tied to the degree of satisfaction with present conditions and the degree of positive hope of future improvement that can be inculcated in the electorate.[3] Evidently, the youthful voters have not identified with political extremes in proportions similar to their more elderly co-nationals. Yet, it is apparent that those among the youth who are poor, who are least satisfied with their compensation, and who are least inclined to view the future as promising are the ones who already have moved in an extreme direction. If the incidence of young voters who fall into this category is appreciably increased we would expect the strength of the Left to increase proportionately at least.

Nor can one place strong reliance on basic political values as a steadying influence. The young voters are fairly confused regarding the values they hold as important. It is reasonable to suppose, for example, that they would accept another Fascist regime with little protest. In any event, they seem not to have the dedication to democratic values that would help to keep the political system free, let us say, in a period of severe economic crisis. One should also bear in mind our previous finding that it is the least well informed, most generally disgruntled type of voter who becomes a political activist or card-carrying member — and that these activists incline primarily to join the Communist party.

Thus, while the blanket indictment of Italian youth as "politically irresponsible" is not supported by our data, we find much that raises grave questions about the probable political direction that youth would take under conditions of social and economic adversity. It seems essential not merely that more be done to strengthen the democratic values of these voters; it is crucial as well for Italian democracy that the conditions that give rise to long-range political radicalism be minimized or removed.

---

[3] For this reason, the migration from country to city, and from North to South, [sic] . . . is probably of considerable importance to political stability in Italy.

14. Social Trends and Electoral Behavior in Britain

MARK ABRAMS

The British type of parliamentary system has frequently served as model both for American reformers dissatisfied with the complexities and obscurities characteristic of the American party system, and for Europeans viewing with envy an allegedly "politically mature" electorate using the ballot to hold the government accountable. The analysis presented by Mr. Abrams indicates that the attitudes of British voters toward their parties and the electoral process are apparently not too different from those of American voters, in spite of the profound structural differences between the systems; and that, therefore, the traditional view of British citizens as exercising "rational choice" between clearly distinct party programs has to be revised.

Before attempting to link the two parts of the title to this paper I would like to discuss them separately. For the great majority of British citizens electoral behaviour consists almost entirely of voting for a party candidate or not voting at all at a Parliamentary General Election, and it is with this form of behaviour that I shall be mainly concerned.

We know from official statistics for all contested constituencies the total turnout, but for anything more revealing than this we are dependent upon the findings of sample surveys. From these, however, we are able to establish with a fair degree of reliability the turnout rate for various sections of the electorate and to see that within the total figures there are considerable and politically important variations. The survey figures used here are drawn very largely from two nation-wide inquiries; one was carried out in the summer of 1959 shortly before the General Election of that year and used a probability sample of just under 1,000 adults; the second was completed in January 1960 (i.e. shortly after the Election) and this used a quota sample of 750 adults. Both surveys asked about voting behaviour at the 1955 General Election and the later one also enquired about the 1959 election. The fact that both surveys were within two or three months of the 1959 General Election meant that few respondents thought in terms of supporting the Liberal Party.

In 1955, with an electorate of 34 million in Great Britain (the survey area) 26.1 million votes were cast, i.e. 77 per cent of the electorate voted. By 1959 almost 2½ million of this electorate had died. Nearly two-thirds of these casualties came from a section of the electorate with usually a low turnout

SOURCE: Reprinted by permission from Mark Abrams, "Social Trend and Electoral Behaviour," *British Journal of Sociology*, XIII (September, 1962), pp. 232–249. Text is abridged.

(i.e. those aged 70 or more), and we would therefore expect that a survey among the survivors in 1959 would show for them a turnout of approximately 80 per cent at the 1955 Election. In fact, in both the 1959 and 1960 surveys, of those old enough to have voted in 1955, some 85 per cent said they had voted at that General Election.

Inflation of this kind and of this order is, unfortunately, not uncommon in surveys which question people about their voting behaviours at past elections. Bearing this in mind one may cautiously but reasonably conclude that:

1. There was in 1955 very little difference in turnout between men and women.
2. The turnout was lower among young electors (aged 34 or less) than among older voters (aged 50 or more).
3. The turnout was slightly lower among semi- and unskilled manual workers and their wives than it was among skilled workers and middle-class electors.
4. The turnout was much lower among people who between elections have not made up their minds to vote for either the Labour Party or the Conservative Party. Among supporters of the two parties, Conservatives had a slightly higher turnout.
5. The turnout was very much lower among people who are not members of a political party, do not support one of them, and do not even feel that they 'lean' towards one of them. These completely non-political electors form roughly 12 per cent of the electorate (i.e. over 4 million electors); but in spite of their detachment half of them do, in fact, vote at a General Election. The difference in total votes between the two major parties in both the 1955 and 1959 General Elections was little more than 1 million.
6. But apart from this fringe of detached electors it is clear that among the

Table 1   *1955 Turnout Rates in Various Sections of the 1959/60 Electorate*

Sections of Survivors of 1955 Electorate	Claimed Turnout in 1955	Size of Each Group in the 1959 Electorate
	(%)	(%)
Men	86	47
Women	85	53
Aged under 35	76	26
Aged 35–49	81	30
Aged 50 or more	86	44
Middle class	87	32
Skilled working class	87	33
Semi- and unskilled working class	83	35
Conservative intending voters in 1959/60	91	38
Labour intending voters in 1959/60	89	40
Other electors in 1959/60	67	22
Party members in 1959/60	95	15
Party supporters in 1959/60	92	45
Party "leaners" in 1959/60	83	28
No party identification in 1959/60	51	12

rest of the electorate there is, in every sub-group, a turnout of at least 80 per cent — and in some the rate is over 90 per cent.

Side by side with this very high turnout rate outside the small detached fringe there is one other remarkable feature of British electoral behaviour — the average person's high stability of party voting from one General Election to another. Table 2 is based on the earlier survey and shows, for those old enough to vote in both elections, the 1955 voting behaviour of the 1959

Table 2   *Voting Behaviour of 1959 Electorate Aged 25 and Over*

Party Supported in 1955 Election	1959 ELECTORATE		
	Conservative	Labour	Rest of 1959 Electorate
	(%)	(%)	(%)
Conservative	87	3	22
Labour	3	86	31
Liberal	1	*	11
Abstained	9	11	36
Total	100	100	100

* Less than 0.5 per cent.

Table 3   *General Election Behaviour of 1960 Conservatives**

	1959	1955	1951
	(%)	(%)	(%)
Voted Conservative	86	75	69
Voted Labour	3	10	11
Voted Liberal etc.	1	1	1
Don't remember	†	4	7
Information refused	1	1	1
Abstained	9	9	11
Total	100	100	100

* Excluding at each election those too young to vote.
† Less than 0.5 per cent.

Table 4   *General Election Behaviour of 1960 Labour Supporters*

	1959	1955	1951
	(%)	(%)	(%)
Voted Labour	89	88	86
Voted Conservative	3	1	1
Voted Liberal etc.	*	1	—
Don't remember	—	2	4
Information refused	1	1	1
Abstained	7	7	8
Total	100	100	100

† Less than 0.5 per cent.

Table 5   *General Election Behaviour of 1960 Rest of Electorate*

	1959	1955	1951
	(%)	(%)	(%)
Voted Conservative	23	17	9
Voted Labour	26	31	37
Voted Liberal etc.	11	12	10
Don't remember	2	10	20
Information refused	14	15	15
Abstained	24	15	9
Total	100	100	100

electorate; almost 90 per cent of the 1959 Conservatives had voted Conservative in 1955; and almost 90 per cent of Labour supporters had voted Labour in 1955.

In Table 3 there is shown for those who supported the Conservatives in the 1960 survey their answers to a series of questions that asked them how they had voted in each of the three preceding General Elections (1959, 1955, 1951). Table 4 gives the answers of 1960 Labour supporters and Table 5 gives the answers of those who in 1960 supported neither of the two main parties.

From these tables it will be seen that:

(a) Among the Conservatives, the party that had grown in electoral popularity over the period (and therefore had probably attracted into its ranks former opponents and waverers), nearly three-quarters of the 1960 supporters were people who were Conservative voters three General Elections earlier.

(b) At the beginning of 1960 support for the Labour Party had probably reached its lowest point since 1945; it is therefore not surprising to find that at the time of the survey older Labour supporters were almost entirely people who had voted Labour throughout the 1950s and stood fast even after three successive electoral defeats.

(c) Even among the 1960 fence-sitters there was a high degree of long-term consistency in their detachment; probably half of them had not voted for either of the two major parties at any of the three elections.

Taken together the two features of British electoral behaviour so far discussed — the very high turnout and the high stability of party loyalties — might suggest that most British electors are keenly interested in politics, and that the supporters of the two main parties see the Conservative Party and Labour Party as sharply unequal in their ability to handle the nation's problems. Neither of these conclusions would appear to be justified.

The first of these possibilities was examined in a survey carried out by Research Services a few months after the last General Election. In the summer of 1960 we interviewed a quota sample of 1,500 persons aged 16 and over; this sample was selected so that in many of its main socio-demographic traits — age, sex, occupation, income, terminal education age, etc. — it matched the total adult population of England and Wales. The main purpose of the inquiry was to measure the extent to which people discussed the sort of material that normally appears in their newspapers and their interest in such material. At one point in the interview they were asked: 'How would you describe your interest in politics?' And their answers were recorded in terms of four levels of interest — very interested, interested, not really interested, not at all interested. Only 15 per cent of all respondents said they were very interested in politics.

Between various sections of the sample there were, however, considerable differences in the responses to this initial question. The proportion claiming to be very interested in politics was much higher among men than among women, higher among people aged 45 or more, among those who had received some higher education, and among middle-class adults. But even in these groups the proportion claiming to be very interested was quite small; it was usually below 20 per cent, and only among men did it rise to 21 per cent.

Within the sample of male respondents the other features of the pattern already described broadly repeated itself. Thus, among middle-class men aged 45 and over, and with some higher education, 22 per cent said they were very interested in politics; and among working-class men aged below 45, and with no higher education, only 13 per cent claimed to be very interested.

Table 6   *"How Would You Describe Your Interest in Politics?"*

	Total Sample	Men	Women	AGE Under 45	AGE 45 and Over	Middle Class	Working Class	TERMINAL EDUCATION AGE Under 16	TERMINAL EDUCATION AGE 16 or More
	(%)	(%)	(%)	(%)	(%)	(%)	(%)	(%)	(%)
Very interested	15	21	8	10	19	17	14	14	19
Interested	37	39	35	41	34	52	30	32	53
Not really interested	33	29	38	35	31	22	38	37	22
Not at all interested	15	11	19	14	16	9	18	17	6
Total	100	100	100	100	100	100	100	100	100
Number	1,496	762	734	736	760	472	1,024	1,147	349

Since a claimed high interest in politics is largely concentrated among men, we have in the rest of this account of the survey restricted ourselves to the replies from the men in the sample.

To assess the quality of claimed interest in politics, all respondents were asked about their attendance at meetings during the twelve months preceding the interview. Over the year, of all the men with little or no interest in politics, only 6 per cent had been to a political meeting. Among those 'interested in politics' as few as 1 in 6 had taken part in a political meeting at least once in twelve months. Only among the 21 per cent of men who claimed to be 'very interested in politics' was there anything like large-scale attendance; and even among this minority less than half claimed they had attended a political meeting during the year. (It should be remembered that the year covered included the 1959 General Election.)

The answers to one of the questions included in the survey carried out just before the 1959 General Election similarly suggest that it is not false modesty which leads so many people to disclaim any lively interest in politics. Here each respondent was asked to name three leaders of the Conservative Party, three leaders of the Labour Party and one leader of the Liberal Party.[1] Within these limitations only 30 per cent of all respondents gave at least five correct names, and 20 per cent were unable to provide even one correct name. Moreover, this total position was not the outcome of a mixture of complete knowledgeability among the 15 per cent of the sample who were party members and complete ignorance on the part of those who felt they did not even 'lean' towards one of the political parties. Knowledge and ignorance were well distributed among all sections of the electorate. Even among party members nearly 40 per cent could think of only three or even fewer correct names, and among those totally detached from party sympathies as many as 30 per cent were able to produce four or more correct names.

Table 7   *Able to Name Party Leaders*

	TYPE OF RESPONDENT				
	Party Member	Party Supporter	Lean towards a Party	Others	Total
7 correct*	9	5	4	3	5
6 correct	16	11	8	8	11
5 correct	18	13	17	6	14
4 correct	18	13	12	13	14
3 correct	11	13	12	13	12
2 correct	8	15	12	12	13
1 correct	9	13	11	11	11
None correct	11	17	24	34	20
	100	100	100	100	100

* Within the limits set, i.e. three from each major party and one Liberal; most people were defeated by the task of naming a Liberal leader.

It seems reasonable, in the light of this and much similar evidence, to conclude that our high turnout and persistent party loyalty do not stem from a widespread, deep and informed interest in politics. What about the other possibility — that they are the products of a sharp awareness on the part of the electorate that the two main parties differ substantially in their competence to manage the nation's affairs? Here again, the two surveys conducted round the 1959 General Election lead one to doubt this explanation.

In the 1960 inquiry respondents were given a card listing sixteen political

[1] The definition of a "leader" was generous; we accepted as correct the names of 19 Conservative Ministers, 18 Labour Front Benchers and 3 Liberal M.P.s.

ends and party traits and told: 'Here are some of the things that have been said about the two main political parties. Would you tell me, for each statement, whether you think it applies more to the Conservatives, or to the Labour Party? You may say that some of the statements apply to both, or do not apply to either party.' For four of the statements roughly half or more of the respondents indicated that they were not aware of any difference between the two parties (these were concerned with the prevention of a nuclear war, fair treatment for all races, a concern for the nation as a whole, and the maintenance of world peace). On a further eight issues between 33 per cent and 45 per cent of the respondents were unable to detect any difference between Conservatives and Labour. And on only four of the statements was there a clear-cut attribution of the goal to either Conservatives or Labour by at least two-thirds of the total sample. (These were: stands mainly for the middle class, would give more chances to the person who wants to better himself, would make the country more prosperous, and stands mainly for the working class. The first three were clearly recognized as marks of the Conservative Party, and the last was seen as overwhelmingly a Labour Party preoccupation). In short, a clear-cut partisan view of the two parties seems to be limited largely to class images and the opportunities for personal and general material advancement.

Naturally, the supporters of each party are able to discern a greater degree of conflict between the two parties, and this discrimination is greatest among those respondents who in 1960 supported the Labour Party — even after its three successive defeats. But even among those die-hards between 44 per cent and 55 per cent of them said they could see no difference in the competence of the two parties when handling seven out of sixteen listed traits and objectives. And these seven included such apparently important items as fair treatment for all races, concern for the nation as a whole, and the prevention of nuclear war. Indeed, these Labour stalwarts were able to discriminate sharply between the two parties on no more than three or four of the listed issues; three-quarters or more of them were able to identify one or other of the two parties as standing mainly for the working class, concerned to help the underdog, or ready to raise the standard of living of ordinary people. Usually they thought it was the Labour Party which distinctively had these interests at heart.

The Conservatives, thanks largely to the broadmindedness of those of its supporters with comparatively recent roots in the party, showed a greater readiness to attribute competence and good intentions to both parties when they came to consider the prevention of nuclear war and fair treatment for all races. On another six issues between 35 per cent and 46 per cent of them were unable to discriminate between the two parties. But, unlike Labour supporters, nearly all Conservatives claimed to be able to recognize a difference between the Conservative Party and the Labour Party when it came to finding a party which would make the country more prosperous, would satisfy the man with ideals, and would really respect British traditions.

Not surprisingly, it was among the 17 per cent of respondents who refused to support either main party that readiness to discriminate between Conservatives and Labour was lowest. In commenting on thirteen of the sixteen listed statements roughly 50 per cent or more of these fence-sitters said that either party would be equally competent or equally incompetent.

Table 8   *Political Ends: Proportion Saying "Applies to Both"*
(or to Neither and Don't Know)

Statement	All Respondents	Cons.	Supporters of Lab.	Rest
	(%)	(%)	(%)	(%)
Would really work to prevent nuclear war	63	67	52	74
Believes in fair treatments for all races and creeds	63	62	54	69
Would do most for world peace	49	46	49	63
Is out for the nation as a whole	49	39	54	68
Has a clear-cut policy	44	31	50	66
Would try to abolish class differences	42	43	36	50
Really respects British traditions	41	29	51	55
Would extend the Welfare services	39	44	31	38
Is out to help the underdog	37	42	22	50
Is most satisfying for the man with ideals	36	29	36	56
Would raise standard of living of ordinary people	35	35	26	53
Has united team of top leaders	33	20	44	48
Stands mainly for the middle class	31	32	26	41
Would give more chances to person who wants to better himself	31	27	28	53
Would make the country more prosperous	29	16	38	48
Stands mainly for the working class	19	24	8	27

Further evidence that a large part of the electorate are prepared to attribute good intentions and reasonable competence to both parties is provided by the findings of the 1959 pre-General Election survey. Informants were asked: 'Do you think the Conservative Party's policies would ever endanger the country's welfare?' Two-thirds said they thought they probably would not. Even among Labour supporters over half were of this opinion, and only 10 per cent were reasonably sure that Conservative policies were a potential danger to the nation's welfare.

Not quite the same high measure of forbearance was extended to the Labour Party when informants were asked: 'Do you think Labour Party policies

Table 9   *"Do You Think the Conservative Party's Policies Would Ever Endanger the Country's Welfare?"*

	Conservatives	Labour	Others	Total
	(%)	(%)	(%)	(%)
Probably would	2	10	6	6
Might	9	32	25	22
Probably wouldn't	87	52	57	66
Don't know	2	6	12	6
Total	100	100	100	100

would ever seriously endanger the country's welfare?' But even so, almost half the sample said they thought they would not. Even among Conservative supporters over a quarter thought the danger unlikely and only one-third considered the threat to be probable. These views are all the more striking when it is seen that over a quarter of Labour's supporters thought their Party's policies might seriously endanger the nation's welfare.

Table 10   *"Do You Think the Labour Party's Policies Would Ever Seriously Endanger the Country's Welfare?"*

	Conservatives	Labour	Others	Total
	(%)	(%)	(%)	(%)
Probably would	34	3	10	16
Might	37	24	34	31
Probably wouldn't	26	68	42	47
Don't know	3	5	14	6
Total	100	100	100	100

One remarkable feature of this unwillingness on the part of the 1959 electorate to translate party defeat into national disaster was the above-average magnanimity of working-class Labour supporters: 54 per cent felt that Conservative Party policies would probably not endanger the country's welfare. At the same time middle-class Conservatives failed to match this tolerance; only 24 per cent of these said that Labour policies constituted no probable threat to the nation's welfare. In other words, within the Labour Party middle-class deviants are slightly more fearful than others of Conservative policies; but within the Conservative Party the middle-class regulars are more suspicious than others of their opponent's policies. In other words, while mutual tolerance is generally quite high there seems to be a little more of it among working-class party supporters than there is among middle-class party supporters.

However, too much should not be made of this appearance of middle-class political truculence. A survey carried out by us in the summer of 1960 was specifically concerned with the intra-party groupings of middle-class people who were under 45 years of age and had a terminal education age of at least 16 years of age. After they had indicated the party they supported they were then asked to indicate their relative position within the party. Almost one-quarters of the Conservatives said they were on the left flank of their party

Table 11   *Location within Party. Middle Class under 45 Years of Age*

	Conservatives	Labour	Liberals
	(%)	(%)	(%)
Left	23	34	28
Centre	59	39	38
Right	18	27	34
Total	100	100	100

nd over a quarter of the Labour supporters considered themselves to be on the ight flank of their party. In each case the biggest single group chose for hemselves a central position.

It seems reasonable to conclude that normally there is comparatively little ension between the mass of supporters of the two main parties and that herefore voting stability and high turnout must spring from other causes.

The early-1960 survey throws some light on one of the main causes of oting stability. Respondents were asked how their parents voted before the var. The replies suggest that most people acquire their party loyalties by nheritance.

Of all the fathers described by informants, 32 per cent were known by their ffspring to have been Conservatives, 31 per cent Labour, 10 per cent Liberals,

Table 12   *Inter-Generation Voting Behaviour*

Respondents' Party Choice	FATHERS' PRE-WAR VOTING BEHAVIOUR				
	Conservative	Labour	Liberal	Not Known	Never Voted
	(%)	(%)	(%)	(%)	(%)
Conservative	71	28	36	48	44
Labour	15	61	24	31	44
Other*	14	11	40	21	12
Total	100	100	100	100	100

Includes Liberals, don't knows, and would abstain.

per cent had never voted, and of the remaining 22 per cent the present espondents said they had never known their fathers' political loyalties. Among he children of Conservative fathers, over 70 per cent are now Conservatives nd only 15 per cent support Labour. Among the children of Labour fathers, ver 60 per cent are now Labour supporters and only 28 per cent are Conservatives. Only the children of pre-war Liberals and the children of ecretive fathers received no clear-cut guidance on political thinking for the ost-war world. At present, just over one-quarter of them are completely etached from both the main parties, another 30 per cent vote Labour and 45 er cent are Conservatives. (It is possible that both these rootless groups are otential defectors from their present parties.)

While these figures show the considerable importance of parental sociali-ation in the acquisition of party loyalties they also make clear that the natching between generations is not complete. Rebels, especially in the ouseholds of Labour fathers, have appeared in the postwar years. The recent urvey among third-year students at four London colleges shows, for one small roup, the inner pattern of this breakaway movement. All the students in the urvey could be considered, because of the jobs they will take up after raduating, to be middle class. Not all of them, however, came from middle-lass homes. Of the 740 students of British nationality, 23 per cent in giving heir fathers' present occupation described them in these terms as working lass. This quarter of the students could therefore be regarded as having moved up the social scale. The relationship between fathers' and children's social class and politics is shown in Table 13. Of all the students with working-class parents, 65 per cent said they knew the political loyalties of their fathers; over half (55 per cent) of these fathers were described by their offspring as Labour supporters, but little more than two-fifths (43 per cent) of these children of working-class Labour-voting fathers currently support the Labour Party; another one-fifth support the Conservative Party. This inter generation move to the right is clearly associated with upward social mobility there is no rightward move of comparable dimensions among the children of middle-class Labour-voting fathers. In this group more than half (54 per cent) follow in father's Labour footsteps, and only one in six has become a Conservative.

Table 13   *Social Class and Inter-Generation Voting Behaviour: London University Students*

| Students' Party Ties | STUDENTS WITH MIDDLE-CLASS PARENTS WHO VOTE: | | | | STUDENTS WITH WORKING-CLASS PARENTS WHO VOTE: | | | |
	Cons. (%)	Lab. (%)	Lib. (%)	D.K. (%)	Cons. (%)	Lab. (%)	Lib. (%)	D.K. (%)
Conservative	52	16	18	32	43	20	33	35
Labour	15	54	22	22	5	43	17	22
Liberal	15	12	60	24	32	10	50	19
Other and D.K.	18	18	–	22	20	27	–	24
Total	100	100	100	100	100	100	100	100

It seems reasonable to conclude, therefore, that while current political loyalties have been mainly determined by parental socialization, complete repetition between the generations has been prevented largely by upward social mobility which has generated a net movement towards the Centre and the Right. . . .

15. The Political Ideas of English Party Activists

RICHARD ROSE

Professor Rose examines the hitherto largely untested but widely held impression that party activists, recruited from the presumably most highly ideological stratum of the electorate, are, as a rule, more extreme-minded and intransigent than either the voting public or the parliamentary party leadership. Through an analysis of resolutions submitted to national party conferences, he finds that, in Britain at least, ideological extremism is rather limited in both party organizations and that motives that induce individuals to become party activists are apparently by no means exclusively ideological, even in parties where ideology has traditionally played a large part.

If a democracy is to function successfully, the great mass of the population need instruments for communicating their views to political leaders. The chief channels for communication are parties and pressure groups. English politics provides much scope for study of these conduits, because both parties and pressure groups are highly organized and well articulated. Although the part played by party activists in policy formulation is only one small aspect of this network, the study of that part throws considerable light upon the interplay of parties and pressure groups, and challenges as well some prevailing notions about the policy demands of party activists.

Party activists in Britain have only comparatively recently been regarded as potentially capable of participating in discussions of public policy. Both the Conservatives and Liberals originated as small coteries of parliamentary notables who controlled, or were independent of rank-and-file party workers. Writing in 1908, A. Lawrence Lowell characterized the two party organizations as shams — the Liberals, with their formal devices for rank-and-file policy-making as an opaque sham, and the Conservatives as transparent shams.[1] He noted that in 1903 Conservative Party members were so deferential that when the Cabinet was split on tariff reform the annual membership conference "shrank from saying what it thought." Both Conservative and Liberal parties have maintained this aloofness from activists in matters of policy discussion up to the present day. The official report on Conservative Party re-organization

SOURCE: Reprinted by permission from *The American Political Science Review*, LVI June 1962), pp. 360–371.

A. L. Lowell, *The Government of England* (London, 1921 edition), Vol. I, pp. 578, 84. See also M. Ostrogorski, *Democracy and the Organization of Political Parties* (London, 1902), Vol. I, p. 161 ff.; J. L. Garvin, *The Life of Joseph Chamberlain* (London, 932), Vol. I, ch. 14; W. S. Churchill, *Lord Randolph Churchill* (London, 1906), esp. chs. 6–8.

prepared after the 1945 *debacle* noted that the size of the annual party conference made it "a demonstration of strength and enthusiasm" and made impossible "the more intimate circumstances necessary to thoughtful debate."[2] Since the farcical intervention of activists in policy-making at the 1958 Liberal Assembly, Jo Grimond has successfully emphasized the need to keep Liberal policy-making in the hands of a small circle.

The Labour Party, in theory and to some extent in practice, has always stood for participation by rank-and-file party members in policy-making. A current party pamphlet states: "The right to a voice in determining policy is important to any member . . . The individual member has a chance to use the machinery of the party to secure support for ideas on every aspect of party policy."[3] In recent years a harassed Labour leadership has begun to stress Robert T. McKenzie's thesis that it is unconstitutional for party members to make policy to which MPs are bound, because MPs must be responsible to those who elect them and not to that allegedly unrepresentative fraction who constitute active party members. The Labour leadership is reverting to the Burkean position maintained by many Conservatives, that an MP owes his constituency party supporters nothing more than his informed and independent judgment.[4] Except for Ralph Miliband, who has argued that the influence of the active Labour minority should not be reduced because of the apathy of the majority,[5] there is a consensus among students of British politics that party activists cannot and should not make party policy, or even influence it greatly.

It does not follow, however, that the views of party activists are of no interest. There are several reasons for analyzing them. First, activists may be mobilized to support a faction within the elite when there occurs what Michels treated as "The Struggle Among the Leadership Themselves."[6] Sometimes, a section of the counter-elite and of the activists appear to work together and respond to a common stimulus. Second, activists are a major channel of communication between MPs and party leaders and the electorate at large. Third, they are presumed to be the last stronghold of ideologists within the party system. Last but hardly least, there has never been any systematic study of the policy views of activists in Britain, although there has been no lack of generalizing on this subject.

Many students of political parties, most notably Duverger, have claimed that the views of activists differ significantly from those of most party voters; hence,

---

[2] *Final Report of the Committee on Party Organization* (National Union, London, 1949), p. 27.

[3] S. Barker, *How the Labour Party Works* (London, 1955), p. 6.

[4] See R. T. McKenzie, *British Political Parties* (London, 1955), esp. chs. 1, 10; *Report of the Fifty-Ninth Annual Conference of the Labour Party* (London, 1960), p. 159 ff., and Morgan Phillips, *Memorandum on the Constitution of the Labour Party* (London, 1960).

[5] "Party Democracy and Parliamentary Government," *Political Studies*, Vol. 6 (1958), pp. 170–74. Wilfrid Fienburgh, then research secretary of the Labour Party, implicitly took this position in "Put Policy on the Agenda," *Fabian Journal*, No. 6 (1952), pp. 25–27.

[6] *Political Parties* (Dover edition, New York, 1959), p. 164 ff. McKenzie ignores this phenomenon.

he description of an activist as a militant.[7] (American experience would
.uggest that many active party workers are far from being ideologically militant,
>ut this has not until recently been thought relevant to European politics.)
such leading writers on British politics as Bagehot, Lowell and McKenzie
iave also argued this with reference to Britain.[8] Leon Epstein has explained
he alleged extremist views of these activists as follows:

> The voluntary and amateur nature of these associations ensures that they
> attract zealots in the party cause, and particularly so at the local leadership
> level, where there are many routine political chores which only the devoted
> are likely to perform. Principles, not professional careers, are what matter
> here.[9]

Nigel Nicolson, the victim while a Conservative MP of a constituency associa-
ion which disowned him because of his centrist views, has argued that the
:xtremist outlook of activists threatens to endanger parliamentary government,
)ecause Parliament is losing power to Cabinet and Cabinet is dominated by
>arty. Nicolson claims that parliamentary leaders rightly see problems in terms
>f "the intrusive grey," whereas activists see things in black and white terms.
Political activity only intensifies their militant beliefs. Hence, in the constitu-
:ncies, warfare between the parties is "a grim reality."[10]

To use the terminology of Martin Lipset in *Political Man*, the influence of
ictivists in party policy-making is said to give heavy emphasis to ideological
:leavage without a compensating statement of consensus, whereas both the
heory and practice of British government value consensus much more than
:leavage. It is theoretically possible that constituency parties may act as a
;afety valve through which extremist pressures escape, but this argument has
iot been advanced. It is the crux of Nicolson's case that the steam being
;enerated by extreme-minded activists threatens to scald the engine drivers of
lemocracy and endanger all the passengers.

I

Party activists have the same formal method of influencing policy in both
>arties — sending resolutions to the annual party conferences.[11] This is not

---

[7] *Political Parties* (London, 1954), p. 101 ff. *Cf.* A. Leiserson, *Parties and Politics* (New
York, 1958), pp. 191, 274.
[8] Bagehot, quoted in N. Nicolson, *People and Parliament* (London, 1958), p. 166; A. L.
Lowell, *Public Opinion and Popular Government* (New York, 1914), p. 92; R. T.
McKenzie, *British Political Parties* (London, 1955), pp. 196–7, 506. See also T. E. M.
McKitterick, "The Membership of the [Labour] Party," *Political Quarterly*, Vol. 31
(1960), p. 316 ff.
[9] "British MPs and Their Local Parties: The Suez Case," *American Political Science
Review*, Vol. 54 (1960), p. 385. Epstein wrongly suggests that rank-and-file extremism
strengthens the position of party leaders. This is because he generalizes from the extremist
position of the leadership on Suez; the instance is, however, exceptional.
[10] N. Nicolson, *People and Parliament* (London, 1958), p. 169. His fear is not new.
Cf. Ostrogorski, *op. cit.*, Vol. I, p. 493 ff.
[11] See S. Barker, *How the Labour Party Works* (London, 1955), p. 7 ff.; *Party Organization* (Conservative & Unionist Central Office, London, 1961), p. 23 ff.; R. T. McKenzie,
British Political Parties (London, 1955), pp. 231–58, 532–46.

sufficient proof of policy concern, but it is almost certainly a necessary condition which activists must meet if they wish their views to be considered by the national party leadership. The other major channel — lobbying one's MP — is informal and indirect. Furthermore, half the constituencies have an MP from the opposition party. There are no inhibitions surrounding conference resolutions. If anything, there is an expectation that resolutions will be used by extremists to voice complaints to and about leaders.

The circumstances in which policy resolutions are drafted, debated, and approved differ widely from constituency to constituency. Resolutions are likely to originate in committee meetings of local parties; alternatively, suggestions or amendments may be made at party meetings, where attendance will invariably be only a small fraction of a constituency party's membership, and an extremely small fraction of the party vote in the constituency.[12] Thus, the method and setting facilitate domination by a small group determined to foster a particular set of ideas. The extent to which policy is discussed in local parties appears to vary considerably.[13] Motives for tabling resolutions may be mixed and several. Expressions of opinion may spontaneously originate within the caucus from concern with an immediate event in the news. MPs or candidates may stimulate resolutions favouring views they wish to advance. Sometimes resolutions are presented in efforts to gain publicity, either for the local party or for the person who may be chosen to move it in an auditorium crowded with delegates.

The resolutions analyzed herein are those submitted to Conservative and Labour annual party conferences from 1955 to 1960 inclusive. No list of resolutions was published for the cancelled 1959 Conservative conference. The omission of one year's total from the sample is offset by the fact that there is no limit on the number of resolutions which a Conservative constituency may forward. In the Labour Party, a constituency normally may send only one resolution, and occasionally an amendment. Because of alterations to constituency boundaries prior to the 1955 election, the analysis could not be accurately carried further back in time.

Each resolution has been assigned to one of four categories — Right, Left, Partisan, or Non-Partisan. Resolutions in the first three categories contain a distinctive element of a partisan ideology; those in the last tend to reflect pressure group concerns or general cultural values not integrally a part of party ideology. The definitions follow, with examples taken from conference programs.

Partisan: Enunciation of an agreed party policy which is opposed to that of the other party and which has an ideological basis.

---

[12] *Cf.* reports of low participation by trade unionists in discussions of union policy, in B. C. Roberts, *Trade Union Government and Administration in Great Britain* (London, 1956), p. 95 ff.; M. Harrison, *Trade Unions and the Labour Party Since 1945* (London, 1960), ch. 3.

[13] *Cf.* D. V. Donnison and D. E. G. Plowman, "The Functions of Local Labour Parties," *Political Studies,* Vol. 2 (1954), p. 156 ff.; A. H. Birch, *Small-Town Politics* (Oxford, 1959), p. 44 ff.

Conservative example: "That this Conference congratulates the Government on its economic policy, which has resulted in full employment, stable prices and the highest standard of living in our history, but urges the removal of the many impediments still hindering the spread of ownership throughout the community." (No. 177, 1960)

Other favored Conservative themes include: requests for maximum economy in public expenditure, denunciation of further nationalization, protection of property rights in land compulsorily acquired by the state, support for the Commonwealth, and approval of the tripartite division of secondary education.

Labour example: "This Conference believes that a substantial measure of public ownership is essential for the nation's well-being. It therefore instructs the NEC to prepare for presentation to the 1961 Annual Conference a practical programme of public ownership for the next Labour Government, based on the needs of the economy, workers and consumers' interests." (No. 203, 1960)

Labour resolutions in this category often deal with: world disarmament through the United Nations, support for colonial freedom and attacks upon the Conservative colonial policy, attacks upon advertising, the need for economic planning and controls, demands for an end to profiteering in land prices and support for a comprehensive secondary education system.

Non-partisan: Enunciation of a policy which is not the subject of controversy along party lines, either because it reflects the views of pressure groups working within both parties or because it is generally regarded as desirable within the culture. A non-partisan resolution is not necessarily non-political.

Conservative example: "That this Conference is of the opinion that in view of the statement made at the time of the General Election that old age pensioners were to share in the prosperity of the country, an increase in their pensions should now be made." (No. 126, 1960)

Other popular themes for non-party resolutions at Conservative conferences include: assistance for particular industries or for agriculture, calls for more teachers and smaller class sizes, demands for more roads and safer roads, tax relief for homeowners, changes to strengthen local government in its work, changes in electoral law to simplify the job of party workers, and improvements in party organization.[14]

Labour example: "This Conference urges the Government to grant an immediate increase for old age pensioners." (No. 344, 1960)

Among a welter of Labour themes that were basically non-ideological were: assistance for shipbuilding, coal, other industries and for agriculture, calls for more teachers and smaller class sizes, requests for more hospitals and removal of alleged anomalies in welfare services, changes to strengthen local govern-

---

[14] Resolutions dealing with the mechanics of party organization have been scored non-partisan because they show bureaucratic rather than ideological concerns. Interestingly, a number of resolutions ostensibly dealing with party principles are also non-ideological. They simply stress the need for unity on principle, or promoting principles, without any indication of which particular principles (if any) should be emphasized.

ment in its work, more roads and safer roads, better railway services, and relief of the housing shortage and need for slum clearance.

Right-wing Conservative: A policy statement which calls for widening the gap between the two parties through adoption of a reactionary variant of party policy.

Example: "That in the opinion of this Conference the monopoly of omnibus transport in large cities and towns should be abolished and that responsible operators be allowed to compete, thereby giving the public a better service." (No. 48, 1960)

Right-wing Conservatives concentrate upon: pleas for weakening taxes which tend to redistribute income, requests for laws to curb trade unions and strikers, demands for a return to flogging and heavy reliance upon capital punishment to fight crime, the absolute reduction of government spending and services, the denationalization of various industries, and reducing benefits available through welfare services.

Left-wing Labour: A statement calling for a radical transformation of the domestic mixed economy welfare state, or of the existing system of international relations, in order to make the breakthrough to a Socialist society. Such statements are usually out of harmony with the declared policy of the leadership.

Example: "This Conference instructs the National Executive Committee to appoint a sub-committee to investigate and report to the 1961 Annual Conference the most practical way in which all the means of production, distribution and exchange can be brought under public ownership, ensuring that the workers and consumers alike can participate in the management of each industry." (No. 206, 1960)

Under this heading come resolutions: asking for unilateral nuclear disarmament, demanding large-scale extension of nationalization and/or workers' control, reaffirming Socialist principles in terms of root-and-branch rejection of a capitalist-influenced society, and those calling for compulsory closure of the public boarding schools.

Left-wing Conservative/Right-wing Labour: Statements of policy which deviate so markedly from conference policy that they tend to be in harmony with the policies of the opposing party.

Conservative example: "That this Conference requests the Minister of Housing and Local Government to examine the position of the tenants of furnished accommodation with a view to introducing legislation to guarantee an adequate standard of furnishings and fittings, and a reasonable security of tenure." (No. 331, 1960)

Labour example: "This Conference moves that the Labour Party, being a social and democratic movement, seeks to determine by means of a social-political survey, such questions as the image of the party in the minds of the electorate, their social habits and background, and their wishes concerning the fundamental issues of the day, with the aim of studying the results of such an enquiry and deciding to what extent they should influence future party policy." (No. 424, 1960)

The number of these resolutions is so few that one cannot generalize much. In the Conservative Party, left-wing resolutions seemed to come either from constituency parties in working-class areas, which voiced Labour-inclined views on social services and economic policy, or from constituencies where progressive Conservatives had some sympathies with Labour's overseas policy. Labour deviation seemed largely motivated by a desire to repudiate traditional Socialist ideology, with an occasional repudiation resulting in virtual alignment with Conservative positions.

Any system of categorizing data is open to criticism. The headings here employed have been designed to group together views which signify, either explicitly or by their nuance, association with one or another faction within the two parties. This is the standard used by many speakers on resolutions at party conferences, who discuss them in terms of left/right tendencies, and the same standard is characteristically employed in descriptions of conference debates by journalists.

II

The analysis immediately reveals that the description of local parties as a force constantly pressing extremist views upon national party leaders is false. The total proportion of ideological (*i.e.*, left-wing, right-wing and partisan) resolutions is 54 per cent; those which are nonideological constitute 46 per cent of the total (Table 1A). In other words, constituency parties are nearly as apt

Table 1A   *Total Scores for All Constituency Resolutions*

Type	No.	%
Extremist (Right, Con.; Left, Lab.)	1398	30
Partisan (Con. and Lab.)	1013	22
Misplaced Partisanship (Left, Con.; Right, Lab.)	97	2
Non-Partisan (Con. and Lab.)	2090	46
Totals	4598	100

to be voicing views derived from general cultural values or from interest group links as they are to voice those clearly associated with a partisan ideology.

When the scores are analyzed according to parties, one finds that the Conservatives are more inclined to press non-partisan resolutions on their leaders than are Labour constituencies. But the differences are not great and Labour parties do not show strong partisanship; 42 per cent of their resolutions are non-partisan, compared with 50 per cent of Conservative ones (Table 1B, 1C). The variation in the number and orientation of resolutions from year to year appears to reflect the temper of the times. A party's adversity would seem to stimulate extremist views.

An analysis of the number of resolutions submitted by individual constituency parties reveals the existence of wide variations in concern with policy. Approximately one-third of Conservative constituency parties did not present a single resolution in the five-year period studied; only 26 per cent forwarded

Table 1B   *Total Scores of Conservative Constituency Resolutions**

Year	Right	Partisan	Left	Non-Partisan	Total
1955	50	52	17	173	292
1956	137	109	10	137	393
1957	130	60	6	216	412
1958	90	141	12	204	447
1959	(No resolutions published)				
1960	98	41	17	259	415
Totals — No.	505	403	62	989	1959
Per Cent	26	21	3	50	100

* This table, like 1A and 5A, includes resolutions filed by Welsh constituency parties and minor federated bodies, as well as those from English parties. Welsh resolutions are omitted from all other calculations because the party system there is not quite the same as in England; minor parties are twice as strong. The federated bodies are omitted because they are not comparable to Labour ones. Omitted groups have similar scores to those fully analysed. Scotland and Northern Ireland are not included in any Conservative tabulations, because these parties are separate and have their own conferences.

Table 1C   *Total Scores of Labour Constituency Resolutions**

Year	Left	Partisan	Right	Non-Partisan	Total
1955	123	98	5	198	424
1956	109	119	5	169	402
1957	127	140	4	172	443
1958	173	89	6	160	428
1959	152	73	3	186	414
1960	209	91	12	216	528
Totals — No.	893	610	35	1101	2639
Per Cent	34	23	1	42	100

* This table, like 1A and 5B, includes resolutions from Welsh and Scottish constituency parties, and from trade unions and other affiliated bodies. There is no significant variation in scores as between those groups fully analysed and those omitted elsewhere.

an average of one resolution or more a year (Table 2A). This disinterest in pressing policy views cannot be attributed to poor party organization, because virtually all English Conservative constituencies are sufficiently well organized to have a full-time party agent. It may well be related to the deferential relationship which exists, socially as well as politically, between party leaders and members. Balfour is reported to have said that he would as soon take orders from his valet as from a Conservative Party annual conference.[15] Perhaps some party members would equally regard it as wrong to depart from the obligations of their station in life.

In the Labour Party, concern with matters of policy is more widely diffused, as one might expect from a party which has always boasted of its ideological

[15] Quoted in R. T. McKenzie, *British Political Parties* (London, 1955), p. 82. See also Earl Balfour, *Chapters of Autobiography* (London, 1930), p. 158 ff.

Table 2A *Frequency Distribution of Resolutions Filed by Conservative Constituency Parties*

Number of Resolutions	Number of Parties*	% of All Parties	Cumulative Percentage†
0	165	32	32
1	90	18	50
2	49	10	60
3	42	8	68
4	29	6	74
5	23	5	79
6	22	4	83
7	14	3	86
8	15	3	89
9	12	2	91
10	7	1	92
11–20	33	6	98
21–30	4	0.8	98.8
31–40	3	0.6	99.4
46	1	0.2	99.6

* Bolton West and Huddersfield West, are omitted from this and subsequent calculations because they do not nominate parliamentary candidates, standing aside in favour of the Liberals.

† Percentages do not add up to 100 because of rounding off.

Table 2B *Frequency Distribution of Resolutions Filed by Labour Constituency Parties*

Number of Resolutions	Number of Parties	% of All Parties	Cumulative Percentage*
0	28	6	6
1	48	9	15
2	62	12	27
3	72	14	41
4	94	18	59
5	102	20	79
6	96	19	98
7	7	1.4	99.4
8	2	0.4	99.8

* Percentages do not add up to 100 because of rounding off.

basis. The gap between individual constituency parties is not so great, because of the limit of one resolution and one amendment for each party at each conference. (Table 2B) Although the Labour Party has more constituencies which will sometimes file a resolution, there is little difference in terms of heavy activity, insofar as different regulations permit of comparison. Among Conservative constituencies, 74 per cent file resolutions less than once a year on average; in the Labour Party, the proportion is 79 per cent.

Concern with questions of policy is not the same as partisanship. In order to isolate those constituencies which reflected particularly strong partisanship, the groups were divided into four categories, according to the extent to which they varied from the average party score. In the Conservative table, partisan views are those scored right or partisan; in the Labour table, those scored left or partisan. From this we find (Tables 3A, 3B) that the proportion of

Table 3A   *Partisanship in Conservative Constituency Parties**

Category	Number	Per Cent
No Partisan Resolutions	164	35
Low (1–34%) Partisanship	113	24
Average (35–64%) Partisanship	120	26
High (65% or more) Partisanship	71	15

* Constituencies which submitted only one resolution in the period, and that one partisan, have been omitted, because this was regarded as insufficient evidence for categorization.

Table 3B   *Partisanship in Labour Constituency Parties**

Category	Number	Per Cent
No Partisan Resolutions	88	18
Low (12.5–40%) Partisanship	83	17
Average (41–75%) Partisanship†	208	42
High (above 75%) Partisanship	113	23

* Constituencies presenting only one resolution, and that partisan, have been omitted from this table.
† This category is not as large as it appears, for only seven parties could have scored between 41–49.9%.

constituency parties which regularly press partisan views is less than one-quarter in each party. There is a skewed distribution among the Conservatives, for 59 per cent of the constituencies show less than average partisanship. Absence of partisanship does not, of course, mean absence of ideological commitments; it is evidence that parties so labeled are little interested in advocating ideological views. There is more interest in proclaiming partisan views in the Labour parties.

The incidence of ideological partisanship is certainly no cause for concern; few could criticize party activists for pressing party policy upon their leaders, when the leaders accept the ideas, as well as many voters. Ideological extremism is a far greater force for social cleavage, but it is extremely limited in both parties. (Tables 4A, 4B) Even though the definition of high extremism in the Conservative Party does not require a consistency to express extremist views as much as half the time, only 11 per cent qualify for that appellation — and only 6 per cent are both extremist and quite active in pressing views. Although more Labour constituencies are extremist than Conservative, they form only 18 per cent of the total. The median Labour constituency will only forward

Table 4A   *Extremism in Conservative Parties**

Category	Number	Per Cent
No Extremist Resolutions	314	66
Low (1–16.5%) Extremism	20	4
Average (16.6–37.4%) Extremism	92	19
High Extremism (37.5% or more)	52†	11

* Those constituencies submitting one extremist resolution and filing only one or two in the period are omitted.
† Consists of 24 parties submitting up to 5 resolutions each in the period and 28 parties submitting more than 5 resolutions each in the period.

Table 4B   *Extremism in Labour Parties**

Category	Number	Per Cent
No Extremist Resolutions	191	38
Low Extremism (20% or less)	47	9
Average (25–50%) Extremism	172	35
High (above 50%) Extremism	87	18

* Those constituencies submitting only one resolution, and that extremist, have not been categorized.

Table 5A   *Topics for Conservative Resolutions*

Topic	Right	Partisan	Left	Non-Partisan	Total
Economic Affairs	121	142	28	64	355
Housing	22	35	4	107	168
Industrial Relations	73	37	7	16	133
Party Organization	5	8	3	112	128
Education	33	18	2	72	125
Pensions	6	2	–	104	112
Taxes	56	17	–	29	102
Compulsory Purchase	16	79	–	4	99
Crime	63	13	4	11	91
Transportation	5	1	–	82	88
Election Law	–	–	–	85	85
Commonwealth, Colonies	31	14	4	7	56
Local Government	–	–	–	51	51
Welfare Services	21	–	–	29	50
Agriculture	5	–	–	42	47
Foreign Policy	6	16	5	5	32
Defence	1	18	2	7	28
Immigration	21	–	–	–	21
Party Principles	9	2	–	6	17
Miscellaneous	11	1	3	156	171

one extremist resolution in a six-year period, and the median Conservative one will not even forward a single extremist resolution in a five-year period.

The foregoing tables indicate that party workers on opposite sides of the political fence are not so partisan as electoral contests suggest, and not so extremist as some theorists suggest. A breakdown of resolutions by subject matter and by policy orientation provides a list of areas of common agreement within both parties (Tables 5A, 5B). A notable feature of Conservative

Table 5B   *Topics for Labour Resolutions*

Topic	Left	Partisan	Right	Non-Partisan	Total
Foreign Policy, Defence	594	145	14	20	773
Economic Affairs	117	141	10	188	456
Housing and Land	10	85	–	80	175
Party Organization	14	4	1	130	148
Pensions	2	1	–	143	146
Welfare Services	7	31	–	94	132
Education	17	19	–	64	100
Commonwealth, Colonies	8	82	3	1	94
Local Government	7	43	–	44	94
Socialist Principles	57	15	2	5	79
Transportation	4	3	–	56	63
Party Unity	18	2	1	31	52
Industrial Relations	6	13	–	–	19
Miscellaneous	32	26	4	245	306

resolutions is concentration upon domestic issues, notwithstanding the importance of international affairs to the government and to the electorate. Only 3 per cent of resolutions concerned foreign policy and defence questions, compared to 29 per cent in the Labour Party. The latter devotes less attention to politically important domestic questions. The virtual absence in both parties of expressions on highly explosive racial, religious and constitutional questions should not be overlooked.

Analysis by topics suggests that the partisanship and extremism of party activists is not so strong in several fields as the pull of interest group or general cultural standards.[16] In four areas of public concern — education, welfare services, transport and pensions — partisan standards are applied less than half the time by activists in both parties. When facing these questions they may ask for 'more schools' or 'higher pensions'; this is a cry of beneficiaries and benefactors, not of ideologues. This non-party emphasis is the more striking because there are clear ideological differences between the parties on education, welfare and transport. For instance, although the method of organizing secondary education is a point of sharp difference between the parties and affects the whole electorate, 64 per cent of Labour resolutions and 56 per cent

[16] Cf. S. H. Beer, "Pressure Groups and Parties in Britain," *American Political Science Review*, Vol. 50 (1956), pp. 1–23.

of Conservative ones steer clear of all partisan controversy on education. The proportion of ideological resolutions rises in areas of economic policy, where interest group and ideological standards are likely to be the same for most activists; partisan ideology is thus intensified. For instance, all of the 19 Labour resolutions on industrial relations were partisan, and only 12 per cent of the 133 Conservative resolutions on this topic were nonpartisan.

Some activists appear more concerned with the mechanics of party organization than with party policy. This shows in Conservative resolutions on party structure and on election law, and in organizational resolutions in the Labour Party, and resolutions asking for party unity — without any sign of preference concerning the program upon which unity should be based.

III

Examination of conference resolutions has shown that constituency parties differ considerably in their political attitudes. The question is then raised: Do they differ in relation to other measurable social or political factors? Unfortunately, the data available for cross tabulation is strictly limited,[17] but sufficient exists to test several important hypotheses.

One hypothesis concerns the relationship between party strength and attitudes of activists. It has been argued[18] that in areas where the strength of both parties is nearly equal, policies will tend to converge. In safe seats, extremist policies may be more readily found. The most important index of party strength is the margin by which a constituency is won or lost at the general election. A safe seat may conveniently be defined as one in which the winner had a majority of more than 10 per cent; a marginal seat as one in which the majority is less than that; and a hopeless seat as one in which a candidate lost by more than 10 per cent.[19] Nearly 85 per cent of English seats were either safe, marginal or hopeless at both the 1955 and 1959 elections. In what follows only these three major groups are discussed, because the numbers in the others are so small as to be of negligible significance. Safe Labour seats may be assumed to be heavily working-class; safe Conservative seats are likely to be disproportionately middle-class, though manual workers may still form a numerical majority in the constituency. It is probable that these differences in turn are reflected in the composition of party activists in different areas, although there is no conclusive evidence on this point.

The analysis shows no relation between partisanship in policy outlook and safety of seat in Conservative constituencies, and only a limited relationship in the Labour Party. (Tables 6A, 6B) In both parties there is a clear but strictly limited relationship between ideological extremism and electoral sup-

---

[17] For instance, census data cannot be related to parliamentary constituencies because of boundary differences.

[18] E.g., Sir Ivor Jennings, *The Queen's Government* (Harmondsworth, 1960), pp. 60–61.

[19] On electoral swing and margins of victory, see D. E. Butler, *The British General Election of 1955* (London, 1955), p. 202 ff.; D. E. Butler and Richard Rose, *The British General Election of 1959* (London, 1960), p. 236.

Table 6A   Partisanship, Extremism and Electoral Support for
Conservative Constituency Parties

Category	Number of Seats	Total Resolutions	% Partisan	% Extreme
Safe	213	788	48.4	29.3
Marginal	123	512	49.8	25.0
Hopeless	110	193	49.7	20.2

Table 6B   Partisanship, Extremism and Electoral Support for
Labour Constituency Parties

Category	Number of Seats	Total Resolutions	% Partisan	% Extreme
Safe	110	383	50.6	28.2
Marginal	123	462	55.2	32.7
Hopeless	217	829	60.0	37.4

port. In the Conservative Party, safe seats display on average 9.1 per cent more extremist resolutions than hopeless seats. In the Labour Party, hopeless seats adopt 9.2 per cent more extremist resolutions than safe seats. A further check was made to test this finding because of its importance. Constituency parties were divided according to degrees of partisanship and extremism, as in Tables 3A–B, 4A–B, to see whether each group had a fair cross-section of parties with strong, medium and weak electoral support. This was the case.

In both parties the variation between these two factors was of the order of one resolution in ten. But it takes a Conservative constituency party on average about 14 years to submit ten resolutions, and a Labour party about 12 years. The major conclusion must be that policy views are randomly distributed among constituency parties without regard to their electoral strength, for the statistical differences are of negligible political significance. One may note but hardly stress that parties in the most markedly middle-class areas are slightly more extremist on both sides than in working-class areas.

The author began his investigation with the hypothesis that the smaller a constituency party's membership, the higher the incidence of extremism. This was based upon the assumption that the number of extremist party supporters is very small, and that they could more easily dominate a small party. This hypothesis could only be tested for the Labour Party. There are 140 English parties which affiliate to headquarters on the minimum membership of 800; the extremism score for this group averaged 36 per cent. For the 61 parties with above average memberships ranging from 2,000 to 3,000, the extremism score averaged 34 per cent; for the 35 parties reporting membership above 3,000, the figure was 30 per cent. Similarly, parties with high extremism scores average 22 party members for every 1,000 electors, compared to a figure of 26 for those with average scores, and 25 for those with no extremist resolutions. The differences are hardly of a size to lend much support to the hypothesis.

Constituency parties may also seek to influence policy by pressing MPs or prospective candidates to act as spokesmen for the local party caucus. Candidates are selected by small groups representing less than 1 per cent of the electorate, and these nominations cannot be effectively challenged. In a normal election, nomination is tantamount to election in at least three-quarters of the constituencies; nomination is virtually tantamount to election for life in upwards of half the constituencies. Most students of British politics have commented upon the failure of constituency parties to exercise their considerable potential powers over candidates in such a way as to produce MPs with views like their own.[20] This generalization needs testing by reference to extremism scores because these writers have usually assumed that constituency selection committees are dominated by extremists. The wide range of opinion within both parliamentary parties might reflect an absence of policy concern in the selection process — or it might reflect a tendency for constituency parties to adopt candidates with views compatible with their own.

The emergence of unilateral nuclear disarmament as a major factional issue within the Labour Party provides one test for the coincidence between extremism in candidates and in parties. We find that there is some relationship between extremism in a constituency party and a candidate who is extreme on this issue. Parties showing high extremism constitute 18 per cent of all local parties, but 29 per cent of those nominating unilateralist candidates. Unilateralist candidates are least likely to be found where extremism is low or non-existent (Table 7). Like many statistical findings, this one is only

Table 7   *Extremism and the Nomination of Unilateralist Candidates by Constituency Labour Parties*

Category*	Number of Candidates	Number Unilateralist	Per Cent Unilateralist
No Extremism	191	14	7
Low Extremism	47	5	11
Average Extremism	172	31	18
High Extremism	87	20	23
Totals	497	70	14

* Constituency parties submitting only one resolution, and that one extremist, have not been categorized.

important if it is an indication of a trend. Further checks showed no tendency for unilateralist candidates to be nominated particularly for hopeless seats, nor were they especially favoured in the adoption of new candidates. Counterbalancing this absence of association was the tendency of constituencies with trade union sponsored candidates to score below average on extremism. Of 102 constituencies categorized, only 5 per cent were extremist, and 55 per cent had submitted no extremist resolutions in the period.

A similarly meaningful issue was not available for testing Conservative MPs. A rundown of the 16 Conservative MPs who took extremist positions on

[20] See especially John Biffen, "The Constituency Leaders," *Crossbow*, Vol. 4, No. 13 (1960), p. 30.

the Suez affair showed that two-thirds of their constituency parties scored below average on extremism. A check was made on Conservative parties which had Privy Councillors as MPs; it was assumed that the responsibility of these MPs, and their closer identification with generally moderate government policies, would damp down party extremism. In fact, the distribution of extremism scores among the 46 parties categorized was virtually identical with the distribution for all Conservative constituency parties. The most significant relationship found had on the face of it no connection with policy. It was that safe Conservative seats choose 84 per cent of their candidates from those with expensive public school educations, and only 31 per cent of the time take men with local connections. In hopeless seats, only 44 per cent have been at public schools, and 60 per cent of candidates have local connections. Marginal seats fall between these two groups. (No such pattern exists in the Labour Party.) One might speculate that the return of members of a national social-political elite by safe constituencies tends to increase the independence of MPs from constituency parties, for such persons are more likely to be independently minded, or influenced by a national peer group, than to submit to pressure from lower status activists.

IV

The fundamental conclusion which arises from this study is that attitudes on questions of policy are randomly distributed among constituency parties and, it may be tentatively assumed, among party activists as well. One cause of the diversity would appear to be the plurality of motives leading individuals to become active in party politics, together with the plurality of functions which local parties may perform.[21] The following list of motives is not exhaustive, nor is any particular one meant to exclude the operation of others within the same individual.

Motives for Volunteer Political Work

A. Overtly political
  — desire to advance party program
  — desire to modify party program to bring it more into line with one's own ideological beliefs
  — desire to modify party program to bring it more into line with the program of one's interest group
  — local government concerns
  — sense of civic duty
  — *ex officio* involvement — *e.g.*, as trade union official.
B. Non-political
  — occupational careerism

---

[21] A. Leiserson, *Parties and Politics* (New York, 1958), is notable for the allowance he makes for diversity. See also Robert E. Lane, *Political Life* (Glencoe, 1959), for much evidence on motives for political participation.

— status seeking
— gratification of desire for power
— pleasure from group activities
— pleasure from a 'sporting' contest
— friendship with active party workers.

The functions which constituency parties fulfill are also numerous. Some have a bearing on national party policy, but others do not:

Functions of English Constituency Parties

— propagate national party policy
— advise upon national party policy
— organize and conduct election contests
— nominate parliamentary candidates
— manage local government affairs
— act as pressure group for local interests
— provide social facilities for the community
— finance and maintain local party office.

An immediate consequence of this diversity is the flexibility which it gives to party leaders. At annual party conferences leaders are not faced with a mass of extreme-minded activists, demanding the adoption of socially divisive policies as the price of continuing to do menial work.[22] Opposition comes from only a fraction of the rank-and-file. Another portion is likely to support the leadership and a significant group may have no clear views, or even interest, in questions of party policy. In such circumstances support of the rank-and-file assembly may be gained simply by giving a clear policy lead. Lacking firm anchorage in an ideological position, constituency parties may be willing to trust their leaders wherever they lead. The pressure from above, the effect as it were of the gardener's lawnmower upon the grass roots activists, is considerable. The classic illustration occurred when the Conservative government was able to keep the party virtually united behind it when it unexpectedly attacked Egypt, and again when it abruptly accepted a cease-fire there in 1956. This flexibility is less in the Labour Party; a small contributing factor is the greater attachment which activists have to ideological standards.

Robert T. McKenzie has suggested that representative democracy presupposes a near identity in views between persons at different levels in parties, and half-suggested that democratic parties should have views tending towards identity.[23] Hence, his polemics against the participation of alleged extreme-

---

[22] Some British politicians still regard local party organizations with the respect they received in the days of open voting and bribery. The Nuffield studies find no evidence to support this. See most recently D. E. Butler and R. Rose, *The British General Election of 1959* (London, 1960), pp. 143, 232 ff.

[23] See especially "Parties, Pressure Groups and the British Political Process," *Political Quarterly*, Vol. 29, No. 1 (1958), p. 12 f.; and "The 'Political Activists' and Some Problems of 'Inner Party' Democracy in Britain" (mimeo, International Political Science Association, Paris, 1961), p. 5 ff.

minded activists in party policy-making. But on the basis of their resolutions, constituency parties do not seem to be pulling the parties apart. While recognizing the simplifications involved, one might consider party differences as being ranked on a scale from 0 to 100, with 0 being extreme right-wing and 100 being left-wing extremism. Simple consensus based upon an identity of views within and between parties would occur if all opinion rested at 50; more realistically, consensus would result if the center of gravity of opinion [24] within both parties was at 50. But a situation of balanced disagreement would operate if one of the parties centered at 60 and the other at 40, assuming a normal distribution frequency. An imbalance would result only if one party tended towards the center while the other balanced near an extreme. Balance, of course, is not a good in itself. Theoretically, a balance would occur if one party rested at 90 and another at 10. Furthermore, balance could produce stagnation when a radical shift in one direction was required by objective social circumstances. If we distribute resolutions along such an axis, we see that much of the weight of constituency views is closer to the center than to the extremes. The leftward bias is largely the result of the greater frequency of Labour resolutions. When a correction is made for differences in expressing views as between the parties, the point of balance turns out to be three per cent to the left of center.

Table 8   *Distribution of the Policy Views of Activists**

Scale	0 Right Conservative	25 Partisan Conservative	50 Non- Partisan	75 Partisan Labour	100 Left Labour
Number of Resolutions	505	438	2090	672	893
Per Cent of Resolutions	11	10	45	15	19

* Resolutions showing misplaced partisanship are assigned to the partisanship category for the other party.

There has been no systematic investigation of political attitudes in an effort to find out what differences, if any, exist between voters, activists, MPs, and leaders in parties. There is evidence to indicate that the spread of opinion is wide at all levels of both parties. For instance, a 1959 national survey found that 45 per cent of Conservative sympathizers accepted the *status quo* in the nationalized industries, and 40 per cent wished to denationalize one or more industries. In addition, 42 per cent of Labour sympathizers were opposed to further nationalization, whereas 36 per cent supported it.[25] In 1960, when 34

---

[24] Cf. D. E. Butler, "The Paradox of Party Difference," *American Behavioral Scientist,* IV:3 (1960), pp. 3–5, where the concept of centers of party gravity is developed.

[25] See D. E. Butler and R. Rose, *The British General Election of 1959* (London, 1960), p. 244, and also p. 71. The opinion surveys regularly reported in the monthly *Gallup Political Index* (London) by the British Institute of Public Opinion, and by Mark Abrams, in M. Abrams and R. Rose, *Must Labour Lose?* (Harmondsworth, 1960), also bear out the point that party sympathizers are divided into partisans, extremists, deviants and indifferents on almost all issues. Cf. also S. E. Finer, H. Berrington and D. Bartholomew, *Backbench Opinion in the House of Commons 1955–59* (London, 1961).

per cent of constituency party resolutions were extremist, 33 per cent of Labour MPs voted against Hugh Gaitskell in a contested election for the parliamentary party leadership. During the past decade the resignations of such leading Cabinet ministers as Aneurin Bevan, Lord Salisbury and Peter Thorneycroft have provided public evidence of the frequent suspicions of sharp divisions within a theoretically united Cabinet. Thus, it appears that the dilemma which David Butler has posed for party leaders — "their most loyal and devoted followers tend to have more extreme views than they have themselves, and to be still farther removed from the mass of those who actually provide the vote" [26] — does not really exist. Differences in policy exist within parties, and conflict is sometimes great, but this is not conflict between a monolithic bloc of activists and a monolithic leadership. Rather, it would seem that factional disputes divide parties vertically, joining some Privy Councillors, MPs, lobbyists, activists and voters into a faction which is in conflict with another which also contains members drawn from all ranks of the party.

---

[26] D. E. Butler, *The British General Election of 1955* (London, 1955), p. 5.

Part 3

POLITICAL TRANSMISSION BELTS—PARTIES

In every democratic system — that is, every system in which positions of political leadership are filled by legitimate competitive contests (elections) — organizations that select candidates, narrow choices, provide cohesion to the governmental decision-making process are requisites for its functioning. These organizations, however structurally diverse they are and however different the emphasis they put on the various functions just mentioned, are commonly referred to as "parties."

Besides these minimal functions, which parties fulfill everywhere a democratic system continues to operate, democratic theory has assigned to parties a number of additional functions that should properly be called tasks deriving from democratic norms. Parties have in the past presented normative democratic theory with an even greater problem than pressure groups. Pressure groups could be accepted as legitimate representatives of admittedly segmental interests, which made no claim to exercise governmental power for "the whole." But parties carried within themselves a theoretically unresolvable contradiction: to represent — by definition — only a part of the people and yet to aim at the exercise of political rule over, and in the name of, the entire people.

In the radical-democratic theories derived from Rousseau, parties are either denied all legitimacy, because they interpose themselves between "people" and "state" and "distort the popular will," preventing it from developing a genuine "general will"; or they are accepted as part of an essentially plebiscitary system, in which their main function is seen as mere transmission of "popular will" to the seat of government. This theoretical justification was — and to some extent remains — particularly strong in "parties of the Left," and there it is frequently reinforced by the Marxist assumption that "the people" is really identical with "the working class," thus resolving the contradiction between "part" and "whole." This view of party rendered central the question of "inner-party democracy," for the transmission belt could only function as such if the party machine did not assume dominance over its members, but provided them with the genuine opportunity to shape the decisions of the party as expressed in its program and political actions.

But even the "representative" theory of democracy, as primarily developed in the liberal interpretation of the British model, made demands on the functioning of parties that went far beyond the minimal ones described. The party was expected to be based on "principle" (Burke's famous dictum), which involved a conception of the "general welfare"; a party could not expressly represent merely a section of the electorate if it wanted to be morally legitimized in exercising power over the whole. Furthermore, if it were to be voted for rationally, it had to present its program in a clear and coherent form; and if it were to be held accountable for its performance by the electorate, this program had to be distinct from that of its opponent or opponents, and the party unequivocally capable of executing it, so that responsibility could be clearly exercised and seen to be exercised. While this second, "representative" theory put less emphasis on "inner-party democracy" — or even, as R. T. Mackenzie has done, considered it incompatible with the government's accountability toward the electorate in general — it demanded that parties be unified around programs and disciplined in their execution. A further, often scarcely articulated premise — and one that is incapable of precise conceptualization in political theory — was that the opposing party programs had to be embedded in a "consensus over essentials." Thus each opponent should be able to accept each other's goals as at least reconcilable with his own vital interests, and thus a legitimate, if different, articulation of the "common good."

Nowhere has this set of demands been fully translated into reality — and only in Britain, as several contributions here reprinted indicate, has it been even approximated. Since Robert Michels published his *Political Parties* more than half a century ago, the discussion over inner-party democracy as an unrealized dream has not ceased. The expectation — so seriously and unrealistically put forward by a committee of the American Political Science Association in its report "Toward a More Responsible Two-Party System" — appears as far from realization as ever, and this not only in the United States. For the developments of the past two decades, as summarized by the late Otto Kirchheimer in "The Changing Structure of West European Party Systems," have seen a widespread transformation of former "parties of principle" into "catch-all parties," functioning primarily as aggregating agents for an increasingly homogeneous electorate. Party programs grow less distinct, "ideological ballast" has been cast off, as by the German Socialists in their "Godesberg Program." The very structure of the traditional mass membership party, which appeared to Duverger shortly after the War as the most progressive party model, has been cast in doubt. Instead of a British-type system of responsible and disciplined parties developing in the United States, one could instead speak of a movement (though still halting and contradictory) toward the "Americanization" of European parties.

One of the results of this development has been that the immanent contradiction between "part" and "whole" has been programatically resolved by the growing consensus and the consequent ability to make and accept political compromises. But another consequence — much less desirable from the viewpoint of democracy — has been the danger of further alienation of the mass electorate from the political game played by the parties. This increasing "privatization" is relatively harmless as long as the decision-making process functions effectively and the major demands of the mass electorate, particularly for economic prosperity, are being met. In reading the following selections it should be remembered that they were, without exception, written during a period when prosperity was, by and large, a fact — a period the end of which may have been initiated by the incipient economic recessions in Germany and Britain, and the far-reaching crises to the American system in the face of the twin challenges of the Vietnam War and the spreading Negro rebellion.

Because political parties are so closely connected with the history and structure and functioning of each political system, they exhibit great individual divergencies that make rigorous comparisons on other than the most abstract or the most superficial level difficult. This may help to explain the absence of genuinely comparative studies. The items chosen to be presented here are primarily case studies that appeared to bring out clearly problems of party policy formation, intra-party power constellations, and party dynamics that are in the forefront of discussion about the changing functioning of political parties in Western mass democracies. Nevertheless, the inclusion of analyses dealing with two "parties of integration," the British Labour party and the Austrian Socialist party, and several "parties of aggregation," the German Christian Democratic Union, the Italian Christian Democrats, and the Japanese Conservative party, should give rise to preliminary generalizations that could be the basis for more precisely formulated comparative hypotheses.

16. Who Makes Policy in the British Labour Party?

LEON D. EPSTEIN

The British Labour Party serves as a prototype of the "left" party based on the principle of "inner party democracy." This principle implies that the parliamentary leadership is accountable, above all, to the mass of party members, considering itself bound to respect and transmit the will they express through the formal channels established in the party constitution. Professor Epstein's case study indicates that neither of the two extreme views—that the parliamentary leadership is a mere executant of party decisions or that it is free to reject any directives it receives from the party Conference—meets the actual situation.

I

Introduction

Mass-membership parties, by existing at all, raise the question of their authority to make policy for public officeholders elected under the party label. The question is inevitable since a party's mass membership tends to be recruited on the basis of ideological, or at least issue-oriented, convictions. Activism in this kind of organization is motivated mainly by partisan zeal and not by patronage. The zeal, it is true, need not be extremist. It may only be intense in its devotion to the party's cause. Yet it would be expecting a great deal of self-restraint by a membership so recruited to believe that it would always contentedly accept party policy as defined by its public office-holding leadership. Such contentment would, of course, be ideal from the leadership's viewpoint. What public officeholders, or aspiring public officeholders, find useful is a mass-membership party that raises money for campaign expenses, solicits votes door-to-door, and generally helps to win elections. Policy determination does not fit in this scheme of things. In fact, a mass organization might well be regarded as so extreme, inflexible, or ignorant as to produce policy embarrassing to an officeholding leadership. Just as troubling is the possibility, opened by policy-making in mass organizations, that an intra-party opposition could use causes popular among activists as the basis for attacking officeholders otherwise committed. Generally, it is plain that a party leadership has an interest in remaining free from policy-making by its own supporters. The leaders themselves must believe that they know best either what is feasible or what is likely to attract the electorate, particularly the marginal portion of it.

SOURCE: Reprinted by permission from Leon D. Epstein, "Who Makes Party Policy: British Labour, 1960–61," *The Midwest Journal of Political Science* (May, 1962), pp. 165–182.

Broadly, there is also the problem of whether it is more or less democratic to have party policy determined by the activists of a mass organization. To be sure, it does seem more democratic if viewed strictly as a matter of numbers within a given party. The activists as a group, even as only crudely represented by several hundred or a few thousand delegates, are plainly more numerous than the officeholding leadership. But public officeholders can claim that they represent the much larger number who cast their votes for party candidates without joining the party. To this group, if not to the electorate as a whole, it can be argued that the leaders are rightly responsible, and that they, therefore, should frame policy in line with the assumed wishes of their electors rather than with the wishes of zealous and probably untypical partisans.

This general problem of the relation of mass-membership organizations to policy-making is by no means new to the student of European politics. It is American experience on this score that is limited, since parties with large numbers of dues-paying activists are recent phenomena existing in only a few states. But early in the century the experience of continental socialist parties provided Michels with material for discussing the position of parliamentary leaders as part of his more general presentation of the domination of party by its leadership. Much more recently the subject has been treated by Duverger generally, and by McKenzie with reference only to Britain. The Michels view, supported in modified form by McKenzie, is that in actual practice parliamentary leaders, rather than their mass organizations, do establish policy. Duverger is less definite on this point; in fact, he believes that British Labour M. P.s at least, have a fairly marked subordination to the party and the trade unions.[1] The question, therefore, cannot be said to be settled.

Here it is proposed to state the question mainly in the form of how workable it is in a competitive democratic system for a mass-membership organization to impose its policy on a public officeholding leadership, and to examine the question in the specific circumstances of British Labour party experience in 1960–61. There are several reasons why the Labour party should provide a leading example of the general problem. Unlike the British Conservative party, whose parliamentary leaders, heavily influenced by an older aristocratic tradition, deliberately created a mass organization to help win elections, Labour formed its extra-parliamentary organization first in an effort to secure parliamentary representation. Thus elected officeholders were viewed as servants of the external movement. Reinforcing this outlook was an egalitarianism characteristic of British working-class politics. Still more crucial is the historical presence of leftist pressure in the external organization of the Labour party. It is this pressure which, in 1960–61, brought into the open the vexed relations between office-holders and their followers. Significantly, this experience occurred after a long period of opposition had weakened the hold of the leadership. For this and other reasons, the party difficulty emerged in the

---

[1] The most relevant passages of Robert Michels, *Political Parties* (Glencoe: Free Press, 1949 reprint of 1915 ed.), are at pp. 141 and 181; of Maurice Duverger, *Political Parties* (New York: John Wiley, 1954), at pp. 192 and 197; and of Robert McKenzie, *British Political Parties* (London: Heinemann, 1955), at pp. 15–17 and 587–88.

usual form of a moderate leadership confronted with the more extreme policies advanced by delegates of the mass organization.

The line of conflict, however, must not be understood as a simple matter of a completely right-wing parliamentary party versus a mass of zealous left-wingers in the constituency associations. The parliamentary Labour party has itself had a substantial left-wing minority, constituting nearly one third of the Labour M. P.s, and the constituency unions have not all, by any means, been dominated by the left-wing. Many of the latter may often be intensely partisan but not extreme ideologically.[2] Most important, in any case, is that the constituency association activists provide only about 13% of the total votes represented at the annual party conference; almost all the other votes are cast in overwhelming blocs by the large trade union delegations.[3] Although these bloc votes are also those of Labour's extra-parliamentary mass organization, they belong to a membership indirectly affiliated to the party and not necessarily to zealous constituency party activists. Consequently it is really extreme or leftist sentiment in the unions that can threaten a moderate party leadership. The constituency parties are not always irrelevant, since their votes may be decisive if the major unions are divided against each other, but they cannot make even conference policy on their own.

Subject to this qualification, the 1960–61 conflict over defence issues between Labour's parliamentary and extra-parliamentary parties provides a most significant example of the difficulties for democratic practice and principle that are raised by the claims of an extra-parliamentary organization to determine the policy of the party's legislative officeholders. Rarely, in the experience of Labour or of another party anywhere, have the difficulties been so sharply exposed and illustrated. The issues at stake were of such moment that they had to be faced. The differences in viewpoints on the issues seemed honestly irreconcilable and incapable of being compromised. The party conference adopted a policy that its proponents wanted to force on the parliamentary party. And the leaders of the parliamentary party, backed by a majority of Labour M. P.s, refused to adopt that policy, but adhered instead to the policy which the Labour party had presented to the electorate during the 1959 campaign. The question of principle thus raised by the conflict is plain enough. Ought the parliamentary party to yield its judgment to that of its own organized following? Closely connected was the practical question whether the parliamentary party could afford politically to ignore its own external organization, or, conversely, to ignore the collective commitment of Labour M. P.s to their largely unorganized voters.

---

[2] The point is convincingly made in a paper by Richard Rose, "The Policy Role of English Party Militants," mimeographed for International UNESCO Seminar, Bergen, Norway, June 1961.

[3] The figure of 13% is for 1960, admittedly a low point of individual membership in constituency associations. The percentage has, in fact, been declining in the last decade. The absolute number of individual memberships has dropped off while the absolute number of affiliated trade-union memberships has increased. Thus in 1952 individual memberships, through constituency associations, then at a high point, constituted 17% of the total membership. Figures are in the *Report of the National Executive Committee to the 60th Annual Conference* (London: Labour Party, 1961), p. 34.

II

The 1960–61 Experience

The events of 1960–61 were dramatic and exciting. Their immediate background began with the general election of October 1959. The fact that Labour suffered its third successive defeat intensified the stress that had long existed between the Left and the Gaitskell leadership. Each side had its own explanation of the party's electoral misfortunes. The Left thought the party had not been forthrightly socialist enough, and Gaitskell thought that the party had suffered too much from the disadvantage of an old-fashioned socialist reputation. Gaitskell, emerging from the general election with the laurels of a vigorous television campaign, took the intra-party offensive by a move to modify the party constitution's famous Clause IV which, since 1918, had generally committed Labour to the objective of "the common ownership of the means of production, distribution, and exchange. . . . ." Opposition to changing the sacred text rose rapidly, and it became plain by March 1960 that what Gaitskell had originally wanted could not be achieved at the annual conference. Accordingly the National Executive decided to let Clause IV stand. The only bow in the Gaitskell direction was an NEC restatement of party objectives so worded as to indicate that Labour's commitment to common ownership, in varying forms, was to be based on what was required to give the community power over the commanding heights of the economy.[4]

Gaitskell's tactical retreat on Clause IV took place as the more immediately important defence issue came to the fore. Here Gaitskell and his friends had to fight because their opponents sought to commit the party to unilateral nuclear disarmament and to a large dose of neutralism. Clause IV did not have to be changed so much as the unilateralists had to be defeated. Labour leaders could continue to lead a party still vaguely committed to public ownership. Probably the leaders themselves believed in some public ownership sometime, and the amount and the timing were not fixed by Clause IV of the constitution. But a party commitment to unilateral nuclear disarmament, and broadly to an anti-NATO position, would be an embarrassment of a much more serious kind. Thus the leadership abandoned its Clause IV fight in order to concentrate its forces where there was both more serious concern and more chance to win. The Left could not be defeated on Clause IV once it had become apparent that the leadership's usual trade-union allies were either opposed to, or uninterested in, changing the constitution. But it seemed, very early in the spring of 1960, that the leadership might hold the line against unilateral nuclear disarmament.

---

[4] The party constitution is published in the *59th Annual Labour Conference Report* (London: Labour Party, 1960), pp. 303–08. The NEC statement on Clause IV is in the same volume, pp. 12–13. It can fairly be said that Gaitskell's retreat on Clause IV did represent a defeat of the leadership by the militants. Its significance, however, was lessened by the fact that it was a defeat that the leadership could accept without suffering the same kind of consequences for parliamentary policy implied by an acceptance of unilateralism, and by the related fact that it was a defeat that the leadership chose not to suffer in a conference vote. The freedom of the leadership to choose those issues on which it will fight is of undoubted importance to its position even though its evident inability to win on every issue indicates a limited power.

Then when it became likely, before the 1960 Scarborough conference itself, that the unilateralists had captured enough unions so as to defeat the leadership, Gaitskell understandably chose to continue to fight. He did so, incidentally, without the considerable help he had received, on similar defence issues in 1957 and 1958, from Aneurin Bevan, who as the erstwhile left-wing leader had greatly strengthened Gaitskell once he made his peace and joined the shadow cabinet. But Bevan, ill from the winter of 1959–60, died in July of 1960.

With the prospect of a conference defeat on what it regarded, and had to regard, as a major policy issue, the Labour leadership tried to prepare for the consequences by announcing its reactions in advance. It sought, in particular, to make the point that the parliamentary party could exercise a practical independence of conference policy-making. The conference, it was admitted, could instruct the external party's National Executive Committee, which in turn was to consult with the parliamentary party about the timing and methods of giving effect to conference resolutions. But the parliamentary party, it was asserted, was not bound by conference resolutions as by an election manifesto.[5] On this score, the leadership found protection in the party constitution, which contains no clear-cut and general doctrine of conference supremacy. Clause V of the constitution provides only that the conference should decide the proposals to be included in the "Party Programme," that a two-thirds conference majority is required for the inclusion of any proposal, and that the NEC and the PLP Parliamentary Committee should decide which items from the "Party Programme" are to be included in the general election manifesto. Otherwise the constitution is silent on the broad subject of policy-making, and certainly on the specific subject of conference resolutions in relation to parliamentary party policy between general elections. The closest to a mention of the matter is the statement in Clause VIII that the NEC has the power to confer with the PLP at the opening of each parliamentary session as well as at other desired times.[6]

At odds, however, with this absence of constitutional authority for conference supremacy was the Labour tradition that had often led even party leaders, implicitly if not explicitly, to honor the principle of policy-making by the annual conference. Practice on specific matters may well have diverged, but the tradition was so much a part of Labour's belief in itself as a uniquely democratic movement that it had seldom been openly challenged within the party. In fact, Labour's most successful leader, Clement Attlee, had proclaimed the tradition in writing (but not by his actions as prime minister).[7]

It is not surprising that the unilateralists, anticipating their Scarborough

---

[5] The assertion was made in a party *Newsletter* by Morgan Phillips, Labour's general secretary. Quoted in the London *Times*, August 10, 1960, p. 5.

[6] Party constitution, cited in note 3.

[7] Attlee's proclamation of conference supremacy, including the issuance of instructions to the PLP, was made originally in his book, *The Labour Party in Perspective* (London: Gollancz, 1937), p. 93, and republished in 1949. The context of this, as well as of similar statements by Labour leaders, was a discussion of the Labour party as a more democratic organization than the Conservative party. This too was an important article of the Labour faith.

victory, should have wanted to fix the traditional principle as a matter of current practice, just as Gaitskell on the other side now had an incentive to restate the principle so as to free the PLP from any commitment to the expected unilateralism of the conference. Consequently the question of conference authority was, along with unilateral nuclear disarmament, a subject of contention between Left and Right at Scarborough. Two resolutions on the subject were to be proposed to the conference. Both "reaffirmed" the authority of the annual conference in policy-making, and were disliked by Gaitskell. On the eve of the conference, however, the NEC (overruling Gaitskell) decided to accept and support the less stringent of these resolutions. Plainly some of Gaitskell's own usual supporters on the NEC realized that they could not secure the defeat, in a conference vote, of this resolution, and that unless it were accepted the more drastic one might be passed.[8] The NEC tactic, in accepting the less stringent resolution, was to explain and interpret its consequences in a limited way. This took subtlety and ingenuity since the resolution seemed most straight-forward in its claim for the policy-making authority of the conference. The exact words were:

> This Conference re-affirms that the policy of the Labour Party to be pursued nationally and in Parliament on questions of principle shall be determined by Annual Conference. While acknowledging that the day to day tactics in Parliament must be the job of the Parliamentary Labour Party, this Conference declares that Labour Policy is decided by the Party Conference which is the final authority.[9]

The mover of the resolution, himself a left-wing M. P., was not less straightforward in his claims for the resolution. Indeed he insisted that the resolution was necessary precisely because there were rumors that the PLP might not follow the policy to be adopted by the conference. The only substantial qualification he would admit to conference authority was the plainly essential one that M. P.s could not be subject to detailed instructions.[10]

Yet, despite the words of the resolution and its mover, the NEC did significantly modify the resolution's import during the debate. This modification was accomplished by A. L. Williams, the party's national agent and deputy general secretary (acting for the ill general secretary, Morgan Phillips). In a speech concluding the conference debate on the issue, Williams largely avoided the resolution itself and concentrated on what he contended were the established conference-PLP relations. These he stated in such a way as to emphasize the absence in the party's constitution of authority for the conference to instruct the PLP. Williams contended that policies adopted by the conference, except for those which become part of the "Party Programme" and subsequently of the electoral manifesto, were only expressions of opinion for the PLP to take into account. Outside the manifesto, the PLP rightly made its own policy, not just in day-to-day tactics but on larger issues as well.

---

[8] Manchester *Guardian,* October 3, 1960, p. 1.

[9] *59th Annual Labour Conference Report,* cited in note 4, p. 159.

[10] *Ibid.,* pp. 159–60.

Having said all this, Williams might logically have concluded by opposing the resolution at issue as he did oppose the stronger resolution. Instead he announced that NEC did not wish to stand against the milder resolution, given an understanding that it in no way changed the relations as he had described them and that nobody had the power to instruct the PLP.[11] Contradictory as this understanding seemed to the chief point of the resolution, it was accepted by the mover of the resolution as well as by the NEC. The mover of the resolution, it is true, accepted with uncertainty and with the qualification that the NEC, on its side, accept the meaning of the words of the resolution. But this was good enough to settle the matter for conference voting. The resolution was passed by nearly a two to one majority, and the stronger resolution was overwhelmingly defeated.[12] For the year that lay ahead, however, nothing was really settled. Each side, the one asserting conference authority over PLP policy and the other seeking to avoid it, could still claim to be acting in accord with party principle. The resolution really went one way, and the NEC's interpretation in the opposite. Immediately, perhaps, the NEC had secured a tactical advantage from the Williams dicta. At least, the leadership had been saved from any clear-cut proclamation of conference supremacy.

This was fortunate since, as expected, on the next day the Scarborough conference did vote, on a series of motions, for unilateral nuclear disarmament with definitely neutralist implications. Although the margins were small (typically about 300,000 votes out of over 6,000,000 cast by conference representatives), there was no doubt about the leadership's defeat. The NEC's own defence policy statement, with its commitment to NATO and to the American-provided nuclear deterrent, was rejected. Adopted instead was one resolution demanding "the unilateral renunciation of the testing, manufacture, stock-piling and basing of all nuclear weapons in Great Britain,"[13] and another urging, not only a complete abandonment of a nuclear deterrent policy, but specifically the cessation of aircraft patrols operating from British bases with nuclear weapons and opposition to the establishment of missile bases in Britain.[14] These specific demands were aimed directly at continued British cooperation with the American nuclear deterrent policy. Any doubts that there might have been about this intention, despite the blunt language of the resolutions, were surely removed by the sponsoring speeches.

Nor did the party leadership seek to obscure the significance of the change in established defence policy that was being adopted by the conference. On the contrary, Gaitskell himself most definitely stressed the anti-NATO and neutralist implications of the resolutions, charging that they represented "the suicidal path of unilateral disarmament which will leave our country defence-

---

[11] *Ibid.*, pp. 165–67.

[12] *Ibid.*, p. 168.

[13] *Ibid.*, p. 176. This resolution was moved in behalf of the Amalgamated Engineering Union.

[14] *Ibid.*, p. 178. This resolution was moved by Frank Cousins for his Transport and General Workers' Union.

ess and alone." And with great emphasis Gaitskell also argued that he and he PLP would reject this path even if, as expected, the conference adopted it. He pointed out that the vast majority of the PLP was utterly opposed to unilateralism and neutralism, and that this was a matter of conviction as well as of electoral commitment. "What sort of people do you think we are? Do you think that we can simply accept a decision of this kind? Do you think that we can become overnight the pacifists, unilateralists and fellow travellers that other people are?" Rather, he added in a phrase subsequently much quoted, "We will fight and fight and fight again to save the Party we love."[15]

Gaitskell did fight during the next year, successfully as it turned out, to reverse the conference decision, but first he had to fight to save his own leadership of the PLP. What was ordinarily the formality of re-electing the incumbent party leader at the opening of each fall's new parliamentary session was in 1960 to be a genuine contest. Much of the controversy about policy had always involved the leadership question – Gaitskell himself suggested that some conference delegates might be voting unilateralist mainly to strike at him[16] – but now seemed the time to propose an alternative to Gaitskell in the PLP, where of course the leadership had to be decided. It was fair to assume that Gaitskell's intra-party political strength was at a low point after both his tacit defeat on Clause IV and his open defeat on defence policy. Although these defeats were in the extra-parliamentary party, they were bound to leave their marks on the PLP. Even fairly moderate Labour M. P.s might wonder whether Gaitskell was not too intransigently right-wing to lead the whole of the party, and especially to conciliate the major trade-union champion of unilateralism, Frank Cousins. The way now appeared open for a significant challenge, not from a unilateralist, but from one willing to compromise, or at least to cover over, the differences between Gaitskellites and unilateralists, between the established PLP defence policy and the neutralism of the conference.

The challenge to Gaitskell, after some preliminary jousting, did come from an apostle of party unity, Harold Wilson, whose campaign in late October was based on the belief that a compromise defence position could be found, that the PLP and the conference could thus be brought back into agreement, and that there could be avoided the intra-party strife promised by Gaitskell's campaign to reverse the conference's 1960 decision.[17] Wilson, a well-established member of the shadow cabinet, had long sought to be acceptable to both Left and Right, but this was his first open bid for the leadership. He secured 81 votes against Gaitskell's 166.[18] The group of 81 was probably the maximum anti-Gaitskell strength; it included at least ten or twenty who were not unilateral-

---

[15] *Ibid.*, p. 201. Gaitskell's reference to fellow travellers was an unpopular note in an otherwise dramatically successful performance. Even his friends, who could hardly have doubted the accuracy of the fellow-traveller label for many of their opponents, thought that Gaitskell had made a tactical error by seeming to be a "Red-baiter" in a political culture resistant to straight anti-Communist appeals.

[16] *Ibid.*

[17] London *Times*, October 21, 1960, p. 12, and October 26, 1960, p. 12.

[18] *Ibid.*, November 4, 1960, p. 12.

ists. There were now really three PLP groups: unilateralists, who were mainl'
confirmed leftists on domestic issues too; straight Gaitskell supporters, wh(
usually shared their leader's moderate or revisionist views but who were no
always personally loyal to Gaitskell even while supporting him out of wha
might have been ideological and party necessities; and compromisers, lik
Wilson himself and R. H. S. Crossman (the new chairman of the externa
Labour party), who wanted the PLP to go part way to meet the unilateralis
demands of the Scarborough conference despite the absence of any firm
unilateralist convictions of their own. They simply were willing to pay a pric(
for unity that Gaitskellites refused. The fact that Wilson lost the leadershi]
contest meant that the policy difference between PLP and conference woul(
persist, open though ashamed, through the 1960–61 parliamentary session.

The awkwardness of this situation was soon apparent. It was now peculiarl'
difficult for the Gaitskellite leadership, although in control of Labour'
parliamentary executive committee, to achieve cohesion in PLP voting o:
defence issues. The convinced unilateralists and even some of the compro
misers could and did claim conference authority for refusing to vote with th(
PLP majority for any motion implying support for a nuclear deterrent policy
The major revolt took place on 13 December 1960 when 72 Labour M. P.
deliberately abstained from an official Labour motion.[19] The idea of discplinin;
so many M. P.s although technically within the PLP's power, was practicall
out of the question. And it would have seemed presumptuous to proponent
of conference authority who thought, in defiance of parliamentary custom, tha
there should be a way to discipline Gaitskell and his majority of Labour M. P.s
A less substantial revolt took place on 8 March 1961 when 24 Labour M. P.
voted against the air estimates.[20] When five of these 24 repeated their offenc
on a later service estimates vote, the whip was withdrawn on the leadership'
recommendation.[21] No disciplinary action was taken, however, against any o
the other rebels even though most of the 24 M. P.s had also been among th
72 rebels of December. Thus the Gaitskellite majority, still declaring th
PLP's adherence to nuclear deterrence, was prevented from maintaining th
usual united party front on a major policy issue. This was hardly behavio
designed to win the confidence of an electorate accustomed to a parliamentar'
party cohesive enough to support the policies of leaders who were potentia
government ministers.

In the meantime, with the PLP struggle continuing, the fight over confer
ence policy was carried to the units of the external party organization tha
would decide the way delegates would vote at the 1961 conference. This wa
where Gaitskell meant to "fight and fight again." Practically speaking his figh
would succeed or fail well before the 1961 conference met at Blackpool i:

---

[19] 632 H. C. Deb. 219–354 (December 13, 1960). The complete list of 72 abstainer
was in the London *Daily Herald,* December 15, 1960, and the London *Daily Telegraph*
December 14–15, 1960.

[20] 636 H. C. Deb. 639–40 (March 8, 1961).

[21] *Report of the National Executive Committee to the 60th Annual Conference,* cited i:
note 3, p. 74.

October. The crucial stage was to convince enough constituency parties and trade unions to shift from their previous unilateralism. The unions required the most early attention not only because they had the bulk of the conference votes but also because they committed their delegates on major issues, for both the TUC and Labour party conferences, in their own union conferences in the spring, Gaitskell's counter-offensive assumed an organized form. His supporters, calling themselves the Campaign for Democratic Socialism, stated as early as January 1961 that they had the support of over 2000 key party workers.[22] It was notable that this was the first time that Labour's right wing had seen fit to organize its following. Previously the party organization itself was assumed to be in right-wing hands, while the Left organized its own groups in order to secure an alternate means of influence. In a way, therefore, the Campaign for Democratic Socialism involved an admission — really obvious after the Scarborough conference — that much of the party, in its trade-union and constituency units, was at least temporarily in the hands of the Left.

Gaitskell himself carried the fight to the constituencies, trying especially to explain why compromise for the sake of unity was impossible. "How," he asked, "can you have a compromise between those who say that the West must arm and those who say it must not?"[23] Plainly he was sharpening the issue between himself and the unilateralists instead of trying to conceal it. He thereby cut off his chance for subsequent retreat into compromise if unilateralism triumphed again at the annual conference. On this hard line, Gaitskell persevered despite heckling at local meetings. On one occasion, he was howled down.[24] No demonstrations from his own party members convinced him that unilateralism was popular among unorganized Labour voters.

Before trying to secure prospective conference votes, the Gaitskellites needed a defence policy statement to present first to the unions in the spring and then to the party conference. This statement, it was agreed in January, would be the joint product of the PLP's executive committee, the TUC's general council, and the external party's National Executive Committee. On each of these bodies, there was an anti-unilateralist majority. This was true, it should be emphasized, even of the NEC, the bulk of whose members elected by trade unions (in contrast to those elected by constituency parties) were anti-unilateralists. This meant that some of the trade unions at Scarborough had chosen anti-unilateralists for the NEC while voting for unilateralist policy resolutions. The apparent contradiction, however, is not inexplicable, since trade unions had a variety of reasons other than defence policy for determining their NEC members. Intra-union and inter-union politics well removed from unilateralism could have been responsible for the composition of the NEC.

Accidental or otherwise, having an anti-unilateralist majority on the NEC as well as on the TUC General Council was of the utmost importance for embattled PLP leaders. If they had instead to deal primarily with unilateralist representatives of the external party, their task might have been impossible

[22] Manchester *Guardian*, January 13, 1961, p. 2.
[23] *Ibid.*, October 24, 1960, p. 1.
[24] London *Times*, November 7, 1960, p. 8.

both in composing the defence statement and in other respects. As matters actually stood, however, when each of the three groups named four of its members to the joint committee of twelve charged with preparing the state ment, Gaitskell had eight supporters.[25] They drew up his kind of statement after rejecting both a unilateralist proposal and the compromise that urged ending the need for American nuclear bases in Europe and Britain. Even so there was a hard passage for the Gaitskellite statement when it was subsequently submitted to the NEC. Before the NEC gave its approval, 13 of its members voted for the compromise against 15 who held fast for continued British provision of bases.[26] The statement thus just barely emerged without any retreat from the principle of NATO cooperation. Particular projects of cooperation, it was noted, Britain should be free to decide according to the circumstances of each case.

In this virtually uncompromised form, Gaitskell now had what was called the party's "Policy for Peace" to present to the critical trade-union meeting in the spring. By early May he had won enough union support to know that he would have an anti-unilateralist majority at the October conference. Both the Union of Shop, Distributive and Allied Workers (USDAW) and the Amalgamated Engineering Union (AEU) reversed their 1960 positions and agreed to support the new defence statement. The AEU vote, incidentally, was close: 28 to 23.[27] Not all of Gaitskell's triumph in winning the support of these and other unions was necessarily the result of changed convictions on defence policy. By 1961, it could have been evident to union leaders that by voting unilateralist they would also be voting for a change in leadership. Whatever they thought of Gaitskell personally, they might believe that he possessed certain electoral advantages as a moderate and as a well-known personality. These were advantages which a trade unionist, concerned with the future of his party, would hesitate to help destroy through a left-wing revolt.

Regardless of the reasons, however, Gaitskell went to Blackpool in 1961 with the new prestige of winning the fight he had had to begin a year earlier. In fact, he seemed to be winning handsomely since the new defence statement was approved by a vote of four and one-half million to one and three-quarters million. A unilateralist resolution was defeated by about the same margin.[28] The reversal of 1960 voting was impressive. Similar support was also given the leadership on its moderate statement of domestic policy, "Signposts for the Sixties," although here there might have been discerned some concession to the Left's belief in nationalization of industry.[29] There were, however, two more definite exceptions to the Gaitskellite triumph at the Blackpool conference, and both of these involved defence questions. One was a resolution against the training of German troops on British soil, and the other was against the

---

[25] Manchester *Guardian,* January 26, 1961, p. 1.

[26] *Ibid.,* February 23, 1961, p. 1.

[27] *Ibid.,* May 3, 1961, p. 1 and May 5, 1961, p. 1.

[28] London *Times,* October 5, 1961, p. 9.

[29] *Ibid.,* October 4, 1961, pp. 18–19.

establishment of American Polaris submarine bases in Britain. In carrying both resolutions by a little over three-quarters of a million votes, the Left won significant consolation prizes to set against their defeat on the central unilateralist question. Gaitskell had argued against both resolutions, partly on the ground that the training of German troops and the establishment of Polaris bases were compatible with the continued British cooperation in NATO pledged by the general defence statement, but he was careful to indicate that one might vote against both projects without necessarily being against the principle of NATO. Thus Gaitskell prepared for an expected defeat on these items by regarding them as particular NATO projects about which opinions might differ among those accepting the general statement's commitment to NATO.[30] He was not going to be denied his triumph over the unilateralists by making his main fight on issues where his opponents had emotional advantages. He concentrated instead on the issue defined in advance as the basically important one.

Consequently Gaitskell was conceded to be the victor at Blackpool despite the two particular setbacks. This is a fair enough judgment with respect to settling the leadership for the time being. In terms of the substance of Labour's defence policy, however, the commitment to NATO cooperation might not be worth much as a general principle if it could be denied to particular projects because of their emotional objectionableness. Even with respect to the leadership question, the votes against Polaris and German troops could turn out to be a truer measure of future strength against Gaitskell's defence policy, and so against Gaitskell, than the major defence statement on which the leadership's full effort had been mobilized to save its position in 1961. It would be best, therefore, to summarize the Blackpool conference by saying that it re-established Gaitskell for the present, meaning through the next general election in all probability, but that there was immediately no rout of his enemies. Anti-Gaitskellites, for instance, still won six of the seven constituency party places on the NEC. Nor were the vital trade unions, despite their re-election of right-wingers to the NEC, securely in the Gaitskell ranks. The largest, Frank Cousins' Transport and General Workers, remained unilateralist, and some other large unions had only narrowly agreed this time to accept the official defence statement. On their adherence, or rather on that of the handful of men who headed these unions, Gaitskell's continued conference support depended. The defection of a few large unions could again set the conference against the PLP.

III

Conclusion

Labour's experience of 1960–61 is interesting enough to be told for its own sake, but the object in presenting the facts here has been to provide a basis for generalizing about their significance for any mass-membership party operating in a political democracy. Before thus attempting to generalize, however, it is

---

[30] *Ibid.*, October 5, 1961, pp. 8–9.

necessary to decide just what significance the 1960–61 experience had for the Labour party itself. In particular, did the experience confirm the doctrine, most fully propounded by R. T. McKenzie, that the Labour party conforms (and should conform) to the British constitutional practice of parliamentary party freedom from external organizational control?[31] Certainly this doctrine would have been struck a mighty blow if Gaitskell and the PLP had bowed to the will of the 1960 Scarborough conference, adopting or even compromising substantially with the unilateralist position. On the other side, therefore, the fact that Gaitskell and the PLP did no such thing does seem in accord with the orthodox doctrine. McKenzie himself thought so, and he asserted as much in the summer of 1961 when he restated his belief that "final authority in the determination of policy must rest, whatever the party constitution may appear to imply, with the parliamentary party and its leaders."[32]

While surely not refuting this doctrine, Gaitskell's responses to Scarborough did not, however, altogether confirm PLP supremacy. He did, it is true, continue to lead the PLP on a course at odds with significant conference resolutions. Thus at least he established the principle that PLP leaders do not have to resign or change position as a result of a single conference defeat even on a major policy question. But he did work to reverse his defeat at the next conference. And however much his subsequent Blackpool success strengthens the view that PLP leaders are much more likely to influence, than to be influenced by the mass organization, nevertheless the strenuous effort by PLP leaders in this case to exert such influence did imply an important respect for conference resolutions. Of course, the leadership may not have regarded such resolutions, even if still unfavorable after a second conference, as so important as to force the PLP into line. They may have seemed only important enough to be worth trying to change so that the Labour party would appear before the nation as a united political force. Uncertainty on this point cannot be fully resolved on the basis of the 1960–61 experience. Unfortunately for political science, Gaitskell's success at the 1961 Blackpool conference prevents us from knowing what would happen if the PLP were faced with two successive conference defeats on a major issue.

All we know is what happened after one such defeat. And it is well to emphasize that even this defeat, at Scarborough, was not accompanied by any complete loss, on the part of PLP leaders, of the levers of control in the external party organization. Both the NEC and the TUC general council, as noted earlier, remained anti-unilateralist. Therefore, it is not really fair to say

---

[31] McKenzie, *British Political Parties* (London: Heinemann, 1955). The doctrine of the book is not stated in as rigid a form as McKenzie's critics often assume. He grants that the Labour conference can exert an influence, greater when the party is in opposition (p. 455). The same point emerges in an exchange with a critic soon after the appearance of the book. See Saul Rose, "Policy Decision in Opposition," *Political Studies*, IV (June 1956), 128–38, and R. T. McKenzie, "Policy Decision in Opposition: A Rejoinder," *ibid.*, V (June 1957), 176–82. [reprinted below]

[32] *New Statesman*, LXI (June 30, 1961), 1044. The statement was part of McKenzie's reply to an attack on his doctrine by R. H. S. Crossman in a review of two other books on political parties. *Ibid.*, pp. 1007 and 1010 (June 23, 1961). Correspondence on the subject continued in the *New Statesman* through July, and that part of it which involved

that in 1960–61 the PLP resisted the will of the external organization as a whole. It resisted only a majority, small and temporary, of conference votes. Most of the trade unions, which provided this unilateralist majority, were not, even in 1960, in the firm control of unilateralists or anti-Gaitskellites. If they had been, it is indeed doubtful whether Gaitskell and the PLP could have effectively maintained themselves. To be sure, this is another way of saying that it is doubtful whether Gaitskell and the PLP could have maintained their position against a second successive conference defeat since such a defeat would have come if most of the trade unions had been firmly in unilateralist or anti-Gaitskell hands.

Although we cannot know what would have happened in the event of a second successive conference defeat for the leadership, the speculative possibilities are worth considering. The orthodox answer is that Gaitskell and the majority of the PLP could still not be expected to accept unilateralism, in defiance of their convictions as well of the assumed convictions of most Labour voters, and that it was equally absurd to expect Gaitskell to turn over the PLP leadership to a unilateralist since the PLP was not unilateralist. The implication is that it was impractical for any conference to impose its will on a genuinely reluctant parliamentary party. And it would follow, as McKenzie argued, that Labour should abandon any pretence to conference policy-making for the PLP. Its unworkability should be frankly admitted.

The opposing point of view has been put with force by R. H. S. Crossman, chairman of the Labour party in 1961 and a parliamentary proponent of a defence compromise. Viewing recent events in the summer of 1961, he suggested a counterthesis to McKenzie's. "Sovereignty in the Labour Party," Crossman said, "is divided between the parliamentary and the extra-parliamentary party, with the latter the final authority on policy issues. If either tries to subject the other, the result is a deadlock, which must at all costs be resolved at the next conference." [33] In Crossman's perspective, then, a second conference defeat for the parliamentary leadership would bring either unconditional surrender, resignation, or a party split.[34] The last of these three alternatives, which seems the likeliest, is not really different in result from the orthodox view that the imposition of conference authority is unworkable. Producing a party split, in which part of the PLP adheres to conference views and the other part goes its own way, does illustrate a kind of impracticality in party arrangements. It hardly seems a successful way to operate a party.

Essentially it is the unworkability of external party policy-making that Labour's recent experience reflects. There is no way in which public office-holding representatives, responsible to their own convictions and to the electorate, can be forced to accept policies to which they are opposed. They

Crossman and McKenzie is referred to subsequently. Another major participant was Henry Pelling, whose latest book on the Labour party was one of the subjects of Crossman's original review. Pelling argued that McKenzie gave too little attention to the importance of the trade unions in determining Labour party policy, whether through the conference or otherwise.

[33] *Ibid.,* LXII (July 7, 1961), 12.

[34] *Ibid.,* LXII (July 21, 1961), 82.

may get the external organization to change those policies if, like Gaitskell in 1960–61, they have sufficient intra-party power to do so. They may, although Crossman does not allow for this, simply maintain their own position despite continued conference defeats. Or they may resign, as Crossman suggests, but this seems almost certain to involve a party split. What seems impossible, contra Crossman, is that an officeholding leadership could surrender by accepting a conference policy it had fought on principle. To do so would involve, as Gaitskell appreciated, an abdication on the part of those publicly elected to exercise responsibility in policy-making. Surely a permanent party split is likelier, given continued conference defeats, and this represents institutional failure.

Seen in this way, it is hard to believe that the traditional Labour party ideal of policy-making by a mass-membership organization is a practical working model for a party in a modern democracy. It is not only the British constitutional system stressed by McKenzie, that operates against the idea of an external party dictating to elected legislators. On this score, the British system does not differ fundamentally from the arrangements of other western democracies. Popularly elected office-holders everywhere are supposed to be responsible, individually or collectively under their party label, to the voters. Practically they have to be thus responsible, given honest and competitive elections, if they want seriously to gain and hold power. Only totalitarian parties, which do not need to win such elections, or small and devout ideological parties, which do not hope to win, can afford to treat policy-making as fundamentally an affair for party members.

17. Policy Decision in Opposition

SAUL ROSE

Two distinct questions are frequently discussed when the decision-making process in political parties is examined: Is this process "democratic"; that is, does the mass of party members have a significant—if not decisive—influence on the formation of party policy proposals? And, secondly, ought the party leadership in a parliamentary democracy consider itself accountable to the extra-parliamentary body of party members and functionaries, or exclusively to the voters? In the following exchange Mr. Rose and Professor McKenzie express divergent views on both these questions.

Three years' experience at Transport House from 1952 to 1955 as Secretary of the International Department of the Labour Party have instilled in the writer an appreciation of the danger of generalizing about the Labour Party. Any general statements made in this article are therefore to be understood with the qualification that they relate to those three years when the Labour Party was in opposition. During the period after the war when Labour was in office, the way in which policy decisions were made was certainly different. Even in opposition, it would be rash to assume that an analysis based on earlier years remains valid. In the interests of brevity and clarity no attempt is made to deal systematically with the process of policy formulation, as distinct from policy decision, although the two processes are interrelated.

To see how Labour Party policy is decided it will be useful to look first at the way in which policy is ascertained. Students of politics have a special interest in the process by which decisions on policy are reached; but a far more frequent question in practical.politics is 'What is the policy?' It is a question which may be asked by supporters or opponents or by the elusive floating voter, by affiliated organizations or by foreign visitors. It arises also in the preparation of official publications.

In principle, there should be an answer. To reply that the Labour Party has no policy on a particular issue may sometimes make an impression of careful deliberation or open-mindedness; but if it happened too often, the Opposition would be in danger of forfeiting its claim to be an alternative government. Also, a noncommittal answer is not likely to be much help to a local party agent who is being harried by opponents. Consequently, whenever the question is asked, the headquarters staff set out to find an answer. If all

SOURCE: Reprinted by permission of The Clarendon Press, Oxford, Copyright owners, from *Political Studies, IV* (June 1956), pp. 128–138.

research fails, that may provide a reason, supposing the matter is sufficiently important, for seeking a policy decision.

Usually the question relates to matters which are currently in the news and the reply is ready to hand. But there is always a first time for any question, and then the answer has to be sought. It is normally to be found among the following sources:

1. Annual Conference decisions.
2. Resolutions of the National Executive Committee (NEC).
3. Motions of the Parliamentary Labour Party (PLP).
4. Declarations by official spokesmen in the House of Commons.
5. Public statements by the Leader or Deputy-Leader.

These sources are not listed in order of precedence, nor could they be, for reasons which will emerge. Yet the way in which policy is decided hinges on the relations between them.

I

Annual Conference

The Party Constitution assigns wide functions to Conference in respect of policy. One of the Party Objects is 'To give effect as far as may be practicable to the principles from time to time approved by the Party Conference.' Further, 'The Party Conference shall decide from time to time what specific proposals of legislative, financial or administrative reform shall be included in the Party Programme. No proposal shall be included in the Party Programme unless it has been adopted by the Party Conference by a majority of not less than two-thirds of the votes recorded on a card vote.' Finally, 'The work of the Party shall be under the direction and control of the Party Conference which shall itself be subject to the Constitution and Standing Orders of the Party.'

According to the Constitution, therefore, Conference is the supreme authority on policy. It has been questioned whether this is so in practice. Mr. R. T. McKenzie, in his book *British Political Parties* contends: 'Like Bagehot's constitutional monarch, the annual party conference has the right to be consulted, the right to encourage, and the right to warn.'[1] Whatever may have been the case when Labour was in office, this contention is a considerable underestimate of the role of the Labour Party Conference in opposition.

The Leader of the Labour Party gave a different interpretation in his exchange of letters with Mr. Churchill concerning the Laski episode. Mr. Attlee wrote: 'Within the programme adopted by the annual party conference, the Parliamentary Labour Party has complete discretion in its conduct of Parliamentary business and in the attitude it should adopt to legislation tabled by other parties.'[2] As will appear, this is not only a more

---

[1] R. T. McKenzie, *British Political Parties* (London, 1955), p. 583.
[2] *The Times,* 3 July 1945.

authoritative but also a more accurate statement of the relation between Conference and the PLP. The PLP has complete discretion — within limits laid down by Conference. Although Conference cannot give positive instructions to the PLP, it is nevertheless a higher authority than the PLP inasmuch as it determines the bounds of the PLP's actions. In practice, this applies not merely to the Party Programme but to Conference decisions generally.

To attempt to give the reasons would lead too far afield into the history and structure of the Labour Party. Nor does it really require explanation that the terms of the Constitution have some bearing on the actual position. It is not without significance that the PLP has each year to give an account of itself to Conference, nor that parliamentary candidates must undertake to 'accept and conform to the Constitution, Programme, Principles and Policy of the Party'. A rift between the PLP and Conference would be a free gift of political capital to the Party's opponents which it is obviously desirable to avoid. Moreover, in considering the relation between the PLP and Conference, it is sometimes overlooked that Conference decisions are mandatory upon the National Executive Committee and the Party headquarters.

The important fact is that Conference decisions are generally regarded as binding, at least to the extent that they are not to be contravened. Arguments may develop about differing interpretations of a Conference decision, or it may be contended that the situation has changed so radically as to make the decision no longer applicable; but no other organ of the Party claims the authority to override Conference. For example, the PLP decision concerning Western European Union in November 1954 was argued largely in relation to the resolution adopted at the previous Scarborough Conference. There was room for differences of interpretation, and the argument persisted; but the question of a West German defence contribution in some form was generally regarded as settled by the Conference.

At Scarborough, as at previous Conferences, there was not the impression that Conference was merely being consulted, warning, or encouraging. Conference was taking a decision which was hard fought and hung in the balance until the last. Some interesting remarks were made by Mr. Morrison about the situation that would arise if the NEC were defeated:

> If the Executive motion were lost today we should be in a chaotic situation in the House of Commons. . . . If the Party is in a state of confusion about this, with a sharp division between the Parliamentary leaders and the Party you will hear about it in the Election and it will not be very convenient. Supposing a Labour Government is returned, which is quite possible, are we going to be faced as a Government, as Mr. Attlee said, with a situation in which we are tied and fettered and cannot think in relation to the facts of a changing situation?[3]

There is an implication here, as there was in Mr. Attlee's speech, that the Conference decision would be binding on a Labour Government. Resisting the temptation to pursue that speculation, it may be said that, *a fortiori*, it would be binding on the Party in opposition. Had the vote gone the other

[3] *Labour Party Annual Report,* 1954, p. 108.

way, it is difficult to see how the PLP could have avoided voting against the Western European Union agreements. At the very least, the opponents of German rearmament would have had the endorsement of Conference for doing so, and would hardly have missed the opportunity. This was the expectation at the time, so much so that speculation centred, not on the consequential action of the PLP, but on the position of the Leader and Deputy-Leader in the event of defeat at Conference. It would be superfluous to multiply illustrations. There would be no need to labour the point had it not been challenged. Participants seem to have fewer doubts than observers that Labour Party Conferences really take decisions which determine policy.

There remains the argument that, nevertheless, the parliamentary leaders can be sure of having their way through their control of the NEC and the support of the block vote of the big trade unions at Conference. Mr. McKenzie puts it as follows:

> To summarize (and to put the matter bluntly), the parliamentary party for the most part receives the advice it wants to hear from the NEC and the party conference, first, because the PLP normally dominates the NEC by a system of overlapping membership, and second, because the PLP leaders are usually in effective control of the conference since the block votes of the big trade unions are almost invariably cast on the side of the parliamentary leaders of the party.[4]

The presentation of this argument is somewhat confused. The NEC faces Conference collectively, without distinction between the parliamentary leaders and the rest. The argument is presumably that the parliamentary leaders normally control the NEC and the NEC in turn usually controls Conference by means of the block vote of the big trade unions. On this interpretation the NEC acts as a connecting link — one might almost say transmission belt — between Conference and the parliamentary leaders. This makes a tidy pattern — much more tidy than the reality.

II

The National Executive Committee

Much has been said and written about the effect of the block vote and the 'steamroller' of the big trade unions. What is sometimes lost sight of is that it is not very extraordinary that the majority of Conference supports the NEC most of the time. It would be more surprising if it did not — however that majority may be constituted.

The NEC cannot count on automatic support, from any section of Conference, for any policy that it may choose. On the contrary, estimates of the feeling within the Party and probable Conference reactions play a considerable part in shaping proposals made by the NEC. This may be stigmatized as juggling with the Conference votes; it may equally be regarded as an essential part of the democratic process by which the leadership and the

---

[4] *British Political Parties,* p. 424.

rank and file are kept in step. Results are not guaranteed: it is not very exceptional for the NEC to be defeated at Conference or be obliged to make concessions. The support of the big trade unions is by no means invariable. Of the big six — Transport and General Workers, Mineworkers, Engineers, General and Municipal Workers, Railwaymen, and USDAW — the T & G, NUM, and G & M are to be found more often in support of the NEC than the other three. In the vote on the German question at the 1954 Conference the big six were divided, three for the NEC and three against. To cite another example, at the 1953 Conference Arthur Deakin threw his not inconsiderable weight against the NEC on education policy, and had the issue been pressed it is likely that the NEC would have been defeated.

To attribute NEC majorities at Conference to the consistent backing of the big trade unions is a superficial and partial analysis. It omits the important point that the object of the NEC is precisely to secure majority support at Conference, and that support is normally obtained, both from the trade unions and the constituency parties, in the policy-making process. The association of the trade unions with policy-making is provided by trade union representation on the NEC (although trade union members do not sit as representatives of their respective unions), meetings of the National Council of Labour, and a variety of consultations, formal or informal, with the TUC, all of which help to define the majority view. The participation of constituency parties in policy-making operates through somewhat different channels. The combination of these two continuing processes results each year in Conference decisions which, if the NEC is successful in its policy-making, should normally go in its favour.

The NEC's role is not confined to guidance of Conference. It also makes declarations of policy between Conferences. It regards itself as having the right and the duty to interpret Conference decisions or, if need be, to decide new policy. For example, the Margate (1953) Conference declared that 'there should be no German rearmament before further efforts have been made to secure the peaceful reunification of Germany.' After the Berlin Conference the NEC came to the conclusion that 'further efforts have been made and have been frustrated by the Soviet Union,' and accordingly declared in favour of a West German defence contribution. Such decisions are subject to Conference approval and could be repudiated by the subsequent Conference. This is less likely to happen in respect of policy decisions if only because, in the interval, the decision will probably become a *fait accompli* or the situation will change so as to present the question in a different form. The NEC decision in favour of the European Defence Community was not challenged at the 1954 Conference, although it had provoked strong reactions when it was made. By the time of the Conference the breakdown of EDC had caused the decision to lapse, and the debate on German rearmament took place on an emergency NEC resolution, adjusted to the changed situation, and a counter-motion from the floor.

The NEC has therefore considerable power to decide policy, but is very much aware that it is subordinate to Conference. Occasionally this is carried to the point that the NEC implements Conference wishes which have not formally been expressed. The much-publicized visit to China in 1954 provides an illustration. At the 1953 Conference there was a resolution on the agenda asking for a goodwill mission to be sent to Russia and China. The resolution was not reached at Conference, and was therefore automatically remitted to the NEC. Usually the NEC seizes the opportunity to bury such resolutions. But in this case the NEC had decided before the Conference to accept the resolution in principle, and there was no reason to suppose that Conference would not have carried it. It was therefore decided that an inquiry should be made through the Chinese Minister in Switzerland. The mission followed when an invitation was received from China several months later.

III

The NEC and the PLP

The Constitution prescribes that 'The Executive Committee shall, subject to the control and directions of the Party Conference, be the Administrative Authority of the Party.' In this, its position differs from the PLP which is not subject to positive instructions by Conference. It might be supposed therefore that the PLP has superior authority to the NEC in deciding policy. In fact, however, their relationship tends to fluctuate. Since both the NEC and the PLP have the right to interpret Conference decisions, the clearest indication of their relative authority would emerge where there is a conflict of interpretation. This very rarely happens, for reasons which will be indicated. But there is one instance which occurred in 1954, relating to National Service.

On 2 March 1954 Mr. Shinwell, on behalf of the PLP, moved an amendment to the Government motion on National Service, regretting that the Government '. . . in particular, has made no proposals for a reduction in the length of National Service.' Ordinarily, this would have meant that the Labour Party had decided in favour of a cut in the call-up, and the Labour League of Youth, naturally jumping to that conclusion, embarked on a campaign to the effect that 'Two years is too long.' At that time, however, a tripartite committee drawn from the NEC, TUC, and Parliamentary Committee was considering the question of National Service, and had not yet reached a conclusion. The PLP had 'jumped the gun.' Neither the NEC nor the TUC was prepared to be presented with a *fait accompli* in this fashion, so the policy remained in suspense. The PLP amendment did not receive the customary publicity in Party literature, and the League of Youth campaign with some difficulty was called off.

The tripartite committee eventually recommended that there should be a committee of inquiry into the National Service Acts, and this recommendation was endorsed by the NEC. At the 1954 Conference, therefore, the NEC opposed resolutions calling for a cut in the period of National Service, and succeeded in having them all remitted. On 28 April 1955 a motion on National Service was again moved in the House of Commons on behalf the PLP by Mr. Shinwell. This time it read: '. . . the time has now arrived for a review . . . of the operation of the National Service Acts in the light of existing circumstances and commitments and, in particular, as to whether the period of

National Service should still remain at two years.' In this instance, therefore — a very exceptional one — of conflict between the PLP and NEC, the PLP fell into line with the NEC and TUC. Subsequently, the General Election Manifesto produced by a joint meeting of the NEC and Parliamentary Committee stated: 'A Labour Government will at once submit all problems of defence to a searching enquiry. In particular, it will review the period of National Service.'

The role of the NEC in preparing an election manifesto also seems to suggest that in policy decision it carries somewhat more weight than the PLP. According to the Constitution, 'The National Executive Committee and the Executive Committee of the Parliamentary Labour Party shall decide which items from the Party Programme shall be included in the Manifesto which shall be issued by the National Executive Committee prior to every General Election.' Mr. McKenzie asserts: 'It has already been noted that the NEC and PLP must *jointly* decide which items shall be included in the manifesto and there can be little doubt that the influence of the PLP in these discussions is overwhelming, if for no other reason than that the NEC normally includes a majority of PLP members.'[5] This assumes a dichotomy between M.P.s and the rest, for which there is no warrant. It is equally true, and more relevant, that in a joint meeting between the NEC and the Parliamentary Committee the NEC has a majority.

What happened at the last election was that a draft manifesto was prepared by the Office. This was considered and revised by the NEC. At that stage the members of the Parliamentary Committee were invited by the NEC to attend a joint meeting to consider the revised draft. The presence of the additional members from the Parliamentary Committee at that meeting did not significantly affect the draft, to which only minor alterations were made. Unquestionably, at the last election, the NEC had the primary role in determining the election manifesto.

This is not to say that the NEC has primacy over the PLP in policy decision — merely that the relations between those two bodies are not so simple as some writers have portrayed them. Ordinarily, while Parliament is sitting, policy is expounded by the Parliamentary Committee and official spokesmen on behalf of the PLP. But the role of the NEC is enhanced when Parliament is not sitting, since it usually meets at least once a month except August whereas the PLP does not meet during recess. The NEC has sole responsibility for policy *vis-à-vis* Conference at which members of the PLP are present merely *ex officio* without voting rights. Judging by recent experience, the NEC has the major role in formulating the election manifesto. Finally, there is a tendency for the NEC to take a hand in policy when the PLP appears deadlocked or acutely divided, as over German rearmament.

How are the policy decisions of the NEC and the PLP kept on the same track? That a divergence can occur has been shown in the matter of National Service. Usually the two bodies do not find themselves considering the same questions of policy simultaneously. If a question which is currently being

---

[5] *British Political Parties,* p. 486.

considered in Parliament is raised in the NEC, the Leader or Deputy-Leader or a member of the Parliamentary Committee would indicate the position, and it would usually be left to be dealt with by the PLP. If the NEC felt strongly that it should have a say in the matter, a joint meeting with the Parliamentary Committee or some other form of consultation would be arranged.

There is, however, an instance of the two bodies dealing with the same question simultaneously, which gave rise to some difficulties of co-ordination. After the Berlin Conference the International Sub-Committee of the NEC on 16 February 1954 decided (by a majority) that a statement should be prepared to the effect that the 'further efforts' postulated by the 1953 Conference resolution had now been made. This statement had to be drafted and circulated to the NEC several days in advance of the next meeting which was due on 24 February. Meanwhile, on 18 February the Government announced that there would be a debate on the Berlin Conference — also on 24 February. A parallel decision was therefore required by the PLP. In the first instance the Parliamentary Committee had to make up its collective mind about the recommendation which it would submit to the PLP, and it was obviously desirable that there should be some similarity between that recommendation and the statement which was being prepared for the NEC. The draft of the statement was therefore communicated to the Parliamentary Committee.

The recommendation which the Parliamentary Committee made to the PLP meeting on 23 February was substantially similar to the NEC draft statement, except for the omission of an endorsement of EDC. The recommendation scraped through the PLP by an extremely narrow majority. On the following morning the draft statement came before the NEC and was adopted textually, except for the section relating to EDC which was omitted. This amendment was designed to bring the statement into line with the decision of the PLP (and also to facilitate the acceptance of the rest of the statement). This would appear to confirm the superior authority of the PLP. But the story is not yet ended. The section relating to EDC which was omitted in February was adopted by the NEC in April, because it was scarcely feasible to favour a West German defence contribution without pronouncing on the question of EDC. Policy was decided, therefore, in the case of EDC by the NEC, in the case of WEU by the PLP.

This episode suggests that the relationship between the NEC and PLP does not lend itself to a simple formula. It also indicates that there is no automatic transmission or parallelism between them. What would have happened if the PLP decision had gone the other way is a matter for speculation. Probably, as the majority in the NEC was also narrow; the question would not have been pressed to a decision. On the other hand, had the NEC meeting taken place before the PLP meeting, it is likely that PLP majority in favour of the Parliamentary Committee's recommendation would have been larger.

It has been alleged that the parliamentary leaders are able to control the NEC because of the preponderance of M.P.s on that body. This contention rests on three fallacies. The first is that the policy cleavages in the NEC occur between the parliamentary and non-parliamentary members. During the years 1952–5 there were divergences in plenty, but none that conformed to this pattern. Secondly, there is no automatic tendency for M.P.s on the NEC to support the parliamentary leaders. On the contrary, the regular opposition was the Bevanite group, all of whom were M.P.s. In the year 1952–3 there were 17 M.P.s in a total of 27 NEC members. This is arithmetically a majority; but of those 17, six were constantly in opposition. This wipes out the majority which, for the purposes of the argument, has to be restored by including trade union representatives on the NEC as constant supporters of the parliamentary leadership. The argument therefore starts out from the premiss of a parliamentary majority on the NEC, and ends by depending on trade union support for control by the parliamentary leaders. Moreover, the Bevanite M.P.s sometimes showed a tendency to arrogate more power to the NEC as against the PLP because of their stronger representation on the NEC than on the Parliamentary Committee. Indeed, it might be asserted that the arithmetical majority of M.P.s on the NEC is less significant than the minority of women members, inasmuch as the influence of the women's viewpoint has sometimes been perceptible.

The third fallacy is that the parliamentary leaders direct the NEC. Precisely who are meant by the parliamentary leaders in this context is obscure. Sometimes it appears to refer to the Leader alone; sometimes to the Leader and Deputy-Leader; sometimes to the members of the Parliamentary Committee on the NEC. Whichever is meant, it may be stated that (1) there has been no regular harmony of views between members of the Parliamentary Committee on the NEC; (2) the Leader and Deputy-Leader have not always seen eye to eye; (3) it has not been unknown for the Leader's views to fail to gain acceptance by the NEC.

IV

The Leader

As has been indicated, one of the sources for ascertaining policy, and therefore one of the authorities in deciding policy, is a public pronouncement by the Leader whether inside or outside Parliament. This also applies to pronouncements of the Deputy-Leader, though perhaps to a less extent. It holds good for official spokesmen in the House of Commons, but not for members of the Parliamentary Committee as such, who are apt to contradict one another.

The reason for the authoritative character of the Leader's declarations is evident. The object of the Party is to make him Prime Minister. What he says must therefore carry great weight. Does this mean that policy is what he says it is? His pronouncements are one of the sources of policy. What if they conflict with another authoritative source, such as Conference? It need hardly be said that this is a very exceptional occurrence. But there was a problem which arose in 1955 concerning Formosa.

The essentials of the problem were that the 1953 Conference had adopted a resolution, at the instance of the NEC, which stated that 'Conference declares that the problem of Formosa should be referred to the people of Formosa. Formosa should be neutralised for a period, and Britain should be prepared to contribute to an international naval force for this purpose. Thereafter, the people of Formosa should be enabled freely to determine their own destiny.' There the matter rested until, early in 1955, a crisis over Formosa appeared in the offing.

The Leader, in an interview given to the *Daily Herald*,[6] took the view that Formosa was an integral part of China. The implication of this was that as the Labour Government had recognized the Peking Government, the Labour Party also recognized Peking's claim to Formosa. Some members of the NEC were not slow to draw this conclusion. Others, including some 'parliamentary leaders,' took the view that, although Formosa had been recognized as an integral part of China during and after the war, the 1953 Conference decision related to the new state of affairs resulting from the civil war and asserted the right of the people of Formosa to decide whether the island should be part of China or not. This was the view which prevailed. The statement issued by the NEC in February 1955 reiterated the 1953 Conference decision. This illustration seems to throw a somewhat different light on the alleged nullity of Conference in policy decision and on the control of the NEC by the parliamentary leaders.

In conclusion, another statement of the obvious seems necessary: that the position of the Leader depends very much on who the Leader is. As Professor W. J. M. Mackenzie has pointed out,[7] there is no adequate basis for generalization about the Leader. With a Leader other than Mr. Attlee the position might has been more important or less important: what seems certain is that it would have been different. The assumption of the argument for the supremacy of the parliamentary Leader or Leaders in relation to the NEC and Conference is that the Leader(s) has a particular line of policy for which he requires to muster support. As is well known, that was not Mr. Attlee's usual method. He preferred to let the discussion proceed and take the sense of the meeting.

To sum up, policy decision in opposition has not been confined to or controlled by the parliamentary leaders alone. Theirs is an influential role, but so is that of the NEC and of the 'rank and file' at Conference. At different times one or other of these bodies emerges into greater prominence. In the nature of things, the bulk of policy decisions is made by the PLP. Yet many of the major decisions flow from Conference or from the NEC. It is illusory to seek one focus of power, and explain the rest as a façade. Perhaps, after all, what the Labour Party believes itself to be is a better guide to what it is.

---

[6] *Daily Herald*, 31 January 1955.

[7] *Political Studies*, vol. iii, No. 2, p. 157.

18. Policy Decision in Opposition: A Rejoinder

ROBERT T. McKENZIE

In this rejoinder to S. Rose's criticism of the central thesis of his book on British political parties, Professor McKenzie emphasizes—in his view— the exceptional nature of the period during which Mr. Rose was able to make his observations. He sees a return to a "single focus of leadership" both as likely and desirable.

Those who have worked in or managed party central offices in Britain have been disappointingly reticent; they have written almost nothing which contributes to our understanding of the operation of party machinery in Britain. Members of Parliament, perhaps for different reasons, have been hardly more helpful; they have been ready enough to contribute their political memoirs and autobiographies but, significantly, they have found it unnecessary in explaining the course of British politics, to make more than casual references to the extra-parliamentary machinery of their respective parties. It is therefore most encouraging to discover that Mr. Saul Rose, on his return to academic life, is prepared to share with us his observations on what he calls 'the policy decision process' within the Labour Party during the three years in which he served as the party's international secretary. In his recent article in *Political Studies*[1] Mr. Rose appears to differ at certain points with my own interpretation of this process;[2] I think the difference between us is easily explained and that the explanation may help to illuminate certain significant developments which have taken place in recent years within the Labour Party.

It is important, first, to note that we were dealing (Mr. Rose in his article, I in my book) with different periods in the history of the party. He limited himself exclusively to the years during which he worked at Transport House (1952–5). I was concerned, almost as exclusively, with the period from the formation of the Labour Representation Committee in 1900 to the Labour Party's return to opposition in 1951. I attempted to generalize about the relationship which had evolved during this period between the Parliamentary Labour Party (PLP) and its leaders, on the one hand, and the extra-parliamentary organs of the party (especially the annual conference and the National Executive Committee, or NEC) on the other.

My argument, very briefly, was as follows: in its early years the Labour Party adopted a form of organization which appeared to vest control of the

SOURCE: Reprinted by permission of The Clarendon Press, Oxford, Copyright owners, from *Political Studies,* V (June 1957), pp. 176–182.
[1] "Policy Decision in Opposition," *Political Studies,* June 1956, pp. 128–38.
[2] *British Political Parties,* chaps. vi–ix, *passim.*

Party (including its parliamentary representatives) in certain bodies outside Parliament, and which was therefore grossly inappropriate to the system of parliamentary government as it had hitherto operated in Britain. But in the course of half a century the parliamentary leaders of the party managed to devise means of escaping the rigid system of extra-parliamentary control laid down in the Party constitution. Attlee and his principal colleagues were, as a result, able to provide ministries, during the period 1945–51, which were no more subservient to the party organization outside Parliament than were Conservative and Liberal governments. Thus the Labour parliamentarians, who were originally expected to serve as little more than spokesmen for the party organization outside Parliament, had achieved sufficient authority within the party to enable them to provide both a strong government and a coherent and effective 'Shadow Cabinet' when in opposition. In either case it was essential that the party Leader and those associated with him on the party's Front Bench should play a far more prominent role in policy-making than was, in theory, assigned to them under the party constitution. They would, of course, have to carry with them their supporters both in Parliament and in the extra-parliamentary organs of the party; but the parliamentary leaders of the Conservative and Liberal parties face the same necessity. This is a more cumbersome process in the case of the Labour Party, because the party's constitution formally vests control of policy in an extra-parliamentary body (the annual conference); but the downfall of Austen Chamberlain and the Conservative 'Coalition' Ministers in 1922 (to take but one example) demonstrates the probable fate of any group of parliamentary leaders who fail, on some decisive issue, to carry their parliamentary party and their mass organization with them. None the less, this proposition stands: the Cabinet and parliamentary system of government require that the parliamentary leaders of any party must bear the prime responsibility for decision-making on major matters of policy. And I have argued that, in the course of the first half-century of the Labour Party's existence, its parliamentary leaders did in practice acquire such responsibility.

Mr. Rose, in his article, demonstrates that during the three years in which he worked at Transport House there was not, as he puts it, 'one focus of power' in the Labour Party; the leading parliamentarians did not, he emphasizes, function as a united team which could play a dominant role in initiating policy and thereafter win support for their policies at the annual conference and on the NEC. He remarks (p. 138) that the parliamentary leaders played 'an *influential* role, but so [did] the NEC and the "rank and file" at conferences.' At different times during the period 1952–5, he adds, 'one or other of these bodies emerges into greater prominence.' He quotes one instance in which the annual conference came close to overthrowing a major policy-decision of the parliamentary party (respecting German rearmament in September 1954); and he shows how, on other occasions, the PLP and the NEC acting, as he seems to suggest, with equal authority on behalf of the Labour Party, took decisions on major matters of policy which varied from each other in important respects. After reviewing the events of 1952–5,

Mr. Rose concludes that it is 'illusory' to seek 'one focus of power' within the Labour Party.

Ignoring for the moment this final conclusion, I would accept (with minor reservations) Mr. Rose's interpretation of events during the period 1952-5. But surely he had failed to note that he is describing the symptoms of the grave illness that beset the party after 1951. I traced the long process by which the parliamentary leaders of the party learned to operate the party machinery in a manner that left them comparatively free to fulfill their parliamentary tasks, whether in office or in opposition. Mr. Rose is describing the disruption of the authority of the parliamentary leaders during the period of profound instability within the party after 1951. A number of factors (with which he does not deal) combined to produce this result. As Attlee's remarkably long span of leadership drew to its close, a ferocious struggle for the succession ensued; sporadically the party attempted to address itself to the problem of re-thinking' its socialist philosophy and this resulted in a 'left-right' split which helped to bedevil the contest for the leadership. In addition, almost all of the able group of parliamentarians who had worked with Attlee (some of them for almost two decades to provide a stable, moderate, and comparatively united Front Bench either died in office (Cripps, Bevin) or disappeared for age or other reasons from the Parliamentary Committee or the NEC or both (Morrison, Dalton, Shinwell, Arthur Greenwood, Chuter Ede, Tom Williams). For the first time in the history of the party, almost all of the 'constituency' places on the NEC (most of which for many years had been held by M.P.s who were in broad agreement with Attlee) were captured by 'rebel' M.P.s who were at odds with the Leader and the Deputy Leader of the party on major matters of policy.[3]

This is the background of the 'policy decision' process during 1952-5 which Mr. Rose describes. One did not need to be a sympathizer with the Labour Party to experience a deep sense of anxiety about its internal condition during those years. It is inevitably a matter of national concern if the leaders of one of the two major parties become so preoccupied with internecine party conflict that they cease to fulfil their duties as Her Majesty's Opposition, and if they fail to behave collectively like a potential government. There can be no doubt that this was the condition of the Labour Party during much of the life-time of the 1951 Parliament. From the resignation of Aneurin Bevan and his colleagues from the Cabinet in the spring of 1951 until Gaitskell's election as Leader in December 1955, the virulent contest for the succession, and its concomitant 'ideological' dispute, was reflected in the work of every organ of the party.

Once Attlee's parliamentary team (and their powerful allies among the trade union leaders) had lost their grip on the affairs of the party, there was,

---

[3] This helps to account for the fact that, after 1951, the presence of a majority of MP's on the NEC no longer operated as a factor tending to ensure that the NEC's views conformed with those of the parliamentary leaders. That this had been the case during the period 1937-51 is, I submit, beyond dispute.

as Mr. Rose correctly observes, no 'one focus of power' within the party. It was obviously to be expected that 'at different times one or other of the [party] bodies emerged into greater prominence'; the explanation is straight- forward enough: guerrilla warfare was in fact raging between the 'Bevanites' and their principal rivals for control of the party. When the Bevanites were defeated in one arena, they renewed the battle in another. For years on end the PLP, the NEC, and the annual conferences were convulsed in turn. It was not at all clear, as I think Mr. Rose's analysis shows, where effective policy decisions were made in the Labour Party or indeed, as some would add, whether they were being made at all. And it is certainly arguable that this state of affairs helps to explain why Labour suffered so humiliating a defeat at the end of the period Mr. Rose describes, in the election of May 1955. Conservative good luck and good management no doubt helped to explain why they became, as a result of their gains in that election, the first party since 1841 to increase their parliamentary strength in three successive elections. But surely the incoherence of the Labour Party, the obvious fact that there was no 'one focus of power' within the party, contributed to this result?

Fortunately it is no longer so 'illusory' as it was during 1952–5 to seek 'one focus of power' within the Labour Party. It is obviously too early to write with confidence, but it would appear that the parliamentary leaders of the party have begun to behave collectively more like a potential government than they have at any time since the collapse of the second Attlee administra- tion. By electing Hugh Gaitskell as Leader in December 1955, the party has identified the man who will almost certainly occupy the office of Prime Minister when next the pendulum swings in the direction of the Labour Party. In addition, the PLP has wisely adopted (since July 1955) a modified version of the 'Shadow Cabinet' system which greatly enhances the Leader's authority and underlines his own status as 'Shadow Prime Minister.' Already, as was to be expected, most of the ablest of the 'rebels' have made their peace with Gaitskell. He is still in a far more exposed position than Attlee was during most of his long career as Leader; Gaitskell has not yet been able to build up a team of 'moderates' with the parliamentary skills of Morrison, Dalton, and Attlee's other principal allies. The personal idiosyncrasies of certain of Gaitskell's new lieutenants may lead them, yet again, to exploit the opportunities for trouble-making provided by the party's ramshackle constitu- tion. But Gaitskell seems likely to prove a 'strong' Leader. (Significantly, his version of socialism, based on the doctrine of 'equality,' appears to have been accepted as the starting-place for the long-overdue re-examination of the party's social doctrines.) If the party's prospects of winning the next election (which at present look fairly bright) were suddenly to dim, then civil war might break out again. But, this possibility apart, it seems likely that at the next election the voters will be offered the prospect of a reasonably stable alternative government, should they wish to dismiss the Conservatives.

Yet the Labour Party will continue to be in jeopardy so long as it clings to a party constitution which is based on an archaic doctrine of intra-party democracy which is in fact incompatible with parliamentary government. In its original form this constitution was devised when Labour had only a

handful of M.P.s, and no apparent prospect of taking office; it was understandable that the founders of the party, who had had experience only of
trade union organizations, co-operatives, or the tiny socialist sects of the day,
should think of a political party as a unitary form of organization in which
the 'leaders of the party' ought to hold themselves responsible to, and serve
as the mouth-piece for, the mass membership of the party in the country.
But such an arrangement was obviously intolerable once Labour became one
of the great parties of the State; then the Leader became a potential Prime
Minister and his Front Bench colleagues a potential Cabinet. If when they
took office they were to conform to the British parliamentary practice, then
of course there must be a single 'focus of power' within the party; the most
likely alternative would be some variation of Joseph Chamberlain's hare-
brained scheme (which he soon forgot) for 'a truly Liberal Parliament outside
the Imperial Legislature' which would formulate party policy and control the
action of Liberal Members of Parliament.[4] Such an arrangement would, of
course, have placed the party above the State and, in practice, no responsible
Labour parliamentarian has ever seriously entertained such a proposition.

Yet, incredibly enough, Labour writers and speakers still expound the
doctrine that the annual conference of their party is, as Mr. Attlee put it in
Labour Party in Perspective, 'a Parliament of the [Labour] movement' which
'lays down the policy of the Party, and *issues instructions* which must be
carried out by the Executive, the affiliated organizations and its representatives
in Parliament and on local authorities.'[5] In office, Attlee and his colleagues
ignored Conference decisions (on such issues as 'equal pay' and 'tied cottages')
with impunity. One would have expected them, on their return to opposition,
to recognize the grave dangers of encouraging the conference to believe that
it has the right to control the actions of a future Labour cabinet. Yet, as
Mr. Rose recalls, in appealing for rejection of a resolution opposing German
rearmament at the 1954 conference, Attlee warned repeatedly that the resolution, if passed, would leave a future Labour Foreign Secretary 'tied and
bound.'[6] One can only assume that in the heat of battle Attlee must momen-
tarily have taken leave of his constitutional senses (or perhaps he had in mind
the consoling reflection that Ernest Bevin, dealing with, for example, the
Palestine question as Foreign Secretary, did not behave as if he were 'tied
and bound' by previous conference resolutions on that subject).

Yet it is disturbing to find that Mr. Rose, with no apparent qualms, cites
this incident at the 1954 conference as proof that 'Labour Party Conferences
really take decisions which determine policy' (p. 131), and that the conference
is 'a higher authority than the PLP' (p. 129). He must not be surprised if
critics of the Labour Party ask, as did Mr. Max Beloff recently, whether 'the

---

[4] Cited in M. Ostrogorski, *Democracy and the Organization of Political Parties,* vol. I,
p. 175.

[5] C. R. Attlee, *The Labour Party in Perspective,* London, 1937, p. 93 (italics mine).
This statement was republished unaltered in 1949.

[6] *Labour Annual Conference Report,* 1954, p. 94. Herbert Morrison, then Deputy
Leader, repeated the same warning at the close of the debate (p. 108).

system [of responsible government] is compatible at all with the existence of a major political party whose centre of gravity is external to the parliamentary process itself.'[7]

Surely it is time that Labour Party spokesmen reconciled themselves to the proposition that a Labour Cabinet (or Shadow Cabinet), working closely with the PLP, must in practice have the prime responsibility for the determination of policy. Of course the parliamentarians will inevitably take into account the views of their organized supporters outside Parliament; if they cannot carry their mass organization with them they face almost certain electoral ruin. But why must Labour spokesmen pretend that the absurd arrangement whereby the annual conference is, in theory, entitled (in Attlee's words) to 'issue instruction' to the PLP, qualifies the Labour Party to claim that it is more 'democratic' than its rivals? Why should the PLP be subservient to a 'higher authority' within the party? The members of the PLP are elected by approximately 13 million Labour voters and if the PLP secures a majority of the seats in Parliament its leaders will be responsible for governing the country. What theory of democracy requires that they should be subject to 'policy decisions' or directives issued by the annual conference of their party supporters outside Parliament? Admittedly, Labour Party members number, on paper, over 6 million. But how many can be considered in any serious sense 'active' supporters of the PLP? Certainly not more than a few hundred per constituency.[8] And, as Mr. Rose must be well aware, it is these party workers, and a similar proportion of 'active' trade unionists, who draft conference resolutions and dispose of the millions of votes of the trade unions and the constituency parties at the party conference. A few hundred thousand people, then, control and operate Labour's mass organization (just as do a roughly similar number in the Conservative Party). These politically active individuals of both parties play a vital role in the democratic process; they select candidates and have a considerable influence (recent attempts by constituency parties to 'bully' M.P.s over Suez suggest they may have too much) on the activities of the M.P.s they elect to Parliament. The views of the party workers, expressed collectively at the annual conference, carry very considerable weight with the party leaders, whether Conservative or Labour, whether in office or out. But do Labour Party Leaders seriously suggest that the representatives of the active membership of the party, meeting in annual conference for a few days once a year, should also have the right to pass resolutions which may leave a future Foreign Secretary 'tied and bound'?

One knows perfectly well, from discussions with Labour Party leaders, and from an examination of the record, that in practice they do not. And it is also perfectly clear that, except in moments of acute schizophrenia within the parliamentary party (as in 1952–5) it would be far more accurate to say that

---

[7] *Manchester Guardian*, 19 October 1956.

[8] Constituency studies suggest that, at the outside, from 500 to 1,000 Labour Party members take some part in the work of their local party at elections; but far fewer play any part between elections. If even 200 party members were continuously active in local Labour parties in every constituency in Britain, this would give a total "active" membership of less than 130,000.

the parliamentary leaders manipulate the party organization than that they are manipulated by it. There is nothing 'undemocratic' about this. Labour's parliamentary leaders have no alternative so long as they are both determined to abide by the parliamentary system and reluctant to attempt to eliminate from their party constitution its anomalous provisions for intra-party 'democracy.'

Labour Party spokesmen have been willing enough, on occasions, to attempt to teach particular local parties a little Burkeian doctrine about the rights and duties of their representatives in Parliament. Perhaps those who write authoritatively on behalf of the Labour Party might propagate among party supporters a more generalized version of Burke: 'Your *parliamentary party* owes you not their industry only, but their judgement; and they betray instead of serving you if they sacrifice it to your opinion . . . authoritative instructions, which the parliamentary party is bound blindly and implicitly to obey, though contrary to the dearest conviction of their judgement and conscience, are utterly unknown to the laws of the land, and against the tenor of our constitution.'

19. Foreign Policy and Party Discipline in the CDU

ARNOLD J. HEIDENHEIMER

The Constitution of the German Federal Republic demands that the internal organization of political parties "must conform to democratic principles"; simultaneously it provides a strong institutional basis to assure the chancellor of a dominant position within the system. Professor Heidenheimer analyzes the conditions—political as well as constitutional —that increasingly limited the domination that Chancellor Adenauer succeeded in exerting over his party. The decline of Adenauer's hold, as well as the rapid political demise of his successor, Chancellor Erhard, indicate clearly that the "power" of a party leader cannot be viewed in terms of institutional supports or personality factors alone.

For the ten years that he has been in office Konrad Adenauer's extraordinary powers as Federal German Chancellor have come to be based essentially on his tremendous personal capacities, articles 65 and 67 of the Basic Law, his status as top-level negotiator with and later confidant and ally of the Western powers, and finally, his supremacy among his party colleagues. In his capacity as leader of the Christian Democratic Union he has proved himself in any crucial test beyond the party's power of influence. It is almost true to say that the C.D.U., and its Bavarian affiliate, the Christian Social Union, have entered the picture only every four years to supply candidates to bolster the Chancellor's majorities in both houses of parliament. Many have regarded this as an insufficient basis for party cohesion, and responsible observers have regularly predicted imminent party splits. Yet as its outward success grew, its many parts and sections — the increasingly unwieldy and heterogeneous parliamentary party (*Fraktion*), the party organization with its static membership, the *Land* parties with extremely diverse denominational and social compositions, the inflated and unworkable party executives — held together to a degree which has continued to perplex all observers aware of the wide and frequently bitter differences which have existed within the party on almost any subject. But the key word is "almost." For the vise which has come to hold the party together and forge at least apparent unity within its ranks, has been loyalty to the party line in one major area of policy. This area is not that of economic policy, on which the party initially won power and from which it has continued to draw the greatest amount of domestic political capital. Rather party unity has been forged around foreign policy, and here its

SOURCE: Reprinted by permission from *Parliamentary Affairs*, XIII (Winter 1959–60), pp. 70–84. Footnotes are abridged.

members have been expected to display loyalty largely for the personal conceptions and tenacious diplomacy of the Chancellor himself.

The C.D.U. solidarity on foreign policy has been shaped partly around the Chancellor's European policies, particularly as Socialist tactics have lent some superficial plausibility to the Chancellor's claim that the creation of a United Europe was a peculiarly Christian task, but mainly around the question of German rearmament within the Western alliance. In the face of repeated Socialist attacks ever since rearmament was first broached in 1950, the C.D.U./C.S.U. parliamentary party came to stand solidly behind the government's policy, and has almost unanimously defended it as the best and only feasible way of meeting the "threat from the East." Those within the party who were critical of the Chancellor on domestic questions found themselves left with little choice but to close ranks in support of a policy to which he was absolutely determined to commit the party's fortunes. Advocates of various unification first" policies within the C.D.U. were pushed entirely into the shadow, becoming, as a perceptive author put it, "sextons at the shrine of German unity." For the overwhelming majority of relatively inexperienced and uncommitted Christian Democratic deputies, who saw their own political futures increasingly tied to the public state of confidence in Adenauer, there was no alternative but to stand solidly behind the Chancellor. When after the first rearmament crisis public opinion polls began to note a swing back towards Adenauer the parliamentary party "thanked the Chancellor for the persistence and toughness with which he [had] pursued his policy. Only in this way could success be achieved."

The crucial character of foreign-policy issues for C.D.U./C.S.U. deputies soon became evident in the contrast between the party's voting patterns on foreign and domestic matters. Discussing party cohesion as displayed in Bundestag balloting during the first two years, Markmann found that the C.D.U./C.S.U. was the least cohesive of the major parties. But all the major questions on which the party was divided lay within the area of domestic policy. "In those votes . . . which related to the Chancellor's foreign policy, the parliamentary party supported its leader single-mindedly."[1] For the first session of the Bundestag taken as a whole, the C.D.U., in contrast to the S.P.D., voted unanimously on only one-fifth of all ballots, but of this small number the great majority concerned foreign policy. Instances of rebellion were few and rather severely dealt with. On the occasion of the first European" vote, that affirming German adherence to the Council of Europe in June 1950, only one C.D.U. deputy voted in opposition. At the time the party cited this as proof that the C.D.U./C.S.U. parliamentary party "refused to force the opinions of its members into a single mold." Later, however, when the same deputy, Matthias Mehs of Rhineland-Palatinate, continued to oppose E.D.C. and other government foreign policy measures, he was disavowed by his local C.D.U. branch and eventually not renominated in 1953. A second rebel, the Bavarian deputy Bodensteiner, resigned in 1952 after his local party

---

Heinz Markmann: *Das Abstimmungsverhalten in deutschen Parlamenten*, Hain Verlag, Meisenheim, 1955, p. 129.

branch had initiated exclusion proceedings against him. In acknowledging Bodensteiner's letter of resignation, the C.S.U. *Land* chairman, Ehard, stated that the deputy's divergent opinions need not of themselves have caused the rupture. "Nevertheless, adherence to a political group, such as a party or *Fraktion*, requires its members to maintain a certain measure of restraint. Lack of such restraint cannot be tolerated for the long term."

Reporting on the parliamentary party's achievements at the party pre-election convention in 1953, Brentano claimed that its decisions were arrived at without imposition of party discipline but also emphasized that "the single-minded support of the parliamentary party" had allowed the policies of the government to win confidence and friendship for Germany in all countries of the free world.[2] When, after the successful outcome of the elections, Adenauer met his augmented parliamentary followers, he took pains to stress, even before the formation of his Cabinet or his own official reinstallation, that "the foreign policy of the next government will be an absolutely undeviating continuation of the present line." The voting record of the C.D.U./C.S.U. during the second session of the *Bundestag* indicated the continued tight hold which the Chancellor kept on his party. On the vital votes on the acceptance of the Paris Treaties in February 1955, in which the granting of German independence was coupled with military obligations under the West European Union, the C.D.U./C.S.U. voted absolutely unanimously, with not a single member voting against or abstaining. On five votes on the Saar statute, held under difficult conditions in April 1954 and February 1955, the C.D.U. parliamentary party registered a total of only six dissenting votes, with eleven abstentions, or a total deviationist vote of only slightly more than one per cent. Five of the six dissenting votes were cast by a single deputy. The party's solidarity was maintained even on questions which directly touched on matters relating to religious conviction. On seven ballots on the introduction of obligatory military service in August 1956, which centred in good part on the problem of conscientious objectors, there was a total of twenty-seven C.D.U. dissenting votes and eleven abstentions. Twenty-two of the dissenting votes and five abstentions were cast on the amending motion of the C.D.U. deputy Nellen, which would have allowed exemption for those objecting to military service on religious or moral grounds. Inclusive of this ballot the total deviationist vote on the military service issue was about 2.5 per cent; exclusive of it it was less than 1 per cent.[3]

As the years passed and as the same deputies began to reflect that they had after all been hearing similar Chancellor speeches from the same back benches for almost a decade, a certain malaise began to develop in the parliamentary party, election victories and German miracles notwithstanding. Even the more patient and disciplined among the C.D.U./C.S.U. flock began to feel that the Old Man was taking their loyalty rather too much for granted. Most restive were those deputies called upon to defend the Chancellor's foreign

[2] *Bundesparteitag der C.D.U.*, Bonn, 1953, p. 39.

[3] Basic Source: *So Haben Sie Abgestimmt: Register und Tabellen der Namentlicher Abstimmungen im Bundestag* (II. *Wahlperiode*), Vorstand der S.P.D., Bonn, 1957.

olicy, for increasingly "since tight party discipline assured the government of
he loyalty of an absolute majority in the *Bundestag*, even on issues which had
ot been fully explained, the Chancellor did not find it necessary to provide
he parliament with more than a minimum of foreign policy information."[4]
Previously in addressing his followers, the Chancellor has frequently made it
lear that he did not consider a full understanding of his policies a necessary
prerequisite for loyalty to them. In September 1951, he had asked a meeting
of Catholic workers to secure for him the confidence of the German people
n the E.D.C. negotiations, "even though not every phase of the political
development may appear clear to someone standing outside." Leading C.D.U.
deputies began to feel that the Chancellor was not only rewarding their
oyalty with ministerial positions, but was increasingly treating them as just
o much more voting cattle "standing outside" the real decision-making arena.

Sooner or later this lowering of morale was bound to affect the party's
performance in public *Bundestag* debates. An extraordinary instance occurred
during the foreign policy debate of late January 1958, when the C.D.U./
C.S.U. seemed totally incapable of answering the brilliant and bitter attacks
of Heinemann and Dehler, the Socialist and Free Democratic speakers.
Observers noted that the parliamentary party leadership "looked up to the
government bench with melancholy helplessness," while even the ardently
pro-C.D.U. press deplored "dull-wittedness, tactical failure and totally inadequate organization." A bare six weeks later the parliamentary leadership saw
themselves drifting toward a similar debacle. Another foreign policy debate
was scheduled, the C.D.U. spokesmen felt themselves inadequately supplied
with information, and both Adenauer and Krone were out of town. In
desperation the Foreign Policy Committee Chairman, Kiesinger, acting in
consultation with the relevant *Bundestag* authorities, arranged for a postpone-
ment of the debate. On his return to Bonn Adenauer bitterly attacked the
parliamentary party leaders for having allegedly gone over his head and
repeatedly humiliated Kiesinger in a stormy parliamentary party meeting whose details were reported at length in the German press. Kiesinger
reacted with vigour, and read out to the meeting a letter protesting sharply
against the manner in which Adenauer and Krone had been issuing unilateral
instructions. Other deputies defended him by declaring that they were not
willing to go into further debates without knowing just what the government
ine was in complex foreign policy situations. The whole incident showed
clearly that many "self-confident men, who during long years of parliamentary
activity had accumulated much experience and rendered much service were
no longer ready to be simply the errand-boys of a single man." Independent
observers saw the beginning of a crisis touching on the authority of the government and party leader as against his own parliamentary party. "Up until
now, this authority had always been sufficient to rally the party on decisive
votes, at least in the area of foreign policy. But now leading deputies are

---

[4] Samuel Wahrhaftig, "The Development of German Foreign Policy Institutions" in
Speier and Davison, ed., *West German Leadership and Foreign Policy*, Row Peterson,
Evanston, 1957, p. 56.

claiming the same expert knowledge and therefore the same authority as the Chancellor."

Foreign Policy and the Succession Struggle

The combination of the Chancellor's increasing absolute power, his refusal to share final responsibility with his own party leaders, together with his paramount preoccupation with maintaining a relatively static position in the one aspect of policy which he cared about, came to produce grave imbalance in the German political process. Although considerable decisions had been taken in the area of domestic policy, these did not loom very significantly in Bonn, for the Federal capital constituted an arena upon which the Chancellor had succeeded in imposing his own perspective. To German politicians of all parties it appeared that for a decade political developments in the Federal Republic had been rigidly controlled so as to conform to the image of Germany which for purposes of his personal foreign policy aims the Chancellor wanted to present to the outside world, with little to show for it in the way of progress toward German unification.

The frustration of the domestic political processes had been initially felt by the Opposition, which soon became embittered by seeing their main forum, parliament, reduced to secondary status both by the government's relative disregard of parliamentary opinion and by the Chancellor's policy of playing a solitary hand in foreign policy discussion. In time, however, leading C.D.U. figures also began to appreciate that not only parliamentary institutions but also their party's prestige suffered from remaining so much in the shadow of the Chancellor. Strong personal motives reinforced such feelings. Adenauer's pseudo-administrative methods of rule frustrated political ambitions. The semi-civil service tenure granted to loyal ministers had made it almost impossible for the mass of parliamentarians to gain advancement, especially as the Chancellor impeded the creation of junior ministerial positions. At the same time the narrow areas of responsibility assigned to ministers in the Adenauer cabinets prevented even them from gaining experience of responsibility broader than that provided by the nominal supervision of a department. Finally, the stubborn unwillingness of the octogenarian Chancellor to allow significant progress toward the aim of choosing eventual successors to his power added to the feeling of rigidity and frustration within his own party. Beneath the surface party groups began to jockey restlessly for an eventual redistribution of intra-party power. Although both suffered from the Chancellor's dominance, Rhinelanders and Bavarians manoeuvered for the creation of cohesive blocs, while the North Germans reiterated their complaints about being underrepresented in the government leadership. Protestants claimed the right under the unwritten parity agreement to provide the Chancellor's successor, while the trade union and other organized party interest groups strove desperately to place themselves into line to fill lesser party positions when and if the Chancellor's retirement should allow a reshuffling in the government and party hierarchy.

It was under these conditions that the question of presenting a C.D.U.

candidate for the Federal Presidency election of July 1959, presented an opportunity for those within the C.D.U. who wanted an unfreezing of the political positions which Adenauer's foreign policy postures had imposed. The policy of this numerically dominant group in the C.D.U. was to attempt to persuade Adenauer to accept elevation to the venerable position of Federal President and to put in his place a younger and more vital candidate who would allow fuller development of domestic political processes. The natural succession candidate of this group was Ludwig Erhard, the symbol of Germany's domestic economic recovery. By the same token, however, the members of Adenauer's personal "foreign policy" camp sought to use the nomination as a means of forcing the leading "domestic" candidate, Erhard, to run for the Presidency, thus removing him as a top contender for the Chancellorship.

The task of selecting a Presidential candidate was, in good C.D.U. tradition, assigned to an *ad hoc* group, a sixty-odd man Electoral Commission which consisted essentially of *Land* party leaders and representatives of both C.D.U. and C.S.U. parliamentary parties. Early in 1959 this body began canvassing the names of "neutral" candidates such as Heinrich Krone, the *Fraktion* chairman. But then in February, due to the agile spadework of Gerhard Schröder, the Minister of the Interior, a loyal and ambitious Adenauer adjutant, the candidacy of Erhard himself was suddenly presented to the Commission. Erhard had been cleverly worked on in an effort to convince him of the positive aspects of accepting the candidature, and when the Chancellor took the unusual step of pressing him to accept in a long-distance telephone conversation, his resistance weakened sufficiently to allow Adenauer to tell the Commission that Erhard would run. At this point, however, the parliamentary party protested *en masse* and, aided by party opinion throughout the country, created an unprecedented wave of protest which allowed Erhard to renege on his earlier decision and to announce his withdrawal from the nomination. For the next two months the Federal Republic witnessed the spectacle of the C.D.U./C.S.U. parliamentary party seeking to force their Chancellor to accept the nomination for the Presidency and to hold him to his acceptance.

The varied motives which united the parliamentary party in this effort found a common denominator in the desire to change the regime in such a way as to give greater play to domestic political forces and to the mundane considerations so important to the practical politician. Dominant in the minds of most back-benchers was the conviction that Erhard, after Adenauer, by far the most popular of C.D.U. leaders, would make the best candidate with whom to enter future general elections. These considerations were reinforced by the calculations of regional party groups and their leaders. Led by the ambitious Franz Josef Strauss, the Bavarians came out strongly for the candidature of Erhard and formed an informal alliance with the North German group which also expected an increase of influence with Erhard in power. Finally the southwestern party groups, led by men as repeatedly rebuffed by Adenauer as Gerstenmaier and Kiesinger, also strongly supported the move. Erhard's candidature was also acceptable to leading ideological groups within the party. Liberals were of course delighted at the prospect of seeing one of their own come to power, but many Catholics also preferred a nominal to an overly fervent Protestant in the leading government position. Finally there were those within the party who, like Krone, were concerned primarily with the problem of ensuring a smooth succession in the party leadership while Adenauer was still alive. This then was the "domestic" alliance which sought to corner the Chancellor.

An intense campaign was launched to persuade Adenauer that his acceptance of the nomination would not only help effect a smooth transition of leadership but would ensure the continuation of his foreign policy. It was suggested that he would as President be not only in a position to supervise the selection of his successor, but would continue to hold great potential power for influencing foreign policy. Specific reference was made to article 59 of the Basic Law which provides that the President shall "represent the Federal Government in matters concerning international law . . . shall conclude treaties . . . shall accredit and receive envoys." Varied and ingenious arguments were presented to bolster the thesis that he could supervise foreign policy as effectively from the President's office as he had from the Palais Schaumburg. It was even suggested that he could on occasion substitute for his State Secretary and personally attend meetings of the Federal Cabinet. By April these arguments were beginning to have their effect, and at a crucial meeting of the C.D.U. Electoral Commission on 7th April, the Chancellor reluctantly gave way to the arguments of Gerstenmaier and others and announced that he would accept the nomination.

Two days later, in a radio address to the German people, the Chancellor explained his decision. The address opened with a long discussion of the forthcoming Geneva conference and other foreign policy matters in the course of which the Chancellor defended his policy and emphasized the supreme importance of foreign policy, which "determines the fate not only of the present, but of future generations." In discussing his acceptance of the nomination for the Presidency, he emphasized that "the position, task and work of the Federal President is underestimated" and said that he agreed with his friends that as a result of his status at home and abroad he would be able to fill the position "in a way corresponding to this high office." He stressed that his decision to step down from the Chancellorship was not the signal of a possible change in foreign policy but was instead "intended to insure the continuity of our policy for years to come." Making it quite clear to the electorate and the world that he was intending to run German foreign policy despite his change of constitutional position, he concluded with a ringing assurance that: "The attitude of the Federal Government in foreign policy questions will not change by one iota either during the present period of conferences or during the coming few years."

But the informal constitutional rearrangement of powers thus worked out between the Chancellor and his parliamentary party leaders soon ran into difficulties. Both domestic and foreign critics quickly pointed out that Adenauer's new views of the Presidency implied not only a complete personal reversal and a severe slight on the incumbent, Theodor Heuss, but also did violence to what little constitutional tradition the Federal Republic had managed to accumulate. Adenauer was accused of a back-door manoeuvre to introduce a Presidential regime on the de Gaulle model. The Opposition contested the C.D.U. argument that Adenauer as the newly installed President would be able to nominate his candidate for Chancellor and argued that this privilege belonged to the incumbent, Heuss. Moreover the timing of Adenauer's decision did not coincide too opportunely with developments in international affairs. The stalemate of the Geneva conference, the continuing impasse over the Berlin problem and signs of an increasingly overt Communist challenge to the *status quo* created problems which the Western leadership, weakened through the loss of the dying John Foster Dulles, found it difficult to cope with.

The attempt to unify C.D.U. opinion on the person of a suitable successor to the Chancellorship thus began under something of a handicap. Although a pro-C.D.U. paper reported that "immediately after Adenauer's decision on 7th April the leaders of the C.D.U. and C.S.U. agreed, in exemplary fashion, to respect the democratic rules of the game and the solidarity of a great party," signs of a bitter conflict became public. Adenauer soon made it clear that he was not willing to see Erhard succeed him, even though the Minister of Economics was rapidly becoming the nearly unanimous choice of the parliamentary party. Instead he sought to further the candidature of the Minister of Finance, Franz Etzel, who had enjoyed great international experience during many years of service with the European Steel and Coal Community and other European organizations. Etzel however, although enjoying a reputation as an excellent administrator and having rendered much service to the party, lacked a public profile. His significant contributions, whether as drafter of the 1949 party programme or as midwife to European economic institutions, had been executed largely behind the scenes. He had been absent from Germany for long periods of time and had been in the cabinet only a year-and-a-half. Even after his endorsement by Adenauer, poll results showed that among C.D.U. candidates for the Chancellorship he was the choice of only three per cent of electors, whereas Erhard was the favourite of no less than fifty-three per cent. Adenauer however was adamant. He was determined to see that "the membership of the cabinet [would] make evident to both domestic and foreign opinion that the foreign policy course would remain unaltered. [He was] also considering which Chancellor-Foreign Minister team would best serve German interests at a possible summit meeting. He [believed] that the choice of Etzel and Brentano would be best suited."

But the parliamentary party, unlike the Chancellor, was much more aware of the 1961 elections than of a possible summit meeting. They were unwilling to see the selection made entirely in the perspective of the Chancellor's foreign policy programme. Since Adenauer's decision to resign had removed many inhibitions, members of the party became quite outspoken in declaring that they were no longer ready to accept his lonely decisions. "The parliamentary party has become noticeably more confident. After all it and not the Federal President will have the vital final decision about the new Chancellor. It is a sign of the times that one hears this said quite openly."

The struggle between Adenauer, his foreign policy intimates and a few party leaders like Schröder on the one hand and the parliamentary party and most of the press on the other soon became increasingly bitter. The attack on Erhard concentrated partly on his lack of organizational genius, but mainly on his alleged inexperience in international affairs. His followers, who had for years carefully sought to broaden his world reputation, refuted this allegation sharply, but the Adenauer camp emphasized certain differences between the Chancellor and his Economics Minister on the question of the Common Market-Free Trade Area and suggested pointedly, particularly to foreign journalists, that Erhard's succession might open the way to significant changes in German foreign policy. The other side, unwilling to build up Etzel's reputation as a rival, concentrated their attacks on Adenauer, particularly by exaggerating the decline of his domestic power and prestige. As leading C.D.U. politicians prematurely rejoiced at the Chancellor's waning political power, the press followed its natural inclination to sensationalize Adenauer's decline and fall, with the result that during the critical final weeks of the intra-party conflict the German public was quite misinformed as to the actual power-relationships in the C.D.U.

Although those high in C.D.U. counsels were aware that the Chancellor had dropped hints that inability to reach an acceptable solution on the Chancellorship question might lead him to an agonizing reappraisal, the parliamentary party, supported by the press, continued to believe that it was winning the battle. The Chancellor was reported as gradually resigning himself to the inevitable, the withdrawal of his candidature was said to be "no longer possible"; the C.D.U. was described as "already acting as though Adenauer no longer held the leadership of the party and the government in his hands." In fact, however, the Chancellor held a trump card which those who knew his capacity for in-fighting believed him to have consciously kept in reserve from the very beginning. When at the beginning of June it proved clear that the parliamentary party would not willingly allow him to nominate any successor other than Erhard, he announced his decision to withdraw from the Presidential nomination and to remain Chancellor until further notice. His decision was assailed at parliamentary party meetings whose rebellious temper Adenauer met firmly with the challenge that his intra-party opponents should try to get rid of him in the only way they could, through the launching of a no-confidence motion in the *Bundestag*. But all the dismay and indignation which his reversal caused in all parties served no purpose. Although a number of C.D.U. deputies urged the parliamentary party to take up his challenge, cooler heads soon prevailed. Responsible party leaders realized how completely the party was now once again in Adenauer's hands. Threats of rebellion notwithstanding, the C.D.U. delegates to the Federal Assembly gave almost unanimous support to compromise party Presidential candidate, Heinrich Lübke, who was elected to the Presidency on 1st July.

While the Chancellor's vitually singlehanded triumph over an aroused majority of his own party illustrated his readiness to write his own rules of the game in the assertion of his tremendous power, the circumstances of the struggle again demonstrated the coupling of the Chancellor's personal will with foreign policy considerations. Few believed the allegations that Erhard and some of the men who might have come to power with him would have radically changed the course of German foreign policy. But the Chancellor was determined to resist any lessening of the discipline which he had imposed on German politicians and the German people as a whole through his adamant preaching of the pre-eminence of foreign policy commitments. Although he did express doubts as to Erhard's abilities within the realm of administration and cabinet leadership, his main efforts went toward casting aspersions on his capacities as the spokesman for Germany in world councils. It was significant that much of the argument on this score, both by Erhard and Adenauer, was carried on through the channels of foreign, and mainly American, newspapers and television networks. Those who wanted politics to reflect a greater emphasis on domestic issues were thus rudely reminded of the facts of political life, as interpreted by the Chancellor. Adenauer had made it clear that no purely domestic political considerations, not even the fate and prestige of his own party, would induce him to allow a significant alteration of the policy priorities which he had established.

20. Intra-Party Conflict in a Dominant Party: The Experience of Italian Christian Democracy

RAPHAEL ZARISKI

The Italian Christian Democratic Party represents a case of an "aggregating" party that has attracted widely diverse and even antagonistic elements of the electorate as voters and members. But, unlike French or American "parties of aggregation," it has developed a highly articulated structure and maintained a remarkable degree of discipline. The author's thesis—which may well serve as a hypothesis for comparative investigation—links the establishment of "dominant" party status with the capacity to contain intra-party factionalism and other disruptive forces.

An interesting development in postwar Italian politics has been the emergence of a dominant party. According to Duverger's definition of the term, a dominant party possesses three distinctive traits. First of all, it is "a party larger than any other, which heads the lists and outdistances its rivals over a certain period of time." Secondly, "a party is dominant when it is identified with an epoch; when its doctrines, ideas, methods, its style, so to speak, coincide with those of the epoch." And finally, "a dominant party is that which public opinion *believes* to be dominant."[1]

The Italian Christian Democratic Party (hereafter to be designated as the DC) appears to satisfy these standards. It has had a plurality of the votes in every general election held in Italy since the Liberation. As a natural consequence of this remarkable string of electoral victories, the DC has held the Premiership and the lion's share of Cabinet portfolios for the past 18 years. Most Italian government agencies, public corporations, and mixed enterprises are headed by Christian Democrats. Moreover, in the process of frustrating Communist expansion, the DC has also been able to contain its own democratic allies — the so-called minor Center parties — which at times appear to be condemned to subsist indefinitely as virtual splinter groups commanding relatively few votes. For these reasons, the DC has generally been regarded as the dominant party in postwar Italy, and the political history of Italy since 1946 is often referred to as the era of Christian Democracy.

While accomplishing this radical transformation of the Italian political spectrum — a spectrum characterized by a pure multi-party system before the Fascist advent to power in 1922 — the DC has succeeded in acquiring an extremely heterogeneous electoral base reminiscent of a two-party system.

SOURCE: Reprinted by permission from *The Journal of Politics*, XXVII (February 1965), pp. 3–6, 19–34. Text is abridged.

[1] Maurice Duverger, *Political Parties* (New York, London, 1951), p. 308.

Christian Democracy has become, in fact, a haven for the most disparate elements: the devoutly Catholic masses of such "white" regions as the Veneto and North Lombardy; industrial workers enrolled in Catholic-dominated unions; industrial entrepreneurs in the Milan-Turin-Genoa "industrial triangle;" small businessmen and artisans; multitudes of small landowners and peasant proprietors; an unusually high proportion of women; and a fluctuating mass of sub-proletarians in the cities and towns of Southern Italy.[2]

The Christian Democratic Party cannot be described as being merely a party which commands the allegiance of the traditional Catholic electorate; for it has polled impressive totals in sections of Italy where its pre-1922 predecessor, the Popular Party of Don Luigi Sturzo, was relatively weak. Nor can it be categorized as being primarily a middle-class party, dedicated to the preservation of the status quo. Nor, on the other hand, is it the militant social reform movement some of its founders had hoped to create. Actually, the DC embraces each and all of these aspects of reality. It has, in short, become an "aggregative" party which seeks to harmonize the claims of conflicting interests, rather than the uncompromising missionary sect which Almond regarded as being typical of Continental European political cultures.[3]

Despite its electoral successes and its motley composition, the DC has erected — and, since 1954, strongly reinforced — a branch-type party structure. That is to say, it has become a highly-articulated party, with local sections, provincial federations, a biennial National Congress, a National Council, a Party Directorate, a Secretariat, and precise regulations regarding the selection, powers, and tenure of the various party organs. It possesses an extensive bureaucracy, including an information and propaganda agency (SPES) and a number of functional party offices. It sponsors and supports a number of permanent auxiliary organizations, including a Feminine Movement, a Youth Movement, a War Veterans Movement, and a National Sports Organization. Other branch-type features of the DC include a party press which publishes one national and five regional daily newspapers plus thirty-four provincial weeklies; a dues-paying membership of 1.6 million; and a fairly rigorous party discipline, which is reflected by party solidarity in virtually all roll-call votes in the two chambers of the Italian Parliament. Thus, it would appear that, in terms of organizational structure, the DC cannot be classed with such "parties of notables" as the French Radicals, the French

2 On the DC electorate, see Giovanni Cervigni and Livio Zanetti, "La grande riserva," "I nomadi della prosperità," and "Mamma DC," *LEspresso*, VI (October 23, 30, November 6, 1960), 6–7, 10–11. See also Francesco Compagna and Vittorio De Caprariis, *Studi di Geografia Elettorale (1946–1958)* (Napoli, 1959), *passim*. On the social composition of the DC membership, see CIRD Working Group, "La Democrazia Cristiana in Italia: I. Composizione sociale, struttura organizzativa, distribuzione geografia delle correnti," *Tempi Moderni*, IV (new series: January–March, 1961), 3–21, especially 5–8, and Luigi Pedrazzi, "Cattolici e democristiani," *Il Mulino*, X (September, 1961), 638–641.

3 See Gabriel A. Almond, "Research Note: A Comparative Study of Interest Groups and the Political Process," *American Political Science Review*, LII (March, 1958), 274–278, and Gabriel A. Almond, "Comparative Political Systems," *Journal of Politics*, XVIII (August, 1956), 399–400, 405–408.

Independents, or the Democratic and Republican parties in the United States. And yet, as we shall see, the DC contains a goodly number of provincial and regional clienteles gravitating around "great notables."

The queries we should like to raise are suggested by the paradoxically disparate attributes displayed by the DC: electoral heterogeneity on the one hand, a highly-articulated branch-type structure and strict party discipline on the other. When a branch-type party in a multi-party system is able to achieve and maintain the status of a dominant party, what effects does this phenomenon have on factional conflicts within the party? What is the impact of such a development on the intra-party processes which do so much to modify the actual workings of a party behind the formal façade of its organizational structure?

It is, of course, a perilous venture to attempt to postulate causal relationships between two phenomena which happen to occur within the same span of time. The expansion of the DC into a party of the masses, its ability to establish a permanent claim to a dominant position in every Italian Cabinet formed during the past 18 years, and its successful colonization of the Italian power structure — these aspects of the DC's emergence as a dominant party are of undeniable importance. But it is difficult to *prove* that they are largely responsible for any changes that may have taken place in the nature of intra-party conflict within the DC or for any basic transformations of intra-party processes. And it is also difficult to assess the relative weight which must be assigned to other factors. But since the emergence of a dominant party is a political change of the first magnitude, there is a strong suggestion that some degree of causal relationship between this factor and the various changes in the intra-party situation must perforce exist, although we can neither measure this relationship nor discount the probable importance of other factors such as historical tradition, the intra-party electoral system, etc. Perhaps, later studies of other dominant branch-type parties in analogous multi-party situations may reveal whether or not our assumption of causality is justified and, if so, to what extent. . . .

The Impact of Dominant Party Status on the DC

One of the most notable changes in the character of factional conflict within the DC over the past 17 years has been a marked increase in the number of contending factions. During the De Gasperi era, from 1946 to 1954, there were usually four or five identifiable factions: the Centrists, the Leftist factions of Dossetti and Gronchi, the trade unionists, and the Rightist faction comprising first the Monarchists and later the Vespisti. By the time of the Trento Congress of 1956, the number of factions had grown to six: Primavera, Centrismo Popolare, "great notables," Iniziativa Democratica, Rinnovamento Democratico, and Sinistra di Base. The split in Iniziativa Democratica resulted in the presence of seven factions at the Florence Congress of 1959. And the emergence of the Tambroniani and Morotei produced a grand total of nine factions by June, 1961. Since then, the Tambroniani have vanished from the scene; but the factional picture is still far more complex than it was in the days of De Gasperi.

It is interesting to observe that this increase in the number of factions took place, for the most part, after 1954 and coincided with a period during which the DC had greatly built up and strengthened its organizational network. The accentuation of the branch-type features of the DC had apparently failed to check the proliferation of new factional groupings within the party.

It should also be pointed out that, by 1960, it had become very difficult to define the ideological shadings and strategic conceptions which distinguished one faction from another. It was possible, of course, to discern the difference in outlook which separated the Left-of-Center factions (Fanfaniani, Morotei, Rinnovamento Democratico, Sinistra di Base) from the Right-of-Center factions (Dorotei, "great notables," Centrismo Popolare, Primavera, Tambroniani). But it was an arduous task indeed to perceive the tenuous line of demarcation between a follower of Fanfani and a follower of Moro, or between some Dorotei and the followers of Scelba. In several instances, the distinctions appeared to rest on little more than conflicts between leading personalities; and some factions (especially the Dorotei) appeared to be ungainly coalitions of provincial and regional potentates, each commanding his own clientele.

The contrast between the relatively clear-cut division which marked the first few DC Congresses (and, for that matter, the congresses of the Popular Party before 1922) and the recent confusing melange of mutually-overlapping factions gravitating around coalitions of leading personalities, is quite striking. In this case, it would appear, our earlier generalization, to the effect that a branch-type party structure is apt to encourage the survival of a relatively small number of factions based primarily on conflicting values and conflicting strategic conceptions, does not seem to be borne out by the data.[4]

The remarkable flexibility of outlook displayed by many DC leaders is also worthy of comment. Some — like Mario Scelba, staunch partisan of the classic four-party Center coalition — showed a high degree of consistency in their policy stands. But many others were unpredictable and volatile. Thus, for example, the late Fernando Tambroni — leader of an extreme Rightist faction of the DC — was considered, in 1959, to be one of the ablest and most imaginative of Fanfani's lieutenants and a faithful advocate of the Left-Center policy. When Tambroni broke with Fanfani in the Summer of 1960, such alleged Fanfaniani as D'Arezzo of Salerno and De Meo of Foggia promptly joined the secession. In most cases (De Meo is a good example), these men had been members of the Fanfaniani faction only because of their ties with Tambroni. In other instances, the desire for Cabinet office was probably the controlling consideration.

We find ourselves confronted, then, with a branch-type party in which factional conflict appeared to be degenerating, to an increasing extent, into a naked struggle for power and perquisites among a number of leading person-

---

[4] See Raphael Zariski, "Party Factions and Comparative Politics: Some Preliminary Observations," *Midwest Journal of Political Science*, IV (February, 1960), 44–45.

alities, each of whom was seconded by a coalition of regional, provincial, and interest-group leaders. Conflicts over ideology and grand strategy still represented significant factors in the situation but were no longer of paramount importance. Ideological and/or strategic commitments were often repudiated when they interfered with a given leader's personal advancement. And several of the major factions (witness the Dorotei and the Fanfaniani) ranked very low in cohesion.

Why did this situation come about? Party structure obviously does not provide us with a satisfactory explanation. The DC was a branch-type party in its structure, although its branch-type features were sometimes rather deceptive in many localities where DC organs were only active during election and pre-Congress campaigns. Thus, we can hardly attribute the lack of cohesion of most DC factions, and the multiplication of thinly-disguised personal cliques, to the existence of the kind of decentralized, caucus-type party with which we are so familiar in the United States.

The Italian election law, which permits a voter not only to cast his ballot for a party list but also to express a preference for three or four candidates from the party list of his choice, has already been cited in an earlier article.[5] Such a legal provision permitted outside pressure groups — Catholic Action, the Civic Committees, the Coltivatori Diretti, or even interested bishops and their diocesan hierarchies — to muster electoral support for Deputies who would uphold their views against the contrary views of the party leadership. As a result, a given Deputy might actually hesitate to back his own Party Secretary for fear of losing preference votes at the constituency level. He would, then, often resist the policies of a Fanfani or a Moro — not, as a rule, by open breaches of discipline in roll-call votes in Parliament, but rather by siding with an opposition faction during a caucus of his Parliamentary Group.[6]

It goes without saying that it would be out of the question for the DC National Directorate, or any provincial Directorate for that matter, to purge the electoral lists of all DC candidates who did not pledge their primary allegiance to the program advocated by the Party Secretary. Any such wholesale purge might entail the loss of the several million votes rallied by the outside pressure groups to which we have referred. A particularly objectionable Deputy belonging to a given opposition faction might be denied renomination perhaps, but *some* candidate adhering to that faction would have to be admitted to the DC lists in virtually every constituency. Thus, Italian electoral institutions tended to weaken the central party leadership of the DC in its power to control recalcitrant Deputies and Senators.

The intra-party electoral system also must bear some share of the responsibility for the ambiguity of factional programs and for the blurring of distinctions between various DC factions. Elections of party officials at the National Congress, and at the provincial and local party conclaves as well, were based

---

[5] *Ibid.*, 39–41.

[6] But open threats by several DC Deputies to violate party discipline were partly responsible for Fanfani's abandonment of his attempts to form a Cabinet in the Spring of 1960. . . .

on plurality voting with panachage. For instance, when the Congress voted to elect 90 of the members of the DC National Council, two thirds of the posts (60) were alloted to the list of candidates which polled a simple plurality, with the remaining positions being distributed among the various minority lists. Moreover, a delegate could, in voting for a list of candidates, cancel some names and add names from other lists.

As Di Capua points out, this system tended to grant exaggerated representation to a faction which, while polling a bare plurality as did the Dorotei at the Florence Congress of 1959, still fell far short of an absolute majority of the delegate votes. It also impelled minority factions to form temporary coalitions at provincial and national congresses with a view to insuring the election of as many of their members as possible. Since this horse-trading process had to begin at the local level (for the aforesaid electoral system was in operation even there), the result could be utter confusion. There were no national resolutions of the different factions to be voted on at the provincial congresses. Instead, there were a great number of generic "local" resolutions and composite inter-factional lists, varying from province to province. During the pre-Congress campaign of 1959, for example, when Fanfaniani and Dorotei were preparing for a showdown fight at the forthcoming Florence Congress of the DC, there were many provincial congresses in which an Iniziativa Democratica slate received a plurality of the votes and elected two thirds of the delegates representing that province at the National Congress. But Iniziativa Democratica no longer existed, of course: in reality, Fanfaniani and Dorotei had formed a temporary coalition with a view to preventing any other faction from gaining a fortuitous and disproportionately-rewarding plurality, and with the informal understanding that the "Iniziativa Democratica" delegates would rejoin their respective factions at the Florence Congress. Often, too, a faction would, in a provincial congress, present a slate of proposed delegates to the National Congress under some mystifying label which failed to give any lucid indication of the policies these would-be delegates proposed to uphold.[7]

And finally, at the Florence Congress itself, there was an open electoral coalition between the Fanfaniani and Rinnovamento Democratico, as well as informal electoral understandings between the Dorotei and Primavera and between the Fanfaniani and the Sinistra di Base. Under these circumstances, it was hardly surprising to discover that the Italian press was not at all clear as to the respective strength of the various factions. Even after the last provincial congress had chosen its quota of delegates, Italian newspapers were full of conflicting estimates regarding the verdict of the provincial congresses; and the final outcome of the Florence Congress was still in some doubt until the balloting for the National Council had actually taken place.

As we can see, then, both the Italian election laws and the internal electoral procedures of the DC had a good deal of effect on the course of factional conflict within that party. But the long years during which the DC had

---

[7] Examples of such labels included: Fidelity to the 25th of May, For Social Development, For Increasing Consensus on the Democratic Development of the State, Unity of the DC, and many others.

dominated Italian political life must also be taken into account. The DC's status as a dominant party over the postwar years had combined with the institutional context and with certain Italian political traditions to help produce a multifactional situation characterized by doctrinal and programmatic ambiguity, by scanty factional cohesion, and by a politics of personality.

First of all, let us stress the fact that the DC had become a truly national party, unlike the Popular Party of 1919–1925. The Popular Party had its major strongholds in some regions where the Catholic Church and its lay organizations enjoyed mass support and where the Catholic tradition was deeply rooted — the Veneto, North Lombardy, and the Marches — but was extremely weak in most of the South. The DC, on the contrary, had been able to expand in all parts of Italy, including the under-developed regions south of Rome.

The DC had succeeded in penetrating the South only by welcoming into its ranks a large number of local notables who headed Right-wing clienteles dependent upon them for patronage and professional services. Many of these Southern notables were spiritually akin to the "askari" of the Giolitti era: they were simply local bosses who cared naught for ideological labels but followed the bigger battalions.[8] They felt much more sympathy for the Monarchists and Neo-Fascists than for the minor Center parties, to say nothing of the Nenni Socialists. It was by wooing these local politicoes that the DC had been able to gain votes at the expense of the Liberals, the Monarchists, and the Neo-Fascists. But these electoral victories carried a high price tag: the Southern clienteles, their ranks swelled by the indiscriminate purchase of party cards for non-existent or inactive members, greatly strengthened the Right-wing factions of the DC. In Naples, in Sicily, in many parts of the South, the influx of new adherents did a great deal to help transform the interfactional conflict within the DC into a value-free struggle for power and patronage.

The DC had not only inherited the Southern electorate which once had buttressed the Giolittian system: it has also become afflicted by that same disease of *trasformismo* which had infected and corrupted Italian governing classes before World War I. Prior to the rise of mass parties, when the Socialists were still electorally weak and the Popular Party had not yet been founded, Italian politics was dominated by "liberals" of various shadings. But such designations as Left and Right were often misleading and irrelevant. A Deputy might be elected to office as a member of the Left and might temporarily "oppose" a Right-wing Cabinet, but would blithely abandon his principles in exchange for a Ministerial portfolio or a public works project in his home district. *Trasformismo* was an old and accepted tradition for a governing party in Italy, and politicians were usually forgiven their frequent peregrinations from one end of the political spectrum to the other.

After World War II, even the possession of doctrinal underpinnings did

---

[8] *Askari* were Italian colonial troops: this derisive term was applied to obedient Southern Deputies. See Cecil J. S. Sprigge, *The Development of Modern Italy* (New Haven, 1944), pp. 79, 85–86.

not prevent many DC leaders from succumbing to the siren call of *trasformismo*. Long years in office had created dazzling opportunities and a host of pragmatic considerations, so that numerous DC Deputies and Senators were, understandably enough, concerned primarily with their own advancement and/or with the achievement of certain projects dear to the hearts of their constituents. Consequently, they were apt to regard values and grand strategy as mere techniques for attaining these limited ends.

The growing importance of personal cliques had also been, to some degree, the product of the great patronage and financial resources available to individual DC politicians as a result of the long period of supremacy enjoyed by their party. Some DC Deputies and Senators had served for many years in one or more Cabinet posts. Others had been able to acquire control (through friendship ties and recommendations regarding appointments) over land reform agencies, agrarian consortiums, rural savings banks, local and provincial credit institutions, social assistance agencies, low-cost housing institutes, unemployment exchanges, or the Cassa del Mezzogiorno (Fund for the South), in their respective constituencies. Still others had achieved special competence and influence in some subject-matter of particular concern to a bloc of their constituents. Maxia of Sardinia, for example, specialized in expediting pension applications; and Pitzalis of Sardinia was the subject of a hyperbolic comment to the effect that, "Not a single teacher is ever transferred except in accordance with Pitzalis's wishes."

According to Scalfari, this situation had permitted some DC legislators to become masters of entire provinces or regions.[9] Thus, Taviana (Dorotei) was said to control Liguria; Cassiani ("great notable") was considered to be the "grand elector" in Cosenza and Catanzaro provinces; Colombo (Dorotei) was regarded as the boss of Lucania; Tambroni (Tambroniani) held the Marches; Mattarella (Dorotei) ruled the Palermo area; and Togni ("great notable") presided over Western Tuscany from Pisa to Lucca. Each of these leading personalities had, by virtue of almost continuous service in the Cabinet, become the center of a network of potent interests. In many instances, as Messina has noted, special ties with the clergy also bolstered a politician's standing. Taviani, for example, was supposed to enjoy the special favor of Cardinal Siri, the Archbishop of Genoa, whereas the more progressive leanings of Salizzoni (Morotei) might perhaps be explained in part by his allegedly close relationship with Cardinal Lercaro, Archbishop of Bologna.

The head of the Primavera faction, Giulio Andreotti, was one of the outstanding examples of the type of feudal potentate to whom Scalfari referred. He had been able to place Primavera men at the head of most public and quasi-public agencies in Latium. Also, his long period in office in successive Cabinets as Under-Secretary for the Theatric Arts, Minister of Finance, Minister of the Treasury, and Minister of Defense, and his close ties with Cardinal Micara, contributed to his seemingly impregnable position in Latium.

---

[9] See Di Capua, "La Democrazia Cristiana in Italia: III. Composizione e funzionamento del Consiglio Nazionale," *loc. cit.*, pp. 16–19, and Eugenio Scalfari, "I feudatari si ribellano al partito," *L'Espresso*, V (October 25, 1959), 6–7.

And in fact, the Primavera faction had its stronghold in Latium and in a few scattered Southern provinces.

Yet Scalfari's view is perhaps a little oversimplified. His "feudal lords" were not all-powerful even in their own provincial bailiwicks. They had to compete for preference votes against other Deputies, who were backed by national pressure groups like Catholic Action, the trade unions, or the Coltivatori Diretti, and they were themselves compelled to cultivate good relations with such groups. And even apart from the role played by national pressure groups in local politics, many of the potentates cited above had powerful rivals in their own "fiefs." These rivals, belonging to other DC factions, also possessed economic and governmental *points d'appui,* also had patronage and influence at their disposal. Thus, Taviani might be strongly entrenched in Genoa, but so was Lucifredi (Centrismo Popolare). Cassiani was at odds with Antoniozzi in Calabria; and by 1963 the once unassailable Andreotti had been stripped of his regional monopoly of power, as the result of a revolt among his followers and of pressure from other factions.

The great "feudal lords" to whom Scalfari referred, could rarely boast unquestioned mastery over their provinces and regions, but they *did* possess a sufficiently numerous clientele to assure them of virtually unlimited tenure. For thanks to the device of the preference vote, which most voters failed to employ, any DC candidate who could obtain a number of preference votes corresponding to, say, 10% of the votes cast for his party in his circumscription, would be able to survive even a severe setback administered to the DC in a general election.[10] So, the situation in many electoral circumscriptions was one of cold war between several DC leaders who belonged (sometimes only as a matter of convenience) to different national factions and who were virtually certain to be re-elected come what may. In a general election there might be a struggle for preference votes to determine which of several provinces was to elect more representatives from a given electoral circumscription, or which of several protégés of the established chiefs was to win a new seat gained, or relinquish a marginal seat lost, by the DC. There would also be a continuous running fight over patronage, public works projects, allocation of national grants, and other pork-barrel matters. But there would be few total victories and almost no irreparable defeats.

Why were so many DC Deputies and Senators able to cling to executive office over such a long span of time and consequently to construct their own personal machines at the constituency level through the generous use of patronage? The dominant position achieved by the DC after 1946 was in large measure responsible. There were many Cabinet and sub-Cabinet posts to distribute (even in the days of the four-party coalition, most Cabinet assignments went to the DC), and there was a natural tendency to appoint men with executive experience and/or legislative seniority. There also developed a tendency to represent all, or almost all, factions in forming a new

---

[10] See Raphael Zariski, "Party Factions and Comparative Politics: Some Preliminary Observations," *Midwest Journal of Political Science, IV* (February, 1960), 44–45.

Cabinet, and to select prominent representatives from the various regions. A circular process was thus set in motion. A politician who, by retaining his parliamentary seat in successive general elections, demonstrated his popularity among a large body of his constituents, would be considered available for executive office; executive office, in turn, would usually assure him of continued success in his local bailiwick. Not all DC veterans were able to survive this winnowing process: many incumbents, who had failed to take advantage of their opportunities for acquiring favor with their constituents or who had alienated the interest groups to which they owed their election, were liquidated in the general elections of 1953, 1958, and 1963.[11] But those who *did* survive were often in a position to defy the central party leadership. For to purge strongly-entrenched provincial or regional potentates would be to risk a grave electoral defeat or even a large-scale secession.

In this last connection, it might be well to mention that the peculiar character of the DC, a party which enjoyed a special relationship with the Catholic Church and with Catholic lay organizations, was an additional factor conditioning internal conflict within the party. One of the reasons that secession was an ever-present menace for the DC was the fact that such ultra-conservative groups as Catholic Action and the Civic Committees played a major role in bringing out DC voters on election day. It was feared, during the prolonged Cabinet crisis of 1960, that these groups — organized as they were on a nation-wide scale right down to the level of the smallest communes — might easily serve as the nuclei for a second Catholic party. It was partly for this reason that the central party leadership hesitated to exert strong pressure against DC Deputies and Senators who were openly threatening to vote against the sort of Left-Center Cabinet envisaged by Fanfani and Moro. Only after the Papacy and (in consequence) the Church hierarchy had abandoned their posture of uncompromising hostility toward a Left-Center Cabinet, did Catholic Action and the Civic Committees lose their virtual veto power over party policy.

The achievement of dominant-party status by the DC appears, nevertheless, to have been one of the prime movers affecting the course of intra-party factional conflict. It also had some impact on intra-party processes. There was a general slackening of discipline in the DC after 1954; and this could be observed, not so much in roll-call votes in Parliament (though even here occasional infractions *did* take place), but rather in the increased freedom with which factions were able to organize and propagate their views. Before 1954, a letter from the Directorate was often enough to persuade a given

---

[11] Less than 10% of the DC incumbents in the Chamber failed to run again in 1958. Some of these were dropped from the lists, others withdrew voluntarily. See *La Stampa* (Torino), April 1, 3, 1958. Of those incumbents who *were* renominated, about 20% failed to retain their seats. But it is interesting to note that, of 41 Deputies who were members of the Zoli Cabinet in 1958, all but two were renominated and re-elected. In 1963, less than 10% of the incumbents failed to run for re-election: several of these, moreover, represented voluntary withdrawals. . . . Again about one-fifth of those who ran for re-election were defeated.

faction to discontinue publishing its newspaper or periodical, or even to induce it to go out of existence. More recently, however, factional conflict was often deplored but tolerated: no concrete steps would be taken to suppress the activities of dissident intra-party opposition groups. By 1960, it appeared that organized factions were here to stay as far as the DC was concerned. And these factions were often powerful enough and bold enough to defy the party leadership with impunity.

Another intra-party development which seemed to merit attention after 1954 was the rising antagonism between the extra-parliamentary party organization (the Secretariat, the Directorate, and the National Council) and the party in Parliament. Right-of-Center DC factions tended to be much stronger in the DC Parliamentary Groups than in the party outside of Parliament.[12] This was understandable; for, as we have indicated, the DC Parliamentary Groups represented an electorate which included some millions of Right-wing voters borrowed temporarily from the Liberals in the North and from the Monarchists and Neo-Fascists in the South. The ex-Liberals in Northern Italy would support the DC as long as it served the interests of businessmen and landowners, while the masses of former Monarchists and Neo-Fascists in the South were simply following the example of local notables to whom they looked for guidance on political matters. In both instances, many DC Deputies and Senators owed their election to these recent and rather unreliable converts to Christian Democracy, and governed their actions accordingly. It was no accident that the rural sections of Piedmont (where Liberalism had held sway before 1922) and most of the South (where Monarchism and Neo-Fascism were competing with the DC for the same strata of voters) were both strongholds of the conservative factions in the DC.[13] But let us once again mention in passing the other source of pressure on DC Deputies and Senators: the conservative elements in the Catholic hierarchy and such lay organizations as Catholic Action.

By contrast with the Parliamentary Groups, the DC National Council, a deliberative organ which met occasionally between Party Congresses, contained until 1962 a slim Left-Center majority.[14] It was only natural, under the circumstances, for the Parliamentary Groups to resist encroachment by the

---

[12] . . . The Left-of-Center factions had a slim majority of 72 out of 142 members of the DC National Council in 1961. But by way of contrast, careful investigation by the author revealed the following figures for the DC Group in the 1961 Chamber of Deputies: Probable Left-of-Center — 74, Probable Right-of-Center — 162, Unknown — 37. These figures were based on data drawn from numerous sources of varying reliability and are therefore to be regarded as approximations. Many DC Deputies succeeded in concealing their factional allegiance from their own Group leaders by the simple expedient of not attending group caucuses at which controversial decisions were to be made!

[13] Pella (a great Notable) and the Coltivatori Diretti were especially strong in Piedmont. Tambroni, Primavera and the Dorotei were especially strong in Southern Italy (including Rome).

[14] See Giovanni Di Capua, "La Democrazia Cristiana in Italia: III. Composizione e funzionamento del Consiglio Nazionale," *Tempi Moderni IV* (new series: July–September, 1961), pp. 15–16.

National Council on what they regarded as their prerogatives. The National Council would be convened only *after* the conclusion of a Cabinet crisis and the formation of a new Cabinet. Party decisions regarding the formation of a new Cabinet, or regarding other basic policy matters, would enlist the participation not only of the DC Directorate (an extra-parliamentary body), but also of the DC members of the Cabinet, the DC President of the Chamber of Deputies, and the leaders of the two DC Parliamentary Groups. And it was painfully obvious that parliamentary resistance could often block the aspirations of even the Directorate itself, if that resistance were sufficiently determined and were backed by powerful interests outside the party.[15]

Some observers suggest that the DC National Council was, by 1961, becoming little more than a way-station on the route of ascent to Parliament, and later to Cabinet status. To a much greater extent than the Party Statute would lead one to believe, decision-making power was coming to rest in the hands of the DC leaders in Parliament rather than in the extra-parliamentary party organs. And as Di Capua points out, the pressure from the electorate and from powerful interest groups outside the traditional party framework was a problem which was being experienced by all Italian parties; but this problem assumed far greater proportions for a vast, heterogeneous party like the DC with its far-reaching governmental responsibilities. In such a party, a Deputy would have to take special pains to cultivate his constituents, and a National Councillor might be impelled to think and act like a prospective Deputy.

Aldo Moro's role in the DC appears to bear out in part Peter H. Merkl's observation regarding leadership in an equilibrial system.[16] In a heterogeneous, dominant party like the DC or the German CDU, where there is a multiplicity of warring factions and groups in a state of shifting equilibrium, the leader must be basically uncommitted to any one group and must play the role of mediator or moderator. Fanfani was ill-cast for this role, whereas both De Gasperi and Moro were successful brokers, winning the confidence of all party factions. It was thus possible for the Dorotei to support the Left-Center experiment in 1962, when it was sanctioned by Moro, whereas they had rejected a much milder version of the same experiment in 1959, when it was sponsored by the overbearing and ebullient Fanfani. Moro's mild and tolerant personality, his concern for maintaining party unity, his ability to smooth the ruffled feathers of factional leaders — all these factors enabled him to acquire an aura of indispensability and to serve as guarantor, in the eyes of his party colleagues, of the democratic nature of the Left-Center course.

---

[15] The objection might be raised that the Naples Congress of 1962 *did* commit the DC, and its Rightist Parliamentary Group, to support a Left-Center Cabinet. But we must bear in mind that the Dorotei had accepted the idea of a Left-Center Cabinet *before* the Naples Congress; and this decision created a pro-Left-Center majority also in the Parliamentary Group.

[16] See Peter H. Merkl, "Equilibrium, Structure of Interests, and Leadership: Adenauer's Survival as Chancellor," *American Political Science Review*, LVI (September, 1962), 634–650 at 638–639.

Conclusions

In the course of our investigation we have speculated as to the effects of 18 years of political hegemony on the internal struggle within a dominant branch-type party in a multi-party system and on the operation of democratic institutions in such a system. We have observed, in this particular case, the appearance of certain phenomena which seem to accompany the condition we have just outlined. These phenomena include:

1. A marked increase, over the long run, in the number of factions struggling for control of the dominant party.[17]

2. A factional situation which is based, to a major degree, on conflicts between leading personalities, and in which considerations of principle and/or grand strategy often play a strictly secondary role.

3. A consequent blurring of the distinctions between the various factions, though it is possible to differentiate the policies advocated by two or more factional blocs (alliances of like-minded factions).

4. Remarkable volatility on the part of many leading and secondary figures in the dominant party: much migration from one faction to another.

5. A relatively low degree of factional cohesion and continuity: frequent splits within the various factions and the frequent formation of new factions.

6. A marked slackening of party discipline and a looser rein on intra-party factional activity.

7. A tendency for the Parliamentary Groups to play an ever larger part in shaping party policy and to compete ever more sharply with the extra-parliamentary deliberative organs of the party.

8. A tendency for broker-type leaders, not too clearly identified with any one major faction, to emerge and perform the indispensable function of mediating factional differences.

A few words of caution are in order, however. Not all the above phenomena may be present in other dominant branch-type parties. . . . Other factors in the Italian situational context probably share some measure of responsibility for the above results. These factors include the Italian electoral law; intra-party election procedures; the survival — in certain underdeveloped regions — of a politics of personal cliques; the persistence — in the Italian political culture — of a tradition of ideological volatility (*trasformismo*) which permits a rapid shift from one set of values to another when career considerations so ordain; and the partial dependence of the dominant party on the support of the Catholic hierarchy and of several outside pressure groups. Only studies of analogous situations can help us determine how much weight must be assigned to these various environmental factors in measuring the impact of a dominant party on the character of intra-party factional conflict.

---

[17] Since the foregoing was written (1963), a major change has been effected in the procedures by which the Christian Democratic Party selects its delegates to the National Congress. This seems to have had the effect of inducing several factions to merge, thus apparently nullifying the hypothesis. However, see the final paragraph of this article.

21. A Profile of the Japanese Conservative Party

JUNNOSUKE MASUMI

A comparison of the organizational structures of the Japanese Conservative party and the Italian Christian Democrats indicates that the system requirements of widely divergent political cultures may create institutional devices that function in basically similar ways. In Japan, too, a highly diverse, aggregative party, riven by ideological and personal factionalism, has been able to establish itself as the governmental party by maintaining a minimum of organizational cohesion necessary to win elections and exercise governmental power within the framework of parliamentary majority rule.

Recently, the Japanese conservative leaders have been discussing possible reforms of the party organization and electoral system. Various issues have been hotly debated. Among the points under discussion are — the functions of the Party Policy Investigation Board, the present structure of party management, the presidential election system, the method of party approval for official Diet candidates, local party organization, political contributions, intra-party factions, and the method of electing Representatives and Councillors. On occasion, these discussions have led to serious intra-party conflicts, but little progress has been made in reaching agreeable solutions. There is no doubt, however, that the conservatives have raised the primary problems requiring resolution. In essence, these issues must be tackled if an integrated party organization is to be created which can cope with the gradual expansion of the Socialist Party. The Socialists also have a "structural reform" plan aimed at strengthening the party so that it may come to power. This plan too has raised internal problems within the party. Thus, at the moment both major parties are struggling to resolve their internal problems.

The struggle between two camps in Japanese politics is not new. The postwar political scene has been dominated by two opposing currents — the conservative and the socialist, often called the "progressive." In the fall of 1955, the conservative elements were finally organized into the Liberal-Democratic Party. This fusion was basically the result of internal and external reactions against the system of political control constructed by Prime Minister Yoshida during the Occupation era. The struggles among the conservatives after the end of the Occupation (1952) were very complicated, but mainly concerned with Yoshida — his methods and the questions of his

SOURCES: Reprinted by permission from Erik Allardt and Yrjö Littunen (eds.), *Cleavages, Ideologies and Party Systems* (Turku, 1964). Footnotes and text are abridged. The original version was published in *Asian Survey*, August, 1963.

resignation and successor. Yoshida had strong support from the Occupation force, but as time went on new postwar political leaders appeared. The termination of Occupation and the emergence of new leaders considerably weakened both the position of Yoshida and as the conservative hegemony over the socialists. At the same time, increasing external pressure came from the socialists, who had steadily increased the number of seats they held in each parliamentary election after 1949, and were watching for the opportunity to gain power by taking advantage of the internal conflicts among the conservatives. The socialists reunited in October 1955. This stimulated the conservatives into forming a huge, diffuse party in November of that year, with the Big Four party politicians — Hatoyama, Ogata, Miki and Ono — as the acting board of directors. With the emergence of a two-party system, there was a perceptible change in the character of the conservative control in the post-Occupation period.

The struggle for increased power between the two parties continues, but the current issue is somewhat different from that of 1955. Concern is no longer limited to the problem of central party organization. Now it includes local organization problems. The basic desire is to integrate local and national organizations so as to prevent the socialists from hurdling the one-third barrier.[1] Consequently, the two parties organizationally are competitive in a more complex manner. What are the reasons behind this change? The expanded organizational problem is a product of socio-economic changes that have recently occurred. These changes were not vital to the parties in 1955, but they have subsequently grown in importance. The present essay is specifically concerned with analyzing conservative electoral organization in a changing society.

Local financial expenditures have increased rapidly in the past thirteen years. With 1950 as 100, the rate of increase was 225 in 1955, 382 in 1960, and 438 in 1962. These increases were the result of greatly increased grants-in-aid from the central government, particularly in recent years. Today, more than 40% of the central budget is spent at the local government level.

It is very difficult even for the expert to estimate the extent to which local governments are under the financial domination of the central administration. But, without financial support from the center, the local governments could not afford to enlarge such public programs as road construction, compulsory education and urban renewal. Local governments have full authority only over approximately 30% of their budgets. This is sometimes referred to as "30% self-government."

As a result, local officials and assemblymen have to be very concerned with the trends of central policy, and have to be adept at maneuvers in obtaining maximum grants for their area. Each prefecture, for instance, maintains an office in Tokyo which has regular contacts with the central government and Diet. In many cases, the personal connections with the official concerned are

---

[1] The one-third barrier refers to the fact that the Socialists have thus far been prevented from obtaining more than one-third of the votes or Diet seats.

too intimate. The main task of governors, mayors and local assemblymen is to adapt their programs to the center's policies, and to push the central offices or the Diet into taking favorable action. In this way, they can also strengthen their own "political territories" by the projects they bring to their constituencies. This is also the case for Diet members, who exert pressure on central officials and party officials, in collaboration with local politicians and officials.

Under these circumstances, the importance of ex-officials in the ranks of the conservative party is understandable. Local officials seek to get grants for their "political territories" so as to influence local elections, particularly for mayors or governors. But often, central officials also, particularly those from the Ministries of Agriculture, Finance, and Autonomy, seek to benefit some area in preparation for their own candidacy to the Diet or prefectural governorship. According to the statistics, seventy-eight ex-central higher officials (26% of the conservative Representatives) were elected in 1958, and eighty-four (28%) in 1960. Twenty-one of the 45 governors elected in the April 1963 elections are ex-central higher officials, while seven are ex-Representatives or ex-Councillors.[2]

Thus, local governments are now more dependent upon the central government, and the conservative administration has gained stronger control over local politics through the adroit manipulation of financial-administrative policy. Power seems to be steadily shifting from the local to the central level. This raises a question: is the power shifting to the conservative party or to the central government? The answer is not simple. At least two opposing trends must be considered. The first is that the conservative party dominates the central government. According to an experienced conservative Representative and Diet official, the Liberal-Democratic Party Policy Investigation Board had grown to be a truly powerful force in the policy-making process during 1952–55.[3] Today, the subcommittee members of the Board are very active and are closely related to key central officials. Consequently, meetings of top party leaders which include some ministers can determine government policy, making the final decisions on the budget and other important issues. In general, it can be said that the traditional power of the central government has declined, and that the conservative party has assumed a major decision-making role.

On the other hand, central officials have become increasingly involved in

[2] See R. A. Scalapino and J. Masumi, *Parties and Politics in Contemporary Japan*, 1962, p. 167; *Shugiin benran* (The Handbook of the House of Representatives), 1961; *Asahi Shimbun*, April 19, 1963. It should be noted that Japanese bureaucracy is a closed society. University graduates who have passed the higher civil service examinations enter the society and advance to the top positions of vice minister and bureau chief in their late forties. Their distinct type of personality and technical competence are probably a result of the long service career in this closed society, and these traits can be distinguished from those of "party politicians." This is the reason why it is important to consider the quotient of ex-official Representatives in the party.

[3] Interviews with the Chairman (a conservative) of the Agricultural Committee of the House of Representatives, and the Agricultural Section Chief, the Diet Registration Investigation Bureau.

party activities, many of them as future members of the Diet.[4] Indeed, most of the leaders of factions within the party, the ministers and top party officials, are ex-central officials of senior rank. In the present government, eight of the sixteen ministers are ex-central officials. The Ministry of Finance alone has provided the present Prime Minister Ikeda, Foreign Minister, Director of the Economic Planning Bureau, Cabinet Secretary General, Director of the Legislation Bureau, Party Secretary General and Chairman of the Party Policy Investigation Board. The influence of ex-officials is now decisive in the conservative government and is a vital factor in strengthening the party. Therefore, it may be concluded that the party controls the central government, but that the ex-central officials control the party.

The conservative government can use financial-administrative policies to strengthen the party's local power. At the Fukuoka election last April, Prime Minister Ikeda urged that "local government [should be] directly connected with the central government." He meant, of course, that the conservative-affiliated candidates should be elected as governor and mayor.[5] This general position of the conservatives toward local elections was first articulated in 1955. The Liberal-Democrats, of course, have not been fully successful in effectuating the policy or strengthening the local party organizations.

A major obstacle comes from the intra-party factional struggles. After the Occupation, real power developed upon the Diet, and Diet members were in a position to pressure the Prime Minister and Cabinet on political appointments as well as on policy questions. The conservative factions, which combined together into a single party in 1955, have maintained an autonomous status, albeit staying within the party ranks. Possibly the survival of the Liberal-Democratic Party is because of continuing socialist pressure. Today, the faction has the status of a semi-official group in the party. Most authoritative sources formally list the members of each faction.[6] Factionalism has weakened the party's cohesion and leadership. It is a primary function of the Prime Minister to create and maintain an alliance among the various factions.

In this respect, it should be noted that the factional networks are not limited to the Diet or the national party organization, but also extend to local levels through personal and interest-group connections. In the 1958 House of Representatives elections, conservatives belonging to more than one faction were successful in 102 out of the 117 constituencies into which Japan is

---

[4] Most retired central officials still obtain leading positions with companies, cooperatives, banks, and national occupational associations which are connected with the central government. The central-government-connected enterprises reportedly number 78 and have about 700 officials, more than 70% of whom are retired central officials. Last April, six Division Directors of the Financial Ministry retired, and one will run in the coming election of the House of Representatives. The remainder obtained jobs in the enterprises mentioned above. *Shukan Asahi*, May 10, 1963, pp. 20–21.

[5] In contrast, the Socialist slogan was "local government directly connected with the people."

[6] For example, *Asahi Nenkan*, 1963. It lists 51 members of the Ikeda faction, 50 of the Sato faction, 32 of the Kono faction, 30 of the Ono faction, 33 of the Miki faction, 27 of the Fujiyama, 14 of the Ishii and two groups, 24 and 18, of the former Kishi faction at the end of 1962. *Nihon no ugoki* (Movements in Japan), No. 55, April, 1963.

divided. The 56 members of the Kishi faction came from 46 constituencies; the 40 members of the Sato faction, from 36 constituencies; the 38 of the Ikeda faction, from 32; the 22 of the Ishii faction, from 20; the 44 of the Ono faction, from 38; and the 36 of the Kono faction, from 35 constituencies. But even the faction leaders do not always control their own constituencies. The first constituency of Gifu Prefecture, for example, elected Mr. Ono, but also elected two socialists, and one member each from the Ikeda and Miki-Matsumura factions. The second constituency of Hiroshima Prefecture elected Mr. Ikeda, two members of the Kono faction and one Ono supporter.[7]

In the 1960 House of Representatives elections, the 55 members of the Ikeda faction come from 48 constituencies; the 48 of the Kishi faction, from 38; the 44 of the Sato faction, from 39; the 32 of the Kono faction, from 30; the 32 of the Miki faction, from 29; the 27 of the Ono faction, from 26; the 26 of the Fujiyama faction, from 24; and the 20 of the Ishii faction, from 19. In this instance, the first constituency of Gifu Prefecture elected Mr. Ono and one of his supporters, but also one member from the Ikeda faction and two Socialists. The first constituency of Kanagawa Prefecture elected Mr. Fujiyama and one Kishi man, together with a Socialist and a Democratic Socialist; and the third constituency of the prefecture elected Mr. Kono, one Kono supporter, one Ikeda man and also one each from the Socialist and Democratic Socialist Parties.

The relationship between Representatives and governors, mayors, assemblymen and local politicians in their constituencies is complicated indeed. For example, an old party politician belonging to the Ono faction has his "political territory" in the rural area around a prefectural capital city. For the assemblymen from this territory, it is very important to have friendly relations with him when they are running for election and in other activities. Yet the Ono man cannot maintain control over his own territory without friendly relations with the assemblymen. However, the intense personal and interest-group relations produce many cases of disloyalty and double-crossing. Meanwhile, in the prefectural capital a younger ex-Finance Ministry official, who is a member of the Diet belonging to the Ikeda faction, has consolidated his territory and is usurping part of the Ono man's territory. The assemblymen from the city are naturally connected with the Ikeda man. Additionally, the governor, a member of the Ono faction, is making tentative overtures toward the Ikeda man, but the relationship between the governor and the city mayor, the Ikeda-man's old friend, has not been very close recently. The shift of the governor's position is being closely watched by the urban assemblymen, who are trying to discern where future power lies. Of course, the actual situation here sketched is much more complicated, but the basic outline we have presented is accurate.

The selection of party candidates is naturally important from the factional viewpoint, since this is the first step towards election. The faction controlling the local party prefers to give the nominations to their loyal followers. Questions of total party interest are only rarely considered. A typical case was

---

[7] R. A. Scalapino and J. Masumi, *Parties and Politics in Contemporary Japan*, 1962, p. 86.

the gubernatorial election in Nara Prefecture, January 1963, in which two conservatives competed. The present governor was not selected by party headquarters, but was supported by most of the prefectural assemblymen and mayors and was the selection of the Prefectural Liberal-Democratic Party Federation. The rival candidate, a former prefectural assemblyman and Representative belonging to the Ikeda faction, was the nominee of party headquarters. The national and local party organizations were opposing each other, and the national party candidate suffered an ignominious defeat.[8]

Even more striking was the election in Kanagawa in April 1963. The prefectural party split over the choice of the gubernatorial candidate. Mr. Sato supported the incumbent governor who had formerly been in the foreign service, while Mr. Kono, head of the Kanagawa Prefectural Liberal-Democratic Party Federation, refused to accept his candidacy and supported the Socialist-sponsored candidate. As a result, conservative party headquarters failed to extend party support to either candidate, and the incumbent won as an independent candidate. In addition, Mr. Fujiyama, head of the Yokohama City (capital of Kanagawa) Liberal-Democratic Party Federation, nominated the head of the Chamber of Commerce and Industry as a candidate for mayor, in opposition to the incumbent mayor who was supported by Mr. Sato and the incumbent governor. The result was that the third candidate, a Socialist Representative, defeated both conservatives.

Faction leaders and their networks are more concerned with their own "political territories" and supporters than they are with the party as a whole. Therefore, the efforts to strengthen the local conservative party organization lead to more fierce internal hostilities, rather than to an attack on the Socialists. The loose alliances among the conservative factions tend to break down because of internal conflicts.

Such situation is closely related to recent socio-economic progress. The character of rural areas has been changing drastically. The population is rapidly flowing out of the agricultural sector, resulting in a shortage of labor

---

[8] *Asahi Shimbun,* January 31, 1963; *Nihon no ugoki,* No. 52. The House of Representatives elections of November, 1963 were called the "unprecedented factional elections." Each faction put up its own candidates and struggled to obtain official party endorsement. The results were reported as follows (*Yomiuri Shimbun,* November 7. See also *Chuo Koron,* November, 1963, p. 46):

Faction	Number of Candidates	Number of Candidates Officially Endorsed	Number of Candidates Who Failed to Get Official Endorsement
Ikeda	60	56	4
Sato	76	65	11
Kono	66	57	9
Ono	49	42	7
Miki	58	52	6

The results of the elections show: the Kono faction increased considerably, i.e., from 33 to 50; the Miki faction gained a slight increase; there was no appreciable change for the Ikeda and Sato factions; and the strengths of the Ono and other factions decreased. (*Mainichi Shimbun,* December 1. See also *Asahi Shimbun,* November 23.)

and a rise in wages. The first as well as the second sons, boys in their twenties and thirties, have begun to commute to non-agricultural sectors, or to leave rural Japan permanently to live in urban areas. This situation, combined with agrarian mechanization, increased cropping and other changes, has drastically altered the traditional rural community life. Moreover, the suburbs of metropolitan centers and medium-sized cities have been shaken by the arrival of salaried people and industrial workers who live in collective housing or apartments separately from the traditional Japanese-style communities. Many big businesses are now building plants with housing attached to rural areas. Generally, the rural areas are rapidly changing due to industrial growth and increased social mobility.

Socio-economic progress has been promoted by the conservative government. For example, the basic agrarian law passed by the Diet in 1961, despite Socialist resistance, is a modern statute in accordance with sound economic principles. The Law of the New Industrial Urban Construction (1962) and the Law of the Industrial Development in Underdeveloped Areas (1961) aim at the construction of industrial centers throughout Japan. These policies were initiated and drafted by big business, ex-officials from the Ministries concerned with economics now in the conservative party, and the central agencies concerned. Meanwhile, national and local politicians and local governments are busily seeking special grants-in-aid, public investments, and plants for their areas under the new policies. To the extent that they are successful, they will increase their dependence on the central government and accelerate the dismemberment of their traditional political territories. It is paradoxical that the new conservative policy spoils the traditional conservative wards, but from another standpoint the new policies force those who desire power to create a new type of ward.[9] This may cause antagonism between the progressive ex-officials from the Ministry of Finance and other strongly conservative ex-officials. Probably, this is connected with the conflict between the so-called "Left" and "Right" wings of the party.

What is the impact of these changes on "political territories"? According to experienced campaigners in the prefectural assemblyman elections, one medium-sized city (about 300,000 population) can be divided into three types of districts from the standpoint of the campaign: the old city section, the suburban section, and the rural section. The city is divided into 42 voting districts (elementary school districts). The rate of increase in the number of electors from 1959 to 1962 in the No. 1 school district was 0%; No. 2. 3%; No. 3. 7%, etc. These are the old city districts, each of which has an average of about 9,000 votes. The suburban section includes districts 14, 15 and 16 which increased 35%, 28% and 21%, respectively, in the same period, having

---

[9] The amalgamation policy of 1953 is important in terms of the changes taking place in political wards. The number of cities, towns and villages was reduced to about one-third over a period of ten years, from 9,868 in 1953 to 3,449 in 1963. In addition, the number of the local assemblymen decreased from 52,655 in the 1955 elections to 41,737 in the 1959 elections. *Asahi nenkan*, 1960, p. 179. The old political territories were reorganized and amalgamated as a result of the abolition of the old administrative district system.

about 5,000 votes each. Finally, the rural section included districts 36, 37 and 38 which increased 3%, 2% and 4%, respectively, and have approximately 2,000 votes per district.

In the rural section, it is still possible to obtain votes through the district bosses who retain some social prestige despite a certain disintegrative process. Therefore, it is also in this section that blocs of votes are sold to the opposition on the eve of the election. The traditional portions of the suburban section may resemble the rural section in this respect, but the newcomers in co-operative housing and apartments are more difficult to approach in this manner. The shops in the old city section cannot be controlled by district bosses, but are won by door-to-door campaigns, with various individuals such as relatives, friends or business acquaintances being used. However, a campaigner sometimes becomes entangled with the lines of other campaigners for his candidate or with the enemy. Introductions to shop owners involve complicated procedures. Moreover, family members and employees, pressed from diverse sides, often vote for different candidates.

The prefectural assemblyman election campaign may be easier. Door-to-door campaigns are effective, because of the number of candidates and "floating votes." The electors are not as interested as they were in the local (city, town and village) assemblyman elections. In the local assemblymen campaigns, numerous candidates approach voters by means of relatives or business acquaintances. In a town assemblyman election last April, my mother-in-law had three visitors: a grocer suggested a poultryman, an independent conservative candidate; a neighboring widow urged the support of an independent socialist; while a Sōka Gakkai widow recommended a butcher. On election day, two cars were sent to transport her to the voting booth. The grocer's car came a few minutes earlier, and won, although no one can be sure which candidate she voted for. No car was sent for me; probably they carelessly assumed that I was not a "floating vote." A friend of mine placed a Communist poster on his gate to deter visitors and telephones. As expected the campaigners avoided him, though it is not at all certain that he actually voted Communist.

In campaign offices, there are numerous posters written in the finest calligraphy covering all the walls and ceilings. These seek to encourage the candidates and campaigners. Various small interest groups have sent these along with candies or *sake*. It is doubtful, however, how far the members of the groups comply with the official group decisions. The rural interest groups, despite their comparatively small number, are probably important since communal ties are still strong. Some posters indicate endorsements of only certain group leaders. However, candidates must seek the support of as many groups as possible, since the traditional type of stable ward is disappearing. In a sense, these interest groups may be called a new type of "political territory" of varying reliability.

Another new type of "political territory" is the supporting association established specifically for a certain candidate. It cultivates supporters for a long period before the election, and, during the election, manages the campaign office, contacting the Election Management Committee, the police and various bosses; arranging the campaign truck, speakers, post cards, posters, and meetings; mobilizing people for work in the office; and promoting the door-to-door campaign. This does not represent anything very different from the traditional method of campaigning. At present, however, candidates have to develop even more effective, well-organized machines to compensate for the fact that "political territories" or wards are not so easily controlled.[10] Most of the candidates in elections at various levels have this kind of special association, and the leading members of these associations overlap. The association for a member of the House of Representatives sometimes officially nominates candidates for prefectural or city assemblyman from his district. Then, the latter candidates' associations will officially support the Representative in the next election.

The supporting organizations at various levels are combined so as to stand together against the common adversaries. The top leader of these combined organizations is a member of one of the factions within the Diet, and his loyal followers act as agencies to collect votes in his constituency where the traditional modes of behavior are declining. The result of all this is competition among nationally integrated factional organizations, despite the desire and advocacy of some conservative reformers for a unified party organization. . . .

---

[10] According to a survey made at Shimane Prefecture in 1960, 10% of the people in an agricultural village belonged to some supporting association; 13% in a fishing village; and 18% and 22% in two mountain villages, respectively. The Shimane Election Management Committee, *Political Consciousness and Voting Behavior,* 1963, p. 43.

22. The Socialist Party of Austria— A "Party of Integration"

KURT L. SHELL

The Austrian Socialist party represents the very model of an integrative mass party whose traditional structure is becoming dysfunctional under conditions of "bargaining politics." In this excerpt from a study written in the mid-fifties, the author examines the functioning of the inherited rigidly disciplined and ideologically committed party pattern in a period of coalition government.

The Socialist Party has always claimed to be "not a party like the others" but a *Gesinnungsgenossenschaft,* a spiritual community. This claim was based on the assumption that its members were not merely passive sympathizers but activists "filled with socialist class consciousness, acquainted with socialist knowledge, trained for the class struggle in trade unions and politics." The continued adherence to the organizational pattern of the mass party has been justified by reference to this concept of the Party as a spiritual community and the insistence that the Party's main task vis-à-vis its members consisted in their "systematic education to Socialism."

To achieve this objective the Party organized the Central Education Office (*Bildungszentrale,* SBZ) and requires all District organizations and Sections to appoint, wherever possible, special committees to provide the members with systematic socialist education. Compared to the First Republic, the Party faces a considerably harder task, for the Trade Union Federation, as an officially nonpartisan body, now must restrict its extensive educational activities to the narrower field of labor and union problems.

The scheme by which the Central Education Office hoped to implement the ambitious goal of "systematic socialist education" for the masses was — on paper — thorough and comprehensive. The lesson of the R.S.* period, with its insistence on differentiation between "cadre" and "mass," was accepted in the educational blueprint. The "masses" of the Party members were to be influenced toward socialism primarily by appeals to their emotions. The funtionaries — the "officer corps" — were to be inculcated with thorough scientific socialist thinking, a training which was to rid them once and for all of any inferiority feelings toward intellectuals and which was to provide them with thorough practical knowledge as well as character qualities of

---

SOURCE: Reprinted by permission from Kurt L. Shell, *The Transformation of Austrian Socialism* (Albany: State University of New York Press, 1962), pp. 95–111. Footnotes are abridged.

* R.S. stands for "Revolutionary Socialists," the name the party gave itself 1934–38 when driven underground by the authoritarian government of Chancellor Dollfuss.

276

nyielding forthrightness and decency, a training aimed at enabling them to
nake decisions and accept responsibility in all situations.

These goals were to be achieved by series of lectures and courses: non-
ntellectual though informative for the mass of members; systematic and
rganized at various levels of thoroughness for the functionaries. Straight
ctures were to be avoided as much as possible and replaced, for the mass
nembership, by propagandistically more effective means such as films; for
unctionaries, by discussion method (*Arbeitsunterricht*). It was recognized
nat indoctrination lectures failed to foster real understanding and indepen-
ence of thought and action.

The SPOe has almost totally failed to achieve the educational objectives it
et for itself. In the first place, the Party has failed to attract the regular or
ven occasional participation of more than a small fraction of its membership
) lectures or meetings. Though Districts and Sections do not even attempt
) schedule frequent meetings for the rank and file, attendance, by general
stimate, usually hovers at about 10 per cent of the total membership, a 10
er cent which, as a rule, is composed of a hard core of "steady customers."

Personal contact between the average member and the Party organization
, *de facto,* restricted to the monthly visit of the dues-collecting functionary.
lowever, even this opportunity for "discovering the interests, moods, and
motions" of the masses and "spreading enlightenment and influence" is
ardly ever utilized. Because of the limited time at the functionary's disposal
ontact between him and the member consists usually of little more than a
ninimum of casual conversation. In the words of a local report: "No time
emains for personal political information, no time for discussion with the
nember, no opportunity for influencing the way of life of our comrades."

The first conclusion we can therefore draw is that the great majority of
'arty members are not exposed to "socialist education" in any form. Lectures,
ourses, and meetings are, in fact, provided *by* Party functionaries *for* Party
unctionaries. But in the efforts directed at the education of the "cadre,"
chievement falls equally far short of expectation. The bulk of functionaries
o dutifully attend the frequent talks aimed at them by the Education Office.
ut their apathy or even antipathy toward "systematic socialist education" has
ot been overcome. In response to their pressure, information lectures on the
ractical questions of everyday politics have increasingly replaced courses with
neoretical content. And comprehensive cycles of consecutive talks dealing
'ith one subject have given way to separate and coordinated lectures ranging
ver a wide variety of topics.

Contrary to the original intention, the straight lecture has remained the
redominant form of presentation. In part this is due to the attitude of the
udience itself. For the low-level functionaries, short on factual information,
equently painfully aware of their verbal inadequacy, are content to sit in
lence and listen. In harmony with the Party's tradition they come to be told,
) be briefed. To a considerable extent, however, it is the organization of
ne educational enterprise and the spirit pervading it which are responsible
or this passivity. Trained Party speakers are handed centrally prepared
edeanleitungen ("speakers' guides") on centrally selected topics. Equipped

with concise and dogmatic outlines, they travel the "circuit" of Party organizations, repeating mechanically the same lecture in each location, a procedure
hardly designed to stimulate the allegedly desired "independence of politica
thought" among the functionaries. In fact, the Party's tradition of preserving
outward unity and discipline is not favorable to a spirit of free discussion anc
probing inquiry. Though adherence to Marxism as a faith has almost com
pletely disappeared at the top, the Party "line" is still centrally determined
and questions as to its rightness are unwelcome as signs of disunity.

For a small number of functionaries — the speakers and future teachers o
the Party — a more concentrated program of political education has been se
up. It takes the form of training and agitation schools for selected function
aries, which usually last a week. In addition, the Vienna Party School attempt
to present a thorough introduction to social and political theory from the
Socialist viewpoint in three-semester courses. Though candidates are carefull
selected, as a rule more than half drop out before the end of the course, ane
the total number of graduates between 1946 and 1952 was only 137. The
original intention to revive the Workers' University, which before 1934 ha
supplied an annual crop of working-class intellectuals instructed by Otto
Bauer, Karl Renner, Max Adler, and others, has not been carried out.[1]

In the process of realization, the Socialist Party's educational scheme ha
simultaneously undergone a radical contraction and change of objective
Comparing blueprint with reality, we find that the approach and objective
considered appropriate for the mass of party members have, in fact, charac
terized the efforts directed at the "cadre" of functionaries; and that the
"systematic education" which was considered a prerequisite for the exercise
of any party function has been limited to a very small and select group with
sufficient time to attend the three-semester Vienna Party School. Thi
concentric contraction of Party education is merely one aspect of the con
frontation between Party myth and Party reality. According to the myth, the
Party is the spiritual community of all its members. In reality, as ou
examination has shown, this community is almost exclusively made up of the
core of functionaries who alone participate in its activities and who are forced
to acquaint themselves, if only superficially, with its policies.

In spite of the merely passive and formal role which most members play
the need to "organize" continues to be stressed unrelentingly by the Part
leadership. Growth of the organization in terms of numbers has become a
end in itself, largely divorced from the rational objectives that were posited
for it. In playing the traditional game, local organizations, striving to outd
each other in the number of new members, are willing to woo and hol
members at almost any price. The rather rigid procedure adopted in 1945, b
which prospective members were to be carefully screened and undesirable

---

[1] At present, no discernible effort is made by the Party to utilize the talents of the Part
School graduates. It is significant that the Central Education Office has no record of thei
Party careers subsequent to graduation. The evidence here presented shows that the
"training" requirement for Party functionaries — taken at face value by Duverger — is
in fact, almost pure fiction. By no means can it be said that training represents a pre
requisite for leadership selection.

(primarily ex-Nazis) kept out, was not retained for long.[2] Promises and expectations of favors are widely used to gain new members. And frequently concessions regarding the payment of membership dues are made in order to hold wavering members. The contribution asked by the Party is small — even by Austrian standards — and organizations are authorized to reduce it in cases of real hardship. The plea most frequently advanced by those dropping their membership, that "they can't afford" to continue dues payments, must therefore be recognized for what it usually is — a sign of indifference rather than of poverty. The impression that the motives for joining the Party are in many cases purely opportunistic is bolstered by the frequency with which "nonfulfilment of material demands, such as for apartments and jobs" are frankly admitted as reasons for decreasing membership.[3]

In view of the nonparticipation of the large mass of members in the Party's activities, the tenuous influence which the organization wields over them, and the frequency with which immediate personal desires of a material nature are given as reasons for joining or leaving the Party, one must conclude that the membership is, to a considerable extent, made up of political "drift sand," without strong ideological ties to its principles or traditions.[4] This conclusion is borne out by the previously mentioned fact that more than 60 per cent of the Party's members, while "new," are old enough to have joined the Party during the First Republic when it offered more fervor and fewer favors.

The Party as a "Democratic Community"

From its beginning, the commitment to "inner democracy" has been an essential part of the Austrian Social Democratic tradition, which it shared with other Socialist parties. In accordance with this commitment, three broad principles reflecting the nature of the Movement as a "democratic community" have been officially accepted: decisions are to be reached democratically, i.e., through participation and free discussion by its members; these decisions are to be binding on the elected Party leadership; and those who are delegated by the Party to represent it in legislature or government shall consider themselves entirely as the agents of the Party and subject to its continuous guidance.

Underlying this strict insistence on locating power at the bottom of the

[2] The special committees set up to screen each applicant were discontinued in 1949 through a change in par. 3 of the Organizational Statute (O. S.).

[3] Though Sections are required to keep records as to members' "reasons for leaving the Party," such records are, in fact, only rarely maintained, perhaps because the impossibility of obtaining reliable data is recognized. Of the few District organizations which seem to maintain these records systematically, that of Wieden reported that of the 183 persons leaving the Party during the first six months of 1952, 76 left "because of the nonfulfillment of personal wishes" such as those made with regard to employment and apartments.

[4] Little concrete knowledge exists as to the members' motivation for joining. Hindels in "Probleme des Aufstiegs" (Die Zukunft, IX [January, 1954], 5–9) cites the case of two new, perhaps "typical" members. One, an engineer, joined the Party because he was convinced of the necessity for planning; the other — formerly a peasant, now an industrial worker — because he saw in it the strongest opponent of Communism. Neither, Hindels regretfully remarks, has any appreciation of the meaning of "Socialism."

Party pyramid is the egalitarian ethos of the Socialist Movement with its wish to see equality become reality within the Movement's own ranks as assurance of the future classless society.[5] Furthermore, as a "revolutionary" party it has traditionally harbored profound suspicion of the existing state power and of the corruption which power might bring to those coming into too close contact with it. As the repository of the historical revolutionary destiny, the Party had the duty to keep close watch in order to protect its leaders from this threatening corruption. This doctrine of Party supremacy was unconditionally expressed in 1918 when Austrian Socialist leaders were for the first time called upon to accept responsible government offices:

> We are a Party which has to fulfill great historical tasks and which must uphold these tasks, perhaps uphold them in a struggle, as far as this is possible, against its representatives in the government.

The Party's "Democratic Constitution": The Organizational Statute

Apart from basic provisions for the election of Party functionaries at all levels and the convening of annual Party Conferences, the ideal of "inner democracy" has found expression in two clauses of the Organizational Statute. One aims to assure control of the Party and its elected Executive Committee over those of its leaders who become members of the government; the second attempts to prevent concentration of power in the hands of top leaders through the much-feared "accumulation of offices." In addition, committees known as "Control" (*Kontrolle*) are elected at every organizational level alongside the Executive Committee. They are charged with the supervision of the Executive Committee in financial and political matters and are generally intended to serve as channels for criticism and complaints against the leadership.

Adoption, in 1945, of an Organizational Statute which based itself, by and large, on its predecessor of 1926 marked the rejection by the Party Conference of the notions of "democratic centralism" which had prevailed in the organization of the Revolutionary Socialists. In fact, no effort was made by surviving members of the R.S. to insist on reorganizing the Party along the lines followed by the underground movement.

Some changes in the Organizational Statute — heatedly debated at the 1945 Conference — have had the effect of formally strengthening the position of the leadership compared to the Party rank and file. In 1919 the Conference had insisted on the inclusion of a clause which unequivocally provided that those members of the Central Executive Committee who accepted office in the federal government lost their votes and offices in the Party, retaining only advisory membership in the Executive. Though he recognized that other socialist parties had not adopted such rigid procedures, Robert Danneberg put the case for the clause in terms which have lost nothing of their relevance:

> One must say that today's government — a coalition government, not a purely social-democratic one — is by no means an organ of the Party . . . but of this

---

[5] Many symbolic expressions of this insistence on equality can be found: the reluctance to employ the term "leaders"; the use by members of the term *Genosse* ("comrade") and the familiar *du* ("thou") in addressing each other.

state which today even as a democratic republic remains a class state. The Party must control the policy of the Government as well as the activities of the comrades whom it has delegated into the government and who are there overburdened with work.

When the draft of the new Organizational Statute was presented to the 1945 Party Conference, this clause had been altered by the addition that "exceptions which are in the urgent interest of the Party could be made by decision of the Party Executive Committee." In spite of considerable criticism, which in substance was a restatement of the argument put forth by Danneberg in 1919, the clause was adopted in this altered form, one indication, among many, of the fundamental change in the Party's attitude to state power, socialist or otherwise, and of the decreasing influence of the Party militants.[6] The qualification inserted in the clause which makes the loss of vote and office by holders of governmental positions exceptional and dependent on "urgent Party interest" has, in practice, turned out to be a mere formality. Dispensation has been granted automatically by the Party Executive and not a single case is on record in which it was denied. Resentment by militant lower-echelon functionaries has frequently focused on the clause and its application. Membership in the government, carrying with it power to grant numerous political favors, was felt to concentrate inordinate power in the hands of leaders theoretically subject to the Party's will.[7] But on every occasion when the question of amending the clause was formally raised, the Party leadership firmly opposed change and was finally able to obtain the support of the Conference for total elimination. By this action the Party has accepted the reasoning of its leaders — in complete contrast to the attitude prevalent before 1934 — that personal identity of Party functionary and government official alone guarantees that "the will of the Party and the will . . . expressed in the political bodies of the state be identical." Such reasoning avoids the main point at issue: on whose terms this identity of viewpoint is to be achieved and how much latitude the power holders are given in defining it.

Actually, there is no evidence that the reduction of Socialist ministers to nonvoting membership in the Executive would have materially increased the

---

[6] *Cf.* statement by Franz Jonas (*Party Conference Protocol* [in future cited as PCP], 1945, p. 52), in which this change of attitude was expressly acknowledged. Duverger correctly points out that the demand for subordination of the parliamentary representatives to the Party proper and to the Executive elected by the Party comes from the ranks of the militant elements who do not wish to see radical action sacrified to parliamentary compromises.

[7] The following statement is a typical expression of this sentiment: "The mass of our members demand democracy in the Party. . . . What we demand is nothing more than the establishment of a situation whereby in the Party, too, legislature and executive are strictly separated. We believe that the Executive must lay down guiding lines for the members of the government and that the members of the government must follow these guiding lines. We believe that the members of the government, even if they do not possess the power of vote in the Executive, carry sufficient weight on the basis of their influence to persuade the Executive of the rightness of their views. It surely is no accident that so many identical motions [to deprive members of government of the vote in the Executive] have been submitted." (Josef Jackl, *PCP*, 1949, p. 120.)

influence of the rank and file on government policy, or that the Executive is divided between holders of government positions and spokesmen for "the Party." Formally the supremacy of "the Party" remains assured, for the line which Socialist members of the government are to take continues to be discussed and decided by the Party Executive. And in the Executive members of the government form such a small minority that the weight of their votes — the only issue formally in question — is insignificant.

The clause aiming at the prevention of "cumulation of offices" also has its roots in the traditional rank-and-file suspicion of powerful leadership. It was assumed that the democratic ballot would provide a remedy against accumulation of party functions. The offices referred to in the Organizational Statute thus are public offices, appointive and elective. The old Statute, as interpreted at the 1926 Conference, denied the compatibility of elective with higher administrative positions, or of membership in the federal parliament with that in the legislature of one of the *Länder*. Furthermore, it recommended that any doubling of elective public office be avoided. Exceptions to these provisions could be made only by decision of the respective Party Conferences in each individual case. In a significant change, effectively strengthening the position of the leadership, the Organizational Statute of 1945 shifted the power of decision-making with regard to exceptions to the Executive Committees on the national and *Land* levels, respectively. This provision has hitherto remained unamended in the face of recurrent complaints against the prevalence of office accumulation.

In one more respect have formal changes in the Organizational Statute strengthened the position of the leadership and diminished its accountability to the rank and file. Until 1948 it was required that all written motions submitted to the Party Conference be published in the *Arbeiter Zeitung* at least one week prior to the Conference. This requirement was eliminated on the motion of the Party Executive and replaced by a provision for their publication in a special folder to be sent to each Conference delegate. The effect of this change has been to restrict knowledge of these motions, containing the thoughts and criticisms of local Party organizations all over the country, to the small circle of Conference delegates.[8]

Oligarchic Tendencies

The Organizational Statute, in spite of the changes mentioned, remains ostensibly the constitution of a democratic community. The rights of election and free criticism, with the consequent accountability of leaders to the led, are still formally safeguarded by it. Because of the significant difference which

---

[8] Even prior to this official change, the provision was treated as little more than a formality. In 1946 and 1947 the *Arbeiter Zeitung* printed (in small type) only a few selected motions. (Cf. *Arbeiter Zeitung*, November 9, 1946, and October 1, 1947, respectively.) Hindels protested this violation of the letter of the O.S. (PCP, 1947, p. 99). An even more serious violation, according to Hindels, was the fact that the motion submitted by the Sozialistische Jugend (SJ, Socialist Youth) was published in condensed form in the special motion folder transmitted to the Conference delegates. (*Ibid.*)

exists between the concepts of direct and indirect democracy, we have to address ourselves to two separate questions: To what extent are decisions the result of a process of genuine collective deliberation by Party members outside the restricted leadership group making up the Central and *Land* Directorates? Or, in the absence of widespread participation in decision-making, how effective are the formal provisions of the Organizational Statute in enforcing accountability upon the leadership?

According to the theory of "inner-party democracy," the entire membership should participate in the discussion and determination of policy. The apathy exhibited by the mass of Party members reflected in their reluctance to play more than a passive role as dues-payers renders such an expectation entirely unrealistic. The problem of participation is thus limited reasonably to the core group of approximately 50,000 functionaries who, as active party workers, may wish to be consulted before decisions are taken. A large part of this group seems, however, content to react to decisions taken above by approval or criticism, humbly aware of their unpreparedness to participate in the solution of complicated issues; a frame of mind which, in spite of avowals to the contrary, the Party leadership has done little to alter. Meaningful participation, as an insistent demand, is therefore restricted to that group termed the middle range of leadership, numbering perhaps 3,500 functionaries, who form the inner organizational cadre of the Party. The resolutions submitted by District organizations to the Party Conference protesting the lack of inner democracy on the part of the Central Executive are themselves as a rule the product of a small drafting committee whose draft was automatically approved by the District Conference.

The regularity with which functionaries of this stratum complain about the failure to be consulted in important matters is an indication of the absence of direct, or participatory, democracy even within the narrow scope made feasible by the realities of party structure. Specifically, the Executive has been accused of failure to have consulted or even to have properly informed functionaries outside its own narrow circle on salient issues such as the appointment of key officials in the Ministry of Interior, the redrawing of district boundaries, and the wage-price agreement which vitally affected the nation's economic life. While in matters of public policy government by coalition may have rendered widespread consultation difficult and the need for prompt action occasionally may have been genuine, the extension of what has been cynically referred to as "secret democracy" to inner-party affairs shows clearly the progressive concentration of decision-making power in the hands of the Party "peak."

In 1957, however, when the Party leadership prepared the new "basic program" of the SPOe, no attempt was made to impose a draft without consultation. The 1947 Action Program and the 10-Point Program of 1952 had been worked out by high-level commissions and merely submitted to the Conference delegates as motions of the Executive one week prior to the Conference, a procedure much criticized by some delegates. For the "basic program" the leadership returned to the precedent of 1926, when the Linz Program had been adopted after prolonged inner-party debate. A small committee, headed by Dr. Benedikt Kautsky, submitted a draft (*Vorentwurf*) to the regular Conference. Another Extraordinary Conference was set for six months later to adopt the new program after the Party membership had had time to examine and criticize the draft. So lively was the debate, so sharp the criticism, that a new committee (including the members of the old, but adding several new ones, the Party chairman among them) completely rewrote the draft. The interest of low-level party functionaries is attested by the fact that 1,070 resolutions for changes and substitutions were submitted for consideration by the Extraordinary Conference.

No formal machinery exists by which the process of consultation is institutionalized. The only body which meets frequently for deliberative and decision-making purposes is the Executive Committee, though informal discussions between its members and influential Party functionaries undoubtedly are a rule. The circle thus comprehended is exceedingly small and does not, for instance, include the approximately 70 Socialist members of Parliament — many also District chairmen — who therefore frequently complain about being kept in the dark on important matters.

Though we must conclude that regular consultation between the "peak" (the Party equivalent to the Cabinet) and the lower echelons does not exist, it must be realized that there is no lack of informal contact. The structure of the Party is such that most members of the top echelon are simultaneously active in *Land* and District organizations, where they are surrounded by functionaries of the middle stratum. Thus, complaints, wishes, and moods are readily relayed to them through Party channels. How much weight these expressions of opinion will carry at the top depends, of course — as in all pressure group situations — on the leaders' estimate of the power of organized force standing behind any particular demand or criticism. The effectiveness of pressure — consultation without solicitation — is clearly dependent on the degree of accountability enforceable on the leadership. We will now turn to an examination of those institutions set up to enforce such accountability.

The Party Conference (*Parteitag*)

In the democratic mythology of the Socialist Party, the annual Party Conference is conceived as the "parliament" which, faithfully representing the political community's will, combines the functions of constituent assembly, legislature, watchdog over the elected Executive, and last appeal tribunal. This view of the Conference's position and function — an almost pure fiction — has been recently restated with solemn pretense by Dr. Schärf, then Party chairman:

> As in every parliament part of its task is to watch over the activities of the bodies appointed by it, in other words: to receive reports about their work, and after thorough examination to approve, to criticize, or even to reject. Another task is the election of the Party Executive and Party Control. Furthermore, it is of course a task of the Conference to lay down for the executive bodies of the Party . . . guiding principles for their actions. . . .[9]

---

[9] Adolf Schärf, "Nachwort zum Parteitag," *Die Zukunft*, VIII (November 1953), 301–302.

The following analysis will show that every one of the tasks mentioned by Dr. Schärf is beyond the capacity of the Conference to perform adequately and that its attempts to do so have, in fact, degenerated into a routine of "going through the motions" in accord with the letter but not the spirit of the Party's democratic constitution.

The Party Conference meets once a year, usually for three days. The Executive Committee (and particularly some of its members) are in almost daily contact throughout the year. The opportunity for constant observation and supervision of the Executive by the Conference does therefore not exist.

Two institutions are intended to serve the purpose of supervision. Neither, in fact, achieves it. The first is the "Party Control," the other the supposedly binding nature of Conference decisions. As to the Control, it is elected on the same list as the Executive. Its personnel is — like that of the Executive — composed of top-level functionaries, most of them members of parliament. Its annual report to the Conference is limited to a statement of the financial accounts kept by the Party Treasurer. In no instance since 1945 has it voiced any criticism of Executive actions, nor has it reported a single case of a complaint reaching it from an individual member or local organization. This is sufficient proof that its function as watchdog over the Executive has atrophied and that its membership has in fact coalesced with that of the Executive and stands in the same relation to the lower-echelon functionaries and the Conference as the Executive.

In the absence of continuous supervision by an organ of the Conference, there is no assurance that decisions taken by the Conference will actually be implemented by the Executive. Until 1934 the annual report of the Party Directorate submitted to the Conference contained a brief summary of the action taken by the Executive on the motions adopted at the previous Conference. In spite of the specific requirements contained in the Organizational Statute, this practice was quietly dropped after 1945, and the Conference at present receives no itemized report of this kind.

Even if both instruments of enforcing accountability — control and detailed reports — were used as intended, the Party Executive by its decisive influence over the formulation of motions and their disposal by the Conference would be able to escape effective supervision and retain for itself a wide area of maneuver. First, the wording of important motions is, on the insistence of the Executive, so modified as to make action not mandatory but merely a matter of recommendation. Similarly, occasional demands for compulsory consultation between leadership and low-level functionaries in specified instances have been uncompromisingly and successfully resisted by the Executive. Second, the great majority of motions — usually the more controversial among them — are, in the official terminology, "passed on for action to the appropriate bodies," a method of disposition which is popularly referred to as amounting to a "first-class funeral." The Party leadership maintains this extensive control over the fate of motions originating from the Conference floor in part through the institution known as "Committees for the Examination of Motions." These committees, whose roll is made up in advance of the Conference, are largely composed of members of the Party "peak." Toward the end of the Conference their spokesmen report to the Conference the method of disposal for each motion recommended by the committees. The vote on these recommendations, by a show of hands, has almost without exception become a mere formality. Not once since 1945 has the recommendation put forth by the *rapporteur* been turned down by the Conference; and in only one case does the record show a "fighting vote." In many instances the result acceptable to the Executive is achieved by some diplomatic negotiations rather than by auto-cratic rule. The Executive attempts to work out its resolutions so as to "dispose" of those coming from the floor or attempts to negotiate formulations satisfactory to critics and criticized alike. Above all, however, it is the generally prevalent desire to preserve some show of unity as well as the absence, since 1945, of a coherent inner-party oppositional faction, which have prevented the Conference from seriously challenging the leadership.

The inability of the Conference, as constituted, to act as a legislature is shown on those rare occasions when the Executive, for reasons of its own, desires to shift the burden of responsibility for difficult decisions by throwing an as yet undecided issue into the Conference's lap. An example is the fate of the so-called "Hillegeist Plan." Its author had widely canvassed the proposal that in cases where recipients had sufficient additional income, pensions should be accordingly reduced. Hillegeist had even submitted the plan to a plebiscite by the members of the trade union of which he was chairman. The Executive, aware of the wide divergency of views on the proposal within the Party and of the political danger it contained, referred the issue to the Conference for debate and decision. The reaction of the Conference to having freedom and responsibility suddenly thrust upon it was one of helplessness. The debate was marked by apprehension that the revelation of division of opinion within the Party was harmful to it.[10] And vivid applause greeted the statement that "this question ought to be thoroughly discussed and thought through in a small circle; then we can come before you with a completely worked-out plan." The explanation for the contradiction between the obvious reluctance or inability of the Party functionaries making up the Conference to decide a significant issue and their frequently expressed complaint at being invariably faced with accomplished facts has already been indicated. To enable an unstructured assembly of several hundred delegates, meeting for a few days once a year, seriously to debate and to decide a complicated and politically dangerous issue would have been possible only if the Executive had made every effort to prepare the delegates by briefing them on the issue and stimulating prior debate. The traditional stress on an appearance of party unity as well as the centralization of the party machine have accustomed the delegates to receive the decisions which are handed down to them,[11] though there might be occasional grumbles.

---

[10] *Cf.*, e.g., the following statement by one of the Conference delegates: "One thing has depressed us deeply; we have immediately seen that this plan has not been issued as the common plan of the Party Executive and the Trade Unions, but as the individual action of a single representative. I believe that, when something is worked out, it always first requires the approval of the Party Executive." (Josef Greier, *PCP*, 1951, p. 118.)

[11] The fate of the Hillegeist Plan at the 1951 Conference is significant and typical. On

The most important instrument — at least in theory — yet devised to render leaders accountable still remains to be discussed. The Central Directorate is elected by the Conference. Yet Party tradition, which aims at avoiding open contests which would disclose inner-party strife, as well as the method of voting have done much to deprive this weapon of its effectiveness. The voting is done by striking out and substituting names on a list prepared for the delegates by a Conference-appointed Election Committee.[12] The true arena of contest is the Committee room rather than the Conference floor. For not a single candidate proposed by the Committee has been voted down by the delegates since 1945. The only means used by Conference delegates to show disapproval of a candidate has been a sometimes organized campaign to strike names off the list. A comparatively small number of strike-outs is then already considered a serious sign of a candidate's unpopularity.[13] The replacement of a candidate of the "platform" by one from the "floor" could only be the result of extensive prior caucusing by a strong faction. When this condition exists or when strong sentiment for a particular candidate is known to be felt, the Committee will usually avoid a floor fight by anticipating the wishes of the delegates. As the Committee merely acts as the spokesman for the Directorate, the method of election has, in fact, turned into one of co-optation, whereby new members are selected by the incumbent top leaders whose discretion is tempered by the necessity to make concessions to strong informal pressures.

Even though we may accept the conclusion that the Party Conference is not exercising those functions which "constitutionally" are assigned to it, it would be erroneous to assume that it is merely tradition and custom that keep the institution alive. Rather would we suggest that the Conference fulfills certain functions for the Party which are significant even though they may be latent. Its continued existence is necessary to the maintenance of the myth of inner democracy, a myth which, though by now almost as nebulous as the proverbial Emperor's clothes, the leadership dare not discard. Furthermore, the Conference provides the lower functionaries with a feeling of "community" by bringing them into close contact with each other and the otherwise remote top leaders. Finally, the Conference serves as a forum at which, however muted, the sentiments and wishes of the rank and file are brought out into the open.

---

motion of the chairman, the Conference voted to send it back to the appropriate commission, which, in turn, brought forward its own, noncommittal version (Resolution XX, PCP, 1951, p. 277), with a recommendation to "pass the question for consideration and clarification to the Party Executive who, in agreement with the Socialist fraction of the Trade Union Federation and the Socialist Parliamentary Club, will at the earliest moment work out appropriate proposals." This recommendation was duly approved by the Conference.

[12] Its members, as far as I have been able to ascertain, are drawn from the upper-middle range of Party officialdom (i.e., District chairmen, members of the *Länder* Directorates).

[13] The results of the voting are frequently not published. The highest number of such strike-outs on record is said to be 80 or 100. (The first figure was mentioned to me in conversation; the second was reported in *Der neue Vorwärts,* November 13, 1949.) This sign of unpopularity has not, however, prevented the annual renomination and re-election of the candidate concerned.

What is significant about the many utterances by local functionaries is not their specific content but the general current of opinion, the revelation of the kinds of problems which occupy their minds, the virulence and the targets of their criticism; these set for the top leadership the broad framework which circumscribes their area of maneuver. Pent-up emotions and the frustrations of the humble have been able to find an escape valve at the Conference all the more easily since 1945 because of the disappearance of such leaders as Bauer, Renner, *et al.*, who, before 1934, dominated Conference proceedings by their towering intellectuality.

The Composition of the Party Conference

Because the Party Conference is conceived as the central institution of the structure of "inner democracy," it is assumed to be the voice of the "people," i.e., of the mass of Party members. Thus the delegates are in theory supposed to be almost exclusively the representatives of the Party's territorial organizations, elected by, and therefore accountable to, the mass membership. In fact, elected representatives of the District organizations have, as a rule, made up slightly less than two-thirds of the total Conference membership. The remaining third is composed of the members of the Central and *Länder* Directorates as well as the appointed delegates of the "organizations with delegating powers," such as the SJ, Socialist fraction of the TU, and so on. In view of the fact that showdown votes hardly ever occur at the Conference, the presence of a sizable minority of nonelected delegates hardly can be said to affect significantly the nature of the Conference proceedings. Nevertheless, their number is frequently the target of criticism by District representatives who have the uneasy feeling that the democratic character of the Conference is being impaired and that the Conference is being manipulated by functionaries who are not representative of rank-and-file sentiment. The District delegations themselves, however, are hardly qualified to play the role of grassroots representatives of the masses. As a rule, the chairman of the District organization heads the delegation while the remaining quota of seats is rotated among the members of the District Directorate and the Section leaders.[14] The requirement that the delegates be elected by the membership is treated purely as a formality.

Thus, Conference delegates come, by and large, from the upper and upper-middle strata of the Party hierarchy. The majority of them hold public office, elective or appointive.[15] They are mostly "old fighters," their political roots

---

[14] At the 1948 Conference the delegates held the following Party offices (*SPOe-Vertrauensmann*, III [December, 1948], 366): District chairmen and vice-chairmen, 126; members of District Control, 18; leading functionaries in District organizations, 87; Section chairmen and vice-chairmen, 60; Trade Union and plant functionaries, 78; leading functionaries in the Central Organization and the Executive, 43; leading functionaries in *Land* organizations and the Party press, 62.

[15] In 1946, 47 were members of the Central or *Land* governments; and 233 held elective offices or positions of mayor or vice-mayor (71 members of Parliament, 83 members of provincial legislatures, the remainder in local legislative bodies). *SPOe-Vertrauensmann*, II (January, 1947), 11.

firmly embedded in the Social Democratic Party of the First Republic.[16] With few exceptions, delegates are not holders of jobs paid out of Party funds, for, as a rule, District Secretaries are not selected as delegates. The factors inhibiting the delegates' freedom of action and criticism concerning the leadership are therefore of a subtler kind than outright financial dependence. As holders of public offices they must obtain a minimum of central Party endorsement of their candidatures; as occupants of jobs in public or semi-public areas of the economy in which the Party wields great influence, their career chances are likely to be affected by a show of open opposition even when they hold secure positions. As long as the Socialist Party shares governmental power, its leaders must be sought out by lower Party officials for the political favors these are able to dispense; furthermore, in view of the co-optative nature of the process of recruitment for leadership positions, advancement within the Party is difficult in the face of opposition by top leaders.[17] In fact, it is the nonelected delegate from organizations not organizationally subservient to the Party proper, resting on somewhat more independent centers of support, who enjoys greater freedom than the elected District delegate.[18] Although it would be misleading to assume that the factors of dependence have resulted in squashing criticism, they do make its expression an act of some political courage. Party Conferences are not, by any means, well-rehearsed cheering sessions. Indeed, serious criticism as well as a multitude of minor complaints have been voiced at many of the postwar Conferences. Criticism from the floor may reflect divergent viewpoints within the ranks of the top leadership; furthermore, the traditional commitment to "inner democracy" makes it impossible to crush opposition overtly or even to "punish" severe and persistent critics. However much top leaders may wish to escape what they consider factious or irresponsible criticism, Party tradition militates against them:

> A comrade who has become a minister must not thereby become immune against every criticism from the ranks of the organization, as he would like to. For it is we who have decided that comrades shall go into the government and therefore we have the right, if something does not suit us or when we believe that the comrades are following the wrong path, to tell them so, even when they are ministers. . . .

---

[16] At the 1953 Conference more than two-thirds of the delegates were over forty-five (*SPOe-Vertrauensmann*, VIII [December, 1953], 387–88); 80 per cent had been Party members before 1934. (*Ibid.*)

[17] The obstacles which Josef Hindels, the most outspoken critic of the leadership, has encountered — according to his own account — well illustrate this point. For several years Hindels was a paid functionary of the SJ. After leaving the SJ, Party chairman Schärf vetoed Hindels' employment by the Party publishing concern, *Konzentration*. When strong support for Hindels' nomination as a parliamentary candidate developed in one of the Lower Austrian District organizations, Minister Helmer made strenuous and successful efforts to prevent his nomination.

[18] Thus Hillegeist, a powerful trade union leader, frequently has acted as the *bête noire* at Party conferences. Significantly, it was in his union that Hindels found a position after having been denied one by the Party.

23. The Transformation of the Western European Party System

OTTO KIRCHHEIMER

In this sweeping comparative survey, the late Otto Kirchheimer analyzes the change of various European party types toward the model of the aggregative, "catch-all" party. This new party type, which aims at "brokerage" functions pure and simple, is handicapped in its appeal by traditional ideological commitments and elaborate mass membership organizations. It is also endangered by the reactions of voters and particularly opinion leaders socialized into highly "idealistic" political cultures with little tolerance for the deviousness and opaqueness of bargaining politics.

I

Load Concept and Party Failures

I have been intrigued enough by the LaPalombara–Weiner concept of the load to use it as a point of departure for inquiring into the successes and failures of major European political parties as transmission belts between the population at large and the governmental structure.

The British case has a pristine beauty: national unity brought about in the sixteenth century consolidation of the establishment, followed by a seventeenth century constitutional and social settlement allowing for the osmosis between aristocracy and bourgeoisie. The settlement happened early enough to weather the horrors and concomitant political assaults of early nineteenth century industrialism. The fairly smooth and gradual integration of the working classes was completed late enough so that the unnerving cleavage between the political promise and the social effectiveness of democracy (LaPalombara and Weiner's "distribution crisis") lasted only a couple of MacDonald-Baldwin decades. Thus once we omit the 1910–1914 interlude, Great Britain offers a case where problems could be handled as single loads. The time factor thus merges into and coincides with the load factor. The impact of constitutionalism slowly unfolds in the eighteenth century, then follows the acceleration of middle-class and the beginning of working-class integration during the nineteenth century, and the tempestuous combination of the consequences of full political democratization with the demands of a distributionist society after the First World War.

Where do we get if we apply the single-load concept to the French case?

SOURCE: Reprinted by permission from Joseph LaPalombara and Myron Weiner (eds.), *Political Parties and Political Development* (Princeton, N. J.: Princeton University Press, 1966), pp. 177–200. Footnotes are abridged.

If there was a French problem of national identity, it was almost oversettled by 1793, with the revolution only intensifying results in principle reached by 1590. Universal suffrage, that is, political democracy as the constitutional basis of the French state, has been almost continuously on the program since 1848 and was definitely achieved in the early 1870's. Whatever the subsequent upheavals in executive-legislative relations, the popular basis of the French regime has not been contested except for the short-lived Pétainist period. But why did political integration, the business of transforming the state apparatus of the bourgeois society into a cooperative enterprise of all social classes, stop so short of success? Why is it that this goal has been reached only now, to some extent at least, as a simple byproduct of increased material well-being and ensuing lessening of social antagonism in the French species of industrial society? How is it that the political parties contributed so little to the end result?

There are reasons why French society in spite of, or because of, the early introduction of universal suffrage could force its working class to accept a position of stepchildren. They were a minority in a society not particularly favoring disruption of the existing social equilibrium by accentuated industrialization. Yet without such industrialization there was little chance of creating a unified party system. Instead there was a dichotomy between parties of individual representation (with their double basis in the local parish pump and the operations of the parliamentary faction) and the incipient mass party of the working class, the Socialist party of the first decade of the century. Most bourgeois parties remained restricted electioneering organizations with loose connections to still looser parliamentary factions having little radius of action beyond the parliamentary scene (Duverger–LaPalombara–Weiner's internally created parties).[1]

Through the courtesy of Alain these parties were equipped with an ultra-democratic theory of eternal vigilance to be exercised by the proverbial small man over his intermediaries in party and parliament. But the reality was far different. Behind the façade of democratic vigilance political fragmentation excluded the party from advancing from the stage of *ad hoc* parliamentary combinations to permanently organized transmission belts between population and government. Party organizations and party conventions were over-sized *Café de Commerce* confabulations of *raisonneurs* without effective mandate. Thus the bourgeois parties and the parliamentary government they carried saw themselves at every turn of events disowned as mere bubbles blown up by the *pays légal* to be confronted with the *pays réel* discovered from the confluence of thousands of discordant voices. Yet neither the *raisonneurs* nor the more or less benevolent intermediaries of the *Comité Mascuraud* watching over the parliamentary performance of rival political clans in the interest of the commercial and industrial community could substitute for the people at large.

As these parties had to face less of a challenge from class-based integration

---

[1] The internal-external creation dichotomy has to be viewed in the light of presence or absence of a supporting framework of religious or class-motivated parallel organizations. The local committee of the internally created bourgeois party and its financial backers can never serve as such a fool-proof prop of electoral success as can the network of parallel organizations typical of external parties.

parties than did their German neighbors, they could afford to become inoperative in semi-crisis periods. In such periods they were, as office-holding combinations, bailed out in the 1920's and early 1930's by proconsul saviors, Poincaré and his cheap imitator Doumergue. Yet as opinion-transmitting conveyor belts they had more and more to contend with the welter of anti-democratic organizations.

The last democratically legitimized attempt of the Third Republic to integrate the working class into the political system was Léon Blum's *Front Populaire*. Its failure was in part a failure of the parties, in part a consequence of international events. With its failure the Third Republic, with its juxtaposition of bourgeois parliamentary clans and class-based integration parties, was near its end.

How did it happen that the Fourth Republic failed to integrate the Communist party into its political system and allowed both the SFIO (French Section of Workers' International or Social Democratic party) and the MRP (Popular Republican Movement, or Christian Democratic party) to slip into the habits of the bourgeois parties of the previous periods? Should we single out two load factors: the supervening, mutually exclusive international policy commitments of the majority of the French political parties and the Communists, and the crisis of decolonization? Yet the end of tripartism in 1947 need not have arrested the transformation of French parties into organizations able to integrate major social groups into the political system and able to work in coalition — collaboration or in alternative shifts. There is no reason why the challenge of *personalismo* in the form of Gaullism and the challenge of the Communist working class opposition of principle had to lead to an atavistic return to the party system of the 1920's. Decolonization was a challenge which the parties might have faced with clear-cut policy propositions. Working-class integration and decolonization, the former on the agenda for virtually half a century, the latter a limited problem, were burdens which an operative party system could have mastered.

Yet the majority of the French political parties had never progressed beyond the stage of local-interest messengers and parliamentary clubs with or without ideological overtones. They were equally unable to make commitments in the name of their voters or to obtain legitimacy through transforming the voters' opinions and attitudes into impulses converted into governmental action. They therefore had little to do with the continuity of the state, which remained the business of the bureaucracy. Major socio-political options were avoided, or, if and when they had to be faced, they became the work of individual politicians temporarily supported by strong elements in the community. It is doubtful whether even such a combination as that of Caillaux and Jaurès, which appeared likely in the spring of 1914, would have been able to establish the party as an effective transmission belt between population and government and a basis for policymaking. It might have failed because of the bourgeois distaste for devices which would transmit and thereby increase popular pressure on political action. In the single-load job of integrating the *couches populaires* into the French polity the performance of the political party remained unimpressive.

The rise of Italian and German political organizations in the middle of the nineteenth century cannot be separated from the history of belated unification. Unification was a competitive effort between the political endeavors of Cavour and Garibaldi and his adherents in Italy and between Bismarck and the Liberals in Germany. The respective statesmen's timing and actions cannot be understood without the urgency of these competitive pressures. But did the more nimble hand of Cavour provide the party system greater chances than the staccato fist of Bismarck? [2] What did Cavour's and Bismarck's styles of unification mean in terms of party loads and chances?

Could the Italian Left, the *Partito d'Azione,* have tried to find contact with the southern peasant masses? Could it by such contact have established a basis for national loyalty transcending class and region? Or was it inevitable that it had to become part witness, part victim, of a *trasformismo* which remained an essentially commercial operation rather than an instrument of national integration? The possibilities may have been slight, but at any rate the attempt was never even made. In Germany, on the other hand, even the lateness and the Little Germany formula involved in the founding of Bismarck's Reich did not prevent that creation from soon becoming a socially and economically viable unit. All political forces, whether friendly or hostile to the Founding Father, accepted his Reich as a basis of operation. But in terms of the chances of the political parties the outcome was not much different. Italy had found a fictitious solution of its national identity problems, workable in constitutional but not in socio-political terms. Bismarck's heirs, the combined forces of bureaucracy, army, industrialists, and agrarians, upheld for about the same time both in Prussia and in the Empire a constitutional setup which prevented any approach to effective working-class participation in the government. In both Italy and Germany the mismanagement of the crises of national identity and of participation increased the problem load which the nation had to face at the end of the First World War. However, it would be difficult to evaluate the differential impact of these load factors as compared, for example, with France. Here, without any crisis of national identity and without constitutional barriers to working-class participation, the long smoldering participation crisis came fully into the open in the mid-thirties. I would argue that the extent of the 1940 breakdown is clearly related to this crisis of participation.

Is the load concept helpful, then, in analyzing the failure of the continental parties to assume their appropriate roles in the 1920's? May we, for example, argue that the belatedness in accepting a constitutional regime which would have allowed political democracy to become fully effective militated against successful political integration of the working classes into the German political system in the 1920's? The acceptance of this argument hinges on some further differentiation. By "political integration" we mean here the capacity of a

---

[2] A German author has recently put the case as follows: "Bismarck's policy to the Liberals was unfair in that he achieved what the Liberals wanted to have achieved, but he gave them neither the chance nor the means to do it on their own." E. Pikart, "Die Rolle der Deutschen Parteien im Deutschen Konstitutionellen System," in *Zeitschrift für Politik,* 1962, pp. 12–15.

political system to make groups and their members previously outside the official political fold full-fledged participants in the political process. Many a mass party, however, was neither capable of nor interested in integrating its members into the existing political community. The party might even want rather to integrate its followers into its own ranks *against* the official state apparatus.

II

The Antebellum Mass Integration Party

Socialist parties around the turn of the century exercised an important socializing function in regard to their members. They facilitated the transition from agrarian to industrial society in many ways. They subjected a considerable number of people hitherto living only as isolated individuals to voluntarily accepted discipline operating in close connection with expectations of a future total transformation of society. But this discipline had its roots in the alienation of these parties from the pre-World War I political system whose demise they wanted to guarantee and speed up by impressing the population as a whole with their exemplary attitudes.[3]

During and soon after the First World War the other participants in the political game showed that they were not yet willing to honor the claims of the working-class mass parties — claims based on the formal rules of democracy. This discovery was one of the primary reasons why the social integration into the industrial system through the working-class organizations did not advance to the state of a comparable political integration. Participation in the war, the long quarrels over the financial incidence of war burdens, the ravages of inflation, the rise of Bolshevist parties and a Soviet system actively competing for mass loyalty with the existing political mass organizations in most European countries, and finally the effect of the depression setting in at the end of the decade — all these were much more effective agents in the politicization of the masses than their participation in occasional elections, their fight for the extension of suffrage (Belgium, Britain, Germany), or even their *encadrement* in political parties and trade union organizations. But politicization is not tantamount to political integration; integration presupposes a general willingness by a society to offer and accept full-fledged political partnership of all citizens without reservations. The consequences of integration into the class-mass party depended on the responses of other forces in the existing political system; in some cases those responses were so negative as to lead to delayed integration into the political system or to make for its disintegration.

---

[3] The German end of this story and Bebel's emergence as commander-in-chief of a well-disciplined counter-army have often been commented upon. It has recently been discussed in Guenther Roth, *The Social Democrats in Imperial Germany*, Ottawa, 1963. Similar observations on the social integration function of socialism are equally valid for Italy. As essentially hostile an observer as Benedetto Croce notes these factors in his *History of Italy, 1870–1915*, New York, 1963; Robert Michels in his *Sozialismus in Italien*, Karlsruhe, 1925, p. 270 *et seq.*, provides ample documentary proof.

Now we come to the other side of this failure to progress from integration into the proletarian mass party and industrial society at large[4] to integration into the political system proper. This is the failure of bourgeois parties to advance from parties of individual representation to parties of integration, a failure already noted in France. The two tendencies, the failure of the integration of proletarian mass parties into the official political system and the failure of the bourgeois parties to advance to the stage of integration parties, condition each other. An exception, if only a partial one, is that of denominational parties such as the German Center or Don Sturzo's *Partito Popolare*. These parties to a certain extent fulfilled both functions: social integration into industrial society and political integration within the existing political system. Yet their denominational nature gave such parties a fortress-type character seriously restricting their growth potential.[5]

With these partial exceptions, bourgeois parties showed no capacity to change from clubs for parliamentary representation into agencies for mass politics able to bargain with the integration-type mass parties according to the laws of the political market. There was only a limited incentive for intensive bourgeois party organization. Access to the favors of the state, even after formal democratization, remained reserved via educational and other class privileges. What the bourgeoisie lacked in numbers it could make good by strategic relations with the army and the bureaucracy.

Gustav Stresemann is the politician who stood at the crossroads of this era, operating with a threefold and incompatible set of parties: the class and the denominational democratic mass integration parties; the opposition-of-principle parties integrating masses into their own fold against the existing order; and the older parties of individual representation. Forever on the lookout for viable compromises among democratic mass parties, old-style bourgeois parties of individual representation, and the powerholders outside the formal political party structure, Stresemann failed. For the party of individual representation from which he came could not give him a broad enough basis for his policies.

Not all bourgeois groups accepted the need for transformation to integration parties. As long as such groups had other means of access to the state apparatus they might find it convenient to delay setting up counterparts to existing mass parties while still using the state apparatus for keeping mass integration parties

---

[4] Integration into industrial society: while the worker has accepted some aspects, such as urbanization and the need for regularity and the corresponding advantages of a mass consumer society, powerlessness as an individual and the eternal dependence on directives by superiors make for strong escapist attitudes. The problems are discussed in detail in André Andrieux and Jean Lignon, *L'Ouvrier d'aujourd'hui*, Paris, 1960. The ambiguous consequences to be drawn from these facts and their largely negative impact on the political image of the workers are studied in detail in H. Popitz, *et al.*, *Das Gesellschaftsbild des Arbeiters*, Tuebingen, 1957.

[5] Another exception was that of parties such as the German Nationalist party of the 1920's, whose conservative predecessor in the days before World War I had already profited from the ability of the agrarian interest representation (*Landbund*) to funnel enough steady support to its companion organization in the political market. See in general: Thomas Nipperdey, *Die Organisation der deutschen Parteien vor 1918*, Düsseldorf, 1961, Vols. v and vi.

from becoming fully effective in the political market. Yet after the Second World War the acceptance of the law of the political market became inevitable in the major Western European countries. This change in turn found its echo in the changing structure of political parties.

III

The Postwar Catch-All Party

Following the Second World War, the old-style bourgeois party of individual representation became the exception. While some of the species continue to survive, they do not determine the nature of the party system any longer. By the same token, the mass integration party, product of an age with harder class lines and more sharply protruding denominational structures, is transforming itself into a catch-all "people's" party. Abandoning attempts at the intellectual and moral *encadrement* of the masses, it is turning more fully to the electoral scene, trying to exchange effectiveness in depth for a wider audience and more immediate electoral success. The narrower political task and the immediate electoral goal differ sharply from the former all-embracing concerns; today the latter are seen as counter-productive since they deter segments of a potential nationwide clientele.

For the class-mass parties we may roughly distinguish three stages in this process of transformation. There is first the period of gathering strength lasting to the beginning of the First World War; then comes their first governmental experience in the 1920's and 1930's (MacDonald, Weimar Republic, *Front Populaire*), unsatisfactory if measured both against the expectations of the class-mass party followers or leaders and suggesting the need for a broader basis of consensus in the political system. This period is followed by the present more or less advanced stages in the catch-all grouping, with some of the parties still trying to hold their special working-class clientele and at the same time embracing a variety of other clienteles.

Can we find some rules acording to which this transformation is taking place, singling out factors which advance or delay or arrest it? We might think of the current rate of economic development as the most important determinant; but if it were so important, France would certainly be ahead of Great Britain and, for that matter, also of the United States, still the classical example of an all-pervasive catch-all party system. What about the impact of the continuity or discontinuity of the political system? If this were so important, Germany and Great Britain would appear at opposite ends of the spectrum rather than showing a similar speed of transformation. We must then be satisfied to make some comments on the general trend and to note special limiting factors.

In some instances the catch-all performance meets definite limits in the traditional framework of society. The all-pervasive denominational background of the Italian *Democrazia Cristiana* means from the outset that the party cannot successfully appeal to the anticlerical elements of the population. Otherwise nothing prevents the party from phrasing its appeals so as to maximize its chances of catching more of those numerous elements which are not disturbed by the party's clerical ties. The solidary element of its doctrinal core has long been successfully employed to attract a socially diversified clientele.

Or take the case of two other major European parties, the German SPD (Social Democratic party) and the British Labour party. It is unlikely that either of them is able to make any concession to the specific desires of real estate interests or independent operators of agricultural properties while at the same time maintaining credibility with the masses of the urban population. Fortunately, however, there is enough community of interest between wage-and-salary earning urban or suburban white- and blue-collar workers and civil servants to designate them all as strategic objects of simultaneous appeals. Thus tradition and the pattern of social and professional stratification may set limits and offer potential audiences to the party's appeal.

If the party cannot hope to catch all categories of voters, it may have a reasonable expectation of catching more voters in all those categories whose interests do not adamantly conflict. Minor differences between group claims, such as between white-collar and manual labor groups, might be smoothed over by vigorous emphasis on programs which benefit both sections alike, for example, some cushioning against the shocks of automation.

Even more important is the heavy concentration on issues which are scarcely liable to meet resistance in the community. National societal goals transcending group interests offer the best sales prospect for a party intent on establishing or enlarging an appeal previously limited to specific sections of the population. The party which propagates most aggressively, for example, enlarged educational facilities may hear faint rumblings over the excessive cost or the danger to the quality of education from elites previously enjoying educational privileges. Yet the party's stock with any other family may be influenced only by how much more quickly and aggressively it took up the new national priority than its major competitor and how well its propaganda linked the individual family's future with the enlarged educational structures. To that extent its potential clientele is almost limitless. The catch-all of a given category performance turns virtually into an unlimited catch-all performance.

The last remark already transcends the group-interest confines. On the one hand, in such developed societies as I am dealing with, thanks to general levels of economic well-being and security and to existing welfare schemes universalized by the state or enshrined in collective bargaining, many individuals no longer need such protection as they once sought from the state. On the other hand, many have become aware of the number and complexity of the general factors on which their future well-being depends. This change of priorities and preoccupation may lead them to examine political offerings less under the aspect of their own particular claims than under that of the political leader's ability to meet general future contingencies. Among the major present-day parties, it is the French UNR (National Republican Union) a latecomer, that speculates most clearly on the possibility of its channeling such less specialized needs to which its patron saint De Gaulle constantly appeals into its own version of the catch-all party. Its assumed asset would rest in a doctrine of national purpose and unity vague and flexible enough to allow the most variegated interpretation and yet — at least as long as the General continues to function — attractive enough to serve as a convenient rallying point for many groups and isolated individuals.

While the UNR thus manipulates ideology for maximum general appeal, we have noted that ideology in the case of the *Democrazia Cristiana* is a slightly limiting factor. The UNR ideology in principle excludes no one. The Christian Democratic ideology by definition excludes the non-believer, or at least the seriously non-believing voter. It pays for the ties of religious solidarity and the advantages of supporting organizations by repelling some millions of voters. The catch-all parties in Europe appear at a time of de-ideologization which has substantially contributed to their rise and spread. De-ideologization in the political field involves the transfer of ideology from partnership in a clearly visible political goal structure into one of many sufficient but by no means necessary motivational forces operative in the voters' choice. The German and Austrian Social Democratic parties in the last two decades most clearly exhibit the politics of de-ideologization. The example of the German Christian Democratic Union (CDU) is less clear only because there was less to de-ideologize. In the CDU, ideology was from the outset only a general background atmosphere, both all-embracing and conveniently vague enough to allow recruiting among Catholic and Protestant denominations.

As a rule, only major parties can become successful catch-all parties. Neither a small, strictly regional party such as the South Tyrolian People's party nor a party built around the espousal of harsh and limited ideological claims, like the Dutch Calvinists; or transitory group claims, such as the German Refugees; or a specific professional category's claims, such as the Swedish Agrarians; or a limited-action program, such as the Danish single-tax Justice party can aspire to a catch-all performance. Its *raison d'être* is the defense of a specific clientele or the lobbying for a limited reform clearly delineated to allow for a restricted appeal, perhaps intense, but excluding a wider impact or — once the original job is terminated — excluding a life-saving transformation.

Nor is the catch-all performance in vogue or even sought among the majority of the larger parties in small democracies. Securely entrenched, often enjoying majority status for decades — as the Norwegian and Swedish Social Democratic parties — and accustomed to a large amount of interparty cooperation, such parties have no incentive to change their form of recruitment or their appeal to well-defined social groups. With fewer factors intervening and therefore more clearly foreseeable results of political actions and decisions, it seems easier to stabilize political relations on the basis of strictly circumscribed competition (Switzerland, for instance) than to change over to the more aleatory form of catch-all competition.

Conversion to catch-all parties constitutes a competitive phenomenon. A party is apt to accommodate to its competitor's successful style because of hope of benefits or fear of losses on election day. Conversely, the more a party convinces itself that a competitor's favorable results were due only to some non-repetitive circumstances, and that the competitor's capacity of overcoming internal dissension is a temporary phenomenon, the smaller the over-all conversion chance and the greater the inclination to hold fast to a loyal — though limited — clientele.

To evaluate the impact of these changes I have found it useful to list the functions which European parties exercised during earlier decades (late in the nineteenth and early in the twentieth centuries) and to compare them with the present situation. Parties have functioned as channels for integrating individuals and groups into the existing political order, or as instruments for modifying or altogether replacing that order (integration-disintegration). Parties have attempted to determine political-action preferences and influence other participants in the political process into accepting them. Parties have nominated public officeholders and presented them to the public at large for confirmation.

The so-called "expressive function" of the party, if not belonging to a category by itself, nevertheless warrants a special word. Its high tide belongs to the era of the nineteenth-century constitutionalism when a more clear-cut separation existed between opinion formation-and-expression and the business of government. At that time the internally created parliamentary parties expressed opinions and criticism widely shared among the educated minority of the population. They pressed these opinions on their governments. But as the governments largely rested on an independent social and constitutional basis, they could if necessary hold out against the promptings of parliamentary factions and clubs. Full democratization merged the opinion-expressing and the governmental business in the same political parties and put them in the seat either of government or an alternative government. But it has left the expressive function of the party in a more ambiguous state. For electoral reasons, the democratic catch-all party, intent on spreading as wide as possible a net over a potential clientele, must continue to express widely felt popular concerns. Yet, bent on continuing in power or moving into governmental power, it performs this expressive function subject to manifold restrictions and changing tactical considerations. The party would atrophy if it were no longer able to function as a relay between the population and governmental structure, taking up grievances, ideas, and problems developed in a more searching and systematic fashion elsewhere in the body politic. Yet the caution it must give its present or prospective governmental role requires modulation and restraint. The very nature of today's catch-all party forbids an option between these two performances. It requires a constant shift between the party's critical role and its role as establishment support, a shift hard to perform but still harder to avoid.

In order to leave a maximum imprint on the polity a party has to exercise all of the first three functions. Without the ability to integrate people into the community the party could not compel other powerholders to listen to its clarions. The party influences other power centers to the extent that people are willing to follow its leadership. Conversely, people are willing to listen to the party because the party is the carrier of messages — here called action preferences — that are at least partially in accord with the images, desires, hopes, and fears of the electorate. Nominations for public office serve to tie together all these purposes; they may further the realization of action preferences if they elicit positive response from voters or from other powerholders.

The nominations concretize the party's image with the public at large, on whose confidence the party's effective functioning depends.

Now we can discuss the presence or absence of these three functions in Western society today. Under present conditions of spreading secular and mass consumer-goods orientation, with shifting and less obtrusive class lines, the former class-mass parties and denominational mass parties are both under pressure to become catch-all peoples' parties. The same applies to those few remnants of former bourgeois parties of individual representation which aspire to a secure future as political organizations independent of the vagaries of electoral laws and the tactical moves of their mass-party competitors.[6] This change involves: (a) Drastic reduction of the party's ideological baggage. In France's SFIO, for example, ideological remnants serve at best as scant cover for what has become known as *"Molletisme,"* the absolute reign of short-term tactical considerations. (b) Further strengthening of top leadership groups, whose actions and omissions are now judged from the viewpoint of their contribution to the efficiency of the entire social system rather than identification with the goals of their particular organization. (c) Downgrading of the role of the individual party member, a role considered a historical relic which may obscure the newly built-up catch-all party image. (d) Deemphasis of the *classe gardée,* specific social-class or denominational clientele, in favor of recruiting voters among the population at large (e) Securing access to a variety of interest groups. The financial reasons are obvious, but they are not the most important where official financing is available, as in Germany, or where access to the most important media of communication is fairly open, as in England and Germany. The chief reason is to secure electoral support via interest-group intercession.

From this fairly universal development the sometimes considerable remnants of two old class-mass parties, the French and the Italian Communist parties, are excluding themselves. These parties are in part ossified, in part solidified by a combination of official rejection and legitimate sectional grievances. In this situation the ceremonial invocation of the rapidly fading background of a remote and inapplicable revolutionary experience has not yet been completely abandoned as a part of political strategy. What is the position of such opposition parties of the older class-mass type, which still jealously try to hold an exclusive loyalty of their members, while not admitted nor fully ready to share in the hostile state power? Such parties face the same difficulties in recruiting and holding intensity of membership interest as other political organizations. Yet, in contrast to their competitors working within the confines of the existing political order, they cannot make a virtue out of necessity and adapt themselves fully to the new style of catch-all peoples' party.[7] This

---

[6] Liberal parties without sharply profiled program or clientele may, however, make such conversion attempts. Val Lorwin draws my attention to the excellent example of a former bourgeois party, the Belgian Liberal party, which became in 1961 the "Party of Liberty and Progress," de-emphasizing anticlericalism and appealing to the right wing of the Social Christian party, worried about this party's governmental alliance with the Socialists.

[7] However, even in France — not to speak of Italy — Communist policies are under pressure to accommodate to the new style. . . .

conservatism does not cost them the confidence of their regular corps of voters. On the other hand, the continued renewal of confidence on election day does not involve an intimate enough bond to utilize as a basis for major political operations.

The attitudes of regular voters — in contrast to those of members and activists — attest to the extent of incongruency between full-fledged participation in the social processes of a consumer-goods oriented society and the old political style which rested on the primordial need for sweeping political change. The latter option has gone out of fashion in Western countries and has been carefully eliminated from the expectations, calculations, and symbols of the catch-all mass party. The incongruency may rest on the total absence of any connection between general social-cultural behavior and political style. In this sense electoral choice may rest on family tradition or empathy with the political underdog without thereby becoming part of a coherent personality structure. Or the choice may be made in the expectation that it will have no influence on the course of political development; it is then an act of either adjusting to or, as the case may be, signing out of the existing political system rather than a manifestation of signing up somewhere else.

IV

The Catch-All Party, the Interest Group, and the Voter: Limited Integration

The integration potential of the catch-all mass party rests on a combination of factors whose visible end result is attraction of the maximum number of voters on election day. For that result the catch-all party must have entered into millions of minds as a familiar object fulfilling in politics a role analogous to that of a major brand in the marketing of a universally needed and highly standardized article of mass consumption. Whatever the particularities of the line to which a party leader owes his intraparty success, he must, once he is selected for leadership, rapidly suit his behavior to standard requirements. There is need for enough brand differentiation to make the article plainly recognizable, but the degree of differentiation must never be so great as to make the potential customer fear he will be out on a limb.

Like the brand whose name has become a household word, the catch-all mass party that has presided over the fortunes of a country for some time, and whose leaders the voter has therefore come to know on his television set and in his newspaper columns, enjoys a great advantage. But only up to a certain point. Through circumstances possibly outside the control of the party or even of the opposition — a scandal in the ranks of government, an economic slump — officeholding may suddenly turn into a negative symbol encouraging the voter to switch to another party as a consumer switches to a competitive brand.

The rules deciding the outcome of catch-all mass party competition are extremely complex and extremely aleatory. When a party has or seeks an almost nationwide potential constituency, its majority composed of individuals whose relation to politics is both tangential and discontinuous, the factors which may decide the eventual electoral outcome are almost infinite in number and often quite unrelated to the party's performance. The style and looks of the leader, the impact of a recent event entirely dictated from without, vacation schedules, the weather as it affects crops — factors such as these all enter into the results.

The very catch-all character of the party makes membership loyalty far more difficult to expect and at best never sufficient to swing results. The outcome of a television contest is dubious, or the contest itself may constitute too fleeting an exposure to make an impression that will last into the election. Thus the catch-all mass party too is driven back to look out for a more permanent clientele. Only the interest group, whether ideological or economic in nature or a combination of the two, can provide mass reservoirs of readily accessible voters. It has a more constant line of communication and higher acceptance for its messages than the catch-all party, which is removed from direct contact with the public except for the comparatively small number intensively concerned about the brand of politics a party has to offer these days — or about their own careers in or through the party.

All the same, the climate of relations between catch-all party and interest groups has definitely changed since the heyday of the class-mass or denominational integration party. Both party and interest group have gained a greater independence from each other. Whether they are still joined in the same organization (like British Labour and the TUC [Trades Union Congress]) or formally enjoy complete independence from each other (like the German SPD and the DGB [Workers' Federation]), what matters most is the change of roles. Instead of a joint strategy toward a common goal there appears an appreciation of limited if still mutually helpful services to be rendered.

The party bent on attracting a maximum of voters must modulate its interest-group relations in such a way so as not to discourage potential voters who identify themselves with other interests. The interest group, in its turn, must never put all its eggs in one basket. That might offend the sensibilities of some members with different political connections. More important, the interest group would not want to stifle feelings of hope in another catch-all party that some moves in its direction might bring electoral rewards. Both party and interest group modulate their behavior, acting as if the possible contingency has already arrived, namely that the party has captured the government — or an important share in it — and has moved from the position of friend or counsellor to that of umpire or arbitrator. Suddenly entrusted with the confidence of the community as a whole, the government-party arbitrator does best when able to redefine the whole problem and discover solutions which would work, at least in the long run, in the favor of all interest claimants concerned.

Here there emerges a crucial question: What then is the proper role of the catch-all party in the arbitration of interest conflicts? Does not every government try to achieve best tactical position for exercising an effective arbitration between contending group claims? Is the catch-all party even needed in this connection? Or — from the interest viewpoint — can a society dispense with parties' services, as France now does?

A party is more than a collector of interest-group claims. It functions at the same time as advocate, protector, or at least as addressee of the demands of all those who are not able to make their voices felt as effectively as those represented by well organized interest groups: those who do not yet have positions in the process of production or those who no longer hold such positions, the too young and the too old, and those whose family status aligns them with consumer rather than producer interests.

Can we explain this phenomenon simply as another facet of the party's aggregative function? But functionalist phraseology restates rather than explains. The unorganized and often unorganizable make their appearance only on election day or in suddenly sprouting pre-election committees and party activities arranged for their benefit. Will the party be able and willing to take their interests into its own hands? Will it be able, playing on their availability in electoral terms, not only to check the more extreme demands of organized groups but also to transcend the present level of intergroup relations and by political reforms redefining the whole political situation? No easy formula will tell us what leader's skill, what amount of pressure from objective situations has to intervene to produce such a change in the political configuration.

In this job of transcending group interests and creating general confidence the catch-all party enjoys advantages, but by the same token it suffers from an infirmity. Steering clear of sectarianism enhances its recruiting chances in electoral terms but inevitably limits the intensity of commitment it may expect. The party's transformation from an organization combining the defense of social position, the quality of spiritual shelter, and the vision of things to come into that of a vehicle for short-range and interstitial political choice exposes the party to the hazards of all purveyors of nondurable consumer goods: competition with a more attractively packaged brand of a nearly identical merchandise.

V

Limited Participation in Action Preference

This brings us to the determination of action preferences and their chances of realization. In Anthony Downs's well-known model action preference simply results from the party's interest in the proximate goal, the winning of the next election. In consequence the party will arrange its policies in such a way that the benefits accruing to the individual members of the community are greater than the losses resulting from its policy.[8] Downs's illustrations are frequently, though not exclusively, taken from fields such as taxation where the cash equation of political action is feasible. Yet Downs himself has occasionally noted that psychological satisfactions or dissatisfactions, fears or hopes, are elements in voters' decisions as frequently as calculations of immediate short-term benefits or deprivations. Were it different, the long-lasting

---

[8] "It always organizes its action so as to focus on a single quantity: its vote margin over the opposition in the test at the end of the current election period." In A. Downs, *An Economic Theory of Democracy*, 1957, p. 174.

loyalty of huge blocks of voters to class-mass integration parties in the absence of any immediate benefits from such affiliation could scarcely be explained. But can it be said that such short-term calculations correspond much more closely to the attitudes connected with the present-day catch-all mass party with its widely ranging clientele? Can the short-term benefit approach, for example, be utilized in military or foreign-policy issues?

In some countries in the last decade it has become the rule for catch-all parties out of office simply to lay the most recent shortcomings or apparent deterioration of the country's military or international position at the doorstep of the incumbent government, especially during election campaigns: thus in the United States the Republican party in 1952 with regard to the long-lasting indecisive Korean War, or in Germany more recently the Social Democrats with regard to Adenauer's apparent passivity in the face of the Berlin Wall. In other instances, however, the opposition plays down foreign or military issues or treats them in generalities vague enough to evoke the image of itself as a competitor who will be able to handle them as well as the incumbent government.

To the extent that the party system still includes "unreformed" or — as in the case of the Italian Socialist party — only "half-reformed" class-mass type integration parties, foreign or military issues enter election campaigns as policy differences. Yet even here the major interest has shifted away from areas where the electorate could exercise only an illusory choice. The electorate senses that in the concrete situation, based in considerable part on geography and history, the international bloc affiliation of the country rather than any policy preference will form the basis of decision. It senses too that such decisions rest only partially, or at times nominally, with the political leadership. Even if the impact of the political leader on the decision may have been decisive, more often than not election timetables in democracies are such that the decision, once carried out, is no longer contested or even relevant to voter choices. As likely as not, new events crowd it out of the focus of voters' attention. Few voters still thought of Mendès-France's 1954 "abandonment" of Indo-China when Edgar Faure suddenly dissolved the Assembly in December 1955. While a party may benefit from its adversary's unpopular decisions, such benefits are more often an accidental by-product that the outcome of a government-opposition duel with clearly distributed roles and decisions.

A party may put up reasonably coherent, even if vague, foreign or military policies for election purposes. It may criticize the inept handling of such problems by the government of the day, and more and more intensively as it gets closer to election day. But in neither case is there a guarantee of the party's ability to act as a coherent body in parliament when specific action preferences are to be determined. Illustrative of this dilemma are the history of EDC in the French Parliament and the more recent battles within the British parties in regard to entrance into the Common Market (although the latter case remains inconclusive because of De Gaulle's settling the issue in his own way, for the time being). Fortuitous election timetables and the hopes, fears, and expectations of the public do not intermesh sufficiently with the parliamentary representatives' disjointed action on concrete issues before them to add up to the elaboration of clear-cut party action preference.

The catch-all party contributes general programs in the elaboration of domestic action preferences. These programs may be of a prognostic variety, informing the public about likely specific developments and general trends. Yet prognostics and desirability blur into each other in this type of futurology, in which rosy glasses offer previews of happy days for all and sundry among the party's prospective customers. These programs may lead to or be joined with action proposals in various stages of concretization. Concrete proposals, however, always risk implying promises which may be too specific. Concretizations must remain general enough so that they cannot be turned from electoral weapons to engines of assault against the party which first mounted them.

This indeterminacy allows the catch-all party to function as a meeting ground for the elaboration of concrete action for a multiplicity of interest groups. All the party may require from those who obtain its services is that they make a maximal attempt to arrive at compromises within the framework of the party and that they avoid coalescing with forces hostile to the party. The compromises thus elaborated must be acceptable to major interest groups even if these groups, for historical or traditional reasons, happen not to be represented in the governing party. Marginal differences may be submitted to the voter at elections, or, as older class-mass parties do on occasion, via referenda (Switzerland and Sweden). But expected policy mutations are in the nature of increments rather than major changes in intergroup relations.

It is here that the difference between the catch-all and the older form of integration party becomes most clearly visible. The catch-all party will do its utmost to establish consensus to avoid party realignment. The integration party may count on majority political mechanisms to implement its programs only to find that hostile interests frustrate the majority decision by the economic and social mechanisms at their disposal. They may call strikes (by labor or farmers or storekeepers or investors), they may withdraw capital to safe haven outside the country, they may undermine that often hypocritically invoked but real factor known as the "confidence of the business community."

VI

Integration through Participation in Leadership Selection— the Future of the Political Party

What then remains the real share of the catch-all party in the elaboration of action preferences? Its foremost contribution lies in the mobilization of the voters for whatever concrete action preferences leaders are able to establish rather than *a priori* selections of their own. It is for this reason that the catch-all party prefers to visualize action in the light of the contingencies, threats, and promises of concrete historical situations rather than of general social goals. It is the hoped-for or already established role in the dynamics of action, in which the voters' vicarious participation is invited, that is most in evidence. Therefore the attention of both party and public at large focuses most clearly on problems of leadership selection.

Nomination means the prospect of political office. Political office involves a chance to make an impact via official action. The competition between those striving to influence official action puts into evidence the political advantage of those in a position to act before their political adversaries can do so. The privilege of first action is all the more precious in a new and non-repetitive situation where the political actor can avoid getting enmeshed in directives deriving from party action preferences. Much as the actor welcomes party support on the basis of revered (but elastic) principles, he shuns specific direction and supervision. In this respect the catch-all party furnishes an ideal background for political action. Where obtaining office becomes an almost exclusive preoccupation of a party, issues of personnel are reduced to search for the simplest effective means to put up winning combinations. The search is especially effective wherever the party becomes a channel by which representatives of hitherto excluded or neglected minorities may join the existing political elite.

The nomination of candidates for popular legitimation as office-holders thus emerges as the most important function of the present-day catch-all party. Concentration on the selection of candidates for office is in line with an increasing role differentiation in industrial society. Once certain levels of education and material welfare are reached, both intellectual and material needs are taken care of by specialized purveyors of communications and economic products. Likewise the party, which in less advanced societies or in those intent on rapid change directly interferes with the performance of societal jobs, remains in Western industrial society twice removed — through government and bureaucracy — from the field of direct action. To this state of affairs correspond now prevailing popular images and expectations in regard to the reduced role of the party. Expectations previously set on the performance of a political organization are now flowing into different channels.

At the same time, the role of the political party as a factor in the continued integration of the individual into the national life now has to be visualized in a different light. Compared to his connection with interest organizations and voluntary associations of a non-political nature and to his frequent encounters with the state bureaucracy, the citizen's relations with the political party are becoming more intermittent and of more limited scope.

To the older party of integration the citizen, if he so desired, could be closer. Then it was a less differentiated organization, part channel of protest, part source of protection, part purveyor of visions of the future. Now, in its linear descendant in a transfigured world, the catch-all party, the citizen finds a relatively remote, at times quasi-official and alien structure. Democratic society assumes that the citizen is finally an integral and conscious participant in the affairs of both the polity and the economy; it further assumes that as such he will work through the party as one of the many interrelated structures by which he achieves a rational participation in his surrounding world.

Should he ever live up to these assumptions, the individual and society may indeed find the catch-all party — non-utopian, non-oppressive, and ever so flexible — an ingenious and useful political instrument.

What about the attitude toward the modern catch-all party of functional powerholders in army, bureaucracy, industry, and labor? Released from their previous unnecessary fears as to the ideological propensities and future intentions of the class-mass party, functional powerholders have come to recognize the catch-all party's role as consensus purveyor. In exchange for its ability to provide a clear-cut basis of legitimacy, functional powerholders are, up to a point, willing to recognize the political leadership claims of the party. They expect it to exercise certain arbitration functions in intergroup relations and to initiate limited political innovations. The less clear-cut electoral basis of the party's leadership claim and the closer the next election date, the smaller the credit which functional powerholders will extend to unsolicited and non-routine activities of the political powerholders impinging on their own positions. This lack of credit then sets the stage for conflicts between functional and political leadership groups. How does the catch-all party in governmental positions treat such conflicts? Will it be satisfied to exercise pressure via the mass media, or will it try to re-create a militant basis beyond the evanescent electoral and publicity levels? By the very structure of the catch-all party, the looseness of its clientele, may from the outset exclude such more far-reaching action. To that extent the political party's role in Western industrial society today is more limited than would appear from its position of formal preeminence. Via its governmental role it functions as coordinator of and arbitrator between functional power groups. Via its electoral role it produces that limited amount of popular participation and integration required from the popular masses for the functioning of official political institutions.

Will this limited participation which the catch-all party offers the population at large, this call to rational and dispassionate participation in the political process via officially sanctioned channels, work?

The instrument, the catch-all party, cannot be much more rational than its nominal master, the individual voter. No longer subject to the discipline of the party of integration — or, as in the United States, never subject to this discipline — the voters may, by their shifting moods and their apathy, transform the sensitive instrument of the catch-all party into something too blunt to serve as a link with the functional powerholders of society. Then we may yet come to regret the passing — even if it was inevitable — of the class-mass party and the denominational party, as we already regret the passing of other features in yesterday's stage of Western civilization.

Part 4

POLITICAL TRANSMISSION BELTS—INTEREST GROUPS

Hardly any area of political life has received more attention from political scientists recently than that which is variously referred to as "lobbies," "pressure groups," or "interest group politics." This focus has been particularly true of American scholars; and their influence on political scientists abroad has been noticeable in the rapidly increasing attention paid to the concept of "group politics" by British, continental and non-European political scientists.

The reasons for the long neglect and the sudden rise to prominence — first in the United States and subsequently abroad — are not hard to find. The traditional theory of pure democracy — closer to Rousseau than to Madison even in the United States — was hostile to "intermediaries" between "the people" and their government. Public policy was to reflect the citizens' concern for the common good. And if transmission belts were required to connect the people and the government, it was held that these should be responsible political parties, making their appeal to the electorate and receiving the legitimation from the voters on the basis of free, equal, and universal elections. Even parties, by their very nature, were long suspected of being detrimental to the common good; a suspicion which, particularly in continental democracies, has by no means completely disappeared, and finds expression today in de Gaulle's open contempt for them.

But the conviction that a responsible party system represents an indispensable feature of an effective democracy can be said to have established itself firmly in most Western democracies. Thus the Bonn Basic Law of 1949 breaks new ground in specifically mentioning the parties' essential function "in the forming of the political will of the people." The same recognition has however, not been officially or constitutionally extended to interest groups Nevertheless, they have increasingly come to be seen as functioning to "aggregate" and "express" the "will of the people" as importantly and frequently as political parties.

That it was in the United States that this recognition first came, and was first made the subject of extensive scholarly study, is probably primarily due to the decentralized nature of the American political system, characterized by checks and balances, separation of powers, federalism — and the concomitant lack of cohesion of American parties. Policy formulation and legislation in the United States has always been the result of complex interactions between elected and appointed officials and interest-group spokesmen. To understand a piece of legislation, it was never sufficient to look at the program (platform) of a party and the outcome of an election.

British and Continental democracies have by and large been characterized by formally unified political systems, with single centers of governmental authority and political parties with high degrees of cohesion and discipline. Therefore, the role of interest groups in these countries has long remained neglected or deprecated. The statement by Professor Beer a little more than a decade ago — that interest groups were as frequent in Britain as in the United States, and more powerful — caused a small sensation. Yet at least the first part of his contention has become a commonplace of scholarly discussion, not only in Britain but in practically all Western democracies. It was soon found, however, that the mere discovery of the existence of interest groups in all democracies did not by any means settle the large number of questions related to their functions: What distinguished them in their behavior from political parties, particularly where parties formed themselves as interest representatives, such as agrarian parties or even labor parties emerging from trade union movements? What was their actual impact on policy formation, and how did it relate to the structure of the political systems within which they operated? At what stage of the policy process, and by what strategies, was their influence executed? Finally — and most difficult to answer — were they a boon, or a threat, to the effective functioning of modern democracy; in other words, is their (probably increasing) role in the policy-making process to be welcomed, deplored, or viewed with indifference?

The following selections provide a spectrum of analyses from several Western democracies and, more revealingly, from rather diversely structured systems. While in all of them influential interest groups are an unquestioned fact of political life, these democracies nevertheless reflect widely differing degrees of institutionalization and acceptance.

The range is wide — from Austria's semicorporatist system of interest representation in official "chambers," to the impatient toleration of pressure group activity by de Gaulle's regime. Thus, the articles should provide material for further hypotheses on the changing functions of interest groups in democratic systems, as well as arguments for the never-ending normative discussion about the merits and drawbacks of interest-group activity in furthering democratic objectives.

24. Parties, Pressure Groups and the British Political Process

ROBERT T. McKENZIE

McKenzie sets out to correct the standard account of the British political system, which has long concentrated on the formal institutions of government and the party system. He attacks the notion that parties and elections can or should be the only instruments of transforming the "will of the citizenry" into governmental policies. Interest groups, he argues, act as correctives to electoral anomalies, the inability of the electoral process to take account of the varying significance of issues to different segments of the electorate. Yet he is not oblivious of the dangers that organized interests pose to traditional and legitimate values of a democratic system.

Samuel Beer, perhaps the ablest American student of British politics, has commented: 'If we had some way of measuring political power, we could possibly demonstrate that at the present time pressure groups are more powerful in Britain than in the United States.'[1] The realisation that this may be the case, appears to have grown rapidly in Britain in recent years and, in most quarters, the reaction to it has been gloomy;[2] indeed, among many publicists the gloom has given way to outright despair. Thus, according to Paul Johnson, assistant editor of the *New Statesman*, 'Acts of policy are now decided by the interplay of thousands of conflicting interest groups, and Cabinet ministers are little more than chairman of arbitration committees. Their opinions play virtually no part in shaping decisions which they subsequently defend with passion . . . When everyone's wishes count, nobody's opinions matter.'[3]

There are no doubt many explanations of this despairing (and, I would argue, belated) recognition of the powerful role played by interest groups in

---

SOURCE: Reprinted by permission from *Political Quarterly*, January–March 1959, pp. 5–16. This version was slightly revised by the author.

[1] Samuel H. Beer, "Pressure Groups and Parties in Britain," *The American Political Science Review*, March 1956, p. 3.

[2] Thus even so well informed an observer as W. J. M. Mackenzie concludes that the dominant role of organised groups in British public life means: "We are gradually shifting back into a situation in which a man is socially important only as a holder of standard qualifications and as a member of authorised groups, in fact into the new medievalism which was the promised land in the days from the younger Pugin to William Morris." W. J. M. Mackenzie, "Pressure Groups in British Government," *British Journal of Sociology*, June 1955, p. 146.

[3] P. Johnson, "The Amiable Monster," the *New Statesman*, 12 October 1957, p. 468. In the same vein, Bernard Hollowood has remarked that "Parliament has become the abused referee of the big power game and . . . the unhappy millions on the terraces are powerless, almost voiceless spectators," in "The Influence of Business and the City," *Twentieth Century*, October 1957, p. 253.

Britain. There can be no question that their activities and their influence have increased in recent decades. This surely was inevitable; once it had been largely agreed by all parties that the governments (national and local) should collect and spend over a third of the national income, tremendous pressures were bound to be brought to bear to influence the distribution of the burdens and benefits of public spending on this scale. And further: a new and powerful factor was injected into the equation when the trade unions, since the Second World War, won recognition (in Sir Winston Churchill's phrase) as an 'estate of the realm.' The highly articulate middle class (by whom, and for whom, so many of our journals of opinion are written) developed an acute sense of claustrophobia as they watched the giants around them, organised business, labour, the farmers, and the rest, struggling among themselves (and often with the government of the day) for an ever larger share of the national income.

An Unexplored Field

These developments since the Second World War provide reasons enough for the new and acute awareness of the role of pressure groups in Britain. But in addition it must be noted that the standard accounts of the British political system (whether in the school texts, or in the academic journals) have done little or nothing to inform even the comparatively well-educated section of the British community about the realities of the sort of pressure politics which has always been a major factor in political life in this country. An American writer on this subject quotes a British information officer lecturing in America in 1954 as saying that there is 'a complete absence of pressure groups and lobbies in Britain.'[4] Unfortunately such a remark cannot be dismissed as a misguided effort in national propaganda; it was no doubt an honest expression of a widely accepted myth about the British political system.

Twenty years ago Sir Ivor Jennings demonstrated the vitally important part played by pressure groups in the parliamentary arena: 'much legislation,' he wrote, 'is derived from organised interests . . . most of it is amended on the representation of such interests, and . . . often parliamentary opposition is in truth the opposition of interests.' (*Parliament*, p. 503) But, strangely, no scholar for twenty years took the cue, even though the first book on the role of groups in the political process, A. F. Bentley's *The Process of Government* (Fisher Unwin), had appeared in 1908.[5] Indeed, it is only in the past three years that learned articles have begun to appear on the problems of definition and methodology and on the activities of particular interest groups. If the scholars and serious publicists have been so remiss, perhaps even the well-

---

[4] Cited in F. C. Newman, "Reflections on Money and Party Politics in Britain," *Parliamentary Affairs*, Summer 1957, p. 309.

[5] Since this essay was written several books devoted to the study of interest groups in Britain have appeared, including S. E. Finer, *Anonymous Empire*, Pall Mall (London, 1958); J. D. Stewart, *British Pressure Groups*, their role in relation to the House of Commons, Clarendon Press (Oxford, 1958); Allen Potter, *Organised Groups in British National Politics*, Faber (London, 1961).

informed citizen can be forgiven for harbouring the illusion that pressure groups are a uniquely foreign political phenomenon accounting for the 'pathological state of American democracy' and the *immobilisme* of France.

The Respective Roles of Pressure Groups and Parties

A starting point in clarifying the situation in this country, is to examine the respective roles in the British political process of political parties and of pressure groups. One source of confusion about the role of party has arisen from Burke's much quoted observation that a party is 'a body of men united for promoting by their joint endeavours the national interest upon some particular principle in which they are all agreed.' [6] This remark has been leaned on much too heavily; it provides no explanation at all of the function of party in a democratic society; and even as a description of parties it is misleading because it places far too great a stress on the role of principle (and by implication on the role of ideology and programme).

Yet some exponents of democratic theory, starting, it would appear, from Burke's definition, have implied that political parties serve (or ideally ought to serve) as the sole 'transmission belts' on which political ideas and programmes are conveyed from the citizens to the legislature and the executive. According to their ideal political model, a group of citizens first organise themselves into a political party on the basis of some principle or set of principles; they then deduce a political programme from these principles and their candidates proceed to lay this programme before the electorate; if the party secures a majority in Parliament it then implements the 'mandate' given it by the electors. If issues arise not covered by the 'mandate' then it is for the M.P.s to use their own judgment in deciding what to do; they are to deliberate, one gathers, in a kind of vacuum in which no external pressures (either from the constituencies or from organised interests) play upon them.

According to this democratic model, it is the exclusive function of the parties to canalise and to transmit the will of the citizenry to their elected representatives who then proceed to transmute it into positive law. The existence of organised groups of citizens, standing outside the party system and pressing the legislature and the executive to adopt certain specific policies, is either ignored or treated as an unfortunate aberration from the democratic ideal.

This conception of the democratic process is, in fact, completely inadequate and grossly misleading even if one applies it in this country, where parties are based on rather more specific sets of principles than they are in many other countries. (Although even in Britain it would not be easy to list the respective 'sets of principles' on which the members of the Conservative, Labour and Liberal Parties 'are all agreed.') Max Weber offered a better working definition of parties when he described them as 'voluntary associations for propaganda and agitation seeking to acquire power in order to . . . realise objective aims or personal advantages or both.' The 'objective aims' may be of greater or lesser

---

[6] *Thoughts on the Present Discontents*, Oxford University Press, World's Classics ed., Vol. II, p. 82.

importance in providing the basis of association and the motive force for the activity of a particular party. But there is little doubt that it is the 'collective pursuit of power' which is of overriding importance. It is obvious too that during the pursuit of power, and after it has been achieved, parties mould and adapt their principles under the innumerable pressures brought to bear by organised groups of citizens which operate for the most part outside the party system.

I would argue that the basic functions of parties in the British political system are to select, organise, and sustain teams of parliamentarians, between whom the general body of citizens may choose at elections. The 'selection' and 'sustaining' of the teams is mainly the job of the party outside Parliament; the 'organisation' of the teams (and the allocations of roles, including the key role of party leader and potential Prime Minister) is the function of the party within Parliament. It does not matter whether the party is organised on the basis of a set of principles on which all its members are agreed, or whether, alternatively, it represents merely an organised appetite for power. In either case parties play an indispensable role in the democratic system by offering the electorate a free choice between competing teams of potential rulers. In Britain, the parties do profess their loyalty to differing sets of principles and these help to provide an element of cohesion for the parties themselves, and they have the further advantage of offering the electorate a choice, in very broad terms, between differing approaches to the social and economic problems with which governments must deal.

None the less, elections in this country are primarily rough-and-ready devices for choosing between rival parliamentary teams. Under our electoral system (with its disdain for the principles of proportional representation and its penalisation of minor parties) the winning team of parliamentarians rarely obtains half the votes cast. (Indeed only three governments in this century have managed to do so). And even when, as in 1951, the winning party, the Conservatives, obtained fewer votes than their Labour opponents, no one challenges their right to rule the country.

Pressure Groups as a Corrective to Electoral Anomalies

It is, in part, one suspects, because of the tacit recognition of the enormous and legitimate role played by organised interests that the public acquiesces in the apparent anomalies of our electoral system. It did not much matter that a Conservative Government took office in 1951, having obtained fewer votes than the Labour Party which it ousted; the Conservatives would be less sympathetic to the aspirations of the principal supporters of the Labour Party (the trade unions), but the new Government was bound to be aware that they could not administer the economic affairs of the country unless they paid very close attention to the demands and the opinions of the trade unions. The trade unions for their part showed no disposition to sulk in their tents when the party of their choice was defeated in the election (although it had obtained more votes than the victors). The trade unions could not be expected to play a dominant role in determining the policies of the new government; but they could be confident that most of the channels of communication between the trade unions and the newly elected executive would remain open and that their views would carry great weight with the new administration.

I have suggested that any explanation of the democratic process which ignores the role of organised interests is grossly misleading; I would add that it is also hopelessly inadequate and sterile in that it leaves out of account the principal channels through which the mass of the citizenry brings influence to bear on the decision-makers whom they have elected. In practice, in every democratic society, the voters undertake to do far more than select their elected representatives; they also insist on their right to advise, cajole, and warn them regarding the policies they should adopt. They do this, for the most part, through the pressure-group system. Bentley, in the first trail-blazing analysis of pressure groups written fifty years ago, no doubt over-stated his case when he argued that individuals cannot affect governments except through groups; therefore, Bentley claimed the 'process of government' must be studied as 'wholly a group process.' But there can be no doubt that pressure groups, taken together, are a far more important channel of communication than parties for the transmission of political ideas from the mass of the citizenry to their rulers. It is true that a larger proportion of the electorate 'belongs to' political parties in this country than in any other democracy. (The Conservative and Labour Parties together claim membership of over nine million, rather more than one in every four of the voters.) But the number of *active* members who do the work of the parties in the constituencies, who draft the resolutions debated in party conferences and so forth, is not more than a few hundred per constituency. This stage army of the politically active, numbering a hundred thousand or so in each party, invariably claims to speak in the name of the millions of inactive members of the party and, indeed, on behalf of the twelve or thirteen million who normally vote for each party at an election. Further, they alone choose the candidates for their respective parties, and this is of course a vitally important function, since nomination is tantamount to election in two-thirds or three-quarters of the constituencies in Britain. But it is perfectly clear that when most citizens attempt to influence the decision-making process of their elected representatives, they do so through organised groups which we call 'interest groups' or 'pressure groups.'

The Articulation of Group Demands

David Truman, in the *Governmental Process* defines interest groups as 'shared-attitude groups that make certain claims upon other groups in the society.'[7] And he adds that when they make their claims through or upon any of the institutions of government, they may be called *'political interest groups.'* In popular parlance they become *'pressure groups,'* which is an acceptable enough term, so long as the word 'pressure' is not permitted to carry a too pejorative connotation. Pressure groups differ from parties in that they seek to influence the policy decisions of politicians (and administrators)

[7] D. B. Truman, *The Governmental Process*, Knopf (New York, 1962), p. 37.

without themselves seeking to assume direct responsibility for governing the country.[8] And the *pressure groups system,* in the language of the sociologist, is the set of institutional arrangements in any society which provides for the 'aggregation, articulation, and transmission' of group demands, when these demands are made through or upon governments.

Three Categories of Pressure Groups

Many attempts, some of them very elaborate, have been made to classify pressure groups. But a very simple and workable threefold classification is possible: first there are the *sectional groups,* which include all those whose basis of association is the common economic interest or vocation of their member (e.g. the Federation of British Industries, the National Farmers Union, the Trades Union Congress, the National Union of Teachers, etc.). Their principal function is to advance the interests of their members and to provide them with a variety of services; but inevitably, in the course of their work, they spend a great deal of their time attempting to influence the decisions of elected representatives in one or another of the organs of government.[9] Secondly, there are the *promotional groups;* they are not usually organised on the basis of a common economic or vocational interest, but are devoted to the advancement of a particular cause such as prison reform, the abolition of capital punishment, the defence of animal welfare, the strengthening of Sabbatarian legislation, etc. These first two categories include almost all groups which are of major political significance within the pressure-group system. But it is possible to designate a third category: *all other groups* which are not included within the first two. This may seem an odd method of classification, but it is very nearly true that every group within a society, however non-political its purpose occasionally attempts to influence public policy. For example, a Ramblers Association 'comes alive politically' on the rare occasion on which Parliament discusses Bills dealing with land use or national parks. The philatelists' associations admittedly would rarely be classified as pressure groups, yet they too no doubt occasionally make representations to Governments with respect to the policies pursued in issuing stamps. It is difficult indeed to think of any groups which would not under certain circumstances attempt to bring pressure to bear on the elected decision-makers.

David Truman and others have devised another category to which they

---

[8] It is admittedly comparatively easy to make this distinction in a preponderantly two-party system of the sort that exists in Britain and the United States; but it more difficult in certain Continental countries, where minor parties, which would elsewhere be content to function as pressure groups, offer candidates at elections even though they have no prospect, or even expectation, of winning full responsibility for governing the country. And of course it is arguable that in this country the Scottish and Welsh Nationalists are little more than pressure groups seeking to publicise their cause by offering candidates at elections. For a further discussion of this question see Allen Potter, "British Pressure Groups," *Parliamentary Affairs,* Autumn 1956, pp. 418–19.

[9] These sectional interest groups are the organisations, in Franz Neumann's phrase, "by which [social] power is translated into political power," *The Democratic and the Authoritarian State,* Free Press of Glencoe (Glencoe, Ill., 1957), p. 13.

attach considerable importance: *potential interest groups.* An example of what they have in mind is the category of people, largely unorganised, who are deeply devoted to maintaining the 'rules of the game' by which political democracy is sustained. When interest groups or political parties seriously transgress these (largely unwritten) rules, then this potential interest group is likely to spring into life. The first indications of its existence might take the form of letters to *The Times* drawing attention to certain dangerous developments in the eyes of the letter writers. Subsequently, if the situation is considered serious enough, *ad hoc* organisations would no doubt be set up to recruit support for those who shared the anxieties of the founders. A specific example of such a potential interest group taking tangible form occurred when the BBC announced its decision to reduce the hours of broadcasting on the Third Programme. It soon became apparent that we had amongst us, perhaps without realising it, a potential pressure group devoted to the defence of high standards in sound broadcasting. Indeed, the more one contemplates the British political scene, the more extraordinary it seems that students of the political process in this country should have so largely ignored the role of pressure groups. There can be few countries in the world in which the inhabitants so readily and so frequently organise themselves into groups for the purpose of influencing or changing the minds of their elected representatives.

Political Affiliation or Neutrality?

Certain of the great sectional groups choose to work through one or other of the great political parties in addition to bringing external pressure to bear on them. Thus, a large proportion of the trade unions are directly affiliated to the Labour Party and a number of unions also sponsor Labour candidates. But, as was noted above, the Trades Union Congress as well as individual unions reserve the right to deal directly with Governments, whether Labour or Conservative. The relations between the business community and the Conservative Party are more obscure, in part because the Conservatives do not permit direct affiliation of organised groups, and also because they do not publish their accounts. It can be taken for granted, however, that business men, as individuals and in groups, provide the greater part of the Conservative Party's revenue.[10] Yet the great associations representing the business community, such as the Federation of British Industries, expect to be and are intimately consulted by Labour governments. The Federation explains its own purpose in these words: '*whatever the government in power*, (the Federation) seeks to create conditions in which each firm has the maximum opportunity to turn its own ideas and resources to the best account in its own and the national interest.'[11]

---

[10] It is important to remember, however, as F. C. Newman has pointed out that in the case of both parties, "it is the programme that attracts the money, the money does not structure the programme," in "Reflections on Money and Party Politics in Britain," *Parliamentary Affairs* (Summer 1957), p. 316.

[11] *The F.B.I., what it is, what it does,* p. 1 (italics mine). For a very valuable examination of the structure and functioning of the F.B.I., see S. E. Finer, "The Federation of British Industries," *Political Studies* (February 1956), pp. 61–84.

Certain other associations, such as the National Union of Teachers, have also sponsored individual candidates for one or other or both parties. But, as the experience of the National Farmers Union suggests, most interest groups in recent years have tended to avoid a too close association with a particular party. This is partly no doubt because both parties, during their terms of office since the Second World War, have shown their willingness to serve, up to a point as brokers reconciling the interests of rival pressure groups.

There is no doubt widespread fear that parties will in fact degenerate into nothing more than brokers serving competing interest groups; and it is this fear which underlies much of the hostile comment on the activities of pressure groups, and which inhibits a realistic evaluation of the positive and legitimate function of these groups in the political process. It may well be that much writing on pressure groups too casually assumes a happy state of equilibrium. (Bentley argues that 'the balance of group pressures *is* the existing state of society.') There is no doubt that governments which indulge in 'piecemeal surrender to interest groups' become incapable of devising a coherent social policy. In the extremity, of course, government action could become merely the resultant of the forces that play upon the decision-makers.

The Experience of Sweden

But the danger can easily be exaggerated. Sweden can be described even more aptly than this country as 'a pluralist society' yet it is far from the 'pluralist stagnation' which some critics of the interest-group system fear. Gunnar Heckscher (who is both a professor of politics and a Conservative member of the Swedish Parliament) recently commented that 'It is now regarded as more or less inevitable' in Sweden that certain of the powerful interests groups 'should exercise a power almost equal to that of Parliament and definitely superior to that of the parliamentary parties.'[12] Yet he does not see in this situation any really serious ground for concern; nor is there, he says, any demand in Sweden that action should be taken to curb the powerful organisations. Heckscher attributes the comparatively good health of the Swedish body politic to the 'strong sense of responsibility among group leaders' and the 'politics of compromise' which govern the relations between the great groups themselves, as well as their relations with governments.

Despite the political and social tensions in contemporary Britain, surely much the same comment can be made about the situation in this country? Vague as the phrase may be, the concept of the 'national interest' is still to the forefront in the course of almost every big sectional dispute in this country. Business, Labour, the farmers, the university teachers, still consider it expedient to argue their case, at least in part, in the terms of the national interest.

---

12 G. Heckscher, "Interest Groups and Sweden," a paper presented to the *International Political Science Round Table*, Pittsburgh, 7–14 September (duplicated), p. 8. See also his "Pluralist Democracy; the Swedish Experience," *Social Research* (December 1948), pp. 417–61. It should be noted, in connection with Heckscher's remark quoted above, that there are five parties in the Swedish Parliament, and in such circumstances it is perhaps less surprising than it would be here to remark that certain of the great sectional groups are more powerful than the parliamentary parties.

Governments may from time to time give in to one or other of the great pressure groups, also in the name of the 'national interest.' But they also on occasion stand out boldly against the claim of pressure groups on the ground that to give way would be to *betray* the national interest.

The Effect of Pressure Groups on Government

If governments may have appeared in recent years to be more pusillanimous than heretofore, it may be in part because since 1950 we have been living in an unusual period of knife-edge parliamentary majorities; and during such periods Governments are bound to spend a good deal of time peering over their own shoulders. It is too often forgotten that a uniform 1 per cent shift from one party to another means a turnover of 18 seats, and hence a drop of 36 in the ruling party's majority. (Thus if at the next election the Conservatives suffer a net loss of 2 in every hundred of those who supported them in 1955, then their Government will be defeated.) One of the most effective ways of minimising the influence on governments of at least some pressure groups, if this is considered urgently necessary, would be to provide one party or another with a sweeping parliamentary majority.[13]

There are of course other grounds for concern, quite apart from the possibility of inhibiting effect of the pressure-group system on governmental decision-making. Many fear that the powerful groups are becoming more powerful and the less well-organised groups relatively weaker. Samuel Eldersveld, writing of the situation in the United States, discussed the possibility that the interest-group system is resulting, not in increased political competition, but in imperfect competition, leading to oligopoly.[14] And he adds that the 'diversification of power sources (in America) means that the decision-making process is more indirect, non-public, and obscure.' The same fears are often expressed in Britain. Are there not a very few great interest groups, it is suggested, whose leaders form a kind of inner circle of 'oligarchs' which deals frequently and intimately with senior ministers? And is it not the case that this handful of people decide the fate of the whole community, which is for the most part, unaware even of the issues they are deciding? Again, it would be foolish to ignore evidence of the trend in this direction; equally foolish to ignore the countervailing forces. Certainly it is true that the leaders of big business, big labour, and the farmers have greater ease of 'access' to senior ministers, whichever party is in office. But it would be inaccurate automatically to equate 'access' with 'influence.' (To take a slightly frivolous example it seems likely that a Conservative Government would be more willing

---

13 The Conservatives in the 1959 election secured a majority of 100 and in the course of that Parliament did act more boldly than hitherto in, for example, attempting to introduce an incomes policy despite trade union hostility; in promoting the Beeching plan for the reorganisation of the railways, despite much resistance in the rural areas; and in the sponsorship of legislation to abolish resale price maintenance against the strong resistance of the small shop-keepers who traditionally support the Conservative Party.

14 S. J. Eldersveld, "American Interest Groups," a paper presented to the *International Political Science Round Table*, Pittsburgh, 7–14 September 1957 (duplicated).

to defy the trade unions and a Labour Government the business organisations, than either of them would be likely to defy the Sabbatarian groups, which are not thought to have very ready access to ministers.) And further, it must be remembered, that intimacy of contact involves the recognition of mutual responsibilities. Ministers may explain the situation to interest group leaders frankly and then ask their cooperation 'in the national interest.'

The Unorganized, Inarticulate Sections

There remains, however, the problem of the ill-organised (or even unorganisable) section of the community. Is there not danger that they will either be ignored or trampled upon by the really powerful interest groups? Certainly the danger is real. But it is the politicians' ultimate worry to see to it that the 'little men' (each of whom has as much political influence in the polling booth, at least, as anyone in the land) do not revolt against their policies in such numbers as to bring about their electoral ruin. This surely is one ultimate safeguard of the ill-organised. Indeed, it is arguable that in the long run Governments are at least as frightened of the unorganised consumers (in their capacity as voters) as they are of the highly organised economic interests. None the less there is an area of public policy in which the absence of organised groups represents a serious problem. Thus, for example, Governments under pressure from shop employees and certain categories of shop-owners, may contemplate further restricting shop hours; there is no one to speak for the shoppers. Or again, Governments may be fearful of liberalising licensing hours because of the pressures they would set in motion against themselves from the highly organised temperance forces; there is no organised body to speak for the drinkers. Here, it seems to be, the public opinion polls have a legitimate and important role to play. The evidence they can produce of the shoppers' attitude to proposals for restricting shop hours, or the drinkers' attitude to licensing laws, should be *one* of the factors taken into account by the decision-makers, in addition to the views of the organised interests, in arriving at their policy decisions.

But with reservations such as these, it seems to me reasonable to conclude that the pressure-group system with all its dangers, is both an inevitable and an indispensable concomitant of the party system. It provides an invaluable set of multiple channels through which the mass of the citizenry can influence the decision-making process at the highest levels. Is it possible that the widespread uneasiness about pressure groups in Britain today is really a result of the shift in the balance of power between the classes? In the paper quoted above, Eldersveld remarked that in 'the fluid politics' of America there is no longer 'a decisive ruling class' but rather a set of 'multiple elites.' The same development has obviously occurred in this country; and it is clear that the new elites are struggling to assert their strength in part through the pressure-group system.

25. Pressure Group Politics in Britain

HARRY ECKSTEIN

The following selection is taken from the Postscript to Professor Eckstein's study of British medical interest-group politics. Here he sums up his major empirical findings, which indicate that the view popularized by Professor Samuel H. Beer—that pressure groups in Britain are exceedingly important, yet largely exempt from public accountability—is correct. At the same time, however, the decisions reached by this process do not appear to be contrary to the (hard-to-define) public interest. In fact, the process itself seems to make a system with strong parties work more effectively and even more democratically.

In the simplest terms, group influence is enlarged by anything which restricts the influence on policy-making of anything else. This either is or comes close to being a tautology, but is none the less worth stating. For example, the influence of groups certainly is enhanced by the lack of any wide public interest in an area of policy, simply because such lack of interest, apart from minimizing group competition, tends to neutralize some of the more important centres of influence which compete with private groups as such. Parties, to be sure, do sometimes propose policy merely for the sake of having a programme, but generally they concern themselves with issues which are of wide public concern. That goes also for the press, especially the popular press, and for Parliament. Here once again consensus is a matter of crucial importance, but not consensus alone. Public interest and the chief organs which express and arouse it may also be diverted from an area of policy by the feeling that the subject involved is not the public's business, e.g. by the conviction that it is a field only for the technically competent. We can see both considerations at work in the striking shift from near-impotence to near-omnipotence which occurred in the BMA's position between the passage of the National Health Service Act and the Appointed Day. There occurred in this period a corresponding shift from profound to much shallower public interest (at any rate, until the Appointed Day itself drew near) and from considerations of general policy to considerations of detail; in fact the very fact that Parliament drew up such a very skeletal piece of legislation in the Health Service Act denotes its willingness to abdicate its own influence (and the influence of Party) to that of technically specialized groups.

Similarly, group influence is enhanced by anything which restricts the interest of formal governmental institutions other than Parliament, especially the administrative departments. Interdepartmental interest is, of course, tepid

SOURCE: Reprinted by permission from Harry Eckstein, *Pressure Group Politics* (Stanford: Stanford University Press, 1960), pp. 155–163; and by permission of George Allen & Unwin Ltd., London. Footnotes are abridged.

where policies impinge relatively little on a variety of administrative concerns; with the exception of its financial aspects this has been so in the case of medical policy. It is also diminished by the factors which diminish broad public interest itself: by agreement and the recognition of technical incompetence. Finally, it is diminished, even where interdepartmental concerns are impinged upon, by the presence of a powerful Minister as spokesman for the policy concerned.

The group theory of politics emerges from this discussion as a powerful heuristic tool, but only for the analysis of certain kinds of political systems and certain kinds of policies within such systems. It is most useful of all wherever there exists a great amount of agreement on basic political issues and a high degree of concern with narrowly delimited policies impinging upon technical, especially professionalized, fields. This is hardly surprising, either in itself or in the light of the conditions . . . under which private groups tend to become politically active as pressure groups. But it does help us to understand the enormous influence of pressure groups on British medical policy; and perhaps it helps us to understand also why the group approach to politics has been influential mainly in the Anglo-Saxon countries and scored its greatest triumphs in the age of the social welfare state.

Pressure Groups and the Democratic Process

Much of what I have said about the group theory of politics is also relevant to an even older issue: whether pressure groups in democratic systems are a good or a bad thing, conducive or not to the 'national interest,' aids or hindrances to the operation of democratic procedures. It has proven extraordinarily difficult to deal with these questions; and most positions taken on them in the past do more to beg them than to answer them. Nor do these questions answer themselves in light of what has been said here about the conditions under which intensive pressure group activity emerges. For something may very well be both a symptom of health and corrosive of health; such neat, uncomfortable contradictions do sometimes arise in nature no less than in Germanic ideologies. The position on the question suggested by this study, however, is much more reassuring. In a nutshell, the study suggests (to me at any rate) that the influence of private groups is greatest when, from the standpoint of democratic values, it matters least whether it is great or small.

Those who abominate pressure groups as influences which distort democratic processes do so for very simple reasons. They believe that pressure group activity leads to the satisfaction of particular interests to the detriment of general interests. They also believe that it shifts the arena of decision-making from the public limelight to the 'backstairs,' where collusion and manipulation become possible because normal democratic controls do not operate — collusion not only against the public at large but frequently also against the rank and file of the pressure groups themselves. 'Light! More light!' exclaims Professor Finer at the end of his otherwise dry and laconic study of the British 'lobby,' while Mr. Mackenzie, in concluding his ground breaking essay on British pressure groups, conjures up the awful prospect of a 'new medievalism,' where a man 'is socially important only as the holder of standard qualifications and as a member of authorized groups.'[1] These writers do not argue that pressure groups have no uses at all, or that nothing can be done to make them more 'responsible.' They do imply that the uses of groups like the BMA are vitiated by the 'too-close embrace' of Ministry and Association: by the latter's ability to force its sectional interests, through all too confidential negotiations, upon the Government. Is this a legitimate criticism?

It is true that relations between the BMA and the Ministry are, more often than not, highly confidential, even secret; but is it really obvious that this is a bad thing? As in the conduct of foreign relations, something is certainly to be said for secrecy in this case, at least at certain stages of the negotiations. We know from experience that the exposure of negotiations to the public while they are in process is one way to make them fail; the Ministry tends to assume a pose calculated to avert awkward interventions by Parliament or other departments; the BMA's leaders act so as to appear to be stubbornly pushing the members' 'interests'; all the latent pressures and limiting factors which prevent free accommodation between Ministry and Association tend to become mobilized. Even where outside interventions do not actually occur they tend to be anticipated, the results being the same. If it is at all desirable that there should be exchanges between the Ministry and the Association aiming at agreement, then it is desirable that their transactions should be confidential — perhaps not always and at every stage, but surely to a large extent.

Anyhow, who would take much interest in these transactions? Negotiations nowadays tend to be confidential not so much because of any anti-democratic collusion among the negotiators, but, much more important, because very few people really care about them. Nor is that really a bad thing. It is the result of the same factors which maximize pressure group activity and pressure group influence: a high degree of consensus on fundamental policy and the shift of disputes (partly because of fundamental agreement, partly for other reasons) to technical issues which most people do not and need not understand. Whenever any fundamental, widely interesting matters have arisen between the Ministry and BMA — money matters, questions of good faith towards the doctors in the Service — the normal machinery of publicity we associate with democracy has in fact swung into action and negotiations have been well aired (to their detriment). In other cases, we are almost always told the broad course and outcome of negotiations, if not the more intimate details, and this regardless of the state of public interest; the difficulty is not so much that information is not available but that it is uninteresting, not of public concern, and therefore largely ignored by Parliament and the Press. This also is not symptomatic of any malaise in the machinery of democracy but a sign of health, for enterprises like the National Health Service would be notorious only if they were highly controversial — or very badly managed.

Of course, even when negotiations are widely publicized we rarely learn who is really 'responsible' for decisions. The originators of positions, the makers

---

[1] W. J. M. Mackenzie, "Pressure Groups in British Government," *British Journal of Sociology,* June, 1955, p. 146.

of compromises, the mediators and the recalcitrants remain anonymous. It is always the Minister who appears before the House and the Chairman who appears before the Council or the ARM to take responsibility, although we know that they enter personally into very few negotiations, and even then, generally speaking, only when they have broken down. The real work is done by the shadowy junta of Assistant Secretaries. But if that is bad, then the whole British parliamentary system is an abomination, for one of its basic suppositions is that it is enough that *someone* should be accountable for decisions, not that it must be the person actually responsible. Like secrecy, this doctrine also has great utility: it produces decisions rather than procrastinations; like secrecy, too, it never keeps real controversies from being really argued.

In this case at least, the empire of the lobby is anonymous, when it is and to the extent that it is anonymous, because of constitutional processes and public apathy; and so much the better. But is it constructive, in a broad national sense, in the decisions it produces? Does it promote general or sectional interests?

That decisions relating to medical policy are made in Britain by the interaction of 'authorized groups' is undeniable. In negotiations about such policy the general public plays no role, except only when its views are 'represented' by the Treasury. But that again is not very serious: what views, after all, are there to represent? More seriously, even medical views are stated only through the medium of the oligarchy, which is itself a kind of specially 'authorized' group *vis-à-vis* the Ministry and not ordinarily representative, in the strict sense, of the profession. But does that matter any more than the relatively free hand of the Ministry? The power of the oligarchy, as we have seen, rests to a large extent on apathy, and apathy in turn reflects not merely the individualistic habits of the profession but also the uncontroversial character of the oligarchy's attitudes. Whenever the leaders have been seriously out of tune with a large proportion of the members on seriously controversial issues, the members have generally managed to exert some independent weight. Only rarely, to be sure, have they been able actually to convert the leaders, who have generally continued to play an autonomous role in negotiations (e.g. in the earlier negotiations over the National Health Service); but, on the other hand, the dissidents have been able to give to the Ministry tactical advantages (playing off one section of the profession against another, for example) which have had important effects on negotiations. As in the case of secrecy, which is great only when public interest is slight, so also here the discretion of the oligarchs is greatest when it matters least. Of course, nothing like a direct flow of views from the rank and file ever takes place; but then it never does.

Perhaps one may more reasonably object to the virtual exclusion from medical negotiations of 'unauthorized' groups like the Medical Practitioners Union (which has two members on the GMSC, where they exert little influence) and the Socialist Medical Association. Neither, however, is very significant numerically, while still other medical corporations, like the Royal Colleges, do play a role when their interests are aroused, infrequently though that is the case.

However, the fact that medical policies are not made by collusion among a few specially privileged leaders — at any rate not more than is inevitable in the nature of the case — does not mean necessarily that the policies are always in the general interest. But how can one readily determine whether they are in the 'general interest' or not? If we could know objectively what the general interest is, no difficulty about this would arise; but I for one have no idea how to determine an objective general interest. Only three questions, it seems to me, allow one to deal with the problem with any precision at all. We can ask, first, whether the policies adopted seem to be what most people seem to want, taking the public interest to be any action broadly desired by the public. The answer in that case is simply that most people appear to have no strong preferences, if any preferences at all, on the sort of subjects negotiations between the BMA and Ministry have covered. There may be a 'latent' general interest in these negotiations, but on the level of manifest and broad social purposes medical negotiations have been virtually irrelevant. We can ask, second, whether public medical services would have been more effective — whatever that may mean: a lower death rate? less suffering? more cures for less money? — if the BMA had been less effective, less intimately involved in medical policy-making. The best answer to that probably is that without such intimate involvement there might be no public medical services at all; but, apart from that, how could one possibly tell what policy could have been under other conditions? Third, we can ask whether, due to BMA pressure, the medical services have been withdrawing too large a share from total national wealth, relative to other services: whether they have encroached unduly on the generalizable resources of society. The answer to that is that since the inception of the National Health Service the cost of medical services has declined in relation to national income and the cost of many other services. On what ground, then, other than some nebulous neo-Rousseauism, could one argue that general interests have been prejudiced among the admittedly sectional interests at the Ministry?

To argue that the activities of the BMA and similar pressure groups prejudice democratic processes is to have a very innocent and academic notion of what democratic processes are all about. The relations between the Ministry and the BMA are a good example of both the limits and potentialities of such processes. Apathy (but apathy rooted in agreement) and technicality keep the bulk of their transactions on medical policy within the 'anonymous empire'; the power of the BMA as a 'veto group' undoubtedly gives it weight beyond its numbers, and perhaps also beyond its expertise. Yet there are important counterweights against its power, most clearly of all when the Treasury intervenes; and, if we take the distribution of the national income as an index, countervailing forces more than sufficiently do their job. Moreover, when a public interest may be said to exist concretely, not just abstractly, the normal machinery of responsible democratic government swings into action, exposing confidential transactions to publicity and tapping previously silent reservoirs of opinion. That, in any possible world, is all one can reasonably expect democratic machinery to do.

I rather think therefore, that political scientists who demand more light on pressure group activities demand it chiefly in their own interest as political scientists, and demand it not in any absolute sense but in a more easily accessible form. One can, to put the matter in a nutshell, get practically all the information one needs — to be an adequate citizen or an adequate political scientist — about medical politics in Britain, but not, as I know as well as anyone, without difficulty. The chief barrier, significantly, is not the conspiratorial silence of the pressure groups, but the institutionalized secretiveness of the administrative departments.

The Functions of Pressure Groups

In the language of contemporary 'functional' theory, pressure groups then are not manifestly dysfunctional in regard to democratic processes; they do not undermine them. They are in fact an inevitable term in the syndrome of an effective democratic system — alongside two-party systems and their functional equivalents, a wide range of fundamental political agreement itself, and a governmental machinery which can adjust rapidly to changing circumstances and act efficiently to realize shared social purposes. Indeed, it could be shown without great difficulty, if it were to the purpose here, that all these terms are related to one another as well as to the existence of effective democratic government. But do pressure groups really make any positive contributions to democratic government? Granted their inevitability, are they in any sense indispensable as well?

That pressure groups do useful work in the formulation and administration of specific policies like contemporary British medical policies is hardly open to question; I have tried to indicate these useful functions throughout the study. The BMA provides information to decision-makers, gives technical counsel, participates (however indirectly) in administration itself, helps to win and organize support, and acts as a communication channel for the grievances, large and small, which arise even in the best administered human enterprises. But groups like the BMA perform also functions of a more general character in democratic systems, functions not related to the contingent characteristics of any specific range of policy.

In the first place, pressure groups perform an important 'integrative' function in the political system. Any political system which values responsiveness to its members faces the problem of how to integrate the manifold goals of individuals (manifold even in the most consensual systems) into manageable ranges of alternatives for action. The widely varying perspectives and purposes of individuals must somehow be 'aggregated' if they are effectively to inform policy at all. We have always thought that this task of creating public opinions — integrated, supra-individual perspectives and goals — is primarily the function of political parties, and no doubt it is their pre-eminent function. But it is a function also of less fully politicized groups like the BMA. These groups aggregate specialized ranges of opinion on specialized subjects, and do so effectively in so far as their members identify themselves — their interests and goals — with those of the groups. Parties, in their very nature, tend to aggregate opinion on a very broad scale, rather infrequently, and for limited purposes, such as elections. This applies especially to parties like those in the Anglo-Saxon countries which must appeal to a very large electorate and are confronted less frequently with the need to define their position than parties in complex multi-party systems.[2] Pressure groups, on the other hand, constantly define opinion for government and do so on a level upon which parties only infrequently touch.

In certain political systems, therefore — especially two-party systems — pressure groups may be said to have still a second general function alongside their integrative function: a 'disjunctive' function. Two-party systems (perhaps any party system other than the most splintered of multi-party systems) tend perhaps to integrate political opinions all too well. In attempting to win mass support, necessarily from a large variety of groups, they do not so much 'aggregate' opinions . . . as reduce them to their lowest and vaguest denominators, sometimes distorting the perspectives and goals they seek to mobilize out of all recognition. One may doubt whether such systems could persist if groups did not have readily available outlets other than the parties through which to pursue their political goals.

The integrative function of parties in two-party systems is certainly important for the existence of stable governments and the simplification of issues at elections, so that easy choices may be made by the electors. The disjunctive function of pressure groups is equally important to prevent the alienation of groups from systems which persistently distort their goals; in that sense they are an indispensable element of stability in such systems. Disjunction can, of course, go too far; but the crucial fact that pressure groups are mobilized to the greatest extent where political agreement has the greatest range, mitigates the potential divisiveness of pressure group politics.

In the light of this, the case for pressure groups in democratic systems is even stronger than I had previously made it. Democratic systems seem to work most effectively, from the standpoint of action, where parties work least effectively, from the standpoint of representation. For in democratic systems parties must perform simultaneously two functions which are, on the evidence, irreconcilable: to furnish efficient decision-makers and to represent accurately opinions. The best way to reconcile these functions in practice is to supplement the parties with an alternative set of representative organizations which can affect decisions without affecting the positions of the decision-makers. This is the pre-eminent function of pressure groups in effective democratic systems, as the competition for power is the pre-eminent function of the parties.

---

[2] I have in mind here the fact that parties in systems like the British tend to define their position chiefly in preparation for elections. Those in multi-party systems must also do so in the constantly repeated manoeuvring for coalitions.

26. Pressure Politics in the Fifth Republic

BERNARD E. BROWN

Comparative analysis need not be cross-national. If we wish to examine the relation between the structure of a political system and the functioning of its political process, it may be equally useful to compare the changing pattern under two institutional settings within the same system. The French system under the constitutions of the Fourth and Fifth Republics gives Professor Brown the opportunity to examine the old thesis that the power of pressure groups declines as the strength and centralization of government increases. The conclusions he reaches point to a much more complex relationship, indicating shifts in relative position and strategies rather than a simple quantitative change.

The thesis of an inverse ratio between strength of the government and power of pressure groups is venerable. It has gained widespread acceptance among American political scientists, since it seems to explain the susceptibility of individual congressmen to pressure group demands, and the relative independence of the president. Some observers discern in this difference between Congress and the president an argument in favor of cabinet government along British lines. Other critics are content merely to ask for greater centralization of the political parties in the United States, which would have the same happy result as the introduction of a cabinet system: pressure groups would be drawn to a central point, and would therefore find it difficult to have their way.

The advent of the Fifth Republic offers a unique opportunity to test the validity of these observations. One of the chief advantages claimed for the new regime by its founders is that the strengthened executive is better able to withstand the egoistic pressures and demands of organized interest groups. Conforming to the ideas of General de Gaulle and Michel Debré, a president chosen by a restricted electoral college (in the future by universal suffrage) now enjoys autonomous political power, while the position of the cabinet has been improved. Restrictions have been placed upon parliament as regards the procedure for voting censure, length of sessions, control over its agenda and role of the standing committees. In practice, decision-making power has been concentrated in the presidency ever since General de Gaulle's inauguration as president in January, 1959. Without entering into the polemical debate over the merits and demerits of these innovations, it is instructive to see what has happened to the pressure groups in these changed circumstances. Are they less important, as important or more important under the Fifth Republic than under the Fourth?

SOURCE: Reprinted by permission from *The Journal of Politics*, XXV (August 1963), pp. 509–525. Footnotes are abridged.

In order to answer that question definitively it will be necessary to undertake a large number of monographic studies of both individual groups and the decision-making process. It will probably be many years before sufficient information is available to satisfy the exigencies of the theorist and historian. However, at the time of this writing the Fifth Republic has been functioning for over four years, and a certain amount of experience is available for appraisal — tentative and limited as it may be. It may be possible to discern some trends by focusing attention on key groups. Fortunately, we now have at our disposal a new edition of the basic work on French pressure groups by Jean Meynaud, the leading authority on the subject. On the very first page of the 1962 edition the reader is warned that it is too soon to measure the impact of the changes brought by the Fifth Republic. Although it is not impossible to note signs of adaptation or continuity, Meynaud observes, our description or judgment of recent events may be distorted by political bias. But Professor Meynaud is far too modest. In the course of his new survey of French pressure groups a vast amount of material is presented — and there are both "descriptions and judgments" which highlight the changes ushered in by the Fifth Republic.[1]

From Meynaud's survey it is evident that in many respects the pattern of pressure group activities has been altered under the new regime. Organized groups now pay less attention than formerly to parliament, its specialized committees, and the political parties — for the simple and understandable reason that the role played by these agencies in the policy-making process has diminished. Thus, notes Meynaud, a number of important measures have been virtually imposed upon a hostile or unwilling parliament, for example the creation of an independent nuclear striking force. In other cases parliament has been utterly unable to obtain even partial satisfaction in areas where once it ruled supreme — as in its failure in November, 1959, to reestablish pensions for veterans. The decline of parliament would therefore appear to mean, inevitably, a decline of pressure groups. "It is clear," says Meynaud, "on the whole, that this diminution of the prerogatives of the assemblies compels the groups to direct their interventions towards the centers of power whose influence has been maintained or is on the ascendant." [2]

The major "ascendant power" in the Fifth Republic has been the president, who appears to be in a strong position with regard to the pressure groups. General de Gaulle has apparently adopted policy concerning Algeria, national defense, the budget, and price-levels without even consulting organized interests. On several occasions he has proudly noted his independence of interest groups. In a letter of March 18, 1960, to Chaban-Delmas, explaining

---

[1] Jean Meynaud, *Nouvelles études sur les groupes de pression en France* (Paris, 1962) and his earlier work, *Les groupes de pression en France* (Paris, 1958). In a recent article, however, Professor Meynaud specifically undertakes the task of contrasting and evaluating the role of pressure groups under the Fourth and Fifth Republics. See, "Les groupes de pression sous la Vᵉ République," *Revue Française de Science Politique* (September, 1962), 672–97.

[2] Jean Meynaud, *Novelles études sur les groupes de pression en France* (Paris, 1962), p. 253.

his refusal to convoke a special session of parliament demanded by a majority
of the deputies for a debate on agricultural policy, General de Gaulle wrote:
"Fully cognizant of the capital importance of the subject which the signatories
justly believe should be considered by the public powers as soon as possible,
it seems beyond question to me that their claims, as formulated, result largely
from urgent demands on the part of the leaders of a professional group. Now,
whatever may be the representativeness of this group as regards the particular
economic interests which it defends, it is nonetheless — according to the law —
bereft of all authority and of all political responsibility." [3] Whatever the merits
of the constitutional question raised by General de Gaulle's refusal to convoke
parliament, the letter of March 18 is a significant indication of the chief of
state's deep hostility towards organized groups.

Perhaps the best example of the Fifth Republic's firm stand with regard to
pressure groups is the financial reform of December, 1958. As Meynaud points
out, all the devaluations from 1936 to 1957 failed because the government was
unable to impose collective discipline upon the producers and trade unions.
Each devaluation was followed by inflation. In 1958 the government was able
to resist the demands of the groups temporarily hurt by devaluation, and
consequently was able to achieve a sound fiscal reform. "Technically,"
observes Meynaud, "the operation was and remains a success." [4] Thus, the
framers of the Fifth Republic seem to be vindicated by the success of the
1958 reform — a strong state was able to defend the general interest against the
egoistic groups.

However, a note of caution is sounded by Meynaud throughout his book:
group pressures result from the very movement of social life. Transformation
of institutions does not annul the pressure or activities of groups; the latter
merely search and use other techniques. "In order to bring about a radical
change, it would be necessary to modify completely the social constitution of
the country: at this price only would it be possible to establish a different
system of relations between socio-economic forces and the public powers." [5]
Indeed, in a number of respects there are some striking *similarities* between
the Fourth and Fifth Republics as regards the role of pressure groups.

In spite of the hard line taken by the government since 1958 towards
pressure group claims, on numerous occasions concessions have been made:
regarding the interpretation of "exterior signs of wealth" in calculating income
taxes; charges for drugs under the national health service; increase of the
minimum wage; reestablishment of some veterans pensions which had been
eliminated as part of the fiscal reform of 1958; revival of the agricultural price
index; and the promise to hold a round table on the problems of viticulture.
Meynaud speculates that the regime may have been compelled to make these
and other concessions because of the need to secure widespread support for

---

[3] *Année Politique*, 1960, p. 640.
[4] Jean Meynaud, *Novelles études sur les groupes de pression en France* (Paris, 1962),
p. 382.
[5] *Ibid.*, pp. 232–24. For examples of similarities between the Fourth and Fifth Republics
as regards pressure groups: *ibid.*, pp. 200, 238–39, 261–63, 276.

General de Gaulle's Algerian policy — and for the Republic itself, in view of the uprisings of January, 1960 and April, 1961.

In many respects interest groups have the same opportunity for exercising influence under the Fifth Republic as under the Fourth. There are approximately five thousand assorted advisory councils, committees or agencies in which organized groups participate. A number of these agencies perform price fixing and other official functions, so that the groups may make suggestions and argue their case *within* the government. The existence of an Economic and Social Council with only minor modifications under the Fifth Republic provides yet another legal outlet for group activities and influence. Most important of all, those organized groups which had ready access to the administration under the Fourth Republic continue to enjoy the same privilege under the Fifth. Both before and since 1958 certain departments within the civil service have tended to be receptive to the viewpoint of various groups (business, labor, farmer, secular organizations, teachers, bankers, veterans, and so on). That is, the groups not only compete with each other in a conflict arbitrated by the government; to a certain extent the administration as well as the parliament is caught up in the struggle and becomes a part of it. Criss-crossing relations among civil servants, parliamentarians, party leaders and organized groups continue, though the exact balance among them has doubtless shifted. By and large the wealthier groups, especially those able to present well documented studies to buttress their claims, have a distinct advantage over such poor or noisy groups as the home distillers. The fact that a number of top civil servants resign their posts and take jobs with both large enterprises and professional organizations (the practice of "pantouflage") facilitates the dialogue.

Before attempting to draw further conclusions about the role of pressure groups in the Fifth Republic, it might be instructive to study a few selected groups in more detail. Attention will here be drawn to three groups or sets of groups concerning which considerable information is available for the period before 1958: the alcohol lobby, the secular and religious organizations, and the army.[6]

The State and the Groups: Three Cases

The Alcohol Case

The nature of the alcohol problem in France is now so well known that it needs no extensive description here. Briefly, for many years the *Service des alcools* has purchased far more alcohol (distilled primarily from beets, apples, molasses and wine) than the economy could absorb. In effect the state monopoly was a device whereby the alcohol producing groups (in particular the

---

[6] For further bibliography and a more extensive treatment of each of these groups, see my earlier articles: "Alcohol and Politics in France," *American Political Science Review* (December, 1957); "Religious Schools and Politics in France," *Midwest Journal of Political Science* (Spring, 1958); and "The Army and Politics in France," *Journal of Politics* (May, 1961).

wealthy and powerful beetgrowers) compelled the rest of the nation in large part to subsidize their activities. Although most of the alcohol purchased by the state eventually was sold to industry, a portion of these stocks were used in the manufacture of alcoholic beverages. To make matters worse, a large number of people (from two to three million) enjoyed the historic right to distill ten liters of pure alcohol a year without payment of tax — and in fact at least twice that amount was distilled and put into circulation fraudulently. Overproduction of alcohol coincided with the existence of a serious problem of alcoholism. However, the two to three million home distillers, the 150,000 beetgrowers, the winegrowers, the proprietors of bars, and the commercial distillers constituted a powerful political force with a direct interest in maintaining the alcohol statute. Several cabinets under the Fourth Republic experienced great difficulty in attempting to bring about needed reform.

Under the Fifth Republic it appears that the basic problem of huge deficits and overproduction has been solved — though other problems are bound to arise as the Common Market takes shape. In 1958 and 1959 the *Régie* actually showed a modest profit, which was used to facilitate the conversion of apple orchards from alcoholic to non-alcoholic production. A number of measures were also adopted by both parliament and the cabinet to meet the menace of alcoholism: a decree of 30 August 1960 finally suppressed altogether the principle of tax exemption for home distillers — but maintained it as a personal right only for those who actually enjoyed that right in 1959–60 and for their "surviving mate." The privilege of home distilling will therefore be progressively restricted. A decree of 29 November 1960 also envisages measures to limit the number of bars in order to reduce temptation in the vicinity of hospitals, youth centers, and the like. On the surface, then, it appears that the Fifth Republic has successfully withstood the pressure of the alcohol lobbies, and resolved one of the problems which had plagued the Fourth Republic.

In all fairness, however, this judgment should be modified somewhat. The determination of the state to place the *Service des alcools* on a paying basis — that is, to put an end to the huge deficits resulting from subsidy of alcohol producers — dates at least from 1956, if not earlier. The Mendès-France government, by a decree of 13 November 1954, determined to abolish the privilege of the home distillers within one year — though every parliament thereafter succeeded in postponing its application. In 1956 the Socialist Finance Minister, Paul Ramadier, ordered an end to the practice of adding alcohol to gasolene. Above all, a vast program was launched to inform the public of the waste involved in the alcohol statute and also of the dangers of alcoholism. Given the decision of the financial experts that alcohol production could no longer be subsidized, reform was inevitable, and indeed some key measures were taken under the Fourth Republic. The Debré government had as much trouble in securing approval from parliament for its decrees against the home distillers as had any of its predecessors. The debate in the National Assembly in December, 1959, was as raucous and as shameful as any under the Fourth Republic. Most of the deputies defended the distillers and denied that their activities were responsible for alcoholism. A number of amendments to the government bill were voted which watered down the original proposal. M. André Liautey, former deputy and leader of the distillers' organization, was ordered to leave the public gallery because he was giving signals openly to the deputies! In the confusion following the debate, the distillers even believed that they had won a victory by securing a condemnation of the 1954 Mendès-France decree. The government measure was later defeated by a vote of 155 to 55 in the Senate. Finally, in July, 1960, the National Assembly voted a text authorizing the government to take measures against ,alcoholism, which provided the legal basis for the decrees of 29 November 1960 limiting the right of distillation. However, the distillers and their defenders put up a fine fight in parliament, comparing favorably with their efforts before 1958. Indeed, the situation as regards the home distillers was roughly comparable both before and after 1958. The distillers, because of their numbers and geographic distribution, enjoyed wide support among the parliamentarians. But, they had a bad press and were resolutely opposed by the financial and health experts. Their privileges were chipped away by a combination of executive decrees, technocratic pressure, and hesitant parliamentary compliance. The influence of the distillers has declined under the Fifth Republic, but that decline has been gradual rather than sharp.

A similar observation can be made about the wealthiest and most powerful of the alcohol groups — the General Confederation of Beetgrowers (CGB). Under the Fourth Republic the beetgrowers were active politically, and probably were instrumental in the overthrow of the René Mayer cabinet in 1953 (though obviously their opposition was only one element in a complex political situation). Under the Fifth Republic the influence of the CGB has been greatly reduced — but again, the decline began before 1958. Under both Republics the beetgrowers enjoyed the support of a large bloc of deputies, who acted on their behalf in debate and in negotiations with the civil service. The beetgrowers also may count on receiving a sympathetic hearing from the minister of agriculture. Traditionally, the minister attends the annual session, and a dialogue takes place between him and the president of the CGB. The minister invariably assures his listeners that their interests are understood and vigorously defended. But the beetgrowers are unable to make any headway at all with the finance minister or the director of the *Service des alcools* — who are unalterably opposed to the accumulation of huge deficits simply in order to encourage beet culture.

The Debré cabinet made a firm resolve to rationalize the alcohol industry, and this inevitably led to measures against the beetgrowers. One of the key moves was the creation of a committee in November, 1959, headed by Jacques Rueff and Louis Armand, with the task of proposing reforms to eliminate obstacles to economic expansion. The committee's findings regarding the beet industry were hardly to the liking of the CGB. It held that the fixing of quotas for sugar limited competition and checked expansion, and termed the manufacture of alcohol from beets "economic incoherence." The committee's recommendation would have the effect of converting beet production largely into sugar — or even reconverting the land altogether to other culture. The pattern of relations between the beetgrowers and the government was about the same under both the Fourth and Fifth Republics – a network of friendly contacts with parliamentarians and the minister of agriculture, but hostility on the part of most civil servants and especially the financial departments.

The long-range problem confronting the CGB is painfully evident: consumption of beet alcohol by industry will decline because of technological developments. In 1961 chemical industry spokesmen announced that within a few years they would be able to do without alcohol altogether – indeed, must do so in order to meet competition within the Common Market. The *Service des alcools* thereupon informed the CGB that it must prepare for a large reduction in purchases of beet alcohol.

These developments have led to a change in the tactics of the CGB. Inasmuch as the challenge is mainly from the technical and financial experts within the administration, the CGB is strengthening its own technical and research agencies. It has presented its principal demands in a form most likely to appeal to economists and civil servants. It now calls for a "sugar law," that is, a comprehensive statute or decree which would establish a target for production, a favorable price and a "trustworthy" administration. In a sense, the proposed sugar law (or five-year charter) reflects the new tactics adopted by many groups under the Fifth Republic. The emphasis is on a rational, long term plan, calculated in terms bound to appeal to civil servants. However, the chances of reversing the long range trend towards a rationalized economy are now slight – not only because of the stronger executive in the Fifth Republic, but also because of pressure within the Common Market. The decline in political influence on the part of the alcohol groups is due to a variety of reasons, and not merely to the advent of a new regime.

The Parochial Schools Case

A slight change in the nature of pressure-group activity is also evident as regards the emotion-laden issue of relations between the state and privately run (in practice predominantly Catholic) school systems. The advocates and opponents of state aid to private schools are organized in powerful pressure groups: the *Ligue française d'enseignement* (which claims over two million adherents of member organizations) and the *Secrétariat d'Etudes pour la liberté de l'enseignement* (an apex organization, headed by Edouard Lizop, which includes representatives of the Catholic parents and teachers associations). In 1951 an intense battle over the question of subsidies resulted finally in the passage of the *loi Barangé* – a professedly temporary measure granting subsidies to both public and private schools, but a clear victory for the private school defenders. A key role in the drafting of the bill, and in planning parliamentary tactics, was played by the *Secrétariat*.

The Debré government expressed the hope in 1958 that issues could be "depoliticized." It was argued that pragmatic solutions should be worked out wholly apart from ideological considerations, making possible eventually a new national consensus. State aid to private schools was one of the divisive issues which the prime minister was determined to resolve. Roger Frey, Minister of Information, commented: "In the atomic age, this scholastic quarrel is completely outdated." The technique of "depoliticization" used by the government was to appoint a special committee, headed by Pierre-Olivier Lapie (a former socialist deputy) to take testimony from leading educational and political figures, and to make recommendations. The committee formula had been used under the Fourth Republic as well. In spite of pressure from both the *Secrétariat* and the *Ligue*, the Debré government refused to introduce legislation or in any way commit itself before receiving the Lapie committee's report. The Ministry of National Education drew up a bill on the basis of the committee's recommendations. After considerable discussion within the cabinet, and a stormy debate in parliament, a text finally was passed by a vote of 427 to 71 (the opposition including 10 Communists, 44 Socialists, 8 Radicals, 3 UNR, 2 Independents and 4 non-inscrits). The Senate likewise approved, after hearing the prime minister call for an end to the quarrel: "It is fitting that the present legislature mark on epoch in the history of public education and of school pacification, that pacification which we could have inscribed in the very title of our bill. It is necessary that the France of the second half of the twentieth century place itself above slogans which no longer represent anything." [7] The solution offered by the Debré law of 31 December 1959 was to present private schools with four alternatives: to demand full incorporation into the state system; to maintain complete independence from the state (without subsidies); to negotiate a contract of "association"; or to negotiate a "simple contract." Both contracts would require various degrees of state supervision or control, but with the state paying the salaries of private school teachers and meeting other expenses.

In the debates leading to both the Barangé law of 1951 and the Debré law of 1959 the *Secrétariat* and the *Ligue* were exceedingly active. In both 1951 and 1959 the *Ligue* and the *Secrétariat* mobilized public opinion, worked actively with friendly deputies, and exerted considerable pressure on the cabinet. The chief channel of action for the *Secrétariat* remained the Parliamentary Association for the Liberty of Education (APLE), which played such an important role in 1951. Immediately after the results of the 1958 election were known, the APLE issued a press communique: it had received 323 signed membership forms from newly elected deputies, "which now guarantees a majority of more than two-thirds of the deputies from the Metropolis desirous of applying a rapid solution to the scholastic problem." [8] Within a short time the Association boasted a membership of 380 deputies and 160 senators. The executive committee elected early in the parliamentary session included an Independent (Boscary-Monsservin), a UNR (Durbet) and an MRP (Thibault). The APLE formed a kind of brain trust, in collaboration with the *Secrétariat*, which functioned throughout the session. In view of their healthy majority in the Assembly, the friends of private schools viewed the coming debate with confidence.

The *Ligue's* political position after the 1958 election was precarious. It took no stand in either the referendum or the election — hardly surprising since its main support comes from such divergent groups as the Communists, Socialists

---

[7] See *Année Politique*, 1959, p. 155.
[8] See the association's journal, *Liberté d'Enseignement*, November 1958, II, p. 3.

and Radicals. Immediately after the election the General Council of the *Ligue* issued a moderately worded plea for "scholastic peace," by which it meant, naturally, an end to the "outmoded system of confessional separation." When the government's intention became clear, however, the *Ligue* was defiant. Albert Bayet, the *Ligue's* president, vowed to defend *laïcité* to the end. "From now on the motto of the *laïques* is the very same that, for four years, they opposed to the alleged government of Vichy: *Résistance!*" [9] The brute fact remained: over two-thirds of the deputies had joined the Parliamentary Association for Liberty of Education. The only recourse for the *laïques* was to mobilize public opinion. A plan of action was drawn up, with the cooperation of the secular political parties and trade unions, for a series of political campaigns and mass rallies. But the secular forces were hopelessly outnumbered in parliament, and lacked the support of the government and the president of the Republic. Only a few ministers (notably Chatenet and Jeanneney), and some civil servants within the Ministry of National Education, could be counted on.

There was one important difference between the 1951 and 1959 situations: the Barangé law was virtually drafted in the office of the *Secrétariat*, and parliamentary strategy was also planned there. The Pleven cabinet in 1951 in effect invited the Assembly to work out its own solution, within certain broad limits. But the Debré government in 1959 jealously guarded the right to draft and present a text. In his declaration of 23 July 1959 to the National Assembly, the prime minister affirmed that "the responsibility of taking a decision devolves upon only the public powers, that is to say, government and Parliament." As for the "interested organizations" (obviously the *Secrétariat* and the *Ligue*): "if they want to be wise, they should remain quiet." And he added that even if they were unable to do so, they would have no influence whatsoever upon the government.[10]

But neither side remained quiet. The laïques stepped up their public campaign, and the friends of the private schools continually pressured the government to go beyond the terms of the Lapie report. In spite of the prime minister's resolve to adopt a purely governmental measure, during the course of the debate he was compelled to make some significant concessions to the advocates of state subsidies. The original version of the government bill was opposed by Lizop, who declared at a press conference that private schools would refuse to negotiate contracts under the conditions stipulated in the bill — which he feared would lead ultimately to the simple incorporation of private schools into the state system. The prime minister thereupon accepted an amendment which eliminated confusion concerning the right of Catholic teachers to profess their religious doctrines — and the Minister of Education, M. Boulloche, promptly resigned. The president of the APLE, M. Boscary-Monsservin, announced that the bill was now satisfactory in view of the "clarification."[11]

Since December 1959 the *Secrétariat* has become a defender of the status

---

[9] *L'Action Laïque* (March, 1959), p. 2.

[10] *J. O., Assemblée Nationale*, 23 July 1959, p. 1458.

[11] *Liberté d'Enseignement* (January, 1960), and *Année Politique, 1959*, pp. 149–55.

quo, while the secular organizations have taken the offensive. In 1960 a campaign was begun for a mass petition demanding repeal of the Debré law. On 19 June 1960 a great rally was held at Vincennes, where the petitions were consolidated into one document, with almost eleven million signatures. The *Ligue* has vowed to take its vengeance, and to bring about the nationalization of private schools at the first opportunity. But it suffers one great weakness: even if the secular parties regain their representation in a future parliament, the divisions between Radicals and Socialists on the one hand, and Communists on the other, would make effective collaboration unlikely.

Thus, viewing the process whereby the Debré law came into being, it appears that the organized groups played a smaller *direct* role than in 1951. Perhaps a major reason was the determination of the government to resolve the "scholastic problem" by granting subsidies and establishing some state control. The views of the President of the Republic were crucial: as early as 1950 General de Gaulle had expressed himself in favor of state aid to parents so that they might educate their children in the manner considered appropriate by them. It was not only difficult for the *Secrétariat* to intervene directly in the law-making process in 1959 — it was in a sense unnecessary. The government did the work for the organization. The *Ligue* could not intervene for the simple reason that the secular parties had virtually had their representation wiped out in the 1958 election. Hence, it may be concluded that the strengthening of the executive under the Fifth Republic did in fact result in a shift of tactics on the part of the secular and religious organizations. But both groups continued to act upon public opinion, organize friendly deputies, and gain the ear of the executive. The *Secrétariat,* in particular, had the opportunity to work *within* the parliamentary majority and the cabinet — tactics which proved remarkably effective.

The Army

Let us now consider a third type of pressure group active under both republics: the army. Professor Meynaud has excluded the army from his survey of pressure groups, arguing that the participation of the military establishment in politics should be viewed as an attempt to conquer or seize power.[12] For our purposes, however, it would be useful to view the army as an organization whose members at times develop and act upon political attitudes. In this respect they share at least some of the characteristics of pressure groups, especially as regards the distribution of power between the state and those with claims upon the state. General de Gaulle himself considered the "weak state" under the Fourth Republic to be the principal cause of a general loss of national integrity, leading to egoism on the part of special groups and "trouble" in the armed forces. As he put it in his press communiqué of May 15, 1958: "The degradation of the State leads infallibly to the estrangement of the associated peoples, uneasiness in the army, the

---

[12] Jean Meynaud, *Novelles études sur les groupes de pression en France* (Paris, 1962), pp. 279–81.

disintegration of the nation, the loss of independence." The army wants only to obey. But to obey requires the existence of a chief, a commander, a source of authority and of orders. The Fourth Republic did not give a firm lead — because of ministerial instability, the weakness of the executive, and divisions within parliament and public opinion. In General de Gaulle's view, the Fifth Republic remedied this defect. A strong executive, far above political bickering, is able to define a coherent national policy. The army's duty is to carry out that policy, fully confident that the objectives are consistent with national honor. In his address to army officers at Strasbourg in November, 1961, General de Gaulle declared: "Once the state and the nation have chosen their road, military duty is marked out once and for all."

But it did not work out that way. Within a period of twenty months — from the announcement of the self-determination policy in September 1959 to the putsch of April 1961 — there were four major conspiracies, all involving the army to some degree: in October 1959 an uprising in Algeria was to coincide with a coup d'état in Paris — but the action was called off at the last minute; in January 1960 barricades went up in Algiers, but the government succeeded in surmounting the crisis; in December 1960 an attempt was made to draw the army into opposition during De Gaulle's visit to Algeria; finally in April 1961 four retired generals took command of a full-fledged military insurrection. After the collapse of the putsch, the Secret Army Organization (OAS) carried on a permanent conspiracy against the Gaullist regime, and received considerable support from army officers and veterans. As two well-known journalists put it, perhaps in exaggerated fashion, military opposition under the Fifth Republic replaced political opposition under the Fourth Republic.[13]

If anything, the army's political role was even greater after De Gaulle's return than before; the putsch of 1961 was an initiative of elements within the army, whereas in 1958 the army followed the lead of civilian insurgents. Important elements within the army were opposed to any policy envisaging independence for Algeria for political negotiations with the rebels, whether that policy emanated from a weak prime minister or a strong president of the Republic. Military intervention in politics was precipitated not by the weakness of the government in Paris, but rather by the development of a political consciousness on the part of a portion of the officer corps and within certain élite formations. Insofar as the army can be viewed as a pressure group, its relations with the state are far more complex than intimated by those who criticized the shortcomings of the Fourth Republic.

Conclusion

In its dealings with organized groups, the Gaullist regime has proclaimed its determination to vest policy-making power entirely in the hands of the state. The prime ministers and the president have all spoken harshly of those groups — army officers as well as home distillers, beetgrowers and butchers — who seek to influence political decisions. It should be pointed out, however,

---

[13] See Jacques Fauvet and Jean Planchais, *Le Fronde des généraux* (Paris, 1961), p. 7.

that hostility to pressure groups is not specifically Gaullist. A profound tradition in France, going back to Rousseau and the Jacobins, condemns all intermediary bodies between the individual and the state.

In fact the pressure groups have not been reduced to impotence under the new regime. The position of the groups has undergone a complex evolution since 1958. Some groups have clearly declined, others have merely changed their tactics and continue to enjoy considerable influence, while still others have become more powerful. In general, those groups which relied principally on contacts with parliamentarians have lost ground. However, the Fifth Republic continues to be a parliamentary system, that is, the cabinet is responsible to the National Assembly, and even the home distillers can still put up a good fight when given the opportunity. In addition, those groups which enjoyed close relations with the Left parties have also suffered, since the Communists, Socialists and Radicals fared poorly under the single-member-district system. The main losers are the trade unions and secular organizations. The shift of power to the prime minister, president and civil service has generally brought, not a diminution of pressure group activity, but rather a corresponding shift in tactics or techniques. Thus, the friends of the religious schools, as well as agricultural and business spokesmen, found themselves within the majority or the cabinet. It was no longer necessary, then, to apply pressure noisily; there was rather an opportunity to press for political or administrative action from the inside. In those areas of policy which were taken over by the president of the Republic himself, pressure groups were in some cases completely frozen out (like the associations in favor of European unity). However, some financial, business and religious groups enjoyed exceptional opportunities to gain the ear of the decision maker through various loyal "companions." The most profound change of style was brought about by the increased importance of the civil service. Wealthy organizations hired researchers, economists and even ex-civil servants in order to present their case to the appropriate department in the most effective possible manner. According to one acute observer, the growing power of financial interests and technocrats is a striking feature of the Fifth Republic. He contends that increasingly there is a dialogue between the "men of the big lobbies" and the technocrats, who speak the same language and usually come from the same social class.[14]

The creation of more centralized political institutions in 1958 thus did not in itself bring about a reduction in the power of pressure groups. It rather compelled the groups to adapt and respond to a new situation, as a result of which their influence in many cases actually increased. Political structure may well determine *how* groups press their claims and *which* groups are to be favored. But there is no simple equation between centralization of political power and subordination of pressure groups to that power.

---

[14] P. Viansson-Ponté, "Vers une nouvelle France," *Le Monde,* 9 May 1962.

27. Austria: Representative Democracy or "Chamber State"?

HERBERT P. SECHER

The frequently discussed "new medievalism," which some observers of contemporary political developments perceive in the encroachments on the democratically elected power holders by large "corporatist" interest-group organizations, has probably found its clearest expression in post-war Austria. The "Chambers"—officially representing major groups in society, somewhat like medieval estates—are powerful participants in governmental decision making. Yet, as Professor Secher shows, the Chambers' power appears dependent on Austria's strong political parties, which act as equilibrating and integrating agencies; and which are ultimately legitimized in this function by the mass electorate.

Austria is a country with a still rather brittle democratic tradition. Its characterization during the interwar period as the epitome of the *Parteienstaat* indicated the extent to which the symbols and practices of parliamentarianism had been undermined by the unbridled group egotism of class-parties and economic organizations. Parties and interest organizations operated with the goal of capturing legislative and executive organs, using them for their own exclusive purposes, thereby obviating the need for developing institutionalized procedures for "access" to the decision-making organs. Parties as well as interest groups were imbued with a sense of "solidarity of the chief economic classes," an attitude which not only fostered class antagonism but also thoroughly subordinated even separately organized interest groups to the strength and discipline of the parties! At best the interest groups were regarded as auxiliaries that enabled the parties to circulate policies and decisions more widely among their following. By the same token, however, this nearly complete identification of party and interest group gave the latter strong leverage within the parties, a fact which was exploited by the interest groups with considerable skill.

This dovetailing of party and interest groups has been continued with minor modification in the political pattern of the Second Republic. Two giant parties and four large interest groups determine the current political structure, sharing between them the power to make decisions that fashion official government policy. These are the Socialist Party of Austria, the Austrian People's Party, the Austrian Trade Union Federation, and the Chamber of Commerce, that

SOURCE: Reprinted by permission of the University of Utah, copyright owners, from Herbert P. Secher, "Representative Democracy or 'Chamber State': The Ambiguous Rôle of Interest Groups in Austrian Politics," *The Western Political Quarterly*, XIII (December 1960), pp. 890–907. Without tables. Footnotes are abridged.

of Agriculture, and of Labor. Though there are other interest groups, none equals the magnitude of organization and political power of these four. It is proposed to examine the nature and role of the legally recognized functional representative bodies and determine to what extent the current framework of government, as well as the peculiarities of the party system, have modified their organization and functioning and what, if any, are the trends in their development.[1]

I

Beginning with the re-establishment of the Second Republic under the sponsorship of the Allies, the two major parties have governed jointly under an agreement — first kept secret but later publicized officially as the Coalition Pact — which permitted no major piece of legislation, no important administrative regulation or appointment to be made by one coalition partner without the consent of the other. Over the years there evolved a system of public administration and economic controls whereby the organization of the most important administrative posts in the government was shared by the two parties in direct proportion to their popular strength at election time. Both parties having remained at nearly equal strength since 1945, the distribution of cabinet offices was arranged in such a way as to assure either party of at least a deputy secretaryship in strategic ministries. Depending on the proportion of popular votes cast for either one of the parties, the distribution of cabinet posts is merely readjusted to reflect the new balance of political power. Under the circumstances the "arithmetical accidents" of election results have to a large extent been replaced by a weighted index of votes which is used to fix quantitatively the position of either party within a controlled framework of political collaboration.[2] The bedrock of party collaboration is provided in the articles of the coalition pact which states that "government proposals that have the unanimous consent, both in substance and in form of the representatives of the coalition parties in the cabinet, are binding for the representatives of these parties in the National Assembly." The pact goes on to state that such cooperation must extend through the legislative session, and that new elections can be called only upon prior agreement by both parties.

The nature of this agreement has contributed enormously to the growth and influence of the two major parties. Through the maintenance of superb discipline and strict internal responsibility these parties are able to determine

---

[1] The Austrian Trade Union Federation (Österreichischer Gewerkschaftsbund, OeGB) is not a "public-legal" (öffentlich-rechtlich) institution, but a club based on voluntary membership. Though it is undoubtedly the most formidable of all organizations in Austria — covering over two-thirds of all non-self-employed persons — a separate treatment of its organization and special powers is not included in this paper, since that would lead too far afield. Furthermore, the relationship between OeGB and SPOe is so close that they can hardly be discussed separately. See H. P. Secher, "The Socialist Party of Austria: Principles, Organization and Policies," Midwest Journal of Political Science, III (August 1959), 277–99.

[2] In 1956 a slight popular and parliamentary majority gained the OeVP seven cabinet posts out of twelve and the chancellorship. After the . . . election of May, 1959, in

the course of political decisions from their headquarters or in joint conference with each other's top leaders. Their representatives in the parliament, informed of the decisions reached by these leaders, merely add their ratifying signatures in the form of unanimous acceptance. The problem of access to the formal decision-making organs, a major problem of organized interest groups in democratic countries, can be said, therefore, to exist hardly at all in Austria. Under the system of well-organized, highly disciplined political parties that operates today in Austria, special interests must have a strong foothold in one party in order to wield any kind of political leverage. Thus, as will be indicated below, all three chambers, as well as the trade-unions, act primarily as appendages to the political parties. Their formally separate existence is indeed merely the result of the medieval corporate structure which, in the feudalized atmosphere of dynastic Austria determined the formation of economic organizations (guild, leagues, etc.). It is, therefore, frequently charged in present-day Austria that the country is really governed as a "democratically disguised chamberstate" in which the national assembly no longer figures as the source of all legislative power but has been replaced, instead, by the triad of party-chamber-trade-union whose oligarchical leadership rules unchallenged and in opposition to the real public interest of the country.

II

The three principal interest groups in Austria are organized so as to reflect the country's division into the three chief economic classes: The Chamber of Commerce, the Chamber of Agriculture, and the Chamber of Labor represent respectively employers, farmers, and workers. The features shared by these three organizations are their position as statutory governmental advisory bodies of elected representatives charged with promoting the interests of their respective groups. Under the laws establishing them these chambers assume the form of public corporations with nearly identical functions. Basically their tasks are: (1) to give reports, advice and recommendations to public legislative and administrative bodies on appropriate matters; (2) to act in the common economic interests of their members; (3) to follow the work of and maintain contracts with the governmental departments most directly concerned with their economic interests; (4) to participate directly and formally in the work of a large number of special government boards having regulatory powers over specific sectors of the economy such as foreign trade, investment policy, scarce raw materials, prices and wages, and housing; and (5) to compile statistical data and to undertake such statistical and other studies as are necessary to carry out these functions. The Federal Chamber of Commerce and each of the provincial chambers of commerce also bargain collec-

---

which the SPOe obtained a popular majority but had to cede parliamentary majority to the OeVP by one seat, this ratio changed to 6:6, with the OeVP, however, still retaining the chancellorship. The ratio of undersecretaryships in the cabinet was changed from 3:3 to 2:2. For a more detailed analysis of the *proporz* — as this phenomenon is known popularly — see H. P. Secher, "Coalition Government: The Case of the Second Austrian Republic," *American Political Science Review*, LII (September, 1958), 791. [Reprinted below, pp. 429–38.]

tively with unions. The Chamber of Labor prepares materials to aid in bargaining sessions but leaves actual negotiations to the unions.

Of the three chambers, the Chamber of Commerce is the oldest as well as the most powerful institution; it is also the only one for which a process of natural historical evolution can be gainsaid. Conceived more than a hundred years ago as a purely entrepreneurial association, it was meant to provide the rising commercial middle class with an effective instrument of representation at the Imperial Court. Both the Chamber of Agriculture and the Chamber of Labor were created much later and essentially as counterweights to the pressures brought by commerce and industry in governmental affairs. Membership in the Chamber of Commerce has always been compulsory, though until the advent of the Dollfuss government certain private organizations of Trade and Industry operated independently. The Dollfuss government eventually arranged for the absorption of these autonomous groups by the chamber and generally introduced a greater degree of centralization into chamber organization. This centralized structure, reinforced by the experiences of the Hitler period during which the Austrian Chambers of Commerce simply became part of the German *Reichskammer,* was again adopted at the time of their re-establishment in the Second Austrian Republic. The compulsory membership was extended to all "physical and legal persons" in commerce, industry, and trade, as well as the fiscal, credit, or insurance businesses. A central governing authority was created, the Federal Chamber of Commerce (*Bundeshandelskammer*), to be elected indirectly by the executive committees of all occupational and professional groups represented in the chamber. The *Bundeshandelskammer* was headed by a permanent secretary who, together with his staff, was also attached to the Ministry of Commerce to supervise the administration of laws that fell within the jurisdiction of that ministry. Their primary task was declared to be that of "obviating unnecessary debate through expert analysis of the laws before they reach parliament."

It should be noted that only at the lowest level of the "occupational and professional groups" are the executive committees elected directly and by secret ballot. The higher governing organs up to and including the chamber presidency are constituted on the basis of indirect elections and the highest organs reserve the right of co-optation. Each of the elective organs from the lowest level to the highest appoints a secretariat which heads up into and is responsible to the general secretary. This constitutes the permanent chamber bureaucracy and it is to this corps of well-paid officials that falls the most important task of the Chamber of Commerce: the reconciliation of the divergent interests among the membership. These conflicting interests are, of course, the result of compulsory membership. This means that the different demands of crafts, industry, wholesalers and retailers, manufacturers and importers, raw-material producers and raw-material processors, and last but not least, of cartelized and non-cartelized branches of industries must be ironed out by the bureaucracy in order to permit the chamber to adopt a uniform stand on questions involving national economic policy. It is almost a corollary of this condition that the chamber increasingly favors restraints on trade or, in its own words, becomes "the guardian of the natural limits of economic competition." "Without chamber organization," it is stated, "the fight of all against all would ensue."[3]

The counterparts of the Chambers of Commerce among the farmers are the Chambers of Agriculture. However, due to the local nature of their interests these chambers were, until recently, established by provincial laws with similar provisions. It is only since 1953 that a National Conference of the Presidents of the Chambers of Agriculture[4] acts as a central co-ordinating body and to a certain extent guides the policies of the provincial chambers. The establishment of the National Conference was a move essentially designed to introduce a certain equality among the various members in their dealing with the federal government. Previously each chamber had had separate and direct access to the Ministry of Agriculture by an arrangement that worked primarily to the advantage of the largest and most influential of the provincial organizations. As pointed out earlier, the regulatory functions of the Chamber of Agriculture parallel those of the Chamber of Commerce.

The third member of the chamber triad, the Chamber of Labor, follows in most organizational essentials the example set by the other two. Here, too, a previously autonomous provincial arrangement has been replaced by a National Conference of Chamber Presidents. However, in this case the preponderant, mammoth membership of the Viennese Chamber of Commerce [sic] continues to act as the central spokesman for the other chambers that have become subordinated to the Viennese leadership. The Chamber of Labor is not plagued by the problem of the reconciliation of interests, since its membership is much less inclusive and therefore much more homogeneous than that of the other two chambers. Substantial numbers of employees in managerial or professional capacities, as well as some agricultural laborers are still specifically excluded from chamber membership.

There seems to be little doubt that the effectiveness of the Chamber of Labor vis-à-vis the ministries and parliament is less than that of either of the other two chambers. What is in dispute is the reason for such lack of effectiveness. The Socialists are quick to charge, for example, that even though all ministries are legally obligated to consult with the Chamber of Labor in matters concerning them, unfriendly ministries can easily get around that by sending important legislation to the Chamber of Labor on very short notice thus not leaving it sufficient time for study. This charge is indignantly denied by the OeVP-controlled ministries whose spokesmen, correctly, point to the

---

[3] H. W. Johnstone, *The Restraints on Competition in the Austrian Economy*, U. S. Dept. of State (1952), Declassified. Based on an analysis of 200 Austrian business enterprises Johnstone discovered that through interlocking directorates, not outlawed in Austria, 20 persons control all forms of commercial and industrial enterprises. About half of that group also occupy either elective or administrative posts in the government.

[4] Unlike the Conference of Presidents of the Chamber of Labor, however, that of the Chamber of Agriculture is constituted merely as a club, i.e., on a voluntary basis: *Satzungen der Praesidentenkonferenz der Landwirtschaftskammern Österreichs* (Vienna, mimeo., 1953). The reconciliation of interests, therefore, does not loom as large in the Chamber of Agriculture as it does in the Chamber of Commerce. It may be doubted that it enters at all due to the commanding position of the Lower Austrian Chamber of Agriculture. The effectiveness of the Presidential Conference has not yet been fully assessed.

lack of autonomy of the Chamber of Labor vis-à-vis the Austrian Socialist party and the Socialist-controlled Austrian Trade Union Federation (OeGB). This political subordination of the Chamber of Labor to SPOe and OeGB is not denied by the Socialists. Indeed, they consider the Chamber of Labor much less a counterweight to the other two chambers but see in its compulsory membership a means of reaching certain strata of workers and employees — domestics, homeworkers, certain agricultural laborers, etc. — that are not within the jurisdiction of the Trade Union Federation or that are still not members of the SPOe. Also, this chamber membership of primarily Socialist voting workers and employees provides the Chamber of Labor with a degree of financial solvency that far surpasses that of either the SPOe or of the Austrian Trade Union Federation. Though not generally known, it is a readily admitted fact that the Chambor of Labor frequently subsidizes the educational activity of the Trade Union Federation. Another advantage accruing to the Trade Union Federation through the compulsory membership of the Chamber is that thereby nearly all gainfully employed persons are brought under the influence and authority of a Socialist-dominated labor organization. It is also known that the legal right of consultation in matters concerning labor legislation is never exercised by the Chamber of Labor without prior approval by the OeGB. For the Socialist party the chamber functions primarily as a research bureau on consumer wants and needs, as well as on financial policies to be adopted by the party.

Theoretically all political parties can offer candidates for the indirect elections in any one of the chambers. Practically it is only one party than can be counted on to dominate each chamber, since the party with a plurality of votes captures all the seats on the governing boards. The electoral groups presenting themselves to the membership do not always run under the same name as the political party. The SPOe uses the name *Freier Wirtschaftsbund* for elections in the Chamber of Commerce and *Arbeiterbauernbund* in the Chamber of Agriculture. The OeVP has its three leagues — OeBB, OeWB, and OeAAB — run separately in each of the chambers. The third political party, formerly VdU, now FPOe, usually runs on a "non-partisan" ticket. Contrary to the truly compartmentalized situation in the First Republic there were some tendencies noticeable to achieve greater representation of the views of one party in the interest group dominated by the other party. Thus, the SPOe at one time granted a representative of the OeAAB a seat on the councils of the Chamber of Labor and members of the FWB were occasionally asked to sit in on meetings of the *Bundeshandelskammer*. The aim here was to give the opposition group a chance to become identified with the decisions of the Chamber — which must always be unanimous — and if the group is really in favor of it, to have it present a "chamber" point of view within the councils of its own party. Generally this arrangement has worked out best in the case of the OeAAB whose position vis-à-vis the national leadership of the OeVP is somewhat stronger than is that of the FWB in the SPOe. It is nearly impossible for any chamber decision to issue contrary to the policies of the dominant party on the governing board. Since under the Austrian coalition agreement it falls to the party executive committees to approve legislation about to be submitted to parliament, decision by the chambers contrary to party policy would never reach the National Assembly. This integrated form of decision-making is made possible by the close overlapping of leadership among chambers, trade unions, political parties, and the legislative as well as executive organs.

III

It was noted previously that the underlying principle of chamber organization was purported to be the "internal solidarity of the chief economic classes." From this principle it did not seem too far-fetched to derive the assertion that the chambers by their activities are simply a realization of the estate and corporate theories of an earlier period. The argument was given even more substance in the beginning years of the Second Republic when on five occasions these groups were called in to negotiate wage limits, maximum agricultural and food prices, pensions, and tax policies without using the available instrumentalities of parliamentary government except for final ratification. It is generally agreed that the chambers reached the acme of their political importance during this era of the so-called "wage-price pacts." These pacts were the culmination of efforts to stabilize the Austrian economy without introducing either a large measure of competition or a centrally administered plan. Production capacity as well as actual productivity and the standard of living were at an all time low; farmers threatened to reduce their already meager deliveries in order to raise prices; labor held fast to a policy of wage standardization and consumer subsidies while business, lacking adequate resources for either capital formation or improved methods of production, took refuge in steadily rising prices. It was a vicious circle in which every one of the major economic groups — business, labor, and agriculture — pursued an essentially "protectionist" policy via its economic interest organization, rather than meet the pressing problems of the national economy in a more equitable manner. Neither a market economy nor a planned economy — and not even a truly "mixed" economy — could be accepted by all of these groups as a basis for future economic development; instead, each group fought doggedly to maintain, in effect, the privileged position of its least productive members. Among labor these were the unskilled laborers; in agriculture, the poor mountain dairy farmers; and in business, these were the small, family or self-employed enterprises. Eventually the political dominance of agriculture (the chancellorship was at that time occupied by the president of the Austrian Farmers League) prevailed and the wage-price pacts were inaugurated, setting primarily maximum agricultural and food prices, but raising wages insufficiently to compensate the consumers for the increased cost of living. For that reason the wage-price pacts must be considered essentially a kind of holding action that had to be repeated annually as long as the only answer to Austria's economic problems was the preservation of the existing size of the gross national product. The pacts were thus necessary evils reflecting the inability as well as unwillingness of agriculture, business, or labor seriously to increase production.

The course of arriving at a typical wage-price pact ran approximately as follows: Legally, the pact went through five separate stages. First, there was the revision of fixed governmental regulated prices, principally those of agriculture. This revision fell under the authority of the ministries of Agriculture and of the Interior. Secondly, rate increases of government-owned public utilities fell under the jurisdiction of the plenary committee of the National Assembly. Thirdly, the Federal Chamber of Commerce and the Austrian Trade Union Federation were authorized to bargain collectively for wage ceilings. Fourthly, an increase in consumer subsidies was subject to the approval of the Federal Assembly (both houses of Parliament in session). Fifthly, the National Assembly entered the process to determine budgetary consequences.

All these measures and steps were, of course, joined intimately one with the other, and the actual mechanics of the pacts proceeded about as follows: Initially, leading officials of the three chambers and the Trade Union Federation established a working committee of technicians representing these organizations to estimate the impact on the various economic groups of price increases and other necessary readjustments. Supplied with this information the actual leaders of the three chambers and the OeGB took over the negotiations. These were, at the time, Herr Ing. Raab, president of the Federal Chamber of Commerce; Herr Boehm, president of the OeGB; and Herr Kraus, then minister of Agriculture. It should be observed that these three individuals did not operate on the same legal or constitutional level. The farmers negotiated through their ministry rather than through the chamber. Business negotiated through the chamber and not through a ministry, while the workers and employees, as consumers, negotiated neither through *their* Ministry of Social Administration nor through the chamber but through the OeGB which, legally, is merely a voluntary organization or "club."

After these preliminary negotiations by the interest groups the pact was submitted for formal consideration to the Economic Advisory Commission and then to the cabinet. These two bodies then referred it back again formally to the expert opinion of the chambers. Only after this step did the pact finally reach the Parliament for discussion by the parliamentary representatives of the parties. Having been duly passed by both houses it was sent to the Allied Council for final approval and eventual publication.

Now this procedure loses much of its complexity when it is remembered that in all instances the actual negotiating partners were the two government parties through their chief representatives. Thus, there were *either* the president of the Federal Chamber of Commerce, Herr Raab (also acting in his capacity as party chairman), *or* the ministers of Finance and of Commerce, both also members of the boards of the Chamber of Commerce as well as members of the executive committee of the OeVP and of the parliamentary party. The chancellor, Herr Figl, as president of the Farmers League, usually entered on the cabinet level. Depending on the combination of men present this was either a cabinet committee, parliamentary club, or a meeting of representatives of the interest groups. On the other side, it was the head of the OeGB, Herr Boehm, or the vice-chancellor and chairman of the SPOe, Herr Schaerf, who together with the Socialist ministers of the cabinet and the president of the Viennese Chamber of Labor formed and reformed as either parliamentary club, cabinet committee, or interest group committee. In reality there were no levels to be observed and in the last analysis the negotiations were carried on between Raab and Boehm, possibly with the consultation of Schaerf. That the legal steps were observed at all was due to certain regulatory features of the pact that required parliamentary involvement. Specifically, the increases in rates of public utilities and certain tariffs were subject to the approval of the plenary committees of the National Assembly, a practice that still dated from the time when the railroads were privately operated and subject to government supervision.

Mention was made above, somewhat tangentially, of the Economic Advisory Commission. At the time of the wage pacts that body could easily be considered the core of political decision-making which further buttressed the power of the chambers. The creation of the EAC was actually the result of American insistence at the start of Marshall Aid in order to facilitate relations with an Austrian government already marked by more than the normal diffusion of responsibility. To this commission were appointed the presidents of the Federal Chamber of Commerce, the Vienna Chamber of Labor, and the Lower Austrian Chamber of Agriculture. In view of the OeVP domination of the agricultural and commercial chambers, the Socialist president of the Austrian Trade Union Federation was added in keeping with the political balance already implicit in the coalition agreement. From 1947–48 until 1952 this body, lacking any real constitutional basis, became the true center of power for economic decisions. Practically all economic legislation originated from it being passed on to the cabinet and hence to Parliament for final ratification. Because of the rather shaky constitutional authority of the commission it was eventually decided to include in it the ministers of Agriculture (OeVP), Commerce (OeVP) and of Nationalized Industries (SPOe), thereby giving the commission the character of a cabinet committee with proper observance of the *proporz* principle. However, since ultimate authority remained with the original representatives of chambers and trade union, the commission can best be characterized as a functional, i.e., in this case, economic committee of the respective government parties.[5]

After the stabilization of the currency and revitalization of the economy through Marshall Aid the importance of the commission declined considerably. A consequence of the replacement of the agrarian wing of the OeVP by its business wing in furnishing the leading positions in party and cabinet after the election of 1952, was the relaxation of some of the most stringent regulatory aspects of the Austrian economy.

The new coalition government, now under the chancellorship of Herr Ing. Raab, head of the OeVP business wing, embarked upon a liberal economic policy whose strict observance was made possible by the party's firm control of

---

[5] No instance is known of a bill agreed upon by the Economic Advisory Commission which parliament failed to enact or, conversely, of a bill on which the EAC failed to agree that was nevertheless passed by the National Assembly. *Cf. Neue Wiener Tageszeitung,* June 7, 1951, p. 4, and July 6, 1951, p. 3.

the Ministry of Finance. From now on the Socialists were in effect excluded from the process of economic and financial decision-making as part of the bargains struck to perpetuate the coalition. However, as the success of the new economic policies of the first Raab coalition became manifest, the Socialists regretfully contemplated the anomaly of their position, which prevented them, although partners in the coalition, from taking any credit for the improving economy. The party had to be content with the fact that the general expansion of productivity gave it at least the opportunity to insist on larger social welfare benefits and higher wages. Under the circumstances the SPOe had to defer its demands for a greater share in economic policy-making to a period of not quite such obvious prosperity.

Thus, between 1953 and 1956 the chambers and the Austrian Trade Union Federation functioned again primarily within their recognized legal framework. But in the latter year the SPOe, taking advantage of the mounting inflationary spiral, renewed its pressure for more participation in the formation of economic policy. Through the instrumentality of the OeGB it was now urged to reactivate the EAC but with greatly expanded functions, which in effect were to assure to workers and employees "the right to codetermination at the highest level." Further, this strengthened commission would become responsible for a "joint economic policy" that was to be the result of true co-operation between the two coalition partners. This proposal necessarily raised some questions regarding the relation of the Commission to established governmental institutions. If the commission were to be provided with such far-reaching powers as to enable it to issue binding decisions the principle of the corporate state would be given at least quasi-constitutional sanction. That the Socialists actually advocated such an arrangement is not particularly surprising once their difficult position is recognized. The SPOe wanted a way out of the dilemma which forced it to agree officially to the government's economic policy under the limitations of the coalition pact without being able to take credit for the success of that policy. In effect, the SPOe was offering its full co-operation on matters of financial and economic policy in return for the establishment of an authority where Socialist-dominated interest groups would have a permanent role in the process of decision-making. The resulting "joint economic policy" would then be truly binding on the government.

Naturally the conservative partner of the coalition received these proposals with considerable coolness. However, due to the continued inflationary trend of the general economic situation and mindful of the experience of the wage-price pacts, it was decided at least to reconvene the commission in its original advisory capacity. A subcommittee was immediately established which dealt with the problems of price and wage stabilization. This subcommittee, essentially a replica of the full commission, made its recommendations to the commission which then transmitted them formally to the cabinet. Again, neither the cabinet nor the National Assembly was expected to make any real changes in the recommendation so that in effect the subcommittee continues to act as the real authority in problems concerning wages and prices. The arrangement thus perpetuates on a somewhat minor scale the practices first introduced by the wage-price pacts.

IV

The relaxation of economic controls and the steadily rising level of prosperity in the country generally have done much to reduce the authority exercised by the chambers in the shaping of economic policies. This is particularly true in the case of the Chamber of Commerce which has always been the strongest and the most authoritarian of the three chambers. In the rather balmy environment of the prosperity of recent years the Chamber of Commerce has experienced a certain amount of difficulty in maintaining its role as the uniform spokesman for all economic interests. Consequently, not only the external jurisdiction of the Chamber of Commerce underwent a serious challenge by its sister groups, but its internal organization also has been subjected to strong criticism. For the first time since the legal establishment of the chambers an attempt was made to obtain a definite delimitation of their jurisdiction and prohibit their expansion into areas of the economy not already under their authority. To this end suit was initiated by the Viennese provincial government before the Constitutional Court against the Federal Chamber of Commerce, which, under the guise of claiming an infringement of the federal principle and an unlawful delegation of powers, really challenged the whole concept of authority underlying chamber organization.

The Constitutional Court decided in the main *against* the claims of the Viennese Government that the very existence of the Federal Chamber of Commerce was in effect *ultra vires*, but it did invalidate certain individual sections of the law creating the Chamber of Commerce. This meant that several occupational groups were removed from the compulsory membership clause and in future would be able to organize as free and voluntary associations. Since many of these groups fell into the category of the nationalized industries — at that time still fully responsible to the Socialist-controlled Ministry of Nationalized Industry — and of municipally-run enterprises, this decision can be considered at least as a partial victory of the Chamber of Labor and its Socialist backers.

Internal criticism has been directed against the so-called integrating function of the Chamber of Commerce bureaucracy. This is the task which enjoins that bureaucracy to balance or compromise the selfish demands of the divergent interests within the chamber through suggestion, persuasion, cajolery, or eventual sanctions. It means that any statements, policy directives, or administrative decisions issued by the Federal Chamber of Commerce present the result of a sifting process at all levels of the organization and take into consideration the wishes of as well as the conditions prevailing in each particular branch of industry and business that falls under chamber authority. Regardless of the chamber bureaucrat's specific job within the hierarchy he must be prepared to act responsibly to the policies laid down by his immediate appointed superiors as well as responsively to the interests of the elected representatives of a specific occupational or business group. In other words, he performs within the chamber a primarily political function, knowing that any outspoken defense of an individual group interest may meet with resistance at the next higher level where that group may no longer be strongly represented. Like any politician he must have the courage to make unpopular decisions, but also like any politician he may find it easier to follow the lead of the largest and most powerful interest within the organizations.

As long as the Austrian economy was recovering from the ravages of the war and coping primarily with the problems created by scarcity, this function of the chamber bureaucracy was comparatively simple. But as soon as a measure of prosperity was again being achieved and the Austrian economy was beginning to lose at least some of its more static characteristics, the large business interests, who were in control of the higher governing boards of the chamber, were shaping chamber policy to suit their own much more competitive position rather than that of the smaller businesses represented in the organization. As a result, there occurred at the time a much publicized "exodus" by groups of artisans, craftsmen and small tradesmen. These groups did not really leave the chamber — impossible under the compulsory membership law — but they frequently engaged in independent actions, such as negotiations of wage agreements or even the rendering of expert opinions without notifying the chamber. Of course, in cases of outright violations there were disciplinary measures available with which to bring these errant groups back into line. Of much greater import was the desire of certain larger business groups to escape the restraining hand of the "integration of interests" and establish their own voluntary associations which could state the demands of the groups much more freely than was possible under chamber tutelage. Since these groups still had to retain their individual membership in the Chamber of Commerce this amounted to double representation which some of the smaller interests could ill afford. Typically, the interests that did take such a step were the Union of Austrian Industrialists, the National Association of Austrian Businessmen, and the Manufacturer's League. But even these "separatists" had to work with the OeVP, i.e., its Business League, if they really wanted to create political pressures and to keep the league strongly interlocked with the chamber leadership. Thus, recommendations that did not receive the approval of the chamber would hardly receive the legislative backing of the OeVP, a fact soon enough recognized by the separatists. Nevertheless, their actions have been viewed with considerable uneasiness by the chamber leadership who suspect that at some future date these voluntary groups may also try to obtain more effective political representation. As one of the prominent men in the chamber hierarchy remarked, not without some exasperation, "if the Austrian businessman had at his disposal within the government the kind of independent political instruments that are available to his American or English colleagues his need for a compulsory, uniform, and centralized interest organization would largely be obviated." [6]

It would, therefore, be rather premature to interpret these stresses and strains within the Chamber of Commerce as a sign that this organization is about to crumble away and become fragmented into its various component groups. The centripetal forces, especially in the form of the really large and cohesive chamber bureaucracy, are still very decidedly in control. Again, it is the very character of the rival organizations which acts as deterrent to a

---

[6] Personal conversation and letter of June 4, 1959.

weakening of Chamber of Commerce power. As long as the Austrian Trade Union Federation, the Chamber of Labor, and even the Chamber of Agriculture exist as large, homogeneous bodies, businessmen, artisans, and craftsmen will tend to identify themselves primarily as employers, hesitating to abandon the only organization which can effectively counterbalance the combined weight of the others. The reproach met with by the Chamber of Commerce that it is not as influential and outspoken as it ought to be in certain circumstances is probably a fair indication that the Chamber is seriously concerned with its "integration of interest" role. Since it is obviously not possible to represent only one interest common to all members there always will be cases in which a group will feel slighted by chamber action.

Another factor of great importance in assessing the strength of the Chamber of Commerce to the small businessman has always been its so-far-unchallenged ability to keep out unwelcome competition in a particular area of enterprise. This is coupled with the chamber's function as a court of arbitration in questions involving the expansion of business operations to include goods and services that were not originally enumerated in the trade license. In the case of small businesses that puts the power of life and death into hands of the chamber organization.

The criticism leveled against the chambers for not heeding the interests of any one of a number of groups suggests that the chamber probably takes its role as conciliator seriously. The publicity surrounding internal chamber dissatisfaction moved the General Secretary to declare on one occasion that "any failure by the chamber to fulfill its primary task of 'interest reconciliation' would have as an unthinkable consequence the turning away of these groups from the chamber in order to seek direct support from the legislature and the executive. Such a development would increase the danger that the reconciliation of interests would take place without an adequate consideration of the point of view of those who alone are capable of understanding their own problems, the businessmen." [7]

V

It would appear that holding fast to the concept of "internal solidarity" could only encourage a certain torpidity of the body politic and economic. If this were true, then the political process of the Second Republic might very well have shown again the frustrations of its prewar predecessor. That this is not the case is amply borne out by the record of adjustments, and compromises which must be arrived at within the framework of the coalition but, due to the unanimity rule of the coalition pact, are often obscured from public view. Thus, at the unofficial level of pre-parliamentary conferences and

[7] *Berichte und Informationen*, VII, April 30, 1953 (354). *Cf.* the statement by Dr. M. Kink in a lecture to the Danubia-Europa Institute which this writer attended: "The Chambers of Commerce will lose their right to economic self-regulation if they become seeped through with primitive individualism . . . only if the chambers prove . . . their devotion to the public interest — even where they must act in the interest of only one occupational group — will they be able to fulfill their mission for society at large."

exchanges between party and interest group representatives a good deal of political horse-trading is possible and is indeed carried out. Ultimately it is the threat of dissolving the coalition which brings about concessions by either side that were originally regarded impossible of attainment. Generally, this can be taken to mean that the visible pattern of politics in the Second Republic no longer conforms to the real alignment of interests since it is carried on under cover of all-inclusive political and economic organization. As both parties and interest groups become less class-oriented, oppositional tendencies within each camp become more outspoken. It is only strong party discipline which gives the rather misleading impression that the contending fronts run regularly between "red" and "black." The official bi-polarity merely hides the many combinations of interests that are not only possible but actually do exist presently in Austrian politics.

Thus, both agriculture and industrial labor are substantially in agreement on the need for a regulated economy. On the other hand, agriculture's demands for higher prices usually meet with the resistance of labor and industry. The big commercial and manufacturing interests disagree with the large exporting interests on questions concerning tariff regulations, with the trade unions usually on the side of the former. The Austrian Trade Union Federation in turn must deal with the conflicting demands of industrial unions and white-collar unions, the latter nearly always obtaining the support of the Chamber of Labor. Workers, employees and self-employed in small businesses are equally interested in maximum old-age security benefits and other social welfare measures — a fact which brings them continually in conflict with Industry and Export who maintain that they must foot the bill for such measures with higher prices. Within business groups there is the always latent conflict between importers in favor of a liberalization of the market, and exporters and other commercial interests favoring further restrictions. And, of course, there is the tug-o'-war between cartelized and non-cartelized branches of industry. Again, though the leadership of the Chamber of Labor is primarily consumer-oriented in its recommendations to the SPOe, as well as strongly attracted to Keynesean theories in its financial blueprints, there are enough old-time Socialists in the party bureaucracy who advocate increased socialization rather than deficit financing to cure the ills of the economy.

The consumer-producer conflict also manifests itself within the Chamber of Agriculture in the frequently very strained relations between farmer consumer co-operatives and farmer producer co-operatives. Since the latter are usually much stronger than the former they are able to dominate the Chamber of Agriculture using it primarily as a producer protective association. In this capacity the Chamber of Agriculture must be able to deal, internally, with the conflicting demands issuing mainly from the large wheat farmers of Lower Austria and the smaller cattle raisers of Styria, and externally, with the Chamber of Commerce's attempt to forestall competition from these co-operatives with its own business enterprises. For example, the Chamber of Commerce would have liked nothing better than to be able to include certain farm co-operatives in the provisions of the Prohibitory Law. That would have made it possible to deny trade licenses to such co-operatives whose activities were an infringement on already existing business enterprises. Politically, this means that the two leagues representing these interests within the OeVP, the Agrarian League (OeBB) and the Business League (OeWB), continue to regard each other with open suspicion. The strain engendered thereby occasionally reaches such proportions that, it is rumored, the Agrarians threaten to join forces with the Socialists — the feared "red-green" coalition. The third faction of the OeVP, the Workers and Employees League (OeAAB), represents primarily the consumer's point of view which, needless to say, brings it into frequent opposition to the other two groups. Much as it may echo many of the welfare policies of the SPOe and even strongly support the deficit financing schemes of the Chamber of Labor against the balanced budget concept of the government, the OeAAB's militant Catholic social reformism and its rather small membership prevent any effective political exploitation of its policies within the OeVP.

The observable tendencies within the Austrian political process indicate an equilibrium of group interests that seems to range from precarious to well-balanced. It is possible to recognize the replacement of the negative immo-bilism of the First Republic by more positive interaction. But it must be noted that this development is still taking place at the expense of so-called "neutral" institutions, i.e., executive, legislature, etc., by making them merely formal instrumentalities of party and group power. Desirable as it may be to have the various political and economic groups join frequently and intimately in the making of decisions, there remains the danger that the absence of a really strong common institutional denominator — be it in the form of tradition, symbol, or office — may undo much of the positive collaboration that has marked the post-World War II years. The coalition very possibly has served to encourage a flexible pluralism while keeping it within bounds of manage-ability. Co-determination is precisely not the issue in Austria that it is in West Germany, because of the ability of all groups and especially organized labor to participate in the making of economic decisions affecting their immediate well-being. The currently much-debated role of functional repre-sentation organs and agencies in the Federal Republic of West Germany or in Switzerland shows that Austria is only practicing what in these countries is still obscured by a pseudo-parliamentary ritual.

Any assessment of the Austrian example must take into consideration that both republics were the artificial creations of two world wars and that espe-cially in the Second Republic the parties qua parties were the initiators of governmental authority. Their organization, their functions predated the "state" in every respect. Just as the political parties took over the control of so-called "neutral" institutions such as the legislature and the executive, so did the economic interest groups, in the absence of a strong state and as it were, by default of the parties, transfer to themselves the regulatory functions of the welfare state. In a sense the execution of these tasks was the most important and significant function of these groups and accounts largely for their growing organization and power. It was, however, the intimate dovetailing of party and interest group personnel that, in the last analysis, permitted compromises to be reached on the basis of political as well as economic considerations. From the point of view of party pressure group interaction, the Second Republic probably comes as close to being an example of an "osmotic relationship" as is possible to find on the continent today. The interest groups and the parties may appear to have rejected the "state" as an intruder — but by their planned and unplanned co-operation they have, in effect, succeeded in preparing the ground for a better articulated political community and for the emergence of a generally respected and acceptable Austrian national state.

28. Group Theory and the Italian Political Process

JOSEPH LaPALOMBARA

Besides providing important insights into the methodological problems of interest group research and the difficulty of testing empirically propositions about the relative power of such groups, Professor LaPalombara adds renewed emphasis on the importance of the state bureaucracy as a far from passive participant in the decision-making process. He thus suggests a corrective to the "parallelogram of pressures" view of politics espoused by adherents of classical "group theory."

Before illustrating some of the problems and results of my field research, it may be appropriate to say something more about the setting within which the research was conducted and the methods utilized for the collection of data. I owe much to Gabriel Almond's article on political cultures as a convenient way of conceptualizing about and describing in broad detail the setting in which Italian interest groups are compelled to act.[1] In Almond's terms, Italy manifests an uneven development of her several political cultures. The society is notoriously fragmented; several political sub-cultures exist of which the major ones are those identified with Catholicism, a secular middle class, and a modernizing and innovating class. Each of these sub-cultures is atomized still further along ideological lines; each tends to have a total and highly articulated design for society as a whole and therefore for the political institutions within it. Although there are some peripheral points at which the views of the sub-cultures tend to merge, these are clearly exceptional; these major groupings are not compatible with each other. The sociologists would say about the society that it is not well integrated; the political scientists might speak of a low degree of consensus when measured, say, against the standard of the United States or Great Britain.

It is of vital importance to understand that formal interest groups in Italy frequently organize *within* these sub-cultures; very few of them cut across subcultural lines, even when the logic of a common economic interest would appear to compel such unification. For their own purposes, Communist-inspired or dominated groups often call for such unity of action and organization, but they are almost always repelled. Even within each of the sub-cultures, the groups are further fragmented. It is not uncommon, for example,

SOURCE: Reprinted by permission from Joseph LaPalombara, "The Utility and Limitations of Interest Group Theory in Non-American Field Situations," *The Journal of Politics*, XXII (February 1960), pp. 36–49. Text and footnotes are abridged.

[1] "Comparative Political Systems," in H. Eulau, S. J. Eldersveld and M. Janowitz, *Political Behavior* (Glencoe, Illinois, 1956), pp. 34–42.

357

to find Communist, Catholic, Socialist, Liberal, Republican and Neo-Fascist rough equivalents of the American League of Women Voters. Or, within the Catholic sub-culture, one can discern functional groups that separate the wealthy from the poor, radical workers from conservative workers, agricultural day laborers from tenant farmers, from small property-holding farmers, and so on. In a context such as this, it is difficult to isolate what may be the "basic" or "fundamental" interest around which the groups are organized.

All of which results in an enormous proliferation of groups — of countless interest groups in a society where they have gone almost completely unnoticed by political scientists. In Rome alone we were able to identify some 3,000 formal national groups from which we drew both our mailed-questionnaire and interview samples. Of course, as our questionnaire responses show, most of the formal groups are only sporadically involved in the political process. Nevertheless, it is noteworthy that not more than a handful of the groups responding to our questionnaire indicated patterns of action that categorically excluded political intervention. For the rest, intervention ranged all the way from an occasional memorandum to a parliamentary committee or administrative agency to frequent and regularized contacts with political party and public officials in every branch of government.

This fragmented nature of Italian society is responsible, I believe, for the relatively important role that violence, and the threat of it, play in the general tactics utilized by interest groups, in support of their demands. The group leaders who were queried on this phenomenon tended to see their activities as part of a basic struggle among the sub-cultures to impose hegemony over each other. For these leaders, domination by the opposition was generally taken to mean not merely difficult access to the key centers of policy making, but outright denial of any access at all to the group members of the sub-cultures not in power. As it turns out, this judgment is definitely not exaggerated; for the group leaders themselves freely indicate that, wherever and whenever possible, they seek utterly to exclude their opponents from the policy making areas. In a setting such as this, the threat or use of violence may be the only logical recourse open to a frustrated interest group.

Given this kind of general setting, it would be foolhardy to try to speak with authority about the characteristic patterns of interest group action in all sectors of Italian politics. My field effort focused primarily on the interaction between interest groups and the Italian bureaucracy, and the research was limited to a small number of groups and just a few administrative agencies. Special attention was given to Confindustria (Italy's equivalent of the N.A.M.), the trade unions and Catholic Action in its various organizational manifestations. Their relationships to the Ministries of Industry and Commerce and of Labor and Social Security were intensively explored. Information was obtained through the following devices:

1. Content analyses of the major publications of the three groups over periods ranging from 10 to 50 years.
2. Mailed-questionnaires to 129 formal groups. The questionnaires elicited information about internal organization, membership, leadership and intervention in the political process. Sixty-eight groups responded.

3. Analyses of newspapers and other periodical literature dealing with the three groups, the issues in which they were openly involved, and the bureaucratic agencies and personalities with whom they interacted.
4. Informal discussions with approximately 100 informants or "knowledgeables" from the fields of government, business, organized labor and the professions.
5. Three-hour focused interviews conducted with 125 group leaders, bureaucrats, party officials and selected members of the legislature.

Perhaps the most frustrating general finding of this study is that, except on the basis of highly unreliable impressions, it is impossible to measure the *relative influence* that groups exert over administrative decisions. The methods employed yielded essentially unsatisfactory results. For example, when respondents (group leaders and public administrators) are asked to differentiate among groups in terms of the power exercised in various administrative agencies, not very impressive results are obtained. For one thing the concept "power" (or "influence") is not easy to define, and, even after the interviewer suggests a definition, he cannot be certain that the respondents adhere to a specific denotation in their evaluations. The most that one can get from analyzing interview materials is a rough classification of responses. Thus, when the agency in question was a sub-division of the Ministry of Industry and Commerce, we obtained this pattern of response:

1. Bureaucrats in administrative agencies other than the ministry identify the unions as weak, Catholic Action as relatively strong, and the power of *Confindustria* as overwhelming.
2. Communist and Socialist trade union leaders describe themselves as weak (but see below!), the Catholic unions as just a little stronger, *Confindustria* as strong and the power of Catholic Action as overwhelming.
3. Catholic trade unionists view themselves as stronger than the Communists and Catholic Action, but weaker than *Confindustria*.
4. Other group leaders and political officials generally identify the unions as weak, Catholic Action as strong, and *Confindustria* as overwhelmingly powerful.
5. Bureaucrats in the ministry involved identify only Catholic Action and the Catholic unions as in a position "to interfere" with orderly bureaucratic processes.
6. *Confindustria* leaders describe themselves as weak, identify the Communist unions as similarly situated and ascribe overwhelming power to the Catholic unions and to Catholic Action.

Interestingly, group leaders tend to argue with the interviewer that their organizations are weak, but only to a certain point. That is, the articulation of weakness to the outsider tends to cease whenever the respondent is probed on the reactions of group members to such a situation. Thus Communist trade unionists insist that, even in the Ministry of Industry, things are not completely black for them. The only exception to this pattern worth mentioning is a leader of the Christian Democratic Association of Direct Cultivators, who describes his organization as a pressure group, claims that it wields enormous power and boasts that 62 Christian Democratic deputies owe their election to it.

Similar patterns of subjective evaluation are obtained regarding a long series of questions pertaining to the relative power of groups in administrative agencies. Only to a very limited extent do the replies of the various categories of respondents tend to vary as the focus of attention shifts from one bureaucratic agency to another. Out of the total responses emerges, first, widespread recognition that organized groups do seek to intervene in the administrative process, and second, the tendency of many respondents (both group leaders and bureaucrats) to ascribe dominant influence to Catholic Action and to *Confindustria*.

The difficulty with such ascription is that it is not at all corroborated by other measures. For example, we attempted to identify over a time the positions of the various groups regarding a series of issues that came before the administrative agencies, and to gauge whether the final decision (where we could identify one) corresponded to one position or another. This analysis shows that on almost every major issue in which it expressed itself over several years *Confindustria* was defeated by the groups with which it competes.

The same analysis conducted for Catholic Action, however, raises enormous difficulties. The organization is so vast, so subdivided into many smaller units, some of which compete among themselves, that it is difficult to know when one has isolated a consistent Catholic Action position. But even here, the current and historical data can be marshalled in support of the proposition that, as far as administrative decisions go, Catholic Action does suffer defeats and, in any case, probably enjoys much less influence than Italians generally ascribe to it.

One might conclude at this point that the subjective evaluations were simply in error and that the second type of measure is more reliable. We think not, and for several reasons. First, it is apparent that group representatives often overstate their demands. This is invariably the case with their public demands, if interview responses mean anything. Thus, it is difficult to know exactly what the interest group really wanted or expected to get. Second, it is also evident that how these groups fare in any of the administrative agencies will tend to vary with the nature of the issue involved, and, alas, with a host of other intervening variables such as the temper of the Minister of the Treasury, the political deals that may be evolving in the legislature, the struggles within the dominant party, the unlikely alliances between Communist and Christian political leaders to name only a few about which we have any information at all. Third, a focus on issues that engender controversy and open opposition tends to lead one away from the many matters that are regularly handled quietly and on a routine basis. The way in which such less controversial issues are disposed of may reflect differing degrees of influence of the very groups about which we are attempting to make a total judgment. And last, this kind of analysis cannot shed any significant light unless a very careful accounting is given of the role of the bureaucrats themselves in these controversies.

Frankly, then, I come away from this experience with the feeling that we can describe relative group influence only in gross and therefore possibly misleading terms. For example, it is my impression that one of the very weakest interest groups in Italy today is *Confindustria,* about whose alleged enormous prowess millions of words have been printed in Italy. I believe that a complete analysis of our data will eventually bear out my assertion, and I recognize that, in making it, I am open to the criticism that I speak of relative group strength on the basis of pure impression. We know enough, in any event, to caution that it is not sufficient to support a claim of group influence in administration to show that an interest group maintains certain relations with the bureaucracy. It is the existence of these relationships between group leader and bureaucrats that has led some theorists to comment on the power of groups over bureaucratic decisions. Let us examine some of these relationships as they apply to Italy.

For example, it is sometimes suggested that the growth of the welfare state — or of economic planning — has intensified the contacts between group representatives and public administrators, especially in those administrative sectors that deal with economic regulation and welfare services. As Samuel Beer articulates it:

> . . . the structure of the welfare state and the controlled economy associates pressure groups more closely with the administration and makes pressure groups more concerned with the decisions made at the administrative level.[2]

Perhaps such a shift in the locus of interest group activity has occurred at the time and for the reason suggested. However, it is also possible that the welfare state has brought many new groups into existence and that the intensity of group activity in general has increased in all branches and at all levels of government. The kind of shift in emphasis probably began historically when delegated legislation became a major phenomenon, and as groups discovered that administrators have discretion in the implementation of legislative policies, notwithstanding what the juridical scholars may say.

Nor is it to be assumed that the nature of a group's interest will determine where it will concentrate its efforts to intervene in the political or governmental process. In Italy it is not clear that groups with strong economic interests gravitate toward the bureaucracy and groups with strong ideological content toward the legislature, as some writers expect. To be sure, Communist and Socialist groups are generally more visible in the legislature. Their leaders tell us, however, that this is not so much a matter of choice as it is the result of their not finding adequate access in administrative agencies where both management groups sporadically and Catholic groups always and with great determination seek to freeze them out.

With the industrialist and employer associations, on the other hand, there is an apparent preference for the administrative arena. Again, however, our findings show that the unwillingness of these group leaders to appear "in public" is largely a result of the trauma they suffered when the fascist regime

---

2 Samuel Beer, "Pressure Groups and Parties in Britain," *American Political Science Review,* L (March, 1956), p. 15.

they so openly supported disintegrated. Italy's industrialists, for example, have carried this political shyness to the point where *Confindustria* has only three members in the national legislature who openly speak on behalf of the confederation. *Confindustria* leaders complain bitterly about their disadvantage alongside other organized groups with strong direct legislative representation. However, *Confindustria's* incredibly amateurish and abortive attempt to reenter the legislature in the elections of 1958 will cause both group leaders and the industrialists they represent to retreat once more into the more reassuring, even if not exclusively preferred labyrinth of Italian bureaucracy.

Because they are the easiest to identify, large-scale interest groups appear to dominate the Italian bureaucratic scene. Yet, we find that, with most of the administrators we interviewed, the associations are of less importance than the more specialized groups that the associations confederate. Thus, members of the Ministry of Industry are more concerned, they say, with, for example, the National Association of Automotive Industries or the National Association of Transport, than they are with *Confindustria* in which both organizations have membership. Similarly, Ministry of Labor bureaucrats show greater concern about the needs and demands of, say, the National Federation of Metal-mechanical Workers, than they do for the confederations in which these units have membership. This is true notwithstanding that the constitutions of almost all confederating associations stipulate that they and not the member units will carry on negotiations with governmental agencies or with other groups.

It is this identification between the governmental and the interest group specialists that leads Meynaud to suggest that the more recent and specialized ministries (labor, industry, commerce, *etc.*) are likely to be more susceptible to group pressures than older ministries such as war, the interior, and foreign affairs. There is no questioning the existence of this identification in the Italian ministries of industry and labor; respondents on both the interest group and bureaucratic sides articulated at great length about the advantages of dealing with persons who speak one's same professional language, who "really understand" the nature of the problems to which both sides address themselves. Supportive evidence for this point is also suggested by the fact that the most proletarian of trade unions will go to great lengths to insure that their representatives to bureaucratic agencies be university graduates whose status (and, perhaps, socio-economic background) is equal to that of the public administrators with whom the groups must deal.

I will defer until later the inferences that we might draw from patterns such as this. Here I wish particularly to add that we conducted a few interviews in the ministries of the interior and of foreign affairs specifically for the purpose of probing the relative susceptibility of the administrators there to group pressures. We also raised this issue with many of our "knowledgeables." Needless to say, we found that these ministries, too, have their clienteles, even highly specialized ones such as the National Association of Municipal Authorities that interact regularly with Ministry of the Interior officials, and all sorts of interest groups (European federation, protection of emigrants, *etc.*) that are in regular contact with the Ministry of Foreign Affairs. These group representatives, too, tend to speak specialized languages that relate to the activities of the public administrators with whom they are in contact. On the basis of our limited findings, I would suggest that hasty conclusions about the newer and more specialized ministries be avoided. It may well be that the proposition is valid for Italy. But it is also possible that not enough attention has been paid the older agencies where, superficially, it may appear that the major functional interest groups are inactive.

We also discovered in Italy a vast network of quasi-corporative relationships between certain interest groups and the administrative agencies. Similar arrangements exist in France and Great Britain, and the practice has been described as providing the privileged groups with built-in access to critical points in the administrative decision-making process. In many of Italy's ministries, group representation is accorded on advisory committees that are expected to aid the minister and other top-level administrators in the formulation of general policy. Additionally, some groups have representation on specialized committees that set prices for consumers goods and scarce natural resources, for gas and electricity, and so on. Other similar agencies consult on matters of foreign commerce, including import-export priorities and regulations. There is no doubt of the intrinsic importance of the activities engaged in by these special committees. *Confindustria,* for example, maintains a card file on all of its leaders and members who hold positions on such committees, both nationally and locally. *Confindustria* leaders are quick to explain that such representation provides an excellent way for the agencies involved to hear the opinions of the parties affected by policy, as well as a way of assuring that the administrators will not succumb to the demands of a single interest group.

In general, representation on these ministerial committees is accorded to the industrial, agricultural and labor associations in the country, with the exception that Communist and Socialist groups in any of the areas have been barred for some years notwithstanding that in several sectors they have the largest organizations. Needless to say, the leaders of these groups complain about this. Interestingly, so did about half of the bureaucrats who were queried on this point. They generally offer as an explanation of their position the view that the representation is meaningless, and possibly harmful to the bureaucracy when it involves representatives of groups that recruit a small minority of the total organized persons in a particular area. This is especially the case where administrative regulation of the groups is the central function of the agency. Not having the regulated individuals represented when, in theory, they are supposed to be results in considerable difficulty for the bureaucrats.

What is one to say about this kind of group representation? In one or two areas, notably the Interministerial Committee on Prices, administrative bias in favor of the industrial representatives and their organizations has been so blatant as to result in the refusal of trade union and other group representatives to attend meetings. However, we have found this to be a glaring exception. For most of the other committees, we found each group represented articulating the view that the other groups were unduly advantaged, that the administrators were playing favorites, that it was really a hopeless task to try to deal rationally with the Italian bureaucracy.

This suggests that, perhaps, no group is dominant. It also indicates that corporative representation cuts two ways for the interest groups. On the one hand, they have ready access to the agencies and they can make their demands heard. They also have inside information that permits them to handle more readily and expertly than unrepresented groups administrative matters that concern or affect them. On the other hand, the fact that they accept representation means that they share part of the responsibility for the policies that evolve. According to most respondents, such representation generally results in the making of more moderate demands than might otherwise be the case. In several instances we find that the group representatives to some of these committees are under great cross pressure and that, often, they tend to side with the administrative agency against their own groups!

This leads me to emphasize what may, perhaps, be well known to all who have looked in on pressure group behavior in administrative settings, and that is that administrative officials are anything but passive actors in the so-called group process. Instead, we often find them competing with group representatives in order to press a point of view that is unsupported by any of the formal groups that interact with the agency.

At times these bureaucrats reveal an amazing capacity for manipulation. For example, one of the officials in the Ministry of Industry has close personal relations with several of *Confindustria's* leaders. During his interview, he indicated that not a day goes by without his talking with his contacts in *Confindustria* and with officials of the trade or industrial associations that relate to the activities of his division. He added that he never makes a major decision without consulting with representatives of these organizations. Yet, when probed about these contacts, it became apparent that the administrator was engaged in this activity as a means of getting commitments to his policies or, as he put it, as a means of preventing the groups from causing trouble later. When we interviewed the group of representatives about their relations with the agency, they described the public official as a "very difficult" person to deal with but also as someone who knew what he was doing and who generally "got things done."

This story could be repeated for most of the administrators who were interviewed in our study. The fact that the bureaucrats speak the same language as do the group representatives, that they may have the same kinds of university degrees and come from the same social stratum of the society seems not to justify the conclusion that the administrators are prey to the demands of special interests.

I am not trying to force the judgment here that Italian administrative agencies are invulnerable to the pressures of special interests. Our study will spotlight, for example, many of the structural weaknesses of Italian bureaucracy which tend to make the administrators overly dependent on some of their clientele groups. The almost complete lack of research facilities and activities in the ministries is one of these structural shortcomings. Administrators frequently complain that they must rely for statistical and other information on which policy must be based on the research activities of the unions, *Confindustria* or Catholic Action. Even when the memoranda containing research "findings" are suspect, the administrators often have no way of demonstrating this. At best, and this is a very limited practice in the ministries we observed, the bureaucrat might go out of his way to solicit other memoranda from groups that clearly compete with the organizations from which their statistical and other technical data usually come. The thing that struck me was that administrators complained, almost to a man, about this dependence.

Much of what we have found fits not so much the interest group "theory" of politics as it does the kind of propositions about organizational behavior that have been expounded by Simon, Selznik and others. To be sure, there are points at which elements of interest group "theory" writ large enter the writings of Simon. However, much value would seem to lie with a research focus that is institutionally circumscribed and which seeks to delineate, or at least to outline, the major behavioral contours that are likely to be associated with the institution or organization itself. Thus, when examining bureaucracy and bureaucratic behavior there is no need for following the proclivities, say, of the neo-Bentlians who would make the bureaucracy an arena for group conflict and the bureaucrat a mere pawn in the "process of government." One can conceptualize about characteristics regarding *all* large-scale organizations insofar as they must reach decisions and implement them, without regard to whether the actors in them are the objects of interest group strategies.

Our data clearly point up the fact that a person who enters a bureaucratic agency is to some degree socialized by it; that is, he takes on some of the values of the administrative agency itself. This identification with his agency, as well as the ideal requirements of the role he occupies, will in some measure curb what might otherwise be a tendency to become an instrument of interest group desires and manipulations.

The bureaucrat also tends to develop certain skills that permit him in turn to manipulate the interest groups, and to play them off against each other for his own purposes. It is for this reason that administrators often welcome group clienteles and, where such do not exist, will seek to create them.

Understanding this, the general interest group "theorists" will observe that, in these instances, the administrative agencies are not merely arenas but an integral part of the battle; the administrators, not merely mediators but participants (in interest group terms) in the struggle to have one's own values or views predominate. But we need not posit the bureaucracy, or any single unit or individual within it, as a competing interest group in order to recognize and explicate the bureaucrat's role in the governmental process. Certainly we could do more research than we have in the direction of exploring the possibility of the highly individualized art of administrative decision-making. Such research is doomed to foredrawn conclusions, however, if our conceptual apparatus makes even the suspicion of such behavior unthinkable and the holder of such a view appear to be hopelessly naive.

In our field interviews, I was impressed by the frequency with which the bureaucrats interviewed sought to explain their policy positions or behavior in terms of a "national interest" or a "general welfare." To be sure, such responses were never accepted at face value, but in many instances (too many to ascribe merely to a chance factor) probing failed to turn up the reference or other group interests that the administrators were serving in the name of a mythical national interest. This failure raises for us, as it has for others who have studied the administrative process, perplexing questions not simply about administrative behavior but about the concept of the "public interest," its meaning, its role and its susceptibility to empirical analysis.

One way out of difficulties such as this is to speak of the administrator as using the "community," the consumer, his fellow administrators, or all those living or dead with whom he feels allied as a reference group. I am increasingly suspicious of such convenient escape hatches. Procedures such as this loom not so much as scientific insights but as self-fulfilling prophesies — or as the kind of cynicism that I touched on earlier. They also point up once more the possibility that simplistic interest group "theory," in seeking to account for all political behavior may not be useful in providing satisfactory explanations for any political behavior in particular. It is to the latter that the field researcher's attention must be directed, and, for the time being at least, only limited propositions about groups appear to have any utility at all.

Part 5

THE CHANGING PATTERN OF DEMOCRATIC POLITICS

As Professor Lipset points out in his contribution reprinted below, affluence and bureaucratization are relatively recent phenomena in Western democratic politics. It should be pointed out that the data here presented were compiled and analyzed in a period marked by the emergence of these characteristics, which are obviously related to both objective and subjective changes that differentiate these societies from those of the interwar period. These changes have been summarized and discussed under the terms "decline of class structure" and "end of ideology."

One does not have to be a Marxist to find in the dynamics of class structure — which brought to parliamentary democracies the heritage of anterior, rigidly stratified systems, and the differential experiences of groups holding diverse positions vis-à-vis the capitalist process of production — the most important single key to democratic politics prior to 1945. The emergence of the industrial proletariat, prior to or contemporary with the establishment of parliamentary democracy based on universal suffrage, created the most salient cleavage on which Western democracies foundered or threatened to founder. Its most dramatic expression was the polarization of democratic politics in radical mass parties of Left and Right, the fragmentation of the political center, and thus the incapacity to form stable governments or to play the classical game of government and opposition. Even in England, Harold Laski in the mid-thirties saw the parliamentary system as threatened by collapse: Laski believed that the prerequisite to its traditional function, a basic consensus between the two contending parties over the fundamentals of the socio-economic system, had disappeared with the Labour party's commitment to Socialism, and the radical elimination of the existing "owning class" claim to privilege and power.

A brief period following the end of World War II appeared characterized by two contradictory tendencies: on the mass level, profound weariness, distrust of ideologies, preoccupation with rebuilding private security out of the chaos of destruction; on the level of political institutions, a re-emergence of strong ideological commitments, their center of gravity well to the left on the prewar spectrum. The ultra-nationalist, fascist, even the traditionalist, conservative right wing seemed truncated as a consequence of its identification with the revealed inhumanities and dysfunctional irresponsibility of the defeated regimes. The choice appeared to lie only between radical and moderate shades of socialism, united in their insistence to permit no return to prewar conditions.

Even parties of the Center, like the German CDU or the MRP in France, committed themselves to socialism in some form and abjured the bourgeois-capitalist past. Communist and socialist parties, at first intent on preventing a recurrence of fratricidal strife that might open the way to right-wing victory, formed common fronts, though complete mergers did not take place where they were free to decide. Three factors impinged on this initial situation and profoundly altered its atmosphere: the negative image that the Soviet Union projected through its Stalinist practices in occupied territories; the American "containment" policy, taking the form of aid in the rehabilitation of non-Communist economies, and the progressive integration of the Western nation-states into an anti-Communist treaty system; and the re-establishment or continuation of traditional parliamentary forms of democracy, forcing party leaderships to adjust to the predominant temper and wishes of the electorate.

After 1948 — and the temporal coincidence with the Cold War is not accidental — the pattern of democratic politics as analyzed in these pages developed rapidly. Its predominant features were the surprisingly quick recovery of the European economies with American aid — followed by a decade of dramatically rising production levels and living standards; the establishment of comprehensive social security and welfare systems, which, combined with a deep commitment to full employment, provided the mass of the working population with a novel feeling of economic security; the dwindling or isolation of Communist parties that were identified with inhumanities and inefficiencies of the Soviet system. Domestic politics centered increasingly around the division of the "cake" provided by the national economy. With the near-disappearance of right-wing movements and the gradual "depolitization" of the Catholic Church, the traditional ideological battles either became obsolete, or were projected into the field of foreign policy, where they took the form of simplified "friend–foe" thinking, rendering genuine politics unnecessary.

Whether this change is best described as "de-ideologization" is arguable because of the multiple and controversial meanings of the concept of ideology. But critics as well as defenders of the "end of ideology" thesis agreed that a significant change had occurred on the levels of mass attitudes, parties, and governmental processes. Stanley Hoffmann describes this change in the governmental process as the "dispossession of parliament not only by the civil service and interest groups but also by the executive." More than a decade ago Otto Kirchheimer spoke of the "waning of parliamentary opposition," and used postwar Austria as a prime example of a development he considered significant far beyond the confines of that small country. Indeed, if "the system" was fixed by technological imperatives and was alterable only through bargaining practices between expert elites, then the Austrian pattern of "proportional democracy," in which the major social groupings shared political power, controlling shares of the executive and government as "antagonistic cooperators," seemed more appropriate than the old model where "ins" confronted "outs." Gone also was the traditional sharp line between "public" and "private," as parts of the economy were nationalized and those remaining in private hands were subject to governmental supervision — not to mention the vast sector including arms production, and nuclear and space technology, where governmental and nongovernmental agencies and enterprises were inextricably meshed.

Obviously this is a simplified picture, which describes only a part of the diverse and contradictory reality. Old structures and old patterns do not disappear at once; societies are not turned to homogenous, fully integrated wholes in a couple of decades, particularly when they vary in tradition so greatly from nation to nation.

To the "resilience of old patterns of behavior" that Professor Hoffmann emphasizes, there has recently been added a new pattern, already significantly affecting the politics of several Western democracies but as yet insufficiently reflected in the scholarly literature. It has been referred to as "the new Radicalism," a movement that has sprung up with such surprising simultaneity that one is forced to view it as a serious political factor that is functionally related to the "stabilized system" against which it reacts. It is concentrated among the young; it is located outside the existing political parties, or is only in tenuous contact with their left wing; and it is, by and large, hostile to the present pattern of parliamentary democracy. Its lack of a mass base has not prevented it from beginning to have an impact on the democratic process, for it rejects the "numbers game" of electoral democracy, and exercises power directly against sensitive points in the organization of mass democracy. Small groups held together by determined rejection of "the establishment" have proved quite capable of using such power effectively.

Again, the emergence of this "New Radicalism" is not accidentally contemporary with the destruction of the rigidly polarized fronts of the Cold War period. The "thaw" has not only affected the Communist bloc. It has unfrozen forces of harsh discontent in "affluent societies" — forces that are difficult to comprehend with the apparatus of traditional scholarship, but that may shortly put in question many of the findings and generalizations here presented. A decade hence, the familiar landscape of democratic politics may once again appear profoundly altered.

29. The Changing Class Structure and Contemporary European Politics

SEYMOUR MARTIN LIPSET

Professor Lipset sees "Marxist sociology" validated at the expense of "Marxist politics." Postwar changes in the class structure—the "base" in Marxist terms—have led to the moderation of political demands. In an admittedly uneven process, "modernization" has in Europe brought with it progressive integration of formerly antagonistic classes and groups around a commonly accepted system of "welfare democracy." Although the paper supports the so-called "end of ideology" thesis, Professor Lipset does not overlook the fact that the continuation of stratification, inequality, and privilege in even the most "advanced" European nations still provides the major source of political conflict.

During the 1950's commentators on both sides of the Atlantic began to depict western society by terms such as "The End of Ideology," "the post-industrial society," and the "post-bourgeois society." While emphasizing different themes, these commentators agreed that the growth of bureaucracy and "affluence" in western industrial democratic society has made possible a social system in which class conflict is minimized. Domestic politics has become the politics of collective bargaining. True, an argument does remain as to the relative income at any given moment of the rural sector, of different groups of workers, of private corporations and so forth. But each group accepts the others' right to legitimate representation within the structure of representation and discussion.

Such a pattern in European society is relatively new. Much of the history of industrial society was a story of class-conscious politics and violent controversy between proletarian and bourgeois ideologists. Marxists viewed such tensions as inherent in a capitalist culture. That the United States, the most powerful capitalist state, lack a strong socialist movement was viewed as a cultural lag, an inheritance of the period of an open land frontier that served as a "safety valve" for the tensions of industrialism. Presumably once this safety valve was gone, the European model of class-conscious politics would emerge.

In fact, history has validated a basic premise of Marxist sociology at the expense of Marxist politics. Marxist sociology assumes that cultural super-structures, including political behavior and status relationships, are a function of the underlying economic and technological structure. Hence, the most developed industrial society should also have the most developed set of political

SOURCE: Reprinted by permission from *Daedalus, Vol. 93, No. 1* (Winter 1964), pp. 271–296. Footnotes are abridged.

and class relationships. Since the United States is the most advanced society technologically, its superstructure should be more likely to correspond to the social structure of a modern industrial society than the "less" developed economies of Europe. In addition, one might argue that the absence of a traditional feudal past should mean that the United States has been most likely to develop the pure institutions of a capitalist industrial society. Hence, as an unpolitical Marxist sociology would expect, instead of European class and political relationships holding up a model of the United States' future, the social organization of the United States has presented the image of the European future.

The linkage between level of industrial development and other political and social institutions is obviously not a simple one. Greater economic productivity is associated with a more equitable distribution of consumption goods and education — factors contributing to a reduction of intra-societal tension. As the wealth of a nation increases, the status gap inherent in poor countries, where the rich perceive the poor as vulgar outcasts, is reduced. As differences in style of life are reduced, so are the tensions of stratification. And increased education enhances the propensity of different groups to "tolerate" each other, to accept the complex idea that truth and error are not necessarily on one side.

An explanation for the reduction in the appeal of total ideologies (*weltanschauungen*) as simply derivative from the social concomitants inherent in increasing economic productivity is clearly oversimplified. T. H. Marshall has suggested that such extreme ideologies initially emerged with the rise of new strata, such as the bourgeoisie or the working class, as they sought the rights of citizenship, that is, the right to fully participate socially and politically. As long as they were denied such rights sizable segments of these strata endorsed revolutionary ideologies. In turn, older strata and institutions seeking to preserve their ancient monopolies of power and status fostered conservative extremist doctrines.

The history of changes in political ideologies in democratic countries, from this point of view, can be written in terms of the emergence of new strata, and their eventual integration in society and polity. The struggle for such integration took the form of defining the place in the polity of the old pre-industrial upper classes, the church, the business strata and the working class. The variation in the intensity of "class conflict" in many European nations has been in large measure a function of the extent to which the enduring economic struggle among the classes overlapped with the issues concerning the place of religion and the traditional status structure. Such controversies usually were perceived in "moral" terms involving basic concepts of right versus wrong, and hence they were much more likely than economic issues to result in sharp ideological cleavage and even civil war. The continuance of extremist movements in nations such as Germany and the Latin countries of southern Europe may be traced to the force of moral sentiments inherent in concerns for traditional status or religious privileges. Where such issues were resolved without becoming identified with the economic class struggle, then as Marshall suggests intense ideological controversy declined almost as soon as the new strata gained full citizenship rights.

Still a third factor related to the general decline in ideological bitterness has been the acceptance of scientific thought and professionalism in matters which have been at the center of political controversy. Insofar as most organized participants in the political struggle accept the authority of experts in economics, military affairs, interpretations of the behavior of foreign nations and the like, it becomes increasingly difficult to challenge the views of opponents in moralistic "either/or" terms. Where there is some consensus among the scientific experts on specific issues, these tend to be removed as possible sources of intense controversy. As the ideology of "scientism" becomes accepted, the ideologies of the extreme left and right lose much of their impact.

But whatever the long-run sources of the reduction of the appeal of total ideologies (and there are short-run factors as well, such as the impact of wars both hot and cold), the fact remains that there has been a reduction in the intensity of class-linked political struggles in most of Europe. This paper surveys developments in the economies, social structures and political parties of European societies which are relevant to an analysis of such trends. Within the context of a broad comparative analysis it also deals with the sources of deviations from these trends. The analysis thus seeks to define the elements in the changing structures which make for a lessening or persistence of class ideologies in different parts of Europe.

I

Class and Political Consensus after 1945

The "miracle" of the postwar economic growth of Europe has been well documented. A combination of circumstances — the depression crises, prolonged experience with state economic intervention and planning under fascism or wartime regimes, the sharp increase in approval of socialist or welfare state concepts during and immediately following the war and the need for some years after the conflict to plan for and even furnish the capital for capital investment — resulted in a far greater amount of planning and government involvement in spurring economic growth than had existed in any democratic state before 1939. The nationalization of businesses in France under the first de Gaulle regime surpassed the most grandiose ambitions of Third Republic Socialists, and systematic planning emerged in the early fifties. The Austrian economy is characterized by large-scale government ownership. Italy retained and even expanded the considerable government economic sector developed under Fascism. In Germany, the numerous dependent war victims and the presence of refugees from the East, comprising more than one quarter of the population of West Germany, involved the state in welfare and other expenditures that took a large share of the gross national product for many years. And in Britain, the Labour government undertook an elaborate program of nationalization and welfare expenditures.

In almost all of these nations, therefore, two general events of considerable significance for class behavior have occurred. On the one hand, many of the political-economic issues that occasioned deep conflict between representatives of the left and of the right were resolved in ways compatible with social-democratic ideology. On the other hand, the dominant strata, business and other, discovered that they could prosper through economic reforms that they regarded a decade earlier as the rankest socialist measures. The socialists and trade unionists found that their formal structural objectives, in many cases, had been accomplished with the cooperation of their political rivals. The need for government planning for economic growth and full employment was generally accepted; the obligation of the state to provide welfare services for the ill, the aged and other dependent groups was viewed as proper by all parties; and the right of the trade union and political representatives of the workers to participate in decisions affecting industry and politics also was increasingly coming to be accepted. Domestic politics in most of these societies became reduced to the "politics of collective bargaining," that is, to the issue of which groups should secure a little more or less of the pie.

The transformation in class attitudes as reflected in political and interest group behavior is most noticeable in northern non-Latin Europe and among the socialist and Roman Catholic political parties. Large-scale extremist or avowedly authoritarian parties have almost completely disappeared north of France and Italy, with the exception of Finland and Iceland. The Norwegian and Austrian socialists who subscribed to a relatively left-wing Marxist view before World War II are now clearly moderate social-democratic parties. The latter take part in what has become a stable coalition regime with the bourgeois People's party. The parties of the three German-speaking nations, Switzerland, Austria and Germany, have given up any adherence to Marxism or class war doctrines and are little concerned with any further expansion of the area of state ownership of industry. The 1959 Godesberg Program of the German party explicitly revoked the traditional policy of public ownership of the means of production. An indication of the mood of European socialism may be found in a description of an international socialist conference:

> In July, 1958, the socialist international held a congress in Hamburg. The name of Karl Marx was mentioned exactly once. The old slogans of the class struggle and exploitation had disappeared. But the words "liberty," "democracy," "human dignity" came up again and again. . . . The principal theoretical speech was made by Oscar Pollack [famed theoretician of prewar Austro-Marxism]. His theme was, "Why is it that we cannot get the working classes excited about socialism any longer?" The answer that Pollack gave is that their lot is so improved, in a way which would have been incredible to nineteenth-century Socialists of any variety, that they are no longer easily moved by the slogans of class struggle and socialism.[1]

On the right, one finds that those parties which still defend traditional European liberalism (laissez-faire) or conservatism (social hierarchy) are extremely weak. The Scandinavian Liberals and Agrarians now accept much of the welfare state. Many Scandinavian bourgeois politicians, in fact, propose

---

[1] Bertram D. Wolfe, "A Century of Marx and Marxism," in Henry L. Plaine (ed.), *Darwin, Marx, and Wagner* (Columbus: Ohio State University Press, 1962), pp. 106–107.

that their countries adopt Swiss and Austrian political practice, a permanent coalition of all parties in which collective bargaining issues are fought out and compromised within the cabinet. The Roman Catholic parties, on the whole, have accepted the welfare state and economic planning, and have even supported increases in government ownership. They willingly participate in coalitions with socialist parties in many countries. Roman Catholic trade unions, once the bitter rivals of the so-called free or socialist unions in most Roman Catholic countries, either participate in the same unions as the socialists, as in Germany and Austria, or cooperate closely with the socialist unions, as in the Benelux nations. Issues concerning the relationship of church and state, particularly as they affect education and family legislation, still separate the left wing of the Roman Catholic parties from the Socialists, but these are not of grave moment as compared to their agreement on economic and class matters. In Germany the traditional base of the opposition to a democratic regime, the regions beyond the Elbe, the homeland of the Junkers and feudal social relationships, is no longer part of the nation. West Germany today is physically and socially largely comprised of regions and classes which historically have shown a willingness to sustain modern socio-economic and political systems. Although once playing a major role in politics, the civil service and the army, the old aristocracy today participate little in these institutions.

Reactionary parties in postwar Europe have tended on the whole to be peripheral movements based on the outlying regions and strata which have not shared in the rapid economic growth, which find themselves increasingly outside of the new cosmopolitanism and which have lost out in the relative struggle for influence and status.[2] Thus in Norway the Christian party, which seeks to further traditional values, is clearly a provincial party based on the lower middle classes of the rural and provincial communities. Poujadism was the classic case of a movement appealing to the *resentments* of declining strata; its base was the backward parts of France which had been losing population, and the petit bourgeoisie whose relative position in French economy and society had worsened with the growth of the metropolis and large business and government. In Italy, the Monarchists and Neo-Fascists have

[2] Parenthetically, it may be noted that similar processes are operative on the left. The only significant exceptions within European socialism to increased political moderation have been the enhanced strength of "radical wings" within the socialist and labor movements of Great Britain and Belgium. These movements have long been among the most moderate in the European left, and their dominant tendency has not changed, so that the growth in left strength is not very important. However, it should be noted that the growth in "militancy" within these parties and unions seems to constitute a form of proletarian Poujadism. Both nations lag behind the other industrialized nations of Europe in their growth rate, their standards of living have increased more slowly than those of most other European countries, and the felt need to renovate their economies — these are the two oldest industrial countries on the continent — by building new plants or changing policies in old ones poses serious threats to the established way of life of many workers and union leaders. In Wallonia, the ancient industrial section of Belgium, the socialists and unions waged a major general strike in 1960–1961 designed basically to stop the shutdown of marginal coal mines, and the location of new and efficient factories in Flanders. Since the strike, the "left-wing" socialists have formed the Walloon Popular

recruited strength from roughly comparable groups, a pattern that has also characterized the support of the Austrian Freedom party.

Not unexpectedly, studies of the attitudes and behavior of the entrepreneurial strata in various parts of Europe suggest that the managerial groups in the traditionally less developed countries of Europe, such as France and Italy, have been the most resistant to yielding their historic autocratic and parternalistic view of the role of management. "In general, France and Italy have been characterized by a large number of small enterprises, looked on by the family as a source of personal security and conducted in an atmosphere of widespread absence of trust." The resistance to accepting trade unions as a legitimate part of the industrial system is greater in these nations than anywhere else in democratic western Europe. And consequently the presence of extreme views of class and industrial relations among leaders of workers and management has contributed to resisting the pressures inherent in industrialization to stabilize such relationships. The available evidence would suggest that Italian industrialists may be more resistant to accepting a *modus vivendi* with trade unions and planning-welfare state than are the French, although, as shall be noted, the relative situation is reversed among the worker-based Communist parties of these countries. It is difficult to account for these variations other than to suggest that Fascism as practiced in Italy for two decades conditioned many Italian businessmen to a pattern of labor-management relations that they still long for. Conversely, however, Fascism spared the Italian Communists the experience of having to repeatedly purge the various levels of leadership of a mass party. The party could emerge after World War II with close intellectual links to its pre-Fascist, and more significantly pre-Stalinist, past and with a secondary leadership and rank-and-file whose major formative political experience was the Resistance rather than the Comintern.[3]

Class conflict ideologies have become less significant components of the political movements supported by the middle classes in Germany, Italy and France. In Germany and in Italy, the Christian-Democratic type parties, with their efforts to retain the support of a large segment of the unionized working classes, have made a trans-class appeal in favor of moderate changes. As compared to pre-Fascist days, they have gained considerably at the expense of older, more class-oriented, more conservative parties. The classically liberal

---

Movement seeking to divide Belgium into a federal state with two autonomous regions, an action which would enable a Walloon government to defend the Walloon economy. Similar Poujadist processes have occurred in Britain, although their impact is not as visible, since the backward sections of the British economy are not concentrated within one ethnic-linguistic region as they are in Belgium. The powerful resistance among many British union leaders and members to Britain's entry into the Common Market is, to a considerable extent, motivated by their fear of the possible effects on their jobs and unions resulting from the modernization of the national economy which would be necessitated by the need to compete within the Market. As in Wallonia, this essentially Poujadist reaction has taken the form of an alliance between trade union leaders and "left-wing" intellectuals who formulate the opposition on traditional left socialist grounds.

[3] The differences between Italian and French Communism are discussed in more detail below.

Free Democratic and Liberal parties receive about 7 per cent of the vote in each country. In France, the Christian Democrats (MRP) were not able to retain the massive upper and middle class conservative vote which the party inherited in the first elections of the Fourth Republic, as a result of the traditional right's being discredited by its involvement with Vichy. And large-scale anti-labor and anti-welfare state parties arose in the late forties and fifties. The Gaullism of the Fifth Republic, however, has replaced such parties in the affections of the conservative and business part of the electorate. Gaullism is oriented to a trans-class appeal designed to integrate the lower strata into the polity, and it supports economic and social reforms which foster economic growth and reduce class barriers.

Looking at the policies of business toward workers and their unions, it would appear that Germany first, and much more slowly and reluctantly, France and Italy, in that order, have been accepting the set of managerial ideologies characteristic of the more stable welfare democracies of northern and western Europe. Curiously, the one country for which research data exist which bear on the relationship between degrees of modernization and bureau-cratization of industry and the attitudes of industrial managers is contempo-rary Spain. An as yet unpublished study of the Spanish businessman by Juan Linz indicates clearly that the larger and more modern a factory, the more likely is its manager to believe in, or accept, modern personnel policies with their denigration of the particularistic rights of *patrons* and their assump-tions concerning universalistic treatment of subordinates. It is interesting to note that whether a manager is an owner or not seems to have little bearing on his attitudes on such issues. If the Spanish pattern occurs in the other Latin countries as well, it would suggest that those who argue that significant changes are occurring among managers in France and Italy are correct. As yet, however, little systematic comparative data exist on the subject, and many of the available analyses rely heavily on published statements of, or interviews with, the officials, that is, ideologues, of business associations. The latter tend to mouth, and probably even believe, the traditional *laissez-faire* and anti-labor ideologies which many of their members no longer follow in practice.

II

The Integration of the Working Class

But if the evidence drawn from developments in various parts of the continent suggests that the secular trends press for political moderation, for the politics of collective bargaining, it is also important to note that these trends do not imply a loss of electoral strength for working class-based parties. In fact, in all European countries varying majorities of the manual workers vote for parties which represent different shades of socialism. As the workers have become integrated into the body politic, they have not shifted from voting socialist to backing bourgeois parties. If anything, the opposite seems to have occurred. In the Scandinavian nations, for example, "all evidence indicates that social class explains more of the variation in voting and particularly more of the working class voting than some decades ago. This has occurred simultaneously with the disappearance of traditional class barriers. As equality has increased the working class voters have been more apt to vote for the worker's own parties than before."[4]

A comparative look at the pattern of working class voting in contemporary Europe reveals that with the exception of Holland and Germany, the leftist parties secure about two thirds or more of the working-class vote, a much higher percentage than during the depression of the 1930's. The two exceptions are largely a by-product of the Roman Catholic-Protestant cleavage in their countries. The traditionally minority German and Dutch Roman Catholics have considerable group solidarity, and the Christian Democratic and Roman Catholic parties in these countries secure a larger working class vote than occurs anywhere else on the continent. Close to 70 per cent of German Protestant workers vote Socialist, as do "humanist" and moderate Calvinist Dutch Workers, as opposed to the conservative Dutch Calvinists, who are more like the Roman Catholics. The leftist working class-oriented parties have increased their strength in much of Europe during the 1960's. It is clear, therefore, that the easy assumption made by many, concerning American as well as European politics, that greater national affluence would mean a weakening of the electoral support for the left is simply wrong. Regardless of how wealthy a nation may be compared to its past, all democratic countries, from the still impoverished lands of the Mediterranean basin to Sweden, Australia or the United States, remain highly stratified societies in which access to education, economic opportunity, culture and consumption goods is grossly unequal. The nature of such inequalities varies greatly; in general the poorer a country, the greater the gap in the standard of consumption between the classes. However, in all countries the more deprived strata, in income and status terms, continue to express their resentments against the stratification system or perhaps simply their desire to be represented by politicians who will seek to further redistribute the goods of the society, by voting for parties which stand for an increase in welfare state measures and for state intervention in the economy to prevent unemployment and increase their income vis-à-vis the more privileged strata.

Greater national wealth and consequent lower visible class differentials, therefore, do not weaken the voting strength of the left as compared with the right; rather, their effects become most evident in the decline of ideological differences, in changes in the policies advocated by different parties. The leftist parties have become more moderate, less radical, in the economic reforms which they espouse. A look at the political history of Europe indicates that no mass lower class-based political party, with the single exception of the German Communists, has ever disappeared or significantly declined through losing the bulk of its votes to a party on its right.[5]

---

[4] Erik Allardt, "Traditional and Emerging Radicalism" (mimeographed paper), p. 5.

[5] Although the German Communists secured about 16% of the vote in 1932, they were never as large as the Social-Democrats. The latter always retained their status as the predominant party of the workers. Hence even the German case is not a real exception.

The loyalties once created in a *mass* left-wing party are rarely lost. The most striking testimony to this has been the ability of the Finnish Communist party to retain mass support and even to grow since World War II, in spite of the Russian invasion of the country in 1940, the subsequent war of 1941–1945, and the Russian annexation of Karelia. The Communists are able to secure a quarter of the vote even though 10 per cent of the population are refugees from the Russian-annexed territory. The support for the Communist party goes back to the Finnish Civil War, which followed the Russian revolution, when the Social-Democratic party, the largest party under Czarist rule, divided into two roughly equal groups in reacting to Bolshevism. And although the Communist party was illegal for much of the period between the wars, it seemingly lost little backing. In recent years, it has grown somewhat during a period of rapid economic development and a sharply rising standard of living.

But if workers have remained loyal to the parties of their class on election day, they show much less commitment to these parties the rest of the year. All over Europe, both socialist and Communist parties have complained about losses in membership, in attendance at party meetings and in the reading of party newspapers. Such changes attest to the growth of what French intellectuals are increasingly coming to describe as the problem of *dépolitisation*. Another phenomenon illustrating these trends is the growing tendency of all the working class organizations to place less emphasis on traditional *political* doctrines and to put more stress on representation of concrete interests. Roman Catholic trade unions also are increasingly reluctant to intervene directly in politics.

In discussing the implications of changes such as these, a number of French political analysts have argued that what is occurring in France, and presumably in some other countries as well, is not so much a decline in political interest (*dépolitisation*), as of ideology (*déideologisation*). Thus René Rémond, in introducing a general symposium on these issues, points out that while political parties have suffered a considerable decline in membership, this has not been true of other French associations; that in fact there has been a considerable increase in the number of voluntary associations in France. Such groups, while nonpartisan, play important roles in politics in representing the specific interests of their members. André Philip has even suggested that contemporary France finally is developing the social infrastructure recommended by Tocqueville as a condition for stable democracy, widespread support for secondary associations. He suggests that this is another consequence of modernization, since the pattern of commitment to one group which represents the individual totally is a characteristic of the early phase of development. In a modernized society, any given group or party will report a relatively low level of direct participation by their members or supporters since the segmentalized individual involved in many roles must support diverse groups, and hence seemingly takes on the role of spectator in most of them.

It would seem as if much of France has taken the plunge of finally dropping its historic commitments to total *weltanschauungen* and seeing the problem of progressive social change as a pragmatic and gradual one. And insofar as

Frenchmen are able to see some of the changes and policies which they advocate being adopted, even by a government which many of them distrust, their motivation to continue to participate in such pragmatic parapolitical activity continues.

There are many ways in which the more pragmatic orientation of Europeans manifests itself, but the changes in trade union behavior are most noticeable. As already noted, in a number of countries socialist and Roman Catholic unionists are cooperating as they never did before World War II. The fact of such cooperation reflects the extent to which both have moved away from ideological or political unionism toward pragmatic or even, in the American sense of the term, "business unionism." In Italy and France, the trend toward a *syndicalisme de controle* is furthered by the emerging patterns of plant unions and supplementary factory contracts. Such organization and negotiation for the first time involve the unions in dealing with the concrete problems of the factory environment such as job evaluation, rates, productivity and welfare. The pressures in this direction have come primarily from the non-Communist unions, though the Communist unions have also increasingly come to accept such institutions, more in Italy than in France. The increase in economic strikes as distinct from political ones, though often resulting in an overall increase of the strike rate, has been interpreted by some observers as reflecting the integration of the workers into the industrial system; an economic strike is part of a normal bargaining relationship with one's employer. Some have suggested that the Italian strike wave of 1961 and 1962 was perhaps the first of this type since the war in that country.

The two major strikes of 1963, those of the coal miners in France and of the metal workers in Germany, are also notable for the extent to which each resembled a typical American strike flowing from a breakdown in collective bargaining. Each strike was ended by a negotiated settlement in which the unions secured more than they had been offered initially. Neither turned into a political strike, though the governments were directly involved in the negotiations. Essentially there was general recognition on both sides that the strike was a normal part of the collective bargaining process, although de Gaulle showed some initial reluctance to concur. Note further that in France the Communist-controlled CGT initially called for a two-day protest strike, while much less politicized miners' unions affiliated to the Socialist Force Ouvrière and the Roman Catholic CFTC called a trade union strike, one that would last until settled by negotiation. The Communists were forced to change their tactics, to shift from a political protest to an economic strike. These strikes in Italy, Germany and France may signify the beginning of a new era in labor relations — one in which strikes are recognized as part of the normal bargaining relationship rather than an embryonic civil war the outbreak of which is threatening to leadership on both sides.

The relative weakness of traditional leftist ideology in western and southern Europe is suggested also by various attitude surveys. These studies indicate that the actual sentiment favoring a "socialist solution" to economic or social problems is much lower than the Socialist or Communist vote. It again demonstrates that people will vote for such parties without commitment to the once basic ideological values of these parties.

In Britain today, where public opinion polls and local election results indicate that the Labour party has an overwhelming lead over the Conservatives, only 18 per cent of the electorate say that they favor more nationalization. Among Labour party voters, 39 per cent support increased nationalization, 46 per cent would leave things as they are, and 15 per cent would actually favor some denationalization. Conversely, only 43 per cent of the Conservatives advocate denationalization.[6]

A comparative analysis of attitudes toward ownership of industry in seven European countries based on interviews in the spring of 1958 reported strong sentiment favoring public ownership of industry only in Italy, the nation which has the largest support for radical ideologies in the form of large Communist and left-Socialist parties.[7]

In France, where about half the workers have voted Communist in most postwar elections, with another 20 per cent going to the Socialists, and a large majority voting for the Communist-controlled CGT trade union federation in Social Security Board elections, opinion data suggest that the workers are not as hostile to the existing institutions as this record might imply. A detailed survey of French workers in 1956 reported that 53 per cent thought there was "confidence" in the relations between employees and management, as contrasted to 27 per cent who said there was "distrust." Over four fifths believed their employer was doing his job well; nine tenths thought the quality of the work done at their plant was good; only 13 per cent thought there was a great deal of waste in their firm; 57 per cent stated that they had a chance for a promotion at their work; and 86 per cent reported they liked their jobs. Though the Communists had secured the vote of a majority of French workers shortly before this survey, only 12 per cent of those interviewed stated they were very much interested in politics, about the same percentage as that which reported strong interest in trade union activities.[8] And when asked in which country "the workers are best off," 54 per cent said the United States as compared with 14 per cent who answered the Soviet Union.[9]

How many of the French Communist voters actually adhere to a class war perspective and a generally Communist view of politics is a question that is impossible to answer. French experts who have examined the available evidence from studies of workers' attitudes differ in their interpretations. Thus Raymond Aron suggests that the polls indicate that about two thirds of French

[6] *Gallup Political Index*, Report No. 38, March, 1963, p. 34.

[7] See studies completed by Affiliates of International Research Associates and reported in DIVO Institut, *Umfragen: Ereignisse und Probleme der Zeit im Urteil der Bevölkerung* (Frankfurt: Europäische Verlagsanstalt, 1959), p. 77.

[8] "The French Worker: Who he is, how he lives, what he thinks, what he wants." *Réalités*, 65 (April, 1956), 8–18.

[9] The findings of a study conducted for *Réalités* by IFOP, the French Gallup Poll; see also Charles Micaud, *Communism and the French Left* (New York: Frederick A. Praeger, 1963), pp. 138–139.

Communist supporters are "convinced Communists," while Mattei Dogan believes that less than half of them think of political action and the class struggle in the Marxist sense of the term.[10]

The weakness of a sharp class conflict view of politics in Germany is borne out by a 1960 opinion study which asked a sample of the electorate their opinions concerning class solidarity and party voting. Less than one fifth took a purely class view of voting behavior, that is, that workers should always vote for the Socialists, and middle class people always for the non-socialist parties. The majority agreed with the statement that workers or middle class people might vote for either tendency, depending on the political situation and the issues involved. Over three fifths of those in middle class occupations, although predominantly non-socialist in their voting habits, agreed with the opinion that the division between the bourgeoisie and the workers was no longer strong and that a doctor or a professor might vote either Christian Democrat or Social Democrat, depending on the particular issues of a campaign. Conversely, only 30 per cent of the workers thought that a worker must always vote for the Social-Democrats, while half of the worker respondents agreed with the statement that a worker should choose between the parties according to the issues.[11]

The ideology of the "open society" in which competent individuals can succeed seems to have permeated much of Europe, a phenomenon which may also contribute to a reduction of class tension. Thus surveys in a number of countries which inquired as to the chances of capable individuals rising socially in their country found large majorities which reported their belief that the chances were good. The percentages of respondents saying that chances were good were 90 in Norway, 88 in England, 72 in West Germany, and 70 in Belgium. The one European country covered in this study in which the proportion of those who were optimistic about mobility was less than half was Austria, but even there the positive answers outweighed the pessimistic ones, 49 per cent to 34 per cent. Italy and France were not covered in this comparative study. However, another set of surveys which inquired as to careers one would recommend to a young man found that the Italians ranked second only to the English in suggesting high status professional occupations (62 per cent). The strongest French preference seemed to be for careers in the civil service, an orientation which distinguished them from all other European nations except the Belgians. It should be noted also that the Italians and the French were least likely among the citizens of eleven European countries to recommend a career as a skilled worker or artisan to a young man.[12]

---

[10] Aron, France Steadfast and Changing, pp. 39–40; Mattei Dogan, "Il compartamento politico degli operai francesi," Tempi Moderni, 9 (April, 1962), 26–27. Dogan reports that in 1952 the majority of workers supporting the Communists told interviewers that "the doctrine of this party was not the main reason for their vote" (p. 25). See also Micaud, Communism and the French Left (New York: Frederick A. Praeger, 1963), pp. 140–141.

[11] Viggo Graf Blücher, Der Prozess der Meinungsbildung dargestellt am Beispiel der Bundestagswahl 1961 (Bielefeld: Emnid Institut, 1962), pp. 73–75.

[12] DIVO Institut, Umfragen: Ereignisse und Probleme der Zeit im Urteil der Bevölkerung (Frankfurt: Europäische Verlagsanstalt, 1959), pp. 120, 124.

There is some direct evidence that modernization results in a positive attitude by workers toward their occupational situation. A French study of the consequences of modernization in textile factories in northern France brings this out clearly. The author notes that the workers view the effects of technological innovation as a "good thing," that they see it as resulting in an increase in employment, greater possibilities for social mobility and increased earnings.[13] The findings of French factory surveys with respect to worker reaction to modernization are paralleled in a report on the comparative strength of the Communist party in five large Italian factories which varied in their degree of modernization. The less modernized the plants the larger the proportion of workers who belonged to the Communist party, holding size of plant constant.[14]

But if workers react positively to working in modernized, more bureaucratic work environments, if they see these as offering greater opportunity for higher earnings and mobility, if job satisfaction is actually higher in many of these, the fact remains that when one looks at the sources of left-wing strength, either in voting or in union membership, and in the extent to which men agree with "anti-capitalist" attitudes, such strength is to be found disproportionately in the larger factories and the larger cities.[15] This seeming contradiction points up an interesting relation between the variables linked to the overall characteristics of a national political class culture and the same variables operating within a given society. As noted above, nations with a high level of industrialization and urbanization tend to have a low level of ideological conflict. But within nations, whatever the level of intensity of political controversy, larger factories and cities tend to be the strongholds of the left politics dominant in the country, Communist, Socialist or Democratic.[16] Trade unions also are generally stronger in large factories in large cities. It would seem that while greater industrialization and urbanization with consequent greater national wealth make for a more stable polity, *within* any system these social factors are conducive to fostering working class political and trade union strength.

How might we account for this? In part it may be related to the fact that the large factory environment sustains fewer informal relations between members of different classes, reducing the possibility that the members of the lower class will be influenced personally by the more conservative and more prestigeful members of middle and higher classes such as owners, managers and supervisors. And the more concentrated the members of a lower class are in a social environment, the easier it is for common class attitudes to spread among them and for representatives of class-oriented parties or other organizations to reach them and activate their anti-elitist sympathies.

---

[13] Claude Durand, "Positions syndicales et attitudes ouvrières à l'égard du progrès technique," *Sociologie du travail*, 4 (1960), 351.

[14] Mario Einaudi, J. Domenach and A. Garoschi, *Communism in Western Europe* (Ithaca: Cornell University Press, 1951), pp. 43–44.

[15] Mattei Dogan, "Il compartamento politico degli operai francesi," *Tempi Moderni*, 9 (April 1962), p. 26.

[16] See Lipset, *Political Man*, pp. 263–267.

But though the emergence of large social environments that are class homogeneous facilitates the spread of lower class-based movements, the same factors operating in the social structure as a whole become linked with other tendencies operating to reduce class friction. On the working class level these involve a rise in standards of living, educational levels and opportunity for upward social mobility within industry. In all countries with large Communist movements (Italy, France and Finland), within any given structural environment, the better-paid workers are more moderate in their political views than the poorer ones. Modernization reduces the sources of worker hostility to management by altering the sources of managerial behavior. These trends involve a decline in the family-owned corporation and in the domination of the economy by the *patron* type who sees himself as all powerful, and the rise within the management strata of a corporate leadership characterized by a division of labor and by the requisite of formal higher education. Accompanying the growth in large systems is a consequent increased emphasis on universalistic and achievement values, on judging individuals on the basis of their specific roles as worker or manager. As management's resistance to formalizing the labor-management relationship gradually declines, union labor's commitment to an ideological view of unionism, as distinct from a business or pragmatic view, is also reduced.

III

The New Middle Class—The Base for Employee Politics

The emergence of the new middle class — the increasingly large layer of clerks, salesmen, technicians, middle management, civil servants — has served to introduce as a major factor in the European polity a group which itself is so exposed to conflicting pressures from the left and the right that it can contribute to stabilizing class tensions. A broad middle class has a mitigating position because it can give political rewards to moderate parties and penalize extreme parties on both sides — right and left. Its members wish to obtain more for themselves and their offspring; they advocate universalistic equality in the educational and other aspects of the status-allocating mechanisms; they often uphold the extension of the welfare state. Yet their position among the relatively privileged in status and possession terms makes them supporters of political and social stability, of the politics of collective bargaining. And the larger a proportion of the electorate and the labor force formed by the new middle class, the more both the left and the right must take this group into account in determining their own policies. The political and trade union influence of the new middle class is largely thrown on the side of pressing for greater opportunity, not greater social equality. The unions of the middle class are interested in maintaining, or even extending, the income gap existing between themselves and the manual workers. They often abstain from affiliating to the same central federation as the manual unions, and many of them are led by men who back "liberal" rather than labor parties. In some countries of Europe, and in Israel in recent years, there have been strikes by unions of salaried professionals in order to widen the gap between themselves and manual workers. However, interest in income differences apart, these rapidly growing new middle classes press the political system toward consensus because as employees they favor many of the same statist policies that were long pressed by the representatives of the manual workers. Otto Kirchheimer in fact has argued that it is the very growth of these strata, who form the mass base of the "bourgeois" parties, that is largely responsible for the decline of ideology.[17]

It is important to recognize that the bourgeois parties are no longer bourgeois in the classic sense of the term. That is, the proportion of those who are self-employed, or who have close ties to the self-employed on the land or in the town, is an increasingly small part of the electorate. Most large parties now represent employees, manual or nonmanual. And while these strata differ in their orientations to many issues, they are also united on many welfare concerns. Recent Swedish political history is an apt illustration of this point. The dominant Social-Democrats were experiencing a secular decline in support, largely, according to survey analyses, because the white-collar segment of the population was growing relative to the manual sector. The party introduced a major reform, an old age pension of 65 per cent of salary, in large part because their electoral researches had suggested such a proposal would be popular not only with their traditional manual supporters but with many white-collar workers. The proposal ultimately carried in referendum, and the party increased its national vote substantially. Even more significant, perhaps, is the fact that the Liberal party, which accepted the general principle of the enlarged pension, gained enormously at the expense of the Conservatives, who took a traditional position against high taxes and against increases in the functions of the state. This suggests that the political struggles of the future will increasingly take place between parties representing the status concerns and economic interests of the two employee strata, and that the parties drawing heavily from the self-employed will continue to lose influence.

IV

Communism Resists the Trend

The dominant structural trend in Europe involves the final triumph of the values of industrial society, the end of rigid status classes derivative from a pre-industrial world, and increasing emphasis on achievement rather than ascription, on universalism rather than particularism, and on interaction among individuals in terms of the specific roles played by each rather than in terms of their diffuse generalized statuses. The heightening standard of living of the masses gives them greater market power and enables them to affect much of culture and societal taste. All these changes imply the emergence of a somewhat similar social and political culture, one which increasingly resembles

---

[17] Otto Kirchheimer, "The Waning of Opposition in Parliamentary Regimes," *Social Research*, 24 (1957), p. 148.

the first advanced industrial society to function without institutions and values derivative from a feudal past, the United States. And as has been indicated earlier, this should mean the end of class-linked severely ideological politics.

Yet there is one major force which in a number of countries has rejected this view of European social change and which has done its best to block these trends — the Communist party. It is clear that the very existence of powerful Communist movements in countries like France and Italy has been a major force perpetuating the institutions and values of the old society. In countries in which the Communists are the large working class party, in which they secure around a quarter of all votes, it has been difficult to elect a progressive government to office. If governments must secure a majority from the non-Communist three quarters of the population, they have to rely in large part on the conservative and traditionalist elements. The fact that one quarter of the electorate, constituting one half or more of the social base of the "left," have been outside of the political game inevitably gives a considerable advantage to the conservatives. In effect, by voting Communist, French and Italian workers have disfranchised themselves. Thus not only does a mass Communist party serve to fossilize the ideological orientation characteristic of a pre-industrial society among the working class, it contributes to preserving premodern orientations on the right.

A series of political developments — the revival of French Communist support recouping most of the electoral losses it suffered between 1956 and 1958 as a result of the Hungarian revolution and the Gaullist coup, the continued massive strength of Finnish Communism and the fairly continuous slow growth in the vote of the Italian Communists — each of which has occurred during long periods of prosperity and economic growth — would seem to contradict the thesis that economic growth and an improvement in social conditions enhance the prospects for political stability. In these countries economic modernization has seemingly not been followed by a reduction in ideological tensions.

The countries with large Communist parties, however, remain among the less modernized of the big nations; their industry tends to be less centralized in large plants. Thus in the mid-1950's the proportion of German employees in plants with more than 1000 workers was twice as high (38.9 per cent) as it was in France (17.6 per cent), while only 12 per cent of the employed Germans were in plants with fewer than 50 workers, in contrast to 37 per cent of the French.[18] Note too that the European countries in which Communism is strongest are among those with a relatively small proportion of their total population living in metropolitan areas. The rank-order correlation between the proportion of Communist votes in a nation and urbanization as of the early 1950's was —.61, while the comparable correlation between left extremist voting and an index of industrialization was —.76.[19] Insofar as the general

---

[18] For Germany see the *Statisches Jahrbuch,* 1959, p. 179, and for France in 1954 see Institut national de la statistique et des études economiques, *Mouvement Economique en France de 1944 à 1957* (Paris: Presses Universitaires, 1958), p. 42.

[19] William Kornhauser, *The Politics of Mass Society* (Glencoe: The Free Press, 1959),

pattern of politics, class relations and other social attitudes is affected by the degree of bureaucratization of industrial and community life, it is clear that the nations with large Communist movements are on the whole among the less developed in these respects of the nations of Europe.

The comparative analysis of the consequences of economic growth on class relationships in relatively industrialized societies is further complicated by the fact that processes endemic in such improvement affect those workers who are accustomed to the industrial system differently from those who are drawn into it. For the former, increased bureaucratization of industry should make for improvement in income and the conditions of work, and thus should serve to moderate their propensity toward extremist politics. For the latter, the experiences of dislocation inherent in social and geographic mobility, particularly the shift from rural or small-town background to crowded urban slums, and from the pace and discipline of rural work to that of the factory, may increase their potential for support of political radicalism. The need to adjust quickly to new social conditions and cultural norms makes individuals receptive to new values and ideologies which explain the sources of their discontent in revolutionary terms. It should also be noted that the decline in the number of the chronically unemployed — from 2,500,000 in 1950–1951 to around 800,000 in 1962 — in Italy may have increased rather than decreased the vote available to the extreme left. There are two empirical generalizations about the political behavior of the jobless and the formally unemployed that hold true in a number of countries. First, the unemployed are much more likely than those regularly employed to be uninformed and apathetic about politics. Their insecurity would seem to reduce their availability for any "outside" interest, including the act of voting. Second, employed individuals who report a past experience of unemployment, or areas which were once centers of high rates of unemployment, are much more likely to exhibit leftist voting propensities than those with more fortunate economic histories.[20]

The most comprehensive analysis of the sources of, and changes in, the support of a mass European Communist party, that of Erik Allardt in Finland, strongly suggests that economic growth in the less industrialized regions of a rapidly developing nation heightens the possibilities for extremist class-conscious politics. He points out that the characteristics of Communist strength in regions in which Communism has gained greatly since World War II, the north and east, are quite different from those in the areas in which it has always been strong, the south and west. The latter are the original industrialized sections of the country. His detailed statistical analyses point to the conclusion that "increase in Communist strength in all areas is related to changes which in one way or another are likely to uproot individuals."[21]

---

pp. 143, 150. The degree of urbanization was measured by the proportion of the population living in cities with over 20,000 population, while industrialization was measured by the proportion of the labor force in nonagricultural occupations.

20 Lipset, Political Man, pp. 187, 198, 236; see also S. M. Lipset, Agrarian Socialism (Berkeley: University of California Press, 1950), pp. 176–177.

21 Allardt, "Traditional and Emerging Radicalism," p. 21. In an earlier study Allardt has demonstrated that areas with the highest proportions of unemployed during the depression

Ecological analysis indicates that increases in the per capita income of the poorer regions are correlated highly with gains in Communist support. Allardt's analysis also suggests some of the factors underlying the continuation of Communist strength once attained. Stable Communist strength, that is, little fluctuation up or down, is associated with the older industrial areas in which the party has been strong since the Russian revolution and which also give strong support to the Social-Democrats. In such regions, the Communists have erected an elaborate network of party-linked voluntary associations and leisure activities, so that, as in parts of France and Italy, one almost has a functioning Communist subculture unaffected by political events.

As already noted, it is doubtful that structural changes alone will result in the decline of a mass Communist party. Where the party is strong it endeavors, as in Finland, to isolate its base from serious influence by non-Communist sources. There are plenty of social strains inherent in the situation of the worker or poor peasant to reinforce acceptance of leftist doctrine, and a mass movement can claim that any improvements are the result of its agitation. The Communist sector of the electorate will join the democratic political game in the foreseeable future only if their party, as a party, does it. There is little doubt that if the various European Communist parties were genuine national parties — that is, if their behavior were largely determined by experiences within their own countries — they would have evolved in much the same way as the European Socialist parties. And consequently, it is necessary to recognize that any predictions about their future behavior must be part of an analysis of developments within the Communist-controlled nations. If the break between the Soviet Union and China permits genuine autonomy for all national Communist parties, then the pattern of independence from Russian control emerging in Italy will probably occur elsewhere as well.

The doctrinal base for such a change in the role of Communist parties has already been advanced by various Yugoslav and Italian Communists. The former have argued that there is a world-wide pressure for socialist innovations which is inherent in the nature of large-scale capitalist economic institutions. They accept the proposition that Communist movements and ideologies as they emerged in eastern Europe and Russia are appropriate for underdeveloped countries which have not had the experience of large and legally instituted labor, political and union movements nor the experience of political freedom. The more developed nations not only can avoid the experiences of the less developed Communist societies, but they can and are moving toward socialism while preserving political freedom. It has even been suggested that in the United States, socialist adjustments and institutions exist even though Americans refuse to accept the term socialism to describe the changes occurring within their society. Co-existence is possible, say these Yugoslavs, not only because war is impossible in an atomic age, but because there is no basic cleavage between the Communist and the capitalist world, since the latter is ceasing to be capitalist in any traditional meaning of the term. Hence Communists in the developed countries will not have to make a revolution or come

---

gave the highest support to the Communists in 1951–1954. See Eric Allardt, *Social Struktur och Politisk Aktivitet* (Helsingfors: Söderstrom and Co., 1956), p. 84.

to power in their own right. By collaborating with other "progressive forces," they can hasten the emergence of socialist institutions.

The Italian Communist party has gradually modified its ideology so that some sophisticated observers would now describe it as a left social-democratic rather than a Communist party. Like the Yugoslav party, it no longer sees a fundamental dichotomy between capitalism and socialism, but rather argues that "there exists in the capitalist world today an urge towards structural reforms and to reforms of a socialist nature, which is related to economic progress and the new expansion of the productive forces." [22] And its leader, Palmiro Togliatti, has gone on to argue the need to "correct" Lenin's position that "bourgeois state apparatus cannot be used for building a socialist society," in the light of "the changes which have taken place and which are still in the process of being realized in the world." It denies the need for one-party dictatorship in Italy, and it has accepted Italian membership in the Common Market. Communist municipal office-holders work closely with business groups in fostering the interests of their cities, and party-controlled labor unions play a somewhat more responsible role in collective bargaining and Italian life generally than has been true for Communist unions in the past. The Chinese Communists correctly point to the Italian party as the foremost example of reformist heresies among the nongovernmental parties. If the Italian electorate has not turned away from the Communists, the Communists have moved to the right. Thus the effect of a reduction in social strains among sections of the Italian workers may be reflected in the changed behavior of their party and unions.

But if the experiences and the behavior of the Italian party suggest an adaptation to the emergence of stable political institutions and economic modernization in Italy, the French Communist party simply has not behaved in the same way and its policies seemingly challenge the underlying interpretation here. The French party also had to react to the end of Soviet domination of party life and to economic modernization in France. But where the Italian party and its union federation, the CGIL, modified their programs and explicitly decided to cooperate "with what they termed the representatives of neo-capitalism," the French party refused. It continued to insist that capitalism could not reform itself, that the workers could not make long-term improvements in the social situation, and that the unions must remain primarily political instruments. The Italian party decided to join forces with modernization, the French party to resist it. The reasons for the differences between the parties are complex and I cannot detail them here. Briefly, they would seem to relate to the fact that the French party was Stalinized and proletarianized in its leadership and membership during the 1930's and 1940's, while Fascism enabled the Italian party to escape some of these consequences; after 1944 it recruited and retained many non-Stalinist intellectuals in its organizations. Palmiro Togliatti, the leader of the Italian party, though an official of the Comintern during the 1930's, more closely resembles the pre-Stalin leaders of

---

[22] Quoted in The Editorial Department of Hongqi, *More on the Differences between Comrade Togliatti and Us* (Peking: Foreign Languages Press, 1963), p. 13.

Communism than those like Maurice Thorez, who won and maintained leadership as a result of following Stalin's every turn. The variations in the Italian and French political systems have meant that elected local Communists have had more real power and involvement in running municipalities and other institutions in Italy than in France. The Italian Socialists, in part because of their long and mutual Fascist experience, have been much less hostile to the Communists than have been the French Socialists. Hence the Italian party has never been as isolated from non-Communists as the French. These differences between the French and Italian Communist parties may be related to the facts that the Italian party has lost fewer members than the French (both parties have lost a considerable portion of their membership as compared with their post-war high point), and that the Italian party has done better at the polls.

Communist parties without a Moscow-centered world party would be like national Roman Catholic churches without a pope, without the need to follow a dogma decreed from a single source. And many observers predict that the individual parties will follow the road of Protestantism, of deviation, of variation, of adjustment to particular national conditions, much as the Social-Democrats did half a century or more earlier. Those parties which operate within democratic societies will be under constant pressure to modify their totalitarian structures, as in fact the Italian party seems to be beginning to do.

Given the history of the Communist movement, the training which its leaders have received in totalitarian methods and the use of conscious deception, the acceptance (even though now critical) of the experiences of one-party regimes as a positive model, no one who cares about freedom can accept a Communist party as an equal player in a parliamentary game. On the other hand, the possibility that changes in the Communist world are permitting sufficient independence and variations among Communist parties to allow some of them to react to the forces which press them to act as regular participants within political democracies should not be ignored. The more positively involved are Communists and their *followers* in a political system which in fact is paying off socially and economically,. the more difficult it will be for a given Communist party to renew an alienated stance among its supporters should the leadership decide to do so. Hence the possibility may be held out that the vicious circle of Communist-reactionary resistance to modernization in Latin-Europe may be breaking down, not only as a result of the decline of the reactionary groups, but because of changes within Communism. Even Communism may be yielding to the pressures making for a decline of ideology and of class war.

V

Continuing Sources of Strain

There are many sources of political strain within stable democratic societies. The stratification systems of all inherently involve a grossly inequalitarian distribution of status, income and power. Even the very "affluent" United States contains a large minority living in poverty by its own standards. A look at consumption standards for Europe finds that very large minorities or majorities in different European countries still lack many items which are available to all but a few in the United States. Status inequality would seem to be experienced as punitive by the lower classes in all systems. But while all societies present some ideological justification for enduring consumption and status inequalities, the concept of mass citizenship that arose with the industrial revolution undermines the stability of class systems because it implies, as T. H. Marshall put it, that "all are equal with respect to the rights and duties with which the status is endowed." [23] Hence he argues that modern democratic industrial society is historically unique in seeking to sustain a system of contradictory stratification values. All previous societies had class systems that assumed inequality, but they also denied citizenship to all except a small elite. Once full and equal political (manhood suffrage) and economic (trade union organization) citizenship was established, the equalitarian emphasis inherent in the concept sustains a successful and continuing attack on many aspects of inequality. Much of democratic politics involves the efforts of the lower strata to equalize the conditions of existence and opportunity.

The tension between equality and inequality is endemic in modern industrial democratic society. The dominant strata will continue the attempt to institutionalize their privileges, to find means to pass on to their kin and offspring the privileges they have gained. This conflict, however, does not mean that one or the other tendency must triumph, or that the strain will destroy or even necessarily weaken the social fabric. The predominant character of modern industrial democracy, as a free and evolving society, is in part a result of the chronic tensions between the inherent pressures toward inequality and the endemic emphasis in democracy on equality.

The current wave of writings that somehow see in the growth of affluence in the western world the emergence of a peaceful social utopia — which will not require continued political struggle between representatives of the haves and of the have-nots — ignores the extent to which the content of these very concepts changes as society evolves. As Marshall has pointed out, ever since the beginning of the industrial revolution almost every generation proclaimed a social revolution to elevate the lower strata. "From the 1880's to the 1940's people were constantly expressing amazement at the social transformation witnessed in their lifetime, oblivious of the fact that, in this series of outbursts of self-congratulation, the glorious achievements of the past became the squalid heritage of the present." [24]

But in spite of the progress leading one generation to proclaim the significance of recent social improvements, only a few years later others are arguing that the present conditions of the poor, of the lowly, are intolerable, that they cannot possibly be tolerated by free men who believe in equality. And as Marshall indicates, such phenomena do not "mean that the progress which men thought they made was illusory. It means that the standards by which that progress was assessed were constantly rising, and that ever deeper probing

---

[23] T. H. Marshall, *Sociology at the Crossroads* (London, 1963), p. 87.
[24] *Ibid.*, p. 268.

into the social situation kept revealing new horrors which had previously been concealed from view." [25] One may ask with Marshall whether the concept of the affluent society will have any longer life than some of its predecessors.

In large measure, the problem of the lower strata is now seen as that of "cultural deprivation." It is clear that in all countries, variation in participation in the intellectual culture serves to negate the dream of equal opportunity for all to mount the educational ladder; consequently, access to the summits of the occupational structure is still grossly restricted. In Sweden, for example, in spite of thirty years of Social-Democratic government providing free access to universities together with state bursaries, the proportion of working class children taking advantage of such opportunities has hardly risen. Few commodities are distributed as unequally in Europe as high school and university education. The simple improvement in economic standards of living, at least at its present pace, does little to reduce the considerable advantages held by the culturally privileged strata to perpetuate their families in an equally advantaged position. And socialist parties in a number of countries are beginning to look for ways to enhance the educational and cultural aspirations of lower class youth. Here, then, is the most recent example of the conflict between the principles of equality inherent in citizenship and the forces endemic to complex stratified society that serve to maintain or erect cultural barriers between the classes. The latter operate as a consequence of the differential distributions of rewards and access to culture, and must be combatted continually if they are not to dominate.

In conclusion, this survey of economic and social developments accompanying the modernization of European society has shown compelling evidence for the moderation of ideological differences in Europe as a consequence of the increasing affluence of European nations, the attainment of economic as well as political citizenship by the workers, the gradual absorption and assimilation of the remnants of European society still living in feudal or otherwise underdeveloped economic and social conditions. The changes in parties of the left, especially Communist parties, to a more moderate orientation toward capitalist society and class conflict have been shown to be also related to broad changes in the international Communist world, as exemplified by the thesis of polycentrism and the reinterpretation of Marxism concerning the possibility of a rapprochement with capitalism. But it has also been pointed out that industrialization does not automatically remove sources of tension. These sources are endemic to an industrial society which permits a relatively open struggle for the fruits of individual effort and which does not automatically give access to opportunity for individual advancement to those on the lower rungs of the status ladder. Finally, it has been shown that much of the anachronistic ideological politics of the "Poujadist" left and right is a response to anachronistic orientations and forms of industrial organization still present in some sectors of European society, as among some peasants and small businessmen in France, or as a result of the preservation of outmoded forms of production and extraction, as in Britain and Belgium. In the latter two nations ideological

---

[25] T. H. Marshall, *Sociology at the Crossroads* (London, 1963), pp. 269–270.

left working class politics, in part, has taken the form of opposition to modernization which might threaten the present security of some categories of workers
and their unions in the interests of improvement of the total economy. In the
long run, however, the remaining bases of ideologically intransigent politics
will continue to decline due to the contradictions between reality and their
definition of the situation, and because of the irrelevance of their call to action
in terms of a situation which will no longer exist.

As a final comment, I would note that not only do class conflicts over issues
related to division of the total economic pie, influence over various institutions,
symbolic status and opportunity, continue in the absence of *weltanschauungen,*
but that the decline of such total ideologies does *not* mean the end of ideology.
Clearly, commitment to the politics of pragmatism, to the rules of the game
of collective bargaining, to gradual change whether in the direction favored
by the left or the right, to opposition both to an all powerful central state and
to *laissez-faire* constitutes the component parts of an ideology. The "agreement
on fundamentals," the political consensus of western society, now increasingly
has come to include a position on matters which once sharply separated the
left from the right. And this ideological agreement, which might best be
described as "conservative socialism," has become *the* ideology of the major
parties in the developed states of Europe and America. As such it leaves its
advocates in sharp disagreement with the relatively small groups of radical
rightists and leftists at home, and at a disadvantage in efforts to foster different
variants of this doctrine in the less affluent parts of the world.

30. Decline of Ideology: A Dissent and an Interpretation

JOSEPH LaPALOMBARA

Professor LaPalombara asserts that one cannot speak of an "end of ideology" when what has taken place is merely the disillusionment of Marxist intellectuals and a change in socialist rhetoric. He does not accept the definition of ideology used by Lipset, and does not wish to see ideology—in Marxist fashion—treated as a dependent variable. Taking the example of Italy, he indicates that here ideology has recently been on the increase rather than on the decline.

Introduction

With increasing frequency and self-assurance, the scientific objectivity of American social science is proclaimed by some of its prominent practitioners. Various explanations are offered for the onset of social science's Golden Age, but central to most of them is the claim that modern social science has managed to resolve Mannheim's Paradox, namely, that in the pursuit of the truth the social scientist himself is handicapped by the narrow focus and distortions implicit in ideological thought. Presumably, the social scientist can now probe any aspect of human organization and behavior as dispassionately as physical scientists observe the structure of the atom or chemical reactions. For this reason, it is claimed by some that the ideologically liberated social scientists — at least in the United States — can expect to be co-opted into the Scientific Culture, or that segment of society that is presumably aloof from and disdainful toward the moralistic speculations and the tender-heartedness of the literary intellectuals.

The behavioral "revolution" in political science may have run its course, but it has left in its wake both obscurantist criticisms of empiricism, on the one hand, and, on the other hand, an unquestioning belief in "science." Quite often the latter belief is not merely antihistorical but also uncritical about the extent to which empirical observations can be colored by the orientation to values that one seeks to control in rigorous empirical research.

The claims of modern social scientists are greatly buttressed by the views of Talcott Parsons. In response to criticisms of his work offered by a group of scholars at Cornell University, Parsons asserts that the "breakthrough" in the behavioral sciences occurred in the United States in part because of that country's intellectual openness and receptivity. A critical cause of this latter quality, according to Parsons, is the American intellectual's ". . . relative immunity to the pressure to put problem in an ideological context," and thus

---

SOURCE: Reprinted by permission from *The American Political Science Review*, LX (March 1966), pp. 5–16. Footnotes are abridged.

his refusal to worry too much about "global" problems.[1] For Parsons, science and ideology are simply incompatible concepts.

This is not the place to explore the ideological underpinnings of Parsons' formulations, particularly since the reader can turn for this to Andrew Hacker's somewhat polemical but nevertheless extremely cogent analysis (which Parsons chooses essentially to evade). It is worthwhile noting, however, that Parsons' refusal to be concerned with the "global" questions, and his claims for the scientific objectivity of his emerging general theory, underpin the claims of other social scientists who extol the "scientific" qualities of their disciplines.

One interesting extrapolation from these assumptions about social science objectivity, and of the essential incompatibility of social science and normative orientations, is found in the so-called "decline of ideology" literature. Presumably, social-scientific generalizations have been made about the waning of ideology. The irony attaching to arguments in and against these "findings" is that they have themselves taken on many of the undeniable earmarks of *ideological* conflict. Thus, I wish to acknowledge that my own effort in this paper may be in part — and quite properly — identified as ideological. Indeed, the underlying theme of my argument here is that we have not, in fact, resolved the Mannheim Paradox and that perhaps the future of social science will be better served if we acknowledge this fact and face up to its intellectual and theoretical implications.

More particularly, however, I wish to deal in this paper with these topics: (1) what it is that is meant when social scientists write about the "decline of ideology"; (2) an examination of some empirical evidence from the West that strongly challenges some of the "findings" of these writers; and (3) a somewhat tentative ideological-social scientific interpretation of what these writings may represent in contemporary American society.

The Meaning of Ideology

It is abundantly clear that those who write about ideology's decline, with few exceptions,[2] intend a pejorative denotation and connotation of the term. Taking their lead from Mannheim, these writers contend that ideological thought means at least that such ideas are "distorted," in the sense that they lack "congruence" with reality. Beyond this, however, they seem to support the Mannheim view that the lack of congruence may be either emotionally

---

[1] Talcott Parsons, "The Point of View of the Author," in Max Black (ed.), *The Social Theories of Talcott Parsons* (Englewood Cliffs, N. J., 1962), pp. 313–315, 360–362.

[2] One exception would be Otto Kirchheimer, who was greatly concerned about the possible consequences of, say, the emergence of the "catch-all" political party in a country like the West German Republic. See his, "The Transformation of the European Party System," in Joseph LaPalombara and Myron Weiner (eds.), *Political Parties and Political Development* (Princeton, 1966). *Cf.* his, "The Waning of Opposition in Parliamentary Regimes," *Social Research* 24 (1957), pp. 127–156. I am uncertain as to whether what Kirchheimer describes is a decline of ideology, but it is noteworthy that he was one of those who didn't think that what he saw was "good" for Western societies.

determined, and therefore the result of subconscious forces, or "conscious deception, where ideology is to be interpreted as a purposeful lie." [3]

It can be argued, of course, that one is free to define ideology as it happens to suit one's mood or purpose, and we have a vast literature demonstrating the considerable range of meaning that can be assigned to the concept.[4] But if one elects a definition that is based too heavily on the notion of wilful or unintended deception or distortion, much of what social scientists generally identify as ideological would simply have to be ignored, or called something else. Moreover, if the central purpose of the analysis is to demonstrate something as significant as ideology's decline, it seems to me to be the essence of intellectual legerdemain, or downright slovenliness, to leave the definition of ideology vague, or to confuse the demonstrable decline of something one finds objectionable with presumably empirical generalizations about the gradual disappearance of something which is much broader in meaning.

My usage of ideology is quite close to the definition suggested by L. H. Garstin, in that it involves a philosophy of history, a view of man's present place in it, some estimate of probable lines of future development, and a set of prescriptions regarding how to hasten, retard, and/or modify that developmental direction.[5] While the concept, ideology, is certainly one of the most elusive in our vocabulary, we can say about it that, beyond the above, it tends to specify a set of values that are more or less coherent and that it seeks to link given patterns of action to the achievement or maintenance of a future, or existing, state of affairs. What makes such formulations of particular interest to political scientists is that ideologies frequently insist that in order to achieve or maintain desired ends, deemed to be morally superior and therefore desirable for the entire collectivity, public authority is expected to intervene.

It is in this broad sense, then, that I am using the concept in this paper. This being the case, several caveats are in order. For example, an ideology may or may not be dogmatic; a relative lack of dogmatism does not necessarily make a given set of cognitions, preferences, expectations and prescriptions any the less ideological. An ideology may or may not be utopian. I assume that conservative movements of the last century or two, as well as the so-called

---

[3] Karl Mannheim, *Ideology and Utopia* (London, 1936), pp. 175–176. Mannheim's second chapter in this volume, pp. 49–96, from which the volume's title is derived, is of course the classic statement of the origins of the term "ideology," its particular and general formulations, its relationship to Marxism and its catalytic impact on the sociology of knowledge.

[4] The best recent short review of the literature that I have seen is Joseph J. Spengler, "Theory, Ideology, Non-Economic Values, and Politico-Economic Development," in Ralph Braibanti and J. J. Spengler (eds.), *Tradition, Values and Socio-Economic Development* (Durham, 1961), pp. 3–56, and esp. Part V.

[5] L. H. Garstin, *Each Age Is a Dream: A Study in Ideologies* (New York, 1954), p. 3. I recognise that my usage here is quite broad and that it may be typical of what my friend, Giovanni Sartori, scores as the American tendency to assign to the concept, ideology, a very wide meaning, "without limits." Sartori argues that such definitions are "heuristically sterile and operationally fruitless" (personal communication to the author, November 16, 1965). Sartori may or may not be right: my point here is simply to break away from the extremely narrow definition implied in the "decline of ideology" literature.

Radical Right in the United States at present have strong ideological dimensions, notwithstanding their vociferous denials of utopias. Similarly, Catholicism is no less ideological in many of its political dimensions by reason of its rejection of the Enlightenment's assumptions concerning man's perfectability. An ideology may or may not be attuned to the claimed rationality of modern science; the place of scientific thought in ideological formulations is an empirical question that should not be begged by the assumption that science and ideology are incompatible. Technocrats and others who enshrine the Managerial Society certainly engage in the most fundamental kind of ideological reasoning. Ideology may or may not emphasize rhetoric or flamboyant verbal formulations. The language of ideology is also an empirical question; it will surely be strongly influenced by the socio-historical context in which it evolves, and a decline or, better, change in rhetoric should not be confused with a decline in ideology itself. Finally, an ideology may or may not be believed by those who articulate it. Whether an ideology is cynically used as a weapon or instrument of control; whether it emanates from subconscious needs or drives or is rationally formulated and incorporated into one's belief system; indeed, whether it is narrowly or widely, publicly or privately shared with third persons are also legitimate and fascinating questions that require careful investigation rather than a priori answers.

It seems to me that the "decline of ideology" writers [6] commit one or more of all of the errors implied above. For example, ideology is said to apply to passionately articulated prescriptions, evidently not to those which manifest calm rationality. As Daniel Bell puts it, "ideology is the conversion of ideas into social levers. . . . What gives ideology its force is its passion." [7] Lipset, in his personal postscript on ideology's passing, tells us that "Democracy in the Western world has been undergoing some important changes as serious intellectual conflicts among groups representing different values have declined sharply." [8] In the case of Aron, his passionate and intemperate attacks on the ideas of certain French intellectuals are so extreme as to represent not so much social science analysis as they do a fascinating example of the rhetorical aspect of ideological exchange.[9]

It seems equally apparent that what these writers mean by ideology is not any given set of values, beliefs, preferences, expectations and prescriptions regarding society but that *particular* set that we may variously associate with

---

[6] I refer here primarily to the following: Raymond Aron, "Fin de l'age ideologique?" in T. W. Adorno and W. Dicks (eds.), *Sociologica* (Frankfurt, 1955), pp. 219–233; R. Aron, *The Opium of the Intellectuals* (New York, 1962); Talcott Parsons, "An Approach to the Sociology of Knowledge," *Transactions of the Fourth World Congress of Sociology* (Milan and Stresa, 1959), pp. 25–49; Edward Shils, "The End of Ideology?" *Encounter* 5 (November, 1955), 52–58; S. M. Lipset, *Political Man* (Garden City, 1960), pp. 403–417; Daniel Bell, *The End of Ideology* (Glencoe, Ill., 1960), esp. pp. 369–375; and S. M. Lipset, "The Changing Class Structure and Contemporary European Politics," *Daedalus* 93 (Winter, 1964), 271–303.

[7] Daniel Bell, *The End of Ideology* (Glencoe, Ill., 1960), pp. 370, 371.

[8] S. M. Lipset, *Political Man* (Garden City, 1960), p. 403.

[9] R. Aron, *The Opium of the Intellectuals* (New York, 1962).

Orthodox Marxism, "Scientific Socialism," Bolshevism, Maoism, or in any case with strongly held and dogmatically articulated ideas regarding class conflict and revolution. Thus, "the exhaustion of political ideas in the West" refers to that particular case involving the disillusionment experienced by Marxist intellectuals when it became apparent that many of Marx's predictions were simply not borne out, and when the outrages of the Stalinist regime were publicly revealed. We need not document the evidence for the widespread disillusionment, or for the agonizing ideological reappraisals to which it has led. But, as I shall briefly document below, to limit the meaning of ideology to absolute utopias, to concentrate one's analytical attention upon what some Marxian socialist may be up to, and to equate certain changes in rhetoric with ideological decline is to narrow the meaning of the central concept to the point where it has very limited utility for the social scientist.

The writers I have in mind also seem to see ideology as a dependent phenomenon, whose rise and fall is conditioned by a number of ecological factors, most of them economic. This curious determinism suggests that if there are marked differences in poverty and wealth — or in life styles — ideology emerges; if these differences are reduced, ideology (i.e., class-conflict ideology) declines. Thus, Lipset tells us that "Ideological passion may no longer be necessary to sustain the class struggle within stable and affluent democracies."[10] At another place he says, "As differences in style of life are reduced, so are the tensions of stratification. And increased education enhances the propensity of different groups to 'tolerate' each other, to accept the complex idea that truth and error are not necessarily on one side."[11]

These writers are far too sophisticated to suggest that there is a simple correlation between increases in economic productivity or distribution and decline of ideology. They recognize, for example, that religious and other cleavages may cut against tendencies toward ideological quiescence. Nevertheless, I came away from this literature with the uncomfortable impression that these writers claim that moral imperatives, differences of opinion regarding the "good life," and opposing formulations regarding public policy must necessarily give way before the avalanche of popular education, the mass media and greater and greater numbers of washing machines, automobiles and television sets. How else judge the assertion — as clearly debatable as it is subjective and ideological — that ideology is in decline because "the fundamental problems of the Industrial Revolution have been solved."[12]

There are certainly thousands of European intellectuals as well as tens of millions of other Europeans, who would react to the last quoted statement sardonically, or in sheer disbelief.

Since the generalizations about ideology's alleged decline apply to the West, and therefore to Europe as well as the North American continent, it may be instructive to look at one of these countries, Italy, to see exactly how accurate

---

[10] S. M. Lipset, *Political Man* (Garden City, 1960), p. 407.

[11] S. M. Lipset, "The Changing Class Structure and Contemporary European Politics," *Daedalus* 93 (Winter, 1964), p. 272.

[12] S. M. Lipset, *Political Man* (Garden City, 1960), p. 406.

these generalizations are. It should be noted that the time span I will consider are the years since World War II; my point will be that since generalizations for such a short period are so manifestly inaccurate, it is useless to lend any kind of serious attention to prognostications about where we will be a century or two from now. Keynes, I believe, authored the most appropriate aphorism about the "long run."

Ideology in Italy

The points I wish to stress about Italy can be briefly stated, although their detailed documentation would require more space than is available here. First, notwithstanding the existence within the Italian Communist party of both a "crisis of intellectuals" and a "crisis of ideology," there has recently occurred within that party a new ferment of ideas which in a certain sense has actually enriched rather than diminished attention to ideology. Second, if one bothers to look away from the Communist party (P.C.I.) and toward Christian Democracy (D.C.), it is possible to conclude that ideology in the latter is actually on the upswing. Third, and following from these two observations, the so-called decline-of-ideology theory is simply not valid for the Italian case.[13]

The Italian Communist Party

The most frequent — and most wishful — interpretation of P.C.I. is that it is moving in a reformist direction that will eventuate in its accepting the existing system and limiting its demands to social, political and economic manipulations designed to effect needed, but not revolutionary, reforms from time to time. This view of the party is superficial in the sense that "reformism" dates back to 1944 when Palmiro Togliatti returned from Moscow articulating a moderate line which was as unnerving as it was unexpected. This line was carefully followed in the Constituent Assembly, which drafted the Italian Constitution, and in this broad sense the party has been "reformist" throughout the postwar years.

What has changed in recent years is neither the party's will to power nor its commitment to a basically socialist ideology. Rather, I would say that the changes include: (1) the party's use of extreme rhetoric; (2) its now openly expressed polycentrist view regarding the nature of the international socialist or communist movement; and (3) the party's notions regarding how the class struggle should be conducted in contemporary Italy. The debates and agoniz-

---

[13] A number of colleagues who were good enough to read this manuscript urge that the empirical evidence challenging the "decline" thesis should not be limited to Italy. Roger Masters and Giovanni Sartori point out, for example, that the United States would provide additional supportive evidence. Nils Elvander notes that Tingsten himself, in his analyses of the Swedish Social Democratic Party, became "caught up in the intense struggle against the 'dead' ideology of the party, and when the battle was over he went on declaring ideology dead, not being able to see that it was revitalized again and again" (personal communication to the author, December 19, 1964). I am aware of this additional evidence and simply note that the Italian case is used here as an illustrative rather than exhaustive example.

ing reappraisals that the party has experienced in recent years must be construed not as a sign of ideological decay but, rather, as a sign of ideological vigor which is largely responsible for the party's steady and increasing attraction at the polls.

The list of P.C.I. errors in prognosticating about Italian society is long and impressive; it led observers at Bologna not long ago to comment on what a "grotesque assumption" was the party's belief that only it possessed a scientifically infallible method for analyzing reality. The errors included such things as predictions about the comparative rate of economic growth in Communist and free countries, expectations regarding the European Common Market, impending economic crises in capitalistic countries, etc. One observer of this pattern of inaccurate prognosticating notes that it was not until the middle of 1961 that the "Communists awoke from their dogmatic dream and almost in a flash learned that their judgments did not correspond to reality."[14]

The truth is that the alarm had sounded for P.C.I. several years before, and precisely at the VII Party Congress of 1956. It was here that the party's activities in the underdeveloped South first received a public airing. The critics of the party's "Movimento di Rinascita" in southern Italy openly noted that the movement was in crisis and that the crisis grew out of the party's failure to adapt ideology and consequently policy to the concrete conditions of Southern Italy. Members of the party itself scored it for its "sterile and negative" approach to national problems, for its rigid and doctrinaire adherence to fixed schemes, for its permitting the movement to lose whatever dynamism it may have had in earlier years.

Both Togliatti and Giorgio Amendola (the latter considered the leader of the P.C.I's "reformist" wing) urged that the party must be flexible and overcome the inertia of pat formulations. They admitted that both the party and its trade union wing seemed to be unprepared to confront the great changes in local conditions that had occurred in the years since 1945. It is possible that, within the party's secret confines, this kind of self-appraisal had begun before 1956, but in those earlier days one would not have expected Togliatti to say publicly that the party was not keeping up with basic social and economic transformations in Italy or that it was necessary for that organization to engage in the kind of total re-examination that will finally sweep away "ancient and recent moldiness that impede the action of P.C.I. [15]

To be sure, removing ideological mold is not easy for Communists, who tend to be ultra-intellectual in a society where intellectual elegance is highly prized. One can therefore note in the party's literature the care — and the web-like logic — with which recent changes are reconciled with Marx and Lenin, and particularly with the writings of Antonio Gramsci, the intellectual fountainhead of Italian Communism, and a formidable dialectician whose work is too little known in the English-speaking world. Nevertheless, the party's public

---

[14] G. Tamburrano, "Lo Sviluppo del capitalismo e la crisi teorica dei comunisti italiani," *Tempi Moderni*, 5 (July–September, 1962), p. 22.

[15] Abdon Alinovi, "Problemi della politica comunista nel Mezzogiorno," *Critica Marxista*, 1 (July–August, 1963), 4–8.

posture has changed radically. The most recent and important indication of this change is the party's decision to seek alliances with elements of the middle class — peasants, small landowners, artisans, small and medium industrialists and even with entrepreneurs who are not involved with industrial monopolies. The importance of this change should be strongly emphasized; the P.C.I. has managed in one stroke to shift largely to monopoly capitalism all of the attacks that had previously been leveled against an allegedly retrograde, decadent bourgeoisie. The party's open strategy is to attract to its ranks the mushrooming members of the middle and tertiary strata that large-scale industrial development tends to proliferate. The fire of opposition is no longer directed against proprietors in general but against the monopolists who allegedly exploit all others in society, who are oppressive, and who increase the degree of imbalance or disequilibrium in the social system.

This, then, is not the party of the Stalin Era. Not many who followed the antics of P.C.I. up to the Hungarian Rebellion would have predicted changes in orientation such as the ones so briefly summarized. The fascinating question to pose here, however, is whether what has happened represents a *decline* in P.C.I. ideology, or something else. If by decline is meant the abandonment of some of the rhetoric, the verbal symbols, the predictions and expectations voiced until the late fifties, there seems little doubt about the validity of such a judgment, although the more appropriate word would be *change*. However, if by decline is meant that P.C.I. is becoming bourgeois or "social-democratized," or that it is abandoning any commitment to ideological formulations, I believe one should hesitate before leaping to such a conclusion. As Palmiro Togliatti significantly put it, "There is no experience regarding the way in which the battle for socialism can or must be waged in a regime of advanced monopolistic state capitalism . . . There do not even exist explicit prescriptions in the classics of our doctrine."[16]

Communist leaders who spearhead this reappraisal are not calling for ideological retreat but, rather, for a concerted search for new ideological underpinnings for party policies and actions. In noting that Marxism offers, at best, vague guides to party behavior in modern Italian society, these leaders seem to me to be a long way from abandoning such key concepts as class, dialectical conflict, the exploitative nature of monopoly capitalism, and the fundamental need for effecting structural — not mild, reformist — changes in the social system. They, and the millions of Italians who support them at the polls, are far from concluding, if this is the acid test for the inclination toward ideological decline, that the problems created by the Industrial Revolution have been largely solved.

The effort to attune the party's ideology to present Italian realities is a complementary side of the vigorous campaign for polycentrism which the party has been conducting within the international communist movement. Beginning in 1956, P.C.I. frankly asserted that the Soviet model could no longer be a specific guide to Communist parties in every country and that it would be

---

[16] G. Tamburrano, "Lo Sviluppo del capitalismo e la crisi teorica dei comunisti italiani," *Tempi Moderni*, 5 (July–September 1962), p. 69.

necessary to find a "national path to socialism." Togliatti made this point forcefully in the last book he published before his death.[17] In November, 1961, the P.C.I. Secretariat formulated a resolution which said in part that "There do not exist and there cannot exist either a guiding party or state or one or more instances of centralized direction of the international Communist movement. Under existing conditions there must be and there must increasingly be a great articulation of the movement in a context of full independence of individual parties."[18]

These are brave words, and it is still much too early to conclude with any confidence what the result of the P.C.I.'s campaign will be. What is important is the apparent P.C.I. conviction that it can come up with a new strategy — a new formula for achieving power — for Communist parties operating in Western European and other countries of advanced capitalism. It is important to bear in mind that, in doing this, the party purports to be able to provide an up-dated ideological rationale for action. Some of the "moldiness" of "Scientific Socialism" has certainly been scraped away. What remains, coupled with some of the newer ideas currently in ferment, amounts to much more ideology than one might detect from the simple notation that the language of the late forties and early fifties is no longer in vogue.

Italian Christian Democracy

The genius of Alcide DeGasperi is that for a decade following the birth of the Italian Republic he was able to hold together within the Christian Democratic party (D.C.) strongly opposed ideological factions that managed to play down ideology in the interest of holding on to power. This was no mean achievement. Although the popular image of the D.C. is that of an opportunistic, anti-ideological "brokerage" party, the truth is that, from the outset, strong factions that would have emphasized ideology, even at the risk of splitting the party, had to be suppressed or defeated. DeGasperi's hegemonic control of the organization was secured only after he had managed to beat down early competition for leadership emanating from such ideologues as Giuseppe Dossetti, Amintore Fanfani and Giovanni Gronchi. One might well conclude that, in an age of alleged ideological decline and after a decade of enjoying the many fruits of political power, ideology would have become a much less salient issue within the D.C.

Exactly the opposite tendency is apparent, however. Since the death of DeGasperi, and the advent of Fanfani as a major party leader in 1954, the ideological debate has not only intensified but has also broken into public view, revealing a party organization under deep internal stress. I believe that the facts will clearly demonstrate that since that date the role of ideology within the D.C. has actually increased rather than diminished, and a few central occurrences will serve to bear out this conclusion.

In September, 1961, the D.C. held at San Pellegrino the first of three

---

[17] Palmiro Togliatti, *Il Partito Comunisto Italiano* (Rome, 1961), p. 181.
[18] See "Problemi del dibattito tra partiti comunisti," *ibid.*, p. 16.

annual "ideological" conventions. They represented a long and successful effort on the part of those in the party who had fought for making the party ideologically coherent, something more than the "brokerage" party the D.C. had been under DeGasperi's leadership. Looming over these proceedings were two of the party perennial dilemmas: First, to what extent should the D.C., a party drawing much of its strength from the political right, articulate a left-wing ideology as a guide to policy? Second, how much ideological freedom could the party express *vis-à-vis* a Catholic Church to which it must necessarily remain fairly closely tied? Those who favored stronger articulation of a coherent left-wing ideology were strongly spurred by an undeniable gradual movement to the left by the Italian electorate, by the increasing willingness of the Italian Socialist party to consider active coalition with the D.C., and certainly not least by the kinds of ideological changes in the Vatican triggered by the innovating papacy of John XXIII.

Speakers at the conferences reviewed the party's ideological history, noting that at war's end it appeared that the party would lead the country left and that, in those years, DeGasperi himself stated that the old order based on the domination of rural landowners and urban industrialists would not remain intact. But it was lamented that whenever the D.C. confronted issues concerning which the party's ideology seemingly required socialist solutions, ideology was arrested in favor of not pushing to the breaking point the ideological centrifugal tendencies within the organization. As Franco Malfatti, one of the followers of Giuseppe Dossetti and Amintore Fanfani, points out, the revolutionary tone of early D.C. pronouncements was gradually transformed into the muted notes of a purely formalistic democracy and of a great concentration of governmental power at Rome.[19]

As the D.C. moved self-consciously toward the "Opening to the Left" which would bring the Socialists into the government, the party's ideologues would no longer accept the DeGasperi formula whereby all concern about or dedication to ideology was to be obscured in favor of the overriding value of party unity. At San Pellegrino, Malfatti put the new posture of the ideologues pointedly. "The problem of [party] unity," he said, "is a great one of fundamental importance but it is also a problem that runs the risk of losing all its value if used as a sedative, or as the Hymn of Garibaldi, every time there is conflict between clerical and anti-clerical elements."[20] If the party wished to be free of all internal ideological conflict, nothing would remain of it except an agreement "to hold power for power's sake."

According to Achille Ardigò, a sociologist and long-time member of the party's national executive committee, the major milestones in the D.C.'s ideological evolution are the following: First, the development of the concept of the political autonomy of Catholics, unconstrained by specific direction by

---

19 Franco M. Malfatti, "La Democrazia Cristiana nelle sue affermazioni programmatiche dalla sua ricostruzione ad oggi," in *Il Convegno di San Pellegrino: Atti del I Convegno di Studi della D. C.* (Rome, 1962), pp. 325–841.

20 Franco M. Malfatti, "L'Unità della D. C. e il problema delle tendenze," *Cronache Sociali*, 3 (February 15, 1949), p. 15.

clerical forces. Second, the growth of the idea of the autonomous function of intermediate groups (such as family, community and social class) against the excesses of the centralizing, modern liberal state. Third, the defense and consolidation of liberty, in a government of laws, through an alliance of the democratic forces of the nation against political and ideological extremes. Fourth, the materialization of the ideology of the "new party" led by Amintore Fanfani. Finally, the emergence of a new concept of the state as an artifice of harmonious and planned development — the idea of the state as an instrument of dynamic intervention in the economic sphere and of the modification of the rights of property in favor of the well-being of the collectivity. It is the evolution of this last, self-consciously ideological stage that permitted the party's recent shift to the left and the acceptance of coalition with the Socialists.

One can identify many reasons for this shift to the left, including Italian voting patterns that have clearly led the D.C. in this direction. To the many social and economic pressures leading to the emergence of a Catholic Socialism, one would have to add the liberating impact of John XXIII's revolutionary encyclical, *Mater et Magistra*. In the light of this radical departure from the conservative, often reactionary, political utterances of Pius XII, it is easy to understand why the D.C. left should be spurred to a more purposeful and ideologically rationalized attack on Italian society's ills.

It is important to recognize that the San Pellegrino meetings mean not that the D.C. has moved left on a purely opportunistic basis, but, rather, on the basis of a "rediscovery" of the ideological formulations laid down by Dossetti and others in the late forties. To be sure the current ideology is not socialism and, indeed, leaders like Aldo Moro have been careful to distinguish D.C. ideology from socialism and communism. Nevertheless, the D.C. is today a dramatically less catch-all party than it was under DeGasperi. It now has a somewhat official and publicly articulated ideology. If ideology is in fact in significant decline elsewhere in Europe,[21] Italy will certainly have to be excepted from such easy generalizations. In the P.C.I., ideology has changed and appears to be vigorously reasserting itself; in the D.C. the era of suppressed ideology has passed, and ideological debate and commitment are clearly resurgent.

How, then, explain the imperfect, distorted and erroneous perceptions of the decline-of-ideology writers?

Interpretations of the Decline-of-Ideology Literature

Several interpretations of the decline-of-ideology writings are possible, and I shall touch here on only two or three. First, one might simply dismiss this literature as reflecting a much too narrow focus on certain undeniable changes in the rhetoric, and even in the perceptions and prescriptions, of some

---

[21] Exactly how much of the West is to be included in the generalizations about ideology's decline is never made too clear. Lipset, for example, is careful to hedge his European generalizations by frequently excepting Italy and France. My point would be that if these two countries are excepted, as they should be, one can scarcely pretend to speak

contemporary Marxists. I say dismiss, rather than accord them serious intellectual attention, because: (a) the narrow focus fails to include a broader
conceptual framework that would permit comparative analytic attention to
other aspects of Marxian and non-Marxian ideologies, and (b) many of the
observations limited to the crisis or travail experienced by Marxists since the
Hungarian Rebellion and the XX Congress of the CPSU amount to nothing
more than propaganda slogans.

Second, it is possible to sidestep the fascinating subject of broader comparative ideological analysis and concentrate instead on the central proposition that
runs through much of this writing, namely, that ideology tends to wane as
societies reach levels of social and economic modernization typified by several
Western countries. It seems to me, however, that any attempt to assess these
writings in such terms is fraught with a number of difficulties that can only
be briefly mentioned here. For example, one will have to come to grips with
Mannheim, who remains, after all, the first and most prominent scholar to
touch on almost every aspect of the arguments mustered by contemporary
writers, including the proposition that the birth and death of ideology depends
on certain social, economic and "ecological" factors.

But, Mannheim, as I have noted, intends a pejorative definition of ideology,
thus greatly narrowing its application. For systems of ideas that are *not*
incongruent with empirical realities, he uses the term "utopia." However, if
I read him correctly, Mannheim's final test for deciding whether a system of
ideas is ideological or utopian is almost invariably *post facto* — in the sense that
what one identifies as yesterday's ideology becomes tomorrow's utopia when it
can be shown that, somewhere in space and time, prescriptions or transcendent
ideas turned out not to be incongruent with potential "social realities." The
pragmatic test is deceptively simple: If it works, it's utopian; if it doesn't, it's
ideological. Outside of ascribing super-rational powers to the "omniscient
observer," there is no readily apparent way of identifying the very thing one
wishes to measure, except after the fact.

Beyond this conceptual problem, there are others implied by the "more
modernization-less ideology" formulation. Such generalizations involve secular
trends that span centuries. Thus, even if one can reach an acceptable working
definition of ideology, the matter of measuring these trends — to say nothing
of projecting them into the future — seems to me to involve a degree of precision in historical data gathering and measurement that is only a little better
today (and in some ways much worse) than it was in Mannheim's time.
My own impression about such long-range trends is that, despite some interest-

---

with justification about *European* trends. See Lipset, "The Changing Class Structure
and Contemporary European Politics," *Daedalus,* 93 (Winter, 1964), *passim.* Moreover, there is also rather persuasive evidence that Lipset's generalizations are not currently valid, if they ever were, for a country like West Germany. See H. P. Secher,
"Current Ideological Emphasis in the Federal Republic of Germany," a paper delivered
at the 1964 Annual Meeting of the American Political Science Association, Chicago,
September 9–12, 1964. Note particularly the extensive, German-language bibliography
on this subject contained in the footnotes of this paper. In any event, the burden of
Secher's argument is that German ideology is on the upswing, both in the SPD and in
the Catholic sectors of the CDU/CSU.

ing changes in the symbology of ideology, we are far from seeing the end in Europe of ideology as I have defined it or, indeed, of ideology defined as dogmatic, inflexible, passionately articulated perceptions of reality and prescriptions for the future. Furthermore, since the long-term trend line is not unequivocally established, we cannot say whether short-term phenomena are part of a downward plunging graph line or merely a cyclical dip in a line which may be essentially flat or rising.

It also seems to me that the proposition we are discussing here suffers all of the limitations (which I have detailed elsewhere) that one can identify with a good deal of the recent writing about political development. This formulation seems to rest on the assumption (or hope) that socio-economic-political development is moving in a deterministic, unilinear, culture-specific direction, whereby the future will consist of national histories that are monotonous repetitions of the "Anglo-American" story. In short, the decline-of-ideology writers seem to believe that "they" are becoming more and more like "us."

This leads to a possible third interpretation of the literature, namely, that most of this writing is not social science but, ironically, simply more ideology. The French scholar, Jean Meynaud, reacts in this summary way to the "decline" writers: "In reality, the deep intent of this theory is to establish that in wealthy societies socialism is definitely eclipsed. With many persons it [the theory of decline] is a rather banal aspect of anti-communism or, if one prefers, of a new version of conservative opportunism." [22] This view is strongly echoed by William Delany who says, "The end of ideology writers write not just as sociologists or social scientists but as journalists and an anti-totalitarian ideological cabal. Their work is ideology but, like almost all Western ideologies since the 18th Century, with a heavy 'scientific' component to give respectability and a sense of truth." [23]

These are admittedly harsh judgments. And yet, when one confronts the waning-ideology literature with actual developments in Western Europe, the gap between fact and "scientific" findings suggests exactly such evaluations. Indeed, it is entirely possible that, in the case of some of the decline writers, what they see may be little more than autobiographical projections, which may be fine for some novelists but is clearly quite sticky for social scientists. In any event, in so far as social science analysis of ideology is concerned, it is more than a little difficult to agree with an appraisal of the social sciences which begins by confiding that the American social scientist has been co-opted into something called the "establishment," and then goes on to say about "establishment" members:

> Theirs is an alienation brought about by "superior wishes," that is, by the ability to penetrate the ideologies of others and thereby to emancipate themselves. In this group is the social scientist, who is the objective observer. He penetrates all of the disguises created by the untrained mind or the ideological

---

[22] Jean Meynaud, "Apatia e responsibilità dei cittadini," *Tempi Moderni*, 5 (April–June, 1962), p. 33.

[23] William Delany, "The End of Ideology: A Summation" (paper delivered at the 1964 Annual Meeting of the American Political Science Association), p. 16.

mind and attaches himself to the image of the wise. He represents the "establishment."[24]

I suppose that, if there is an American "establishment" and if the social scientist has come to play such a prominent role in it, one would expect that in the rationalization and defense of his well-ordered world the social scientist's words are likely to take on typically ideological overtones. In any event, it is difficult to imagine how the social scientist in the United States would now go about rebutting the reiterated Russian claim that Western social science is not much more than thinly veiled bourgeois ideology.

This leads to a few concluding remarks about the extent to which phenomena associated with the alleged decline of ideology reflect in great measure certain kinds of adaptations to the crisis confronting Western intellectuals. The Italian case will serve as one concrete illustration of this, although similar patterns can also be explicated for other Western countries.

At the end of World War II, Italian intellectuals — like their counterparts elsewhere in Western Europe — felt deeply involved in a concerted and apparently promising effort to transform Italian society. This was a period in which "The sacred texts were dusted off and the people were enlightened in order to create the maximum degree of consensus and to realize the maximum degree of support and conversions."[25] But romantic notions of socialist revolution — widely fostered by intellectuals — were of very short duration. Failure of Italian society to move directly toward socialism caught many intellectuals flat-footed. They remained tied to a permanent anti-Fascism which led them to ritualistic rhetorical statements about Italian society's ills and the paths to salvation. For almost fifteen years, these intellectuals repeated with startling monotony themes and prescriptions which were simply out of joint as far as the changing conditions of Italian society were concerned. In this sense, certainly, Aron and others are right in scoring the stultifying consequences of doctrinaire ideological formulations.

These were years of demoralization for intellectuals who expected revolutionary change and were treated instead to a great deal of temporizing under DeGasperi; but the intellectuals were also blinded to certain social and economic changes that made the traditional rhetoric of Marxism alien to growing numbers of Italians. The irony in all of this is that the intellectuals were the last to appreciate the need for new rhetoric and, indeed, for new ideological formulations. They had been preceded by political leaders not only in the Communist party, but in the ranks of Christian Democracy as well. The politicians evidently quickly understood that no large-scale intervention of the public sector in any kind of development was likely to proceed for long without some kind of *ideological* justification.

To some extent, the isolation of intellectuals from social realities was encouraged by the P.C.I. In keeping the party's intellectuals organizationally separated from mass members, the P.C.I. was able to capitalize on a tendency

[24] David E. Apter (ed.), *Ideology and Discontent* (London, 1964), pp. 37–38.

[25] Antonio Carbonaro and Luciano Gallino, "Sociologia e ideologie ufficiali," *Tempi Moderni,* 4 (January–March, 1961), p. 31.

which is deeply rooted in Italian culture. As Guiducci points out, Italian intellectuals were strongly influenced by the Crocian idea that they were a caste apart, superior to and removed from the masses, and thus failed to maintain an open and realistic contact with the broader population. Even in a context of deep ideological commitment, they managed to adhere to "a position which is traditional with the Italian man of culture, estranged as he is from reality, tied as he is to a culture which is literary and humanistic in the narrowest sense of the words." [26]

The striking thing about Italy in recent years is that the country's intellectuals (largely of the left, but also of the right) seem to be emerging from the kind of isolation Guiducci mentions. Their confrontation of the realities of Italian society has not led, however, to a decline of ideology. Rather, I would suggest that what has happened involves in part ideological clarification and in part the framing of new ideologies to which striking numbers of Italian and European intellectuals now adhere. These new ideologies in a profound sense involve substituting new myths for old. The new myths, which form the core of the ideological structure of many intellectuals, are those of the welfare state and of economic planning. As Henri Jarme rightly puts it, "The myth of planning is only the socialist variant of the myth of progress." [27] But such myths, if Italy is any test, attract more than segments of former orthodox Marxists; they are woven as well into the kind of new ideology that Christian Democrats create.

To be sure, the emergence of new myths creates new symbols and vocabulary. This sort of change should not be construed, however, as an end of ideology. As Giovanni Sartori notes, "Granted that in an affluent society the intensity of ideology will decrease, a lessening of its intensity should not be confused with a withering away of ideology itself. . . . The temperature of ideology may cool down but this fact does not imply that a society will lose the habit of perceiving political problems in an unrealistic or doctrinaire fashion; and it implies even less that a party system will turn to a pragmatic approach." [28]

Two points are relevant here. First, it is obvious that many Italian intellectuals seem to have rediscovered a valid — or at least personally satisfying — function in society, namely, providing an ideological rationale, as well as rational alternatives, for economic planning activity. Second, in achieving this redefinition of role, the intellectual seems to have reaffirmed his responsibility for creating the ideological system within which contemporary activity is justified. Needless to say, some of these intellectuals will phrase ideology in the language of science and rationality, whether they are in favor of radical change or of the preservation of the status quo. There is certainly little

---

[26] Roberto Guiducci, *Socialismo e verità* (Turin, 1956), pp. 23 ff.

[27] Henri Jarme, "Le Mythe politique du socialisme democratique," *Cahiers Internationaux de Sociologie,* 33 (July–December, 1962), p. 29.

[28] Giovanni Sartori, "European Political Parties: The Case of Polarized Pluralism," in J. LaPalombara and M. Weiner (eds.), *Political Parties and Political Development* (Princeton, 1966).

evidence in Italy, in any event, that, say, a commitment to social science miraculously resolves the nagging problem of Mannheim's Paradox, nor, indeed, that it should.

When we turn to the decline-of-ideology writers, it is possible to detect that they, too, are in search of a definable role in contemporary American society. Whether that role involves the use of social science to criticize America's failings, or to extol its consensual or managerial character is a fascinating empirical question. But surely the exploration of this problem would require of a mature social science a certain amount of caution and humility regarding the danger of translating highly selective data gathering or personal predilections or ambitions into sweeping historical projections and "scientific" generalizations. Clifford Geertz, I believe, has put this most succinctly: "We may wait as long for the 'end of ideology' as the positivists have waited for the end of religion." [29]

---

[29] Clifford Geertz, "Ideology as a Cultural System," in D. E. Apter (ed.), *Ideology and Discontent* (London, 1964), p. 51.

31. Some Further Comments on "The End of Ideology"

SEYMOUR MARTIN LIPSET

In a brief rejoinder Professor Lipset expresses doubts on the significance of a single example and insists that, whatever term may be applied to the phenomenon, an empirically testable and tested development, involving the reduction of intense political conflict, has characterized a number of Western democracies in the postwar period.

I am somewhat puzzled by Professor LaPalombara's critique of the decline or end of ideology thesis which points out that deideologisation is itself ideological behavior in a pure sense. This is obvious to most of those who have written on the subject. In an article cited in other contexts by Professor LaPalombara, I, for one, have written as follows:

> As a final comment, I would note that not only do class conflicts over issues related to division of the total economic pie, influences over various institutions, symbolic status and opportunity, continue in the absence of *weltanschauungen,* but that the decline of such total ideologies does not mean the end of ideology. Clearly, commitment to the politics of pragmatism, to the rules of the game of collective bargaining, to gradual change whether in the direction favored by the left or the right, to opposition both to an all powerful central state and to laissez-faire constitutes the component parts of an ideology. The "agreement on fundamentals," the political consensus of western society, now increasingly has come to include a position on matters which once sharply separated the left from the right. And this ideological agreement, which might best be described as "conservative socialism," has become the ideology of the major parties in the developed states of Europe and America. As such it leaves its advocates in sharp disagreement with the relatively small groups of radical rightists and leftists at home, and at a disadvantage in efforts to foster different variants of this doctrine in the less affluent parts of the world.[1]

It should be clear that if one says that he prefers a system with a low degree of ideologically intense political conflict rather than a high degree, he is making an ideological choice. However, as I read the rather lengthy literature by experts on various countries, e.g., political scientists, such as Herbert Tingsten, Otto Kirchheimer, Hans Daalder, Otto Brunner and Giovanni Sartori, journalists like James Reston or George Lichtheim, or sociologists like Raymond Aron, T. H. Marshall, or Stein Rokkan, they are concerned with one of three tasks, often with all three: (1) describing the decline in their own or

SOURCE: Reprinted by permission from *The American Political Science Review,* LX (March 1966), pp. 17–18.

[1] S. M. Lipset, "The Changing Class Structure and Contemporary European Politics," *Daedalus,* 93 (1964), p. 296.

various countries; (2) analyzing the social determinants of such changes; and (3) analyzing the presumed consequences of the changes. Thus, much of the literature involves stating specific testable propositions of the following sort:

a. Less intense conflict encourages greater respect for the rights of political minorities.

b. Intense ideologisation, sharp conflict, is characteristic of polities in which new emerging classes or strata denied political, social, or economic rights, are struggling to achieve these rights, but declines when these classes are admitted to full citizenship.

One may prefer sharp ideological conflict, yet recognize that the social conditions which foster it are weak under specified conditions. Curiously, many who argue that a prediction of the decline of ideological bitterness in industrially developed states reflects conservative political preferences do not also suggest that support of the thesis that stable western-type democratic constitutionalism is difficult, if not impossible, to sustain in impoverished "new states" or post-revolutionary societies bent on rapid industrialization means that one is opposed to political democracy. Some who make this latter argument are, in fact, opposed; others, however, are not. The propositions themselves must be testable if they are intended as scientific statements and not propaganda.

There are many researchable questions. Is it, or is it not, true that there has been a decline in the intensity of, in the depth of ideological cleavage in industrialized western society as compared to its industrializing past? Is it, or is it not, true that there is less bitter political cleavage in the wealthier as compared to the poorer democracies? Is it, or is it not, true that strata or ethnic groupings which have been admitted to citizenship in Marshall's sense are less likely to support intensive ideological politics than when they were denied citizenship? [2] Most recently, we have had implicit answers to these questions from a major spokesman from the Chinese Communist Party which reaches the same conclusions about comparative political behavior as have been posited by those who have written about "the end of ideology" in western society. Lin Piao, Vice-Chairman of the Central Committee of the Communist Party of China, and Vice-Premier, stated in a recent major policy speech:

> The countryside, and the countryside alone, can provide the revolutionary bases from which the revolutionaries can go forward to final victory. Precisely for this reason, Comrade Mao Tse-tung's theory of establishing revolutionary base areas in the rural districts and encircling the cities from the countryside is attracting more and more attention among the people in these regions.
>
> Taking the entire globe, if North America and Western Europe can be called "the cities of the world," then Asia, Africa and Latin America constitute "the rural areas of the world." Since World War II, the proletarian revolutionary movement has for various reasons been temporarily held back in the North American and West European capitalist countries, while the people's revolutionary movement in Asia, Africa, and Latin America has been growing vigorously. In a sense, the contemporary world revolution also presents a

---

[2] *Class, Citizenship and Social Development* (Garden City: Doubleday, 1963).

picture of the encirclement of cities by the rural areas. In the final analysis, the whole cause of world revolution hinges on the revolutionary struggles of the Asian, African and Latin American peoples. . . .[3]

The general question, whether the emphasis on systematic and integrated total ideologies has been experiencing a secular decline concomitant with social and economic development can not be resolved, of course, by reference to opinions, whether these be of scholars or revolutionaries. Neither can it be challenged by pointing to specific episodes which go in the opposite direction implied by the general thesis which refers to long-term historic trends. With this generalization as with all others, what is needed is hard research. And I would call attention to three studies which have attempted to systematically examine trends in the ideological behavior of political parties over time with the explicit purpose to test the "decline of ideology" thesis in Norway, Japan, and the Netherlands. Each concludes that it is valid for the politics of the country under investigation.[4]

I do not want to join issue with Professor LaPalombara on specific details of current Italian politics. I would only note a few facts. First with respect to the Christian Democrats, they are now sitting in a cabinet with Pietro Nenni's Italian Socialist Party. For the D.C. and the P.S.I. to join as coalition partners represents a considerable concession, a considerable moderation of historic ideological conflicts in Italian politics. Second, although the Italian Communists clearly remain committed to socialism, the party ideology is more moderate. Professor LaPalombara refers to a decline in "the party's use of extreme rhetoric," but he prefers to see this as a sign of "ideological vigor." The thesis that ideological tensions are moderating does not imply that class or party conflict is declining. Professor LaPalombara, here as elsewhere, is attacking a straw-man. No one has said the P.C.I. is "abandoning any commitment to ideological formulations."

Since he ends his article approvingly citing Giovanni Sartori that "Granted that in an affluent society the intensity of ideology will decrease," I simply do not know what he is trying to say, unless it is that political life is much too complex to be subsumed in a simple image like the "decline of ideology," that all political groups have ideologies and that over any given limited period of time the character of partisan ideologies will vary greatly. If this is what he means, then I am certain that almost everyone who has written about the end of, or decline of ideology will agree.

---

[3] Lin Piao, "Long Live the Victory of People's War," Peking Review, 8 (September 3, 1965), p. 24.
[4] See Ulf Torgersen, "The Trend Towards Political Consensus: The Case of Norway," Acta Sociologica, 6 (1962), 159–172 [Reprinted below, pp. 413–24.]; Masaaki Takane, "Economic Growth and the 'End of Ideology' in Japan," Asian Survey, 5 (1965), 295–304; A. Hoogerwerf, "Sociaal-Politieke Strijdpunten: Smeuland Vuur," Sociolgische Gids, 10 (1963), 249–263. I am indebted to Hans Daalder for calling my attention to the latter study, which, like the others, shows that the party programs of the different political parties have been converging since the last war.

32. The Trend Towards Political Consensus: The Case of Norway

ULF TORGERSEN

Torgersen's case study of Norwegian party development both strengthens and weakens the "end of ideology" thesis. It supports the generalization of de-radicalization with empirical data, but it also suggests that the period of radical politics was itself exceptional and should not be used as an absolute or "normal" yardstick. "De-ideologization" thus means to Torgersen a return to consensus after a transient period of disturbance, rather than a move toward a new equilibrium.

This paper takes its point of departure in the current concern within political science and political sociology with a phenomenon, or rather a cluster of related phenomena, which has been very noticeable in many post-World War II western political systems. This is the trend towards decreasing political conflict and increasing political consensus. This trend has been given various names. Words like "the end of ideology," "*fin de l'âge idéologique*" and "*Entideologisierung*" have been applied, but there is little doubt that the problems referred to are essentially similar. I think that within this over-all cluster of problems one can further make a distinction between four analytically separate, though empirically intertwined problems:

— first, there is the problem of the decreasing differences between the platforms and programmes of the various parties. This is a problem concerning the major alternatives of political choice existing within a political system;
— second, there is the question of the character of the intellectual and academic discussion in the various countries, of the extent to which new aspects of politics, or new perspectives on politics have tended to change its focus and character,
— third, there is the problem of mass activity, of the extent to which the disappearance of a "hot" political climate has had the consequence of sapping the strength of the parties, and leaving them as pretty empty organizational shells, since what they offer is just the difference between "tweedledee" and "tweedledum," in a society where other and more exciting ways of spending one's leisure time have emerged,
— fourth, there is the problem of the possible restructuring of the channels of political influence; there have been cases in which the parties in a country (a very good case in point is Austria) have established elaborate agreements between themselves in order to share power. A related problem concerns the extent to which the parties appear to the various groups which want to

SOURCE: Reprinted by permission from *Acta Sociologica*, VI (1962), pp. 159–71. Footnotes are bridged.

influence the decisions of the central authorities to be the appropriate channels of pressure.

In this paper I want to make a brief excursion into all these four related topics with reference to one country, Norway. To this I will add a few comments, on the whole speculative, on the possible preconditions of the current state of affairs.

Decreasing Differences between the Parties

If in one short word one wants to characterize the political situation in present-day Norway, *depoliticization* seems to be the one that fits best.

The trend in this direction is not exclusively a post-war phenomenon. But it is in the post-war period that the tendencies towards a decline of the previously strong political tensions and the bitter conflicts between the left and the right, really have gained momentum. Without doubt the war had a noticeable effect in establishing cross-party ties, stemming from loyalties from the underground activities. The period immediately after the war was characterized by a minimum of political conflict, and it was supposed that this was something that had come to stay. This was not exactly what happened. The election in 1949 showed a rather marked increase in political conflict between the parties, but I think that rather than interpreting this event as an indicator of anything else it should be seen as an event necessary for displaying to the electorate the distinctiveness of the parties. The events that have followed the 1949 election have rather emphasized this interpretation. The development has been more and more in the direction of decreasing political conflict. This had led to the situation that many areas of decisions have been "taken out of politics" – such as foreign politics and defence politics – and it has led the parties to compete for a position in the centre of the battle, and to try to move away from any position that might be interpreted as *extreme*. The parties have differed somewhat in their strategies for reaching this highly desired goal: each of the parties have their own special groups that must not be forgotten in the general concern for getting the vote of the "marginal voter." This means that the character of this endeavour and the internal problems that stem from this, vary from party to party, but the essential problem is the same.

The *Labour party* was before the war a party inclined toward a Marxian interpretation of society and politics. The new programme adopted in 1949 showed how far the party had moved in the direction of a broad "people's party" covering all social groups. The party has largely dropped its plans for nationalization. This development may have been facilitated by the fact that nationalization was in the more revolutionary period described as "state capitalism," an especially wicked variety of capitalism. The party thus had had no important history of socialization plans: its very "revolutionary" past eased the transformation to a purely pragmatic orientation. The party still maintains that the goal is "socialism," a noun usually defined in a rather loose way, but that there are many means of achieving it, and that nationalization is not among the best, as a committee on that question expressed it some years ago. It is also highly indicative of the present temper within the Norwegian Labour party that when a member of the opposition urged the Labour government to throw away old-fashioned ideas just as the British Labour party was in the process of doing, the Prime Minister replied that this really had been done years ago by the Scandinavian socialist parties.[1] The party has not been able to transform itself without some internal conflicts. In 1957 a small splinter party seceded, but stayed a minute sect, and in 1961 another splinter party, this time with a lot more backing, was established, mainly as a result of the ambiguous stand taken by the Labour party on the question of nuclear weapons in Norway. Generally the Labour leadership has shown great flexibility in adapting to the various strains of the geographically and socially highly heterogeneous party.

The *Conservative party* has also travelled towards the centre, but from the opposite direction. In 1949 the party fought the election battle under the slogan "Let us change the system," but the lack of success forced the party to take up other lines of propaganda. More deep-seated forces were at work, too. The Conservative party has since the war been going through some rather crucial changes: besides the business element the element of white collar workers has become increasingly more important. The attempt to win over this rapidly growing social class to conservative policies has forced the party to softpedal the liberalist and all-out business orientation, and to stress the essentially reformist and welfare state-accepting character of the party. It has grown more "me-too-ist" in the more recent political campaigns, and has more or less said that "anything you have done I'd have done better." This change of strategy has meant a certain alienation from the business elements in the party, and a very hostile attitude between "Libertas," essentially a business-financed fund for anti-socialist information, and the Conservative headquarters. This has partly been tackled through attempts to consolidate the organization and to bureaucratize the party, in order to make it more independent of business sources of financing, but the issue is not quite solved.

A similar problem exists within the *Agrarian party*. For quite a long time after the war the Agrarian Party was close to an activist line of policy, and took a rather conservative stand on many issues. Gradually, however, this line has been abandoned and the leadership within the party has shifted to men who have been more conciliatory in their attitudes to other parties and perspectives. The party has changed its name to the *Centre party*, and has recently been involved in negotiations with the other "parties of the centre," in order to see what could possibly be done in order to solidify themselves as a "third force" in Norwegian politics. So far very little has come of it.

The *Liberal* party is one of these parties, and it has all the time emphasized its middle-of-the-road character. But this party is exactly the party which has suffered the greatest losses in the more recent elections. Torn between the various demands from the city liberals, the farm interests and the fundamentalist anti-alcohol section of the party it has been able to please no one completely, and its political importance has declined. The other of these parties

---

[1] *Stortingstidende*, 13 October 1960, p. 123.

is the *Christian People's party*, which represents the more fundamentalist sections of the population. It made some headway just after the war, but seems to have been on the decline recently.

The *Communist* party has been declining gradually since the war, and thus testifies to the reduction of the extreme positions in political life.

This development towards the political centre has not gone on unnoticed by the politicians themselves. The parliamentary records and the newspapers abound in statements to the effect that the post-war period has eliminated really fierce political fights. "The area of political disagreement has been greatly reduced," said one of the Conservative leaders. "The most important feature is that we have been able to work out certain norms that are acceptable by everybody." [2] One of the leaders of the Liberal party expressed the notion that the party programs "were essentially similar." The Labour Prime Minister said in 1957 that there were many areas "where there is no deep disagreements between the parties," and recently stated this even more emphatically: "When it really comes to brass tacks, it appears as if we don't have very much to fight about, really. Quite obviously none of the parties are very excited about being too different from the others." [3] A clearer and more explicit description of the present absence of political conflict would be hard to find.

Politics and the Academic Debate

Let us now turn away from the debate going on in the political arena to the, presumably, more reflective and at any rate more detached orientations of men with primarily intellectual concerns. Again we find the same general pattern of decline of excitement about what is usually called the "old" issues of politics; if there is any great concern with political issues, these are likely to be rather different from the "old" ones. Just to emphasize the lack of concern with the old questions: in a recently published jubilee-book of graduates from the University of Oslo, the graduates were asked about the present applicability of the distinction "bourgeois" — "socialist." Only about 10 per cent answered, but among those who did answer there was almost complete unanimity about the outdated character of the distinction, which was supposed to have mainly historical interest.[4]

As I mentioned, this reduced concern for the traditional lines of political cleavage may have different results, and it may be hard to say which one is the most common. Partly the result is reduced concern for politics. The content of the leading Norwegian periodical *Samtiden* has since the war gradually shifted from social problems to highly personal and philosophical problems, in a way similar to the change following the decline of interest in political questions among intellectuals in Norway at the turn of the century.[5]

---

[2] *Sjur Lindebrække: Tillit og tillitspolitikk,* Kragero, Naper, 1953, pp. 11–12.

[3] *Stortingstidende,* 14 October 1960, p. 204.

[4] *Studentene fra 1935,* Oslo, 1960.

[5] A content analysis of the subject matter of the articles of the journal mentioned for the years 1946, 1950, 1954 and 1958 shows that the proportion of articles dealing with a

In part, interests among academics have turned in new directions. If one looks at the Conservative Student Association at the University of Oslo, it is quite evident that there has been a very clear change of emphasis and leadership. While in the period up to well past 1950 the organization was mainly interested in the "old" questions, and mainly run by students from the Law School, which is the traditional Conservative stronghold at the University of Oslo, the interest has since gradually changed to other fields, and the activities of the Conservative students are now much more literary and philosophical. This change, which has meant that students of liberal arts have become more important within the association, is a change which is partly associated with the decline of interest in politics *proper*, but it also ties in with the more general development within the Conservative party. The Conservative groups that fight the business elements within the Conservative party through appeals to Burke, and who have had considerable success, have had close connections with this student association. One might question the logical connection between Burke and a switch to white-collar appeals, but as a fact it cannot be doubted.

The Socialist student organizations exhibit somewhat different features. One of them is independent of the Labour party: it was expelled some years ago. It is essentially Socialist on the questions of domestic politics and usually demands more nationalization, but the most important issues are foreign policy issues. The other organization belongs to the Labour party and follows very much the same policy as the party.

The Channels of Influence

The decreasing difference in the actual programmes of the parties has led to none of the consequences that have occurred in Austria. The co-operation of the parties has not been formally established, but there is hardly any reason to assume that this is of any real importance; for all practical purposes the co-operation between the party leaders has been as effective as it could possibly be.

This means that even if there is no "charter of interparty co-operation" there is just as much "waning of opposition" as in the cases described by Kirchheimer. This is in a way a direct consequence of the ideological similarity: the standard argument of the Labour party against the Conservative opposition is now not that they have hatched wicked plots and sinister schemes, but that they in fact do not have any other programme at all, and the standard retort is that this is because the Labour party has improved in a Conservative direction. Leaving aside the question of the amount of truth in these statements, it is pretty evident that this makes for rather amiable parliamentary conditions. Indeed, cross-party friendships in Parliament have become much more frequent in the recent years than they were immediately after the war, and it has made for

---

social, economic, political or military subject had declined from 47% in 1946 to 30% in 1958, while the proportion of articles dealing with literary, religious, psychological or philosophical subjects increased from 40% to 53% in the course of the same period.

rather smooth between-party co-operation. This has also had another effect: it now happens very rarely that a Cabinet minister stakes his position on one particular piece of legislation or other measure that has to be accepted by Parliament. This has happened in *one* case after the war, apart from the cases in which the whole government threatened to go, and caused general surprise and a reaction which heralded the resigning minister as particularly brave and principled.

It is probably part of a relatively stable and conflictless democracy that the different party élites feel as loyal to each other as to their own followers: such cross-party loyalties help to check their inclination to exploit situations for short-term gains for their own party. Some sociologists have in this seen the outstanding characteristic of what they call "pluralistic politics" as against "ideological politics." [6] We do not disagree in principle in this conclusion but we must ask ourselves exactly how much a society can have of such cross-party loyalties before it saps the sources of a vital political system: the activity of the citizens in political organizations. We shall look a little closer into this problem in the next section of this paper.

Mass Mobilisation for Political Purposes

We have so far described some trends within the strata of the population closest to politics, among the people most likely to express their conception of how it really works, but we have said next to nothing about corresponding trends in the broader activities of the rank-and-file voters. The questions most central in this respect are the following:

— to what extent has the decreasing political tension brought about a decrease in *electoral turnout?*
— to what extent has the decreasing political tension tended to reduce people's involvement in the *organized party activity?*
— to what extent has the decreasing political tension worked to limit people's *participation in the electoral contest,* e.g. their attendance at meetings, their turnout at rallies and so forth?

We shall try to give a brief overview of the trends visible within these areas. The evidence presented will in some respects be incomplete, and in other ways quite circumstantial; nevertheless we think it gives at least some credence to the conclusions that we will suggest.

---

[6] Edward Shils, *The Torment of Secrecy,* Glencoe, Free Press, 1956, part IV. It is in itself a remarkable fact that so many of the criticisms of present-day political consensus are couched in terms of "system-needs." It is very common to find arguments to the effect that a certain amount of conflict is necessary if democracy is to prevail, that there really should be more issues (without any specification) and that there should be higher political interest among people (without mentioning issues). This tendency is highly reminiscent of the character of much contemporary American political debate, where "ideology" has become something of a *Schimpfwort,* rather regardless of the substantive content of the ideological position.

Table 1 summarizes the trends in electoral turnout from 1945 to 1959. For a variety of reasons, turnout was generally low throughout the country at the first post-war elections in 1945. There was a steep increase from 1947 onwards, then a culmination in 1949 and 1951, and since that time either stagnation or some decline. There are important differences, however, between the largest cities and the rest of the country.

In the case of *parliamentary* elections voting reached a peak in 1949 and has since dropped back several percentage points. This drop is most marked in the largest cities: in Oslo 4.8 for men and 3.4 for women, in Bergen 6.4 and 5.4, in Trondheim 5.8 and 3.5, in Stavanger 6.1 and 1.1. The decline was less marked in the smaller cities and in the countryside. This difference comes out very clearly in the *local* elections. For these the peak year was 1951. The decline from 1951 to 1959 was for Oslo 4.2 and 3.4, for Bergen 3.2 and 4.2, for Trondheim 3.3 and 2.6, for Stavanger 3.3 and 3.4. By contrast there was a slight *increase for the men and quite a marked one for the women in the rural communes*. We may interpret this as evidence that there are two opposite movements at work in the system: in the centre there is increasing *depolitization* and some slight decline in the level of mass mobilisation while in the periphery there is still at work a process of *increasing politicization* through further party efforts. For further details on turnout levels in the rural communes the reader is referred to the paper by Rokkan and Valen.[7]

Is this same trend discernible in the fluctuations in party membership?

There is no indication of a general trend: the situation differs from party to party. For the *Labour party* the records indicate (*Table 2*) a gradual decline in membership figures since roughly 1949. That year the membership reached

Table 1   *Electoral Turnout 1945–1959*

		Parliamentary Elections (%)				Municipal Elections (%)				
		1945	1949	1953	1957	1945	1947	1951	1955	1959
All Cities	Men	82.0	87.8	84.9	83.1	73.8	80.9	81.0	77.4	77.7
	Women	79.5	85.2	83.2	81.9	67.2	77.5	79.5	77.0	76.8
Oslo	Men	87.3	88.5	85.0	83.7	73.4	83.5	83.2	79.7	79.0
	Women	83.5	86.1	84.0	82.7	66.1	79.3	81.7	79.9	78.3
Bergen	Men	81.8	86.3	82.0	79.9	72.9	78.7	77.4	72.9	74.2
	Women	86.8	84.5	81.7	79.1	65.7	76.3	77.1	72.1	72.9
Trondheim	Men	81.0	86.7	82.6	80.9	69.2	75.4	78.6	75.0	75.3
	Women	78.8	83.3	80.8	79.8	59.8	69.5	76.8	74.7	74.2
Stavanger	Men	86.0	87.6	89.2	81.5	75.5	78.4	80.9	74.2	77.6
	Women	80.6	83.2	80.1	82.1	70.3	77.4	80.1	74.8	76.6
Rural Communes	Men	77.2	83.5	80.7	79.2	70.3	73.0	73.1	71.8	73.3
	Women	68.0	74.8	72.8	73.2	56.7	62.1	64.4	65.2	68.0

[7] S. Rokkan and H. Valen, "The Mobilization of the Periphery," *Acta Sociologica*, VI (1962).

an all-time high; never before and never since has the party had so many members. From that year on we have witnessed a pretty regular decline; the figures for 1959 indicate 162,093 members, and this is most likely to be somewhat inflated, particularly because of multiple affiliations. The sources do not allow assessments of how much of the decline has been in collective membership and how much in individually affiliated members. Data from the Oslo branch of the party indicate a stronger decline in individual membership than in collective membership. The decline in absolute membership figures implies an even more distinct drop in the percentage of the Labour voters who are party members (see Table 2). This is less marked for Oslo, where, however, the same general trend appears to be present. The relative decline is even more marked in the percentage of individual members: in 1949 there were about 7300 out of 119,000 or about 6% in 1957 5700 out of 129,000, or less than 4%. It is well known that the Labour party looks with considerable worry on this trend. The drop in membership does not, however, seem to be associated with any marked turn away from Labour at the polls: on the contrary, despite this decline in membership, the Labour party has since the

Table 2   *Reported Membership in the Labour Party 1946–1959* *

	THE WHOLE COUNTRY			OSLO		
	Total Individual and Collective Members	*Total Labour Votes*	*% Members*	*Total Individual and Collective Members*	*Total Labour Votes*	*% Members*
1946	197,638			46,934		
1947 (municipal el.)	202,043	550,477	36.7	55,618	91,065	61.1
1948	203,094			59,426		
1949 (parliamentary el.)	204,055	803,471	25.4	61,948	119,741	51.7
1950	200,501			65,504		
1951 (municipal el.)	179,361	659,290	27.2	62,710	107,249	58.5
1952	178,102			62,915		
1953 (parliamentary el.)	178,004	830,448	21.4	62,499	119,784	52.2
1954	174,575			61,272		
1955 (municipal el.)	174,080	696,411	25.0	60,892	110,266	55.2
1956	170,823			59,195		
1957 (parliamentary el.)	163,991	865,675	18.9	57,339	129,456	44.3
1958	165,455			57,267		
1959 (municipal el.)	162,093	729,503	12.2	x	118,849	48.2

* SOURCES: Figures for the whole country are from the annual reports of the Norwegian Labour party, issued under the title Det norske arbeiderparti: *Beretning*, for the years in question. The figures for Oslo were obtained from the annual reports from the Oslo Labour party, issued under the title Oslo Arbeiderparti: *Beretning*. For both figures members of youth organizations are included. Computations of the member-voter ratios therefore are not *quite* exact, as the membership figures include individuals below voting age. For 1959 the computation for Oslo is based on the 1958 figures.

end of the war almost invariably solidified its position in the electorate, both in the capital and in the country as a whole.[8]

The lack of relationship between this decline of party activity and the results at the polls is brought out very clearly in the case of the Labour youth organization. There is very little reason to believe that the Labour party has any particularly weak positions among the young voters. And still it is the youth branch of the party that has suffered the most drastic decline. In Oslo, the number of youth members dropped from 1800 in 1949 to 500 in 1957, and similar tendencies have prevailed in many other areas of the country.

If we turn to the *Conservative party,* we find a different picture. According to the figures reported by various agencies within the Conservative organization, the party has had an extraordinary growth during the first decade of the post-war period. This growth is supposed to have increased the figures for the Conservative party proper (here Women's Conservative Associations and Young Conservatives are not counted) from 39,655 in 1949 to 66,385 at the end of 1952, to 72,905 in 1958 and 71,343 in 1960. Added to this growth comes the membership for the Conservative Youth organization: it claims to have reached the figure 20,000 members in 1950 and has stuck to that figure ever since, the latest record known to the author being for 1958. For the Oslo branch of the Young Conservatives a similar stagnation seems to have occurred: in 1951 they claimed to have 16 locals in Oslo, with a total membership of about 3200, in 1954 they reported 3000 members in 12 locals, in 1957 2800 and in 1959 3000 members. These figures certainly are higher than those reported by the Labour Youth Organization, though there may be reason to assume that the concept of membership here may be somewhat more elusive. Without arguing about this, we will, however, call the attention to the stagnation in the figures. For many years the Conservative organization has keep as their official figure a total of 100,000 for all categories of members and used this to indicate their strong position among the voters. The party has also recently given figures for the total number of members of voting age: in 1956 93,000, in 1957 95,976, in 1958 96,931, and in 1960 97,509. This is a slight increase, which roughly matches the increase in votes. On the whole, I think that there is fairly good reason to assume that there has been a stagnation in absolute figures, and probably a loss in relative terms in the last five years.

For the *Communist party* there has most certainly been a marked decrease since 1949, but to buttress this with exact figures is extremely complicated, due to the high level of secrecy of internal party affairs.

For the other parties, the Christian People's party, the Liberal party, and the

---

[8] This was written before the national election of 11 September, 1961. At this election the Labour party lost votes for the first time after the War. This was primarily due to the emergence of the left-wing *Socialist People's Party.* The results were as follows:

	Total Votes		Per Cent of Votes Cast
1957: Labour		865,675	48.3
1961: Labour	860,526		46.8
Socialist People's	43,996		2.4
Total		904,522	49.2

Agrarian party, we have not been able to get hold of membership over any length of time.[9] On the whole, there is reason to believe that the proportion of the members relative to the voters is likely to have declined somewhat during recent years. The absolute figures reported by the parties are either declining or stagnant, while the number of voters have increased for both of the parties we have evidence for.

Very much the same factors that seem to reduce people's willingness to *join* parties seem to be present when it comes to attending the campaigns put up by the different parties before the elections. This is of course partly a two-way causation as the decrease in the organization strength reduces the capacity for arranging meetings, organizing rallies and so forth. As a consequence, the number of meetings arranged by the parties before the elections have tended to decline pretty clearly since the 1949 election campaign.

The data supporting this assumption are somewhat scanty, and some of the evidence is rather circumstantial. But there is a remarkable similarity in the conclusions which can be drawn.

The Labour party arranged during the 1949 campaign roughly 5000 meetings throughout the country. In 1953 there were only 3200 meetings and in 1957 (the King died so the plans were not actually carried out) the plans included some 2000 meetings. Indeed, the reduction is even more marked, since among these meetings are also counted "discussion" meetings, where more than one party is present. Such meetings hardly ever occurred before 1953, when they were used occasionally, but with fairly great success, as it meant more of a show for the audience, and there were plans for quite a number in 1957. This means that an increasing proportion of the meetings we have given figures for cannot be classified as purely Labour meetings.

The Agrarian party arranged about 2000 meetings in 1949, and had planned roughly 1000 meetings for 1957.

That this decline in meetings had started in 1953 is also indicated by some other data: The Conservative party in the province of Rogaland arranged 54 meetings in 1949, 50 in 1953, while the corresponding figures for the Labour party are 168 and 130. The Conservative party in the province of Buskerud had more than 50 meetings in 1949, in 1953 less than 30; the figures for the Labour party were 160 and 100 respectively.

Concluding Remarks: The Consensus and Its Preconditions

We have given a somewhat perfunctory analysis of the political conditions in post-war Norway, but we have not touched on the question of the origin of these conditions or the likelihood that they will remain stable. It goes without saying that our treatment of that subject will be even more cursory: what we can do is primarily to offer some comments on the theories presented in accounting for similar phenomena in other western political systems. The essence of my criticism, so far as Norway is concerned, is that too much

---

[9] The figures for 1957 are given in S. Rokkan and H. Valen, "The Mobilization of the Periphery," *Acta Sociologica*, VI (1962).

emphasis has been placed on the purely social and economic aspects of the historical development and too little on the character of the political institutions.

The starting point for my considerations along these lines is a dissatisfaction with the tendency to look at modern western history as if it is approaching some absolute zero. In the case of Norway, this perspective is simply grossly misleading. The normal state of affairs in this country during the last 150 years has not been a high-pitched ideological crisis; on the contrary, this situation has been rather unusual, more unusual, maybe, than in most other countries. Consensus rather than dissensus has been the prevailing condition. Just to give a brief summary: political consensus was the rule almost until 1880. With the exception of the period following 1814 and the short rupture of political peace resulting from labour unrest in 1848, there was substantial agreement on most questions until well into the 1870s. Then there was a tense period until 1884, followed by a cooling-off period that ended sometime before 1905. This was followed by a relatively peaceful period until the end of World War I, when the labour movement was radicalized, and finally joined the Comintern in 1920. 1884 and 1919–1920 were probably the tensest moments during the last 150 years; here I leave aside the exogenous conflict with Germany. The situation of the twenties changed very soon, however. The radicalization of the Norwegian Labour party is very well known to most political sociologists, but what they invariably fail to notice is the extremely speedy de-radicalization that brought the party from membership in Comintern to the Cabinet in the course of four years. Any analysis which limits itself to the strictly social variables, such as "speed of industrialization," will rightly assess the basis for the radical upsurge, but such an approach will fail to come to grips with the problems contained in the limited level of revolutionary activity displayed (concrete plans for revolutionary activity, such as real preparation for armed conflict hardly existed) and in the rapid decline of the revolutionary wave.[10]

In this respect it is helpful to look back at the other event just mentioned, the crisis in 1884. At this time, the political system was changed from one dominated by civil servants to a parliamentary system, but without leaving any unresolved deep conflicts, and without essentially threatening the legitimacy of the system. In a sense, there is a basic similarity between these two events:

---

[10] In the analysis of the radicalization of the Norwegian labour movement, all writers are relying, directly or indirectly, on the work of the Norwegian historian Edvard Bull, who was the first to speculate on the conditions making for this development. But they often omit a factor of a more political character, studiously emphasized by Bull: in Norway there were few ties between the Liberal and the working-class movements since parliamentary government had been established already in 1884, without the support of the working-class, while in Sweden and Denmark a Liberal-Labour alliance had to fight together against the establishment to gain full political rights. This politically necessary alliance probably did as much as the purely social-structural conditions to "domesticate" the workers in Denmark and Sweden and thus added to the contrast with "radical" Norway. The importance of an electoral system that gave the Labour party a considerable underrepresentation in parliament is another "political" factor, that should not be forgotten in the concern with social-structural explanations.

in both cases the tension was reduced after a reasonably short time. The political system was in both cases able to incorporate new movements and new elites in an extremely rapid fashion.

These remarks are meant as a reminder that too much attention to the social basis of new political movements is in a way to ignore "politics," because it tends to divert the attention from the fact that a social movement is not just an expressive act by some social collectivity, it is just as much an organized effort to get something, and the chances that groups will get these things depend upon the character of the political action of those whose co-operation is needed if they are to be able to get it in a relatively peaceful fashion. To try to explain social movements by leaving out the policy of the "established elites" and the political institutions is like trying to explain the moves of one of the two players of a game of chess, while closing one's eyes to what the other player is up to, and to the rules of the game.

The implication of this is that it helps little to study social movements, comparatively or otherwise, if this is not done in the sense of a study of their interaction with the established social institutions or elites. In the Norwegian case this has mainly this relevance to the problems just stated: because of the weakness of ascriptive values in the Norwegian civil servant upper class, and later in the business upper class, their ability to withstand the pressures from below and their tendency to co-opt the new elements have been rather marked traits of their political strategy, and their relatively un-military orientation — due to the absence of military traditions and of a strong army — has reinforced this tendency to appease rather than to fight back. Only when such considerations are included in the reflections about the causes of de-politicization can we hope to come to grips with the question. And the consequence of such an analysis must be a deep concern not only with the character of the new social movements, but with the broader capacity — if so metaphysically tinged phrases can be accepted — of the political system to weed out the sources of conflict by appropriate "action."

It will be seen that one of the explanations that arise from this is that Norway is relatively free of internal political tension because it has been that way all the time. If this is to push the problem one step back, the answer is that this is the nature of historical explanation. I have not here given any really sufficient account of the possible sources of this peaceful state of affairs. Rather I have sketched some of the possibilities that should be looked into because the usual explanations are seen to be deficient. They may describe the potential social movements, and they may throw light on qualities pertaining to the early phase of such movements. But a broader and in a sense more "political" orientation is needed in order to account for their future fate, as in the case of the Norwegian trend towards political consensus.

33. Coalition Government in Austria

HERBERT P. SECHER

The "permanent" coalition that governed postwar Austria for twenty years came to serve as a kind of model for the new style of politics perceived by political scientists. The role of parliamentary opposition was exchanged for that of a partner in government and administration, providing opportunities for mutual control and participation in shares of power and patronage. Originally rooted in the need to preserve Austria's position under Four-Power occupation, the coalition both reflected and was the cause of a newly emerging spirit of compromise that had been quite uncharacteristic of Austrian democracy. Even when the coalition collapsed under the weight of accumulated frictions, this neither seriously affected the newly gained consensus nor ended Proporz *in the public sector of administration.*

The Second Republic of Austria is now well into its thirteenth year of national existence. The First Republic, thirteen years after its creation, showed all the signs of political disillusionment and impending dissolution. The Second Republic, in happy contrast, presents to the foreign observer a picture of political stability, economic prosperity, and sound foreign relations almost unequalled in this part of Europe. Much of the credit for the unusual state of affairs must be attributed to the two major political parties, the *Oesterreichische Volkspartei* (OeVP) and the *Sozialistische Partei Oesterreichs* (SPOe) which, uninterruptedly since 1945, have collaborated in the political resuscitation of the state that was once characterized as having "a strong tendency toward nonexistence."[1] Collaboration has taken the form of a coalition government which, from its inception as a temporary expedient, has become permanent and is now generally considered to be the *sine qua non* of Austrian politics. By tacit agreement the question of continuing the coalition has been removed from the sphere of political controversy. The evolution and nature of that coalition is the subject of this essay. In the language of economic organization the coalition is a cartel formed to mitigate party competition.

SOURCE: Reprinted by permission from Herbert P. Secher, "Coalition Government: The Case of the Second Austrian Republic," *The American Political Science Review*, LII (September 1958), pp. 791–808. Footnotes are abridged.

[1] R. Lorenz, *Der Staat wider Willen* (Vienna, 1938).

I

Introduction

It is a truism that parties are instruments for the reflection of the public will. But types of reflection differ widely and seem to depend importantly on the degree of stratification prevailing in a given country. After World War I continental Europe particularly witnessed the entrenchment of class-oriented parties, the result of sharply stratified societies; parties of that sort displayed a much greater cohesiveness than their more loosely organized counterparts in countries that still maintained great flexibility in their social spectrum. Yet for a variety of reasons before, during and immediately after World War II a social levelling occurred there in the wake of resurgent industrialization, and with a consequent relaxation of purely class-oriented political discipline. In the postwar era of expansion many of the slogans, ideas and organizational tools suitable to an age of scarcity lost their attraction. But the much-vaunted trend toward a "two-party system" can hardly be said to have taken the direction that was once forecast for it under these conditions. Doubts about the compatibility of party and democracy can be sensed almost everywhere — both in popular opinion and in academic circles — despite the fact that democratic procedures are being scrupulously observed.

Such attitudes are particularly outspoken in central European countries, where popular government has been traditionally embarrassed in its efforts to steer a safe course between the extremes of oligarchical and plebiscitary rule. There the role of parties in the making of public decisions is under suspicion because of their strength and consequent ability to compete with the "neutral" power of the state. Democratic consensus there is identified more often than not with the absence of any party, rather than with the shaping of agreements out of the variety of popular and partisan opinions. The Second Republic of Austria is a fair example of this sort of attitude — the more so that its independent political existence is comparatively brief and its experience with democratic methods limited. The reluctance and even fear to see one party in control of the government has been so persistent in Austria because republican experience was mainly one of political struggle that involved the rationality of representative institutions in deadly combat with the emotional appeal exercised by plebiscitary forces.

It is hardly exaggeration to consider the First Republic a prime example of Braunias' Parteienstaat.[2] In Austria, the constructive principles of representation and integration had indeed vanished. There was no discernible desire to establish a community of people, or even to create a unity of purpose. Since all voters had been politically organized, elections no longer served the purpose of presenting alternative policies to the electorate; the functioning of an election depends on the recognition of the majority principles, and no party then wanted to be bound by the chance of electoral arithmetic. The almost military discipline imposed on parliamentary representatives had made them "party agents subject to recall" without notice. In a system devoid of common

---

[2] K. Braunias, *Das Parlamentarische Wahlrecht* (Berlin, 1932), Vol 2, p. 22 ff.

symbols of loyalty and authority, the parties of the First Republic exhausted themselves in a mortal struggle for the dominance of one class over another.

It is relevant that these parties themselves had their origin in a time of failing symbolism — the decline of the dynastic concept that once cemented the Austro-Hungarian Empire. The parties — or movements — that dominated Austrian political life at that time were the Austro-German remnants of the economic and social forces that had been given political substance with the granting of universal suffrage in 1907. It was then generally assumed that these "inter"-national movements within the monarchy would act as a unifying force able to counteract the national separatism that was fast gaining ground in the far-flung Empire. But a viable basis for common political action was already disappearing during the last decade of the Empire, and the emergence of economically based but nationally oriented political parties merely brought the differences into sharper relief. The essential quality of the Austrian party system under the Empire — its extreme nationalism — spelled the doom of parliamentary government as well as of the Habsburgs themselves. What the First Republic inherited was the class rivalries of the Empire without the unifying concept of the monarchy which, for a time at least, had kept these conflicts from getting out of control.

Three major political movements during the inter-war years claimed the allegiance of the electorate: Political Catholicism, Democratic Socialism, and German Nationalism, represented respectively by the Christian-Social party, the Social Democratic party, and the Pan-German party. The core of the Social Democratic party was composed of industrial workers in Vienna and other industrial areas, while the chief support for the Christian Socials came from the peasants in the provinces, the middle classes of the cities, and the members of the former Imperial bureaucracy. Certain Protestant academic circles, anticlericals, liberal Catholics, and the diehard elements of German nationalism rallied around the Pan-German party and some minor splinter parties.

The small size and poverty of the country sharpened the bitterness of political strife that was born of class conflict and continuously imperiled the basis of social order. No attempts were made to create the symbols that are fundamental for the harmonious coexistence of differing social and economic groups; instead, each faction sought to make the acceptance of its own philosophic or economic egotism the basis for any kind of negotiations. The goal of complete dominance for its particular Weltanschauung was characteristic of all groups competing for power. In pre-Hitler Austria, two such exclusive political systems, one of an almost romanticized materialism and the other of a somber religious orthodoxy, stood face to face. In 1934 the latter forcibly suppressed the former, only to be ousted again by another system even more rigid and exclusive in doctrine and political organization.

With such a legacy of civil strife, the task confronting the new political leaders in 1945 was formidable indeed. Could the heritage of a generation be discarded and the once bitterly feuding social and economic groups become sufficiently realistic and undoctrinaire, sufficiently endowed with a sense of the state, as opposed to that of the party, to prevent the revival of political rifts that could only invite totalitarian solutions? It is this process of transferring loyalty from party to state which has constituted the outstanding problem confronting political leadership in the Second Republic. To the solution of that problem the whole concept of the coalition is basically oriented.

II

The Origin of the *Proporz*

The coalition itself originated in those confused and insecure days following the occupation of Vienna, when both victors and vanquished cast anxiously about for persons to whom the onerous task of forming a government could be entrusted. Eventually, the leaders of the three parties whose establishment had been licensed by the Allied authorities formed an *ad hoc* committee. Since no election seemed to be possible within the immediate future, this committee was eventually expanded into a regular cabinet, with its posts distributed among the three "democratic" parties — Socialists (SPOe), People's Party (OeVP), and Communists (KPOe). The idea was to share equally in the responsibilities of government during this transitional period until an election could be called. It was agreed to fill every ministerial office with representatives of all three parties: a minister from one party and at his side under-secretaries from the other two parties. Decisions were to be arrived at jointly, the under-secretaries being required to countersign all orders of the ministers. This improvisation, except for the removal of the Communist Party (which left the government in 1946), has survived the results of four national and two presidential elections that have provided clear popular majorities for one or the other of the two major parties.[3] And there is currently no indication of a possible discontinuance of this system in the foreseeable future.

What were the consequences of this kind of cooperation on the shaping of the political process?

---

[3] Following are the results of the Parliamentary elections since 1945:

	1945	1949	1953	1956
OeVP	1,602,227	1,846,581	1,781,777	1,999,986
(seats)	(85)	(77)	(74)	(82)
SPOe	1,434,898	1,623,524	1,818,517	1,873,295
(seats)	(76)	(67)	(73)	(74)
KPOe	174,357	212,651	228,159	192,438
(seats)	(4)	(5)	(4)	(3)
VdU(FPOe)	—	489,273	472,866	283,749
(seats)		(16)	(14)	(6)

The second conservative party, the VdU (since 1955, FPOe) has no share in any proportionate arrangements. The slow absorption of its electoral following by the two major parties has minimized its political effectiveness. The *Koalitionspakt* (see below) serves effectively to prevent a coalition of the conservative parties, or Marxist parties, and of course, the memory of the First Republic serves as a warning against relegating one or the other of the two major parties into the "permanent opposition." (In Germany the unwelcome consequences of such a "permanent opposition" are again making themselves felt quite strongly.)

First of all, from the very beginning, the primacy of the party over any kind of representative institution was virtually assured. Since no under-secretary or minister could refuse his signature unless he was willing to risk rejection of his party's demand in another department, the area of ministerial or cabinet authority was sharply circumscribed. Individual responsibility was immediately moved into the background as the parties assumed command of policy formulation. In effect, decisions were concentrated more and more in the hands of the two major party leaders — who, as chancellor and vice-chancellor, occupied seats in the cabinet and whose absolute authority within their respective parties made it impossible for them to compel the carrying out of decisions reached bilaterally. It was of the greatest importance in determining the bargaining power of either of these leaders, vis-à-vis his opposite, and in buttressing his authority within the party, that he be able to control the disposition of the requisite positions in the newly forming hierarchy of the government service.

Legally, the distribution was launched with the passage of the *Civil Service Transitional Law*,[4] which was intended to govern the filling of those positions that had been left vacant by the removal of regular NSDAP members and their known sympathizers. The law gave preference to those who had never been Nazi party members and also to those who had proven their anti-Nazi sympathies by having been actually persecuted politically. It prescribed that a proven Austrian democratic attitude was to be considered more important than expert qualifications.

The language of this law worked rather markedly to the disadvantage of the Socialists. Very few, if any, of them had been members of the government service during the First Republic and consequently they had no prior rights to assert. Socialists had therefore to compete on the basis of legal equality with those Austrians whose "democratic" attitudes had not prevented them from faithfully serving the Dollfuss regime but who then had been dismissed by the succeeding Hitler regime. For this reason the SPOe considered it vitally important to safeguard its own political interests by insisting wherever possible on the appointment of active SPOe members to positions — high or low — in the government service.

The ability of each party to press its demands depended on the strength of its popular and parliamentary support, and, accordingly, was subject to adjustment at election time. The first such adjustment took place after the November 1945 election when the Communists found their vote reduced and hence their representation and positions within the government. Eventually, a regular formula was worked out for distributing government positions in proportion to the party strength as it appeared after an election. The tenacity with which each party fought for its proportionate representation in each branch of the government earned the system the appellation of *Proporz* or, more popularly, St. Proportius.

Though the system of *Proporz* was never given any official sanction as a

---

[4] *StGBl.* No. 134, Gesetz vom 22 August 1945, zur Wiederherstellung des oesterr. Beamtentums (*Beamten–Ueberleitungs Gesetz*).

means of regularizing and formalizing appointment procedures, it developed almost effortlessly from the granting of hiring autonomy to most government departments. This made it possible for department heads to surround themselves largely with advisors and subordinates of their own party. As long as the OeVP remains the majority partner in the coalition it has, of course, more ministers under its control and therefore greater access to new positions. By maintaining high educational requirements for certain areas of the civil service, the OeVP also still has the edge over the SPOe, since the bulk of university graduates are OeVP members or affiliated with that party. In any case, it is now generally conceded that no action involving a public position can be taken without party affiliation playing a major role. In time it has become possible for each party to build up a loyal following within specific areas of governmental administration. An unofficial yet strictly observed axiom of Austrian politics requires that no party be dislodged from its sphere of influence regardless of electoral results without its prior consent and then only on the basis of return guarantees.

The nature of these respective spheres and the guarantees that support them are laid down in a document, the *Koalitionspakt*. A published version of this pact was made available for the first time after the election of 1956, and it reflects precisely the bargaining strength of the two government partners.[5] The pact provides that, ". . . in the relations between the OeVP and SPOe, the proportionate result of the election of May 13, 1956, is to be considered as binding. This *Proporz* is to be applied in all proposals concerning administrative positions in the nationalized enterprises. This is valid also for all appointments to the boards of directors and the supervisors of the nationalized banks." [6]

The basis of uninterrupted government cooperation is laid in the article which provides that ". . . government proposals that have the unanimous consent, both in substance and form, of the representatives of the coalition parties in the cabinet, are binding for the representatives of these parties in the National Assembly." [7] The pact further states that such cooperation must extend throughout the duration of the current legislative session and that new elections can be called only upon prior agreement by both parties.[8]

The effect of the coalition pact and its operational instrument, the *Proporz*, on the political life of the country has been twofold and somewhat paradoxical. On the one hand they have served to increase the power and organization of

---

[5] For the official version of the *Koalitionspakt*, see *Wiener Zeitung*, June 27, 1956; an unofficial final version, together with the original demands put forward by the SPOe, can be found in IX. *Taetigkeitsbericht der sozialistischen Abgeordneten und Bundesraete* (Vienna, 1956).

[6] *Wiener Zeitung*, June 27, 1956, par. 2.

[7] *Ibid.*, par. 5.

[8] *Ibid.*, par. 3. The pact also provides for the creation of a Coalition Committee in the National Assembly, which is to secure a harmonious cooperation of the parties. It is composed of five representatives from each of the two government parties. Its chairmen are the chancellor and vice-chancellor, and the two party whips must also belong to it. (Par. 4.)

the political parties since only the parties provide access to positions of responsibility and control. On the other hand, the continued cooperation and finding of compromises to keep the coalition a going concern have contributed greatly to the reduction of the ideological temperature that was once high enough to break out into civil war. This was expressed concretely in a statement by the president of the National Assembly, who declared that "the consistency with which the two major parties currently reach agreement on decisive issues and the established practice of ensuring this concurrence by a preceding pact are in perfect conformity with the domestic political conditions prevailing in Austria." [9]

The acceptance and workability of the proportionate principle in the filling of government positions as well as the continued adherence to the coalition concept indicate a very realistic compromise between two parties that have recognized the dangers inherent in a deep ideological separation. Because these two parties have become entrenched, however, in distinct areas of the economy and of the government over the past dozen years, it is generally realized that their removal from these spheres of influence might bring in its wake an organizational collapse of the parties. Since the government obviously could not be run if each party insisted rigidly on its doctrine as well as on political dominance in its respective sphere, both parties have willingly paid the price of progressive ideological dilution for the maintenance of their organizations in positions of power and authority.[10] Consequently the two parties no longer confront each other from behind barricades of hostile ideas but instead are able to view sympathetically each other's demands for buttressing power — and meet these demands through strict adherence to the *Proporz* principle. Yet either party, despite the loss of its ideological values, is able to boast of increased organizational strength and, of course, an expansion of party-bureaucratic influence to the point where it is no longer possible for any decision to be made that has not been previously approved by the party executive committees.

III

The *Proporz* in Operation

The process of accommodation between the two party giants can be observed in innumerable instances. Not only are all governmental positions from ambassadors to garbage collectors distributed in exact proportion to the strength of the two parties, but decisions affecting both social and economic

---

[9] *Die Presse,* June 8, 1957.

[10] See the program decided upon by the OeVP at a special party conference on January 28, 1952, in which mention of the Catholic principle of *Solidarismus,* once espoused enthusiastically by the party in 1945, was relegated to the preamble; the rest of the program dealt with socio-economic problems. *Oesterr. Monatshefte,* March 1952. At the Party Conference of November 1957, the SPOe officially broke with its traditional Marxist past by proposing for adoption a new set of party principles — the first since the *Linzer Programm* of 1926 — admittedly patterned after those of the British Labor Party, and citing the errors of Marxian analysis. *Arbeiter Zeitung,* November 22–24, 1957.

policies are also made with reference to the existing distribution of power between the parties. Examples of that kind can be found continually in the daily operations of the government, though here only the most characteristic cases will be singled out.[11]

An almost classic case of the kind is displayed in the attempts to reorganize the governmental broadcasting facilities which until 1955 had been nominally under the control and supervision of the occupation authorities. After the witdrawal of the occupation forces, supervision over these stations was lodged in the hands of the provincial governments. This led to some duplication and inefficiency in both personnel and programming, as well as to the political identification of the various *Land* stations with the party in power, especially in the case of the Vienna station, the largest and best equipped of the system. Between 1955 and 1956 the legal status of the broadcasting system was highly uncertain since neither the provinces nor the central government seemed to have any legal basis for exercising their authority. One of the goals of the 1956 election therefore, as stated by both parties, was a clarification and final settlement of that issue. The SPOe at first went on record as advocating a tightly centralized system, organized preferably as a public corporation but under the jurisdiction of the Ministry of Transport, a Socialist enclave. Later this plan was modified to permit participation by the provinces in the capitalization of the corporation, in a 40:60 ratio, and the creation of a governing board composed equally of representatives from the Ministry of Transport (SPOe) and the Ministry of Education (OeVP).

The OeVP was divided in its attitudes toward reorganization. In the provinces, of course, there was a strong preference for a decentralized system, since the OeVP controlled all but one of the provincial governments. However, this met with strong opposition within the party from the Vienna headquarters, which feared that such a separation would play directly into the hands of the SPOe since that party could then easily get control over the biggest broadcasting plant, the one in Vienna.

With the defeat of the SPOe in the 1956 election, its plan for nationalization of the entire broadcasting system under the authority of the SPOe no longer provided a feasible basis for negotiations. The resulting *Koalitionspakt*, in fact, stipulated that the Cabinet — under OeVP control — would now be charged with the reorganization of the broadcasting system. A cabinet subcommittee, composed of the Chancellor (OeVP), the Vice-Chancellor (SPOe), and the Ministers of Education (OeVP) and of Transport (SPOe) was formed and proceeded to work out the details of the new organization. After protracted negotiations that extended for over a year — and in which the SPOe picked up added bargaining strength through its victory at the presidential election in

---

[11] In the province of Styria the following recent cases have turned on the principle of *Proporz*. Until December 31, 1957, OeVP and SPOe appointed beginning school teachers on the basis of their party membership. *Presse* 6/26/57. The principle applies equally to appointments of principals of secondary schools in the City of Vienna. All social welfare funds — milk subsidies, public housing loan funds and aid to private housing construction — are administered according to the *Proporz Die Wochen Presse*, 2/23/57. The position of vice-president of the Vienna municipal police was left vacant for eight months due to

May 1957 — a scheme was eventually worked out that proved acceptable to the coalition partners.

The Austrian broadcasting system was now reorganized as a limited liability corporation responsible to, and under the ultimate authority of, the central government but providing for financial participation and a controlling voice by the provincial governments. A board of directors was constituted, its membership of 26 members distributed proportionately among the parties according to their representation in the plenary committee of the parliament, i.e., 13:12:1. The chief concerns of this board of directors were to be financial. A four-man executive committee was entrusted with the actual management and decisions on policy; to it were appointed two SPOe and two OeVP representatives. The statutes further provided for an Advisory Council on Programming, to which would be sent representatives of the trade unions, chambers, cultural and scientific associations and the arts — equally divided in their party allegiance. Proof that the OeVP still represented the majority of the electorate was shown in its ability to insist on the appointment of an OeVP man as general manager of the corporation.

The broadcasting problem was thus solved in a manner that reflected accurately the distribution of power between the two parties. The OeVP was able to insist on the organization of a "privately" incorporated system which was ultimately subject to the authority of the cabinet in which the OeVP had a majority, while the SPOe was able to assure for itself sufficient positions of control and responsibility to make certain that neither radio nor television would reflect one-sidedly the views of the majority party. It is improbable that the Austrian broadcasting system could be turned again, under these circumstances, into an instrument of "governmental policy," even in the unlikely event of the dissolution of the coalition.

Equally illustrative of the careful division of spheres of influence according to the proportionate strength of the parties is the manner in which the Austrian airlines were organized. The controversy surrounding the founding of Austria's airline system was also a legacy of the occupation. Soviet Russia, in agreeing to the state treaty which saddled Austria with heavy reparations, had sweetened the pill by magnanimously granting to Austria the right to fly, with her own planes, to and across the Soviet Union. This made Austria the only country outside the Iron Curtain to enjoy this privilege, and under the conditions of the cold war then prevailing it was undeniably a unique commercial opportunity, a fact immediately recognized by the then Minister of Transport and Nationalized Industries, Dr. Waldbrunner (SPOe). When, under SPOe sponsorship and with the financial aid of the Scandinavian Air Lines (SAS), a holding company was formed and incorporated as *Austrian State Airways*, he forthwith issued to it a license granting exclusive operating rights.

Proporz considerations. Since seniority was involved, all promotions down the line had to satisfy the proportional arrangement. *Die Wochen Presse,* July 1, 1957. Most recently the question of political allegiance was raised in the filling of vacancies on the Supreme Judicial Bench of the Provinces. All four of the Superior State Judgeships during the preceding year were listed simultaneously in order to achieve an equitable distribution between the parties. *Berichte und Informationen,* 594 (1957), p. 2.

The objectives of the Socialist minister were, of course, not hidden from the OeVP. Interested parties in the conservative camp countered by sponsoring the formation of a private airline to be known as *Air Austria* whose financial backers were the Dutch KLM and certain private interests in Austria. Since the company could not operate without a license, it applied for one to the Ministry of Transport and Nationalized Industries, only to be informed that such a license would not be forthcoming. However, *Air Austria* (OeVP) had practical advantages over *Austrian Airways* (SPOe) in being able to establish itself in a hangar on Vienna's principal air field and in having access to enough working capital to start the buying of some machines and the training of pilots. The anomalous as well as the comical aspects of the situation were reminiscent of the plots of some old-style Viennese operettas: the company with the license but without capital confronting the company without license but with the necessary funds.

It was fairly clear that Waldbrunner's aim was a completely nationalized airline system that would fall easily within the sphere of interest of the SPOe. Whether this scheme could have succeeded can no longer be stated with certainty; undoubtedly Waldbrunner's position in this as well as in a similar matter involving rights to oil deposits seemed strong enough to make any merely temporizing settlement impossible.[12] If the OeVP wanted to challenge the SPOe on this matter, elections that would measure again the "proportionate" influence of the respective parties seemed the only possible answer. National elections were called accordingly for May 1956. The result, somewhat unexpectedly, was a reduction in the popular support of the SPOe — and the consequent obsolescence of Waldbrunner's grandiose plans for nationalization of both air and oil.[13] Instead, on the basis of the *Koalitionspakt*, the parties now began to negotiate for the creation of a corporate structure that would assure both coalition partners influence and control proportionate to their showing in the May elections.

A compromise finally emerged in July 1957, after thirteen months of on-again-off-again negotiations held against the background of threats of a dissolution of the coalition. It was agreed to merge the "paper" airline with the "squatting" airline as the OeLAG (*Oesterreichische Luft Verkehrs A. G.*),

---

[12] The 1955 State Treaty establishing Austria's independence also provided for the return to her of formerly Western-owned oil fields that had been under Russian domination. It was the intention of Waldbrunner's ministry, which had been entrusted with temporary administration of these enterprises, to nationalize them completely. Since these oil fields were located in the OeVP-governed *Land* of Lower Austria, the *Land* government claimed them as *Land* property. It created an oil enterprise of its own, *NIOGAS*, backed by OeVP-oriented financial interests, and declared its intention to issue operating rights to United States and British oil companies. This scheme understandably aroused the opposition of the SPOe, which charged the OeVP with wanting to bring Austria again under the domination of foreign capital and to compromise its neutrality. *Arbeiter Zeitung,* February 2, 1956. For the highly complicated legal tangle that surrounded the returned oil properties (no less than 17 treaties were applicable) see *Die Presse,* January 20, 1957; also *Wiener Zeitung,* December 2, 1955.

[13] The jurisdiction of Socialist Minister Waldbrunner was reduced from Transport and Nationalized Industries to Transport and Electricity. The nationalized industry complex,

Austrian Air Transit Corporation. This privately incorporated company was to be capitalized according to a 60:40 ratio, representing the interests of the OeVP and SPOe groups respectively and together making up 70 per cent of the total investment; the rest — 30 per cent — was to be raised from foreign sources. The Austrian share thus was split 42 per cent to 28 per cent of the total, the former representing the investment interests of the three nationalized banks (*Creditanstalt, Laenderbank,* and *Oesterreich. Creditinstitute*) all under OeVP control, and of a number of large industrial firms that were well known backers of the conservative party. The latter represented the funds of the *Arbeiterbank,* Vienna Municipality, Austrian Travel Bureau, Vienna Municipal Insurance Company and others — all institutions under direct SPOe control.[14]

Both parties were highly satisfied with this settlement, the OeVP because it held majority control, and the SPOe because it had been able to reserve for itself at least a partially controlling interest in a commercial enterprise whose continued importance and almost certain profitability were virtually assured. It also proved that outright nationalization was no longer necessary to provide the party with a determining influence in the economy.

Two other major examples can be cited to illustrate the pervasive influence of the *Proporz.* One is the arrangement that made possible the emission of "People's Shares" — a form of denationalization of the banks — and the other is the creation of the military establishment permitted to the newly neutralized Austria by the former occupying powers.

Among the issues with which the OeVP had entered the 1956 national election was the denationalization of the banks. This was not regarded very seriously by the SPOe: such a step could hardly be taken, even in the event of an OeVP victory, without bringing into question the further continuance of the coalition — a risk neither partner was willing to take. The *Koalitionspakt* contained no reference to any such plan. Even the declaration of government policy endorsed by the SPOe made only passing reference to the eventual issuance of "People's Shares."

Events took an unexpected turn, however, and both parties were forced to deal with the problem much sooner than they had anticipated. The action which triggered the People's Share problem was the threat, in October 1956,

---

including oil, was transferred to the authority of a cabinet committee under the chairmanship of Chancellor Raab, which gave the OeVP a permanent one-vote majority. The authority of this committee also extended, as a board of directors, to a newly chartered corporation charged exclusively with the exploitation of Austrian oil deposits, in which the government held a majority interest. *Koalitionspakt,* IV and V, *Wiener Zeitung,* June 29, 1956. If this seems like a crushing defeat for the SPOe, it must be pointed out that despite the substitution of collegial for one-man rule in the nationalized industries, the SPOe influence on the managerial level went unimpaired. And in the case of oil, the SPOe at least secured a share in the control of these deposits. Neither arrangement would have been likely under a "normally" operating parliamentary system. For a detailed account of the administrative reorganization pursuant to the provisions of the *Pakt,* see "Das kleinere Ministerium und die grosse Holding-Gmbh," *Berichte und Informationen,* 519 (1956), p. 7.

[14] *Wiener Zeitung,* July 11, 1957.

of a general strike by public employees. They demanded that scheduled salary increases be moved up from the date originally promised, July 1957, to January 1957. The gap which this step would leave in the budget was estimated at about 600 mil. A. S. Chancellor Raab and his finance minister, Herr Kamitz, moved quickly and without prior consultation with the coalition partner. Having first secured a promise of support from the six-man FPOe, the OeVP laid before Parliament a resolution demanding the sale of government shares in the nationalized banks to cover the prospective budget deficit. But the risk which the OeVP seemed to be taking deliberately, of dissolving the coalition, was really no risk at all. The SPOe, like its coalition partner, stood committed to the salary raises for public employees. The treasury was undeniably empty and the SPOe was in no position politically to insist on its own plan for covering the deficit — raising taxes — since that would have alienated a considerable portion of its own supporters.

After a hastily called meeting of its central committee, the SPOe declared its willingness to agree in principle to the OeVP proposal, provided that a majority of the shares of the nationalized banks should remain in public hands. Privately, many SPOe leaders expressed the opinion that in conditions of prosperity and full employment it would not make too much difference who owned a minority interest in the nationalized enterprises. The SPOe and the OeVP now entered into negotiations over the "proportionate" division of the capital of the three large nationalized banks.

On the basis of a separate coalition agreement, the two parties in December 1956 introduced jointly a bill that provided for full payment of public salaries by January 1957 and also contained provisions for meeting the consequent budgetary expenses. Thirty per cent of the capital of the nationalized banks was to be issued as non-voting shares of six per cent preferred stock, and these would be available to the public as "people's shares." Another 10 per cent of bank capital would be sold as regular Founders' shares with full voting rights, but only to *party-controlled enterprises,* on the basis of a 60:40 distribution between the OeVP and SPOe respectively.

In order to arrange for the sale of these securities, the Ministry of Finance initiated the creation of two investment trusts, A and B, each representing the financial interests of one party. Investment trust A is dominated by agricultural cooperatives and a number of provincial private banks, all closely identified with the OeVP; they in turn, offered these securities for sale to other OeVP-dominated interest groups, *e.g.,* the Chambers of Commerce, Association of Manufacturing Industries, and remaining agricultural cooperatives. Investment trust B was controlled by the *Arbeiterbank* and the Central Savings Association of the City of Vienna, both SPOe-operated enterprises. This trust would then sell exclusively to the OeGB (Austrian Trade Union Federation) and to the Consumer Cooperatives, both SPOe-controlled institutions.

The agreement was hailed by both sides as a triumph of compromise and as an illustration of the beneficent workings of the *Proporz* in yet another sphere of public life. In March 1957 the first People's Shares went on sale; the first person to appear for his "People's Share" was a trolley-car conductor whose membership in the SPOe dated back to the time of the "class struggles" in the First Republic. Within a few weeks the People's Shares were oversubscribed and ceased to be a political issue.

But undoubtedly the greatest triumph of the *Proporz* was achieved in connection with the new military establishment of the liberated Second Republic. After the bitter experiences with the army of the First Republic a long controversy between the parties over ultimate control of the new army seemed almost unavoidable. Especially in view of the tensions then agitating the West German neighbor, equally busy with the task of creating a new military establishment, the efforts in Austria were watched with apprehension by both foreign and domestic observers. But no friction developed between the parties. With spectacularly diplomatic smoothness, even the minor points were very soon settled. After ten years of practice in operating the *Proporz* machinery, this should hardly have been cause for surprise.

As the majority party, the OeVP could claim for itself the office of Minister of Defense. The occupant of this post was no newcomer to either politics or administration. Herr Graf, secretary of the OeVP, had been in charge of the federal police force (*Bundes-Gendarmerie*) built up during the occupation. This force fell under the jurisdiction of the Minister of the Interior, Herr Helmer, a Socialist who had already proven during the 1950 Communist riots that he could and would fully cooperate with his assistant secretary from the other party. Graf's lines of communication to the SPOe were, therefore, of the best, and it was even rumored that the SPOe insisted on his appointment to the Defense Ministry over that of others.

The new minister, in turn, was given a Socialist undersecretary, Dr. Stephani, who, unlike his superior, had an excellent war record — as a decorated captain in the German tank corps — and who had joined the SPOe only after the war. Together, the former concentration camp inmate and the former *Wehrmacht* captain prevented a struggle from developing over the control of this new power factor in Austrian politics.

The re-establishment of the army was aided by the fact that the constitution vests the authority of Commander-in-Chief in the President, who is elected by popular vote. In 1956 that office was held by Herr Koerner, Socialist, onetime general of the Imperial Army, and one of the organizers of the *Schutzbund*, the SPD party's paramilitary organization of the First Republic. Under his influence the Second Republic avoided many of the mistakes that had frustrated the creation of a popular army in the early days of the First Republic. Together with military experts, Koerner insisted on the principle of a single Chief of Staff, and was able to convince both parties of the advantages of such an organization. The Law of September 7, 1955, providing for the creation of a defense establishment, declared that "the Minister of Defense exercises his authority via the commanding officers and *their* superior officer."[15] Thus was implied the creation of an office of Chief Inspector General of Troops who is in effect a single Supreme Chief of Staff. It is his responsibility to select the higher rank command and staff officers. The man appointed to this position

---

[15] *BGBl* 181/1955.

of supreme command was Colonel Fusseneger, son of a former officer in the Austrian Imperial Army, himself a career soldier in the army of the First Republic, and later in the German *Wehrmacht*. What made Colonel Fusseneger so eminently acceptable to both parties was his "clean" record during the First Republic. Through a combination of happy circumstances, he had managed to be absent whenever the army became involved in conflict, armed or otherwise, with the civilian part of the Austrian population.

In appointing Fusseneger as Chief of Staff, the Second Republic showed once again that it had learned a lesson from the First Republic. The suspicious founders of the shaky constitutional edifice in 1920 refused to grant to its army a supreme military commander. As a result, the Austrian army became the plaything of the parties, until, eventually, the conservative Christian Socialists captured completed control and successfully fashioned it into the exclusive instrument of that party. The natural reaction of the Social Democrats was to turn their backs on the military, castigating it as an instrument of class oppression, and to devote themselves to the perfection of their own military arm.

Even within the short time since the new Austrian army has been in operation, it is agreed by all competent observers that Colonel Fusseneger, unimpeded by party bickerings, has succeeded in creating an impeccably organized and well-disciplined conventional defense arm that has earned him the confidence and admiration of both government parties. During the period of the Hungarian revolution his organization received its "baptism of fire" by conducting itself in such a manner as to avoid all semblance of partisanship or aggressiveness, in a situation that was fraught with explosive international potentialities.

IV

Conclusion

The creation of a civil service and an army which, though not necessarily "neutral" or "nonpartisan" in the usual tradition, are at least fully acceptable to both government parties is an achievement that cannot be overestimated in view of the turbulent history of the Austrian Republic. It bespeaks a spirit of cooperation that by now extends into the most delicate areas of public policy, *e.g.*, that of Church-State relations. This relationship is even now undergoing a process of accommodation that may have far-reaching consequences for Vatican policies in other countries.

Provided the practice of *Proporz* can be continued without major impairment of the state's services, it may well constitute the only effective instrument for injecting into Austrian politics that sense of state over party, the absence of which contributed to the downfall of the First Republic. The sudden discontinuance of the *Proporz* at the present time would almost certainly work incalculable damage to both government parties and seriously undermine the sense of trust in the idea of coalition which is held responsible by Austria's leading politicians as well as their followers for the current economic prosperity, social tranquility, and political stability.

Nevertheless, these leaders are not unaware of the disadvantages wrought by their "peculiar institution." Efforts at reducing the area in which the writ of the *Proporz* runs are under way. Thus it has been suggested that regular civil service examinations should be introduced for positions that require expert technical qualifications. Reference to such reforms was made by the new President, Dr. Schaerf, former chairman of the SPOe, in his inaugural speech, and since then they have received the endorsement of other well known personalities in both parties. This, it is generally agreed, is at least a beginning which may prove eventually that the practice of the "Holy Proportius" will not have been in vain, but, on the contrary, can be considered as having justified itself as a contributing factor in successfully launching Austria on its second attempt at an independent national existence.

Despite the unifying effects of the trying experiences of the last two decades, Austria is still groping for national unity. Given the present size and still largely compartmentalized spheres of influence of the two government parties, it is doubtful that anything but their continued cooperation can provide a basis for popular acceptance of the Austrian state. A disruption of that condition, especially in view of Austria's exposed international position, might again herald that "tendency toward non-existence" that stalked the political efforts of the First Republic. It is possible, of course, that the present system could, under these circumstances, lend itself more easily to the establishment of one-man rule in a period of real internal crisis. Yet it is not without significance that so far this arrangement has weathered several crises without taking this ultimate step and without the participation of either the extreme right or left. Equally, this unique political collaboration can be given at least part of the credit for having maintained Austria's continued separation from the Communist-dominated East European bloc of nations.

34. Consensus and Cleavage in British Political Ideology

JAMES B. CHRISTOPH

Basic consensus was re-established in Britain through the integrative experience of the wartime coalition against Nazi Germany and the acceptance by all parties of the major features of the welfare state. The major problem became how to meet the challenge of productive efficiency—one that neither party, bound by mutual concern for established values and aversion against too-ruthless rationalization, and hemmed in by various powerful veto groups, was equipped to meet. The dividing line between "modernity" and "tradition"—between "expertise" and "amateurishness"—cuts across traditional ideologies, and raises, in Britain as elsewhere, serious questions as to the relevance of parliamentary politics.

One of the most perplexing questions to students of politics since the mid-1950s has been whether western societies are now approaching, or have reached, a condition called "the end of ideology." Numerous answers have been propounded, both by those who regard such a development as desirable and by those who view it with disquietude. But difficulties have arisen because exponents of one view or the other have had recourse to markedly different, and often shifting, concepts of the terms "ideology" and "end." If this important controversy is to be saved from sterility, social scientists must both reflect more upon the nature of the terms employed and descend from the level of sweeping cultural generalizations to examine the condition of ideology in particular political settings.

It is my purpose here to try to shed some light on the debate by surveying the state of political ideology in present-day Britain from the standpoint of two different uses of the term. My position is that if we adopt one view of ideology, we find that British politics are profoundly non-ideological; but if we define the concept in different but still meaningful terms, we discover that in fact it does play an important role in the British system. In other words, by compressing extant concepts of ideology into two distinct molds we may be able to fashion tools for judging the ideological condition of countries such as Britain. These I will designate the *Weltanschauung* and the "attitude structure" versions of the term.

The first refers to the more traditional meaning of ideology, the alleged decline of which has occasioned the debate of the past decade. It has been characterized as a "comprehensive, consistent, closed system of knowledge, to

SOURCE: Reprinted by permission from *The American Political Science Review*, LIX (September 1965), pp. 629–642. Footnotes are abridged.

which its adherents turn to get answers to all their questions, solutions to all their problems."[1] Its connotations are familiar: commitment (both intellectual and emotional), orientation toward action, distortion or simplification of reality, hostility to critics and opponents, and goal-orientation (often of the millennial variety). Perhaps its best-known paradigms are classical Christianity and classical Marxism.

The conception of ideology as attitude structure is more difficult to set forth because it falls short of the total belief system and tight logic of a "world view." Like a *Weltanschauung*, it partakes of a generalized view of man; it has moral and normative content; it "places" the individual in relation to his fellows; and it calls forth commitment and points to desirable actions. It consists of many separate but related attitudes which function to relate, and give meaning to, the different political events experienced by the individual. On the other hand, this concept of ideology is less apt to provide its holders with a total explanation of life or a full vision of human destiny. It is more earthbound, culture-bound and diffused, both in its sources and its scope. Ideology in this sense refers to a more or less institutionalized set of beliefs about man and society. It is likely to be a composite of prevailing generalized views of man, the goals that he does and should seek, the means he uses to achieve them, the outlook for progress under present or alternative institutions, and so forth. Because such ideology may have many sources, it is less likely than the "big" world views to be intellectualized, comprehensive, systematic or consistent, and more likely to be fragmentary, limited, even inconsistent. Yet when political man operates with reference to this organized bundle of views, he may derive from it some of the certainty and security that accompany a commitment to fuller, better articulated ideologies. While undoubtedly many would reject this use of the term, it is noteworthy that most of those who have attempted to measure the presence and effects of ideology in the Anglo-American polity have favored this definition, or one similar to it.

Without attempting here to defend my preference for viewing ideology in this two-fold way, I would assert that an awareness of the distinction is necessary for any exploration of the state of ideology in Britain today. In addition, I make two other assumptions that need to be stated explicitly. First, I am assuming that the pertinent kind of ideology for this discussion is one with a fairly direct *political* implication, *i.e.*, one which relates to questions involving the relations of rulers and ruled and the principles of governance. While these aspects of ideology may be torn from a larger context (general belief systems), no attempt will be made to delve into such related problems as the psychological functions served by the holding of ideologies. Second, I proceed on the assumption that a country's ideology is not wholly concentrated among its intellectuals and political leaders, but in a participant political culture like the British also operates in and is expressed by the lives of "average people." For this reason, it will be necessary to examine (in Lane's terms) both *forensic* ideologies — the articulated, differentiated, well developed political arguments put forth consciously by the elite — and *latent* ideologies — the loosely struc-

---

[1] Herbert J. Spiro, *Government by Constitution* (New York, 1959), p. 180.

tured and often unreflective statements of the common man — and to see how they relate to each other.

I

The Rejection of Total Ideology

The kind of ideology associated with a complete world view emerged and flourished under certain historical and social conditions. Many of these conditions were indeed present during the period from the seventeenth to the nineteenth centuries, the so-called "age of ideology," [2] just as they appear to be present today in a number of the new developing countries. Ideology in this sense seemed to flourish especially in societies that experienced the upheavals of modernization in violent and concerted forms — that pitted classes and religious groups against each other in passionate struggle, that aroused a strong sense of deprivation among underdogs and losers, and that fragmented the community into subcultures alienated from the value patterns of the dominant political system. Put another way, total ideologies were most likely to gain ground in societies with political systems that failed both the test of effectiveness (success in solving the problems put onto them) and the test of legitimacy (widespread agreement on the propriety).[3] Where these conditions are lacking, or disappearing, it has been argued, ideology of this variety cannot really flower. Recent critics have extended the argument to read that when a society achieves modernity (seen as a matter of industrialization, urbanization, secularization, economic prosperity, middle class expansion and working class access to political power), then the passionate attachment to total ideology not only subsides, but becomes dangerously dysfunctional to the system.

I have no desire to put an oar into the choppy seas of this latter controversy. My point is simply that Britain has not provided the conditions favoring the growth of this kind of ideological thinking. The British have shown a marked disinclination to take up total ideologies for a host of reasons, many of which are familiar and only a few of which can be mentioned here. In the past three hundred years Britain has avoided, or seriously blunted, the traumatic revolutions that many other countries have undergone, and the main changes in its political, economic and social systems have occurred gradually. The mounting demands of disadvantaged groups have been met in a piecemeal way, with the result that with the exception of the Irish (whose fate was finally settled by truncation) no major group has failed to be integrated in some way into the political system. As is well known, neither the communists nor the fascists have gained substantial followings or political leverage. The non-revolutionary character of the British working class is equally well known; and while a distinct working class subculture may exist, as Williams and Hoggart have argued, it does not involve working class alienation from the values of the political system. Social mobility in Britain may not be as great as elsewhere,

---

[2] Frederick M. Watkins, *The Age of Ideology — Political Thought, 1750 to the Present* (Englewood Cliffs, N. J., 1964).

[3] Seymour Martin Lipset, *Political Man* (Garden City, 1960), chs. 2–3.

but it has always been present and visible, and with the postwar changes in the educational system and the rapid expansion of white collar occupations, most Britons see it as increasing.

Another explanation for the lack of enthusiasm for total ideologies is imbedded deep in British political culture: it is the much-cited attachment to precedents and usage in preference to the logic of rational blueprints. In a system where there is widespread agreement on fundamental institutions and on a considerable range of current policies, it is possible to operate without continual reference to eternal verities, large schema, or articulated belief systems. The tendency to settle issues on the basis of accepted usages and through the means of implicit "understandings" is indeed great, to the frustration of those who plump for a fuller rehearsal of arguments or an enlightening confrontation of basic doctrine. Whether the source of this political style is the common law tradition, the evolutionary character of the British constitution, the norms of parliamentary and bureaucratic behavior, or the social homogeneity of the ruling elite is impossible to ascertain, and really beside the point. Political styles develop from many sources. They are bound to be both causes and effects of other phenomena. What can be asserted is that British political leaders have become habituated to thinking in terms of concrete problems and familiar responses; and that this — when coupled with a general complacency toward the outputs of such behavior — serves as a barrier, a disincentive, to the adoption of total ideologies. Thus, however circular the logic may seem, the British tend to be immune to extreme ideological views because they have not been used to thinking along these lines, and they have no strong motivation to abandon the habit.

The point can be put more strongly. Pragmatic norms in Britain have been elevated into something approaching a national cult — so much so, I would argue, that we can speak without sophistry of an ideology of pragmatism, which serves as a foil to the ideology of total ends. For many Britons pragmatism is not simply a descriptive term for the way they approach or grapple with political problems; it is also a particularly British virtue and an object of pride, which they would not trade for what they consider to be the inflexible, irrevocable, and inhumane (in the sense of denying the variety of human nature) qualities of this or that "world view." Thus pragmatism easily becomes imbued with nationalistic affect, and preference for it is supported by other values into which Britons are socialized. The content of this socialization is both positive and negative in character: positive in the sense that Britons learn, both from formal teaching and from informally picking up the views of those around them, that the success and stability of the British parliamentary system is due in large part to the pragmatic frame of mind displayed by its practitioners; and negative in the sense that they also learn that the turbulent, unstable and often grotesque pattern of Continental politics derives from the European habit of looking at the world through the distorting spectacles of total ideologism. What they have learned may be a caricature, but it has had consequences. It has, for example, affected the British Labour Party's relationship with the European socialist movement; it has been partly responsible for the lack of enthusiasm for venturing too fully into experiments in European integration, and undoubtedly it has helped strengthen Britain's relationships with the United States and the older Commonwealth — peoples reputed to be fellow pragmatists under the white skin.

These conditions, and many more, add up to a general climate in which the total ideological structuring of politics is difficult to achieve. The skeptic might counter that the case has yet to be proved, that these generalizations are no more than the accumulated clichés of historians and journalists, who have selected their examples to suit their preconceived case. Fortunately, political scientists have begun to amass more empirical data bearing on the subject and tending to confirm these assertions. Thus far, to be sure, no one has made a comprehensive, systematic exploration of the distribution of ideological propensities among the British people or the political elite. We have, for example, no British counterparts of the extensive surveys of political attitudes made by the Michigan Survey Research Center and by McClosky, Prothro and Grigg, or of the intensive psychoanalytical probing by Lane into the political ideologies of a handful of east coast residents. Nevertheless, in the past several years a small number of rigorous empirical studies of the character and distribution of British political attitudes have appeared, and in an indirect way they offer evidence as to the role of ideology in contemporary British political thinking, both at the mass level and among political activists.

If it can be shown that the mass of Britons are not alienated from the system in which they live, that they look tolerantly on those who hold different political beliefs, and that they tend not to be polarized on policies presumed to be highly charged with ideological affect, then we can reasonably conclude that total ideology has not taken hold of them. And if we can demonstrate further that this same pattern prevails among the political elite as well, we will have further confirmation of the generalization.

Data on Alienation

In an ambitious cross-national survey carried out in 1959, Almond and Verba found that the British ranked comparatively low on social and political alienation and high on willingness to trust and cooperate with other people. For example, 84 per cent of the British sample agreed with the statement, "Human nature is fundamentally cooperative," compared to 80 per cent of the Americans, 58 per cent of the Germans and 55 per cent of the Italians. Another query designed to measure generalized trust ("Most people can be trusted") drew affirmative replies from 49 per cent of the British, 55 per cent of the Americans, 19 per cent of the Germans, and five per cent of the Italians.[4] Almond and Verba not only find in the United States and Britain a widespread belief that people are basically cooperative, trustworthy and helpful; they also show that in these countries social trust is translated into politically relevant trust, thus reducing the alienation of people from the system. From spontaneous and unstructured responses to another survey question designed to test

---

[4] Gabriel A. Almond and Sidney Verba, *The Civic Culture* (Princeton, 1963), p. 267, Table 4.

emotional attachment to certain aspects of the nation, the same investigators found that the features mentioned as objects of pride most frequently by Britons were their country's governmental and political system (46 per cent), its social legislation (18 per cent), and its position in international affairs (11 per cent). (Only three, one and two per cent, respectively, of the Italians who were asked the same question named these areas as objects of pride. They chose instead the physical attributes of their country [25 per cent], contributions to the arts [16 per cent], and "nothing" [27 per cent].)[5] These are admittedly fragments of indirect evidence, but they seem to point to the presence in Britain of the kind of social and emotional climate in which total ideologies are not apt to flourish.

Intensity of Partisanship

A related consideration is the strength of partisan feeling that runs through a country. If we assume that in the modern state the political party is likely to be a major channel for the expression of ideological thinking, then one would expect to find in countries characterized by *Weltanschauung* politics a high degree of hostility among one party's followers toward rival partisans. Here again, recent surveys of British attitudes show this to be far from the case. While the images of their own and the opposite party's supporters held by Britons are somewhat sharper and more polarized than in the United States, they fall far short of intense hostility. Almond and Verba did find that 28 per cent of Conservative party supporters, and 29 per cent of Labour party supporters, believed that "selfish people" support the opposite party; that nearly one-fourth of the Conservative respondents viewed Labourites as "ignorant and misguided," and that 10 per cent of the Labour respondents characterized Conservatives as "militarists and imperialists." On the other hand, almost no followers of either party (three percent in each case) accepted the view that the followers of the other were "betrayers of freedom and welfare." [6] Furthermore, when asked the hypothetical question, "How would you feel if your son or daughter married a supporter of the Labour (Conservative) party?", only 12 per cent of Labourites expressed displeasure at the thought of intermarriage, and 87 and 97 per cent, respectively, professed indifference.[7]

An even stronger indication of the tolerance of the British electorate toward political opponents is found in the results of the survey made in 1960 by Mark Abrams for *Socialist Commentary* magazine. On the basis of that poll, Abrams reported that

> . . . between 40 per cent and 50 per cent of Labour supporters thought that the Conservatives could do as well as their own party in standing for the nation as a whole, in giving fair treatment to all races, in respecting British traditions, and in working for world peace and against nuclear war. Of those who opposed

---

[5] *Ibid.*, p. 102, Table 1.

[6] *Ibid.*, p. 126, Table 2.

[7] *Ibid.*, p. 136, Table 8.

Labour, at least 40 per cent were prepared to describe Labour as equally quali-fied with the Conservatives in giving fair treatment to all races, working for peace, and opposing nuclear war.[8]

The same survey revealed that supporters of both parties, as well as uncom-mitted voters, when asked to choose the characteristics they looked for in a good party leader, picked identical traits in the same order and nearly the same degree — the top three being strong leadership, willingness to make unwelcome decisions, and honesty and sincerity.[9]

Policy Attitudes

This tendency toward doctrinal flexibility within the electorate can also be demonstrated by referring to policy attitudes which, in view of their historical importance to the parties, are apt to be imbued with considerable ideological affect. Consider the concept of nationalization, which for many years was linked by the Labour movement with the ideas of economic rationality and social equality, and which was painted by Conservatives as the epitome of economic tyranny and socialist inefficiency. The *Socialist Commentary* poll found "no homogeneous, blanket attitude toward public ownership," and concluded that "views on this subject are apparently not the outcome of either blind faith or blind rejection."[10] When asked to assess the condition of the nationalized industries, Conservative and Labour voters made practically identical judgments, discriminating mainly on the grounds of performance rather than ideology. For example, among Conservatives favorable attitudes toward public ownership exceeded unfavorable ones for four of the industries (electricity, gas, atomic energy and the airlines), while more Labour sup-porters termed the nationalization of coal and the railways a failure than a success. Eighty-four per cent of Conservatives and 58 per cent of Labourites expressed themselves as opposed to any further nationalization. Finally, when asked more generally how much government regulation of industry they thought was necessary, 10 per cent of the Conservatives and only 18 per cent of the Labourites chose "a good deal," while at the other pole 25 per cent of the Conservatives and 10 per cent of the Labourites replied "practically none." Majorities in both parties accepted the need for a fair amount of regulation, and within each there was goodly support for the "wrong" ideological position on this issue.[11]

Low tension between party supporters also tends to characterize foreign policy attitudes. This is borne out by the analysis made by Davis and Verba of British mass opinions during the period 1947–56 on selected foreign policy issues, many of them presumed to be vested with ideological affect. The polls

---

[8] Mark Abrams, Richard Rose, and Rita Hinden, *Must Labour Lose?* (Harmondsworth, 1960), p. 19.

[9] *Ibid.,* p. 25.

[10] *Ibid.,* p. 31.

[11] *Ibid.,* pp. 31, 35–36.

they examined dealt with respondents' orientations toward the following issues: internationalism, armament, colonialism, the choice between the United States and the Soviet Union, European alliances, the Far Eastern policy.[12] On only 13 per cent of the questions was there a low degree of interparty agreement, as compared with 59 per cent high agreement; and had the Suez crisis not been included, the interparty differences would have virtually disappeared. Davis and Verba conclude that "for the most part adherents to any one political party generally express the same sorts of opinions on international issues as adherents to another party; and a high degree of unity within a party is not so much evidence that the party tends to unify the sentiments of its supporters as that it expresses the sentiments of a highly unified nation."[13]

Insofar, then, as the attitudes of the mass public reveal the extent of ideological modes of thinking, these varied data show not only that a good deal of pragmatism does prevail, but also that the conditions associated with the politics of total ideology — distrust of and hostility to opposing views, a considerable alienation from societal values, and marked polarization on policy questions — are not characteristic of contemporary Britain. It is still conceivable, of course, that these attitudes are not shared by the elite among political activists, and we must now turn briefly to an examination of this possibility.

Again it must be noted that full and systematic data on the basic beliefs of British political leaders are lacking. Nevertheless, several important studies of elite opinion in Britain have appeared recently. They indicate that ideological views at this level too, while more substantial and coherent than within the general public, are not especially prevalent and tend to keep conflict within manageable bounds. The studies that I shall cite here are those of constituency party attitudes and back-bench opinion in the House of Commons.

For some time it has been assumed that the real seat of ideologism in the British political system is the parties' constituency associations. The argument runs something like this: while the top parliamentary leaders of the major parties must blunt any ideological tendencies they might have, for electoral reasons as well as because they are dealing with the realities of governing, the activists who man the local parties are not under these constraints and thus are more likely to be involved in politics for reasons of ideological principle. They work zealously for their party not to advance their own careers, but to further the abstract principles in which they believe passionately. They are more likely to be purists or extremists, more reactionary than the national leadership if they are Conservatives, more radically socialist than the national leadership if they are Labourites. Several demonstrations of this pattern appeared in the 1950s, notably the continuing support for Bevanism in the constituency Labour parties and the stiff punishment meted out to leftward deviating Conservative M.P.s by Conservative associations when their Members failed to support the government on issues such as capital punishment and Suez.

---

[12] Morris Davis and Sidney Verba, "Party Affiliation and International Opinions in Britain and France, 1947–1956," *Public Opinion Quarterly*, Vol. 24 (Winter, 1960), pp. 590–604.

[13] *Ibid.*, p. 601.

These gave the impression that the constituency parties are apt to be composed of die-hard, dogmatic, irresponsible ideologues, who are neither representative of grassroots partisan thinking nor, unless they are kept at arm's length from policy-making, assets to responsible party leadership.

This argument has some validity, although a closer look at the local parties shows it to be quite exaggerated. In a painstaking study of resolutions sent by local parties to the annual conferences from 1955 to 1960, Rose has shown that the image of local parties "as a force constantly pressing extremist views upon national leaders" is overdrawn.[14] He found, for example, that the total proportion of resolutions containing ideological elements was 54 per cent, while the remaining 46 per cent dealt with nonpartisan questions of little ideological content — expressing mainly views derived from general cultural values or specific interest groups demands. Furthermore, most of the resolutions Rose classifies as ideological were simply in line with the standard programs of the parties (e.g., concerning support for or opposition to the present organization of secondary education, the need for or danger of more economic planning, and so on) and were a far cry from the categories of total ideology. Rose also analyzed the resolutions for their "extremism" content, i.e., whether they deviated markedly from the prevailing doctrine of the party in the direction of purism. He found that in the period in question 66 per cent of Conservative and 38 per cent of Labour associations had submitted no extremist resolutions whatever; while in 11 per cent of Conservative and 18 cent of Labour associations, over half the submitted resolutions were of this variety.[15] Rather than finding these attitudes to be geographically concentrated in a few constituency parties, however — which might function as party subcultures — Rose determined that they were randomly distributed around the country. So he concluded that there is much less hot partisanship in the local parties than has been thought, and that the supposed doctrinal differences between these parties on the one hand, and either rank and file party voters or parliamentary leaders on the other, are really not great.

We have also recently been given a glimpse of the attitude structure of the House of Commons in the research of Finer, Berrington and Bartholomew of Keele University.[16] Recognizing that strict party discipline and caucus decision-making have made it virtually impossible to penetrate behind the unified ranks of the Division List into the real attitudes in individual M.P.s, the Keele group turned instead to an analysis of another expression of parliamentary opinion — the Early Day Motion — which is both publicly available and amenable to statistical treatment. Motions of this type can be made by any M.P. and customarily are signed by those who agree with their expressed sentiments — occasionally as many as 300 Members. They are rarely debated, and support for them is not subject to the party whip. By tradition they are

---

[14] Richard Rose, "The Political Ideas of British Party Activists," *American Political Science Review*, Vol. 56 (June, 1962), p. 364 [reprinted above].

[15] *Ibid.*, p. 366.

[16] S. E. Finer *et al.*, *Backbench Opinion in the House of Commons, 1955–59* (Oxford, 1961).

never signed by the Government or its Whips, and seldom by members of the Opposition front bench; hence their description as "spontaneous unwhipped back-bench manifestos." Obviously any study of these motions is subject to the difficulty that these expressions are often casually made and are not always representative of total parliamentary attitudes. Still, when examined in quantity they afford a rough-and-ready profile of one type of leadership attitudes.

The Keele study focused on nearly 300 Early Day Motions signed by Labour and Conservative M.P.s from 1955 to 1959. They included 111 cross-bench motions and 178 motions signed by members of a single party, again revealing the absence of watertight exclusiveness among dedicated partisans. On the Labour side, the study showed — both in the subject of the motions and in the extent of their support — a fairly unified set of concerns and positive correlations between different attitudes. Thus on the seven sets of attitudes which the authors group as "the syndrome of socialism" — humanitarianism, civil liberties, foreign policy, welfare, cost of living, health and education — all attitudes were correlated, on the average, to the degree of .267.[17] But when examined separately, as pairs, these attitudes showed marked differences in their distribution among various types of M.P.s (such as trade-union sponsored, cooperative sponsored, and constituency-party supported Members). In particular, a group of about fifty Labour M.P.s consistently supported all the motions with maximum zeal, forming "the permanent core of the otherwise fluctuating Left." In the judgment of the Keele group, the data from the Early Motions bear out the view that British socialism, at least as represented by Labour backbenchers, does not repose on a single coherent universalistic body of doctrine but instead is better described as "a set of propositions or attitudes, which when all or many of them are simultaneously held, constitute socialism."[18]

The Keele group's data for the Conservatives tend to confirm the impression that it is extremely difficult to find clear-cut ideology or even persistent left-center-right factions in this party. While positive correlations were established among a few issues (e.g., attitudes toward Suez policy and penal reform, social progressivism and concern for civil liberties, devotion to national sovereignty and attachment to the Commonwealth), numerous ideological inconsistencies emerged: e.g., many Conservatives displayed enthusiasm for both social reform at home and militant policies abroad, for both world government and intervention in Suez. In contrast to the attitudes of Labour backbenchers, those of the Conservatives did not scale statistically and could only loosely be termed a syndrome. If these data are persuasive, then apparently the average Conservative M.P. does not approach his tasks from a prepared emotional or intellectual position, but rather, as the Keele group has put it, "the Conservative party acts or thinks as unrelated, *ad hoc* groups of Members, groups whose members join together to contend for one specific objective, and then fall apart once the goal has been attained or has been by-passed by events."[19]

---

[17] *Ibid.*, pp. 56–58.
[18] *Ibid.*, p. 48.
[19] *Ibid.*, p. 110.

II

The Equilibrium of Consensus and Cleavage

If Britain lacks the normal concomitants of the politics of total ideology, she is not altogether free of the pull of ideology in the second sense that I have used the term. The British political system manifests certain important beliefs which, though they do not add up to a *Weltanschauung*, nevertheless embody values and principles of action connected to larger views of man, society and the state. These attitudes, however general, affect the functioning of political institutions, and substantial changes in them, when they occur, are likely to be reflected in the balance of the political order. I have mentioned a few of them in the preceding section, in the context of an effort to deny the grip of sterner doctrines on the British people. For example, it seems quite clear that two ideological elements which facilitate democratic politics — a relatively optimistic and trusting view of human nature, and a measure of toleration of political opponents — have a firm place in present British attitudes. In this section I will discuss briefly several more of these elements and show not only some of their consequences for politics, but also some recent additions to more firmly established, historic beliefs. Finally, I will attempt to give the character and flavor of various recent challenges to this bundle of attitudes. No attempt can be made here to present a comprehensive inventory of such beliefs, or to offer empirical evidence of their distribution, salience or intensity.

My argument is not only that certain attitudes in Britain fulfill the functions of an ideology; it is also that they serve as forces making for a balance between consensus and cleavage in the political system. Obviously these attitudes may be deeply held by some Britons and only casually by others. But the overall effect is the maintenance of a moving balance between general agreement on some values and well distributed disagreement on others — the conditions Parsons refers to as a "limited polarization of society." [20]

Consensus

To illustrate both the persistence and changing character of the political belief system, four ideological elements will be cited as fundamentally consensual in nature: the conception of governmental leadership, devotion to procedures, "pragmatism," and the "new feudalism." The first three have been constants in British thinking for many decades, while the last-named has entered the consensual stage only recently.

Britons are widely agreed that the principal duty and task of government is to govern: however important it may be in this age to couple the authority of government with a substantial measure of mass participation, the more populistic elements should not be allowed to paralyze the powers of the Crown.

---

[20] "Voting and the Equilibrium of the American Political System," in E. Burdick and A. J. Brodbeck, *American Voting Behavior* (Glencoe, 1959), p. 92.

This attitude is a mixture of predemocratic attachment to the notion of a natural ruling class and a recognition that democratic government requires stable and responsible leadership, on the one hand, and a commitment to mass participation and the control of governmental experts and elites by amateurs and non-elites, on the other hand. Its importance as an attitudinal underpinning of political behavior cannot be overestimated. Perhaps the most striking characteristic of the modern British parliament is its provision and maintenance of a stable majority that permits the government to rule legitimately. Numerous informal institutions which facilitate the conduct of parliamentary business, such as Cabinet hegemony, party discipline and the circumscribed powers of backbench M.P.s, can be linked directly to a general acceptance of the need for strong leadership. This is not simply the ideology of the political elite, for the norm pervades British society in a wider sense. For example, respondents to *Socialist Commentary's* 1960 poll, when presented with a list of 15 possible characteristics of a good party leader, opted most for "strong leadership" (56 per cent) and "strength to make unwelcome decisions" (47 per cent). Conservative and Labour supporters showed no significant difference in their preference for these qualities.[21] No evidence suggests any weakening in this attitude in recent years; on the contrary, if anything it seems to be increasing in its pervasiveness.

The flavor of ideological commitment attaches also to the place of procedures in the British polity. Whereas they may display flexibility and a willingness to bargain over the content of public policy, the British often show an unbending dogmatism in regard to the process by which policy is established. As Eckstein has aptly observed. ". . . the British invest with very high affect the procedural aspects of their government and with very low affect its substantive aspects; they behave like ideologists in regard to rules and like pragmatists in regard to policies." [22] Numerous examples of this disposition might be cited. The intricate fabric of rules, formal and informal, that bear on the conduct of Parliament has shown amazing resistance to reform, despite the enlarged scope of governmental activity and the agitation for more efficient methods coming from both inside and outside Westminster. Many of them have developed their own mystique and are approached by M.P.s of almost every stripe as akin to absolute values. Interest groups are likely to refuse to accept policies affecting them if they have not been consulted during their formulation. The parties have shown themselves willing to examine critically, and often to abandon, a number of their historic policies; but almost invariably they have held firm in their attachment to time-honored procedures, which are seen as fundamental agencies of legitimation. Thus, the closer it came to actual power, the more the Labour Party divested itself of its radical system-reformers and stressed its adherence to the traditional rules of the game. Conceivably it was their acceptance of the ideology of parliamentarism as

---

21 Mark Abrams, Richard Rose, and Rita Hinden, *Must Labour Lose?* (Harmondsworth, 1960), p. 25. These were multiple responses.

22 Harry Eckstein, *A Theory of Stable Democracy* (Princeton, 1961), pp. 30–31.

much as their growing middle class character that made Labour leaders palatable to large numbers of non-socialists in the electorate.

When important procedural questions on occasion become mixed with arguments over the substance of policy, the temperature of politics rises appreciably; or, alternatively, disputes over procedure tend to elbow out those over content. The heated Commons debates at the time of the Suez crisis are a case in point. A sitting of the House had to be suspended by the Speaker because of an uproar caused by the refusal of the Prime Minister to answer what Labour M.P.'s believed to be a legitimate parliamentary question (whether the country was or was not at war with Egypt), and almost as much criticism was leveled at Eden for allegedly not consulting with his own parliamentary supporters and the leader of the Opposition on government plans as was directed against the wisdom of his decision to take military action. A concentration and fixity of dogmatic concern tend to attach to this one aspect of the political system, then, even if they do not carry over into other areas equally.

A third component of this ideological structure, also deeply embedded in British political culture and high in affect, is the concept of pragmatism, already noted. It has come to be shorthand for the belief that sweeping change is unnecessary and dangerous, that effective change is that which comes gradually and builds on, rather than obliterates, previous forms and practices. The test of any institution or any policy, accordingly, is not its esthetic form or logical consistency but its success in performing the fairly immediate task for which it is designed. Anomalies and loose ends are no problem. The rhetoric of British politics is filled with tributes to this mode of thinking (e.g., "Britain is ruled not by logic but by Parliament" [Disraeli]; "Logic is a poor guide compared with custom" [Churchill]), and no description of the working of basic institutions, from the City of London to the University Grants Committee, seems complete without the proffered explanation that "It may seem odd to you, but it works." Pragmatism is bred into the bones of modern Britons by a self-conscious celebration of its virtues and an insistence that it serve as the most suitable guide to political decision-making.

The attachment to larger principles may often be modified or supplemented by an equally intense belief that translation of these principles into practice should take pragmatic form. The policies adopted by the two major parties toward nationalization and colonialism are illustrative of this tempering. Not only did Labour go slow in implementing the social ideal of public ownership when the party came to power in 1945; it also devoted much of the 1950s to a reappraisal of the place of nationalization in its program, with the resultant de-emphasis — but not extinction — of the older ideal. Conversely, traditional Conservative opposition to nationalization did not prevent the party when in power from retaining in the public sector most of the industries nationalized but its predecessor. Again, though dedicated to ending colonialism and raising the remaining outposts of empire to self-governing status, the Labour Government began gradually by concentrating on the Asian flank, and left to succeeding Conservative governments the continuation of the process, step by step, in Africa and the Caribbean. The defense of these actions, as with nationalization, has been largely in terms of the kind of pragmatic outlook that Britons understand and approve.

Pragmatism, then, is closely related to other basic beliefs — in stability, in peaceful solutions, in mixed institutions, and in the legitimating effect of gradual change. It serves as a brake on rapid, root-and-branch societal transformation. In practice, it may also have the effect of reinforcing a preference for amateurs (who are presumed to be more pragmatic in their outlooks) over specialists and technicians (who are thought more likely to be narrow dogmatists — in Keynes's famous jibe, "slaves of some defunct economist"). As I will show very shortly, critics may be found to argue that pragmatism has been raised into a dangerous cult which the country can no longer afford to perpetuate; but of the pervasive hold of pragmatism on British political thinking there can be little doubt.

These three elements of consensus — belief in leadership, attachment to procedures, and pragmatism — have been present in British political culture for many years. Nevertheless, the composition of the bundle of attitudes that comprise the ideology is not static or immutable. As society changes and the role of government is modified, basic attitudes are also likely to undergo transformation. One of the most important recent ideological adjustments involves changing attitudes toward the private and public spheres of British life. These newer attitudes, sometimes referred to as "the new feudalism," parallel ideologically the development of the welfare state and the highly controlled economy. They are attitudinal adjustments to the new balance of social forces created by corporatist developments in the polity, which have given to many private groups what amounts to veto power over public policy. The vast responsibilities now thrown onto government can be carried out only if important affected groups in society agree to go along. By withholding capital, talents or cooperation such groups could make a shambles of any government's program. The requirements of this quasi-corporatism evoke the danger that Britain might reach what Samuel Beer has called the point of "pluralistic stagnation." One reason why this has not yet materialized is that, as Beer has noted, the Keynesian revolution in economics succeeded after the Second World War in altering popular ideas about the role of government and the pursuit of unlimited private gain. In particular, the almost complete acceptance of the neo-mercantilism associated with Keynesian doctrine, which gives to government the role once played by Adam Smith's "invisible hand," provides new standards for judging group values, demands and behavior. In a sense the ethic of bargaining has displaced what has remained of the ethic of competition, and personal acquisitiveness has given way in large measure to the search for security guaranteed by the community. Put another way, despite the powers of blackmail inherent in the position of interest groups in British society today, the potentialities of this power have generally been held in check by a consensus derived in part from the recognition of governmental responsibility for maintaining the economic equilibrium and in part from the decline of acquisitiveness in favor of the more medieval standard of just rewards. The acceptance of a national incomes policy, for example, depends upon the pervasiveness of this attitude.

Cleavage

Along with these consensual elements, other basic attitudes divide the British community and foster some degree of ideological tension. Some of the forces making for cleavage are built into the political party system; others are less organized and function as generalized outside pressures. Broadly speaking, this constitutes the distinction between party competition on the one hand and intellectual criticism on the other. I shall deal first with ideological differences between and within the two main parties and second with the challenges to the prevailing ideology from the outsiders.

In spite of the growing trend toward interparty agreement on many policies, the Conservative and Labour parties continue to espouse somewhat different conceptions of human nature, society and the state. Their ideological centers of gravity are distinct, and to the extent that activists and supporters are socialized into the historic norms of the parties, significant differences between them will remain. Even when they are forced to support similar programs, it is often for basically different reasons. The ideologies of the parties do not function solely as symbols and myths; they are potentially operative (so long as they have not atrophied completely), and on occasion they fix the boundaries and direction of policy decisions. For Conservatives, the belief in the naturalness and usefulness of inequality, the inevitability of hierarchy, and the positive values of nationalism and empire may have been muted by the necessities of Britain's contemporary situation, but it has not been abandoned in favor of a wholly different value system. Similarly, Labour's attachment to the values of equality, social democracy, classlessness and pacifism, while also tempered by the exigencies of the moment, has remained fairly fixed. As a motivation and a standard for political action, it has not declined to the level of cynical rhetoric. So long as this ideological gap between the parties continues to be perceived by their partisans — and I believe that at the moment it still is — talk of the politics of Tweedledum and Tweedledee is premature.

In addition, each party has within its ranks militant individuals and groups concerned with preserving the party's doctrinal purity and historic values. The persistence of such forces, which may or may not take the form of factions, cannot be disregarded as strictly of nuisance value, for they often represent ideological cleavages within the electorate as well. As ideological pressure groups within the party's structure they may serve to set limits beyond which the leadership ventures at its peril. The Labour Party has long been beset by internal doctrinal cleavages, which not only affect the struggle for leadership but create an image with the electorate. During the 1950s and early 1960s, for instance, the party was almost constantly engaged in internecine disputes between left-wing factions and the dominant right-wing leadership. The splits that occurred over the Bevanite view of socialist priorities, over German rearmament, over the status of the commitment to nationalization, and over nuclear disarmament are familiar examples. In each case the disagreement turned at least in part on the question of how strictly the party should adhere to the historic body of doctrine known as "socialism" and "socialist foreign policy." And while the Attlee-Gaitskell forces were usually successful in fending off the left-wing accusations that they had betrayed the fundamental tenets of the Labour movement, the leadership could not afford to be wholly impervious to the substantial body of opinion represented by the Beavanites and their successors. Nor, as the disputes over the party's constitution and over nuclear weapons revealed, was the moderate leadership able to subjugate the radical wing so completely as to foreclose the possibility of a resurgence of doctrinaire opinions within important sections of the party. When Gaitskell attempted after the 1959 election defeat to persuade the party to amend Clause IV of its constitution in the direction of virtually eliminating the commitment to nationalization, he was set upon not only by the left but also the center of the party, and forced to beat a hasty retreat. The controversy over Clause IV showed convincingly that the ideological reflexes of the party are not atrophied, and that electoral calculation has not completely replaced them as the mainspring of Labour's program.

The Conservative Party is much more homogeneous than Labour in its social composition, its relation to outside groups, and its public loyalty to its leadership. But it is not altogether free of ideological dissension. It has its stalwart and reformist elements, who occasionally succeed in moving the party in one direction or the other, often on the basis of very different views of man and society. These forces are apt to take a rather different form from their counterparts on the Labour side. Whereas in the Labour Party the usual instrument of ideological dissension is the faction, a stable set of politicians organized for political activity, the more common form among the Conservatives is what Rose refers to as a "tendency," a stable set of attitudes expressed in Parliament by less organized, more fluctuating groups of politicians. Thus, as the Keele study of backbench opinion made clear, the Conservative leadership has encountered significant internal party opposition on a number of issues invested with ideological affect, such as crime and punishment, colonialism, and the maintenance of free enterprise (e.g., public vs. private television). However, the M.P.s who pressed dogmatic views on these issues did not form a stable group but tended to fall apart and regroup along different lines when other controversies arose. Single issues, such as the Suez crisis, may split Conservatives into right, left and center groups, with strong ideological disputation between the extremes; but continuing factionalism, with the risk of intra-party polarization, runs counter to the traditional Conservative belief in loyalty to the chosen leadership. The Conservative Party, like Labour, shows both consensus and cleavage on ideological questions. Unlike the pattern in the Labour Party, the Conservative balance is skewed strongly in the direction of consensus, with ideology generally secondary to more tangible interests.

The overall picture of the condition of ideology in Britain shows, therefore, a continuing mixture of consensus and cleavage, of attitudes making for stability and attitudes fostering change. These attitudes are not distributed uniformly through the population or within the political system; but neither are they polarized in separate groups, and they coexist at almost every important level of political structure. In sum, the process of government rests upon a combination of strong commitment and low-temperature pragmatism. "If too much principle can kill a government," Eckstein has observed, "so can the lack of principle at all . . . what is wanted is 'programmatic' government, and this must of necessity blend principle with pragmatic adjustment." [23] The prevailing distribution of attitudes in Britain goes some distance to satisfy this condition.

Critics

The content of British political attitudes has not escaped criticism, especially in the era of the Common Market. If the 1950s were the heyday of the angry young men of letters, the early 1960s spawned a number of critics concerned with the condition of the nation's political values. Some of them, notably the so-called "New Left" and the marching and squatting foes of nuclear weapons, are in the long tradition of radical protest in Britain. Although their targets are contemporary, their moral and social values are not markedly different from those of the 1930s. Rather than focusing on this fairly familiar pattern of out-group protest, I shall concentrate on another group of critics whose concern is less single-minded and whose methods are less spectacular than the "angries" of the traditional left, but whose belief that the nation's values are dangerously outdated is equally strong. I refer to those intellectuals who are devoted to exposing the alleged loss of Britain's *élan vital* and to pleading for the modernization of basic attitudes as well as institutions.

This unorganized group of critics, whom Henry Fairlie has termed disdainfully "State of England" writers, is difficult to fit into ready-made political categories. It numbers, among other, several right-wing Labour M.P.'s, a couple of leftish Oxford economists, a few mildly left-of-center journalists, a professor of government known mainly for works on France, the industrial editor of the *Financial Times,* and Arthur Koestler. What they have in common is a reformist outlook, born of disillusionment with the tenacity of certain historic British attitudes in the postwar world. This has led them to strike out without discrimination against left and right alike — in Crosland's phrase, "the conservative enemy," wherever found. Because they share this motivation, their chief ideas can be lumped together for convenience without serious distortion, so long as it is remembered that what follows is a composite of themes scattered in many writings.

Underlying these critics' attack is the non-Marxian assumption that what ails Britain is not so much its material conditions or its new place in the world as its cultural attitudes. "We are faced," Koestler writes, "with a 'functional' rather than a 'structural' disorder. Structural diseases have objective, material causes, functional diseases have subjective, psychological causes." [24] It is a lack of dynamism, of incentives (in more than the pecuniary sense), of social discipline bred by a sense of community, that lies at the root of the *malaise.* The aftermath of empire, the decline of Britain's power in world affairs, the effects of the welfare state, the challenge of new Europe — all are but proxi-

---

[23] Harry Eckstein, *A Theory of Stable Democracy* (Princeton, 1961), p. 33.
[24] Arthur Koestler, "The Lion and the Ostrich," *Encounter,* July, 1963, p. 8.

mate causes; the real sources of the present difficulties lie deeper, in attitudes toward society and government which stretch back into British history. Paradoxically, it is said, it has been the almost unbroken character of British development, its vaunted evolutionary stability, that now holds back the creation of the types of modern attitudes so badly needed. Having been spared the upheavals of radical social revolution, the interruption of its political regime, the destruction of its land and economy, and the psychological trauma of invasion and alien rule, Britain has not been forced to agonize over, or to reconstruct, its fundamental values. In the view of many of these critics, the very traits so much admired by outside observers — the blending of the pre-industrial and the modern, the conscious preservation of aristocratic institutions, the taste for new wines in old bottles — have unfitted the country for the tasks of survival in a rapidly changing world.

It is hardly surprising that one of the targets of this line of criticism is the alleged historicism of the British, their compulsive fixation, as one writer has put it, on either the glories or the miseries of the past. The consequence in both cases is a retreat into unreality, frustration and passivity. All too many Britons remain, it is asserted, who hanker after the day when Britannia was top-dog and could solve any problem by sending a gunboat. While Suez was supposed to be their lesson, they have refused to hearken to it. More important, others refuse to believe that Britain can learn anything from the rest of the world, in particular from the political and economic experiments now under way in western Europe. Thus Henry Fairlie:

> I am extremely doubtful whether we have anything to learn from either the Fifth Republic in France or the Federal Republic in West Germany about the manner of ordering and sustaining a free society; I am not even sure whether we have much to learn in the matter from the French and Germans as peoples . . . for the moment, I am prepared to wager fairly heavily that our own social and political arrangements will outlast theirs. Any takers?[25]

Still others, it is maintained, are mesmerized by the ancient rituals and dominant values of Oxford and Cambridge — "fairylands in the heart of modern Britain" — the essence of whose magic is that it is pre-industrial.

This satisfied, even complacent, immersion in the British past is coupled, usually at the other end of the social scale, with the equally corrosive tendency of Britons to view the present in terms of the miserable and insecure days of the 1930s, the period when so many leaders of the Left came of age. Here the prime target is usually the trade unions: their restrictive practices, their security-mindedness, their suspicion of innovation, their unwillingness to adopt business unionism and provide their leaders with adequate powers, their division of the industrial world into "They" and "Us," and their "I'm All Right, Jack" response to their own rising affluence. Again, though the causes of this *malaise* are recognized as partly structural, it is argued that at the base of the problem are attitudes derived from situations and days long past. The result of conservatism in this major area of British life is that the unions are proving

---

25 Henry Fairlie, "On the Comforts of Anger," *ibid.*, p. 12.

themselves "the natural allies of the forces of stagnation and conservatism in industry — and not those of expansion and dynamism." [26]

From this target it is but a short step to another: the alleged cult of amateurism and pragmatism. These seeming valuable traits, it is argued, have been transformed into fetishes in contemporary British usage. The amateur has become not the curious and adaptable all-rounder, but the dilettante; and pragmatism, rather than being synonymous with the experimental outlook, has shrunk to cautious, narrow tinkering. Teleology has given way to functionalism, the spirit of inquiry to the norms of adjustment and conciliation. Not surprisingly, the institutions most under fire for the inculcation of these attitudes are the educational system and the civil service, which at their higher levels are seen as extensions of each other. Hence the claim that the dominant humanist tradition of the top public schools and Oxbridge, while perhaps suitable for the days of laissez-faire and empire, is now hopelessly out of keeping with the requirements of industrial society and positive government. The defense of the prevailing values of British education in terms of training the generalist for the tasks of policy-making is really a deception. In the civil service, as in industry and Parliament, the domination of those possessed of (in Balogh's phrase) the "crossword-puzzle mind, reared on mathematics at Cambridge, or Greats at Oxford," is inimical to the kind of rational, comprehensive, long-range planning that British society now requires.

The prevailing low esteem for science, technology and business enterprise particularly agitates the critics, who attribute to it much of Britain's slow economic growth, the "brain drain," and the nervous ambivalence toward the Common Market. This attitude, they argue, is one of the negative residues of aristocratic values in a democratic age. Whereas in the eighteenth and nineteenth centuries the progress of technology and the promise of economic growth were the special ideology of the business class in its struggle with the land-owning aristocracy, over time the ideology faded out as the rising masters of technology and entrepreneurial power gave in to the tempting possibility of emulating the life of the landed squire. "The combination of a sharply divided class society — and the possibility of rising from one class to another held in greater esteem — meant that the ambition of the sons of many manufacturers was to leave their family businesses and to become landowners (or, at least, 'professional men')." [27] Business, manufacturing and applied science continue to exist, but top creative talent refused to associate with these activities, and their controllers became increasingly docile, unadventurous and apologetic. In the view of the non-socialist wing of this school of critics, the reforms needed to achieve greater efficiency and expanded production have been stymied by the unwillingness of Britons to put these values above those of short-run group security and "fair play." "We are unwilling to advance if it means that anybody is going to get hurt. . . . This is in many ways an admirable trait, but it is a sure recipe for national decay." [28] What these writers

---

[26] Michael Shanks, *The Stagnant Society* (Harmondsworth, 1961), p. 93.

[27] Austen Albu, "Taboo on Expertise," *Encounter*, July 1963, p. 46.

[28] Shanks, "The Comforts of Stagnation," *ibid.*, p. 31.

call for, then, is a reorientation of basic values in the direction of recognizing that whatever may have been the contributions in the past of aristocratic, unspecialized and humanistic standards of performance, the new Britain requires the upgrading of those attitudes which will foster technological innovation and organizational efficiency. Such a reorientation hinges upon the ability of Britons to sublimate, and finally eliminate, the class-bound attitudes of the past, which have stood as barriers not only to a democratic life, but also to national growth.

These cries are also echoed by critics of the process of government, especially those who view with misgivings the increased corporatism of policy-making. A notable example is Brian Chapman, whose slashing broadside, *British Government Observed*, significantly is subtitled "Some European Reflections." Although Chapman is critical chiefly of what he believes to be the archaic, nineteenth century character of the machinery of government — its "rich Byzantine structure" — he attributes much of this condition to the lack of doctrinal value attached to the concept of public service in Britain. In contrast to the trends in Continental countries, he asserts, British government remains in the grips of the luxuriant amateurism of centuries past and has not developed a genuine pluralism based upon the sentiment that public office carries with it public responsibility. Its pragmatism is a mask for weak-kneed, expensive abdication to whatever pressures happen to be brought to bear. Thus public policy is "simply equated with finding the least controversial course between the conflicting interests of vociferous private groups. It is not a doctrine of government; it is a doctrine of subordination."[29] Other critics sharing these views have added the argument that a system that acts as much on the basis of "understandings" — unarticulated, unstructured, implicit responses to new situations — does not encourage bold solutions or positive action.

This small sample of the expanding literature of discontent testifies to the survival of ideological concern in Britain today. True, these particular critics are not of a single mind, and few of them present fully drawn prescriptions for reform (aside, perhaps, from a common emphasis on the need to reconstruct the educational system). But they do share two strong interests that have influenced their analysis and their prescriptions. First, they are impressed by many of the recent developments occurring on the Continent, and they would shake Britain out of its traditional belief that nothing positive can be learned from that quarter. Thus they would seem to pin their hope of change in part on the prospects of closer union with Europe, if only because this might jolt the country out of its complacent ways. Second, they believe that the primary force making for attitudinal change will be the rising power of the newer, more modern and classless elements in British society — the managers, scientists, technicians and white collar workers — who have reaped the benefits of the 1944 Education Act, and whose occupational skills and roles have removed them from the attitudes of the older England. In this sense, but not

---

[29] Brian Chapman, *British Government Observed* (London, 1963), p. 61. For a challenge to this interpretation, see D. N. Chester, "British Government Observed," *Public Administration*, Vol. 41 (Winter, 1963), pp. 375–84.

in others, these critics would agree with the diagnoses of the "end of ideology" writers.

None of this cluster of critics offers a new "world view" ideology to the British, but most of them are concerned with the reordering of basic political attitudes in the second sense that I have used the term "ideology." While acknowledging the need to retain many of the historic values associated with the British polity, they would nevertheless adjust the equilibrium of ancient and modern values in the direction of modernity. This can be achieved, they believe, in the best British tradition, without resort to cosmic theories or to the intolerance of closed systems.

35. French Technocracy and Comparative Government

F. F. RIDLEY

This analysis of the role of governmental "technicians" in the French system under De Gaulle helps to throw a good deal of light on the French political process. It also raises more general questions about the functional requirements of the modern industrial state. Does the French "technocratic Establishment" meet an indispensable need for planning, coordination, and impetus? If it does, can it be replicated elsewhere— and how is it to be integrated into a functioning democracy?

I

Introduction

In recent years there has been much discussion of technocracy in France, some academic, more polemical. A number of distinguished 'technocrats' have produced their own statements of faith (e.g. Armand, Bloch-Lainé, Closon). Academic studies have in the main been analytical, but some empirical work has also been done. . . . The subject is an interesting one and one which may appear relevant to the student of politics for several reasons.

The simplest, of course, is as part of the explanation of the French system of government. Most 'Foreign Governments' textbooks now have a reference to French technocracy. But it is not simply a case of understanding France for its own sake. Growing ties with Europe — governmental, industrial, and scientific — make it necessary for an ever wider group of persons to understand the structure of French administration and the character of French administrators (public service and private enterprise).

A consideration of technocracy is also relevant to the simplest sort of comparative study: the description and comparison, or at least juxtaposition, of a number of different political systems. The civil service forms part of the complex of institutions that must be described if one system is to be compared with another. Institutions themselves can only be understood against their wider, cultural background. 'The comparison of one national administration with another involves more than a confrontation of techniques; it involves a confrontation of cultures' (C. H. Sisson). The educational and career systems which lie behind technocracy form an important part of the French cultural pattern. A common criticism of 'old-fashioned' comparative government studies is that they are 'culture-bound' because they deal only with similar 'Western type' systems. This criticism itself overlooks the great cultural differences

source: Reprinted by permission of The Clarendon Press, Oxford, copyright owners, from *Political Studies*, *XIV* (February 1966), pp. 34–52. Footnotes are abridged.

between 'Western' countries. A consideration of French technocracy may draw attention to this. If one is going to compare systems, France and Britain are still two good starting points: sufficient broad similarities allow one to concentrate on the effect of a limited number of significant cultural differences.

Another common criticism of comparative government studies is that they are descriptive rather than 'problem solving'. Underdeveloped countries need public services. And what they need, as Morstein Marx points out, is not merely technical proficiency but 'an administrative system that can sustain the essential presence of government.' In other words, the issue is not merely whether one sort of civil service is more efficient than another (though that is important), but whether it can live off its own resources where 'political' institutions are weak or unstable. It has been suggested that the French model is more appropriate in these circumstances than the British.

But this is a high level of abstraction. We may look at how they do things in France, not because we hope to generalize about the French model but because we hope to adapt some French experience to our own use. A good deal of interest is being shown in various aspects of French administration these days. To some extent one can look at French institutions without asking 'How does it work there; how will it work here?' On may simply be casting about for new ideas. It is unlikely that the two questions will not be asked, however, and the political scientist should ideally be able to give some sort of an answer. In practice he cannot do much more than guess at the extent to which a particular institution depends on the system of which it forms part. Does French planning depend on the character of the French civil service and on the background of French industrialists? Do these in turn depend on class structure, on the organization of higher education, or on other traditions? How far can we go in picking out one institution, how far are all institutions linked together and bound up with even more intangible factors such as national character? A consideration of French technocracy may not be useful in the sense that there is much we can adapt — it may appear too deeply embedded in a complex of political and cultural factors. But it may make us aware of these wider differences and thus help us understand why, for example, a certain type of planning works in France but may well not work in Britain.

There is another field to which the question of technocracy is relevant and that is the study of class and power. The problem of the ruling class, however defined, is central to political sociology and is the starting point of much political philosophy. We compare political systems in terms of who governs and debate political ideas in terms of who should govern. Much theoretical discussion is possible about whether we should talk of ruling classes or power elites ('men whose position enables them to make decisions having major consequences') or something else again. But it is not all that difficult to enumerate the persons or groups of persons who influence French government. In many cases it is a matter of offices and functions; even the 'grey eminences' are not hard to discover. It is another matter to determine the exact influence of any particular group on any particular issue because of the difficulty of obtaining the information necessary for a study of decision-making at the highest level. The relevant question here, however, is whether the technocrats form a class and, if so, in what sense. If they do, is it the ruling class (as the word technocracy implies), a ruling class among others, or are individual technocrats members of a diffuse power elite?

Linked with this is the question of leadership. Where, within a political system, do the centres of initiative lie? Is one system better adapted for dealing with certain problems than another? More specifically, is the French system better adapted because technocrats are more efficient or more dynamic? Here we are back at the level of speculation to which comparative studies contribute little that is 'scientific.' But it is essentially with these important questions that the following is concerned.

II
The Definition of Technocracy

Technocracy means government by technicians. A technocrat is a technician with power (not necessarily, though as generally used, political power). The difficulty is to know what is meant by technician in this context. A technician is a person with a specialized skill in an art, science or craft, a person exercising a function by virtue of his specialized qualifications. In English, the term usually refers to one skilled in the mechanical arts, often to a mechanical skill (as compared to a technologist, a person with an understanding of the skill he exercises). In French, *technicien* is used in a much wider sense. Indeed, its ambiguity leads to some confusion. A skilled politician may be called a 'technician of power' though he would not be described as a technocrat.

The term technocrat is used by French writers in different (and overlapping) ways, often depending on whom it is intended to attract. There are four main usages. First, it is occasionally applied to the members of all the prestige corps of the civil service. Generally, members of the more 'political' corps are exlcuded (prefects, diplomats). The term may then be widened to include the corps of *administrateurs civils,* thus covering all other civil servants equivalent in rank to the British administrative class ('the administrators'). In this sense, however, it is often used with the graduates of the *Ecole Nationale d'Administration* in mind ('ENA is a factory to produce technocrats'), rather than the administrators in the corps of engineers. It is generally applied then to those in the economic and financial services ('the economists'), especially to the members of the *Inspection des Finances.* It may include other influential economists, not in the civil service (academics and politicians). This usage is frequently pejorative and is employed by threatened interests (farmers, small businessmen). Another, probably more frequent, generally favourable use restricts the term to members of the elite technical corps of the state, and especially to those who are *polytechniciens* ('The engineers'). Finally, it can then be widened to include *polytechniciens* and other graduates of the elite engineering schools in executive posts in industry, and further widened to include graduates of lower ranking schools (i.e. all entitled to call themselves engineers). It is often used in this way by those who are thinking in terms of the 'managerial revolution.'

What these uses have in common is that they refer to power elites which are neither 'political' in the accepted sense, nor representative of sectional interests (in this sense, too, the term has been applied to Monnet and the 'men behind the Common Market'). If one is thinking of technocracy in terms of the character of French government, one will examine the higher civil service. If one is thinking in terms of the 'managerial revolution' and the relations between government and industry, one will examine the position of engineers in the public services and in private enterprise.

It has been suggested that higher civil servants can be divided into two broad groups according to how they see the functions of government. First, there are those who believe that its function is to maintain the security of the state, the unity of the nation and a fair balance between interests. Second, there are those who believe that it has a positive, indeed dominant, responsibility for economic development and social progress (leadership, planning, provision of services).

To some extent, this is a question of generations (before and after the establishment of ENA). It is also linked to functions. The prefects and the members of the 'judicial' corps (Conseil d'Etat, Cour des Comptes) are more likely to take the negative view, at least in economic matters. Those in the economic and technical ministries tend to the more positive view. It is the latter who are the technocrats. This gives one a definition in terms of outlook, rather than in terms of qualifications.

There are broadly two paths to the highest civil service posts: through ENA and the elite non-engineering corps or through the Ecole Polytechnique and the elite engineering corps. One may be tempted to think of the former as 'generalists' and the latter as 'specialists,' reserving the term technicien for them. It is not possible, however, to impose these categories on the French civil service.

The graduates of ENA, even the members of the theoretically least specialized corps (the administrateurs civils), are trained as administrators and may regard themselves as technicians in administration. This, of course, raises the old question 'administration: art or science?' Their training does not in fact include much 'administrative science,' but it does include a good deal of administrative practice. The pre-entry university education is also to some extent geared to the public service. There are now some 1,200 ENA graduates. Forty per cent are in the services of the Ministry of Finance and Economic Affairs, which they by now dominate (younger men tend to be appointed to key positions there than elsewhere). This reinforces the tendency to identify ENA graduates as 'economists.' Many have acquired a considerable knowledge of economic techniques. Even if they are not appointed because of their specialized knowledge, they do use a specialized skill in their work. There is no reason why the term technicians should be reserved for a specialist in the mechanical, as distinct from the social, sciences.

On the other hand, the engineers are not narrow specialists. They will have studied literature and classics, as well as mathematics, at school. At the Polytechnique, their studies are almost entirely theoretical (general science). They will not have received a specialist training in what we would call a technology until they reach one of the post-graduate 'schools of application.' There are thus two points to note about the members of the elite engineering corps. First, they are men of 'general culture' (in the sense that the term is applied in Britain to the administrative class). Indeed, there are those who maintain that they are men of greater culture than the graduates of ENA. Second, they are trained from the start to become 'polyvalent' (i.e. 'all purpose' or 'generalist') administrators after a period of field service.

The technocrats may thus include three over-lapping groups: administrators, economists, and engineers.

There is no doubt that the technocrats form part of the power elite. But those who speak of technocracy usually suggest that they occupy the dominant position — that power has shifted decisively away from the politicians (and capitalists). This is much more doubtful. It is generally proved by explaining why it must have happened, rather than by showing that it has in fact happened. The proof is theoretical and the conclusion not tested. (It is hard to see how it could be, except by a large number of case studies of the decision-making process in major political issues.)

The general line of argument runs along well-known lines. First, the politicians have abdicated. The governments of the Fourth Republic were weak and unstable. Ministers often had no policy at all, or they had no authority to enforce it. In any case, their tenure of office was too short. The civil servants kept the government going. They filled the power vacuum. Second, it is argued that politicians are out-dated. 'They are still living in the age of the Roman senate.' The growing functions of government, and their growing complexity, mean that they are no longer able to understand the issues or to take sensible decisions. Only the experts can cope with the problems of the modern world. This argument is grossly exaggerated. If one looks at the major political decisions of the Fourth Republic, there is little evidence that civil servants had a decisive influence. Many of the reforms they advocated were, moreover, held up by politicians representing vested interests.

It has also been suggested that the Fifth Republic is the Republic of the Technocrats. Evidence for this is seen in the appointment of civil servants as ministers, in the influence of economists (e.g. the Rueff Committee) and in the way in which a number of major reforms have been pushed through (e.g. reform of Paris local government). There are certainly links between the Gaullist and the technocratic outlook. It is certainly also true that certain decisions have been 'depoliticized' in the sense that sectional interests have been ignored (no consultation prior to the Paris reforms). But General de Gaulle stands above the technocrats and their power is limited by other forces (the most important, perhaps, being the trade unions).

What is true, however, is that the technocrats have played a leading role in a host of decisions which were not at the time the subject of strong political controversy or where sectional interests were not sufficiently mobilized. In the long run, these decisions may well prove to have been of greater importance than the major 'political' decisions in shaping French society (economic planning, industrial expansion, regional development, reforms in the educational system, promotion of scientific research etc.).

Linked with this is the fact that those spheres of government in which the technocrats have been influential have increased enormously since the war. The government plays a larger role in economic affairs than in Britain. Public enterprise is much more extensive and is still growing (most markedly, in recent years, in the field of petroleum and in regional 'infrastructure' schemes). Directly or indirectly, the state controls a high proportion of all investment. It takes the most important decisions in the planning system. It is in the economic sphere that the power of the technocrats is most marked.

III

The Technocrats as a Class

Talk about technocracy implies that the technocrats (the higher civil service in this context) form a class and, what is more important, act as a class. This immediately leads one to ask how homogeneous the technocrats really are in outlook and interests. It is possible to show several factors of cohesion. Attention at the same time must be drawn to factors working in the opposite direction.

Five main factors of cohesion can be discerned. First, there is common social background. Napoleon's creation of the *Polytechnique* and the 1945 establishment of ENA 'opened the civil service to the talents.' In fact, entrants come overwhelmingly from the upper and solid middle class (partly because of the preparations needed to sit the entrance examination and the absence of a comprehensive system of grants). Second, there is common training. The majority have gone through one of the two paths noted above. Within each system, they obviously acquire a common body of knowledge and a common language. There is also much that is common between them: both instill similar ideas about the role of the state and the functions of the civil service. Third, and linked with the second, is a shared sense of superiority. This has several causes. Graduates of both systems know that they are the intellectual cream of the nation — especially the engineers, who are selected earlier (at university entrance level) by nation-wide competition, and who must graduate among the top twenty of their year to join a *grand corps*; all are the product of a repeated, highly competitive, sifting process. Enormous prestige attaches to the *grand corps*; the intellectual and 'moral' superiority of their members is widely recognized outside the civil service. As servants of the state, they consider themselves a cut above those who work for mere sectional interests. A fourth, and even more important factor of cohesion, is the spirit of camaraderie born of their common education. The economists/administrators will not merely have studied together at ENA; most will have studied together before that at the Law Faculty and the *Institut d'Etudes Politiques* in Paris. The engineers start their common career earlier (at undergraduate level), and there is much greater emphasis on communal life at the *Polytechnique*. It retains some of the military school tradition given it by Napoleon and engenders a special pride. Although there are graduates of the *Polytechnique* who go directly into industry and there are some 'private' students at the 'schools of application' (*Mines, Ponts et Chaussées*), the engineers study in a much more closed society. Members of the same *promotion* (year) at these schools are likely to be on a *tu* basis and maintain this relationship afterwards. There are well organized associations of *anciens élèves* and there is a strong sense of loyalty (partly, no doubt, for the good reason that loyalties lead to jobs). There are probably closer ties between them than between the old boys of British public schools or the *alten Herren* of a German *Burschenschaft*. Finally, cohesion is promoted also by the organization of the civil service into *corps*. Membership of a *grand corps* engenders the same pride and loyalty. It is these corps which fill virtually all key positions. Practical career considerations again partly explain the cohesion of the corps (it is noticeable that the *administrateurs civils* have least sense of identity: this is not only because the corps has least prestige, but also because it cannot offer the same assurance of a successful career).

Five main factors of division can also be observed. First, there is the distinction, which has already been made, between the technocrats and the members of the judicial/political services. Second, there are other conflicts based upon functions, notably between the 'saving' and 'spending' services (*direction du Budget versus* technical ministries). This, to some extent, is a conflict between economists and engineers, but not necessarily so: there was a smilar conflict between members of the Ministry of Finance and the Secretariat of State for Economic Affairs ('accountants' *versus* economists). There may also be differences of outlook between those in the central services and those in the regional services. Third, there are conflicts about spheres of competence. The most obvious example is the rivalry between the *Ponts et Chaussées* and the *Génie rurale*. There are similar rivalries between different divisions within a single ministry. An example was the 'imperialism' of the divisions for higher, secondary, technical and primary education in the Ministry of Education. Fourth, there are also corps rivalries which are concerned with status and access to high posts. Such rivalry exists within the administrators/economists group, between the *administrateurs civils* and the *Inspecteurs des Finances* (more accurately, a one-sided rivalry). Moreover, those who enter ENA from within the civil service tend to come from humbler backgrounds than those who enter from the university and they also tend to do less well at the school and thus enter the humbler corps of *administrateurs civils* on graduating. To that extent, a class division is carried over into the corps. Within the engineers' group, there is rivalry between the *polytechniciens* and the engineers from the less prestigious schools which give more practical training (the *ingénieurs-mécaniciens*). There can also be rivalry between the two groups when they compete for posts (e.g. in the Ministry of Agriculture). Finally, the civil service is not entirely 'depoliticized.' Appointment to key positions, especially in the non-technical ministries, falls outside the normal promotion pattern (though men are rarely appointed to posts which would not normally be accessible to them). The most common path is through a ministerial *cabinet*. Those concerned do not see this as engaging them politically and party affiliations do not usually play a role. But it has been suggested that such men are likely to have a greater political awareness and thus be less technocratic in outlook than their colleagues. This links with a distinction made between the *hauts fonctionnaires* and the hundred or so *grands fonction-naires* occupying key posts. It is the latter who are able to make or influence policy. They may differ in outlook from their colleagues because of the wider perspectives with which they deal.

If one compares the French civil service to the British, there are obvious differences. Paradoxically, the French civil service is both more divided and more united that the British: it is divided by its own organization, which creates considerable rivalries; it is more united because it has a more positive view of its functions. There are many ties which bind the technocrats and in many ways they share a common outlook. But this outlook is very broad (see below), and it does not really give answers to specific questions of policy. The highest civil servants, moreover, are appointed as individuals (though often the advice of their peers is as important as simple ministerial favour.) While technocrat civil servants occupy positions of power and form part of the 'power elite,' it would seem that they exercise that power as individuals, not as a class.

IV

The Technocratic Outlook

It is not sufficient to ask whether technocrats have power, one needs to know whether they use it to pursue policies different from those of other groups in the 'power elite.' Does technocratic government pursue ends different from those of other forms of government? It is only if these ends differ markedly from those the rest of the nation wishes to pursue that technocracy becomes a real problem.

The most hostile critics (the threatened interests) often claim that technocrats are just another 'ruling class' with their own interest to pursue — their own interest being the simple desire to exercise power for its own sake. This may explain the expansion of some sectors of public enterprise, but it does not get one very far. The civil servants are not power-hungry machiavellians. They are, in fact, as disinterested as the British civil servant. But they are probably motivated to a much greater extent by their own views of the ends of society.

The following outline of the technocratic outlook is suggested, though there is, of course, no empirical evidence that the majority of senior civil servants actually hold these views. It is hard to tell, moreover, how far such views reflect the technocratic character of the civil service and how far they are simply a reflection of French traditions of the public service state.

Of only the crudest technocrats could it be said that he believes technical achievements to be an end in themselves, though such views are sometimes attributed to the engineers ('power stations are the cathedrals of our time'). Something approaching this attitude has been found in some sectors of public enterprise, (emphasis on technical, rather than financial, considerations). The technocrat is likely to believe, however, that it is technological achievements which will make the 'good society' possible. He is likely to be an optimist (a 'Victorian' belief in progress). He is committed to economic expansion. He 'accepts the industrial society.' At the same time, he is fundamentally a humanist. Industrial development and material wealth are not ends in themselves. He is concerned with the transformation of society, so that the new wealth may serve the 'full man.' 'He has a high view of his role and an ambition to guide our civilization in a new direction.' Economic development and the transformation of society are questions of organization. 'All conditions for progress are there except one: organization.'

This leads the technocrat to an alternative definition of technocracy to the one given earlier. Technocracy is *gouvernement par la technique,* i.e. the scientific management of society. The technocrat is the heir of Saint-Simon ('industrialism,' 'organizationalism'). 'Technics must replace politics.' (cf. Marx: 'the government of men will be replaced by the administration of things'). The technocrat is a rationalist (heir of the Encyclopaedists). He has great confidence in the possibility of solving the problems of society by a scientific approach. It is not technology (the mechanical arts) but logical analysis that is important ('The Frenchman is a mathematician at heart'). There is a considerable Keynesian influence. There is also a respectable tradition of scientific management (Fayol). Only the technician is capable of this task. This is only partly because he alone has no sectional interests to promote (political or economic) and is thus the only person capable of taking an unbiassed, overall view of social problems. At the same time, he is a pragmatist, hostile to political ideologies or, indeed, to any theoretical systems (for this reason, marxists would deny that he is a rationalist). Technocrat writers frequently make the point that the age of ideologies is dead. The world is changing all the time, and no hard and fast body of doctrines can serve as a guide to its problems. Problems must be solved in a rational, scientific manner as they arise. His training reinforces this approach. The ENA student receives a practical, rather than a theoretical, training. Courses in economics, for example, deal with institutions and policies rather than with economic theories. Engineering (like law) is often considered an ideal education in Europe because it combines a training of the mind (cf. arguments for Classics) with practical application. Although the engineers receive a theoretical training at the *Polytechnique,* they also receive a practical training at a 'school of application.' There is a marked difference between them and the students of the science faculties at the universities (the latter tend to go to research posts).

In the technocratic theory, progress can be achieved only by the 'depoliticization' of problems. Technocrats may criticize politicians on the grounds that they are venal, incompetent or impotent. More fundamental is the thought that politicians are, by the nature of things, committed either to an ideology or to a sectional interest. The technocrat is dedicated to the national interest as against sectional (or even individual) interests. The notion of the general interest is fundamental. There are echoes of Rousseau and the same hostility to *intermédiaires.* There are clear links with Gaullism here. Interests are the great enemy of the rational organization of society. Insofar as politics is the play of interests and democracy is the adjustment of interests, they are antipolitical and anti-democratic. This leads the technocrat to emphasize the role of the state. Only the state can provide the leadership that is necessary, because only the state stands above interests (the state is the organized nation). This is, of course, the traditional view of the public service state (thus it is civil servants who represent the 'general interests of the nation' on the representative boards of nationalized industries). The technocrat is the heir of the *ancien régime* and of Napoleon.

The technocrat has great confidence in himself. This is partly because he thinks of himself as an expert, partly because of the prestige that attaches to his corps, partly because he is a servant of the state. He has a great sense of responsibility, linked as much with the traditions of the public service state as with notions of technocracy. His moral integrity and his claim to moral leadership is widely recognized.

The emphasis on pragmatic solutions, the absence of a 'theory' or 'programme,' explains the earlier point that the technocrats as a group have no common policy on specific issues. It is not simply that they may differ on what is the 'scientific' answer to any particular problem. More fundamental is the fact that the technocratic outlook gives little guidance, except in broad terms, where there is a choice between different ends. This is why technocrats are more likely to influence decisions as individuals than as a group. Nevertheless, it is not sufficient for technocrats to say that all conditions for the good society exist except organization. The question remains: organization for what sort of a society? Have the technocrats a view of the good society? What are their values? A certain common outlook can in fact be detected. Immediately after the war, the question 'organization for what?' raised few problems, at least in the economic sphere (social reforms were born in a political movement — the Resistance — although that had its share of technocrats too). The immediate need was to develop industries: priorities were fairly obvious and could be decided on technical grounds. Increasing prosperity posed new problems. This was apparent in the elaboration of the Fourth Plan — the need to decide the balance between production and leisure, consumption and investment, public and private expenditure, the relative importance of health, education and culture, the emphasis to be placed on regional development. It became more difficult for the technocrats to act as if their decision were purely technical (they could no longer 'live off their own resources'), though some choices were disguised to make them appear technical. The Planning Commissioner admitted this problem when he said that 'choices must be made on the basis of a philosophy.' In fact, the technocrats showed the values to which they were attached and managed to embody them in the Plan. They can be called 'Galbraithians' — critical of public squalor in an affluent society. The emphasis was on social expenditure rather than on private consumption (cf. their emphasis on society as against the individual). Broadly, therefore, they tend to be 'anti-individualist' in economic, though not in political, matters. This is reflected, for example, in the emphasis on large-scale housing projects with flats at subsidized rents, rather than providing mortgages for owner-occupiers. It is suggested that the planners preferred the *architecture de masse* for aesthetic and social reasons. The planners also tend to be 'anti-materialist'; hostility to an American-type society is an aspect of this. Thus the Planning

Commissioner's remarks that emphasis on consumer goods leads to the 'sin of frivolity,' that such material prosperity simply creates a 'spiritual emptiness,' that 'the new abundance must be placed at the service of a full idea of man,' and that what was needed was 'a civilization of the cathedral, not a civilization of the gadget.' There speaks the technocrat who is also a man of 'general culture.' Consumer demand is not to be the guide, but the development of the full man in a civilized society. There is an obvious parallel to Gaullism. While the positive emphasis is different ('France cannot be herself unless she is great'), there is the same tendency to ignore the selfish wishes of the individual.

A major problem of technocracy lies in what has been suggested above. With the growth of planning, and its extension to the social sphere, it becomes increasingly important that those decisions which are not purely technical, but relate to the choice of ends, should be clearly identified and means found whereby the citizen can have some influence on them. It is round this problem that much present discussion ranges (e.g., Mendès-France, *La République Moderne*). It is hard to see, however, how this can be done effectively. Much of the success of the planning system (and of French government generally) has been due to its 'depoliticization.' 'Democratization' may solve certain political problems while creating new economic and administrative problems. In the last resort, of course, it is a question of whether one believes in liberal-democracy (even if people choose to live in an 'uncivilized' society) or if one prefers the rule of the Philosopher-Kings.

V

The Ubiquity of the Technocrats

Technocrats do not merely occupy the highest posts in the government departments. They are found in many other key positions in the public service (an institution with far wider ramifications than in Britain), and they also occupy key positions in private enterprise. The 'ubiquity' of the technocrats is something which has often been described. Members of the *Inspection des Finances* are found in the senior positions of their ministry, at the head of the great financial institutions of the state (*Banque de France, Caisse des Dépôts*) and in private enterprise — a random sample includes the director general, *Union des Mines;* deputy director general, *Chargeurs réunis* (shipping); *fondé des pouvoirs, Wendel* (steel); *associés gérants, Worms* and *Lazards* (merchant bankers); secretary general, *Printemps* (department store). *Polytechniciens-Inspecteurs des Finances* include Giscard d'Estaing (Minister of Finance), Rueff (economic adviser) and Gruson (head of the government's economic research services). *Polytechniciens-ingénieurs des Ponts et Chaussées* include the heads of several divisions of the Ministries of Industry and Transport, heads of several services of the Prefecture of the Seine, chief executives of nationalized industries, the Planning Commissioner (Massé) and senior executives in many private firms, banks, and trade associations. Political power may or may not be in the hands of the technocrats, much of management and administration certainly is.

The French economic system is sometimes described as '*economie concertée*'.

It is based on close collaboration between the state and private enterprise. This is possible largely because of the 'ubiquity' of the technocrats. The majority of members of the specialized committees of the Planning Commissariat, for example, have a similar background and speak the same language. In Britain, there are on the whole three worlds (admittedly a simplification): those of the civil servant, the business man and the scientist. One tends to think of them as having (and recruit them for) different qualities and qualifications. Business managers are often thought to need qualities of character (enterprise, leadership, 'common-sense'), rather than great intellect or technical knowledge. The three groups tend to follow separate careers and are often suspicious of each other. The business man may think of the civil servant as an 'unproductive bureaucrat' and the expert as a 'mere backroom boy' or 'ivory tower intellectual.' In France there is greater unity (social, educational) and career patterns overlap much more. A common career for a *polytechnicien* is a period of field service with his corps (technical work), service in a ministerial *cabinet* (political experience), senior administrative post in a ministry, membership of committees, move to high executive position in public or private enterprise.

This brings one to the question whether the technocrats in these different fields form a single class. Wright Mills suggests that there are close links between the various American elites: links of social origin, wealth, interchange of personnel. Anthony Sampson takes rather the opposite line in his *Anatomy of Britain.* He describes a ring of establishments, overlapping to some extent, but often not aware of each other, so that power is diffused and a sense of responsibility tends to vanish. The Wright Mills model is perhaps closer to the French reality, though the links between the elites are not always the same as in America. Career politicians and capitalists born into the *grande bourgeoisie* may also form power elites, but their role is probably more limited than in Britain and they are closely linked with the technocrats. These are links partly of social origin, partly of technocracy itself. Though the power structure is as complex in France as in Britain in organizational terms, it is probably less complex in social terms. This does not mean that the technocrats form a class, if one thinks of a class as an actor on the stage of history, with an interest and a purpose, a mind and a voice of its own. They do not act as a group. On the other hand, it is true that, as individuals, they do tend to promote each other's, and thus their own, interests, at least 'career-wise'; they have common loyalties and in a vague fashion some share a common outlook.

The outstanding feature of French industrial management is the extent to which it is dominated by engineers. The title 'engineer' may be acquired by training in different schools, with different standards and specializations. It is the degree/diploma awarded for virtually all higher scientific and technical training given outside the universities (where engineering proper is not taught). Most prestige attaches to the engineers of the *grandes écoles* (*Mines, Ponts et Chaussées*) who will have received a solid theoretical education at the *Polytechnique* beforehand (equivalent to B.Sc.). Engineers of the *Ecole Centrale* spend little time on general science, more on technology and practical work, those of the *Arts et Métiers* even more on practical work. Much the same is true of other general and specialized engineering schools.

Some form of further education is virtually a requisite for any 'cadre' post in French industry ('cadre' has many meanings: here it means all ranks above foreman — in large firms generally about 3 per cent. of total staff). As a rule, 'cadres' enter at this level. There is probably less promotion from the floor than in Britain. Class and educational divisions reinforce each other: relatively few working class children receive further education. A large-scale study of the 'cadres' in the metallurgical industries (23,000 men in 500 firms) showed that 85 per cent. had some sort of diploma, the overwhelming majority being engineers of one sort or another.

Those who enter industry after further education choose a subject which is directed to their career. This is true even of those who will enter at the highest level because of their social background and family connexions. The majority of industrial managers have university level education, but they have received it outside the university. If they do study at the university, it will probably be law and/or political science; they do not study in the arts faculties. The British situation, where an arts student decides in his final year to go into industry, rarely arises.

The highest proportion of engineers it probably found in the nationalized industries. This may be partly because the technicians were left in control when the 'business men' were ousted; it may be partly because this sector has been most effectively 'colonized' by the civil service. But in fact many of these industries were already largely run by engineers before nationalization. A study has been made of the qualifications of those in senior management posts. The definition of these posts varied with each undertaking (broadly, it included heads and deputy heads of services in the central offices, heads of regional and local offices and their deputies, and equivalent ranks). In the railways the entire group was qualified, in electricity and gas corporations nearly all. Career patterns were somewhat different at Renault, where almost a quarter had only primary and secondary education (the motor industry is not served by specialized schools and training at work is more common).

	Electricity and Gas	Railways	Renault
Polytechnique	87	112	3
Ecole Centrale	97	29	8
Arts et Métiers	34	1	71
Ecole Sup. d'Electricité	36	3	–
Other Engineering Schools	120	2	21
Science Faculties	3	2	8
Arts Faculties	–	3	–
Law Faculties	–	1	6
Political Science Institutes	9	–	3
Commercial Schools	1	1	6
Military Schools	–	–	3
n.a.	15	5	1

These figures are rather deceptive as a fair proportion will have taken more than one diploma in more than one school. This, of course, is particularly true of the *polytechniciens,* who may also have gone to the *Ecole des Ponts et Chaussées.* In the electricity corporation, moreover, there are actually 82 graduates of the Ecole Supérieure de l'Electricité if one counts those who went there after another school. What stands out is the fact that the *polytechniciens* dominate the railways (75 per cent. of senior ranks); in the electricity and gas corporations (20 per cent.) they provide 5 of the 6 directors and deputy directors general.

The figures are not substantially different in private enterprise. The following analysis is based on a sample of 2,500 men, mainly chairmen and chief executives of large companies, but including some non-executive board members and some heads of medium sized firms (all sectors of industry). These are the true policy-makers. At least three quarters had some form of higher education (exceptions were found in certain areas with strong family traditions, especially in the textile industry). This figure becomes more interesting when one looks at the type of higher education received. Engineering is the prince of subjects. Law and political science, though important, come a long way behind. University degrees in science and the arts are regarded with scorn.

	(%)
Polytechnique	21.4
Other Engineering Schools	34.5
Science Faculties	3.8
Arts Faculties	3.8
Law Faculties	8.8
Political Science	9.6
Commercial Schools	1.7
Military Schools	2.6
Other Schools	1.2
n.a.	3.7

Again the figures are deceptive: about a quarter of the group had more than one diploma.

The *polytechniciens* occupy so many key posts, especially in the largest undertakings, that they tend to set the tone. Of the 10,000 still alive today, only about 4,000 are still in the civil service or army (or retired as civil servants or officers). The remainder are either in public or in private enterprise (banking as well as industry). It is significant that those in the highest posts in the most important concerns generally move there after ten or even twenty years in the civil service. The *belle carrière* is through the civil service. It is noticeable that the most brilliant graduates of the *Polytechnique* enter the civil service as the first stage of their career, the poorest (for whom there are no interesting public service openings) go directly into business where, unless they have family connexions, they tend not to do quite so well.

French industry is increasingly dominated by a number of very large concerns. The public sector (far more important than in Britain) is in the hands of technocrats with a civil service background. In the private sector, there are still important family-controlled concerns but even these tend to have technocrats (engineers of *Inspecteurs des Finances*) with a civil service background as general managers. The technocrats in other firms are more likely to have entered private enterprise directly, but if they are *polytechniciens* they have passed the same stiff entrance examination which makes them part of the intellectual elite, and they will have received the same training as the technocrats in the government service.

Is this a true 'managerial revolution'? Do the technocrats occupy the key positions in industry by virtue of their technical knowledge? This is difficult to answer because of the close links between educational qualifications and social class. Law and engineering are the subjects studied in Europe by young men whose family connexions make it likely that they will go into business. 'Family is important, school is vital' is probably a fair assessment.

Even so, it may be that technocrats are really appointed for reasons other than their technical qualifications. It is often suggested that all that has happened is that the *polytechniciens* have effectively 'colonized' large sectors of industry on the principle of 'jobs for old comrades.'

Almost as cynical, but nearer the truth, is the suggestion that it pays industry to appoint former civil servants (or at least men who have studied with civil servants). In a country where the state plays so important a part in economic affairs, contacts are an obvious advantage. A firm gains if it is directed by a man who can talk to senior officials as an old schoolmate (the *tu* of the *polytechniciens*); the officials may be more sympathetic to a director who is not a 'mere businessman,' but whose own background is one of 'general culture' and public service, whom they can regard as (and who, to an extent, is) a displaced civil servant himself. It is this, of course, which explains the success of the planning system and the difficulty of transplanting it to England. The same type of men sit round the tables as representatives of government and industry, and as experts. The technocrats form a network which binds together most of the organizations which really matter (the trade unions are the serious exception). 'The Plan is the formal expression of the sentiment which permeates this network.'

But, in the last resort, the *polytechnicien* is valued for his own sake. The system of competitive examinations makes it reasonably certain that he will be a brilliant man. Capitalism never struck the same deep roots in France as in Britain, and the notion of the entrepreneur never became as widely accepted. Different qualities have as a result been looked for in a manager (reduced to a simple formula: intellect rather than character). Ideally, the technocrat, especially the engineer who has moved from the civil service to industry in middle life, has the following seven qualities:

1. Intellectual calibre;
2. Technical knowledge and, perhaps more important, an understanding of technical language:
3. At the same time, wider interest and the ability to bridge the 'two cultures';
4. Practical experience in the field at the start of his career;
5. Administrative experience (with an emphasis from the start on his 'polyvalent' character);

6. Wide range of contacts;
7. A sense of moral integrity and some qualities of leadership so as to be in the public service tradition.

With these qualities he will fit the description of the ideal manager in a recent book on management: 'Able to think with crystal clarity, he would combine a thorough technical knowledge of the goods or services with which he is concerned with strong integrity, shrewdness, an enterprising and humane outlook, high enterprise and considerable powers of leadership.'

VI

Assessment

It was suggested earlier that a question of practical interest with regard to elites is that of leadership. Where, in a society, do the centres of initiative lie? In private enterprise, initiative is supposed to come from the entrepreneur. The phrase 'Stagnant Society' has been bandied about a good deal in this country. Many factors are involved, an important one undoubtedly being the character of industrial leadership. It may be that the French pattern of training and recruitment is better adapted to current needs than our own. It is probably true that the French technocrat shows more enterprise than the French entrepreneur (i.e. 'capitalist'). This may be because the technocrat has a more positive outlook; it may be because the entrepreneur, like the British, but unlike the American or German, tends to be somewhat negative. It seems reasonably certain, in any case, that France would not have had its 'economic miracle' without the leadership of its technocrats.

A similar point may be made about the civil service. It is easy to caricature the British civil servant but the picture drawn by C. H. Sisson (an insider) is not untrue. He tends to see the functions of government rather negatively as the adjustment of conflicting interests, rather than as the promotion of new policies. In France, on the other hand, the technocrat-administrator does have a sense of responsibility for modernization, either by direct action or by example and guidance. There is no doubt about the role he has played in industrial and scientific development.

The issue is not so simple, however. Are the technocrats dynamic because they are experts? One's first inclination is to suppose that they are committed to expansion and progress by virtue of their very choice of career, their training and interests. Engineers will naturally want to build bigger and better power stations and progress, to adapt Lenin, is, in large measure, electrification. But the French technocrats are inspired by other motives as well. There is the motive of personal power, which partly explains, for example, the expansion of public enterprise in recent years. Above all, there is the French civil service tradition. Technocrats are committed to active government because they are formed in the French tradition of the public service state. What has happened in France is not simply a 'managerial revolution,' management of affairs taken over by experts. The administrative elite are the heirs of Colbert and Napoleon; they are another facet of the tradition that de Gaulle himself is heir to. They have not obtained power because they are technocrats; they are technocrats because they need expertise to exercise that power.

Technocratic leadership depends on the French educational system and on the general structure of careers. We could not early copy French administrative or managerial institutions, even if we should want to, because we live in a different society with a different culture. That is only saying, of course, what is often said by those who argue that we need to reform our own educational and recruitment systems if we are to modernize Britain. Even this, however, would not necessarily give us anything like the French technocracy. British technocrats would not automatically develop the same sense of responsibility that flows from the French notion of the positive state. One cannot so easily acquire a tradition that has been built up over centuries. We are back at the starting point. What practical lesson can one in fact learn from comparative studies?

36. Europe's Identity Crisis: Between the Past and America

STANLEY HOFFMANN

Professor Hoffmann argues that the "Americanization" of European politics has not proceeded—and is not within the foreseeable future likely to proceed—far enough to eliminate significant differences in structure and values either between individual European states or between them and the United States. Political cultures, historically developed patterns of stratification, resist leveling and foster the maintenance of traditional attachments and propensities. Historical memories survive and affect the style and content of politics. Can it then be said that the values of liberal democracy (rather than mere surface manifestations) have taken hold and are becoming part of national political cultures traditionally hostile to them?

Europe today is prosperous and disunited. What it will be like tomorrow remains a mystery — both because disunity results from conflicting assumptions about Europe's future, and because prosperity tends to become an end in itself. Europe today has no clear identity, no profile other than that which a process of industrialization and a process of economic integration have given it. Europe today has no sense of direction and purpose; this essay laments its absence and calls for its rebirth.[1]

But one cannot be asked to choose his future unless it is first established that freedom of choice exists. The point of this essay is to show that Europe's freedom of choice has been destroyed neither by the advent of industrial society nor by the evolution of world affairs. There is no "determinism" of the economic and social system. Nor has a new "European identity" been fully shaped by the European communities. And yet many Europeans behave as if the future course of Europe had been set, and many Americans believe it too. Whereas the former are divided between happy resignation and bitter protest, the latter show pride and some complacency. There is no justification for either of their attitudes.

One factor is involved in both processes which many see as inhibiting Europe's freedom: Europe's relationship with the United States. This essay

SOURCE: Reprinted by permission from *Daedalus*, Vol. 93, No. 4 (Fall 1964), pp. 1244–1266. Text and footnotes are abridged.

[1] In this essay, "Western Europe" refers to the so-called Six; the problem of Britain would require a separate analysis. Many of Europe's postwar developments discussed here have affected England also — and yet Britain's absence from the so-called "European experi-

is an attempt to explore this relationship. Since 1945 it has been one of double dependence, internal and external. The internal dimension of dependence has been called "Americanization." European societies have been transformed by the eruption of the age of mass consumption. Of course other terms, such as modernization or industrialization, could be used; but "Americanization" for several reasons applies. It was the United States which preached the gospel of prosperity and which goaded the Europeans into creating the institutions that would usher in the new age. It is the United States which serves as the model for the "new Europeans" — the businessmen back from productivity tours, or the shrewd fabricators of mass culture, or the party propagandists who look for inspiration on Madison Avenue, or the scientists and social scientists who envy, learn and use American theories and techniques. It is in the context of liberal policies, rather than in a framework of totalitarianism and public property, that the economic and social revolution has taken place. The external dimension shows dependence in a less intellectual and far more classical sense. For the first time in modern history, Western Europe has become a stake in the international competition, and its role in the world has been reduced to that of a protectorate of an extra-European power. To be sure the protector has been benevolent, often self-denying and inordinately generous; but this changes only the edge, not the essence, of the relationship. Thus, were it not for America's presence, one could hardly speak of Western Europe as an entity: to the extent to which Europe has a face, it is a borrowed one.

It is therefore not surprising that a mirage should have bloomed in the vision many Americans and Europeans have of Europe's future. It is the picture of a European society increasingly similar in its institutions, behavior and values to the "American model" of industrial society; of a European entity gradually growing into a federation, speaking in world affairs with a single voice, which, because of the very identity of Europe's outlook and interests with America's would use orthodox "Atlantic" language. This essay, in discussing Europe's freedom of choice, tries to show that such a picture may well be a mirage. Internally, an "American" Europe need not be Europe's future. There are enough differences between Europe's and America's industrial societies to feed and to preserve a separate identity — if the Europeans so desire. Externally, an Atlantic Europe is not likely to be Europe's future; but there is a choice between a "European" Europe if the quest for a new European role in the world succeeds and no united Europe at all if it fails. Thus, as much as a call to the Europeans, this essay pretends to be a warning to Americans. Being free, the former ought to think and act for themselves. Being different, the latter should not expect Europe to become America's twin.

---

ment," Britain's "special relationship" with the U. S., as well as the important differences between the recent past of England and that of the continental countries (i.e., the illusion of victory vs. the humiliations of defeat) make of Britain's case a special one. Indeed, were "the Six" more capable of defining a new European identity, Britain's painful hesitations about its own might be overcome more easily.

I

"Americanization" with a Difference

The "Americanization" of Western Europe is not a mere cliché. It is a fact recently documented by *Dædalus*. Economic expansion, higher wages, a peasantry whose numbers dwindle and whose production grows, classes that are less different from and feel less hostile to each other, a "service class" on the rise, a drive for mass education, the "end of ideology" in political life, intellectuals reconverted from tragedy to expertise, collective bargaining with the participation of "technocrats" instead of deliberations by a political class of leisurely generalists: all of this does indeed make Europe much more like the United States. Had *Dædalus* included in its issues studies of the new public role of the Catholic Church, the transformation of the family, the phenomenal progress of "mass culture," it would have become even more obvious that Tocqueville's prophecy of the democratic age has come true at last. What Tocqueville did not realize was that egalitarian society would triumph in Europe only after the spread of material prosperity. Nor did he see that those voluntary associations without which he thought liberalism would perish from the twin dangers of social conformity and political centralization would in fact grow out of an industrialization that proceeds in the framework of liberal democracy.

And yet industrial society in Europe may remain quite different from America's, for a reason Tocqueville would have well understood. He knew that a single type of society can be ruled by opposite types of regimes. He knew that the face of the polity in the democratic age is shaped by the relations between classes and the state in the predemocratic age. He would have realized that Europe's current emancipation from its past cannot help being shaped by that past — a past entirely different from America's. There are three areas of significant differences. First, there is the problem of the *polity*: America's industrial democracy was a creation; Europe's industrial society involves a conversion of the previous order. Second, there is the problem of *historical conscience*: the United States, on the whole, is at peace with itself; Europe's transformation entails a catharsis. In each of these areas, America's originality is double; not only does the American experience diverge from Europe's as a whole, but America's is single, whereas Europe's is fragmented into separate national experiences. Finally, and as a result, there is the problem of *beliefs*. America's growth is rooted in a creed; Europe's revolution unfolds amidst the repudiation of past creeds.

Creation vs. Conversion

Tocqueville saw the United States long before the age of mass consumption. Yet much in his description remains valid. Obviously, industrial society in America has been affected by the network of pre-existing institutions, laws, customs and values more than it has affected this network. The ideal type of advanced industrial society or that of capitalism tells us little. They are liquids which take the shape of whatever vase they are poured into, although they give their color to the vase. What matters in America's case — it has become a cliché to say so — is that industrialization proceeded in a society already democratic, freed by its revolution not from a previous aristocratic phase but from outside tutelage, and constantly confirmed in its essence by new waves of immigrants. Moreover, industrialization expanded in and benefited from a single national framework, which survived the great test of secession. In both respects Europe's past has been different. It plagues the present and mortgages the future. The industrialization of nations deeply marked, socially and politically, by their "predemocratic" stage and by the rivalries means the laborious breaking down of class barriers and borders. Consequently, on the one hand they are not "like America" *yet*, for the task of conversion still entails both much destruction of the old and the tough resistance of major residues. On the other hand, the new Europe might not be "like America" *ever*, for the task involves innovations which either confirm old differences or create new contrasts with the United States.

What is being destroyed in Europe's social structure would not deserve being mentioned in a study that focuses on what is likely to keep Europe lastingly distinct from the United States, were it not for three reasons. One has to do with the difference in social structure and values; the elimination of various groups whose economic or political function has disappeared has left a residue of bitterness not only among the victims but also among other groups who shared the values if not the social position of those victims. The second reason has to do with the difference in social structure and with Europe's fragmentation into separate states; the process of elimination has put new strains on already fragile political systems, for it is much more trouble-some to deal with angry farmers, displaced miners or depressed areas when they represent a large fraction of the population or of the space of a country than when they occur in the "wide open spaces" of a sparsely settled continent. The last reason has to do with national differences in Western Europe; the destructions and dislocations brought about by economic change have affected these nations unevenly, depending on the degree of development they had reached at the start of the process. Thus Germany, despite the influx of refugees, has suffered least; France has had serious troubles with shopkeepers, peasants and workers made jobless by progress; Italy is the country in which change has entailed not only "the disintegration of agriculture and of tradi-tional rural communities" through a huge rural exodus, but also a problem of regional imbalance of enormous proportions. Despite the common movement toward industrialization and the efforts made by European communities to ease the journey, the fact that each nation has had to deal with its own incidents and its own casualties of progress has strengthened separateness just as it was being undermined.

It is not only Europe's social structure that is affected by destructions. Partly as a result of those just mentioned the load which Europe's political institutions have had to carry has crushed one vital organ: parliament. The decline of a body that symbolized one important difference between Europe's and America's political systems has, however, not made for any rapprochement. In Europe's cabinet system, parliament was supposedly the fount of all effective and responsible power in contrast with the United States Congress, handicapped by the separation of powers. Today, parliament's share in decision-making and its role in supervising the execution of decisions are far smaller than the share and role of Congress. The dispossession of parliament not only by the civil service and interest groups but also by the executive has been much greater. Congress is now protected by the strict separation of powers, by the fragmentation of the bureaucracy, and by the very looseness of American parties. Whenever the party system worked, parliament's decline has occurred because of the control exerted over the majority by the cabinet or by the majority party's ruling organs; where the party system has failed (i.e., in France), parliament has been demoted to a position legally much narrower than that of the United States Congress. Here again, differences among the Europeans compound the difference with the United States. Outside France, parliament, having lost its role, at least preserves its "myth" — that of the body that speaks for the people and that can overthrow the cabinet. In France's hybrid political system, the president plays the part of the people's voice and combines the advantages of a chief executive in a presidential system with those of a cabinet leader in a parliamentary regime — at the expense not only of parliament's position but also of its reputation. Outside France, it is the strength of the parties that has weakened parliament in parliamentary regimes. In France it is the very weakness of the parties which has brought the demise of the parliamentary regime altogether and which is being perpetuated by the practice of so-called "direct democracy."

Destructions and resistance both mark the attempt at transforming the educational system. Nowhere is the difference between the creation of one national industrial society and the conversion of a variety of "old" national societies into a more democratic one so obvious. The need to abandon a system of secondary schools and universities which were the shapers and guardians of societies in which elites were few, access to the elite was restricted and authority was hardly democratic is widely recognized. Most European writers on the subject agree that the new society requires leaders and executives, technicians and bureaucrats in far greater number, that the old curriculums and structures are obsolete, that the new schools ought to be training centers for teamwork and imaginative cooperation. And yet the result of their efforts is not likely to resemble the United States system of education. The United States was able to let its system grow; the Europeans are obliged to let their old one either continue or collapse because they cannot oblige it to adapt. The resistance of the old structures and of the teaching personnel to change is fierce — in the one sector of society where no reform (however much determined from the top, by fiat, or supported from below, by the rising masses) can be adequately carried out without the help of the very men and women whose whole philosophy is being challenged and who are still in charge of training their own successors. Thus the educators try to block reform either by opposing change altogether or through the familiar device of rejecting anything short of perfection. As a result, the reformers are forced either to back down, delay or compromise, or else to try to win by indirection: by undermining that which cannot be persuaded to reform, by initiating new types of school programs or institutes which besiege or submerge the old establishments. The outcome, in either case, is a fearful mess. The *status quo ante* is obviously impossible, but chaos is not necessarily creative. The new structures and the new personnel suffer from a lack of prestige and a frequently makeshift quality. Here again, national differences complicate the matter. There is a great deal of educational planning in France, none in Germany. Resistance to change is greater in Catholic countries, where the religious schools are particularly devoted to the values of the old society. The Belgian problem has been compounded by the Walloon-Flemish split. Thus the prospects of a unified response to the crisis are slim.

Of course, it can be argued that in the United States also there is a crisis, and that the responses and forms of experimentation are multiple. But whereas it is not impossible to improve and diversify the training of elites within a system of mass education, the forceable transformation of a narrow, rigid, coherent and largely successful system of elite education into a democratic one is a heroic and infinitely more controversial enterprise. In mere financial terms it requires extraordinary budgetary transfers and an entirely new attitude on the part of businessmen or foundations, whose role in education has until now been almost nil. Furthermore, there is a major difference between the experiments of a fantastic number of school districts and state and private colleges and universities, and the laborious decisions taken by a small number of ministers of education in the light of their national situations.

The resilience of old patterns of behavior is also visible in the whole area of class relations. The way in which social groups face each other in the new society remains deeply marked by the past history of social and political contests. To be sure, recent European writings show a longing for the "American model" of group politics, democratic authority, face-to-face discussions and compromises. But the model is not really relevant. Whereas America is a fluid society, Europe remains a set of sticky societies. Mobility within each and between them is less practiced and less highly valued. Such viscosity preserves past obstacles to social harmony and even to further economic development (for instance, in keeping the size of enterprise much below the "American model"). Moreover, despite growing prosperity, inequality remains a major social and political issue: first, because everywhere in Europe the differences in living conditions between the rich and the poor are still huge (the access of the latter to higher education and power is far from assured); second, because the underprivileged groups' attitudes toward inequality remain shaped by the European tradition of global protest against and challenge of the "established disorder"; third, because the discontent and the expectations of the underprivileged are far more focused on the state than in the United States; finally, because of considerable variations from nation to nation. Thus, although one can rightly speak of a moderation of the class struggle and of a decline in revolutionary messianism, the long record of contests between the workers and the upper class and the constant role of the state as a stake and a force in the struggle introduce a lasting distinction between the American and the European cases. In every European country the workers' organizations — unions or parties — are more concerned with the global economic development of society and with the role of the workers in the management of enterprises than are those in the United States. It may well be that this concern now expresses itself in requests for "participation" instead of the old demands for revolution, but even this points to a difference in scope and temper between America's well-established reformism — more fragmentary and more placid — and Europe's new one.

If one examines not merely the political expression of social grievances in the "new Europe" but political behavior in general, one reaches the same conclusion: despite real changes, old reflexes resist. Ideology in politics (and in the writings of intellectuals on politics) may be declining, in part because of the moderation of the class struggle, in part because of a reaction against the ideological excesses of "secular religions," in part because of the increasing irrelevance of "isms" that grew out of the conditions of preindustrial society. But proneness to ideology (in the sense in which a weak body is prone to diseases) and attachment to old ideological symbols persist, even if the symbols have lost much of their "objective" content. Thus in France and in Italy neither the rise in the standard of living within societies still marked by grave injustice nor the relative decline of groups that provided the bulk of the support of the Communist party (proletarian workers, landless farmers) have seriously reduced the electoral strength of the Communist parties. For where ideology was strong it was never exclusively related to the stage of economic development. There simple discontent still expresses itself in ideological terms, and events unconnected with either the old class struggles or the old stable constellations of political doctrines still provoke ideological reactions. Thus in France the division created by the new postwar issues — the Cold War, decolonization, European integration — have been anything but moderate, and the attitudes of the opposed factions anything but pragmatic.

The resilience of old forms of political behavior and traditional styles of political argument explains in large part why the European political problem continues to differ from that of the United States. The American issue is the efficiency of institutions that are stable and legitimate. The issue in the three largest countries of Western Europe is the stability and legitimacy of their institutions. Neither in France nor in Italy nor in Germany are they so secure that they could survive a prolonged period of inefficacy. In none of those three countries could allegiance to the Constitution be the symbol of national integration. Before their alleged death, the ideologies of yesterday left deep scars on the institutions.

Finally, the weakness of representative government, the residues of ideology and the persistence of old habits in class relations all contribute to the preservation of two important differences between Europe's and America's political life. Divided polities in which the state has played a major part in class conflicts and in which a core of efficiency and continuity has been indispensable have produced professional civil services with traditions of their own and also with a natural tendency to persist even if the conditions of their earlier rise and role have changed. The bureaucracy of the European state has preceded the age of democracy; its power and centralization create a problem of control far more acute than in the United States, with its mixture of often rather low-grade professionals and temporary recruits from business or the universities, and its fragmentation of bureaucracy into countless agencies and services. Moreover, the strength and staying power of the civil service continues to limit the scope of representative government, that is, to curtail the chances of what one now calls "participation." Tocqueville is again the more relevant reference: Europe's politics still suffer from that radical distinction between "us" and "them," the subjects and the rulers, the citizens and the state, which has been perpetuated by centuries of absolutism, authoritarianism, and even liberal politics that entrusted the polity to men of knowledge and order only, and thus served the interests of some classes alone.

Indeed, this is a difference which has been confirmed by one of the major innovations of the new Europe. There has been an increase in the scope of the state. The Europeans' conception of public functions has radically expanded in this century, whereas the Americans' has changed but little — there is a gap between the practices in the two areas, and an even greater one in their "public philosophies." In part because of the differences in the background — greater poverty, the ruins of the war, the need both for reconstruction and for regulation of the sudden boom — Europe has allowed more overt intervention of the state in economic and social affairs, has shown greater concern for welfare and balanced growth, has repudiated uncontrolled laissez faire and has tried to avoid the scandal of public squalor in the midst of private opulence. Although the private virtues have been practiced in Europe so much more fervently than the civic ones, by contrast with the United States, the hold of the state on the individual and the subordination of private gratification to collective requirements have been strengthened. Both the bureaucracy and the interest groups (what the French call *les forces vives*) have received a role in the preparation and execution of state decisions that is both greater and more readily recognized than in the United States. This innovation has not only created a new difference between the United States and Europe; it has also consolidated two old ones. On the one hand, the role and prestige of European parliamentarians has declined even further, whereas United States congressmen cling (and sometimes behave according) to a theory of representation that crowds all public concern within the charmed but occasionally vicious circle of Capitol and White House, and makes of the member of Congress the only legitimate spokesman for his constituents. On the other hand, the expansion of state functions has benefited the public "technocrats" and provoked a renewed demand, often utopian in its scope, for "participation," symbol of a growing gap between "us" and "them." Thus the basic relationship of the American citizen to his officials may well be one of apathy, based both on trust or a sense of identity, and on rather modest expectations; the European relationship is often a mixture of apathy based on distance or distrust, and hostility due to heavy dependence as well as fear of arbitrariness.

Another area where innovations have both confirmed and added to the contrasts between Europe and America is that of class relations. Both in France and in Germany the structure and the behavior of labor unions have been molded by the past attitudes of the upper classes and the earlier role of the state, as indicated above. Today the circumstances which shaped these French and German unions have disappeared. And yet, on the one hand, the traditional behavior and organization of the workers have been confirmed by the new events. The French workers' pattern of protest and blackmail of the state developed at a time when the bourgeois, who had adopted many features of the French aristocracy in their fight against it, resisted proletarian demands and slowed down economic growth. Today, despite the change in business attitudes, the new and leading part played by the French state in development has perpetuated what Michel Crozier calls the unions' fascination with Power, and has made blackmail even more useful as a way of affecting the distribution of the national income. Moreover, Communist preponderance among the workers provides a new force of protest against inequities in this distribution and a new focus for business and labor hostility to face-to-face discussions. In pre-Weimar Germany, labor unions were more cohesive and less rebellious than in France because of faster economic development promoted by the aristocratic class and by a "Gnaden-bourgeoisie." Today, the influx of refugee labor has contributed both to the numerical strength and to the cautious behavior of the unions. On the other hand, the innovations have sharpened the difference between Europe and America insofar as they have broadened previous differences among the Europeans, thus offsetting the unifying impact of industrialization. The divisions of French unions and the fact that the biggest one is under Communist control oblige the labor movement to concentrate its efforts on the central level — that of Power. German unions are wholly without Communist influence, and their strength allows them to concentrate on the control of the workers in the factory and on relations with business. Moreover, each European nation has created its own network of procedures — ranging from ineffective to quite effective in the Dutch case — for the settlement of social conflicts.

In one area, old differences have been confirmed and a new one has been created not merely by European innovations but by a combination of destructions, resistance and novelties: I refer to the attitude of social groups and nations toward the new industrial society. What is being destroyed is the former bourgeois "sobriety" which once kept the European way of life far below America's splashes of conspicuous consumption, as well as the former reluctance of bourgeois and aristocrats alike to mass production, which meant dependence on the market. What is, however, resilient is the concern of even hard-working Europeans (businessmen or industrial workers) for "whatever . . . is beyond work": "distraction, pleasure, evasion." There is a desire to put limits on work; there is a determination to preserve "elite cultures" that coexist with but are not submerged by the progress of mass culture and that continue to set standards in the arts. Both show the imprint of the "aristocratic age" in which work was a disgrace for a few, a curse for most, for others a means to rise but not an end in itself, for some a tunnel through which one had to pass before one could cultivate one's inner freedom and fulfill one's deepest aspirations. What is new is the possibility for many more Europeans than in the past to enjoy what is "beyond work" — holidays or paperbacks. As a result an old difference from the United States has been deepened:

despite, and even to some extent thanks to, the progress of mass consumption and mass production, Europeans keep "asking more from life" both in terms of an "insatiable demand" for material goods and "in terms of fulfillment" than the Americans, whose society "remains oriented toward and by work."

Moreover, the contrast between America's rather uniform orientation and Europe's has been increased by new differences among the Europeans. The more European societies become alike in their social structures and economic makeup, the more each national society seems to heighten its idiosyncrasies. Recent surveys among young Frenchmen and Germans who have visited each other's country fail to reveal any "homogenization." Clichés about national character live on, and national disparities get stronger: the spectrum extends from Italy, in which the task of economic and social change is least advanced and where the Communists have a powerful intellectual and political hold, to France, whose economic and social transformation has so far made no constructive impact on the party system, and to West Germany, whose values and politics remind observers far more of the United States, for federalism divides its bureaucracy, the disasters brought by past ideologies have singed all who have not been charred, and the ideal of the *Marktwirtschaft* (although it is *Sozial!*) has more than a few illusions in common with American free enterprise. To be sure, there are regional differences in the United States as well, but how pale they look by comparison! The national state, exorcised daily by the prosecutors of its obsolescence, continues to make a difference. Each European country adjusts its "national character" to the new age in its own style, and particularly its own style of authority.

Pride vs. Purge

It is neither fashionable nor accurate to say that nations have souls. But they do have historical memories — memories of how their citizens behaved toward each other and towards outsiders in moments of stress and crisis. If the concept of industrial society tells us little about the institutions each kind of industrial society will have, it tells us nothing at all about the historical conscience and consciousness of a nation or continent. And yet, since people do not live by economic rationality alone, this is a dimension that cannot be dismissed.

American industrial society has grown in a nation whose rendezvous with history have not been disastrous. It overcame its greatest internal challenge in such a way that its political institutions were strengthened. It survived the depression in such a way that the Presidency emerged as the center of national action and the focus of national expectations. It managed its relations with the outside world, first so as to avoid explicit dependence, and later so that entanglement corresponded with supremacy. Thus it is not surprising that Americans (outside, perhaps, of the South) should feel a special pride in American history, tend to read it — from Wilson to Morgenthau or Niebuhr — in terms of ethical teleology and often indulge, when they speak either of America's development and "purpose" or of the ups and downs of less fortunate nations, in what C. Wright Mills called the national celebration. It is in the literature of the South alone that one finds a deep sense of guilt, resentment, doom and tragedy — and this is of course the literature that appeals to Europeans most.

For however much European societies may have been rejuvenated by post-war changes, their unhappy past clings to them. They may have shed their old skins, but their nerves and blood are still weakened by the diseases of their past. The contrast with the United States is provided not only by a long record of national rivalries and wars that have left traces everywhere, from the history books which are so hard to harmonize this side of expurgation, to the *arrière-pensées* of foreign policy. It is also the depressing story of multiple disillusionment and frustration which every major European nation has experienced in this century. Except in the relations between North and South, Americans of different regions can face each other without deep misgivings and look at their past without shame. Their very mobility has loosened the grip of sectional memories. It remains difficult for a Frenchman and a German (even the postwar young ones) to talk to each other as if the past had never happened, or to think of their own nation's recent history with complacency. The only common heritage of the "new Europeans" is one of guilt and shame. Shame, for having produced the biggest record of atrocities in centuries; shame, for having acted in such a way that Europe has become a stake; guilt, for having so often repressed awareness and atonement; guilt, for having again and again turned the national community into an arena for civil war. The plays that describe the European historical condition most adequately are Camus's allegorical *State of Siege,* which uses Spain to express truths of general European relevance, and Sartre's frantic *Condemned of Altona,* which uses Nazism to speak about Algeria. Both are plays of disillusionment and denunciation. The stinkers and the cowards, the politicians of restoration and the practitioners of torture fill the stage. The pure rebels die, and even the self-torturing guilty rebel Frantz, in *Altona,* finds peace in suicide only. This common experience of failure on a massive scale — World War I with its methodical slaughter, the thirties which debased ideologies intellectually but turned them into deadly weapons, World War II with its atrocities, the traumas of dependence and decolonization — all of it opened a gulf between the continent and the United States, and a gap between the continent and England. For although the British and Americans shared some of those experiences, they did it without humiliation and traversed them without much sense of guilt.

True enough the "new Europe," in passionate pursuit of the pleasures of the present, often appears to have digested its past; some of its statesmen talk as if pride, not shame, were its duty; many of its sons behave as if the new generation had been born without parents. The United States is in the midst of a soul-searching act of its own: the civil rights crisis. But the French, two years after the end of the Algerian war, seem to have forgotten what used to be for so long an all-filling tumult. Nor is Nazism a major issue in German politics. And yet suppression is not oblivion; amnesia is no absolution. At least the United States is willing to face its damned spot. Europe wants to remove the smell of blood; but pretending that there is no stench will not make it go away. In every new debate the old lines of division among Frenchmen reappear: Vichy still produces a presidential candidate, and discussions on foreign aid or military policy bring back the sound and fury of Algerian controversies. Trials and scandals show that however much so many Germans may want to think of Nazism as an accident, something like the aberration of another planet, the temporary filling of the German void by a gang of advanced savages fallen from the blue, it was not a fluke but a cancer whose extirpation leaves scars and whose incomplete postoperative treatment leaves doubts as to whether it will recur. What killed Sartre's Frantz was not just the memory of murder but also the discovery of his nation's refusal to remember, and of its abdication to prosperity.

And so the contrast with the United States continues. What sharpens it is the fact that the United States faces its own blotch as one nation (especially since the North realizes that it has its own share of the responsibility), whereas Europe tries to escape from its past as a set of separate nations. Since Europe's recent history has been both one of national hatreds and one of internal strife, each European nation continues to stew in its own sour juice. Each one has tried a different way of coming to terms with itself. The French have been submitted to de Gaulle's psychological massage. They have been told that they all resisted, that their share in victory was great, that their colonial policies were beautiful, grand and generous, that decolonization was their wish and their pride, that the world's eyes were glistening whenever they met France. This heroic effort at restoring self-respect and denying humiliation has had mixed results. The emperor's beautiful clothes do not hide, even from the French, the dirt and the wounds beneath — and there were twelve years during which the emperor was not even around to parade his mantle. Yet mixed with cynicism there is pride, or at least cockiness and self-assertion. Half-believing in pedagogical flattery is more than disbelieving it altogether.

Germany, on the other hand, has been neither flattered by its leaders (how could it be?) nor asked by them to repent (for one hesitates to plunge a whole nation into repentance when one tries both to lead it to its future and to be a democratic politician depending on votes). The result has been what foreigners and many Germans, too, call either the absence of a face or the lack of a national backbone. The French, even and especially when they disagree about the purpose and mission of France, still feel intensely French. They have accepted, indeed some have blessed, the material aspects of Americanization, but they still talk of a "French way" of using it. Many Germans, having passed through the most searing nationalism ever known to the world, now deny having "ever really understood why nations exist." Hence the birth of new misunderstandings which maintain Europe's historical conscience as it always was: fragmented. The French, on the whole, try to exorcise their past by providing their nation with new reasons for hope or pride (this has been true of all their leaders; the drama resides in their miscalculations — Suez! — and in their conflicting assessments). The Germans, on the whole, have tried to do so by exorcising nationalism altogether. There is no pan-European recipe.

As for Italy, it has come to terms with its past neither in the French nor in the German way. Neither national self-assertion nor "European" good behavior, those two forms of activism, has prevailed. Amenesia, here, has not even tried to be constructive. Hence there exists an intellectual mood of pessimism and protest that reminds one of Germany's twenties or of France's thirties and forties. The nation has neither half convinced itself of its heroic fight against totalitarianism nor acted in such a way that a recurrence of the causes that once produced Fascism becomes unlikely. It is as if Italy had not had its thirties yet. Thus all Europeans have skeletons in their closets, but they are not the same skeletons.

Values vs. Void

Although in the depth of its memories each European nation remains unique, and although the color of its memories makes of the European family an heir to the Atrides, the surface appears much more rosy, more homogeneous and more like that of the United States. The memories, being evaded, do not loom large by daylight. Then too, Americans and Europeans alike celebrate the progress of European pragmatism. Tolerance replaces the class of ideologies; a concern for concrete issues and practical solutions inspires the politicians and the voters alike. Intellectuals try to contribute to the national discussion and settlement of those issues instead of indulging either in global justification or in a total *mise en cause*. The Europe of "carnivorous idols" has become *l'Europe du dossier;* it celebrates technology and compromise, expertise and empirical research. Does not all this show that American values are sweeping the Old Continent?

In my opinion, it shows nothing of the kind. Europe is converting itself to the functional necessities of a new type of social order — it has not converted itself to a new set of values. Europe flees from its past because it cannot look at it honestly — not because of a deliberate and mature repudiation. America's pragmatism, pluralism and "engineering approach" rest on a solid bed of beliefs, those of classical liberalism, which the Declaration of Independence and the Bill of Rights embody and a common loyalty to the Constitution symbolizes. Pluralism can be harmonious or cacophonic. America's is harmonious because of a basic consensus: what is never questioned because it is not merely accepted but cherished is always larger and deeper than what is contested. The engineering approach is that of men concerned with the means because the ends are not in doubt. Empirical research is guided by a formidable body of theory, much of which (despite its value-free pretense) conceals or sublimates a firm conviction in the superiority of America's way of political and social life. The school system produces — consciously and enthusiastically — Americans, that is, men and women capable of cooperating because of a common respect for the values of liberal democracy and a common faith in America's purpose. In no society is conflict more universal, and yet its social theory takes consensus, not conflict, as its conceptual framework. There is logic, not paradox, in this apparent contraction, for conflict flourishes at all levels precisely because it is contained within well-accepted limits and channelled through procedures and institutions to which loyalty is assured. The role of those devices is not to turn conflict into consensus; it is to find for limited conflicts solutions that are inspired by the procedural and substantive consensus which keeps the system going, and which such solutions strengthen in turn. In support of this proposition, we find both the silence of social theory (and the lack of effective procedures) in the one area where consensus was missing — race relations — and the gradual progress of theory and procedures as consensus begins to grow.

None of this is true of postwar Europe. Here there is no agreement on fundamentals. What works in America works because Americans believe in it; what Europeans believe in today is what works. The European consensus is negative: like culture, which a Frenchman defined as "what is left when everything has been forgotten," today's consensus is around "what is left after everything has been discarded." The French who have discovered the virtues of a presidential system, the Germans or Italians who praise liberal democracy often do so not because of any conviction but because everything else has been tried and has failed. The same is true of the intellectuals who repudiate the past tradition of "totalism"; often they do so not because of a deep belief in the intellectual's responsibility as an expert but because of the obvious failure of Grand Intellectuals to bridge the gap between thought and action. There is all the difference in the world between an affirmation and an auto-da-fé. America's intellectual stand has been on the plateau of a democratic *juste milieu*; Europe's road has gone from a mountain range of disparate ideologies to the present naked plain. Intellectuals who believed too fervently and too long that the polity was a battlefield of rival conceptions of good and evil, the *locus sacrus* for saving one's soul, have now fallen into a state of nihilism. It is not a nihilism of despair; this phase is over. It is a happy nihilism, to be sipped in prosperity after all the great nectars of the past have turned sour. It has, of course, its reassuring charms. But it also brings with it three dangers that can be summed up in two words: Europe's silence.

The first danger is a lack of imagination. The old questions were too big, too vague, too murderous. Today there are no questions. In the past European intellectuals seemed to assume either that the worst was certain or that everything had to be subordinated to the triumph of the best. Today they act as if the worst was certain not to happen, and the best required no choice at all. Not long ago Raymond Aron denounced the ideological opinions which sacrificed the present to the future. Today he wants to investigate how the desire to calculate where one is going has come to replace the desire to ask where one ought to go; his and Camus's plea for modesty, against fanaticism, seems to have been interpreted as an appeal against intellectual probing, for the sacrifice of the future to the present. The accumulation of facts and figures, the extrapolation of trends, the discussion of forecasting and planning as if they involved no fundamental choices but only technical problems — better instruments of detection as it were, or better statistics — as if only the point at which the ball will stop rolling along the slope remained to be discovered, all of this betrays an intellectual fatigue that is excusable, given the past, but hardly encouraging. The fact that in a world *où l'action n'est pas la soeur du rêve* attempts at realizing utopian dreams turned life into a nightmare is no reason for chasing all dreams away. Past questions may have led to the wrong answers, but the avoidance of questions is not likely to prove any better. The man who drives himself into a ditch may get killed; so may the sleepwalker.

The European intellectual who today either borrows American theories, often without questioning their relevance, or else assumes that the questions have been already formulated and answered gives up a role which has been both his glory and the only clean feather in Europe's dirty cap: that of raising the fundamental problems about society — its direction, the ethical validity of its actions, the relative worth of the choices open to it. A society without some judge who frets over its behavior, admonishes, advises, at times indicts and at other times approves, tends all too easily to fall into complacency. America is often charged with it; and yet both in domestic and in foreign affairs the issues are more sharply discussed, the choices more clearly spelled out and more hotly embraced than in present-day Europe. The reader of *Dædalus's* "A New Europe?" cannot find a single European answer to such questions as: What political institutions would be most capable of protecting the individual altogether from excessive bureaucracy, from special interests and from arbitrary executive power? Should Europe's industrial society keep trying to regulate demand so as to give precedence to collective equipments (if not cathedrals) and to preserve some realm for quality? Should intellectuals accept as good and final the demise not only of verbal efforts to "change the world" but also of their role of overall social critics?

Here lies the second danger. The refusal to ask such questions means the implicit or explicit acceptance of unquestioned illusions. There are three which are quite common. The first is the technological illusion, according to which the progress of the sciences, material expansion and the spread of specialized knowledge will gradually eliminate that residual category, politics. Authoritative answers will at last be given to social problems that have remained unsolved (that is, political, if one accepts Jouvenel's notion that the political is what is insoluble) only because the material and intellectual elements of a solution were missing. Aron once wrote that the day when intellectuals, having discovered the limits of politics, would become indifferent to it was not yet threatening. He may well have been wrong — or rather, having discovered that politics was not all, many intellectuals seem to assert that it could somehow be reduced to nothing. Alas, there are only too many social problems which cannot be erased either through a welfare calculus or through the tidal rise of the learning process, for instance, all those of political philosophy.

A second illusion is the procedural one. It consists in believing that the method for solving problems is to put around a table all the interested parties, informed of course by the spirit of compromise; participation and goodwill shall provide the answers. This is merely a new version of Europe's traditional attitude toward conflict. The recognition of deep-seated cleavages has always been at the core of Europe's social theory, but the practices of European polities — in part because of the prevalence of nondemocratic styles of authority, in part because of the role of state bureaucracies — have always tended toward the settlement of conflicts not through compromise but by acts of authority. Today the old practices are increasingly discredited (although they still abound), but the same desire to eliminate conflict as one removes a spot on a suit shows in the proliferation of suggestions for orderly procedures of settlement, based on the hope that the procedure would transmit conflicts of values and interests into harmony, painlessly and without friction. A kind of *escamotage* at the bottom has replaced the *escamotage* from the top. Once again the parallel with American beliefs is strong, but once again one has to say that there is no *escamotage* where the conflicts are marginal, often technical, and steeped in a culture that values agreement for agreement's sake. Where social groups remain divided by memories, suspicions and insecurity, where citizens do not recognize themselves in their public authorities, where interest clashes are made more rather than less ferocious by a dearth of ideological beliefs that lends interests a vicarious fierceness, the situation is not auspicious for procedural solutions. There would be less discussion of "democratic planning" in France if one would at last realize that what is involved in a so-called "income policy" is nothing less than a philosophy of social goals. A coherent policy has little or no chance of resulting from interest compromises and conciliation procedures, for the simple reason that groups and parties disagree drastically on ends and means—the real choice remains (once again) between a decision by fiat and the pluralism of cacophony.

There is a third illusion: believing that Europe's undeniable progress since the twenties in the difficult art of making a society aware of its problems and of its collective responsibility for solving them means an increased capacity to identify the problems of the future or a greater relevance to the concerns of less developed nations. It is true that in the areas of social security, planning, and regulation of the economy, European postwar reforms have carried collective consciousness beyond what exists in the United States. The long battle over medicare seems incomprehensible to many Europeans. But nothing yet shows that the techniques developed in order to solve the problems and allay the fears born out of the thirties will prove equally capable of dealing with the next phase. When it comes to automation and the problems of leisure, to the fate of the aged and to juvenile delinquency, all "societies of plenty" find themselves in the same wasteland. If Europe has been more inventive in battling the scourge of poverty, it is because the pressure was so much greater there. But applied Keynesianism is of little help in the new situation.

What is striking in those areas and in many others as well is the third danger of the void: the absence of a European *projet*—that is, of a European social and cultural design. It is easy to argue that there has never been a European design or that those we find in the past are *ex post facto* intellectual reconstructions. But this is not the way in which Europe appeared to non-Europeans; moreover, whoever reads Europe's doctrines of the past century discovers two sets of convictions. One was the conviction of an over-all movement of mankind. This faith was symbolized by all those philosophies of history that our superior "scientific" knowledge ridicules (but that are still represented in much of America's more sophisticated grand theory of today—*vide* Walt Rostow); the movement was marked not merely by the unfolding of material progress but by political progress as well: the drive toward parliamentarism or imperialism, those summits of human ascent, or at least so they seemed at the time. The other was the conviction of a national purpose, carried at times to incredible chauvinistic lengths but nevertheless of value in unifying national elites often deeply divided on other issues. There is little of either left in today's Europe; smart debunking has replaced rash belief. We should not be surprised; the development of a *projet* requires a sense of stability, a belief in man's capacity to set the course of the journey and to get to the destination through his own means. What prospers instead is either the belief that technological forces will drive one to the end of the road or that the best one can do is hold high the lamp so as to illuminate the next steps.

In no area are the absence of questioning, illusions, and the lack of a *projet* more evident than in education. If the resistance of the old system is so self-righteously strong, if the reforms of the new prophets are so timid and tentative, if the attempts at defining a new curriculum are so groping, if the alternative to the old authoritarian relation between students and teachers so often seems to be the collapse of discipline and structure, if the sum total of national destructions does not amount to a European construction, it is because of the void of values. The old system did not merely dispense knowledge to some. It taught a number of alleged truths and served to shape a society according to those truths. There was a basic conviction: in the value and necessity of elites for the government of society; in the superiority of elites trained in the classics or in pure science, steeped in "general education," made capable of rising above ordinary human mediocrity through the enjoyment of personal freedom (money helped). This freedom was to be achieved through and nourished by the knowledge of essential facts and laws of nature or human nature discovered over time by the wise — facts and laws that did not have to be discovered again by each generation but that could be transmitted authoritatively by those who knew them to those who had to be told and who would later on transmit them in the same way. Neither the purpose nor the substance nor the method was in doubt.

In today's enthusiastic rush toward mass education the questions which are not being asked are those about the purpose of the enterprise. Is it to provide the new industrial society with the requisite number of technicians in each branch, or is it to make it possible for a much larger number of men and women to enjoy the kind of knowledge and culture without which liberal values cannot be safeguarded? The choice between economic rationality and a democratic humanism exists, and to avoid stating it may lead to failure on both counts. . . .

37. The Problem of the New Left

TOM KAHN

The movement known as the New Left has in recent years dramatically changed the political climate in Western democracies on both sides of the Atlantic. An unanticipated and new "opposition of principle" has emerged in systems that were assumed to have been integrated around the concept of "welfare democracy." It appears unlikely that the movement will be an ephemeral phenomenon because its protest is oriented not primarily against the traditional targets of poverty and exploitation, but rather against the "alienation" and "manipulation" of the system, and calls for the rejection of both the "elite model" of democracy and the trend toward bureaucratized technocracy. The lack of a mass base may, however, lead to its isolation as a minority student movement—and perhaps to its de-politization. Though the movement naturally differs somewhat from country to country, the fundamental problems of the American New Left, here analyzed by a member of the Liberal Left, are significant for all of them.

What more is there to say, at this date, about the New Left?[1] It has already received extensive coverage in the mass media; it has emerged as an identifiable entity in the mind of Washington; before the year is out, at least half-a-dozen books will have appeared on, or even by, the subject;[2] and it has even been recognized as a proper object of formal study — there is a course on it at the New School.

SOURCE: Reprinted by permission from *Commentary*, July 1966, copyright by the American Jewish Committee. Text and footnotes are abridged.

[1] The term "New Left" is generally used to cover a wide variety of student organizations and youth groups, with an estimated total membership of about 12,000. The two most important are the largely white Students for a Democratic Society (SDS), and the largely Negro Student Nonviolent Coordinating Committee (SNCC), a non-membership organization with a fluctuating staff of between 150 and 250. SDS is best known for its work in trying to organize the poor in such cities as Newark, Cleveland, and Chicago, and, more recently, for its protests against the Vietnam war. SNCC is best known for its work among rural Negroes in Mississippi and other Southern states.

Often subsumed under "New Left" are groups which Paul Jacobs has more accurately described as "the Ancestral Left," youth groups identified with "Old Left" views – e.g., the DuBois Clubs (pro-Soviet), the Progressive Labor Movement (pro-Peking), the Young Socialist Alliance (Trotskyist), and the Young People's Socialist League (democratic socialist) – each with fewer than a thousand members. Even these groups are affected by the action-styles of SDS and SNCC. Finally, various *ad hoc* and local project-centered student organizations are also considered part of the New Left.

[2] See Phillip Abbot Luce, *The New Left*, McKay, 1966; Paul Jacobs and Saul Landau, *The New Radicals*, Random House, 1966.

Yet most liberals come away from encounters with the New Left, whether direct or literary, feeling profoundly ambivalent: the problem is not in determining how much weight to assign the good as against the bad elements embraced by this movement, but in deciding whether to take it seriously at all. To take it seriously requires political measurements of the kind few liberals have had to employ in more than a decade; for it has been at least that long since large numbers of people sought consciously to build a mass political movement for social change. How is such a movement to be constructed? From the rich history of failure of similar efforts in the United States, what lessons can be learned?

One can avoid dealing with this question, and win favor on the New Left, by retreating into sociological formulae which "explain" the motives of the students, the social origins of their rhetoric, the institutional context of their revolt — in short, their emergence as a new social type. (One is apt to forget that technology is creating other revolutionary social types — the modern housewife, for example.) As an avowedly political movement, however, the New Left presumably intends not to be studied as sociology but to transform society — in other words, to make history. Yet the widespread reluctance — shared by members and adult partisans of the movement alike — to analyze its evolving political philosophy, and the preference for sociological description instead, suggest to me an implicit conviction that the New Left will not in fact make history, but rather that it will turn out to be a symptom of history, a fleeting moment in which radical "energies" were released into the larger society. In most discussions of the movement one finds an exhilarated note of romantic defeatism: how can this effort possibly succeed in the face of the corruption of American society, the power of the state, the brainwashing of the people by the mass media, the machinations of the economy?

Now it makes a considerable difference in sizing up the student movement whether one views its "inevitable" defeat as a disaster or as a vindication. My own experience suggests that those who see it as a disaster, or at least as a disappointing setback, are for that reason the least indulgent of the New Left's errors and conceits. And it is for such people — Michael Harrington, Bayard Rustin, and Irving Howe, for example, all of whom are committed to building a movement for social change and who share a conception of the strategy by which such a movement can be created — that the new radicals have reserved their most vitriolic vocabulary. (Staughton Lynd, an influential New Left spokesman, refers to Rustin, a democratic socialist and pacifist, as a "labor lieutenant of capitalism" who is in "coalition with the marines." Tom Hayden, one of the founders of SDS and now head of the Newark Community Union Project, speaks of the League for Industrial Democracy and the liberal-labor-civil rights coalition as playing the same role vis-à-vis the poor in America as the Pope played vis-à-vis the Jews in The Deputy.) No comparable volume of criticism is brought to bear by the New Left on a certain school of generalized radicalism composed largely of journalists, commentators, and stray intellectuals (Nat Hentoff, Howard Zinn, Paul Jacobs, and others) who favorably report from the fringes of activity on the stylistic innovations of the New Left. They are fascinated by the New Left as a milieu, an atmosphere, an élan, a mode of life. They do not clarify strategic problems for the New Left nor participate in the making of political decisions. Although not mentors in the strictest sense, they become champions precisely by virtue of the students' hunger to have their own contours delineated, their unique moods articulated.

All this helps to account for the peculiarly surrealistic quality of the New Left's perceptions of American political life and its own relationship to it. For in the 1960's, in the bastion of world capitalism, where only a beginning has been made toward eradicating racism and toward constructing a welfare state still backward by European standards; wherein the poor remain powerless while General Motors racks up unprecedented profits; wherein the labor movement cannot amass sufficient support to win repeal of 14b; and wherein millions of people are prepared to vote for Richard Nixon and Barry Goldwater — in such a society one again hears, this time from the disenchanted scions of the middle class, denunciations of "the social democrats"!

II

Whatever their differences, every group, without exception, which has called itself Left or radical, has believed that the organized working class, the labor movement, has a unique historical role to play in the creation of the new society. Disagreement as to the precise nature of that role, and as to the political strategy the unions should pursue — such disagreements, however severe, have rested on a common assumption regarding the socially progressive character of the organized working class. The single new ideological feature of the "New Left" — all that seems to me really new about it — is the rejection, implicit or explicit, of this fundamental assumption. The reasoning behind this rejection is not that the labor leadership or bureaucracy represses the workers' instinctive radicalism (the Trotskyist formula), or that the workers have been atomized or culturally degraded by mass society (the ex-radical's formula), but that the organized working class has achieved its goals and has itself consequently become part of the power structure.

If such an attitude is new in the history of radicalism, it is, of course, familiar in the society at large and particularly among ex-radicals. Ironically, it is precisely such ex-radicals who, having bequeathed to the new radicals a legacy of bitterness and cynicism toward the labor movement, and a concomitant intellectual self-centeredness, now wonder why ultra-radicalism pervades the New Left, failing to understand how ultra-radicalism grows out of a sense of alienation from all major institutions.[3] A classic example is John Fischer's "Letter to a New Leftist from a Tired Liberal," in the March 1966 issue of *Harper's*. Criticizing the New Left for its naiveté, incoherence, and anarchism, he explains how he himself was brought to political maturity:

> Consider the labor unions, for instance. To us it seemed self-evident that the quickest route to universal reform was to muster all the unorganized workers

---

[3] A corollary is (Irving) "Howe's Law": where there is no genuine radicalism, there will be no ultra-radicalism.

into strong unions. They would then form the backbone of a liberal political movement, something like the Labor party in England. . . . Under the leadership of the intellectuals, organized labor — with its new-found freedom, leisure and money — would rejuvenate the arts and theater, toning up the soul and muscle of the whole American society. . . . [But] Instead of becoming the stoic troops of liberation, the unions (with a very few exceptions) quickly petrified into lumps of reaction and special privilege. I don't need to tell you that some of them — notably the construction trades — are the stubbornest opponents of integration; how they have no use for intellectuals, no interest in the arts, no cultural aspirations higher than the bowling alley; that none of their aged leaders, except Walter Reuther, has entertained a fresh political idea in twenty years. At their worst, as in the case of the Transport Workers Union in New York, they have turned pirate, using their monopoly power to torture millions of people (most of them workers) into paying ransom.

Fischer, of course, is wasting his breath, because the New Left already shares his disillusionment with labor. What they have not yet acquired, as a protection against ultra-radical alienation, however, is his comfortable position in the intellectual firmament — or his post-idealistic snobbery. But if we substitute "Negroes" or "poor people" for "the unions," we can foresee a time about twenty years hence when an ex-New Leftist, musing on his past, may write a piece similar to Fischer's — that is, if the New Left fails to understand the needs and aims of Negroes and poor people as Fischer patently failed to understand the purpose of unions. None of these groups exists to rejuvenate the arts or to provide salvation for intellectuals. (Given Fischer's notions of a union, no wonder he denounces the TWU without mentioning that prior to the strike, transport workers earned considerably less than the "modest but adequate" budget specified by the U.S. Bureau of Labor Statistics.)

In any case, the disaffection of intellectuals from the labor movement reached a peak in the 50's, and few students of a liberal or radical persuasion during that time held the labor movement in esteem. It was therefore predictable that when the next wave of radicalism emerged, it would view labor as simply another big institution — and the New Left is very much a revolt against bigness. But it is important to remember that the indifference or hostility to labor grew out of a conservative period, when middle-class prosperity was reshaping the ethos of the university, and the McClelland hearings were convincing millions of Americans that Dave Beck of the Teamsters was the prototype of the labor leader. Thus, while much student criticism of labor comes from the Left, it also contains strands of middle-class prejudice — a lack of appreciation for, or identification with, the historic and *continuing* role of the unions in the day-to-day lives of literally millions of working people. Little interest will be found among most New Leftists, for example, in the campaign for a $2.00 minimum wage, or for extension of the Fair Labor Standards Act, although such measures would result in a dramatic upgrading in living standards for masses of Negroes and poor whites who are not likely to be reached by white students working in the ghettos.

The abandonment of the traditional pro-labor perspective confronts a radical movement with a major problem. If not the labor movement, then what social force can be expected to lead the way in transforming society, and how are the students to relate to that force? The Marxian tradition, after all, had not only nominated the working class for his historic role, but also had an analysis of the middle classes which, at least by implication, outlined the relationship of breakaway radical intellectuals to the working class. That role was the ideological education of the workers, by which the latter, in the words of Lenin — himself a middle-class intellectual — could achieve a socialist consciousness.

SDS answered the question in the first draft of the Port Huron Statement (June 1962), a kind of manifesto for the new generation of radicals: ". . . the civil rights, peace, and student movements are too poor and socially slighted, and the labor movement too acquiescent, to be counted with enthusiasm. From where else can power and vision be summoned? We believe that the universities are an overlooked seat of influence." Thus, the new radicals, first coming to consciousness of themselves as a force, saw in their own institutional base the main hope for change. And the statistics lent weight to their argument. The mushrooming of higher education had boosted the university population to four-and-a-half million. Many of these, moreover, were highly concentrated, like factory workers in basic industry, in mammoth institutions — among them the University of Michigan (spawning ground for the early leadership of SDS), the University of California at Berkeley, and the University of Wisconsin, each of which had close to thirty-thousand students. In any one of these institutions, a demonstration by only one per cent of the student body would be impressive.

The strategic importance assigned to the university continues as a strain in radical student thinking, but the emphasis has by now shifted considerably. In part, the intellectual realization grew that students alone, even at maximum strength, had neither sufficient numbers nor enough political power to change American society: the absence of strong institutions and social classes which made student politics a decisive factor in the underdeveloped countries was not characteristic of the United States. (It must also be said that the quest for allies outside the university intensified as the intellectual leadership of SDS was graduated.)

The allies chosen, of course, were the poor. It is interesting to review how this choice was made, since it preceded the elaborate ideological justification for it. For one thing, many white students had already participated in SNCC projects in the rural South, where they had their first taste of real poverty. Beyond this, it is ironic to note that the two individuals who are perhaps most responsible for the shift in strategy are now frequent targets of attack by the New Left, Michael Harrington and Bayard Rustin. Harrington's *The Other America* came out in 1962 and succeeded during the following year or two in putting poverty on the political map. Then, on Thanksgiving weekend of 1963, at a SNCC Conference at Howard University, Rustin received a standing ovation when he urged that white students who had donned dungarees and gone off to Mississippi should consider taking their dungarees into the poor white communities of the nation. The enthusiastic response was probably due in part to the fact that many of the white students present had returned from the 1963 Mississippi Summer Project with the feeling that for racial reasons their effectiveness had been limited. Within the civil-rights movement generally, the traditional notions of protest were being challenged by advocates of a grass roots community organizing approach. The East River Chapter of CORE had been formed out of a split with the New York Chapter on this issue, and the entire national organization was plunged into a debate on related strategic questions.

The idea that poor people must be organized is one thing; what they should be organized for, and by whom, are other matters. In Rustin's view, the poor should be organized into the coalition that mobilized the 1963 March on Washington, won the civil-rights legislation, and helped to turn back the Goldwater threat. Just as the organized participation of the poor in the coalition would help to strengthen and radicalize the latter, so would the strength of the coalition be required to back the poor in winning immediate gains, without which apathy and demoralization would prevail.

As against this perspective, another was developed within SDS – namely, that to bring the poor into the coalition would mean their absorption into the Establishment. The poor, because they have been outcasts, are perhaps the only group in the society not to have been corrupted. Tom Hayden became the leading spokesman for this viewpoint within SDS, contending that American society is quasi-fascist, that the ideology of the coalition is "corporate liberalism," and that the effect of the social legislation of the New Deal and the Great Society is to enslave the poor to a bureaucratic welfarism that leaves them worse off than they were to start with. In an essay in *The Radical Papers,* Hayden writes that ". . . there is much evidence which suggests that the reforms gained [in the past thirty years] were illusory or token, serving chiefly to sharpen the capacity of the system for manipulation and oppression. . . . Except for temporarily boosting income for a few people, this entire reformist trend has weakened the poor under the pretense of helping them and strengthened elite rule under the slogan of curbing private enterprise. . . . A way has been found to contain and paralyze the disadvantaged and voiceless people."

Thus the poor and New Left catalysts, instead of entering into coalition with the liberals, the unions, and the established civil-rights groups, should build counter-institutions, revolutionary enclaves in the garrison state.

It would be unfair to attribute this perspective to the majority of SDS or the New Left generally. In recent months the Hayden-Lynd influence in SDS has waned (no one at the national conference of SDS last December even referred to their trip to Hanoi with Herbert Aptheker). Still, the prolongation of the Vietnam war may win many of them to the Hayden-Lynd *description* of American society, if not to their strategy for changing it. Hayden and Lynd can thus continue to enjoy high reputations among the students for their rhetoric, even while relatively few are following their advice. The SDS December National Council, for example, voted down a series of civil-disobedience proposals advanced by Lynd and the National Coordinating Committee to End the War in Vietnam; yet Lynd continues to be billed as the "leading intellectual spokesman for the New Left" (by, among others, pacifist A. J. Muste's *Liberation* magazine).

Among the majority of the SDSers, as represented by President Carl
Oglesby and the National Secretary Paul Booth, there is a greater open-
mindedness. The slogans "No Coalitions" and "No Compromises," which
filled the air during and immediately following the 1964 Democratic Convention in Atlantic City, have given way to questions: "Coalitions with whom
and under what circumstances?" and "Compromise what in return for what?"
   These practical questions impose themselves even on the most alienated
and romantic elements who are serious about community organizing. Thus,
the Newark Community Union Project — probably the most successful of the
SDS ghetto projects — has found it advantageous to work within the Democratic party. In no area, it must be said, have SDS organizers recruited
more than a hundred or so poor people into ongoing organizational structures.
Inasmuch as most of their projects are barely two years old, final judgments
are premature; but thus far, the major contribution of the New Left has been
to counterpose to the paternalistic social-worker approach to the poor a rugged
willingness to live and work among them. In the process they have helped
make the poor more visible, if not significantly more powerful.
   The same judgment would apply to other New-Left activities: largely
through use of direct-action techniques borrowed from the civil-rights movement, the students have focused attention on problems and contradictions in
American society but lack the political power to resolve them. One exception
would be SNCC, which has clearly brought changes to the Deep South;
another might be the demonstrations at Berkeley, which have reverberated
among policy-makers at other large universities. (In Berkeley, incidentally,
the local SDS people played a relatively minor role, though the national
organization did seek to articulate the students' revolt around the country.)
Again, with regard to the Vietnam protests, the New Left seems to have been
most effective when, as in the teach-ins, it helped mobilize debate among non-
New Left students and faculty. While such expressions of dissatisfaction in
the academic world would have surely impressed, if not stung, the administration, demonstrations dominated by the style of the New Left — a style which
includes an amenability to cooperation with pro-Vietcong elements — have
quite possibly hardened public opinion on the side of the administration.

III

   Activists of the New Left most frequently describe themselves as a-Com-
munist, or as anti-anti-Communist. Their writings speak indiscriminately of
"*the* ideology of anti-Communism," as if the anti-Communism of socialists,
trade unionists, liberals, McCarthyites, Birchers, and Klansmen were cut from
the same cloth. What actually operates here is a kind of reverse McCarthyism
which refuses to differentiate between libertarian and rightist opposition to
Communism. The New Left, precisely by adopting as a cardinal tenet the
thesis that the "Communist question" is irrelevant, raises the Communist
question to a standard by which it will judge others. In actual practice, the
standard works to the advantage of the pro-Communist and the indifferentist,
neither of whom has reason to raise the question.

The result is that an atmosphere strongly reminiscent of the old Popular Front often pervades the New Left. At a recent SNCC teach-in at NYU, for example, a speaker on "red-baiting" warned an audience of eight-hundred that "anti-Communism" was "anti-The Movement." Anne Braden of the Southern Conference Educational Fund argued in a recent pamphlet that anti-Communism, as the weapon that reactionaries have always used to destroy all "progressive" movements in the South, must be resolutely combatted by civil-rights activists.

This atmosphere makes it all too easy to suppose, as some liberals have, that we are witnessing a resurgence of the Popular-Front politics of the 30's and 40's. The crucial difference is that today there is no significant organized Communist movement to which dupes, fellow travelers, or innocents can be attached, or through which large organizations can be manipulated. Popular-front politics in the earlier decades was not, after all, *simply* a matter of atmosphere or milieu; the Communist party, which recruited from this milieu, exercised very real influence and power over intellectuals and activists. The absence of a comparable threat today — the virtual invisibility of the Communist party in this country — means that the New Left can be persuaded of the totalitarian nature of Communism only through ideological education. And this they resist — often with a hostile arrogance that reflects a nervous awareness of their illogical position. The more sophisticated SDS leaders will acknowledge that there is an anti-Communism of the Left and that it is a different phenomenon from anti-Communism of the Right. But, they say, the latter is overwhelmingly dominant and is merely fed by the former. Left anti-Communism should therefore be muted (and anyone gauche enough to violate this implicit understanding can be made to feel quite uncomfortable).

The irrelevance of the "Communist question" was at least a discussable proposition so long as "the movement" confined itself to domestic questions. Anti-Communism, after all, is a position deriving in the first place from an analysis of the social system established and ruled by Communist parties, and in the second place from an evaluation of the role of apologists of this system in countries throughout the world. Thus, the New Left could argue the irrelevance of anti-Communism on the ground that there are no significant numbers of Communists apologists in this country; as for other social systems, "We live here, not in Russia." Once the movement turned toward the war in Vietnam, however, what began as an admissible (if morally and politically dubious) disinclination to develop an attitude toward Communism, became an indefensible double standard. One need not support administration policies in Vietnam to recognize that the United States may not be playing the *only* reactionary or oppressive role in that tragic land. Yet this is the assumption underlying the SNCC statement on the war of last January 6:

> We believe the United States government has been deceptive in its claims of concern for the freedom of the Vietnamese people, just as the government has been deceptive in claiming concern for the freedom of colored people in such other countries as the Dominican Republic, the Congo, South Africa, Rhodesia and in the United States itself. . . . Our work, particularly in the South, has taught us that *the United States government has never guaranteed the*

freedom of oppressed citizens, and is not yet truly determined to end the rule of terror and oppression within its own borders. . . . We ourselves have often been victims of violence and confinement executed by United States government officials. . . . Vietnamese are murdered because the United States is pursuing an aggressive policy in violation of international law. . . . We know that for the most part, elections in this country in the North as well as the South, are not free. . . . We maintain that our country's cry of "Preserve freedom in the world" is a hypocritical mask behind which it squashes liberation movements which are not bound and refuse to be bound, by the expediencies of United States Cold War policies. . . . [Italics mine.]

These lines are not distorted for having been taken out of context; the ellipses do not conceal qualifying statements. The war in Vietnam is viewed solely as an extension of the American system, as defined and understood by SNCC, and there is nowhere to be found an evaluation of "the other side" except as a force for "liberation." One need not look for Communist infiltrators in SNCC to explain its position; the answer lies in the conditions under which SNCC workers must operate in the Deep South. But to acknowledge those conditions should not entail acceptance of the skewed perspective they foster. The U.S. government is not the State of Mississippi, and the Vietcong are not the equivalent of SNCC. "We have seen that the 1965 Voting Rights Act and the 1964 Civil Rights Act have not yet been implemented with full federal power and sincerity," the statement says. That is true, but how can it be used in apparent support of forces which do not rule by free elections? Hanoi has demanded that the NLF be designated (not elected) the *sole* representative of the South Vietnamese. And when is the last time an election was held in North Vietnam, *even* a Mississippi-style election?

The SNCC statement is the most extreme example of a fairly pervasive mode of thought on the New Left. The danger is not that it paves the way for a resurgence of the Communist movement; it is rather that it encourages a stance and a species of reasoning that muddies the democratic vision of the Left. People would fight for the right to vote in Mississippi, and yet support forces which rationalize the denial of that right, sow great confusion as to the depth of the American Left's commitment to democracy. It is the resurgence of that confusion, which once before took an enormous toll of radicalism, that we have to fear.

IV

It is at this point that the sociology of the New Left becomes important. For the New Left is not merely middle-class; it springs largely from the affluent, professional, liberal middle class. Here I am talking about the composition of predominantly white organizations like SDS. The young Negro militants in SNCC, CORE, and other civil-rights groups come mainly from a lower-middle-class stratum which, since the early 40's, has experienced many dislocations and a high degree of mobility. The young Negroes in the movement who have gone through college are the first in their families to have done so. This is not the case with the white radical students, whose parents, by and large, are well-educated.

The class origins of the New Left lie at the root of two characteristics of the movement: its anti-materialism and anti-intellectualism. As to the first, only a childhood of relative economic security could account for the student radicals' insouciance with regard to material circumstances, especially in their ghetto work (which involves living in poverty with the poor). People whose early lives were disrupted or menaced by material deprivation are likely to feel some anxiety at the prospect of living in poverty, even if only as a temporary project. Voluntary poverty, precisely because it is voluntary, is never real poverty. Moreover, because these student organizers of the poor are well-educated, the choice of escaping poverty is open to them, which is not the case with the poor themselves. It may well be that the anti-materialism of the New Left is a strength, a protection against the fatalistic despair that victimizes the poor. But it can also distort the students' relations with the poor. The students are in rebellion against middle-class values and ways of living. The poor, on the other hand, want nothing so much as to get into the middle class, and they are interested in tangible activities toward that end. To be sure, to the extent that poor people struggling for material improvement become politically active and conscious, their values are affected; and as the students work with the poor, they may come to appreciate more fully the urgency of immediate, concrete economic reform. But the point is that between the students and the poor there is no essential identity of interest such as can be assumed to exist between the union organizer and the factory worker.

The anti-intellectualism of the New Left may, in the eyes of the general public, be obscured by the skillful articulateness of the leadership. Still, it is self-admitted:

> The December Conference will . . . be the beginning of an analysis and self-criticism which has been lacking in SDS for the last year: . . . We have slogans which take the place of thought: "There's a change gonna come" is our substitute for social theory, "Let the people decide" has been an escape from our own indecision; we scream "no leaders," "no structures" and seem to come up with implicit structures which are far less democratic than the most explicit elitism. . . . What sociology, what psychology, what history do we need to know the answers? How seriously have we treated those not from the "New Left"? [From the call to the SDS December Conference, 1965.]

What has been articulated is moral indignation, personal alienation, and populist sentiment. Although the new student movement is better educated in a formal sense than its counterpart of the 30's, it has been less competent — and willfully so — in making political and intellectual distinctions. This attribute is rooted in a revolt against the liberal rhetoric of their class, against the apparent fecklessness and hypocrisy of modernistic parents who always *stood* for progressive ideas but never seemed to act or *sacrifice* for them. No one knows for certain how many of the New Leftists are the children of the hundreds of thousands who at one time or another passed through the Communist party, but everyone recognizes as a type the ex-party member who, while maintaining abstractly committed to certain "liberal" ideas, cautiously withdrew from political activity during the McCarthy era, perhaps to save a job or "spare the children." The children, some of whom have grown up to confront terror in Mississippi, now make a judgment, not only on the fuzzy ex-Communist milieu, but on liberals generally, for what was clearly not their finest hour. The judgment is manifest in a weariness with talk; an almost mystical devotion to activism; and, in place of the older generation's apparent failure of nerve, an "existentialism" whose central value is the permanent protest, the continuous personal confrontation with power.

V

All this has been said before, but it does not by itself constitute a sufficient explanation of the political orientation of the New Left. It does not follow that a new student generation, with a given socio-economic background and style, must inevitably wind up with a given politics. Many of the student leaders of the socialist movement of the 1930's, for example, also came from the higher socio-economic brackets, yet had vastly different attitudes toward methods and possibilities of radical social change. The difference, fundamentally, lies in the political context of the 60's, which is sharply dissimilar from that of the 30's and 40's.

Much of what the New Left says and does is inexplicable except in terms of the shifting fortunes of the American radical movement. Seymour Martin Lipset has elsewhere sketched out the historical background of student protest since the days of the pre-World War I Intercollegiate Socialist Society (predecessor of the present League for Industrial Democracy). Some details of more recent history are directly relevant.

The notion of "generation gap" has often been used to cover up or write off very real ideological disagreements between the younger and older radicals. But there is a sense in which the term has a significant application. When Mario Savio, leader of the Free Speech Movement at Berkeley, uttered his now famous warning that the movement should not trust anyone over thirty, he was in effect placing beyond the pale all those who were in college during the years darkened by McCarthyism. The point is, in other words, that there *is* a missing "generation" in the recent history of the American Left — a generation of 30- to 35-year-old radicals who should have served as a link between the New Left and the Old (speaking purely chronologically) but who, because of what campus life was like in the days of McCarthy and Eisenhower, never appeared. (It has been estimated that there were fewer than five hundred members in any socialist youth group during the late 40's and 50's.)

Having begun my own undergraduate career in 1955 (it continued intermittently until 1963), I recall that one of the few exceptions to the non-appearing generation was Michael Harrington, who regularly toured the campuses, a youthful evangelist for socialism. But his labors were Sisyphean, and perhaps no more than two-hundred students were recruited to the democratic socialist movement in those days. Those who were recruited, however, received an intensive political education; and when the possibilities for radical politics opened up again in the late 50's, the Young People's Socialist League (YPSL, the youth section of the Socialist party) was the first of the radical youth groups to expand. The Montgomery Bus Boycott and the Southern school-integration struggle stimulated the 1958 and 1959 youth marches on Washington, in which YPSL's played an outstanding role. By the summer of 1962, a year-and-a-half after the Greensboro sit-ins, YPSL membership had reached eight-hundred, not a large figure to be sure, but the largest since the 40's and, more important, the largest of any radical student group at the time. YPSL had perhaps twice the membership of Students for a Democratic Society, then still known as the Student League for Industrial Democracy (SLID).

Within two years, however, the situation had changed drastically. The "left wing" of the YPSL captured control of the organization and promptly subdivided into four factions; the result was to cut YPSL membership in half and finally to destroy the organization altogether. SLID, meanwhile, had changed its name to SDS and had succeeded in racking up a membership of a thousand; thereafter, it grew almost geometrically.

This is not the place to analyze all the factors which led to the decline of YPSL. The reader may feel that too much space has already been devoted to what was, after all, a tiny organization. But all the radical student groups were then tiny and even today are small. A different evolution of YPSL, in that context, might have altered the present configuration of forces in the radical student movement. Furthermore, the then leadership of SDS was in its domestic political views closer to the position of the YPSL "right wing" (which favored working within the democratic party with the aim of realigning the major parties) than to the "independent labor party" line of the "left wing"; it was also more sympathetic to the former group's emphasis on civil-rights work than to the latter's emphasis on peace activity. But the SDS leaders tended to find both YPSL factions too theoretical, insufficiently pragmatic. Above all, SDS was out of tune with the explicit anti-Communism that characterized all YPSL factions. Most of SDS's present membership of five thousand probably is not aware of this history, but the older leadership is. A former national secretary of SDS recent proclaimed at a Turn Toward Peace debate: "You social democrats who keep raising the Communist question are just a bunch of chiefs with no Indians."

VI

If anti-communism and the Marxian faith in the working class rendered YPSL obsolete in the eyes of the new student radicals, factionalism was seen as its most deadly characteristic. Not only was rampant factionalism the apparent cause of YPSL's decline; it was the underlying reason for the fragmentation of the entire American Left. If the warfare among Communists, Socialists, and liberals could somehow have been avoided, the radical movement of the last generation would not have gone under. Some of the New Leftists will dig deeper and assign specific responsibility, or guilt, in the ideological disputes of the 30's, but in such a way that the errors of the respective political tendencies cancel each other out. Thus, the Communists were wrong for taking their line from Moscow and especially for behaving like New Deal liberals; the Socialists were wrong for being so virulently anti-Communist. (Liberals, of course, were wrong because they were liberals.)

The techniques used by the New Left to fend off factionalism, however, create as many problems as they resolve. Decision by consensus, borrowed from the Quakers, helps to present the expert abuse of parliamentary procedure, but it also discourages the crystallization of opposing viewpoints, seeking the gentle obliteration of differences. A possibly creative by-product of factionalism — ideological education — goes unrealized. Meanwhile, if a minority is unsatisfied with the common denominator, it is permitted to carry out its own program by itself (the inadmissable alternative being to vote it down) — a procedure which discriminates *a priori* against people who believe that an organization ought to pursue an integrated strategy.

The consensus technique is wed to a particular adaptation of "participatory democracy," a term never satisfactorily explained by the New Left but apparently signifying that there should be no "leaders" — "Let the people decide!" One must hope that more serious writing will be done on "participatory democracy," an attractive and important concept, central to radical thought. But is rank-and-file decision-making strengthened by the denigration of leadership *per se?* People who take the lead in formulating problems and proposing solutions are inevitable. Leadership, if not exercised overtly, if made invisible by a distortion of the concept of "participatory democracy," becomes dangerously manipulative. Accountability is obscured rather than democratically distributed.

This is no basis for smugness. If the New Left has not successfully answered the problem of factionalism, who has? There is no formula which does not create new problems; the process is ongoing. And one must respect the fact that the student radicals are immersed in it, and that they have brought to it an energetic idealism which this nation had not seen in many years.

The same must be said in connection with the other problems discussed here. The insistence of the New Left that its own experience be the basis of its ideas is very much in the American pragmatic tradition (just as its style has been richly endowed by the history of American radicalism); and while this insistence can lead to an exasperating provincialism, it may promise a more genuine, indigenous confrontation — one less dependent on the European radical heritage — between American radicalism and social reality.

This new generation of radicals will learn its own truths, puncture its own myths. But if the slate is to be wiped, let it be wiped evenly; if the new radical politics is to be constructed with an eye to present realities, let these realities be objectively analyzed. If we are to recognize the decline of the American Communist movement and the breakup of monolithic world Communism, where does that leave us? How are these facts to be interpreted? Do they justify the view that Communism and anti-Communism are irrelevant? What are the standards by which we can judge whether or not a given political trend in the underdeveloped world is democratic and progressive? (After all, one can defend the right of other people to determine their own destinies without forfeiting one's own right to judge their choice.)

Similarly, the labor movement should be judged in its present reality, shorn of the illusions of yesteryear's radicals, today's tired liberals. If labor has lost much of its old élan and yielded to incredible foreign policies, it nonetheless faces monumental challenges today; no one can afford to be indifferent to its responses, because they will largely determine the shape of the coming political order. The difficulties posed by automation and the changing nature of the work force are enormous. The labor movement may be sluggish in coping with these difficulties, but one cannot be blind to the rapid growth of the American Federation of Teachers, the American Federation of State, County and Municipal Employees, and other white-collar organizing efforts. One-third of the Executive Council of the AFL-CIO, whose leadership is aging, was replaced at the last convention. The point is not only that changes are occurring in the labor movement, but that these very changes relate to a continuing revolution in the socio-economic order in which labor is rooted. The conditions which cause labor to reflect the conservatism of the total society thus compel it also to face up to the problems of change at their most basic level.

VII

The SDS conference in December gave signs that the shrill and easy slogan-eering of the last couple of years may be losing ground to a more concrete and perceptive politics. For the future, however, almost everything will depend on what happens outside the New Left, around it. The New Left can have little direct impact on the administration's policies in Vietnam; yet prolongation or acceleration of the war will have the twofold effect of heightening the alienation and desperation of the movement and simultaneously encouraging right-wing attacks on it. "On the other hand," says Professor Lipset, "should the Vietnamese war end, it is highly probable that the revival of the American New Left in the mid-1960's will turn out to be as ephemeral as the well-publicized growth of campus conservatism in 1960–61." Probably it was awareness of this prospect that caused SDS, at its December conference, to reemphasize grass-roots domestic reform as against pure and simple antiwar activity. Whether the political passions excited by the war can, upon its end, be rechanneled into the daily grind of community organizing, fighting poverty, and making civil-rights victories economically meaningful, is problematic.

Another important factor, aside from the war, is whether students slightly to the "Right" of SDS — moderates, liberals, religious youths — can be politically activated. The extent to which they have already been moved, mainly by the moral dimensions of the Negro struggle, has been obscured by the publicity given the wilder aspects of the New Left. As individuals, many of these students have participated in Southern projects under the aegis of SNCC and Dr. Martin Luther King's Southern Christian Leadership Conference. They have also been troubled by the Vietnam war. But because they have not organized any coherent or distinctive movement of their own, a gigantic vacuum exists — and this explains why the most conspicuously radical elements in the New Left command such disproportionate attention.

The organization of relatively moderate students into their own autonomous movement should be welcomed, indeed encouraged, by the New Left in the same way they encourage such organization among the poor. For it seems clear that if this is not done, the great mass of students will remain apathetic, and the campus radicals will remain isolated, with nothing to fall back on. Efforts in this direction are under way (e.g., the Youth Committee Against Poverty in New York), but not by the leadership of the New Left, which is still suspicious of coalitions with liberals, absorption into the Establishment, loss of style and identity, etc.

The suspicion is far from paranoid; historically, American politics has shown itself uniquely capable of making lapdogs of radicals. But there is little evidence that this danger is ever foreclosed by the strenuous and willful assertion of ultra-radicalism. On the contrary, the latter is the surest path to the isolation and impotence which makes cooptation easy. Accommodationism and ultra-radicalism are only superficially at opposite poles; in reality, they find each other.

To steer clear of both is no simple task, and criticisms of the New Left should be tempered with a humility and a straining toward understanding, recognizing that something valuable and exciting has emerged in American life, and something fragile. But fragility and numerical weakness should not lead to dismissal of its importance. The activists in the New Left do articulate the questioning rebelliousness that pervades, if not a majority, at least a sizable segment of this generation of college youth. This, after all, is the segment from which the adult liberal and radical movements will be recruiting their leadership in the next decade or two. The formative ideological experiences to which that future leadership is now being exposed will clearly affect the political character of American reform in the 70's and 80's. Should today's New Left disintegrate, as a consequence of sectarian or defeatist policies, debris from wrecked hopes would scatter far; and the cynical disillusionment which would follow would darken, not illuminate, the prospects for a Great Society. The importance of the New Left, finally, lies in its relation to these prospects, and no one can deny that the problems it has publicized and grappled with are real — whether in university reform, poverty, civil rights, or foreign policy. A militant and democratic New Left is needed in America.

It will not, however, be strengthened by pampering, but rather by its own experiences and relevant criticism. Among the critics the New Left will encounter several schools, and they need to be distinguished if anyone is to profit from dialogue. There are those who refuse to criticize the New Left because, while they sentimentalize it, they do not take it seriously; they are satisfied that it be *alive* and youthful. There are those who criticize it because they want to destroy it — some because they are reactionaries, others because they have become excessively comfortable in their liberalism. But there are also those, among whom I include myself, who criticize out of a hope growing nearly desperate that this outburst of radical discontent will stick, that it will sink deep roots, that it will energize a new political movement, and transform national institutions — in short, that its legacy to the next generation will be a new beginning, not that tiresome mixture of cynicism and nostalgia that grows out of defeat and hangs over us still.

B C D E F G H I J   5 4 3 2 1 7 0